Through Indian Sign Language

THE CIVILIZATION OF THE AMERICAN INDIAN SERIES

Through Indian Sign Language

THE FORT SILL LEDGERS OF
HUGH LENOX SCOTT
AND ISEEO
1889–1897

Edited by
WILLIAM C. MEADOWS

University of Oklahoma Press : Norman

ALSO BY WILLIAM C. MEADOWS

Kiowa Military Societies: Ethnohistory and Ritual (Norman, Okla., 2010)
Kiowa Ethnogeography (Austin, Texas, 2008)
The Comanche Code Talkers of World War II (Austin, Texas, 2002)
Kiowa, Apache, and Comanche Military Societies: Enduring Veterans, 1800 to the Present (Austin, Texas, 1999)

LIBRARY OF CONGRESS CATALOGING-IN-PUBLICATION DATA

Scott, Hugh Lenox, 1853–1934.
 Through Indian sign language : the Fort Sill ledgers of Hugh Lenox Scott and Iseeo, 1889–1897 / edited by William C. Meadows. — First edition.
  pages cm — (The civilization of the American Indian series ; volume 274)
 Includes bibliographical references and index.
 ISBN 978-0-8061-4727-7 (hardcover) ISBN 978-0-8061-9108-9 (paper)
 1. Indian sign language. 2. Kiowa Indians—Folklore. 3. Kiowa Indians—

Ethnography. I. Iseeo. II. Meadows, William C., 1966– III. Title. IV. Title: Fort Sill ledgers of Hugh Lenox Scott and Iseeo, 1889–1897.

E98.S5S36 2015
419'.54—dc23

2015001528

Through Indian Sign Language: The Fort Sill Ledgers of Hugh Lenox Scott and Iseeo, 1889–1897 is Volume 274 in The Civilization of the American Indian Series.

The paper in this book meets the guidelines for permanence and durability of the Committee on Production Guidelines for Book Longevity of the Council on Library Resources, Inc. ∞

Copyright © 2015 by the University of Oklahoma Press, Norman, Publishing Division of the University. Paperback published 2022. Manufactured in the U.S.A.

All rights reserved. No part of this publication may be reproduced, stored in a retrieval system, or transmitted, in any form or by any means, electronic, mechanical, photocopying, recording, or otherwise—except as permitted under Section 107 or 108 of the United States Copyright Act—without the prior written permission of the University of Oklahoma Press. To request permission to reproduce selections from this book, write to Permissions, University of Oklahoma Press, 2800 Venture Drive, Norman OK 73069, or email rights.oupress@ou.edu.

To
PARKER P. MCKENZIE
November 15, 1897–March 5, 1999

SÉPYÀLDÀ (RAINY MOUNTAIN)
and
YÍSÀUM (THEY VIEWED HIM TWICE)

with my deepest respect

I have been exceptionally fortunate in having the confidence and friendship of all the tribes tributary to Fort Reno and to Fort Sill where I was stationed from February 1889 to December 1897. . . . These and similar occurrences gave me the friendship and confidence of all the Plains Indians of Oklahoma. . . . This all brought about a mutual feeling of confidence and trust and as I was always anxious to obtain their legendary lore and their sign language, I had great opportunities during those nine years of constant association. I have many notes upon many different subjects. . . . Attention is invited to the fact that they are unique as having been obtained directly from the Indians in the sign language of the Plains without the aid of an interpreter. There do not exist elsewhere such documents and probably never will exist. They were obtained from a generation that has gone, of Indians brought up on the warpath, lived to old age with the buffalo.

     Hugh L. Scott (n.d.b: MS 2932)

If you could have witnessed the scenes enacted in many of their lodges during the long nights of the winter . . . when some one of their older and more skillful men, fired with enthusiasm by the memories of his youth, was relating his stories of the warpath and adventure, the ancient customs of his people, or the ceremonies of their religion . . . then only could you realize the great force, the intense meaning, and the exceeding gracefulness and beauty of the sign language of the Plains Indian.

     Hugh L. Scott (1898:220)

Contents

List of Illustrations	xi
Acknowledgments	xiii
Introduction	xv
Kiowa Pronunciation Guide	xix
Abbreviations	xxiii

PART I.
INDIAN SIGN LANGUAGE, SCOTT AND HIS CONSULTANTS, AND THE LEDGERS

1.	Plains Indian Sign Language	3
2.	Hugh Lenox Scott (1853–1934)	41
3.	Iseeo, Other Native Consultants, and the Scott Ledgers at Fort Sill	87

PART II.
THE SCOTT LEDGERS AT FORT SILL

4.	Volume I: Indian Sign Language Notes	159

Buffalo Bull Medicine · What Makes the Wind Blow · Wolf Helped a Man [Version A] · Pipe Stems · Buffalo Tail Shield Medicine · Names of Months, Kiowa · [Tribal Names] · Looking for Buffalo · Holding the Buffalo · Tay-bodle—Tsait-an-te's Shield = Sun Shield · Adobe Walls Fight · Quanah · [Comanche Soldier Bands] · Oath · Leaders · Satanta's Medicine Arrow · How to Find a Village · Buffalo Bull Skulls and Taime · Taime · Dead Man Fainting Trance · Man Having Medicine · Crier or Haranguer · Eagle Catching · Dead Man's Medicine · Docto's Medicine · Going to the Medicine · Catching Wild Horses · Wichitas · Kiowa Bands · Spotted Horse Sun Dance · Sun, Moon, and Morning Star · The Pleiades—6 Boys and a Girl · Customs—Hanging · Kiowa Hair Customs · Glue Making · Wichitas and Iseeo · Accidental Killing · Judges/Oaths · [Miscellaneous: Sweat Houses/Tattoos] · [Kiowa Mourning Customs] · [Defensive Earthworks] · [Sun Dance Bison Hunters] · [Seasonal Changes,

Miscellaneous Signs] · [Ten Medicine Bundles—Water Taboo/Rain Medicine] · [Bison Hunting] · [Tipi Making] · Making Rain · Scalping · Property Rights—Kiowas · Counting Coups · Marrying [a] Younger Sister · Thunder and Lightning · Burials · Abandoning Old People · Holding Camp · Tohausen · Names · Omens · Guarding/Holding the Buffalo · Surrounds, Driving Buffalo into Corrals, Etc. · Ponkas · Mescal [Peyote] · Many Scalps Medicines or Ten Medicines · Cholera · Origin [of] Bear Lodge Tower · Angry Lone Wolf, Stumbling Bear, and Kicking Bird · Buffalo Holes · Medicine Butte · Crane's Friend · Scout (Wolf) · Getting Horses · The First and Only Time Peace Was Made between the Kiowas and Pawnees · Kom-au-dy's Shield · Comanche Bands · Origin of Comanches · Comanche Story: How Kiwash Deceived the White Man · Old Lone Wolf Killing Buffalo · White Buffalo · Origin of Ten Medicines, Also of Kiowa People · Star Woman's Tree River—Salt Fork of Red River · Scinday Stories · Turkey · How Scinday Deceived the White Man · Scinday, the Prairie Dogs, and the Coyote · The Wolf and the Rock · How the Crow Came to Be Black · Antelope · Bonee · Arrows · Scinday and the Boy Who Killed the Eagle · Scinday and the Beavers · Scinday and the Bald Headed Eagle · When the Osages Cut Off the Kiowa[s]' Heads · Peace Made with Cheyennes and Arapahoes · Medicine Bluffs · Buffalo Tree · Bear Lodge and Pleiades · Kiowa Bands · Calumet Dance · Night Arrangement with about Four Wide Lodges Day Arrangement · Crazy People and Mad Wolves · Comanches Cure Snakebites · Caddos · Persimmons · Tree Signs · Navajos, April 22, 1908, at Smeth, Utah · Soldier Bands—Kiowa · Men's Names/Places · Descriptions of Signs That May Be Forgotten · Birds[, Snakes, and Plants] · Names: Men and Places · [People] at Bent's Fort · Signals · Paint Mines · [Rattlesnake Bite] · Four Winds · Names of Mountains · Names of Rivers · [Wichita Stream Names] · Deaf and Dumb [Mute] People · Hairpipe or Bone Necklace · Expressions · Signs "A" to "J" · [More] Expressions · Signs "K" to "N" · Seasons · Ages of Buffalo · Time · Signs "O" to "Q" · Indian Names of Each Tribe · Signs "R" to "Z" · Modern Signs

5. Volume II: Sign Language   327

Comanche Months · Comanche Soldier Bands · Arapahos, August 27, 1897 · Cheyennes · Palo Duro Rock—Cheyenne Oath · What Old Kiowas Say about the Crows · Medicine Lake · Thunder · Scinday and Coon · Sapoul · Scinday's Laws · How the Ant Came to Have Such a Slim Midwaist · Scinday and [the] Pawnee · Scinday and the Fight Tree · Scinday and the Girl · Scinday and the Boy · Scinday and Hashmeats/Why Cat Has No Nose and [a] Short Tail · How the Kiowas and Comanches Made Peace · Giving Names · What Shield Keepers Are Afraid Of · Holding the Buffalo · Electing Chiefs · "Lives A Long Time's" Medicine Road · Where Ten Medicines Came from First · Renewing [the] Parfleches of [the] Ten Medicines · Bear Woman's Road · How the Kiowas Got Their Country [Version A] · Cyclones · Cheyenne Massacre (1837) · How the

Kiowas Crossed the Salt Fork Red River (Elm Fork) at High Water · Sitting Down Rock · Kit Carson Fight · Kiowas and Cheyennes Fight (1837) · Comes Over A Ridge's Owl Medicine · Bull Medicine · War Trails · Told by an Old Quahada Comanche Woman · Indian Women · Porcupine · Kiowa Medicine Dance · How Wild Horse (Kiowa) Was Killed · Scinday and the Ghost (Whirlwind) · Scinday, the Bear, and the Tight Tree · Scinday, Sapoodle, and the "Cheet" Bird · Tattooing · Death of Tsait-an-ke (Sitting Bear) · Komauday's Shield Is Called Sun Dance Shield · Scinday's Race with Sapoodle · Scinday and the Flatulent Root · Scinday and the Elk's Head · Scinday and the White Eagle's Medicine · [The] Blind Man and His Wife · Killing Herders near Fort Sill · Buffalo Cow Woman · Breaking a Chief's Bad Road · Scinday and Porcupine · Why the Kiowas Do Not Have Tails · Scinday and Sapoodle · Kiowa Apaches · Antelope Medicine · Buffalo Surround on Foot · Comanche Separation from Shoshones · Kiowa-Comanche-Cheyenne-Arapaho Fight on Wolf Creek · Pawnees Attack Ten Medicine Keeper and Two Other Lodges · Poor Boy · Wolf Helped a Man [Version B] · Tonkaways · Mirage · Kiowa Mountains [and Tribal Names] · Cheyennes, the Makers of Names · [Sign Language] Phrases · First Mention of Horses · The Sign Language · Adequacy of the Sign Language · Synonyms

6. Volume III: Sign Language and Stories and Fables   435

Kiowa Peace with Caddos · How the Kiowas Got Their Country [Version B] · Antelope Udder (Milk Bag) Heart On the Ground Move Away People · Horse Medicine · How Scinday Broke His Legs and Mended Them · How Scinday Deceived Panther · How Scinday's Lodge Burned Up · [Scinday and the Bison Hunt] · [Scinday and the Antelope Kid] · [Zemacouny and the Kiowa Girl] · Scinday Kills Deer Woman · How Scinday Became Blind · Scinday Let Out the Buffalo · Ring or Spear Game · Boys' Ring Game · Arrow Game · Moccasin Game [Hand Game] · [Another] Arrow Game · [Miscellaneous Tribal Information] · Foreword to the Scinday Stories · Zohn-Al or Awl Game of the Kiowas and Kiowa Apaches

Appendix. Troop L, 7th Cavalry Rosters, Fort Sill   455
References   461
Index   479

Illustrations

FIGURES

Panel of Plains Indian Sign Language signs	12
Strange Owl (Cheyenne) and Bird Rattler (Blood) with Hugh L. Scott performing sign language, 1930, Browning, Montana	29
Scott performing the signs for elk and wolf	30
Captain Hugh L. Scott, ca. 1895	48
Camp of Troop L, 7th Cavalry, near Fort Sill Hotel, 1892	61
Kiowa scout Iseeo in native dress	90
Iseeo on horseback at Fort Sill guardhouse	93
Close-up of Sergeant Iseeo in uniform in later years	115
Funeral of Sergeant Iseeo, March 1927, Fort Sill, Oklahoma	116
Installation of the Parker-Iseeo Post, November 11, 1927	121–22
Mobeadleky (Troop L member) and daughter A-ke-a	129
"Buffalo Bull Medicine," from Scott ledger, vol. I	138
Rabbit (Big Dipper) constellation, from Scott ledger, vol. I	196
Hueco Tanks Fight, from Scott ledger, vol. I	210
Hueco Tanks, cave at the rear right of the canyon	211
Arrow styles, from Scott ledger, vol. I	254
Cutthroat Mountain, from Scott ledger, vol. I	263
Kiowa Sun Dance encampment, image A, from Scott ledger, vol. I	266
Calumet Ceremony arrangements, from Scott ledger, vol. I	269
Mount Sheridan (Bull's Face Mountain), from Scott ledger, vol. I	295
Kiowa Sun Dance encampment, image B, from Scott ledger, vol. II	383
Kiowa Sun Dance fan, from Scott ledger, vol. II	391
Kiowa Sun Dance face paint and lodge interior, from Scott ledger, vol. II	392

Wichita tattoos, from Scott ledger, vol. II 398
Diagram of Kiowa awl game, from Scott Collection 452

MAPS

Core area of Plains Indian Sign Language distribution 8
General locations of major sites mentioned in the Scott ledgers 143

Acknowledgments

I WOULD LIKE TO ACKNOWLEDGE SEVERAL INDIVIDUALS WHO contributed to the completion of this project. Foremost I would like to offer my sincere thanks to Towana Spivey (former director), Judith Crowder, and Wade Popp (curator/museum specialist) of the Fort Sill National Historic Landmark and Museum Archives, for facilitating my research on the Hugh L. Scott ledgers from 1989 to 2012 and for many enjoyable discussions. Towana Spivey provided me with a great amount of time in accessing the ledgers over the years. Wade Popp prepared the photographs of the ledgers for publication. I would also like to thank my uncle, the late Kiowa linguist Parker P. McKenzie (1897–1999), for providing translations and linguistic insights on the Kiowa vocabulary and names contained in Scott's notes (including the Kiowa personal names given to Scott) and for information concerning his observations on the use of sign language among the Kiowas during his youth. Gus Palmer, Sr., Harry Domebo, Oscar Tsoodle, Atwater Onco, Jake Ahtone, Vanessa Jennings, Alice Littleman, Delores Totebo Harragarra, Pearl Potiye Bigbow, Dan Ahhaitty, and the Tonemah Family (Kiowa); Forrest Kassanavoid and Ed Yellowfish (Comanche); and Alfred Chalepah, Sr. (Plains Apache) all contributed information on topics related to editing of this work during my fieldwork interviews. My mother, Vanessa Jennings (Kiowa), contributed to this project by providing me with a home at Red Stone, Oklahoma, from which I often traveled to Fort Sill to work on these notes. Kenny Harragarra (Otoe-Kiowa) volunteered three days of assistance in making handwritten copies of portions of the Scott notes. Dr. Candace Greene of the Smithsonian Institution graciously shared copies of materials (Scott n.d.b) that she had from various museums and provided background information on the history of the Scott manuscripts, the accompanying Silverhorn drawings, and earlier attempts to publish them. Daisy Njoku was extremely helpful in making copies of portions of the Scott notes from the National Anthropological Archives. Dr. Thomas Kavanagh and Dr. Daniel Gelo shared information from their Comanche research to assist me with Comanche lexicon and personal names and in developing biographical sketches of some of Scott's Comanche consultants. I would also like to offer my thanks to Dr. Lorene Stone and Dr. Victor Matthews, deans of the College of Humanities and Public Affairs, Missouri State University, for faculty research funds that allowed me to travel to Fort Sill in July 2006 and March 2010 to complete the final collection of data for this project. At Missouri State University I offer my sincere gratitude to Dr. Frank Einhellig, Provost; Dr. Victor Matthews, Dean of the College of Humanities and Public Affairs; and David Rohall, Head of the Department of Sociology and Anthropology, who strongly supported the development of this project. At Missouri State University Rona Babb and Elise Hargiss assisted in portions of the data entry, and Dan McMurray and Florice Pearce aided in checking bibliographic sources against in-text citations. I would also like to offer my thanks to Dr. Jeffrey Davis for sharing his experiences with the Hugh L. Scott film materials on sign language and documents on the Indian Sign Language Councils, to Dr. Davis and Cody Christopher Klecka for providing an image of Scott signing at this event, and to Kay Yandell for insights on her research (Yandell 2012). At the University of Oklahoma Press I would like to offer my sincere thanks to editors Alessandra Jacobi Tamulevich, Thomas Krause, and Emily Jerman Schuster and for the fine work of copy editor Kathy Lewis and two anonymous readers for their constructive critique of the manuscript and their excellent suggestions to improve it. Finally, my sincere thanks to a number of anonymous donors who contributed subvention funds to lower the cost of the publication of this volume, and thereby lower the sales price to make the volume more available for the public.

Introduction

THIS VOLUME MAKES AVAILABLE A UNIQUE COLLECTION OF ethnographic field notes about Plains Indians written by Lieutenant (later Captain) Hugh Lenox Scott between 1889 and 1897 while serving as an officer in the United States Army at Fort Sill in Indian and later Oklahoma Territory. Fort Sill is unique in that it remains the only active army installation of all the forts on the southern plains built during the Indian Wars, in part due to Scott's efforts. From 1891 to 1897 Scott was in charge of Troop L, 7th Cavalry at Fort Sill. Under Colonel George Armstrong Custer this unit had been entirely wiped out at the Battle of the Little Bighorn in 1876. Ironically, fifteen years later it was reconstituted as an all-Indian unit at Fort Sill, where it functioned from June 30, 1891, to May 31, 1897, under Scott's command. Scott's notoriety came not through his military prowess but through his skill in diplomacy, peacemaking, and peacekeeping with Native American communities, with some of which he held a friendship for over sixty years. Scott collected this body of ethnographic material primarily from a few members of Troop L, in particular a Kiowa named Iseeo and other tribal elders. Iseeo was not only a principal source of much of the information collected by Scott but also aided in collecting stories from other elders and in arranging meetings with tribal elders, sometimes translating their spoken accounts through sign language.[1]

The procurement of these accounts is unique in that they were communicated not through speech or observation but through Plains Indian Sign Language (PISL), in which Scott was highly accomplished, and then recorded in handwritten English. The narratives are thus direct

---

[1] These materials are located in the Fort Sill Museum Archives, Fort Sill, Oklahoma, Collection No. 266, Box 21, ledgerbook volumes I–IV. Additional manuscripts, with some duplication of the Fort Sill materials, are in the collection of the National Anthropological Archives of the Smithsonian Institution and the Library of Congress in Washington, D.C.

translations and transcriptions from Plains Indian Sign Language and retain much of the syntax of that language. These texts are perhaps the largest source of ethnographic data collected before the late twentieth century through Plains Indian Sign Language and recorded in writing.

This project grew out of my periodic examinations of the Scott ledgers at the Fort Sill Museum archives between 1989 and 2012 while conducting research on the Kiowa, Comanche, and Plains Apache communities. From 1989 to 1995 I visited the Fort Sill Museum archives frequently to examine the ledgers. During this time I surveyed the ledgers and developed a table of contents for them by topic and pages. This work was a seminal part of my initial experience in learning how to conduct ethnohistorical research with primary documents and allowed me to develop a grasp of the ledgers' contents and to determine the extent of their use in existing literature, which led to this project.

During this time army policy dictated that an individual could hand-copy notes during visits and could receive up to fifteen pages of Xerox copies per visit, which the museum staff would copy and mail to the researcher. The limited museum budget and facilities for copying materials (the army could not install a Xerox machine for paying customers) made working with the Scott ledgers a very tedious and time-consuming experience. Nevertheless, through the kindness of Towana Spivey, Judith Crowder, and Wade Popp, I continued to work on the ledgers as time permitted, becoming familiar with Scott's handwriting and abbreviation style and collecting handwritten transcriptions and Xeroxed copies of portions of the notes, which facilitated the later editing of these ledgers.

Only portions of the Scott ledgers have been published, in part due to limited access and not being available online. The most significant use of data from these ledgers has been in two articles by Scott (1907, 1911) and more extensively in two books by Wilbur S. Nye (1937, 1962), who was later stationed at Fort Sill. Some of the material published by Nye (1962) was collected from Iseeo by Hugh Scott (cf. Nye 1962:xix, 15–19, 91–93, 127–31, 155–56, 178–80, 222–26, 257–58) or obtained by Nye from Kiowa historian George Hunt, who acknowledged having learned much of it from his uncle Iseeo. William Meadows (1999, 2008, 2010), Candace Greene (2009), Greene and Reuss (1993), and others have used small portions of these notes (or copies in other institutions) in a variety of works on Indians of the southern plains. The majority of data in these ledgers have never been used in popular or scholarly fields and thus represent an important primary source of ethnographic information on Indians of the southern plains.

The focus of this work is primarily ethnographic rather than linguistic. While the history of sign language studies and some aspects of linguistics are addressed in chapter 1, the primary focus of this book is on providing a body of ethnographic data as a reference and resource rather than a formal linguistic analysis of the morphology, grammar, syntax, kinesics, and use of Plains Indian Sign Language. There are two primary reasons for this approach. First, a complete linguistic analysis of such a large body of data is beyond the scope and length of this project. Second, Scott's writing style, which consists of lengthy accounts written in longhand English from signed language, often lacks articles and tense agreement and contains very little punctuation. Thus without some editing, this body of data in the form it was recorded does not lend itself to study by the broader range of scholars interested in the ethnographic and historical information. In terms of linguistic significance, however, Scott's notes may represent the longest texts ever recorded from Plains Indian Sign Language. Thus a future linguistic analysis of the original written texts may offer potential research into varied aspects of this unique form of communication. For the most recent works on the linguistic and historical aspects of Plains Indian Sign Language, see Farnell (1995a) and Davis (2010).

The Scott ledgers contain a wide array of ethnographic, historic, and linguistic data that will be of use to peoples of the Southern Plains Indian cultures, academics from different fields who study these cultures, and lay readers interested in the history of the southern plains. Focusing on Scott's association with Plains Indian Sign Language, this volume completes the earlier historical work on Scott by James Harper (1968) and a forthcoming biography by historian Armand La Potin. This book is organized into six chapters and an appendix. Chapter 1 provides a brief overview of the origins, nature, and history of Plains Indian Sign Language; its study in the field of anthropology; and the nature of Scott's notes. Chapter 2 offers a biographical sketch of H. L. Scott, providing the historical and cultural context. The chapter describes how Scott learned sign language, how he and Iseeo met and communicated, how they served and interacted over nine years at Fort Sill, and how sign language continued to have importance for both men for the rest of their lives and includes an outline of Scott's military-related service. Chapter 3 provides a biographical sketch of Iseeo and his military service, along with briefer sketches of other identified consultants that Scott collected data from. This chapter concludes with an analysis of the content and nature of Scott's Fort Sill Ledgers (tribal focus, topical subjects, unique characteristics, writing style, editorial choices, previous use of material from the ledgers, and suggestions for future use of the ledgers). Chapters 4, 5, and 6 present the ethnographic data contained in volumes I, II, and III of Scott's Fort Sill ledgers. The appendix provides rosters of the Indian members of Troop L, 7th United States Cavalry, at Fort Sill from June 30, 1891, to May 31, 1897.

Kiowa Pronunciation Guide

THIS WORK USES THE PARKER P. MCKENZIE KIOWA ORTHOGRAPHY (Meadows and McKenzie 1999). Because Kiowa is a tonal language, it is necessary to mark syllable pitch and length for accuracy. I use the McKenzie orthography because it was developed by a fluent Kiowa speaker who was intimately familiar with the subtleties of the Kiowa language and because I find it to be the most accurate, thorough, consistent, and easy to use non-IPA (International Phonetic Alphabet) orthography for writing Kiowa. The McKenzie orthography was designed by using the English alphabet to enable writing on a typewriter and then adding handwritten diacritical markings. Today computers and linguistic font programs facilitate the full use of this system.

VOWEL QUALITIES
Tone

All Kiowa vowels contain high, low, or high-low tones. Using the letter *a*, these include: *á* (high short), *à* (low short), and *â* (high-low or rising and falling, also known as a circumflex), as reflected in the words *pán* (sky), *hàu* (yes), and *hîn* (dig).

Length

The length of vowels in Kiowa may also indicate a contrasting element in pronunciation or meaning. A macron above vowels marks length (a drawn-out vowel), such as *ā́* (high or rising, long) in the word *dā́ugà* (song) and *ā̀* (low or descending, long). Length is a critical factor in denoting meaning in

---

Based on the Parker P. McKenzie Kiowa Orthography (Meadows and McKenzie 1999) and Palmer (2009:200–202).

many Kiowa words. Gus Palmer, Jr. (2009) has replaced the use of an overscore with a colon to denote length (*á:* and *à:*). Having already published at length in the original McKenzie system, however, I prefer to maintain a consistent orthography. The diacritics in McKenzie's orthography both reflect the actual direction of the tone and length and are easily replicable in Unicode "Latin" and "Combining Diacritical Marks" font files.

Nasalization

Many Kiowa words are nasalized. An underscore (_) beneath a vowel marks a nasal tone, as in *chê* (horse). The five tone and length forms (*á, à, á̄, ā̀, â*) can also be nasalized (*á̱, à̱, á̱̄, ā̱̀, â̱*), producing ten possible pronunciations of a syllable, although not all correspond to Kiowa words or uses. When nasalization occurs in a diphthong the first vowel in a syllable is underscored, as in *kyôi* (shield), but the entire diphthong is sounded as a nasal.

Consonants

Kiowa contains twenty-two consonantal sounds. Fourteen are consistent with the English alphabet (*b, d, g, h, k, l, m, n, p, s, t, w, y, z*) and are pronounced relatively the same. The remaining eight Kiowa consonants have no direct correlation to Kiowa sounds and are represented by reassigned English consonants to represent variations of *c, k, p,* and *t*, which Parker McKenzie referred to as the "distinctive" Kiowa sounds. The reassigned consonants include *c, q, f, v, ch, x, j,* and *th*. The consonants *k, p, s,* and *t* all have two additional variations in Kiowa: unaspirated (soft) and hard or ejective (plosive), for which English has no counterpart. These variants produce the following four clusters of related sounds.

    c = a soft (unaspirated) (k) sound, as in "Scot."
    k = a regular (k) sound, as in "kite."
    q = a hard or ejective (k) sound, like an aspirated *k*.

    f = a soft (unaspirated) (p) sound, as in "spot."
    p = a regular (p) sound, as in "pack."
    v = a hard or ejective (p) sound, like an aspirated *p*.

    ch = a soft (unaspirated) (s) sound.
    s = a regular (s) sound, as in "so."
    x = a hard or ejective (s) sound, like an aspirated *ts*.

j = a soft (unaspirated) (t) sound.
t = a regular (t) sound, as in "stop."
th = a hard or ejective (t) sound, like an aspirated t.

While both soft and hard sounds can easily be learned with practice, English speakers often do not hear the soft or unaspirated sounds because they do not occur in word-initial positions in English, as they do in Kiowa.

PRONUNCIATION TABLE

Stops	unaspirated	aspirated	glottal	voiced
Labial	P	p^h	p'	b
Kiowa	F	p	v	b
Dental	T	t^h	t'	d
Kiowa	J	t	th	d
Velar	K	k^h	k'	g
Kiowa	C	k	q	g
AFFRICATIVES				
Dental	C	—	c'	—
Kiowa	Ch	—	x	—

VOWELS

Kiowa contains ten vowel elements: six vowels and four diphthongs. The six Kiowa vowels are much like their English counterparts except for the Kiowa vowel a, which falls midway in sound (shown in parentheses below), as in the words "act" and "arm." Unlike English vowels, which can have more than one pronunciation (as with the letter a in "arm," "meat," and so forth), each Kiowa vowel has only one basic sound. The six Kiowa vowels (with their pronunciations in parentheses) are:

    e   (ay) as in "day"
    A   (ah) as in "father"
    au   (aw) as in "caught"
    i   (ee) as in "meet"
    o   (oh) as in "coat"
    u   (woo) as in "boot" but with an initial "w" sound.

Kiowa also contains four diphthongs (syllables containing multiple vowels), with the vowel i (ee) as the second element:

    ai   (ah-ee) as in "bite"
    aui   (aw-ee), which has no English counterpart

oi   (oh-ee) as in "boy"
ui   (woo-ee) as in "Louie" but with an initial "w" sound.

Although Kiowa vowels and diphthongs are affected with varying frequency by nasalization, vowel quality or length, and pitch accent or accentuation, they keep their respective sounds.

W and Y Sounds

The vowel *u* (woo) occurs in Kiowa syllables only after the consonants *g*, *k*, *c*, and *q*. The (w) sound associated with the vowel *u* (woo) always falls before the vowel *u* when voiced. Because it is a constant and in order to reduce repetitious spelling, however, the *w* is retained in pronunciation but omitted in written Kiowa: thus *gu* (gwoo), *gui* (gwoo-ee), *ku* (kwoo), *kui* (kwoo-ee), *cu* (cwoo), *cui* (cwoo-ee), *qu* (qwoo), and *qui* (qwoo-ee).

Palatal Glide (y)

When the consonants *g*, *k*, *c*, and *q* precede the letter *a* and diphthong *ai*, a (y) sound is made. Thus *ga* is pronounced (gyah), *gai* (gyah-ee), *ca* (cyah), and *cai* (cyah-ee), respectively. Although the McKenzie system does not mark the palatal glide or (y) sound where it occurs in written form, it is understood and retained in pronunciation. The following words are examples of the palatal glide:

Kiowa word	Pronunciation	English
Câi-gù	kyây-gù	Comanche
dáu-gà	dáu-gyà	song
qá̰-hį̂	k'yá̰-hį̂	man

A few words, mostly of foreign origin, occur without the palatal glide. They are indicated by the presence of an apostrophe, as in C'aiwau (Caiwau, not Cyah-ee-wau), the Comanche pronunciation of "Kiowa." The reader will notice variation in some Kiowa singular and plural forms. Unlike English, which has singular and plural forms, Kiowa has singular, dual (two), and triplural (three or more) forms (designated by the abbreviations s, d, and t). For a complete account of the McKenzie orthography, refer to Meadows and McKenzie (1999).

Abbreviations

FSA   Fort Sill Museum Archives, Fort Sill, Oklahoma
LOC   Manuscript Division, Library of Congress, Washington D.C.
NAA   National Anthropological Archives, Smithsonian Institution, Washington, D.C.
SDSHS   South Dakota State Historical Society, Pierre, South Dakota
USMA   United States Military Academy, West Point, N.Y.

PART I

Indian Sign Language, Scott and His Consultants, and the Ledgers

CHAPTER 1

Plains Indian Sign Language

SIGNS AND GESTURES DATE BACK TO THE EARLIEST RECORDED times, as both a substitute for and a supplement to speech. The use of signs in addition to spoken language continues today in almost all cultures, especially in situations in which sound is impeded by noise, distance, or a need for silence (Davidson 1950:3; Walker 1953:168). Numerous examples of the use of nonvocal forms of communication to facilitate our social relationships are found in religions, occupations, sports, the stock market, political movements, traffic control, and military activities. In addition to the 6,700 known spoken languages of the world, at least two hundred extant signed languages are known (Davis 2010:183; Gordon 2005). Along with a material culture based on the horse, tipi, bison, feathered headdresses, and animal hides, sign language has long been a distinguishing characteristic associated with historic North American Plains Indians. Although best known and recorded among Plains Indians and those groups bordering the plains region, forms of sign language are documented across most of North America. Sign language is employed both as an alternative to speech and as a primary language used by deaf members in at least forty Native American languages in twelve distinct North American language families (phyla), including some groups in every geographic culture area. While North American Indians are known to have used several forms of sign language, the form known as standard Plains Indian Sign Language (PISL) is the best documented. During its apogee, PISL was used throughout the plains and adjacent regions in a geographic area of over 1.5 million square miles, equal to the European Union's twenty-seven member states combined (Davis 2006:8, 2010:6–8, 171).

Plains Indian Sign Language is the most sophisticated of all known North American Indian nonspeech communication systems. It consists of an extensive vocabulary of physical hand and body signs and movements to signify individual words, phrases, and concepts. Sign language is a communication system independent of spoken language and thus not an alternative system of expression, such as the relationship between a spoken language and its written form. Just as the placement of the tongue and lips determines speech sounds, sign language is produced by placing one or both hands in varied positions (open, closed, fingers extended or curved, and so forth) and motions. Signs are both iconic (physically resembling what they refer to) and symbolic (containing an arbitrary or conventionally agreed upon relation between sign and meaning). While PISL is largely iconic, convention has been a significant factor in its evolution and use. Because sign language can make effective use of icons by devising gestures that resemble their referents, humans of different language groups often resort to the use of gestures to communicate (Taylor 1996:278).

In the late nineteenth and early twentieth centuries several U.S. writers referred to the ability of Native American peoples to communicate over distance through a variety of means known as the "moccasin telegraph." Ethnographic accounts and Indian autobiographies describe the use of varied forms of signal chains using smoke signals, mirrors (heliograph flashes), piles of stones or other materials, bent tree limbs (turning trees), relay runners, animal calls, distanced signaling using the body, robes, horses, lances, or thrown dirt, tracking skills, and sign language (Gelo 2012:381–83; Yandell 2012:535). Yandell (2012:535, 555–56) reports that by the late nineteenth century at least some Indians had expanded the range of their telegraphing capabilities by using telescopes to pass signs to others over several miles. Before the Battle of the Little Bighorn, a number of Crow scouts using telescopes created a "sight chain" by spreading out at several points that enabled them to pass sign-language communications on three separate occasions to the U.S. encampment faster than by horse or foot. Plenty Coups (Linderman 1962) reports numerous instances in which he used a telescope in scouting and identifying game, villages, and enemies. As Jeffrey Davis (1997:115) notes, tribal, regional, historical, and other variants of Native American Sign Language existed, but the best-documented cases are from the Great Plains, southwestern United States, and northwestern Canada.

During the historic period (circa post-1540) so many languages existed in the plains region that verbal communication was often difficult. As Marianne Mithun (1999:1) notes, while the languages of Europe are classified into only three language families (Indo-European, Finno-Ugric, and Basque), North American languages belong to over fifty language families. Although the exact factors leading to the development of PISL are unknown, several elements may have contributed, including communication by and with the deaf, intertribal gatherings and councils, spontaneous signing in interactions between peoples who speak different languages, situations requiring silent communication (such as warfare and hunting contexts), and communication across distances that inhibit adequate verbal communication. Hugh L. Scott recorded several instances of sign language use between tribes during conflict situations. The development of extensive cross-cultural exchange via prehistoric trade networks, travel, and social intercourse, which only increased with the rise of plains equestrianism, also likely contributed to the development and growth of sign language. Because the core demographic area for bison hunting closely resembled the area of sign language use, John Peabody Harrington (1938) suggested that the constant intermingling of diverse groups with different languages in pursuit of this animal prompted the development of sign language. The need for increased cross-cultural communication across greater distances would likely have arisen from this situation and probably contributed to the number of regional sign language systems that developed on the plains. Hunting and warfare situations that required silence provided other uses for sign language but were probably not the primary factors contributing to its development. Jeffrey Davis and Melanie McKay-Cody (2010:150–51) classify traditional Indian sign language into five forms: intertribal communication; storytelling; rituals; distance communications during raids, war, and hunting parties; and use involving deaf family members.

Although some local languages such as Chinook, Comanche, Lakota, and Apache became lingua francas, none was widespread enough to dominate the entire plains region economically, politically, and thus linguistically as languages such as English, Spanish, and Chinese have in other regions. As Davis (2010:12) notes, "The lack of a single dominant group in the Plains cultural area may be a reason for the adoption of the signed language over any particular spoken language." Thus Davis (2005b:49) suggests linguistic heterogeneity as a major factor: "Over many generations, signed language appears to have emerged as a way to make communications possible between individuals speaking so many different mother tongues." These communication systems became known as Indian sign language or, more accurately, Plains Indian Sign Language (West 1960; Taylor 1996; Farnell 1996). PISL became a lingua franca used primarily by hearing American Indians who were already fluent in at least one spoken language. "In brief, primary sign systems are developed, acquired, and used by deaf people as a first language, whereas the so-called alternate sign systems are developed, transmitted, and used by hearing individuals already competent in a spoken language" (Davis 2010:180).

William P. Clark noted the need to learn the cultural context of Indian life in order to comprehend the conceptions of sign language and to become proficient in the language, which has its own syntax. As Clark (1885:18) described it, "articles, conjunctions, and prepositions are omitted, and adjectives follow the nouns. Verbs are used in the present tense; nouns and verbs are used in a singular number, the idea of plurality being expressed in some other way. Abbreviation is constantly practiced." Clark (1885:17–18) provided a hypothetical example of the relationship between speech and sign language.

> I arrived here to-day to make a treaty,—my one hundred lodges are camped beyond the Black Hills, near the Yellowstone River. You are a great chief,—pity me, I am poor, my five children are sick and have nothing to eat. The snow is deep and the weather intensely cold. Perhaps God sees me. I am going. In one month I shall reach my camp.

In sign language this would be conveyed in the following order of syntax;

> I—arrive here—to-day—to make—treaty. My—hundred—lodge—camp—beyond—Hills—Black—near—river—called—Elk—you—chief—great—pity me—I poor—My—five—child—sick—food—all gone (or wiped out)—Snow—deep—cold—brave or strong. Perhaps—chief great (or Great Mystery)—above—see—me—I—go. Moon—die—I—arrive there—my—camp.

Origins

While the exact origin of Plains Indian Sign Language is unknown, both mythological and historical references exist. Native American accounts reference times, past and present, when animals and humans could speak verbally to one another. This also sometimes applied to the use of sign language. Pretty Shield (Linderman 1972:188) provided an account in which a white bear, serving as a spiritual helper to a Crow woman and her child, spoke to her on several occasions but in one instance at a distance "signed to her to come alone to him to hear what he had to say." Another account collected by Scott (vol. I:135, chapter 4 in this volume) comes from one of the Kiowa origin stories and involves the Kiowa culture heroes known as the Twin Boys and the trickster Scinday (Sainday, Sinday, and properly Séndé). This account describes a time when Indians could not speak and used sign language. Like most oral and religious history, this account ethnocentrically places the storyteller's group at the center of the universe. The Twin Boys meet Scinday and travel west with him to his territory. Each boy marries a medicine woman, and Scinday marries the other four. All Indian people descend from these marriages. After Scinday placed the sun in the sky, Indian people began to increase more quickly. Scinday then called a council of all the people together and created hearing and spoken language to supersede sign language.

> one time Scinday called them all together to a big council and told them to come up one at a time. He rubbed some medicine in the palm of his hand, like rubbing tobacco, and spit in it, and put his fingers on it and when a man came up he rubbed his finger on his lips and poked his finger in his ears, bored his ears so he could hear, and then they told him to speak. And when he spoke to suit him he put them aside and did the same to another man, making them to speak and understand different languages. Before that they used only the sign language, but now they spoke different languages—Cheyenne, Pawnee, Sioux, Wichita, Kiowa, Comanche, and Apache, all different.

Historical accounts describing the use of Native American sign language date to the 1520s. Conquistador Alvar Núñez Cabeza de Vaca (Covey 1993; Wurtzburg and Campbell 1995:154–55) reported several instances of groups using sign language during his travels from 1527 to 1535 in what is now the region of Florida to Arizona and northern Mexico and kept notes regarding linguistic affiliations. Pedro de Castañeda in the expedition led by Francisco Vázquez de Coronado also recorded the presence of sign language among several southern plains tribes in 1540–42, and sign language is firmly documented among multiple Texas Indian groups in the 1740s. Conversely, sign language is not recorded in the northern plains until much later and is believed to have spread across the central and northern plains after the 1740s. George Drouillard, the son of a French trader and a Shawnee mother, was hired by Meriwether Lewis as a "civilian interpreter" to accompany the Lewis and Clark expedition of 1803–1806. In addition to being a skilled hunter, guide, and scout, he was hired primarily because he knew sign language, which he is recorded using with the varied tribes that they encountered along the way in several instances.[1] While William Samarin (1987) argues against

---

[1] Drouillard is celebrated in the historical novel *Sign-Talker* by frontier novelist James Alexander Thom (2000).

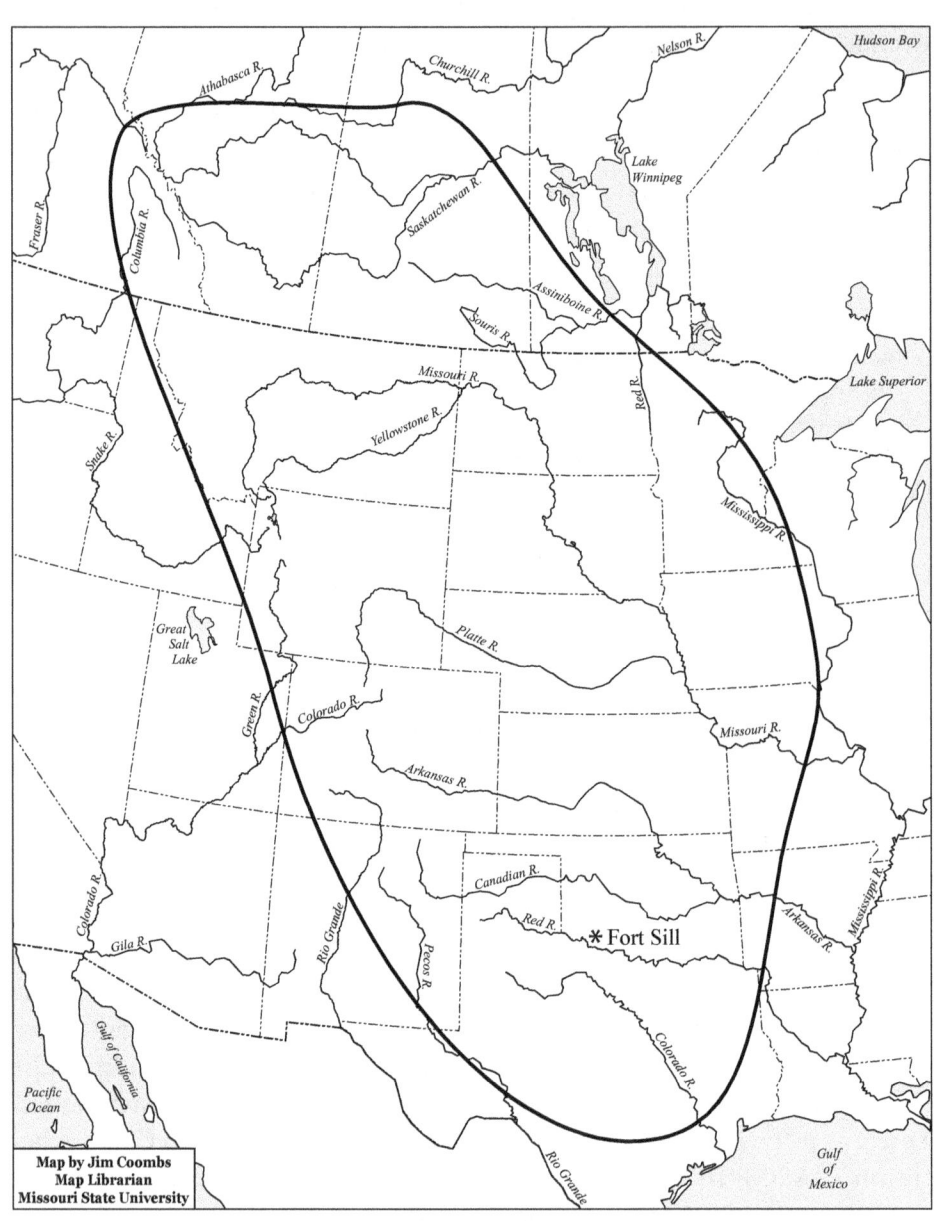

Core area of Plains Indian Sign Language distribution.
Map by Jim Coombs, Maps Librarian, Missouri State University.
Copyright © 2015, University of Oklahoma Press.

the precontact existence of Indian Sign Language, Susan Wurtzburg and Lyle Campbell (1995) provide numerous examples from Louisiana, Texas, and northern Mexico. Subsequent reports of sign language continue into the nineteenth century.

Historical evidence suggests that PISL may have originated in the region of the Texas Gulf Coast and northern Mexico (Clark 1885:11–13; Tomkins 1926:89; Goddard 1979; Wurtzburg and Campbell 1995). According to Jeffrey Davis (2006:6–7), "The generally accepted hypothesis among scholars (see Campbell 1997; Mithun 1999) is that North American Indian Sign Language originated and spread from the Gulf Coast, became the intertribal lingua franca of the Great Plains, and spread throughout the northwest territories of the United States and Canada." Alan Taylor (1996:275) further suggests that trade may have stimulated the development of sign language, as it was clearly a major factor in its diffusion after the arrival of the horse.

Davis (2010:182) suggests that PISL may have originated with the deaf. "PISL has been transmitted from one generation to the next and acquired as the primary and secondary language by deaf and hearing members of these communities. PISL most likely developed from the emergent-signed language of tribal members who were deaf or with deaf family members; and, over time, members of the larger hearing community acquired it as an alternative to spoken language. As PISL was transmitted from one generation to the next, and acquired by both deaf and hearing Indian participants, it was linguistically expanded with greater lexical and grammatical complexity."

Although sign language became the most extensive lingua franca on the plains after about 1740, not all tribes were recognized as equally proficient in its use (West 1960; Taylor 1996:275; Farnell 1996). As Taylor (1996:275) describes, "Kiowas are frequently mentioned in the nineteenth century as excellent sign talkers, and this tribe was certainly a center of dissemination of sign use in the Southern Plains." Geographically the Kiowas held an intermediate position between the tribes of Texas and the tribes of the northern plains. The Comanches, Cheyennes, and Arapahos were also highly regarded as sign talkers by some observers.[2]

Two accounts recorded by Scott state that the Kiowas and Comanches acquired the sign language from the Cheyennes and imply, at least based on their views, that it may have originated with the Cheyennes. According to one account (Scott n.d.a:II:161–64; chapter 5 in this volume) from

---

2   Harrington (1938) notes that the prevalence of sign language among these three tribes figured in a "Ripley's Believe It Or Not" series.

a Kiowa man, "born two summers after the stars fell" (1833, thus born in 1835), who discusses the Kiowas' time in the northern plains, women were well versed in sign language and the Kiowas may have learned sign language from the Cheyennes. "When we live[d] up there and fought the Cheyennes we had different languages and then [the] Cheyennes made the sign language and we used that all the time I was growing up. The Cheyennes know that better than any other tribes, they made [it]. We do not see that now like we used to see it. Women and everybody knew it then." Similarly another account recorded by Scott from the Comanche named Cabaya (Scott n.d.a:I:120, chapter 4 in this volume) states, "The Comanche sign was given us by the Cheyennes without doubt. They made the sign language and gave the names to the Kiowas, Comanches, Apaches, and Arapahoes in signs." As Scott (1898) noted, members of every tribe that he asked stated that PISL was of great antiquity, noted that it was handed down to them as their spoken languages were, and attributed its origins to other tribes. Thus, instead of attempting to link the origins of PISL to a single ethnic group, Scott believed that all tribes that used sign language had some influence on its development.

Farnell (1996) suggests other possible factors that characterized and may have promoted the use of sign language in the protohistoric and historic eras. First, no single plains nation was economically dominant, so neither did any one spoken language dominate. Hence Plains peoples may have maximized the human tendency to resort to gestures in communicating with peers who only spoke other languages. Second, Plains Indians did not view gestures as "primitive" or less sophisticated than vocal gestures (speech), thus considering sign language to be a respectable mode of communication (unlike long-held European views). Third, Plains Indian Sign Language is heavily icon based (signs resembling the objects and actions they refer to) and indexical (using grammatical pointing gestures), often making sign languages easier and quicker to learn than the arbitrary signs (abstract sound combinations) in spoken languages. Fourth, gestures common to two or more groups may have been accepted or rejected in situations with increased intertribal travel and trade. Although no single sign language developed, these processes would have led to a standard sign system in a region, perhaps beginning as a signed pidgin. Frequent users would have extended the vocabulary and created grammatical rules to the point that a fully developed sign language emerged. Skilled sign talkers who were well traveled and frequently represented their respective populations in intertribal contexts such as trade and diplomacy would have fostered this scenario. According to Clark (1885:6) a skilled sign talker was able to recognize signs exhibiting a wide range of variations, "provided that they contain the radical or essential part."

USE

Sign language appears to have been used more extensively by men, probably due to their greater role and visibility in public life and intertribal relations. This perhaps reflects an ethnographic bias of the period, including greater documentation of their use. But use of sign language by women is well recorded in nineteenth- and twentieth-century accounts and in the personal accounts of elders interviewed during my fieldwork since 1989. Signing was also common between members of the same tribe as a part of everyday communication that added meaning to speech in many contexts, especially to accompany storytelling and public oratory (Farnell 1996; Davis 2010:77). Frank Bird Linderman (1972:16) notes how the Crow woman Pretty Shield simultaneously signed to him while speaking Crow to their translator Goes Together, although at times she continued to speak while ceasing to sign. In one instance after she stopped signing, Linderman (1972:51–52) noted that from "the merriment of both women, I guessed that these details were not for me." Pretty Shield continued, commenting: "It was just a women's joke. Now I will go on with my story." Recent reexaminations of the historic and ethnographic record of American Indian Sign Language (Taylor 1996:276; Davis 2005b:61, 2006:4–5) indicate that, in addition to serving as an intertribal lingua franca, signed language was used intratribally and intertribally for numerous discourse purposes, including for storytelling; in gender-specific activities; during periods when speech was taboo, such as mourning; for ritual practices such as chanting, singing, and prayer; and in everyday use between friends and family members.

Sign language was learned at an early age. Clark (1885:9) reported seeing a three-year-old deaf-mute Indian child converse in sign language. Sign language enabled the inclusion of otherwise marginalized community members such as the hearing-impaired, the elderly, and preverbal children. Sign language also allowed speakers from very different verbal languages not only to engage one another but to enrich their intertribal, intercultural exchanges (Yandell 2012:536). Referring to the Kiowas and Plains Apaches (Kiowa-Apaches), Major Stephen H. Long (1823:2:186) noted that the "Kiawa [sic]" and "Kaskaia [sic]," who spoke

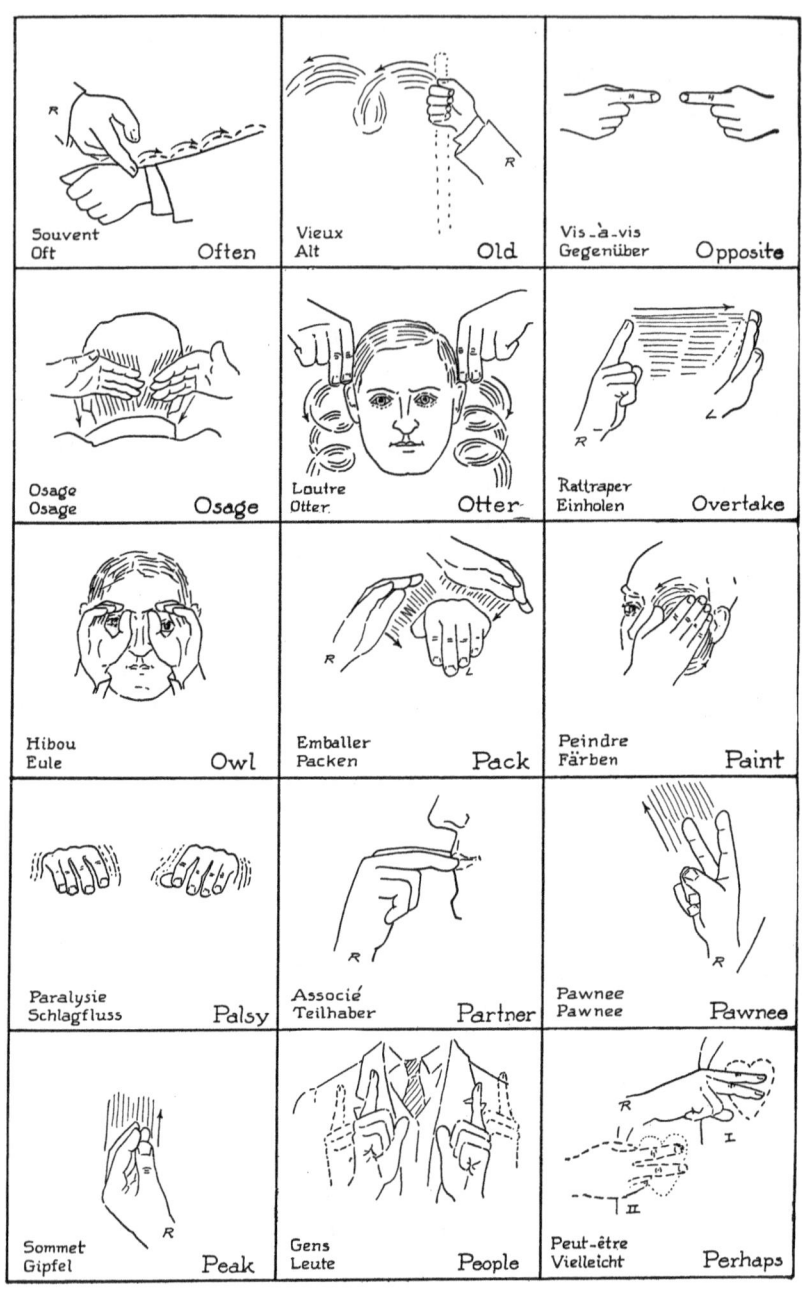

Panel of Plains Indian Sign Language signs.
Line drawing shows beginning of movement of hands;
dotted outline shows end of movement. From William Tomkins,
Universal Indian Sign Language of the Plains Indians of North America
(1926:44). *Courtesy of Dover Publications, Inc., Mineola, N.Y.*

totally unrelated languages but had frequent close contact and interaction, understood one another only through signs.

While many early observers assumed that Plains Indian Sign Language was homogeneous, comparison of published descriptions indicates that PISL was not uniform. In addition to tribal and regional differences in lexicon, individual and tribal variations in body stance, techniques of sign execution, and speed of delivery also existed. In many areas signing was accompanied by speech, paralleling, commenting on, or in some instances differing from the content of the signs. Two northern plains dialects and a southern plains dialect have been identified (West 1960). The use of faster motions, more restrained and smaller hand movements, and single hand and finger positions is characteristic of the southern plains, while the use of the whole hand, both hands, and larger and freer movements is typical of the northern plains (West 1960; Taylor 1996:281–82; Farnell 1996; Davis 2010:12).

Sign language also evolved as new signs were created for new cultural practices and forms of material culture. Clark (1885:15) describes how the introduction of the coffee grinder changed the sign for coffee from representing the grains to the grinding motion of the grinder. Scott collected several new sign language terms for modern items in the 1890s, including Jesus (Cross Man Above), interest (money's child), marshal (prisoner chief), picture (write looking glass), petroleum (fire water), and vaccinate (cut arm in back, place medicine).

One of the least explored aspects of Plains Indian Sign language is its use in military contexts between tribes. The Crow woman Pretty Shield (Linderman 1972:52, 79) described how scouts (regularly employed at distances around a camp while moving) frequently used sign language to relay information back to the main camp. "There was always danger of attack by our enemies, so that far ahead, on both sides, and behind us, there were our wolves [scouts] who guarded us against surprise as we traveled. The men were ever watching these wolves, and we women constantly watched the men." She also described instances of sign use: "I saw . . . one of our wolves signal 'The enemy is coming. Look out for yourselves.'" She added: "But always our chief sent out his wolves . . . to the high places to watch for enemies, so that we women felt safe enough" (Linderman 1972:22, 55, 100).

Intertribal use of sign language between hostile tribes is widely documented. Jack Doyeto (1870–1937), a Kiowa, relates five instances of how sign language was used in scouting and combat situations involving Kiowas,

Comanches, Cheyennes, and Utes on the southern plains.[3] The Crow chief Plenty Coups (Linderman 1962:136, 163, 268) describes using sign language to communicate with Lakotas across a river before fighting and with Métis Indians. Pretty Shield (Linderman 1972:174–75, 241) describes the use of sign language between Crows and Lakotas as well as between Crows on opposite sides of a river. She concluded her life history (Linderman 1972:222–47) with an account of how her husband, Goes Ahead, one of several Crow scouts serving under General George A. Custer, used sign language while scouting before the Battle of the Little Bighorn. As Yandell (2012:552) describes, "In so doing, she repeats one of the few survivor eyewitness accounts of the event, provides an alternative to the nineteenth- and twentieth-century history most Americans are taught, and surprises readers with a vital role of sign talk in the battle, which in most accounts remains almost wholly unexamined." Luther Standing Bear (1988:74–75) noted that sign language routinely prevented war on the plains.

Sign language was not limited to economic, political, and conflict venues but was also important in social contexts where individuals shared aspects of their life experiences and entertained visitors, especially those of different linguistic backgrounds. During his youth Parker McKenzie (1897–1999) described seeing his grandfather Que-ton (Wéjàn) a Mexican captive who lived as an adult among the Kiowas, visit with other warriors of neighboring tribes in the early 1900s. McKenzie described one instance in which his grandfather, along with a number of Comanches, Cheyennes, Plains Apaches, and Kiowas, spent the evening taking turns telling warfare exploits as well as humorous stories and jokes. They all spoke their native languages for members of their own tribe, while simultaneously signing the story for the members of other tribes. When I asked if the timing of the two systems was in sync, he replied, "Let me put it this way; when one of them told a joke, everyone laughed at the same time."[4]

While at Fort Sill, Scott (vol. I:216, chapter 4 in this volume) described four deaf Indians he knew, a Comanche boy, a Kiowa man, and two Kiowa women, all of whom he described as "good sign talkers." Among the Kiowas, sign language was known as *tháumgá* (literally, hand motion/

---

3   Doyeto's references are contained in the following accounts: "Stories of the Early Life of the Kiowas and Comanches," "History of the Second Group of Kiowas on the War Path," "History of the Following Story, a Year after the Battle with the Ute Indians," "History of Indians When Going Out on the War Path, and the Usual Ways They Have in Going from Camp to the Distant Land," and "History of the Vicinity around Now Which Is Elk City (about 4 or 5 Miles south of the city)" (Scott n.d.b: MS 2932, Box 2, Kiowa).

4   Parker McKenzie (Kiowa) to the author, Aug. 28, 1994. See Clark (1885:14–15) for a similar reference.

signal). Parker McKenzie (1991) lists tháumgá as a noun denoting (1) the act of signaling by hand or arm and (2) the sign language. Born in 1897, he stated that usually only the oldest Kiowa men could use sign language fully during his youth; by then most older people used it only partially. McKenzie reported that sign language was used by members of different tribes, to accompany spoken language as a supplement to speech, and by deaf people. Olive Goomdaw (born 1898), for example, was a deaf-mute Kiowa woman who used sign language. Deaf-mutes were known in Kiowa as thàumhátdàu (hand/arm-imitators or gesturers/signalers, meaning hand signalers). Kiowas also used sign language to supplement their speech, even when talking to other Kiowas. McKenzie recalled that his brother-in-law, Bert Geikaunmah (1881–1967), often did this.[5]

Studies of Sign Language

Sign language has interested a wide range of North American observers over the past 250 years. Brief descriptions of PISL have been recorded by early explorers, missionaries, military personnel, government officials, amateur and professional ethnographers, and linguists (Dunbar 1809; Long 1823:1:378–94; Wied-Neuwied 1843; Ruxton 1848; Marcy 1866:32–34; Dodge 1877:394–97, 1882; Clark 1885; Hadley 1890, 1893; Scott 1898; Humfreville 1899:108–11; Seton 1918; Tomkins 1926; Webb 1931; Walker 1953). Many explorers and military officers wrote accounts of their experiences on the plains. As early as 1800 William Dunbar wrote a brief paper focusing on sign languages of Asian and North American Indian cultures that was combined with descriptions of fifty-eight signs from tribes west of the Mississippi River. The paper was read by Thomas Jefferson the following year at the American Philosophical Society and later published (Dunbar 1809).

Major Stephen H. Long (1823:I:378–94) provided a pioneering study by collecting a list of 104 PISL signs and describing the vital role that sign language played during an expedition into the Rocky Mountains in 1819–20. Thomas H. Gallaudet, who co-founded the first school for the deaf in the United States in 1817, used Long's descriptions of Indian signs in support of the use of "the Natural Language of Signs" in teaching and communication with the deaf (Davis 2007:104).

---

5   McKenzie to the author, Aug. 28, 1994. The syllable hát occurs in several Kiowa words associated with mocking, jesting, ridiculing, and making fun of (McKenzie 1991), which in this compound suggests imitating through signing.

More formal efforts to record PISL were not undertaken until the last quarter of the nineteenth century, however, largely by a number of military officers stationed in the American West. These included Colonel Richard I. Dodge, 11th Infantry, U.S. Army; Colonel Garrick Mallery, U.S. Army Signal Corps; Captain William Philo Clark, 2nd Cavalry, U.S. Army; and Lieutenant Hugh L. Scott, 7th Cavalry, U.S. Army. While some of these writings were more systematic and scholarly, others briefly record the officers' experiences with Plains Indians, a common genre of writing in the late nineteenth and early twentieth century.

Richard I. Dodge (1877) published a few comments on PISL in a larger work on Plains Indians and later (Dodge 1882:379–94) provided a brief chapter on Plains Indian Sign Language, attributing its origins to extensive contact with other groups through hunting and warfare. Dodge recognized PISL as a true language, recorded several syntactical patterns and regional and individual patterns in signing, and listed fifty-one signs for tribal names, kin terms, seasons, increments of time, and numbers. However, it is puzzling that Dodge (1877:390) never observed a woman, child, or young man "at all reliable in signs." Captain J. Lee Humfreville (1899:108–11) briefly commented on his experiences in observing and using sign language with Plains Indians. Brigadier General Albert J. Meyer, chief signal officer of the Army Signal Corps from 1866 to 1880, was a surgeon with an interest in sign language. Influenced by the Plains Indian use of distance signaling, Meyer developed a system of military communication by signals (Dodge 1882:316, 379).

Garrick Mallery (1880a, 1880b, 1880c, 1881, 1882) provided the first extensive studies of sign language. Several of his works (Mallery 1880a, 1880b, 1882) provide extensive comparisons of PISL with other verbal and nonverbal codes, descriptions of types of hand positions used in gesture language, and theories on its characteristics, formation, and origins. Published as proof sheets intended for future revisions by individuals who had contributed lists of signs, Mallery's work (1880a) included an alphabetical but unillustrated dictionary of 631 signs with translations, a dictionary of tribal signs, and texts of sign language. Mallery (1880a, 1880b) also provided important lists of individuals and sources of the signs they collected and comparative descriptions of intertribal sign vocabulary. The following year Mallery (1881) published a work based on excerpts from his earlier work (Mallery 1880a) with numerous diagrams of signs, illustrations, and accompanying general material on sign language. Along with Clark (1885), *A Collection of Gesture Signs* (Mallery 1880a) is one of the largest

PISL vocabularies compiled. Significantly, Mallery (1881, 1882) disputed Dodge's conclusion that a single Indian sign language existed, based on a lack of data. Although several regional variations of Plains Indian Sign Language existed in the nineteenth century, Mallery demonstrated that skilled sign talkers were able to understand one another across the plains.

William P. Clark (1885) became fluent in sign language from extended interaction with nearly three hundred Indian scouts (Pawnee, Shoshone, Arapaho, Cheyenne, Crow, and Sioux) placed under his command in the U.S. Army's campaigns against the Sioux and Cheyennes in 1876–77. Many of these scouts communicated with one another entirely in sign language. Clark's assignment to the northwest plains from 1876 to 1880 allowed him to communicate almost constantly with members of several tribes on the plains. In 1881 Clark was instructed by Lieutenant General Philip Sheridan to submit a work on Indian sign language accompanied by notes on the habits, manners, and customs of Indians. Clark subsequently visited several tribes across the plains, working with translators and the most skilled sign talkers in each tribe, to complete his study (Clark 1885:5–6). Presumably this was for the army's future use. With the help of the Indian scouts assigned to him, Clark (1885) produced the first major dictionary of Plains Indian Sign Language. Without the aid of any drawings or photographs, Clark was forced to describe each ideographic sign in English to the best of his ability. Although he was verbose in places, the work was helpful to military personnel interacting with peoples of the plains and recorded a wealth of associated ethnographic data.

Clark's work was submitted to Sheridan at the United States Army Headquarters on July 7, 1884, and published shortly after Clark's death as *The Indian Sign Language* (Clark 1885). The work is largely an alphabetical appendix of over 1,000 signs with English descriptions of how the signs were made and associated ethnographic and historic information, including valuable early historical data on the peoples of the western or high plains. For most entries it also contained comparisons of the accompanying signs made by non-Indian deaf-mutes. Clark proposed that, along with many other cultural aspects, sign language had flourished across the plains as part of a lifestyle based on equestrian nomadism and increased permanent populations that developed during the eighteenth and nineteenth centuries. He also maintained that long-term alliances between groups such as the Cheyennes and Arapahos, who spoke different languages (Arapaho was reportedly difficult for Cheyennes to learn), and among groups such as the Kiowas, who traveled great distances and encountered new contacts, facilitated the use of sign language. Other groups such as the Crows are believed to have become proficient sign talkers through their extensive alliances with eastern plateau tribes. Although Clark's work was not illustrated, Clark and Little Wolf (Northern Cheyenne), who became close friends, planned an additional illustrated work on sign language that unfortunately never was produced due to Clark's early death (Dunlay 1982:97).

In 1893 Scott was ordered by General Nelson Miles to deliver a presentation on Plains Indian Sign Language before a World's Congress of Ethnologists at the World's Fair in Chicago, accompanied by six Lakotas from William F. Cody's Wild West Show. The demonstration was well received: the audience reportedly requested an extension of the demonstration, the only such request to date (Scott 1928:171).

William P. Clark's book on Indian Sign Language was first published posthumously in 1885 by a private press. Despite his commendable efforts, the Bureau of American Ethnology may have wanted a more linguistic and analytical account of the subject. Garrick Mallery of the Bureau of American Ethnology was preparing a manuscript for a new book on sign language when he died in Washington, D.C., in October 1894. Dr. Walter J. Hoffman, Mallery's main research assistant for fifteen years, was the best candidate to continue Mallery's work. After his efforts to complete Mallery's work on Indian pictographs in late 1893, however, Hoffman shifted his focus to completing his manuscript on the Menominees. When his monograph was finished in late 1893, Hoffman left the Smithsonian. After serving in the U.S. consul in Mannheim, Germany, he died in 1899. Mallery's work was never published due to his death, the lack of another scholar to complete the typesetting and the engraving of the illustrations, and a freeze on publications through the Government Printing Office around that time (Davis 2010:51–63). Thus by 1895 both scholars of Plains Indian Sign Language were no longer with the Bureau of American Ethnology. The most experienced candidate familiar with PISL who remained was Captain Hugh L. Scott.

After nine years at Fort Sill, Hugh L. Scott requested a reassignment to Washington, D.C., in the fall of 1897, largely to obtain better educational opportunities for his children. "I went down to the War Department next morning and arranged for a station in Washington in either of two capacities. My choice of them was a detail in the Smithsonian Institution, the Bureau of Ethnology . . . to write a book on the sign language of the buffalo plains" (Scott 1928:208). Scott was reassigned in November 1897 and given access to the Library of Congress and the Geological Survey.

In searching the accounts of the earliest Spanish and French explorers he was surprised at the lack of material on the subject. Knowledge of sign language would provide great advantages, especially for the army's goals of containing Plains Indians on reservations, beginning to assimilate them, and freeing officers from their dependency on translators. Hence the paucity of material on the subject seemed to be the result of almost a century of neglect and not opportunity. As Scott (1928:216–17) recounts:

> I found an enormous quantity of literature carrying only small references to the sign language here and there, but it had all to be searched to glean out the little material in existence. It has always been a deep mystery to me why those explorers did not better appreciate the value of the sign language to their enterprises. The famous explorers Lewis and Clark (1804–1806), who were the first white men to encounter many of the Indians of the Northwest, were directed by President Jefferson to make a comprehensive report of all they saw that was new and interesting. They spent the winter of 1804–05 among the three tribes which inhabited the earthen lodges on the upper Missouri, which spoke three different tongues and received visitors from other tribes, speaking still other vocal languages; they saw the sign language used inter-tribally every day; their man Drewyer learned enough of the sign language for them at different times; yet their references to it in their report are so casual as to do nothing more than prove a knowledge of its existence. Every tribe on the Plains spoke it as an intertribal language with varying degrees of skill, but only three of the early travelers did more than allude to it. The officers of our army lived with it all about them while serving on the Plains for a hundred years, but Captain Philo Clark [William Philo Clark], Second Cavalry, was the only one I ever saw who acquired a reasonable degree of proficiency. I have seen many who had enough interest to learn maybe a dozen signs, but not enough interest to learn to put them properly together, and they never knew that the language had a syntax of its own.
>
> I have often marveled at this apathy concerning such a valuable instrument, by which communication could be held with every tribe on the plains of the buffalo, using only one language, by which an officer could make himself independent of interpreters, render great service to his associates and to his government, acquire a commanding influence over whole tribes and districts, and which possibly might save his life.[6]

Inspired by the work of Mallery (1880a, 1880b, 1880c, 1881) teacher, missionary, and amateur linguist Lewis Francis Hadley switched from

---

6   Some of these observations closely resemble those of Clark (1885:5–20 [especially 11]).

his study of Indian spoken languages to pursue sign language. Seeking a means of writing to educate Indians, Hadley believed that sign language, once transferred to printed form, would provide a means to both educate and missionize Indians. He reported promising results from samples of charts and cards shared with Indians (Foreman 1949:51–53). Hadley published two major works on sign language (1890, 1893) and sought to use carved wood block images of sign language to print the New Testament to aid in missionizing Indians. Although his proposed sign language Bible was never published, he produced two small pamphlets containing the Lord's Prayer and the Sermon on the Mount (Foreman 1949:49). Providing estimates of the numbers of Indians who still had knowledge of sign language as well as extensive diagrams on signs and card sets on biblical subjects, Hadley sought funding for his plans for several years (Hadley 1890; Forman 1949:46–55). Hadley (1893) contained 577 entries illustrated with diagrams and was the second text published on sign language. Unfortunately, Hadley passed into obscurity around 1894; his final years are unknown (Foreman 1949:55).[7]

Ernest Thompson Seton's *Sign Talk* (1918) compiled 1,725 signs in alphabetic order with English translations, many with illustrations. Prepared in consultation with Hugh L. Scott and others, this work was based primarily on Cheyenne forms of PISL and intended for use by the Boy Scouts of America. Scott believed that PISL could provide a form of international communication and that individuals would be more interested in learning the sign language of Indians than the sign language of the deaf (Scott ca. 1930:4; Davis 2007:105–106).

William Tomkins published *Indian Sign Language* (1926), illustrating what are essentially abbreviated versions of Clark's descriptions of movements. Thus his work relies more on succinct ideographic illustrations than on lengthy written description. Still in publication today, his work was expanded from seventy-seven to ninety-six pages and contains an alphabetized sign language dictionary with English translations, text on the righthand pages, illustrations of some signs on the lefthand pages, an additional dictionary of synonyms, and a codification of Ojibway and Sioux pictographic word symbols (Tomkins 1927). The Boy Scouts and other organizations adopted this second edition. Other ethnographic and popular accounts include the works of A. H. Sayce (1880) and I. E. Cody (1952). Although he wrote in English, the Lakota Luther Standing Bear

---

7   For the most extensive accounts of Hadley's contributions and the materials that he produced, see Axtell (1891) and Foreman (1949).

(1975, 1978, 1988) discusses the use of sign language throughout his three autobiographical works.

Other related works include biographies collected through sign language and translated into English (Linderman 1962, 1972; Marquis 1962, 1974). Learning sign language from Indians in Montana in the early twentieth century, Frank B. Linderman (1972) collected the autobiography of Pretty Shield, an elder Crow woman, in 1931. Pretty Shield gave her account simultaneously in Plains Indian Sign Language and in spoken Crow through an interpreter, another Crow woman named Goes Together. Plenty Coups and Pretty Shield both addressed Linderman as "Sign Talker," which appears to have been the name that the Crows gave him. Kay Yandell (2012:533) discusses the interpretive role of "Plains Sign Talk," contributing to "a growing body of scholarship focusing on the inclusion of alternative signification practices within the multimedia matrices of transcultural American literature." Referencing the work of Matt Cohen (2009), Yandell (2012:534) views works like the autobiography of Pretty Shield not just as translation but as transcultural: sign language gave individuals from a wide array of cultures alternative "ways to gain agency across cultural and linguistic divides."

Thomas Marquis, who lived over forty years in Montana, briefly served as agency physician at the Northern Cheyenne and Crow reservations and also learned Plains Indian Sign Language. Marquis established rapport with the local tribes, often giving them food, money, and medical care. Many elders would converse with him in sign language when they would have little to do with other whites. In 1922 Marquis began interviewing surviving Cheyenne, Crow, and Lakota participants of the Little Bighorn Fight, including Wooden Leg (Cheyenne), who also made pencil drawings and sketch maps (Marquis 1962:vii–ix). His autobiography of Wooden Leg was recorded through sign language. Marquis also conversed at length through sign language with Thomas H. Leforge, a non-Indian adopted by the Crows, who was also fluent in Crow and sign language and had served as a scout for George Custer prior to the Battle of the Little Bighorn. Although Leforge was a native speaker of English he and Marquis are known to have regularly communicated through sign language. Once while driving on the reservation in a Model T Ford the two were so engrossed in a sign-language discussion that Marquis rammed into another car (Viola 1999:25). In 1929 Marquis published Leforge's life story, taken through sign language and perhaps some English as well, as *Memoirs of a White Crow Indian* (Marquis 1974).

Realizing that sign language had received little significant academic attention over the past sixty years and fearing its decline, Alfred Kroeber had been urging someone to undertake a field study on the subject for several years in the 1950s. Carl Voegelin of Indiana University responded and arranged for his student Lamont West, Jr., to begin visiting Plains Indian reservations in the fall of 1956. Finding sign language still in use among members of several tribes and in several contexts, Kroeber and Voegelin secured funds from the American Philosophical Society to allow West to continue fieldwork with a selected consultant in the summer of 1957 and for a joint meeting to review and appraise the project that fall.

Kroeber (1958) and Voegelin (1958) each published articles the following year. Kroeber's paper was presented as a return to the earlier work of Garrick Mallery (1881), William P. Clark (1885), and Lewis Hadley (1893) that had ceased with their deaths and with the Bureau of American Ethnology's emphasis on data collection and description over analysis. Mallery and Clark were military officers and Hadley a missionary, so Kroeber also felt that they lacked the background to conduct an appropriate and "intensive scholarly analysis" of the unique language system. Kroeber outlined what he believed to be some of the more promising twentieth-century perceptions associated with sign language and suggested topics and leads that would contribute to a more thorough understanding of the subject. Voegelin (1958) provided a comparison demonstrating the advantages of using a two-level analysis over a one-level analysis of sign language, based on work with William Shakespeare, an Arapaho.

In the late 1950s and early 1960s the focus of anthropological linguistics centered on the documentation of American Indian languages that included a "rhetoric of demise" (Farnell 1991, 1995b:85) regarding American Indian Sign Language and William Stokoe's (1960) pioneering structural linguistic work on American Sign Language in the American Deaf Community. This led anthropologists such as Alfred Kroeber, Erminie Voegelin, and La Mont West, Jr., to revisit Plains Indian Sign Language. Their work fostered the development of a distinct "sign language studies" in linguistics, separate from anthropological linguistics. The work of Kroeber (1958), Voegelin (1958), and West (1960) in describing the distinctive features of conventionalized sign language among American Indians was thus an important by-product of the growth of the field of anthropological linguistics.

Influenced by Kroeber and Voegelin, West (1960) surveyed extant Northern Plains Indian Sign Language use. Through descriptive linguistics

West discovered that sign language remained widespread and had diffused into Canada from British Columbia through Manitoba, where it had been almost or completely unknown in some areas in the nineteenth century. In the twentieth century sign language continued in everyday conversation, as a symbol of Indian identity, as a potentially more appropriate and exhibition-like (suitable for public performances) means of communication than English, and had regional variations (Voegelin 1958; West 1960; Farnell 1995a:303; Taylor 1996:275). West (1960) also differentiated between two dialects of PISL: a north central plains dialect referred to as Plains Standard and a far northern plains dialect referred to as Far Northern or Storytelling Dialect, used primarily in portions of British Columbia, Alberta, Saskatchewan, and Manitoba in Canada. West also collected the largest sample of PISL signs at the time of his work. PISL inventories recorded by scholars have varied from around 1,100 signs (Clark 1885), 3,000 signs (Mallery 1881), and 3,500 signs (West 1960) to smaller collections of 400 to 700 (Hadley 1893; Seton 1918; Tomkins 1926, 1927; Hofsinde 1941, 1956; Taylor 1996:281).

The work of Kroeber, Voegelin, and West produced several significant contributions. Voegelin and West developed an elaborate transcription system and "phonemic-like" inventory for recording PISL, including the first descriptions of the distinctive features of the Plains Indian lexicon in terms of hand/s shape, points of articulation or the areas of the body where a gesture is made, and movement (direction and nature of motion involved). Thus conventionalized signs were described in terms of distinctive signing features, similar to the description of phonetic features or the sounds in spoken languages (Davis 2005b:51, 59).

Other works soon followed. Magnus Ljung (1965) published an article on stratificational analysis in Plains Indian Sign Language. Theoretical interests in identifying distinctive features of signed languages were largely ignored by other anthropological linguists. Then the semiotic studies of Thomas Sebeok and Donna Jean Umiker-Sebeok in the 1970s revitalized interest in sign languages. In 1972 the Sebeoks assisted in the reprint of Mallery (1881), accompanied by reprints of Kroeber (1958) and Voegelin (1958). The most extensive collection of published works on Plains Indian Sign Language is Umiker-Sebeok and Sebeok (1978). This two-volume work provides reprints of the major works on sign language for both North America and Australia as well as new discussions of sign language. As major figures in the study of semiotics at Indiana University, the Sebeoks joined in the resurgence of sign language studies.

In "The Semiotic Character of Aboriginal Sign Language" (introduction in Umiker-Sebeok and Sebeok 1978:xx) they note Mallery's repeated use of the term "semiotics" and his comparison of Indian sign languages with other auditory and visual systems from a "broad semiotic typology." Umiker-Sebeok and Sebeok acknowledge the analysis of PISL signs by John Peabody Harrington (1938) as the closest coherent approach to a semiotic classification of sign types. But they note that professional linguists did not pursue the study of Indian sign language until the 1950s, so their efforts to catch up followed a narrow type of formalism. Thus Indian sign language studies remained largely outside of the tradition of semiotics. No consistent application of a classification of signs incorporating a "coherent and systematic distinction between the interdependent iconic and indexical sign relations" common to sign languages had been undertaken by 1978 (Umiker-Sebeok and Sebeok 1978:xvi).

During this time Alan Taylor (1975) compiled a scholarly account of Plains Indian Sign Language for the Smithsonian Institution's *Handbook of North American Indians* series. Providing a stratificational description of Plains Indian Sign Language, L. E. Newell (1981:189) supported Kroeber's earlier findings that sign language is an independent system of communication and not a secondary form based on a spoken language such as writing. Research into American Indian Sign Language also contributed to informing some of the first linguistic research into American Sign Language (Stokoe 1960, 1972; Battison 1978; Davis 2005b:50). While Stokoe (1960:16) did not embrace the approaches of Mallery, Tomkins, and others, he was aware of the research in PISL from the 1880s to the late 1950s. His influential article "Sign Language Structure" (Stokoe 1980) demonstrated that American Sign Language for the deaf had as much structure as any other language.

Early Visual Sources

Sign language found another arena for use in the burgeoning "western" entertainment industry of the late nineteenth and early twentieth centuries. Several former Indian scouts who knew sign language worked in the myriad of Wild West shows running from 1883 to 1933 and in the early western film industry. Although it is difficult to ascertain how often and to what extent sign language demonstrations were incorporated into these formats, some references exist. Citing Fred Pfening (1955:49), Lester Moses (1996:274) notes that Colonel Tim McCoy's show included "talking in signs to the Cheyenne and Sioux performers." In 1913 William F. Cody was preparing to shoot a film entitled *The Indian Wars on Pine Ridge Reservation, South Dakota*. He telegraphed Indian agent John Brennan at Pine Ridge, telling him of his plan "to have moving pictures taken of Wounded Knee Massacre and last surrender. Also the last grand council, in order to preserve the sign language which took place in 1890 and 1891."[8] Unfortunately, only a few minutes of actual film of the eight-reel epic and the scene list remain, due to the decomposing nature of the nitrate stock on which it was shot. The scene lists do not indicate whether scenes of sign language were filmed or not (Moses 1996:229–50).

THE 1930 SIGN LANGUAGE COUNCIL

In addition to Hugh L. Scott's autobiography (1928), Harrington (1938) provides a significant account of Scott's activities with sign language in his later years. In the 1880s Senator Leland Stanford took snapshots of a horse race in Palo Alto, California, in rapid succession. In the 1890s cardboard zoo tropes began to be published as a supplement in Sunday newspapers. When mounted at home and whirled by hand, these produced pictures in motion. As early film evolved, Scott had secretly planned for many years to use this technology to record Plains Indian Sign Language before it disappeared but had told no one. He had noticed stylistic changes from the older generation of Plains Indians who "talked" with greater motion, more intuitively, and more vividly to those born after about 1870, who performed sign language with fewer of these qualities. While sign language was declining among Plains Indian populations, Scott saw the Boy Scout and Girl Scout movements, which he strongly supported, as potential arenas for perpetuating and preserving this mode of communication and sought a means to film a sample of the oldest and best remaining Plains Indian sign talkers before they passed on (Harrington 1938:132).

In 1919 undersecretary of agriculture Wilburn L. Wilson met Scott at the Crow Indian Reservation in Montana (ironically, Scott was in a dormitory in the Indian school studying a card catalog of sign language). Wilson spent four days with Scott on the Crow and Northern Cheyenne Indian reservations. He marveled at Scott's use of sign language to talk with Indians and later that year observed him again at the Yankton Reservation in South Dakota (Harrington 1938:130).

---

8   Telegram: William F. Cody to John Brennan, Aug. 26, 1913. Brennan Papers, Scrapbook 1, SDSHS. Quoted in Moses (1996:229).

In 1930 Scott persuaded influential friends in Congress to pass a bill appropriating $5,000 to be used at the discretion of the secretary of the interior to create a permanent film record of Plains Indian Sign Language, which was believed to be near extinction.[9] This was to be the first film record of PISL. In a joint agreement between the Office of Indian Affairs, Department of the Interior, Office of Motion Pictures (later Division of Motion Pictures), and (probably reflecting his broad political connections and friendships) the Department of Agriculture, Scott organized the filming to be conducted at the Blackfeet Agency in Browning, Montana, from September 4 to 6, 1930. Scott provided Blackfeet Agency superintendent Forrest R. Stone with a list of elderly sign-talkers that he wanted to attend the council. Stone sent out telegrams to their respective agencies, inviting the agency superintendents, Indian agents, and certain elder Indian men from several northern plains reservations to attend the council (Harrington 1938:140; Davis 2010:75). John Ewers (1978:121) notes that Richard Sanderville (Blackfeet) also assisted in assembling the group. Members would gather at Browning, Montana, to demonstrate their use of sign language. Because the conference was held near the Blackfeet Reservation, several of the participants were from the Blackfeet Nation (Piegan and Blood). Participants officially named in the documentary materials include Hugh L. Scott; Tom White Horse (Arapaho); James Eagle (Arikara); Rides Black Horse (Assiniboine); Mountain Chief (Piegan, Blackfeet); Bird Rattler (Blood); Strange Owl (Cheyenne); Deer Nose (Crow); Bitter-Root Jim, aka Bear Road (Flathead); Drags Wolf (Hidatsa); Assiniboine Boy (Upper Gros Ventre); Foolish Woman (Mandan); Fine Young Man (Sarcee); Big Plume (Sarcee); Dick Washakie (Shoshone), Short Face (Piegan); Night Shoots (Piegan); Little Plume (Piegan); and Iron Whip (Sioux). Richard Sanderville (Blackfeet), a well-known tribal leader, interpreter, and local guide, and Jim Whitecalf (Blackfeet) were asked to serve as off-screen interpreters. A few women and children were filmed entering the lodge and attending but were not introduced or shown signing (Harrington 1938:140; Davis 2010:75). The twenty-one participants represented a dozen spoken languages from seven linguistic families from the Plains, Plateau, and Great Basin culture areas (Davis 2012:75). In addition to Scott, congressman Scott Leavitt, governor Joseph M. Dixon, and Indian agent F. C. Campbell

---

9   Second Deficiency Act, fiscal year 1930, approved July 3, 1930, 71st Congress, Second Session (U.S. Stat. 46, p. 147, 875) (Harrington 1938:132–33; Museum of the Plains Indian Arts and Crafts Center 1979).

also attended (Museum of the Plains Indian Arts and Crafts Center 1979; American Indian Sign Language Conference 2012).

Three large Piegan-style tipis were erected in a row north to south for a mess tipi (dining hall), the council meeting, and a women's quarters, respectively. The fourteen members and Scott sat in circular fashion inside the central lodge, with Scott on the west side. All filming and still photography were conducted during daylight hours with a camera and tripod placed in the door of the lodge. Footage of the council (Scott 1934) shows members of these northern plains tribes and then Scott using sign language. Each member was filmed sign talking, giving his name, tribal affiliation, and introductory comments. Four members gave more substantial stories in sign language (Harrington 1938). While the American interest in Indians (albeit heavily romanticized) continued to grow at this time and Scott made many public appearances in his retirement years, I believe that he had a sincere interest in preserving Plains Indian Sign Language through film. In his introductory remarks at the council Scott addressed the rapid decline of sign language and thus the need to preserve it visually: "The young men are not learning your sign language, and soon it will disappear from this country. It is for us to make a record of it for those who come after us, before it becomes lost forever."

Davis (2010:77) describes the variety of discourse genres discussed and the importance of these films: "The spontaneity and variety of discourse types captured in these films offers the best historical linguistic evidence of American Indians using signed language. The American Indian participants are engaged in lively, natural, and unrehearsed signed language discourse covering a variety of topics, anecdotes, and stories, such as making introductions, and showing name signs for each of the tribes represented, signing traditional cultural and medicine stories, and making metaphorical comparisons." Two reels of film consisting of 1,841 feet of film were shot, all without sound. Filming was conducted over three and a half days (Harrington 1938).

To commemorate the council, Richard Sanderville proposed that a cement block be prepared in order to make the footprints of each council member. Someone insisted that all members be barefooted, although Scott and the other white participants were allowed to wear their shoes. Wooden molds approximately twenty inches square were prepared for each concrete block. The prints were intended to create a memorial for the sign language council, but the reason behind Sanderville's decision to use footprints rather than handprints was not recorded. It may relate to the Plains

Indian emphasis on recording foot tracks to show an individual's travels in the painting of men's warfare scenes on hide and in later ledger art.[10] Sanderville, who drew a diagram of the proposed monument, planned to have the blocks placed in a circle in the exact location of the council tipi in the order and positions in which the council members sat. At the time of Harrington's writing, the blocks were stored in the basement of the Blackfeet Agency Office in Browning. At this time the National Park Service had developed a proposal for an Indian Museum at nearby Glacier National Park and Congress had appropriated funds to the Department of the Interior for its construction. Richard Sanderville reportedly persuaded commissioner of Indian Affairs Harold L. Ickes that a "Blackfoot Indian Museum" belonged on the reservation rather than at nearby Glacier National Park. The site of the 1930 Indian Sign Language Council became the Museum of the Plains Indian, which opened in June 1941 with John C. Ewers as director (Harrington 1938:137–39; Ewers 1978:122; Davis 2010:73).

In 1941 the footprints were recast in bronze, along with a bronze plate containing the name and tribe or title of each individual. On June 30, 1942, the Indian Sign Language Conference marker was dedicated as a permanent memorial on the lawn of the Museum of the Plains Indian in Browning, Montana. The footprints were arranged in a circle in the order that the participants occupied during the original council circle and imbedded in concrete. A large illustrated label depicted all of the 1930 participants. In 1973 the memorial was reinstalled at its present location, directly south of the museum entrance, as part of an extensive Indian Arts and Crafts Board development program (Ewers 1978:122; Museum of the Plains Indian Arts and Crafts Center 1979).

During the winter of 1930–31 Scott worked on the film in Washington, D.C., adding an introduction, translations, and explanations in English as well as six additional reels of silent film depicting a sign language dictionary. Nearly 400 of 1,300 intended signs (about 30 percent of the intended dictionary) were completed, representing 4,753 feet of silent film, due to a lack of funds and other pressing matters (Scott 1934). With a dictionary of 1,725 cards depicting sign language signs and aware that the Depression would make a second congressional appropriation difficult, Scott appealed to the Smithsonian Institution for additional funds to obtain blank film to continue the project. Scott proposed that he and his son would perform

---

10   Although Harrington (1938:138) notes that the practice of making handprints and footprints in cement at Grauman's Chinese Theater in Hollywood, California, began in May 1927, there is no indication that this practice was known by or influenced Sanderville.

Strange Owl (Cheyenne) and Bird Rattler (Blood) with Hugh L. Scott performing sign language at the 1930 Council, Browning, Montana. *Courtesy of National Anthropological Archives, Smithsonian Institution, Suitland, Maryland. John P. Harrington Photographs Collection, NAA Box 1203, Rework on Sign Language File. Photo no. 91-35530.*

the work pro bono and then donate the materials to a public institution. No action was taken before Scott unfortunately died in April 1934. Davis (2010:78) states that Scott used his own finances to finish the film that he had shot just days before he passed away.

Less than two months after Scott's death Matthew W. Stirling, director of the Bureau of American Ethnology of the Smithsonian Institution, invited Richard Sanderville to Washington, D.C., to complete Scott's "Film Dictionary of the North American Indian Sign Language" (Scott 1934), which had been deposited in the bureau's archives. Sanderville worked almost three weeks on extending Scott's sign language dictionary, which received considerable news coverage in the Washington newspapers and magazines such as *Literary Digest* and *Science News Letter* (Sanderville 1934; Ewers 1978:121). Sanderville was a likely choice for several reasons. His father and grandfather had both served as translators. Sanderville,

General Hugh L. Scott performing the signs for elk (*top*) and wolf (*bottom*). *National Anthropological Archives Neg. 42511b (both before 1934).*

who was half Blackfeet, was among the first group of Blackfeet to attend Carlisle Indian School in Carlisle, Pennsylvania. Although he left the school after two and half years due to health problems, he furthered his education upon returning to the reservation then entered government service as an interpreter in 1895. Well-versed in Blackfeet culture, Sanderville later served as a consultant for Ewers and was involved in leading numerous presentations on Blackfeet culture, dancing, and sign language (Ewers 1978:117–22). In addition to being a fluent translator and fluent in sign language, Sanderville had served as a translator during the sign council and was thus intimately familiar with both the proceedings and Scott's objectives. The other members of the council were elderly, and some did not speak English, which would have made travel and the necessary work involved more difficult (Harrington 1938:137–42). Ewers (1978:121) suggests that Scott and Sanderville may have met when Scott, then the retired chief of staff of the United States Army, visited the Blackfeet Reservation during the 1920s as a member of the Board of Indian Commissioners and recognized a mutual interest in sign language.

Scott's sign language materials were deposited by his wife in the Bureau of American Ethnology then transferred to the Library of Congress in 1934. Although Scott was unable to complete his project fully, he did finish processing the film of nearly 400 signs that he had shot. He was the first to film the sign language in a formal manner and left extensive film of the language and ethnographic materials collected through sign language for future generations (Harrington 1938:137–42). Sanderville (1934) added to Scott's contributions in providing the original transcriptions and voice-over translations for the film shot at the Sign Language Council (Film No. 106.14), and performed three additional signed narratives (360 feet in length) with English translations that were filmed (Film No. 106.25) during his work at the Smithsonian (Ewers 1978:121; Davis 2010:78, 80). Davis (2007:113) considers the combined film and written and voice-over translations a "Rosetta Stone" for PISL. Despite Sanderville's invaluable contributions, the final project was not as large as Scott had originally planned (potentially as many as 1,725 signs) but is unparalleled in terms of its visual content and value in recording Plains Indian Sign Language. In addition to the preservation aspects of the project, Davis (2006:21, 25–26) has shown that the films of the signed narratives produced in 1930 and 1934 demonstrate the use of phonological, morphological, and syntactic patterns associated with the use of a "full-fledged conventional signed language" (not simply a collection of gestures) as well as the strongest evidence of a historically signed lingua franca. The project also represents the first known use of motion picture film to create a language dictionary (Davis 2010:78). These materials have recently been digitally remastered and are now available online for public viewing (Davis 2010:72–73; pisl research.com).

Tim McCoy produced a film entitled *Injun Talk* (McCoy 1946), which is now available online on YouTube. In the 1950s he produced a video dictionary of Plains Indian Signs that is similar to Scott's dictionary. A copy of this film is housed in the Sheridan, Wyoming, Library. In the 1970s Station KTUL, Channel 8, in Tulsa, Oklahoma, aired footage of Dick West (Cheyenne) performing the "Lord's Prayer" in sign language as a nightly signoff.[11] Two visual sources of Plains Indian Sign Language are available on YouTube (Foley 2007).

Recent Research

Focusing on the sign language storytelling of two elder Assiniboines in Montana, Brenda Farnell (1995a, 1995c, 1996) discovered that by the 1980s Plains Indian Sign Language was no longer common in the northern plains. Knowledge of PISL persisted primarily among hearing elders and some deaf American Indians, having been largely replaced by the forced accommodation to spoken English. This has also contributed to the decline of many tribal spoken languages. Despite the decline of PISL, Farnell identified fluent signers in several northern plains reservation communities. By the late twentieth century fluent sign talkers were few but present in the Assiniboine, Stoney, Blackfeet, Piegan, Blood, Crow, and Northern Cheyenne communities, usually due to having learned signing at an early age, having a deaf member of the family, or being a group in which storytelling has kept it active. PISL is used most commonly in contexts involving religious ceremonies, drumming, and storytelling. The use of some signs in accompaniment with spoken language has also continued. A renewed interest in PISL was spurred by efforts to revive and maintain ethnic awareness and indigenous languages, with several tribal school systems incorporating sign language into language maintenance programs (Umiker-Sebeok and Sebeok 1978:2:xvii; Farnell 1996).

---

11 For these films and others, see Foley (2007); Northwest History: Plains Indian Sign Language Conference, online at http://northwesthistory.blogspot.com/2007/10/plains-indian-sign-language-conference.html; "Plains Indians Sign Language, Browning 1930," online at http://jeroen arendsen.nl/2007/09/plains-indian-sign-language-browning-1930/; and others. All are available online through YouTube.

Contemporary with Farnell's work, Taylor (1996) surveyed studies of PISL for the languages volume of the *Handbook of North American Indians*.

Over the past century and a half intensive contact with non-Indians has led to a marked decrease of traditional spoken languages and increase of English as the dominant or primary language. As use of English grew, it replaced sign language as the lingua franca between members of different native language groups. Likewise as most deaf members of tribes began attending American and Canadian schools for the deaf, they have primarily been taught American Sign Language (ASL) instead of more traditional varieties of North American Indian Sign Language (NAISL), leading to a marked decrease in use of the latter (Davis and McKay-Cody 2010b:120–23).

Recently Jeffrey Davis (a professor of linguistics in the Department of Theory and Practice in Teacher Education at the University of Tennessee) and others have produced a number of publications on both Plains Indian (Goff-Paris and Wood 2002; Miller 2002; Davis 2005b, 2006, 2007, 2010; Davis and McKay-Cody 2010a, 2010b; McKee and Davis 2010) and contemporary deaf sign language (Davis 2005a, 2005c, 2005d; McKee and Davis 2010). Regarding American Indian Sign Language, the most current and comprehensive of these has been Davis (2010): *Hand Talk: Sign Language among American Indian Nations*. Based on anthropological and linguistic studies of historical and contemporary periods, this work examines the relationship between PISL and the development of anthropology in the United States and provides a more linguistic study of the phonology, morphology, and syntax of PISL. Davis has also developed websites containing a corpus of historical documentary materials from written, illustrated, and filmed sources, including film clips, photographs, and illustrations of American Indian Sign Language at pislresearch.com (Davis 2010; Davis and McKay-Cody 2010b:124).

Davis and McKay-Cody (2010b:123) define primary-signed languages as those that "have evolved within specific historical, social, and cultural contexts and have been transmitted and acquired natively from one generation to the next" and alternate signed languages as those that "have been developed and used by individuals who are already competent in spoken language." Davis (2007) suggests that forms of signing are best understood along a continuum: alternate sign use ranges from accompanying speech, to signing without speech, to signing that functions like a primary sign language. Focusing on contemporary deaf and nondeaf American Indians, several scholars (Davis and Supalla 1995; McKay-Cody 1997; Kelly and McGregor 2003; Davis 2006:5, 2010; Davis and McKay-Cody 2010b) maintain that sign language systems used by nondeaf Indians as an alternative to spoken language become a primary signed language when learned in Indian communities by tribal members who are deaf. As Melanie McKay-Cody (1997:50) describes, when alternate sign language traditionally used by hearing members of Plains cultures was acquired as a primary sign language by deaf tribal members, they "seem to gain a higher level of [sign language] proficiency" compared to hearing members. Her findings suggest that an alternate sign language becomes linguistically enriched when learned as a primary language by deaf Indians (Davis 2005b:55; Davis and McKay-Cody 2010b:123).

While more research is needed, promising results have come from several comparative studies of signed languages (Davis 2007:95). In comparing lexical signs from three sources of Northern Plains Indian Sign Language, Davis (2007) found high percentages of lexical similarity (80 to 92 percent), which suggests that all three varieties of PISL were dialects of the same language. Conversely, a much lower percentage of lexical similarity in comparisons of three sources of PISL and ASL (38 to 55 percent) suggests that the two are unlikely to be genetically related languages, although lexical borrowing between the two languages seems probable.

The possibility that PISL influenced ASL is supported by documentation that depictions of Indian sign language signs were published and distributed to American educators in schools for the deaf through *American Annals of the Deaf* (Long 1908–10) from 1848 to 1890 and that signing American Indians frequently visited residential schools for the deaf in the nineteenth century (Mallery 1880a; McKay-Cody 1997). In addition, J. Schuyler Long (1908–10, 1918) principal of the Iowa School for the Deaf, published one of the earliest works on the American Sign Language "The Sign Language: A Manual of Signs," first as a series of articles in the journal *American Annals of the Deaf* from 1908 to 1910 and later reissued under a longer title as a book in 1918. Long's work included lexical descriptions of ASL, 500 photographic illustrations, and 1,063 root signs. After Long's death, his manual was republished by Gallaudet College and by 1963 had been reprinted nine times as *The Sign Language: A Manual of Signs*. Although Long corresponded with Mallery and Scott, Long's manual contains no reference to PISL. While these data suggest that language contact and borrowing occurred between ASL and PISL, it remains uncertain whether PISL signs were introduced to deaf Americans (Gordon 2005; Davis 2007:104–106).

This growing body of work is especially important in the context of the decline of both spoken and signed American Indian languages. As signed languages decline, tribal members who are deaf are potentially marginalized and isolated within their respective communities (Davis 2005b:51). Damara Goff-Paris and Sharon Kay Wood (2002) and Katrina Miller (2002) have focused on the experiences of deaf Indians. These works also contribute to multiple ongoing language and cultural education programs and to reaching a greater understanding of sign language structures on a multicultural basis. Scholars (Johnson 1994; Farnell 1995a, 1995c; Davis and Supalla 1995; McKay-Cody 1997; Kelly and McGregor 2003; Davis 2005b) have documented historical sign language use in most of the major American Indian cultural areas (Plains, Northeast, Southeast and Gulf Coast, Southwest, Plateau, Great Basin, Subarctic, Mesoamerica) and contemporary use among the following four American Indian language families: ALGIC-Algonquian (Blackfeet, Piegan, Blood, Northern Cheyenne), Siouan (Assiniboine, Stoney, Dakotan, Crow), Diné Athapaskan (Navajo), Keresan Pueblo (Keres), and in Yucatán-Mayan. Current sign language use and maintenance programs have been documented among the Assiniboines, Stoneys, Blackfeet, Piegans, Bloods, Crows, and Northern Cheyennes (Farnell 1995c) as well as at the National Multicultural Interpreting Project at El Paso Community College, the Intertribal Deaf Council in Salem, Oregon, and the Department of Blackfeet Studies at the Blackfeet Community College in Browning, Montana (Weatherwax 2002; Davis 2005b:65–66, 2006:7, 11–12).

Examination of documentary materials on PISL led by Jeffrey Davis has produced several recent findings. Although sign language is documented in several culture areas, this does not mean that various signed languages were mutually intelligible. Establishing whether varieties of the same signed language or distinct signed languages exist will require further research that may offer additional insights into issues such as contact, change, and attitudes in language acquisition. Recent studies support the conclusions of earlier scholars that PISL existed as an intertribal and intergenerational-signed language lingua franca and that dialect difference within the plains did not seriously impede signed communication. PISL was the dominant variety of sign language shared by Plains Indian communities and was learned through language contact. Sign language was used by American Indians as a "complementary alternative to spoken language" and became linguistically enriched and conventionalized over time. The theoretical classifications of "universality" and "iconicity" continue to be addressed in sign language research, resulting in the establishment of higher thresholds to determine lexical similarity and word lists with a low potential for iconicity (Davis 2007:115). The endangered status of PISL calls for promoting language revitalization, especially through the making of documentary sources available in digital formats. Finally, ongoing research into the phonological, morphological, and grammatical characteristics of PISL and other varieties of sign language will provide further insights into the origins, innateness, and resiliency of human language (Davis 2005b:66–67, 2010).

Davis and McKay-Cody (2010b) have also examined how sign language interpreters can work more effectively with deaf members of American Indian and Alaskan Native communities. This involves work in a wide range of communities with diverse cultural backgrounds. Their research suggests working more in internal (emic) contexts through increasing awareness of tribal and community cultural values and practices, gender roles, learning Indian cultural terminology, alliance development, and establishing collaborative interpreting teams with Indian members.

In commemoration of the 1930 Sign Language Conference, an American Indian Sign Language Conference was held at the Museum of the Plains Indian at Browning, Montana, from August 31 to September 2, 2012. In addition to the commemoration and invitations to the descendants of the original conference participants, the program included formal demonstrations of contemporary Indian sign language, a discussion of dialectical differences, signed tours of the Plains Indian exhibits, children's sign language activities, and other events. The conference was co-hosted by the University of Tennessee, Friends of the Museum of the Plains Indian, and the Blackfeet Community College, with support from the Browning Area Chamber of Commerce, Museum of the Plains Indian, Blackfeet Nation, National Science Foundation's Documenting Endangered Languages Program, and others (American Indian Sign Language Conference 2012).

Recognizing that human language is not limited to auditory-oral channels but includes equally rich forms such as visual-gestural modes, linguists continue to explore the gradient and semiotic features of human languages to uncover new insights into the complexities of language and the human mind. This direction is especially relevant because sign language uses the semiotic features of gesture and space, which become codified and conventionalized over time. Research in this area is demonstrating striking similarities in the processes of sign language emergence and transmission (Davis 2010:186). Davis and McKay-Cody (2010b:152–53) are currently conducting further ethnographic and linguistic research into the development and use of sign language by deaf and hearing American Indians.

The use of PISL has declined significantly since the mid- to late 1800s. Most Plains Indians have attended Anglo schools where spoken English was not only required but became a lingua franca among Plains Indian tribes. Likewise, most deaf Plains Indians have attended schools for the deaf, where they learned American Sign Language (ASL), which became the shared form among Indians of many cultures. In addition, Euro-American goals of cultural and linguistic assimilation of Indians and views of sign language as being more primitive than spoken language have contributed to pressures undermining its use. Thus fewer Indians, both hearing and deaf, have continued to learn PISL as a communications system (Davis 2010:13–15). Assimilation-oriented Anglo schools for Indians discouraged and contributed to an overall loss of sign language use. But Anglo schools for the deaf (also established primarily after the Civil War), ironically, became the primary institutions promoting the use and acculturation of sign language, albeit a different system of sign language intended primarily for non-Indians (Davis 2005b:60).

The rapid decline in both spoken and signed American Indian languages over the last century and a half stems from many combinations of historical, governmental, social, cultural, and educational factors. As Lisa Blee (2007:594) notes, with the beginning of the reservation period, which increasingly isolated tribes to some degree from one another, the use of Plains Indian Sign Language for cross-cultural communication declined and was gradually replaced by English as the lingua franca. Increasing intertribal marriages, boarding and later public schools that often discouraged or prohibited the use of Indian languages, and increasingly intertribal traditions such as Native American Church meetings and powwows also promoted the use of English. Although use of sign language has greatly decreased, varying degrees of use continue among American Indian groups today, primarily by some hearing elders and by deaf members. Sign language use has continued to a greater degree on the northern plains, where it can be found in rituals, prayers, legends, conversational narratives, traditional storytelling, and conversational contexts and is still being learned by a few deaf American Indians (Farnell 1995a, 1996; Taylor 1996; McKay-Cody 1997; Mithun 1999; Davis 2010:15; Davis and McKay-Cody 2010b:123–24). Davis and McKay-Cody (2010b:151–52) classify existing uses of Native American Indian Sign Languages into five forms: in storytelling, in Christian religious texts, in the Native American Church, in Hollywood depictions, and with deaf family members.

While little research has been conducted with contemporary Indian communities of the southern plains the same general trends described by Farnell (1995a) appear to have developed there, although I believe that far fewer fluent speakers of PISL remain. In 1927 Lutie Goombi translated Kiowa hymns into sign language during Iseeo's funeral at Fort Sill (Beebe

1931:360). Although it is not the primary focus of my research, since 1989 I have noticed the continued use of a limited number of signs in varied settings, most commonly associated with greetings, asking questions, affirmations, directions, singing, and references to eating. When I was interviewing elders with a tape recorder another family member frequently would enter the room and ask a question by employing certain key signs. For example, mixing traditional PISL and contemporary signs, during one interview a Kiowa man came in and signed to his father (1) question then (2) the motion of turning a key to start a car. The elder pointed to where the car keys were lying, whereupon the son retrieved them and left. During the early 1990s some elders when asked about an individual who had recently died in several instances answered by making the sign for "die" (literally, "going under"; cf. Clark 1885:150) rather than answering verbally, which may relate back to earlier traditions regarding not speaking the name of deceased individuals. The most common sustained use of sign language is now occasional public performances of the Lord's Prayer by groups of young girls in Indian dress at powwows and other special events.[12] Over the years I have interacted with an elder mother of a deaf daughter who describes their sign language as a "pidgin" of traditional signs (PISL) and their own innovations. Members of one Kiowa family related how their mother translated church services via sign language to elderly Kiowas in Hobart, Oklahoma, as late as the 1950s.[13] The most active use of sign language on the southern plains that I am aware of is by Dan Ahhaitty, a Kiowa who lived with his grandparents as a youth. When his Kiowa grandmother remarried to a Cheyenne man, neither spoke the other's language. They communicated through sign language, which Ahhaitty learned. He currently teaches a weekly evening sign language class, which precedes a longer-running class on spoken Kiowa language, at the Jacobson House at the University of Oklahoma.[14] One currently uninvestigated area is the use of sign language in the ongoing Plains Indian Hand Game, where a number of signs are regularly used in play.[15]

---

12   Author's fieldnotes, 1989–2012. See Farnell (1995a:2–3) concerning similar practices and their origins on the northern plains and how sign language has been reappropriated as an acceptable display of ethnic identity and "Indian" traditions.
13   Author's fieldnotes, Oct. 26, 2013.
14   Dan Ahhaitty (Kiowa) to the author, Mar. 7, 2012, Norman, Oklahoma.
15   Signs are used in all major facets of the game, including guessing, hiding, refereeing, scorekeeping, and spectating. A sample of types includes requesting a re-hide, beginning guessing, passing the position of guesser, the end of a game, and several forms of exclamation. Author's fieldnotes, 1989–2014.

Scott's Legacy

Unfortunately Scott's military service prevented him from publishing extensively, especially concerning his planned work on sign language. Scott is only briefly mentioned in Taylor's (1996) discussion of sign language, primarily in reference to Scott's film work with sign language, as mentioned in Harrington (1938). Davis's (2010:72–80) discussion of Scott is largely confined to his role in the 1930 Sign Language Council and the resulting film footage (Scott 1934; Sanderville 1934), with very little information on his background, how he became involved in sign language, or the breadth of his ethnographic notes. In addition, most sources reference only Scott's Library of Congress materials and not his extensive ethnographic notes. Thus one of his largest accomplishments (in addition to the recording of the Plains Indian Sign Language) has been overlooked: the potential use of sign language for ethnographic data collection, especially in the late nineteenth and early twentieth centuries. While most ethnographers approach fieldwork and ethnographic data collection through oral and observational approaches, sign language has rarely been used. The biographical works of Linderman (1962, 1972) and Marquis (1962) are the closest extant examples. Like Clark (1885), Scott realized the potential of sign language to obtain a wide variety of ethnographic data that could be recorded in writing. Once learned, sign language allowed researchers to communicate with plains populations faster than they could learn the respective spoken languages. This unique form of communication permitted Scott to obtain data on varied subjects from different (often neighboring) populations and to be comparative in his analyses, as reflected in numerous notes and commentaries in the margins of his notes.

Scott and Clark were both military officers and technically only amateur ethnographers. The opportunities for collecting ethnographic data would have been greatly increased if more ethnographers had become proficient in PISL, especially in the early days when they were forced to depend on translators or, less commonly, learn a spoken Indian language in the field. While the ubiquitous nature of English and the decline of both Plains Indian spoken languages and signed language have decreased the use of sign language, the materials collected by Scott and Clark are invaluable in showing the potential of this form of ethnographic data collection. Unfortunately, the use of sign language to collect ethnographic data, which allowed researchers to enter and communicate with numerous linguistic communities faster than they could possibly have learned numerous spoken languages, was not employed more extensively by military officers and ethnographers of the late nineteenth and early twentieth centuries. But this means of data collection can still potentially be used, especially by scholars of PISL working with deaf Native American Sign Language speakers and by linguists studying PISL through texts such as those recorded by Hugh L. Scott in this work.

CHAPTER 2

Hugh Lenox Scott
(1853–1934)

HUGH L. SCOTT'S CAREER SPANNED A PERIOD OF TREMENDOUS transition in the United States and in the United States Army, ranging from equestrian prereservation conflict with Plains Indians to the beginning of America as a military world power in World War I. This chapter provides a sketch of Scott's life and military career with particular attention to his introduction to Plains Indian Sign Language in 1876 and his subsequent study and use of it for the remainder of his life. Attention is also given to his years at Fort Sill (1889–97), his association with Troop L, his relationship with Iseeo and other Indians of the southern plains, and how he collected the data in his ledgers. Additional material on Scott and Iseeo's relationship is included in chapter 3.[1]

Hugh Lenox Scott was born in Danville, Kentucky, on September 22, 1853, to the Reverend William McKendry Scott and Mary Elizabeth Hodge Scott. He was named after his maternal grandfather's brother, Dr. Hugh Lenox Hodge, a physician in Philadelphia. Scott's maternal line included many well-educated individuals serving as theologians, ministers, and doctors. His paternal line emigrated from Ireland to Ohio in 1798, where they became prominent farmers. His step-grandmother, Mary Hunter Stockton Hodge, was the daughter of Andrew Hunter, chaplain of the House of Representatives during the War of 1812, and a sister to General

---

1   The primary published source on Scott is his biography, *Some Memories of a Soldier* (Scott 1928). For a military record of Scott (including letters of commendation for gallantry in the field, etc., up to and including the rank of colonel), see USMA (n.d.) Based on the dates of his promotions, the military record appears to have been published between August 1911 and March 1913.

David Hunter, a West Point graduate and influential military leader. Graduating from West Point in 1822, Hunter served at Forts Dearborn and Chicago in the 1820s, was a friend of both Abraham Lincoln and Ulysses S. Grant, and facilitated the enlistment of 1,500 black soldiers in the Union Army during the Civil War. Ironically, Hunter accompanied the 1834 United States Dragoon expedition into what would later become southwest Oklahoma as the captain of Company D, First Dragoons, and was met by the Kiowas and Comanches: Scott would later serve in the same area at Fort Sill (Scott 1928:168).

After graduating from Princeton Seminary, William M. Scott and Mary Hodge married. As a ministerial student and disciple of the Reverend Charles Hodge (1797–1878), William Scott served in several congregations in New York, Ohio, and Kentucky, finally settling in Danville, Kentucky. He was professor of ancient languages at Center College and pastor of the Presbyterian Church. After relocating to Cincinnati in 1856 and Chicago in 1859 for church assignments, William Scott died of consumption in 1861 when Hugh was only eight years old. His mother returned with her children to her family in Princeton, New Jersey, where Scott was brought up Presbyterian. During this time, his maternal grandfather, the Reverend Charles Hodge, who had been the mentor of William M. Scott, served as principal of Princeton Theological Seminary and was recognized as one of the foremost Presbyterian ministers of his time. Hugh Scott's maternal line of educators and growing up in Princeton provided him with an intellectually and physically rich environment. He attended Edge Hill and Lawrenceville Schools near Princeton, where he also hunted, fished, and explored the surrounding countryside extensively. His early affinity for the outdoors not only helped shape his character but proved useful throughout his future military service.

Scott's great-uncle David Hunter, a brother of Charles Hodge's second wife, Mary Hunter Stockton, was instrumental in the young Scott's military advancement. Hunter, who had served as a brevet major general of volunteers in the cavalry and as a departmental commander during the Civil War, arranged for a provisional presidential appointment for his great-nephew to enter West Point in the class of 1871. By 1870 Scott had passed all entrance exams and was preparing to enter Princeton College when he was notified of his appointment to West Point. He continued studying for both programs with a tutor so that he might enter as a sophomore at Princeton if he failed to enter West Point. In May 1871 Scott was taken to visit West Point by his uncle and entered the class of 1872. He became involved in disciplinary issues involving hazing. Although Scott had also undergone the rites of passage, he later refused to turn in his peers. Despite the expulsion of several classmates and being held back one year, Scott graduated, in part due to his family's status and connections, on June 14, 1876. The class members received their diplomas from General William T. Sherman. Scott ranked 36th of 48 in his class, which was high enough for acceptance into cavalry service but only for a position with the 9th Cavalry, a black unit originally stationed at Fort Davis, Texas. Scott requested a second lieutenancy in the cavalry over a full lieutenancy in any other branch and was initially assigned to the 9th Cavalry on June 15, 1876, then serving on the Arizona border. On July 5, while in Philadelphia visiting the American Centennial Scott learned of Custer's June 25 defeat at the Little Bighorn. He immediately returned to Princeton and requested a transfer to the 7th Cavalry. Although it was already July, his assignment as a second lieutenant of cavalry was dated as beginning June 26, 1876. He was assigned to Fort Abraham Lincoln in Dakota Territory.

Over the next twenty-one years Scott served on the western frontier of the United States, primarily in the plains region and with the 7th Cavalry. During this time he saw action in campaigns against the Sioux, Nez Perces, Cheyennes, and other tribes of the plains. During this period Scott developed a keen interest in Plains cultures, desiring to learn as much about their ways of life as possible. While he clearly benefited from the U.S. western frontier and the warfare, both personally and professionally, he would apply those benefits to help Indians in a variety of ways. The key was the manner in which he would communicate with them—through Plains Indian Sign Language.

In the 1870s cavalry detachments regularly used Indian scouts in their campaigns because of their knowledge of scouting, the geographical region, and the habits of the specific tribe being sought. Often the scout was an enemy of that tribe, who worked in advance of the military column scouting for the enemy, trails, game, water, and any other useful geographic or meteorologic information. During his first assignment Scott was taken into a Sioux village. Realizing the political significance of the Lakotas on the plains, Scott (1928:31–32) decided to learn their language two days after arriving at Fort Abraham Lincoln.[2]

---

2   Scott also discusses this in another archival document (n.d.b: "Tales of the Kiowa," pp. 8–9, MS 2932, Box 3).

> Realizing that the Sioux tribe was the largest and most powerful in the Northwest, I thought that their language must be the court language of that section, especially as the Arikara scouts all spoke it, and I made arrangements to have them teach me Sioux. I thought that a knowledge of the tongue would help me in getting command of the scouts, a position sought after by the more adventurous lieutenants with no troop of their own ... one could always be ahead of the command, away from the routine that was irksome, and sure to have a part in all the excitement.

Scott (1928:31) quickly realized, however, that a more pervasive and useful form of communication existed that would better facilitate communication throughout the plains—Plains Indian Sign Language. In discussing the learning of sign language, William Clark (1885:17) noted that to understand and interact efficiently with Indians it was necessary to understand their cultural background and the conceptions behind their way of thinking. "To become, in short, accomplished, one must train the mind to think like an Indian." By permitting more efficient interaction with Indian peoples across the plains, sign language allowed Scott to work to their benefit in shaping army and government actions on a local and (to some degree) national policy level, while simultaneously recording valuable ethnographic material from numerous populations.

> I soon found that the Sioux language was quite limited in the scope of its usefulness, but that the sign language of the Plains was an intertribal language, spoken everywhere in the buffalo country from the Saskatchewan River of British America to Mexico, east of the Rocky Mountains and west of the Missouri, and I began the study of this at the same time with the Sioux, and have continued its study down to this day.
>
> Through my mastery of this means of communication with the natives, I soon became known to commanders of every grade, clear up to generals Sheridan and Miles, who befriended me as long as they lived; they gave me a freedom and scope I have seen extended to none else in the Indian country, perhaps because I was satisfied there and took pleasure in carrying out any work they might have for me. Generals Ruger and Merritt did likewise, and, in fact, I came and went as I pleased without question, but I [was] always pleased to be on deck when I was wanted.
>
> I began then an intensive study of every phase of the Indian and his customs, particularly as to how he might best be approached and influenced, a knowledge that has stood me in good stead many times, has doubtless saved my life again and again, and has also been used to the national benefit by different Presidents of the United States, by secretaries of war and of the interior. (Scott 1928:32)

While operating in the Big Horn Country in the fall of 1876, Scott became well acquainted with various Arikara, Cheyenne, Crow, and Lakota scouts, who often traveled ten to thirty miles ahead of the column. "While traveling with the scouts I lived just as they did, and allowed no custom of theirs to go unnoticed, never resting until I found the motive, which they were often unable to formulate themselves, although they were always the very soul of affability, anxious to impart information whenever possible" (Scott 1928:33). It was during this time that Scott was introduced to the Plains Indian Sign Language.

Scott began accompanying advance scouting parties on patrols, due to his love of the outdoors and adventure as well as to alleviate the boredom of such an isolated post. This provided him with the opportunity to learn the sign language as well as the customs and cultures of several tribes from the Indian scouts. His patience, keen observation, sincerity, and empathy with the plight of American Indians garnered the respect and trust of several tribal communities. Scott reciprocated this trust by often entering villages alone or with a minimum of accompanying personnel, which only added to the Indians' views of his courage and integrity. This mutual trust allowed him access to tribal leaders, some of whom were initially hostile to Euro-American interests. Scott's decision to focus on sign language became a defining moment in his ability to communicate and interact with Indians of the plains and would significantly impact the progression of both his military and ethnographic careers.

Beginning on June 25, 1877, one year to the day after Custer's defeat, Scott participated in the recovery of the cavalry killed in the Little Bighorn Fight. That summer he also took part in disarming a group of Yanktonai Sioux and served in an escort under General Alfred Terry traveling to interview Sitting Bull in Canada that was redirected prior to reaching Sitting Bull's camp. That fall Scott participated in troop assignments to bring in all Nez Perces who had not come in following the surrender of Chief Joseph and the majority of the tribe on October 5. This involved inducing bands of the tribe to surrender and escorting them to Bismark, Dakota Territory, from whence they were to be shipped to Kansas and finally to Indian Territory. Promoted to quartermaster and placed in charge of the escort, Scott rode part of each day in a wagon with the Nez Perce leader Joseph and part of each day in the wagons of Cheyennes and Sioux who were traveling east to Chicago to meet with General Phillip Sheridan, "carrying on my study of Sioux and the sign language, of which I never missed an opportunity to learn more" (Scott 1928:83). Camping at Fort

Berthold, Scott witnessed Joseph addressing a large intertribal council of approximately 1,500 Plains Indians from seven tribes and many non-Indians in sign language. Scott's interest and increasing proficiency in this area soon allowed him to serve as an interpreter, a valuable skill that gained him favor among higher-ranking officers. Within a year Scott (1928:59) had acquired some degree of proficiency in sign language: "I was by that time an interpreter in a small way, knowing enough to get about, but not yet able to interpret in council." This would soon change.

During the winter of 1877–78 Scott continued his study of sign language at Fort Abraham Lincoln. In January 1878 Captain Frederick W. Benteen brought a contingent of Cheyenne prisoners to winter at the post, where Scott met White Bear. "I visited their village every day, subsidizing White Bear, principally with sugar, coffee, and other rations, to teach me the sign language, and we both worked hard at it." Major E. A. Garlington, adjutant at Fort Abraham Lincoln, described Scott's dedication to learning about Indian cultures: he "was very much interested in the Indians and was beginning the study which has placed him at the head of the officers of the army in knowledge of the Indian's character, his human nature, his method and thought of action, and of the sign language. He spent nearly all his time, when not on duty, in the Indian village, became well acquainted with the head men, won their confidence and esteem."[3]

Discovering that the Cheyennes planned to escape to the Yellowstone River Scott reported this to his superior Colonel Samuel D. Sturgis, who sent for the principal chiefs. Scott translated the Cheyennes' direct and defiant statements to Sturgis. Not believing that Scott had translated correctly, Sturgis sent for the Arikara interpreter F. F. Girard and for a Cheyenne man married to an Arikara woman. Reinterviewing the various individuals in order through these two men verified what Scott had already reported, and the escape was prevented (Scott 1928:86–87). Thus, within a year and of half of entering service on the plains, Scott's proficiency in sign language was deemed sufficient to be used by his commanders. In 1878 Scott served as interpreter for the 7th Cavalry in meeting with Lakota leader Red Cloud. Scott was promoted to first lieutenant in June 1878.

In 1909 Brigadier General Caleb H. Carlton wrote: "Lieut. H. L. Scott, on entering the Army in 1876 from West Point, made a specialty of studying Indians, their language, customs, manners, and history" (Scott 1928:211).

---

3 Major, Inspector General, E. A. Garlington, Adjutant, Fort A. Lincoln, to Adjutant General, U.S. Army, June 18, 1879 (USMA n.d.:43–44).

In June 1880 Scott married Mary Merrill, the daughter of General Lewis Merrill, at Standing Rock, Dakota Territory. They would have two sons, David Hunter Scott and Lewis Merrill Scott, and a daughter, Mary Scott Blanchard. In the fall of 1882 Scott was placed in charge of building the telegraph line from Fort Totten to Larimore seventy-eight miles to the east, to meet the Great Northern Railway (Scott 1928:109–10). At Fort Totten, Scott participated in his last buffalo hunt, conducted forced marches across multiple swollen streams when necessary, nearly drowned in a horse-riding accident, and led a 1,500-mile geology expedition with his brother (a geologist and paleontologist) and his class from Princeton University through the Big Horn Basin, Yellowstone Park, and back down the Yellowstone River to Fort Custer (Scott 1928:109–27). Scott also entered camps alone in advance of troops to negotiate with Indians who had left their respective reservations. Captain H. G. Sickel (Scott 1928:212) noted the value of Scott's knowledge of sign language in catching and returning a band of Crow Indians to their reservation in 1883: "The band of Indians was finally overtaken at Mizpah Creek and here Lieutenant Scott's knowledge of the Indian sign language served a good purpose. He was selected for this duty mainly on account of his knowledge, as there was no other interpreter at the post."

In August 1886 Scott was reassigned from Fort Meade to Philadelphia, where he oversaw a cavalry recruiting detail for two years. He considered these two years in the city, away from troops and the unique service for which he had trained himself in the Indian country, to be "wasted" (Scott 1928:126–28). This would soon be remedied. With the end of the wars on the southern plains in 1875 and the northern plains in 1890, the fear of Indian wars began to decline. As the military sought to reduce its size, career officers often found it difficult to achieve promotions. With the settlement of Indians onto reservations, Congress saw no need to maintain a large standing army. Officers in the Indian service were no longer seen as useful, so there was little incentive to promote them.

But Scott would gain the recognition of the military establishment, and in turn promotion, through his unique skill in sign language and in an unconventional manner. Scott would advance in a period of rare promotion by demonstrating his skills as a diplomat and in making and maintaining peace with their former enemy, rather than through combat on the field. His greatest achievements came in the camps and lodges of the Indian peoples and not on the battlefield. Thus, while always emphasizing diplomatic over military solutions, his service shifted from military action to pacification and supervision Scott's diplomatic approach to negotiating with tribal

Captain Hugh L. Scott, 1895–97.
Photo #P12819, The Fort Sill National Historic Landmark, Fort Sill, Oklahoma.

peoples offered another advantage to the military in terms of cutting costs through the prevention of armed conflicts. Scott also began to advocate on behalf of Indian rights and treatment, allowing him to continue making contacts with influential military and government political leaders who would further his career. These contacts would also expose him to the processes of governmental policy making and administration. Combined with his position as a peacetime supervisor of Indians, this presented opportunities to perform this role in other locations while helping to shape future policy toward Indians and other peoples in American territories. While most military officers possessing firsthand experience with Indians were rarely in a position to take action on a policy level, or chose not to, Scott frequently advocated for Indians' treatment, lands, and physical welfare.

Fort Sill

At the end of his assignment Scott was reassigned to Fort Sill in Indian Territory, where he joined Troop M, 7th Cavalry, in July 1889.[4] Although Scott (1928:126–28) initially lamented the assignment, his doubts were soon allayed. "I rather pitied myself for going to a post where the Indians were too tame, but I need not have done so, for I found the Kiowa, Comanche, and Kiowa Apache Indians still as wild as the Sioux and Cheyenne I had left in the north." Here Scott's career would again shift. Although he had already demonstrated his skills in diplomacy with Indian peoples, Scott's tenure at Fort Sill would be his first opportunity to work with Indians in a postwar era of assimilation rather than the more conflict-based northern plains service.

Always drawn to the mountains and exploration, Scott quickly set out on a camping trip to explore the nearby Wichita Mountains, accompanied by a few of the Kiowa and Comanche scouts maintained at the post.

> Whenever I live near the mountains, they call until I go to them. The Wichita Mountains were within plain sight and twelve miles from Fort Sill, and they began to call to me the first day. . . . It was not long before I started with a visiting cousin, accompanied by I-see-o and five of the Kiowa and Comanche scouts, a cook, a packer, and two pack mules, to answer their summons and to learn about the country. We rode all around the Wichita group and through the middle before we got back, the Indians pointing out the sites of historical occurrences and relating their legends in the sign language. (Scott 1928:129)

---

4   Hugh L. Scott (Princeton, N.J.) to Samuel A. Eliot, Chairman, Board of Indian Commissioners (Washington, D.C., Dec. 5, 1927) (Scott n.d.b: MS 4525, Kiowa Agency).

It was on this trip that he met Iseeo, with whom he would have an intimate and long friendship, participate with in several peace-keeping efforts, and, with his assistance, record the majority of his ethnographic notes on the tribes of western Indian Territory. He was also joined on the trip by the Kiowa scouts Mobeadleky (High-Bridged Nose), also known as Kokoyden (Elk Tongue); Kicking Bird II; and Tchaka (Bread); and Comanche scouts Big Cow and Comanche George. The Indians were surprised to meet an Anglo so adept at sign language.

> Having learned the sign language on the Northern Plains, the Indians of the Southern Plains were surprised to see me, a new man from the east, come there with a good knowledge of it, something never seen before, and the Comanche called me at once, "Molay tay-quop," "he talks with his hands" or "sign talker," and it enabled me to get into the good graces of all the Indians of that district almost at once, giving me their confidence and good will within a radius of two hundred miles from Fort Sill. (Scott 1928:129)[5]

Scott soon became involved in mitigating a number of potentially volatile events among the Kiowas. They had last held a Sun Dance, their principal religious ceremony on a pantribal level, in 1887. In 1890 they had requested permission from Indian agent Charles E. Adams to hold another dance but had been denied. When the Kiowas began building the lodge for the ceremony, Adams sent for troops from Fort Sill. Scott was among the troops sent out to prevent the dance. Although they proceeded from Fort Sill to Anadarko, news of their imminent approach resulted in the dispersal of the Kiowa camp, then located near present-day Carnegie, Oklahoma. The troops returned to Fort Sill without ever actually reaching the encampment (Scott 1928:131).

The Ghost Dance

One of Scott's most important roles was in helping maintain peace during the spread of the Ghost Dance among the tribes of the southern plains and in preventing another Wounded Knee Massacre, as occurred in Dakota Territory in December 1890.[6] Scott could not have achieved this without his knowledge of sign language and the help of Iseeo (Scott 1928:146–55). Although the ceremony had been active among the Paiutes in 1870, during

---

5   Molay-tay-quop is probably similar to Mo?otekwapu (hand talk, meaning sign language). Dan Gelo to the author, Jan. 22, 2014.
6   For the seminal study on the Ghost Dance see Mooney (1896).

the summer of 1890 the Ghost Dance doctrine spread across the plains. Wovoka (Jack Wilson) a Paiute from Nevada who claimed to be the prophet of a new messiah, led the movement. It blended elements from ancient northern and northwestern Paiute beliefs with a belief in world renewal through ceremonies and Christian teachings associated with the second coming of Jesus Christ. Through a Paiute-style round dance with dancers performing a circular sideways step while holding hands, instructions from supernatural powers, especially Jesus, could be obtained in periods of trance and unconsciousness. In general the doctrine required faithful dancing, clean living, nonviolence, peaceful adjustment with or avoidance of whites, a return to traditional lifeways and material culture forms (sometimes involving a rejection of white-derived products), hard work, and following the direction of God's chosen leaders. Proper adherence to the doctrine would result in the resurrection of dead relatives, the return of the bison, and a return to the prosperous "golden days" of Indian life. The supernatural removal of whites, through powerful whirlwinds and fire in some versions, would accompany world renewal (Stewart 1987:65–66).

In western Indian Territory the Northern Arapaho chief Sitting Bull brought the Ghost Dance doctrine to the Cheyenne-Arapaho Reservation. By May of 1890 the Kiowa-Comanche-Apaches (KCA) had learned of the doctrine from their Cheyenne and Arapaho neighbors. That summer Poor Buffalo became the first Kiowa convert and was disseminating the doctrine to other Kiowas. Quanah Parker, assisted by David Grantham, sent a letter to agent Adams to inform him of the dance and the Comanches' lack of interest in the movement (Hagan 1976:188–89). Sitting Bull visited the Anadarko Agency three times during the fall and winter of 1890, gaining more converts each time. In the fall of 1890 the first Ghost Dance among the Kiowas was held along the south side of the Washita River in the river bottom just west of the mouth of Rainy Mountain Creek, northeast of present-day Mountain View, Oklahoma. Unlike the Lakota version, the Kiowa dance was pacifistic in nature, with no association between the wearing of Ghost Dance shirts and their ability to turn bullets. Practitioners tended to choose remote parts of the agency for their ceremonies and frequently shifted the location of their activities.

Despite the pacifist focus of the movement, beliefs in the eradication of whites through a cataclysmic wind and fire, large crowds, and wild rumors with threatening overtones associated with the dance intensified, alarming whites and the army. The rumors morphed into hysteria and fear among whites, who feared a general Indian uprising against white supremacy. As the dance grew in popularity among the southern plains tribes the post commander at Fort Sill called in Lieutenant Scott, who had the reputation of having the confidence of the Indians. He was ordered to spend the winter traveling among the Indian camps in present-day western Oklahoma to watch for any individuals who might become disaffected. In December 1890 the War Department commissioned Scott to investigate the meaning and cause of the excitement associated with the movement and the possibility of an outbreak. Being intimately acquainted with members of several plains tribes and expert in their sign language, Scott was well suited for the assignment. To minimize their presence and the threat of military action, Scott's group remained inconspicuous by appearing as a hunting party. Scott assembled a small party including Iseeo and a few enlisted men: an orderly, scouts, a cook, and a driver. They set out to spend the winter among the eight tribes in western Indian Territory. Upon leaving the fort Scott took Iseeo aside and told him the true purpose of the mission, noting that others preferred to send the cavalry out to force the Indians to cease the Ghost Dance if they continued. He explained to Iseeo that he could help by collecting information on the size and extent of the following associated with the religion. Iseeo considered the assignment and accepted (Mooney 1896:900; Scott 1928).

From December 1890 through February 1891 Scott visited the camps, attending a number of dances and talking with the religious leaders. During an attempt to disarm Big Foot's band of Minnecounjou Lakotas use of military force by the 7th Cavalry at Wounded Knee, South Dakota, on December 29, 1890, resulted in the slaughter of over 150 Lakotas, mostly women, children, and elders. Although it was actually intended as a meeting to disarm the camp of Indians, the firing of a single shot resulted in a massacre of the Lakotas. Wounded Knee is often used to mark the end of the Indian wars, yet it remains one of the darkest moments in the history of United States–Indian relations. As news of Wounded Knee spread and the dance went on in Oklahoma, tensions continued to mount. Scott provided valuable reports on the various forms of the dance and "confirmed the War Department in his previous opinion that no danger was to be apprehended, and that the true policy was one of noninterference" (Mooney 1896:900).

Although Scott was assigned to Fort Sill when Wounded Knee occurred, he soon became aware of its outcome. Determined to prevent another Wounded Knee from occurring on the southern plains, Scott wisely pursued a peaceful approach to the situation (Nye 1937:271). As he later reflected (Scott 1928:147),

The excitement became as great among the white communities as among the Indians, the former expecting an uprising, a feeling that was greatly intensified by news of the battle of Wounded Knee in South Dakota with the Sioux, when Sitting Bull was killed near the Missouri River. The press called for the disarming of the Indians all over the Plains. Some of the agents, notably the agent in charge of the Kiowas and Comanches at Anadarko, were insistent upon the use of troops to bring about disarmament and the stopping of the dance, a policy I resisted with all my force.

Supporting a policy of noninterference, Scott persuaded the army to allow the movement to run its course: as the prophecy failed to materialize, the movement's effectiveness and numbers would diminish. As Colonel Wilbur Nye (1937:272) described, Scott "took the position that the dance itself was harming no one, any more than a cadet hop": to use military force would only incite resistance. Scott and Iseeo visited camps throughout the region to monitor their behavior and inform superior officers if events turned serious. In employing Iseeo as an agent, Scott instructed him that he must follow his orders even if they became unpopular with his own people. In the end their efforts were instrumental in preventing bloodshed, for which Scott predicted that the Indians would greatly respect Iseeo (Nye 1937:271–72).[7]

While Scott's party was camped along the North Canadian River eighty miles north of Fort Sill and waiting for Iseeo to complete his rounds of the villages, a Kiowa scout arrived with a message from General Wesley Merritt, commander of the Department of the Missouri, ordering Scott to prepare to disarm the Indians. Scott responded with a note telling Merritt that Iseeo was constantly monitoring the developments and that the dance's doctrine involved no action against whites. He suggested that to wait and let the doctrine fail when the messiah did not appear was more prudent.

The testimony of the Kiowa Ahpeahtone, who had recently lost a son and was especially interested in the aspect of being reunited with deceased relatives, aided in the ending of the dance. In the winter of 1890–91 Ahpeahtone traveled to the northern plains to investigate the dance and finally to Mason Valley, Nevada, to meet with Wovoka about

---

7   Nye (1937:272) claims that Iseeo "was absolutely unable to understand what the Ghost Dance was all about," which seems unlikely. Iseeo was familiar with the varied forms of Kiowa religion, including the Sun Dance and peyotism, and was later a keeper of one of the Kiowa Ten Medicine Bundles. Although Iseeo may not have supported or believed in the Ghost Dance, it would seem incredible that he did not understand the basis of the movement and its prophetic claims, as much as he was involved in visiting leaders and camps performing the dance. In addition, as described in Scott's writings, Iseeo seems to have been skeptical of the other Kiowa "prophet" movements in the 1880s.

the religion. When Wovoka could neither show Ahpeahtone his dead child nor offer proof of a supernatural vision, showed no evidence of the stigmata, and required an interpreter to communicate, Ahpeahtone became disillusioned with him. Stopping at Fort Hall, Idaho, Ahpeahtone sent a telegraph to the Kiowa Agency denouncing Wovoka as a fraud then proceeded south, arriving home on February 19, 1891. When the agent learned of his impending arrival he called the Indians to assemble at the agency to hear what Ahpeahtone had to report, including the Arapaho Sitting Bull. When Ahpeahtone denounced the prophet and his movement, many were stunned and others refused to believe him. Some continued to dance in hopes of the prophecy's reality. But the messiah failed to appear in the spring of 1891, and the prophecy failed to materialize. As winter approached many had deserted the ceremony and fallen into a state of despair (Mooney 1896:907–14, 1898:221–22; Nye 1937:272–74).

In the end Scott was right. When the movement's prophecies did not materialize, people lost interest and ceased participating. Heeding Scott's suggestion, Merritt did not issue any further order to disarm the Indians. A mock dance was later held at Fort Sill by some Comanches, Cheyennes, and Arapahos for the enjoyment of some of the officers and their families, and the dance was revived among the Kiowas in 1894 and continued until 1917. But the second period of the Ghost Dance lacked the dramatic aspects and was conducted without the fear associated with the 1890 dance. Together Scott and Iseeo were able to counsel with tribes and to prevent any bloodshed—not a single shot was fired during the height of the Ghost Dance on the southern plains. Scott received an official commendation for his work (Swett 1935:348–49; Nye 1937:271; Hollis 1977:43). Shortly after the movement died down Scott (1892) published a brief account of the events. The adjutant general of the U.S. Army, Brigadier General Caleb Henry Carlton, described the value of Scott's work in a letter: "The Ghost Dance caused immense excitement in the West. . . . Doubtless, similar conflicts would have occurred between the whites and Indians in the Indian Territory had not Lieut. Scott kept constantly in touch with the tribes. . . . The Department Commander, General Merritt, wrote me that Lieut. Scott's reports were the only reports that gave him a clear and correct knowledge of these Indian affairs."[8] Although Iseeo was instrumental to Scott's success in a peaceful resolution, he unfortunately received no formal recognition. Scott would not forget Iseeo's assistance, however, and his service would later be rewarded in other ways through Scott's efforts.

---

8   C. H. Carlton, Brigadier General, U.S. Army, Headquarters of the Army, Washington D.C., to Adjutant General, U.S. Army, Washington D.C., July 8, 1902 (Scott 1928:210–14).

The Three Kiowa Boys

Another potentially volatile incident occurred on January 9, 1891, that could have resulted in an armed response by the Kiowas. Scott and Iseeo were again able to control the situation (Scott 1928:158–61, 212). By this time several Kiowa children were attending the government-run Kiowa school in Anadarko, including Séth<u>á</u>idè (Small Intestine), Káuiqáunhól (Dragonfly), and Màuchàchê (Muchacho). When Small Intestine, the eldest of the boys and then about fourteen years old, received a whipping from Barton Wheritt, one of the white schoolteachers, he decided to run away from the school and return to his home camp on Stinking Creek some thirty miles away. He persuaded two younger schoolmates to accompany him. As the three boys set out for the Kiowa camp a terrible blizzard set in that night, reported as the worst in that part of the country for many years. After traversing nearly the entire distance the boys apparently drifted off course to the southwest by two to three miles, where they succumbed to the cold and froze to death. A few days later the three boys were found on the slope of a hill southwest of Zodaltone Springs by a dog of one of the boys that led Kiowa searchers to them. When the cause of the boys running away from the school was learned, the Kiowas were justifiably upset. As they began to congregate near the agency, the agent perceived their presence as threatening and feared an outbreak.

When agent Charles Adams telegraphed Fort Sill for assistance, then post commander Colonel Caleb H. Carlton wanted to send a squadron of cavalry to control the situation but was persuaded against doing so by Lieutenant Scott, who told him that he and Iseeo could go and settle the matter. Scott, Iseeo, and post interpreter Horace P. Jones were sent from Fort Sill to investigate and report on the manner. Because of Jones's physical condition, he and Scott rode in a wagon, while Iseeo rode ahead on horseback, carrying a lantern to lead the wagon. The three rode thirty-three miles through mud and snow to reach the agency in a wagon around four in the morning. Shortly after breakfast Iseeo was sent among the camps to gather the chiefs together so that Scott could address them. Scott managed to prevent any retribution. One Kiowa woman was said to have threatened to knife Wheritt if she found him. Wherritt reportedly hid himself for an entire day, leaving the agency that night (Nye 1937:274–75). Agent Adams (U.S. Office of Indian Affairs 1891:351) wrote: "The loss of the three boys who ran away from the Kiowa school and were frozen to death in the snow was an occurrence which might have been productive of most serious results. It speaks well for the Kiowa Indians that it not only was passed without such consequences, but seems to have left no prejudice against the school. It has been most gratifying to me on several occasions during the year to note the growing spirit of self-control among these people, and their desire to stand by lawful authority." Nevertheless, Adams, the school principal, and others called for strong action to be taken against the Indians, in particular a request for the arrest of one of the boy's uncle who had come and whipped the principal with his riding quirt. Reflecting his judicial management of the situation and his coolheadedness, Scott countered that use of force might result in a senseless tragedy. With Iseeo, Scott was able to disperse the mourning group quietly and without incident. Scott telegraphed Fort Sill to report that no troops were needed (Nye 1937:274–75).

The Poolant Incident

In September 1891 Scott and Iseeo were called upon for a third time to prevent a possible armed fight (Mooney 1898:361; Scott 1928:162–64). A Kiowa man named Poolant was killed by a ranch hand after trying to recover a horse that Poolant claimed had been stolen from him from a nearby ranch in the edge of Greer County, which bordered the southwest portion of the KCA Reservation.[9] Tensions quickly mounted between the local Kiowas and non-Indians with the formation of armed parties that eyed one another across the reservation boundary for two days. When word of the incident reached Fort Sill, Scott made a forced march of sixty-seven miles with a small contingent of troops to the camp of Big Bow. Although Nye (1937:275–76) does not mention Iseeo's role in the event, Swett (1935:348) and Hollis (1977:43) write that Scott dispatched Iseeo ahead to counsel moderation. After he reached the camp and reminded the chiefs that Poolant was off the reservation without a permit, was trespassing when he tried to take the horse, and had only himself to blame for his death, the chiefs agreed to settle the matter legally. The ranch hand was tried and acquitted, prompting the ranch owner to give several beeves to the Kiowas in an attempt to settle the matter. Major General Robert Hollis (1977:43) aptly described the judicious strategy that Scott and Isseo used and their reputation among the tribes in western Oklahoma: "The Indians knew Lt. Scott's reputation for fairness and they trusted I-See-O's judgment and counsel. In the end cooler heads prevailed and hostilities were prevented."

---

9 Poolant is the Kiowa Agency spelling of Fólą́jè (Crawling or Approaching Snake).

Troop L, 7th Cavalry (June 30, 1891–May 31, 1897)

Congress rapidly began cutting military spending following the Civil War, as was typical of American armed forces policy. With a downsized army, many troops were involved in the reconstruction of the South, leaving limited numbers of troops to fight a series of ongoing wars against Indians in the plains, Southwest, and California. The image of the martial nature of Indians was now well impressed in the non-Indian psyche. In need of individuals who were familiar with the geography and tribes of the West, the army pressured Congress to pass an act in 1866 allowing the establishment of an Indian scouting corps. It was believed that Indians, especially those with excellent equestrian skills, would make good horse soldiers for the U.S. Cavalry. Numerous civilians, especially those in the Indian Service and pro-assimilation reformers, favored the idea, including commissioner of Indian Affairs Francis A. Walker, who believed that military service would help integrate Indians into mainstream society and provide employment for them. Others stressed that service would offer a constructive outlet for recently defeated young men from some of "the most warlike tribes" and would encourage discipline, obedience, industry, cleanliness, punctuality, and knowledge of English. Some believed that the use of Indian scouts would benefit the army through personnel, provide order among tribes, reduce the number of hostile Indians, and provide time to further teach Indians the ways of white society when not fighting (White 1976:17).

Indians became enlisted personnel but were frequently paid less than regular soldiers. They served as scouts and often as combat troops, both with and independently of Anglo troops. Enlistment was usually dictated by the advent of emergency situations. While expenditures for only 300 Indian scouts were appropriated, this limited number was soon raised in 1876 due to increased conflicts in the plains and Southwest. The Indian soldiers proved themselves in numerous instances between 1876 and 1890. Some American military commanders were confident in the military service and political allegiance of American Indians, believing that they could serve as regular troops and not just as scouts (Holm 1996:94–95).

Major-General John M. Schofield, who succeeded Philip Sheridan as commanding general of the army in 1888, also influenced these developments. Schofield sought to integrate Indians into mainstream American society and believed that the army could greatly facilitate the transition. In 1890 the United States Army developed an experimental military force composed of all-Indian units, based on the success of an army consisting of units of Indian locals by the British. On July 25, 1890, recently appointed secretary of war Redfield Proctor, a pro-assimilation reformer, reassigned all soldiers in Troop L of the first eight regiments of cavalry in the army. After the end of the Sioux War in South Dakota during the winter of 1890–91 the secretary of war wanted to supplement some of the existing cavalry troops with low numbers with Indian soldiers. In 1891 Congress introduced a bill proposing the reorganization of infantry and artillery services and the enlistment of two thousand American Indians. After prolonged discourse the bill was defeated by a small margin in the House of Representatives (Mooney 1898:223; Scott 1928:168; White 1976:17; Holm 1996:96–98; Spivey n.d.).

Nevertheless, on March 9, 1891, Secretary Proctor issued General Order No. 28, authorizing the enlistment of Indians in formerly organized troops and companies, including one company of American Indians for each of the twenty-six regiments of non-Indian cavalry and infantry then serving west of the Mississippi River, excluding black units. This order provided for all-Indian units to be formed in Troop L of each cavalry regiment except the 9th and 10th, which were black, Company I of each infantry regiment except the 6th, 11th, 15th, 19th, 24th, and 25th, which included the black organizations, and some eastern regiments. Officers and noncommissioned officers in the units would be white, although noncommissioned officers would eventually be Indian recruits. That May a circulatory letter was issued, directing that the instruction of Indian recruits begin immediately and include tactical movements, care of quarters and bunks, and athletic exercises. While English was not required for enlistment, the teaching of English was planned as a part of their instruction. Seminal to the success of these units would be the degree of cultural knowledge and understanding of the non-Indian officers presiding over them. Proctor believed that the structured nature of army life would further assimilation goals, which he (in contrast to other reformers) felt must occur gradually and in stages. Many Lakotas enlisted due to need for food and shelter (Mooney 1898:223; Scott 1928:168; White 1976:17; Holm 1996:96–98; Spivey n.d.).

Troop L, 7th Cavalry, was entirely wiped out at the Battle of the Little Bighorn under Lieutenant Colonel George A. Custer in 1876. Ironically, it was reconstituted at Fort Sill in 1891 as an all-Indian unit. Troop L functioned from June 30, 1891, through May 31, 1897, and was composed mainly of Kiowas, Apaches, some Comanches, and a few Cheyennes and Arapahos (Spivey n.d.). In 1891 fifty-four Indians enlisted in Troop L, including approximately thirty-six Kiowas, sixteen Comanches, and two

Apaches. After February 1892 sixty-four additional members joined the unit, including two Kiowas, eleven Comanches, and fifty-one Fort Sill Apaches.[10]

When Captain Jesse Lee of the 9th Infantry, who had been successful in recruiting Lakotas, was sent to Fort Sill to recruit Kiowas and Comanches he encountered resistance. Some Comanche tribal leaders such as Tabenanaka and White Wolf told him to go back to Washington and walked out of a meeting with him. Many Comanches were persuaded not to join by Quanah Parker and Tabenanaka on the premise that Christianity was then teaching them that it was wrong to go to war. In addition Kiowa chiefs including Poor Buffalo also initially discouraged their young men from joining. A month after the Kiowas and Comanches told Captain Lee that they did not want to serve as soldiers, Poor Buffalo invited Scott to his lodge and told him through sign language that the chiefs had changed their minds. A troop was formed and filled shortly thereafter (Scott 1928:168–70). Scott notes that men were also reluctant to enlist due to fear of being forced to cut their hair, whereupon he told them they could cut it or "let it drag on the ground so far as I was concerned, and they all enlisted." The War Department issued an order for all to cut their hair, which was gradually achieved, with eleven members coming forward and asking Scott for a quarter each to get their hair cut. The others gradually followed suit. The last holdout, an Arapaho named Yellow Bull, had one of his braids cut off by some of the Kiowa scouts while sleeping and later had the other side cut to match (Scott 1928:170). Although Iseeo was later photographed wearing traditional braids, a photo circa 1892 of him in field uniform shows that he also cut his hair during his tenure in Troop L (Spivey n.d.). A second photo taken in 1898 also shows Iseeo with short hair and wearing civilian clothes.[11]

None of the Indians spoke English, so Ernest Stecker of Troop M, who also knew sign language, was reassigned as first sergeant to assist with paperwork. Thomas Clancy was assigned as quartermaster sergeant to look after supplies and equipment and Iseeo as first sergeant. Other noncommissioned officers were chosen from the Indian troops (Scott 1928:169). Although Iseeo, who also could not speak English, was initially appointed as a figurehead, he clearly served important roles both symbolically in

---

10 Troop L, 7th U.S. Cavalry (1929). I have been unable to positively identify the tribal affiliation of a few names, so these numbers are close approximations.
11 Cf. "Profile of Aisiai (Many Tipi Tracks)," March 1898, Photo BAE GN01409B 06265500, National Anthropological Archives. Smithsonian Institution, Washington, D.C.

having an Indian in an officer's position and functionally in his dedication to the job and his rapport with Scott and the military. The scouts moved their tipis and came to camp in a designated area on the post. Scott's outdoor orientation, his overall respect for Indian peoples, his familiarity with the members of many tribes and Plains Sign Language, and his increasingly good standing among the tribes of western Indian Territory made him well suited to the assignment.

In 1894 a contingent of Apache prisoners of war arrived at Fort Sill from Florida and Alabama. Initially enlisted in Company I in another infantry unit, they quickly transferred to Troop L. Some Kiowa members of Troop L, such as Wohaw, had also been prisoners of war from 1875 to 1878 at Fort Marion, Florida. As former Fort Sill Museum curator Towana Spivey (n.d.) notes, "The contradiction of Indian Prisoners of War serving in the U.S. Army, carrying weapons, drawing a monthly salary, and being soldiers in every sense, was indeed unusual." Composed largely of Cheyennes and Arapahos, Troop L of the 5th Cavalry Regiment was housed at nearby Fort Reno, some eighty miles to the north. Enlistment in the Indian units did not require knowledge of English due to the presence of interpreters. At Fort Sill the efficacy of relations between officer and enlisted men was enhanced, if not superseded, by Scott's extensive knowledge of sign language.

At Fort Sill regimental headquarters assigned officers to the Indian units, while noncommissioned officers were temporarily appointed until Indian noncommissioned officers could replace them. Indian soldiers received the use of government horses and the standard monthly wage of $13, while scouts received a monthly stipend of $25 for using personal horses. Separate records were kept for Indian soldiers and scouts. Up to ten married men per troop/company could live with their families. Photographs of the Troop L encampment depict several rows of canvas tipis located on the flat ground immediately north of the Trader's Store (Spivey n.d.).

Although usually referred to as scouts, the soldiers of Troop L, which was formed sixteen years after hostilities on the southern plains ended, were actually enlisted regular cavalry in a noncombat era, not scouts. While their duties involved no combat action, Troop L provided valuable service to Fort Sill and the army. Members policed the reservation for trespassers, land squatters, illegal cattle rangers, timber thieves, whiskey peddlers, and any outsiders infringing on the reservation and its resources. Non-Indian soldiers, Indian scouts, and Troop L members provided mounted escorts for payroll wagons and supply trains to guard against criminal elements

Camp of Troop L, 7th Cavalry members and families,
near the Fort Sill Hotel, Oklahoma Territory, 1892.
*Photo #P1046, The Fort Sill National Historic
Landmark, Fort Sill, Oklahoma.*

that frequently roamed through Oklahoma and Indian Territories and oversaw cattle drives that crossed Indian lands from Texas to the north. Individuals found to be illegally present on the post or reservation were escorted to the nearest boundary (Scott 1928:127–40). Troop members were also used for reconnaissance through scouting, as messengers, and to help maintain peace on the reservation. In the most critical times, such as occasions of possible uprisings or armed resistance, Scott often used Iseeo to visit the Indian camps in advance and dissolve the matter diplomatically. Due to their assignments some members developed special skills such as blacksmithing and wagon repair, while others became farmers and ranchers in their spare time. Troop members were also employed for leading hunting parties into the nearly Wichita Mountains to provide wild game to supplement the post diet, to provide fresh deer and turkey for the post officers' holiday dinners and for visiting military dignitaries who desired a recreational hunting trip. Although normal military activities occupied much of their time, the duties were not onerous overall. Much time was spent in camp playing the card game monte (Mooney 1898:223, 362; Nye 1962:261–62; Meadows 1999:378–79; Spivey n.d.).

Rank aside, a degree of mutual respect and friendship developed between some of the officers and the Kiowa and Comanche members of Troop L, as demonstrated in tribal naming practices. In 1891 Tonemah (Tónmàui or Water Drinker) named his son Lieutenant Quay after Lieutenant A. G. Clayton Quay of Troop L. Among the Kiowas the boy was known as Lòtán, the Kiowa pronunciation of "lieutenant." The name "Quay" has continued to be handed down in the Tonemah family to the present.[12] In 1913 Tonemah named another son General Scott Tonemah, based on his association with Troop L. In 1895 another Kiowa in Troop L, E-mau-ah (Sleeping Bear, short for Sétèmmâuà̱, Bear That Repeatedly Arises And Lies Down), named his son Captain Scott Emauah.[13] During Scott's time with the Kiowas he acquired two Kiowa names, both related to personal traits, which is a common basis of naming in Kiowa culture. Há̱ujàqì (Bespeckled, literally, Metal Eyes) refers to Scott's eyeglasses and visual status. Kà̱uàukâui (Baggy Pants, literally, Wrinkled or Floppy Pants) referred to the bulging wide-hipped military trousers of the time.[14] Both articles appear in photos of Scott during this period. While the Indian scouts undoubtedly addressed by standard military protocol of rank, these names were most likely used among the Kiowas themselves in referring to Scott. Shortly after arriving at Fort Sill, Scott was given the name Molay-tay-quop (Sign Talker) by the Comanches (Scott 1928:129). Harrington (1938:132) reports that the Cheyennes sometimes called Scott "Sign User."

Despite optimism difficulties soon developed in the program. While many Indians such as the Lakotas initially enlisted due to conditions of poverty following the recent end of hostilities, their numbers soon dropped off, especially in infantry units, as reservation conditions improved. Indians were also reluctant to enlist if their service meant leaving their families, local community, or hunting and improved agricultural grounds. The limit of ten married men per company meant that few could relocate their families to post quarters. Other issues arose concerning higher pay and

---

12 Author's fieldnotes, Tonemah Family, 1994–96, Tonemah Family Reunion, Meers, Oklahoma, 1995.

13 Kiowa Family Record (1901: Fam. 325): Lieutenant Quay Tone-mah (the name Quay continues in the Tonemah family to the present); Kiowa Family Record (1901: Fam. 350): Captain Scott Em-mau-ah. Kiowa Tribal Census (1920: Fam. 325-1/4); Parker McKenzie to the author, Apr. 17, 1994.

14 Parker McKenzie to the author, Mar. 21, 1993, Apr. 4, 1993. See also Scott (n.d.a:I:194, chapter 4 in this volume).

fewer regulations for scouts, military methods of punishment, compliance with military custom, unauthorized absence, and reluctance to cut their hair or receive vaccinations.

One of the largest problems with the Indian scout troops was their reaction to changes in officers and leadership. As Towana Spivey (n.d.) described:

> Over the years leadership problems sometimes developed at some of the Posts when trusted officers were replaced with new individuals unknown to the Indians, leaving them to wonder what the first officer had done wrong. The Indians' philosophy of following the person, not the rank, became obvious. Discipline began to break down in some of the units at various Posts resulting in negative reports by newly arrived commanders. Eventually, the experiment was deemed a failure throughout the Army and the all-Indian units were inactivated.

By the end of 1894 army administrators viewed the Indian Scout Program as largely a failure, and some units began to be disbanded. Attempts to reinvigorate the units were made by recruiting from eastern Indian boarding schools, where individuals would have a greater degree of assimilation and knowledge of English (White 1976:17–18). In 1897 the War Department disbanded the Indian Scout program. In January 1895 Scott was promoted to captain and continued as commander of Troop L until it was mustered out of active duty. Troop L at Fort Sill was considered to be the most successful Indian unit in the entire army. It was the only Indian unit to serve out its full time and was the last Indian troop to be deactivated on June 30, 1897, when the remaining fifty-three Indians were discharged. During the Army's Indian Scout Program 1,071 Indians served between March 1891 and June 1897 (Mooney 1898:223, 362; Scott 1928:169; Spivey n.d.).

As Jack Foner (1970:129–30) demonstrates, racism, distrust of Indians, and the army's view that incorporating Indians was a form of social experiment were the principal obstacles to the continuation of Indian companies. At Fort Sill Troop L placed above the middle of all the army organizations with the rifle, was fourth of eighteen cavalry troops in the Department of the Missouri with the revolver, and was considered a success in every aspect by the War Department except one: it was a success as long as Scott remained with it and its officers could not be replaced, as was typical in white units. Despite the formation of four companies of Indian cavalry, three of infantry, and satisfactory results, the companies were viewed as a disappointment overall and were disbanded. This change was not the result of the Indians' service, which received high marks, but due to the attitudes toward Indians in the officers' corps and the loss of support with a change in the secretary of war (Mooney 1898:223; Scott 1928:168–69; Holm 1996:96–98). Scott (1928:170) recorded his view of the program's undermining by higher-ranking personnel: "The truth was that the army was angry at General Schofield for mustering out white men of the two troops in each regiment, and did not want the experiment to succeed. Innumerable obstacles were thrown in my way by unthinking officers, and support in Washington was withheld by a change of the secretary of war."

Nevertheless, Troop L as a whole was viewed successful by the War Department, and in Scott's (1928:170) view the experience was beneficial to its participants.

> The men of that troop nevertheless are men of power and influence now in the Kiowa reservation and dictate its policies, and I have been told by a number of agents that the marked difference between this agency and those surrounding it was caused by the discipline, instruction, and general improvement brought about by service in that troop, and that it would be of advantage to the government to have a similar troop at every agency. The men were made to save their money, and by the time that they were discharged they received help from troop funds, so that every one of them had a house on his lot, to which he retired.

Jennings C. Wise (1931:529), who served as a staff officer in the American Expeditionary Forces during World War I and later under John R. Eddy in the Historical Section of the General Staff at the General Headquarters in the United States, which conducted a study of Indian service in World War I, also confirms the success of the Indian scouts' service. Wise attributes the termination of the Indian scouting program to the end of active warfare on the plains and the view that their service as scouts had helped Indians adapt to the reservation and was no longer needed. However, individual Indian enlistments continued.

Studies of Indian scouts and auxiliaries from the 1860s through World War I repeatedly demonstrated that the U.S. government and Indian reformers intended to incorporate Indians in U.S. military service to provide scouts to aid in subduing the remaining autonomous Indians in the plains and Southwest and to promote Indian assimilation into Anglo society through a form of military service acceptable to non-Indians (White 1968, 1976; Dunlay 1982; Tate 1986; Meadows 1999:378–81; Van De Logt

2010). In hindsight this practice had dual results. While it did familiarize a number of younger Indian males with aspects of Anglo-American life, it provided a means for the continuation and retention of both a tribal (ethnic) and warrior tradition and ethos (Meadows 1999:377–401).

Scouting programs of the late 1800s came at a critical period when younger men were faced with having no venue for acquiring and expressing traditional male roles through martial status. This was especially important for younger men whose war records became frozen with the end of hostilities on the southern plains in 1875 and for those who were born too late to have participated in prereservation-era warfare. A review of the ages of Troop L members at Fort Sill (see the appendix) with tribal enrollment records demonstrates that the overwhelming majority of individuals who served in Troop L had limited or no preservation warfare experience. Scouting provided a new means of gaining status in traditional tribal contexts of males distinguishing themselves as warriors, including the wearing of military dress and the sanctioned right to bear arms and enforce law. Although Troop L at Fort Sill saw no combat, many other Indian troops such as the Pawnees, Apaches, Crows, Warm Springs, Sioux, and Cheyennes did, resulting in an overall retention of respective tribal martial traditions that spanned a critical period between the beginning of the reservation era and later service in the world wars. Consequently numerous ceremonies to send off and welcome home veterans, songs and dances with martial themes, and participation in men's ceremonial societies were reinvigorated for a new generation. Many of these cultural practices were repeatedly intensified with later military service in the twentieth century (Meadows 1999:377–401).

The Apache Prisoners of War (1894 to 1897)

Scott was also in charge of Geronimo's band of Chiricahuas and other Apaches who were placed at Fort Sill as prisoners of war in 1894. Already familiar with the tribes and geography of the region, Scott was a logical choice for the assignment. After visiting the prisoners in their incarceration at Mount Vernon, Alabama, he recommended that the band of Eskimazin (sometimes given as Eskiminzin) be returned to Arizona and the others be sent to Fort Sill. Initially the Kiowas and Comanches did not want the prisoners relocated, as they had past animosities with these Apache groups. Scott aided in gaining Kiowa and Comanche consent to allow the Apaches to have land on a portion of the military reserve that would legally revert back to them if the military no longer used it and an executive order to expand the land base to give each individual 160 acres upon allotment. Eventually Eskimazin's band was returned to Arizona, while Geronimo and Naiche's groups arrived at Fort Sill on October 7, 1894. The following spring Scott oversaw the development of communities and headmen as well as house construction. He hired some as scouts, who were issued uniforms. During his remaining four years at Fort Sill, Scott also oversaw the employment of many Apaches in farming and ranching operations, arranging the purchase of a herd of cattle for them. Several Apaches enlisted in Troop L during its last two and half years. Scott saw their mortality decline and their birthrate increase, commended their good behavior, and noted that no complaint from an outsider was ever lodged against the Apaches. During this time Scott was offered the opportunity to transfer to Fort Supply, which was about to be closed, with the Apaches. He declined and actually persuaded General Nelson Miles to have them sent to Fort Sill. Although Scott interacted often with the Apaches, they did not use sign language, requiring an interpreter or an Apache youth who had returned from Carlisle Indian School to facilitate communication (Scott 1928:184–92; Nye 1937:297–99). Consequently Scott's notes contains almost no ethnographic data on the Apaches.

Allotment

Following congressional approval of the Dawes Act in 1886, a commission began visiting various plains tribes to negotiate for the assignment of individual allotments of land and for the opening and sale of the remainder of their respective reservations.[15] In the fall of 1892 the Cherokee Commission, better known as the Jerome Commission, visited the Kiowa, Comanche, and Apache Reservation. Because the terms under the Medicine Lodge Treaty did not expire until August 25, 1898, the KCA were opposed to changes in the existing conditions (Mooney 1898:225).

Scott was highly sympathetic toward the KCA concern about the efforts of the Jerome Commission to persuade or force Indian consent to allotment and their efforts to resist the proposed agreement. He reportedly became aware of a conspiracy planned by John Hill to manipulate signatures in support of the commission and attempted to help the Indians by seeking the aid of a friend who was a lawyer. Both Scott and Indian agent George

---

15   Clark (1999) provides the most extensive work on the allotment of the Kiowa-Comanche-Apache Reservation and the case of *Lone Wolf v. Hitchcock*.

Day spoke during the official negotiations. While they talked in neutral terms for the record, they privately worked to gain Indian consent to the final agreement (Hagan 1976:210–11; Clark 1999:44–45).

As negotiations continued, the Indians furnished a list of white men that they desired to receive allotments. This included whites married to Indians, Indian agent George Day, Scott, the Reverend J. J. Methvin, and others in reservation-related occupations such as interpreters and one tenant farmer. The commissioners added others to the list, viewing it as a small price to pay for persuading a quorum to sign the document (Clark 1999:44–45). During the following eight years the Indians and various lobbyists managed to delay congressional ratification of the Jerome Agreement through impassioned appeals on their behalf. Scott wrote to the secretary of war that the implementation of allotment would result in taking away the last lands held by the wards and turn them "into a band of miserable and degraded beggars."[16]

Finally the commission declared that it had acquired the necessary quorum of approving signatures to take the agreement before Congress for ratification. When the Indians learned of the true content of the negotiations, they denounced their interpreter Joshua Given, a Kiowa, and demanded that their signatures be removed from the agreement. The final meeting between the tribes and the commission ended in a melee of shouting, with the commission instructing the Indians that they had congressional power, that the government had decided to open up the land, and that the Indians must accept the proposal offered or receive less when allotment was enforced. Upon the government denying this, the Indians repudiated the actions of their leaders in council, replaced Lone Wolf with Ahpeahtone, and elected representatives to go to Washington to protest the Jerome Agreement. The party, consisting of Ahpeahtone, Apache John, and Big Looking Glass, Captain Scott, and Kiowa captive Andrés Martínez as interpreter, arrived in Washington, D.C., in March 1894 (Mooney 1898:225; Clark 1999:47–48). During this visit Scott and James Mooney met with commissioner of Indian Affairs Daniel Browning. During one meeting led by Scott and Ahpeahtone and sympathetic to their cause, Commissioner Browning became angry, slamming his fist into his other hand and strenuously declaring: "I will not permit it. I will see justice done to those Indians as long as I am in power." With the help of others, Browning helped postpone ratification for seven years (Scott 1928:201).

---

16   Scott to Daniel S. Lamont, May 11, 1893, in Sen. Doc. 77, p. 5, in Clark (1999:50, 152).

Scott (1928:199–202) reports that the KCA elected him to lead a delegation from the three tribes to Washington to prevent ratification of the treaty by Congress. Quanah Parker, who was in favor of allotment, had received permission to travel to Carlisle Indian School to visit his children but had gone to Washington to arrange for a hearing before the Committee on Indian Affairs, allegedly without knowledge of the local Indian agent. Arriving the same day, Scott and the KCA contingent sat in on Parker's testimony in favor of allotment, after which they requested to be heard. Scott produced credentials from the KCA reservation agent allowing him to be there. According to Scott, when challenged to show credentials Quanah did not do so, being there without knowledge of the agent. When Scott presented the case that the majority of the KCA did not want allotment and that Quanah did not speak for everyone, a heated debate ensued between Scott and the KCA delegation and Quanah and the Oklahoma congressional delegate. Scott (1928:201) reports: "Quanah announced his intention of killing me before I could get back to Fort Sill, and the committee reserved decision." Later Scott, Ahpeahtone, and others met with President Grover Cleveland and Senator Matt Quay of Pennsylvania, father of Scott's fellow officer Lieutenant A. G. Clayton Quay, who also aided in preventing ratification of a bill to allot the KCA Reservation for seven years. Scott notes that in those days he was an enemy of the Indian Department and everyone in it as well as Oklahoma congressional representatives. Scott also appears to have favored Ahpeahtone and contributed to his rise in prominence over Lone Wolf as Kiowa tribal chief in 1894 (Scott 1928:157–58, 201–202).

During every session of Congress between the Jerome Commission's work in 1892 and the passage of the act in 1900, delegations of Indians appeared before Congress and the commissioner of Indian Affairs requesting significant modifications in the agreement (Clark 1999:52). These and other meetings, along with continued lobbying, correspondence, and protests, resulted in a temporary postponement of the agreement. Finally, despite their efforts, allotment was implemented in 1901, resulting in the seminal case of *Lone Wolf v. Hitchcock* in 1903, which established Congress's right of plenary power, to make and break its own decisions and agreements when it deemed necessary.

During his years on the plains (1876–97) Scott witnessed many of the traditional aspects of Plains Indian culture. In the northern plains this included bison and antelope hunts, the return of a successful war party and scalp dance, policed bison hunts and "soldiering" or punishment of those who broke tribal hunting laws by military societies, and traditional games. He personally participated in bison hunts with a gun and a bow and arrow. In the southern plains he witnessed the end of the Sun Dance and the Ghost Dance as well as the six years of the all-Indian Troop L. Scott participated in the capture of bank robbers (the McDonald brothers) and driving a group of criminals out of Norman, guarded against Texas cattle ranchers grazing on reservation lands, helped provide security for the land rush at Purcell, Indian Territory, on April 22, 1889, and was involved in the events leading up to the devastating Jerome Agreement and allotment of the KCA Reservation (Scott 1928:127–207).

While supervising a cattle drive through the reservation near the western end of the Wichita Mountains, a Kiowa reported a golden eagle's nest five miles from their camp. Scott and his cousin climbed above and then down to the nest, where they found an immature golden eagle. They put the eagle in a gunny sack and returned with it, tethering the bird at their camp. Elders warned them that some misfortune might come to them for having taken the young eagle from the nest. Scott soon fell ill with a malarial fever at the camp and had to be brought back seventy-five miles to Fort Sill by army ambulance. The next morning one of the non-Indian troopers drowned while swimming in the North Fork of the Red River. The elders attributed the death to taking the eagle from the nest. Nevertheless, Scott kept the eagle and plucked its tail five times, producing sixty feathers that Iseeo, Elk Tongue, and Chaka made into a long feathered bonnet. Upon leaving Fort Sill in 1897, Scott shipped the eagle to Fairmount Park in Pennsylvania (Scott 1928:139–40).[17]

Frequently living in Indian encampments for extended periods, Scott repeatedly observed many of the daily customs and practices of a variety of tribes. During these years Scott came to know many of the most prominent Indian leaders of their respective tribes and communicated with them in sign language. He resided with some of them for periods in their lodges. In the north this included Red Cloud (Lakota), Joseph (Nez Perce), Two Bears (Yanktonai), Iron Bull (Crow), and Dull Knife, Wild Hog, Old Crow, Two Moons, Little Chief, Hump, Black Wolf, Ice or White Bull, Brave Wolf, and White Bear (Cheyenne). The following incident reflects Scott's attitude toward the Indians of the plains. Although he was warned by his friends not to accompany the Cheyennes who served as scouts on a trip in search of Sitting Bull (who, they felt, would surely kill Scott and cross into Canada to Sitting Bull's camp), Scott (1928:52) felt differently.

---

17 For an account of the capture of the eagle, see Davis (1903:171–72).

But I never felt that way toward them. They were all keen, athletic young men, tall and lean and brave, and I admired them as real specimens of manhood more than any body of men I have ever seen before or since. They were perfectly adapted to their environment, and knew just what to do in every emergency and when to do it, without any confusion or lost motion. Their poise and dignity were superb; no royal person ever had more assured manners. I watched their every movement and learned lessons from them that later saved my life many times on the prairie.

In the south, Scott came to know Quanah Parker (Comanche), Big Bow, Stumbling Bear, Ahpeahtone, Poor Buffalo, Heidsick, Taybodle (Kiowa), the Ghost Dance prophet Sitting Bull (Arapaho), Geronimo and Naiche (Chiricahua Apache), and Chee Dodge (Navajo). He also became well acquainted with nearly every major figure in the United States Army, including Generals Nelson A. Miles, William Tecumseh Sherman, Alfred Terry, Philip Sheridan, Oliver Howard, Wesley Merritt, and Leonard Wood, and many international dignitaries as well as Presidents Theodore Roosevelt, William Howard Taft, and Woodrow Wilson. Scott was also personally acquainted with a who's-who list of western American historical figures (and in some instances was a close friend), including Liver Eating Johnson, Frank and Jesse James, William Buffalo Bill Cody, Annie Oakley, Frederick Remington, and noted scouts and translators Ben Clark and Horace P. Jones.

One of the most humorous experiences that Scott (1928:186–87) recorded during his time at Fort Sill was when he met the noted painter Frederick Remington: "Remington told me that I was the most disappointing man he had ever seen; he had been hearing about me in the Indian country for ten years and now meeting me at last he found me looking like a college professor, I asked him what he expected me to look like, but he avoided specifying. Notwithstanding his disappointment at my appearance, we became excellent and enduring friends."

Scott also helped preserve Fort Sill. With the end of the Indian wars in 1890 President Cleveland's administration chose to close a number of plains army posts in the mid-1890s. Fort Sill was listed for closing due to the presence of Fort Reno only seventy-five miles away. It was favored over Fort Sill by General Merritt, who had been stationed there. Although Sill had better water, it needed significant repairs in terms of the outward progression of the gables and the cracking of interior plaster walls. Considering its better water, more scenic proximity to the Wichita Mountains, significant history, and the need to maintain army troops in the area, Scott set out to save the post from closing. Scott discovered that most of the problems were due to lack of foundations for many of the buildings and saved three hundred dollars on the construction of a water tank to use it for excavations and jacks to insert foundation stones. When the chief quartermaster visited Fort Sill, he found the expenditure satisfying, gave eight thousand dollars the following year for repairs, and promised twenty-five thousand dollars the year after. After examining Scott's use of the second installment, the quartermaster was pleased. Scott was notified that Fort Reno and not Fort Sill would be closed. Scott went on to engineer other repairs to help the post. When J. Franklin Bell became chief of staff, policy changed: more than $1 million was put into Fort Sill to develop a school of fire (Scott 1928:141, 185). Since that time there has been no real consideration of closing Fort Sill, which remains the principal military training site for artillery.

Leaving Indian Territory

After nine years of service at Fort Sill, Scott decided to transfer back east in 1897. Although he did not want to leave the West and his many friends, he realized that his children needed a better locale in order to obtain a good education. In November 1897 Scott sought and received an appointment with the Bureau of American Ethnology (BAE) under Major John Wesley Powell. Scott was assigned to compile and write a comprehensive ethnographic account of the Indian sign language. Why Scott was released from his normal military duty is unclear. With the phasing out of the Troop L programs, additional studies of Plains Indian Sign Language would not appear to be of use to the military. Following the early deaths of W. P. Clark in 1884 and Garrick Mallery in 1894, ending their research, Scott was the most qualified person remaining to research and publish on the subject, which undoubtedly was of interest to the BAE.

Correspondence indicates that Scott left Fort Sill in early December 1897. In a December 12, 1897, letter to Scott, acting agent Frank Baldwin, then at the Kiowa Agency in Anadarko, Oklahoma Territory, refers to a December 5, 1897, letter that he received from Scott, expressing regret that he had not seen Baldwin prior to his departure from Fort Sill due to having been out of the office on assignments. Baldwin's letter and others demonstrate that even at this early date Scott took measures to ensure that subsequent officers at Fort Sill and the Kiowa Agency would take an interest in seeing that Iseeo did not want for anything, "I will certainly do all I can for your old sergeant Is-e-o. If he has any wants or wishes, I hope he will not hesitate to come and let me know what they are."[18] Although Scott would continue to assist Indian peoples in varied ways throughout the rest of his life, this would be the last major assignment in which he worked directly with Indians on a regular basis until after his retirement in 1917.

Scott was given access to the Library of Congress and to the Geological Survey, where he began searching the accounts of the earliest Spanish and French explorers. He had barely gotten started collecting background material for his sign language manuscript when the sinking of the USS *Maine* in Havana on February 15, 1898, and related political and military unrest in Cuba prompted the outbreak of the Spanish-American War. Scott was soon reassigned (Scott 1928:207–29). In May 1898 he was appointed major of volunteers and assistant adjutant general of the 2nd and 3rd Divisions, I Corps. He reported for duty in Havana, Cuba, in 1889. Although he saw no action in that war, Scott was assigned to Cuba as adjutant general, Department of Havana, with the rank of lieutenant colonel of volunteers. In light of the general reduction in U.S. armed forces after 1890, Scott's skills and connections furthered his value to the military as it began to take on a new role as an army of occupation of American overseas territories. The same diplomatic skills that he had honed on the Great Plains of North America, which had brought him to the attention of military leaders such as Philip Sheridan, Nelson Miles, Leonard Wood, and others, would serve him well in Cuba, the Philippines, and then again in the United States. In May 1900 he was promoted to adjutant general of the Department of Cuba. During this time he served as acting governor, aided in establishing the first public library in Cuba, figured prominently in settling political and military unrest in Cien Fuegos, and was actively involved in the transfer of the government into Cuban hands. Scott remained at that post until May 1902, when he returned to Washington, D.C. (Scott 1928:229–72).

In February 1903 Scott was appointed major of regulars and under the Bates Agreement served as military governor of the Sulu Archipelago in the Philippine Islands until 1906. During this assignment he established peace and prevented uprisings among warring regional factions of the Moros (then engaged in an ongoing violent conflict). He put down the slave trade and dealt with the activities of various outlaws and pirates marauding in the region. Scott commanded troops and took part in several

---

18 Hugh L. Scott (Princeton, N.J.) to Samuel A. Eliot, Chairman Board of Indian Commissioners, Washington, D.C., Dec. 5, 1927 (Scott n.d.b: MS 4525); Captain and Acting Agent Frank Baldwin to Hugh L. Scott, Dec. 12, 1897, Box 7, Gen. H. L. Scott Coll., 1893–1902 File (Scott n.d.g).

skirmishes and sieges of Moro strongholds. In one fight he was severely wounded in both hands: despite a doctor's warning concerning the possibility of losing both through amputations, Scott continued with both arms in bandages until he completed his assignment. He lost two fingers from these injuries. He then reorganized the civil government and institutions (Arlington National Cemetery 2010; Scott 1928:252–53, 273–416).

Throughout his service in the U.S. plains, Cuba, and the Philippines, Scott repeatedly exhibited calmness and tact in tense and often potentially lethal situations. Time and again he demonstrated that courtesy, patience, forethought, directness, and leadership by example were the keys to diplomacy. As Paxton Hibben (1928:4) described, "From the outset . . . Scott had one infallible system of dealing with men: he saw the other fellow's point of view, and then put what he, Scott, wanted in terms that the man could not fail to understand." In doing so he is credited with preventing many uprisings and preventing considerable loss of life. His contributions as an ethnographer, often overshadowed by a focus on his military status, shed considerable light on the existing conditions of these regions. Scott provided rich and detailed accounts of politics, economics, health and disease, living standards, civil life, corruptness, tribal customs, and culture change, as well as their causes from both internal and external sources (Scott 1928).

On August 31, 1906, Scott was named superintendent of West Point, from which he had graduated thirty years before. He was temporarily promoted to colonel. His appointment was both liked and disdained by military personnel. He viewed his service at West Point as the most difficult command due to being under constant public scrutiny through the press. He had to keep from being portrayed negatively by the press and to avoid congressional interference. Politicians frequently asked for special favors and used their political influence on the responses they got. During his appointment Scott increased the number of the corps and its barracks, introduced black troops in the cavalry detachment at West Point, eradicated hazing at the academy, supervised the construction of a new chapel, and acquired a new chapel organ. Making use of Sioux moccasin patterns, Scott had more comfortable shoes made for his children. The style was eventually adapted for the shoes used at West Point, thereby solving previous problems experienced by cadets with standard-issue footwear. When Scott's appointment ended on August 31, 1910, he resumed the rank of major of cavalry (Scott 1928:417–60).

Scott spent most of the next four years in New York and Washington, D.C., being periodically sent out for various assignments. He was promoted to regular lieutenant colonel in March 1911 and colonel that August. In the fall of 1911 he was sent to settle a hostile element among the Hopis at Hoteville, Arizona, who were then defying the directions of the Indian Department and their Indian agent. During this assignment he directed his surgeon to record notes given by the Hopi leader Yukeoma. He was given command of the 3rd U.S. Cavalry in Texas, which was active in settling various problems with Indians and Mexicans of that region. Posted at Corpus Christi and Brownsville, this unit was especially active in preventing parties from entering Mexico in defiance of neutrality laws (Scott 1928:471–77).

In March 1913 Scott was promoted to brigadier general and given command of the 2nd Cavalry Brigade, then still assigned to the Southwest. With the Mexican Revolution going on, his unit was assigned to control the Mexican border from Fabens, Texas, to California. During this assignment Scott received a special commendation for his peaceful and skillful handling of disturbances among the Navajos at Beautiful Mountain, Arizona, in November of that year. On April 22, 1914, Scott was named assistant chief of staff, and on November 17, 1914, chief of staff of the army, a position that he retained until September 22, 1917. In April 1915 he was promoted to major general. During his time as chief of staff, Scott continued to exhibit his skills in mediation and conflict dissolution, serving in diplomatic roles with Indians and Mexican border officials in the Southwest. During this time he oversaw the settlement of problems that arose between Anglos and Paiutes near Bluff, Utah, in February 1915 and recovered property "confiscated" by Pancho Villa that August. It was Scott who ordered General John J. Pershing into Mexico on a punitive expedition in 1916. If war was declared between the United States and Mexico, Scott was slated to command the army of invasion (Scott 1928:481–533; Hibben 1928:7; Peery 1935; Arlington National Cemetery 2010). In February–March 1916 Scott served as ad interim secretary of war. His efforts were directed toward preparation for possible entry of the United States into World War I. He was also very influential in gaining early support and acceptance among civil officials regarding conscription for military service and participated as a member of a special diplomatic mission to the Soviet Union in 1917.

Scott retired at the required age of sixty-four on September 22, 1917, but was recalled to inspect the battlefront in Europe and remained on active duty until May 12, 1919. In December 1917 and again in March 1918 he became commander of the 78th Division at Camp Dix, New Jersey.

According to Dan Peery (1935:356), Scott served with the British and French Divisions at the front during World War I but not in active command. In May 1919 he again retired from military service and resumed residence at Princeton, New Jersey. His retirement allowed him to renew his advocacy for American Indians, but now without the constraints of military service and policy. Over the next fifteen years he would serve on their behalf in numerous ways.

Although Scott deeply respected Indian culture, recognized its importance, and viewed it as a subject worthy of scholarship, he did not believe that tribes could sustain their cultures indefinitely in a Euro-American world. While this view is easily considered ethnocentric today, Scott's focus was more concerned with the immediate issues of land and economics. Thus his solution was to find a way to maintain a sustainable land base and adopt agriculture as a means to reaching success, as he undersaw with the Chiricahua Apaches at Fort Sill in 1894. In light of the times—with the loss and fractionalization of land through allotment inhibiting ranching, limited western education, and limited infrastructure in rural reservation locales—arguably the most practical solution short of relying on government annuities was to adopt a degree of agriculture. Although Scott believed that the federal government had an obligation to protect tribal peoples and provide for their welfare, largely by retaining the remaining land base and maintaining health and educational facilities, he did not feel that it was the government's role to be involved in the preservation of their cultures. This issue would ultimately become a factor leading to the reorganization of the Bureau of Indian Affairs (BIA) in 1934. While some scholars might view Scott as paternalistic and ethnocentric, these views must be tempered with knowledge of the context of the times in opposition to modern views in order to avoid being tempo-centric. While Scott was clearly impacted by the larger American romantic views of Indians of his era, his respect for Indians and efforts for their benefit far surpassed those of most Euro-Americans.

From 1919 to 1933 Scott served on the Board of Indian Commissioners, a body of private citizens charged with monitoring the government's administration of Indian Affairs through the BIA. During his service on the board Scott participated in writing and submitting over forty reports advocating improvements for Indians as well as other media opportunities through speeches, conferences, radio and press releases, and attending events such as the Indian Congresses in Montana. He also served as chair of the New Jersey State Highway Commission from 1923 to 1933.

On November 16, 1923, he was made an honorary member of the Oklahoma Historical Society and received its major publication, *Chronicles of Oklahoma*, until his death (Peery 1935:356).

Scott's interest in Plains Indian Sign Language continued throughout his life. This allowed him to enter almost any group of Indians of the plains and quickly befriend them. Beyond the mere novelty of a white man who knew the system, Scott had respect for the Indians of the plains and their cultures, which communicated beyond any verbal or sign system. In 1893 Scott encountered a group of Lakotas during a visit to Buffalo Bill Cody's Wild West show in Chicago (Scott 1928:175): "The Indians were a new lot of young men I had never seen before, but I would be able to gain their friendliness by the sign language within ten minutes. . . . [Cody] took us down to Iron Tail's lodge where the others soon congregated, and I was on excellent terms with them all within five minutes, asking about their relatives who were no longer with the show." In 1911 Randolph Petter at the Cheyenne-Mennonite Missionary in Oklahoma wrote to Scott regarding the Cheyenne names of geographical locations Scott had previously asked about.[19]

One interesting aspect of Scott's later career is that he remained proficient in sign language despite the loss of some of his fingers in the Philippines fighting the Moros. On July 18, 1925, Scott attended the "Fort Union Indian Congress," a council of about four hundred Indians from thirteen northern plains tribes from Montana and North Dakota that gathered at Old Fort Union, Montana, near the headwaters of the Yellowstone. Organized by the Great Northern Railway, the celebration was to commemorate the one hundredth anniversary of the founding of Fort Union and was the centerpiece of a week-long expedition by rail. Scott was billed as the "greatest living authority on Indians, and especially on the Indian sign language" (Blee 2007:594). His address to the council in sign language was showcased as a highlight of the event. The Indians greeted visitors in their native dress and provided presentations of sign language, dances, gift giving (giveaways), horse and "teepee" erecting races, "the best tribal presentation of old time Indian games," and making pipes from pipestone (Blee 2007:593). Scott and James Willard Schultz were chosen as judges for the competitions. A second congress, which also included the Northern Cheyennes from Montana, was held on July 17, 1926 (Scott 1928:84; Hibben 1928:10; Blee 2007). Although the two Indian congresses at Fort Union

---

19 Randolph Petter, Cheyenne-Mennonite Missionary, to Lt. Col. Hugh L. Scott, May 22, 1911 (Scott n.d.g).

were marked by clear ethnocentric qualities, exhibitionism focusing on "past" or "primitive" Indian cultures, and differential political overtones emphasizing both Euro-American ideals of progress and Indian views of cultural maintenance and resilience, the events also had positive aspects. As an outgrowth of a popular interest in Indians the two Indian congresses were some of the first public occasions that recognized Indian cultures as worthy of learning about and saving and not merely as something to be displaced by Euro-American Manifest Destiny (Blee 2007).

In 1928 Scott published his autobiography, *Some Memories of a Soldier*, which remains a valuable if often overlooked ethnographic source in many ways. It offers an extensive description of the inner workings of the U.S. Cavalry on the American plains from 1876 to 1897, including detailed accounts of little-known but common aspects of cavalry life in those days, such as the intricacies of maintaining a supply pack-line, jerk lines, the engineering required to cross dangerous flooded streams, and techniques for traveling undetected. Frequently Scott did not hesitate to offer other possibilities to solve problems, to question authority when prudent, and to offer logic over standard operating procedure in his duties. Scott's work also provides many insights through his criticisms of cavalry policy, methods, and leaders and an extensive account of many of the daily aspects of late nineteenth century Plains Indian culture and Indian scout duties.

As noted by Mooney (1896:655, 785, 895–97, 900, 904, 1898:143, 146, 210), Scott contributed significantly to his work by making available items of material culture and ethnographic data that he had personally collected. This included the Little Bluff Kiowa Calendar that Scott procured in 1892 and worked on translating, the shield of Kiowa chief White Bear that his son of the same name had willed to Scott upon his own death in 1894, and Scott's notes on the calendar, the Ghost Dance, and other related subjects. At the time Mooney's *Calendar History of the Kiowa Indians* (1898) came out Scott was participating in the Spanish-American War. Some degree of incompatibility seems to have developed between the two, at least from Scott's view. He never felt that Mooney adequately acknowledged his own contributions, although Scott was the first person referenced in Mooney's acknowledgments in *Calendar History*. Mooney even included a photograph of Scott in his work (Mooney 1898:147, 224). As Scott noted in one of his letters to Fort Sill: "Mooney's Kiowa Calendar is in the 17th Annual Report of the Bureau of American Ethnology of the Smithsonian, and the Sioux Outbreak and Ghost dance religion is in the 14th Annual Report. I have always felt that Mooney did not treat me well in either, for I made it possible for him to establish himself in the reservation, gathered much of the information, and generally saw him through." Always the gentleman, however, Scott concluded the issue with tact: "He by no means gives me my due in either, but he is dead now and we will say no more about it."[20] As Mooney died in 1921, Scott wrote this draft sometime between 1921 and his own death in 1934. Scott (1911:348–49) also emphasized these contributions in one of his publications.

It is unclear whether Scott truly felt that Mooney had not sufficiently credited him for his help or harbored some animosity, possibly envying Mooney's ability to pursue ethnology full time while his own ethnological pursuits were never fully realized due to his ongoing military service. Scott's well-developed observational and analytical skills indicate that he would undoubtedly have been a skilled ethnologist and contributed greatly had he been able to continue working for the Bureau of American Ethnology.

In a twelve-page entry entitled "Kiowa" Scott again discussed his aid to Mooney at Fort Sill:

> I introduced him, on arrival, to the Southern [Plains] Indians and he always stayed at my house when at Fort Sill. He was taken into the camps at my request, as I desired him to have every facility possible. These mistakes are mentioned here for the sake of accuracy. These mistakes, remembering that we are all liable to error, are only mentioned for the sake of historical accuracy as one mentions the spots on the sun. Because these views are continually quoted by those who came after and should be correct. His Calendar History and other Kiowa work are most valuable and instructive, the fruit of long and patient effort. His early death has left a vacuum that no one can fill.... If it should be reworked that but few annotations here made from Mooney's works, it should be stated that I had been long among the Plains tribes before Mooney came west, in constant communication with different tribes N. & S. [North and South] and I was aware of most of the truths he sets forth before his arrival, some of which I very gladly gave him and which he acknowledges [Bureau of American Ethnology Volume] 17, p. 143. I do not now recall any fact that I obtained from Mooney other than some of the historical matter connected with the calendar, which he obtained in the libraries of Washington, while I was still on the Plains.[21]

Scott's statements are somewhat paradoxical in that they criticize Mooney for mistakes in his research but never specify what the alleged

---

20 Introduction to "Tales of the South Plains" edited by Gillette Griswold, pp. 39–40 (Scott n.d.e).
21 Scott (n.d.b) MS 2932, Box 2, Kiowa, "Notes on Kiowa History and Culture and Relations with Other Tribes."

mistakes are; he simultaneously applauds and commends Mooney's work while dismissing it. In fairness I cannot agree with Scott's critique of Mooney's work. While Scott was in the area slightly earlier (1889–97) than Mooney (spring 1891–1918), Mooney continued to conduct research in Oklahoma until 1918. One only need compare Mooney's Calendar History and his field notes with those of Scott to see the differences. While both collected data that the other did and did not, Mooney obtained far greater data concerning, language, place-names, personal names, genealogies, personal histories, painted tipi and shield heraldry, and men's society memberships. Again pride may be an issue, as Scott seems to have either resented the degree to which he assisted Mooney or perhaps resented that he was not able to research and publish to the degree that Mooney did. In hindsight, both are to be commended for providing very valuable ethnological materials that when combined complement one another in providing a greater understanding of Southern Plains Indian cultures. Despite lacking official recognition as an ethnologist Scott left an important ethnographic legacy through his notes and writings.

Scott's role as a leader and a conscientious peacemaker is reflected in the numerous times he was selected by the War Department to investigate potential troubles among the tribes of western Indian Territory and among the Hopis, Navajos, and Paiutes, and particularly during the Ghost Dance movement. His status is further demonstrated by his selection by the Indians themselves to represent their interests in Washington, D.C. (Mooney 1898:223). In discussing situations that he had successfully negotiated without bloodshed and the double standards in treatment that Indian people often received from state and federal governments, Scott (1928:540) stated: "I am never afraid of what the Indian will do in such flare ups—if I can reach him in time. I am always afraid of what the white men do—legally."

Theoretically, Scott's writings (1898, n.d.c, n.d.d) are examples of social evolutionism, a Eurocentric approach that views human societies as evolving from simple to more complex (often presented in stages: savagery, to barbarism, to civilization). This was a predominant anthropological approach at the time he was collecting his data and is most often reflected in Scott's frequent use of the words "primitive," "savage," and "barbarism" in describing cultural practices of both early humans and Indians. Scott believed that Indians of the plains were simply in a less developed stage of knowledge and technology and not inherently inferior based on race, pointing out that non-Indians shared many traits with non-Indians in the not distant past (Scott 1928:155).

Scott saw sign language as the product of interaction between members of different linguistic families who could not understand the spoken languages of one another. He believed that sign language originated as spontaneous pantomime and developed through local and then broader standardization. Although cognizant of the existence of sign language elsewhere, Scott believed that such sign language was less developed in other areas, which contained more pervasive lingua francas in the form of widely known tribal languages or pidgins based on the political and military predominance of some tribes. He viewed sign language as more common among the nomadic tribes of the plains, in part facilitated by increased travel and contact with others through hunting, raiding, and warfare (Scott n.d.c:88–91). But Scott viewed many aspects of Indian life favorably, describing Indian languages as well developed and calling others to task when they described them as deficient (Scott n.d.c:87).

Scott was highly critical of the impact of Anglo missionaries on Indian cultures. While clearly supportive of helping nonindustrialized cultures to modernize in following his military duties, he sought to implement such change in a humanistic manner aimed at preserving as much of the Indian sense of pride, dignity, and culture as possible. As Scott (1928:313) describes:

> One of the greatest mistakes made by our missionaries in our Indian country is their opposition to everything native—the notion that everything peculiar to the Indian must be broken down and destroyed, and their pride in their achievements of their ancestors must be preached against, derided, and wiped out.
>
> The missionary would be scandalized were the situation reversed; should the Chinese, for example, come over here and say to him: "Your religion is no good, you have got to take mine; your ancestors were nothing but dirty savages; everything you do is wrong. Here, let *me* show you how to act!" Then indeed would he be amazed at his own tactlessness in the mouth of a native.
>
> It is not possible to raise up any people who are destitute of pride; and pride once lost is one of the things most difficult to restore; it lies at the root of all formation of character; its possession is a priceless gift; and no effort should be spared to save it. Nor should any attack be permitted on the religion or customs of races except where those factors bring them in conflict with the law, as did the murder, slavery, and theft which were daily events in the Sulu of that time.

Compared to the majority view of late nineteenth century America, Scott's approach to preserving Indian culture and identity while working to help Indians retain land, rights, and better treatment was ahead of its time and reflects the importance of the principles of what anthropologists now describe as cultural relativism and Native American agency in culture change situations. Scott differed from other evolutionists: while he believed Indians must adapt to the modern world and was thus pro-assimilation, he also found value in many Indian cultural practices and respected the peoples of these cultures.

One of Scott's strengths was in his ability to see both sides of an issue as well as to consider what repercussions might result from a certain decision. This was especially critical in tense situations (such as when the three Kiowa boys froze to death) and allowed Scott to mediate effectively so that situations were resolved without the need of firearms. He treated Indians with respect and trust, giving them the chance to prove themselves by keeping their word once they agreed to a decision or made a promise (Scott 1928:161, 197). This in turn promoted mutual trust and respect between the two sides. As Hibben (1928:9) described, "Scott built up in the minds of the men with whom he dealt the feeling that he had faith in them, that he trusted them implicitly. Because he himself was fine and courageous and honest and sincere they felt that there were meannesses to which one could not stoop with 'Len' Scott." John P. Harrington's description of Scott's personality and demeanor (1938:130) further suggests why he was able to get along with so many people: "General Scott was plain and unassuming. He would talk with anybody. He could hold his own with any ethnologist. As he used to say, he always put the civil above the military and the scientific above all."

Noted journalist and writer Richard Harding Davis was touring the West in the 1890s to write a book, when he spent time at Fort Sill and observed Scott's interaction with Indians and his use of sign language. Davis's (1903:172–74) firsthand account offers another view of how this skill allowed Scott to transcend linguistic and cultural barriers:

> But what has chiefly contributed to make the lieutenant's work easy for him is his knowledge of the sign language, with which the different tribes, though speaking different languages, can communicate one with the other. He is said to speak this more correctly and fluently than any other officer in the army, and perhaps any other white man. It is a very curious language. It is not at all like the deaf-and-dumb alphabet, which is an alphabet, and is not pretty to watch. It is just what its name implies—a language of signs. The first time I saw the lieutenant speaking it, I confess I thought, having heard of his skill at Fort Reno, that he was only doing it because he could do

it, as young men who speak French prefer to order their American dinners in that language when the waiter can understand English quite as well as themselves. I regarded it as a pleasing weakness, and was quite sure that the lieutenant was going to meet the Indian back of the canteen and say it over again in plain every-day words. In this I wronged him; but it was not until I had watched his Irish sergeant converse in this silent language for two long hours with half a dozen Indians of different tribes, and had seen them all laugh heartily at his witticism delivered in semaphoric gestures, that I really believed in it. It seems that what the lieutenant said was, "Tell the first sergeant that I wish to see the soldiers drill at one o'clock, and, after that, go to the store and ask Madeira if there is to be a beef issue to-day." It is very difficult to describe in writing how he did this; and as it is a really pretty thing to watch, it seems a pity to spoil it. As well as I remember it, he did something like this. He first drew his hand over his sleeve to mark the sergeant's stripes; then he held his fingers upright in front of him, and moved them forward to signify soldiers; by holding them in still another position, he represented soldiers drilling; then he made a spyglass out of his thumb and first finger, and looked up through it at the sky—this represented the sun at one o'clock. "After that" was a quick cut in the air; the "store" was an interlacing of the fingers, to signify a place where one thing met or was exchanged for another; "Madeira" he named; beef was turning up of the fingers, to represent horns; and how he represented issue I have no idea. It is a most curious thing to watch, for they change from one sign to the other with the greatest rapidity. I always regarded it with great interest as a sort of game, and tried to guess what the different gestures might mean. Some of the signs are very old, and their origin is as much in dispute as some of the lines in the first folios of Shakespeare, and have nearly as many commentators. All the Indians know these signs, but very few of them can tell how they came to mean what they do.

Scott (1928:145, 155–56) reflected on what he considered the role of the military to "protect" Indian peoples. As he described (Scott 1928:145), "Formerly most all of my studies had gone toward warfare with the Indian, which I used to think, at one time would last during my lifetime, but conditions on the Plains were rapidly changing. Instead of protecting the white man from the Indian, it was now for the soldier to protect the Indian from the white man." Scott's efforts resemble the role of many current applied anthropologists working to help populations adjust in situations of rapid culture-change.

Scott witnessed and participated in nearly all of the major changes on the plains in the late nineteenth century, including the placement of tribes on reservations, the systematic slaughter of the bison, the spread of the Ghost Dance, peyotism and Christianity, the coming of the telegraph and railroad, allotment of Indian reservations, and land rushes (Scott 1928:123–35). He was particularly critical of Anglo hunting of bison, designed to starve Indians into submission rather than for commercial purposes. Scott cites hunts in which sometimes only one of one hundred bison killed would be skinned and the meat taken. As Scott (1928:123–24) notes, "The waste was terrible. . . . But the bison never returned, and many Indians starved to death in consequence; starved to death under the American flag, wards of our government, because our government was too weak and too careless to protect their food from wanton destruction by white men."

Scott frequently took his superiors to task when he saw what he considered abuses of Indians. Scott (1928:134–35) noted the difficulties of maintaining law and order in Indian country by troop commanders who were not given civil jurisdiction to enforce laws by arresting criminals and protecting property, which in turn would have helped the United States maintain its treaty obligations to tribes. He was also extremely critical of dishonest Indian agents who embezzled Indian annuities for personal profit, which only magnified the difficulties that reservation-era Indians were attempting to deal with. When a newly appointed agent began openly committing graft, even to the point of asking Scott and Captain Schuyler how he could conduct his plan, Scott drafted a letter in support of dismissing the agent and sent his cousin as witness with Iseeo to all camps to obtain signatures. The same agent had also sent the Kiowa and Comanche children home when measles broke out at a school in 1892. To make matters worse, he then had both tribes report to the agency and camp together for a payment. The disease spread, resulting in 221 deaths of Kiowa and Plains Apache (Kiowa-Apache) children, approximately 15 percent of their tribal populations.[22] The Indian agent was promptly dismissed. Scott saw to it that he was not reassigned elsewhere, although the man's son-in-law was soon made the agent for the Poncas. When measles broke out in the camp at Fort Sill; Scott, Captain J. D. Glennan, M.D., Lieutenant A. G. Clayton Quay, and Sergeants Ernest Stecker and Thomas Clancy quarantined and cared for the affected individuals, with few losses. In gratitude to Dr. Glennan the Indian parents collected forty dollars as a first payment for his services and asked Scott to buy a horse for him. The doctor already had a

---

22 Based on the date of the measles outbreak confirmed by James Mooney (1898:223, 226), this would have to be agent George D. Day.

horse, so Scott suggested a "piece of silver," which appealed to them. The gift was presented to the doctor, bearing an inscription expressing the gratitude of the Indians of Troop L (Scott 1928:205–207).

Scott was also not afraid to stand up for his principles and in some instances to challenge authority and the military hierarchy. When Governor José Venustiano Carranza Garza of Coahuila forbade the use of Casas Grande railway from El Paso to transport supplies to General Pershing, then four hundred miles into Mexico, the State Department acquiesced to this decision. Scott took it upon himself to order the necessary trucks, staff, supplies, and ammunition to reach Pershing from New Mexico. He would not allow a fellow officer to be stranded and made defenseless due to inconsistencies in supply transportation. Secretary Newton D. Baker assisted in seeing that Congress ratified the expenditure (Scott 1928:518–33).

Less is publicly known about Scott's activities with sign language in the final years of his life after the publication of his autobiography, from 1928 to 1934. Fortunately, Harrington (1938) describes these activities in detail (see chapter 1). The highlight was Scott's coordinating of the Sign Language Council in 1930 on the Blackfeet Reservation in Montana.

Major General Hugh L. Scott died on April 30, 1934, in Walter Reed Hospital in Washington, D.C. He is buried along with many family members in Section East Site S-12, in Arlington National Cemetery in Virginia. As reflected in his admission of black cavalry troops at West Point and his treatment of Indians, Scott was clearly someone who sought respect and equality for all. He is remembered as a man who devoted his life to military service through the promotion of peace rather than war. He is also remembered as a friend of the Indians who did much to aid in their protection and advancement during a period of great cultural change. During his time at Fort Sill, Scott passed up other better-paying job offers that would have removed him from the Kiowa-Comanche-Apache Reservation community (Scott 1928:185–90, 214). These included an offer to become the post commander at Fort Supply (including the reassignment of Troop L), a five-year assignment as military instructor at Girard College in Philadelphia with an $1,000 annual increase in pay, and command of Carlisle Indian School after the retirement of Captain Richard Henry Pratt. When the offer at Girard came via telegraph, Mrs. Scott turned it down in her husband's name, "well aware, that my decision would be on account of my promise to stay with the Indians a certain time, if permitted by the War Department" (Scott 1928:190).

Scott's dedication to the Indian people is also reflected in an official commendation of his service written by then Lieutenant General Nelson A. Miles on July 2, 1908 (Scott 1928:214–15): "After many years of personal service, disregarding personal interest (he had at the time opportunities for other stations much more desirable and lucrative) he remained constantly with these Indians and succeeded in safely leading them in the pursuit of peace and civilization, and left them in a very prosperous condition, far above the average of most other Indians that had been for years under the influence of peaceful control." In light of the fact that Scott's service at Fort Sill occurred prior to allotment and the subsequent disastrous economic effects of that policy, this statement is merited. To this day Scott remains well thought of in western Oklahoma by many Indians and non-Indians.

Hugh L. Scott is commemorated through three namesakes. Scott Middle School in Fort Knox, Kentucky, was named after him. The SS *Hawkeye State*, a transport ship built in 1921, was acquired by the army on July 31, 1941, and renamed the USAT *Hugh L. Scott*. After making four voyages to the Far East, the ship was taken over by the U.S. Navy on August 14, 1942, converted to an attack transport, and commissioned as the USS *Hugh L. Scott* (AP-43) on September 7, 1941. During the North African campaign the *Hugh L. Scott* was off the coast of Morocco preparing to unload troops when it was struck by a torpedo from German submarine U-130 and sunk on November 12, 1942.[23] Scott also remains an important part of the history of Fort Sill, Troop L, and the reservation experiences of the Kiowas, Comanches, and Apaches in the 1890s. Gate Number Three at Fort Sill (now Fort Sill Boulevard) was named Scott Gate.

Finally, Scott's unique service is reflected in the private memorial carved on the backside of his gravestone (Arlington National Cemetery 2010): "His great service to the country was shown in the remarkable control and influence which he exercised in dealings with the Moros, Mexicans, and Indians, which invariably he used in promoting peace. By personal effort he preserved many hostile outbreaks on the part of the Indians. Blessed are the peacemakers."

A chronology of Scott's military and related service follows (Scott 1928; Peery 1935; Arlington National Cemetery 2010; and Bell 2010):

Graduated, United States Military Academy, West Point, N.Y.: 1876.
Second Lieutenant, United States Army: 1876.

---

23 USS *Hugh L. Scott* (AP-43), *Dictionary of American Naval Fighting Ships*, online at www.history.navy.mil/danfs/h8/hugh_l_scott.htm.

First Lieutenant, United States Army: June 1878.
Captain, United States Army: January 1895.
Major, U.S. Volunteers: May 1898.
Lieutenant Colonel, U.S. Volunteers: March 1899.
Major, Regular Army: February 1903.
Colonel, Regular Army: August 1906.
Lieutenant Colonel, Regular Army: March 1911.
Colonel, Regular Army: August 1911.
Brigadier General, Regular Army: March 1913.
Major General, Regular Army: April 1915.
Retired: September 1917.
Recalled: September 1917.
Retired: May 1919.

Major Commands and Positions Held

1898: Acting governor general of Cuba following Spanish-American War.
1903–1906: Served in Philippines, commander of Jolo Military Post, and ultimately military governor of Sulu Archipelago.
1906–10: Superintendent of the United States Military Academy.
1908–15: Office of the Chief of Staff.
1910–14: Mediator, Mexican border and Indian troubles; commander, 2nd U.S. Cavalry Regiment, Mexican border.
1912: Commander, 3rd U.S. Cavalry Regiment.
1913–14: Commander, 2nd U.S. Cavalry Brigade.
1914–17: Chief of staff of the United States Army.
1917: Member, United States mission to Russia.
1918: Commander, 78th Division and Camp Dix, New Jersey.
1919–33: Member, Board of Indian Commissioners, Department of the Interior.

Conflicts and Wars

1876–78: Campaigned in Sioux, Nez Perce, and Cheyenne Indian expeditions.
1903: Wounded at Crater Lake in campaign against Moros, Philippines.
1917–18: Battlefield inspection, World War I.

CHAPTER 3

Iseeo, Other Native Consultants, and the Scott Ledgers at Fort Sill

ISEEO IS THE ENGLISH PRONUNCIATION OF THE KIOWA NAME Áiséàuidè (Many Camp Smokes/Campfires). It is a distinguished name that was passed down through three known individuals in the nineteenth century. The first known to have this name was a noted warrior in the early to mid-1800s. On a prolonged series of raids into Mexico in 1853, he lost his shield during an attempted raid on a town, bringing great disgrace upon himself and the loss of his martial status. He was even denied the right to carry a bow and arrows, leaving him only a lance to bear. Suffering from the social consequences of his son's action, his father secured a headdress from a medicine man for him to wear into combat. It was said that the headdress, similar to that worn by the Ta̱imé Keeper in the Sun Dance, would bring him bravery, cause great success in battle, and enable him to regain his status. On another journey into Mexico, Iseeo made repeated charges on horseback in front of the enemy, proceeding closer to them each time. Carrying only a lance, he dismounted and dramatically charged into the line of Mexican soldiers, killing an officer with his lance. Shot in the knee, Iseeo fell and was blinded when a gun discharged near his face. Inspired by Iseeo's actions, the other Kiowas rallied and overran the Mexican position, eventually killing the entire contingent. Although Iseeo regained his status as an honored warrior among the Kiowas and was presented with another shield, he remained blind and died shortly thereafter from an infection in his knee (Nye 1962:94–102).

The name "Iseeo" later passed to a nephew who was killed in the fight with the Sauk and Fox in 1854 and then to this individual's younger brother (1849–1927), who became a member of Troop L and related much of the ethnographic material recorded by Hugh L. Scott at Fort Sill through sign language.

In 1849 a Kiowa boy was born in the vicinity of Fort Larned, Kansas, to Quo-haw-ty and his wife, Kau-nai-ty. In volume III of Scott's notes Iseeo reports his father's name as "Moving About With Lodges." In the nineteenth century many Kiowas did not name children until they were a few years old, often to ensure their survival. Using the name of a deceased person prompted continued mourning, and the name was not generally used again until it was bestowed upon a living individual. Some children were given names that were believed to ensure their longevity and success in life, especially if they had suffered from health problems or if the family had lost multiple children. George Hunt, a nephew of Iseeo, stated that a child's luck, health, and position depended upon his or her name.[1] To ensure that a sickly child would recover the family might change the child's name.[2] Iseeo, who was not formally named as a child, explained to Scott (n.d.a:II:78, chapter 5 in this volume) how he received his first name:

> My name was first Tah-bone-moh—Sees Big Morning Star [Jábònmàui]. Kom-au-dy was my father's near brother and when I was little I was very sick and dying. I had no name then and was about four years old. Kom-au-dy said, "That is my child, he is very sick. I will call him Tahbonemo-hand maybe he will get well." We all used to have a way and must have it now to get up early and look out the door to the E [east] and if we see the morning star it will soon be day. When I enlisted first for a soldier I took my brother's name Iseeo "Plenty Of Round Fire Places" [Áiseàuidè], which you see when the village has moved away.[3]

Sees Big Morning Star was later enrolled as Tah-bone-mah, Family 328, on the Kiowa Tribal Roll (Kiowa Family Record 1901), which in time became Tahbonemah.

Little is known of Tahbonemah's youth other than that he accompanied a war party against the Navajos into what is now New Mexico, witnessed the Medicine Lodge Treaty in 1867, and participated in a few raiding parties before the Kiowas were confined to the Kiowa-Comanche-Apache

---

1   Kiowa Family Record (1901: Fam. 328); George Hunt to Alice Marriott 1934, Alice Marriott Papers (hereinafter AMP).
2   George Hunt to Alice Marriott, 1934, AMP.
3   Scott (n.d.a:II:78, chapter 5 in this volume). In a 1922 letter Scott provided a different origin for Iseeo's childhood name. "His former name was Tah-bone-moh = Sees the Morning Star. When he was little and sick he used to lie awake and watch for the morning star to rise." H. L. Scott to Major A. V. Arnold, June 23, 1922, 88.063.012, Iseeo (n.d.b). It is possible that both events contributed to the creation of the name by Iseeo's uncle.

Reservation in 1875. Following the conclusion of the Kiowa Sun Dance of 1874 Tahbonemah joined a war party formed by Lone Wolf, who wished to avenge the recent deaths of his son and nephew, and led by Mamanti. On July 12 the party attacked a group of Texas Rangers near Lost Valley, Texas. Riding a large gray horse, a famous racer, Tahbonemah (wearing sky blue paint with dark blue dots) and Quo-to-tai (Cújòtâidè: Bird/Eagle On Top) closed in on Mel Porter, who turned and fired his pistol almost in Tahbonemah's face, finally throwing the revolver at him. Tahbonemah knocked Porter off his horse with his lance and captured the horse but was unable to count coup on him due to heavy fire from the man's comrades, who had taken cover in the adjacent woods. Porter sought cover and escaped with his comrades. The killing of ranger William Glass in this fight would result in the noted incident of Lone Wolf bestowing his name on Mammedaty, who had been the close comrade of his deceased son and who counted coup first in the fight (Nye 1937:192–200; Blaylock 1980). While Tahbonemah had been on horse and war or revenge raids prior to the reservation period (Nye 1962:167, 193), he was not a recognized chief or band leader. Although there is some indication that all Indians did not view Iseeo's later interactions with non-Indians favorably, he ultimately earned their respect for his tenure in the army and the service that he provided during the reservation era and after.

Scott recorded some information about Iseeo's life in his notes. Iseeo received a form of horse medicine (Scott n.d.a: III:7–8, chapter 6 in this volume) from his father, Moving About With Lodges, who died in 1869, that he later used in two instances to win horse races. Other information concerning his participation in war parties, his first experiences in meeting tattooed Wichitas as a child, his observations of a Calumet Dance, his knowledge of botanical medicine for rattlesnake bites, and other incidents are contained in the notes. Iseeo reported (Scott n.d.a: I:63, 176, chapter 4 in this volume) that his wife, Pau-to-mah, was half Wichita and that they lived with the Wichitas for a while after the Kiowas surrendered. Iseeo was not imprisoned at Fort Sill. He is reported as being a member of Kicking Bird's band around 1870. During that same year he joined his wife's people, the Wichitas, and remained with them for some time. The 1879 and 1880 Kiowa censuses list Tahbonemah (#371) residing in a small residence band headed by Tsatoke. Iseeo's 1894 enlistment record at Fort Sill lists him as having been born near the "Head of the Red River," and as 5 feet 6-3/4 inches in height with brown eyes.[4]

---

4   Iseeo (n.d.b) FSA; Kiowa Tribal Census 1879.

Kiowa scout Iseeo in native dress.
Photo #1, Albers Collection, Western History Collections.

Troop L

In 1891, when Troop L was being formed at Fort Sill, Tahbonemah, who was then forty-two years old, wanted to enlist. In addition to his prereservation warfare experience, he had served fifty-four months on the police force at the Kiowa, Comanche, and Wichita Agency between 1881 and 1885 (McKenzie n.d.), which may have influenced his decision to enlist in Troop L. Because Tahbonemah had met Scott the week he arrived at Fort Sill in 1889, had accompanied him on hunting trips, and had already distinguished himself through his service with Scott during several tense situations in 1890, he was already well known around the post and was surely recognized at the time of his enlistment. Whether Scott had any influence on his successful enlistment is unknown. Tahbonemah reported his age as twenty-nine and enlisted under the name of I-See-O after his famous uncle and older brother. While much has been made of Iseeo's age at the time of his enlistment, Honameatah, a son of the late Kiowa chief Little Bluff who also enlisted in Troop L, was six years older than Iseeo.

By the time Troop L was formed Scott and Iseeo were already well acquainted and had developed a friendship. Scott had used Iseeo's service as a horse wrangler, guide, and general aide and, perhaps most importantly, in monitoring the Ghost Dance (Jacobs 1969). Scott soon became impressed with the loyalty and devotion exhibited by Iseeo and appointed him first sergeant in Troop L.[5] Despite the difference in rank their relationship would grow into a deep friendship that greatly influenced the careers of both men. In time Iseeo's service expanded to include seeking out ethnographic information on a wide array of subjects, both by interviewing elders and conveying the information to Scott and by arranging meetings between Scott and highly respected elder men of the tribe. Although some sources state that Iseeo learned some English (which seems possible as he lived so long at Fort Sill), he never learned to speak it fluently. Scott noted that Iseeo did not speak English during the time he was at Fort Sill and conversed with him through sign language (Swett 1935:347; Nye 1937:271). Some verbal communication undoubtedly accompanied the accounts of the pronunciation of Kiowa names, vocabulary, and exclamations used to emphasize storytelling, as reflected in Scott's notes. In addition, during group and interethnic settings it was normal for individuals to speak in their native language while simultaneously signing their account.

---

5   It is interesting that Iseeo, who was made first sergeant by Scott, was given a higher-ranking position than Honameahtah (first a private and later a sergeant), the son of the late chief Tohausen, and others such as Wohaw who had a far better war record than Iseeo.

According to Swett (1935:347–48), Iseeo claimed to have taught Indian sign language to Scott: "I-See-O was Scott's teacher. It was he who taught him the ways of the Indian, his language, and customs. Scott became very proficient in the use of the Indian sign language, and nothing so pleased I-See-O as to tell how he taught Scott the Indian signs. The language is dead, of course, but I-See-O never tired of showing the signs and their meanings." This is only partially true. It is well documented that Scott learned sign language from northern plains Indians beginning in 1876, well before coming to Fort Sill in 1889. Scott also noted how many Indians were amazed upon first meeting him because he knew sign language when he arrived in the southern plains and elsewhere (Scott 1928:32, 175). Because dialectical differences existed in Plains Indian Sign Language (Taylor 1996:281–82), Iseeo probably taught Scott some of the southern plains variations as well as much specific ethnological information pertaining to the Kiowas and neighboring tribes. As Scott (n.d.e:36) noted, "I-see-o instructed me in the lore of the Plains during nine years of almost daily converse in the sign language, as he knew no English and never learned to speak it. . . . Nothing was ever told me as fact that would not be recognized as genuine by the majority of the tribe. . . . And he never told me anything that did not afterward prove to be absolutely true."

After fifteen years of residence on the reservation, which received only twenty inches of rain per year and required fifteen acres of grazing per cow, the Kiowas realized that few could become self-sufficient through farming or stock-raising on a single allotment of 160 acres. During negotiations for the Cherokee or Jerome Commission, Iseeo (then a member of Troop L and opposed to any additional reduction of the KCA Reservation) pointed out the poverty of their neighbors to the north, the Cheyennes and Arapahos, who had recently negotiated the sale of their surplus reservation lands to the United States, as an example of the detrimental results of allotment. Uninterested, the commissioners responded that those tribes exaggerated their poverty in order to beg ponies and cattle from their Kiowa neighbors and that any hunger was due to their own improvidence (Hagan 1976:207). During hearings held by the Jerome Commission in 1892 Iseeo was one of several Kiowas to testify. In one instance he summarized the feeling of many Indians: "Mother earth is something that we Indians love. . . . We do not know what to do about selling our mother to the Government. That makes us scared."[6] Although some tribal members

---

6 Minutes of the council in Sen. Doc. 77, 55th Cong., 3rd sess., Jan. 26, 1899, Serial No. 3731, vol. 7, p. 23, in Clark (1999:33, 150).

Iseeo, Troop L, 7th Cavalry, on horseback at Fort Sill guardhouse.
*Photo #P1472, The Fort Sill National Historic
Landmark, Fort Sill, Oklahoma.*

refused to sign the agreement due to personal belief or peer pressure, Iseeo finally relented (Hagan 1976:211). When he signed in support of the agreement, the 303rd person to do so, he was verbally disrespected for the first time by a nephew.[7] The forced assignment of 160-acre allotments and the sale of many of the excess reservation lands to non-Indians inevitably led the Kiowas, Comanches, and Apaches to the exact poverty that Iseeo, Ahpeahtone, Scott, and others had foreseen (Hagan 1976:213).

7   Minutes of Fort Sill Meeting, Sept. 1892, in Sen. Doc. 77, p. 23; and Minutes of Oct. 11, in Sen. Doc. 77, p. 43, in Clark (1999:41–42, 45, 130, 151–52).

In 1893 General Nelson A. Miles, then department commander in Chicago, sent word to Fort Sill that he wanted some wild game for Thanksgiving dinner. With little time to spare, each troop was allowed to select three men to participate in a morning hunt. First Sergeant Iseeo selected Kicking Bird (the younger), Jim Todome, and Mark Auchiah from Troop L. The Kiowas secured two deer and a turkey, while the white soldiers procured a few quail and prairie chickens, which were packed in ice and sent to Chicago. The following year Miles decided to come to Fort Sill to enjoy a hunt himself and was accompanied by Scott and a contingent of Troop L (Nye 1962:249–52).

When Scott and his family left Fort Sill in late 1897 to return to Washington, D.C., for better educational opportunities for his children, the relocation was difficult for both Scott and Iseeo. Scott (1928:208) described their last meeting prior to his departure:

> Before I left Fort Sill, Sergeant I-see-o came in and sat down by the fire and asked if what he had heard was true; he had heard that I was going away from Fort Sill forever to live in the east. I said, "Yes, it is true." He turned his face away, and I could see the tears run down his profile while he sat crushed in his chair without a word. I tried to comfort him, but he soon got up and went away unable to speak.
>
> I wound up my affairs, gave away the pack of coyote and bear dogs I had bred and trained so carefully, sold my horses, and bade farewell to all my Indian friends.[8]

Scott (1928:208) reflected of the experience of a colleague who had likewise left after a prolonged stay:

> I had seen Dr. McMurdo leave for one of the great northern posts after a long and happy sojourn. He had looked all around at the landscape of mountain and plain for the last time to impress its memory on his mind before getting into the ambulance for the drive of thirty-five miles to the railroad, and now it was my turn to do the same thing; loving every bit of it in sight, I got into the ambulance with real sorrow in my heart. After nine years of service, nine useful years of the strenuous outdoor life on horseback, where we had been so happy, a life of usefulness to white men and red, now I was leaving it. I did not know it then, but it was the end of my happy plains life without anxieties. I expected to go west again when my children were through with school but the Spanish War changed all that. I was to become thenceforth a dweller in cities engaged in administrative work.

---

8   In many Plains Indian cultures crying in public is not unusual and is viewed as a sign of sincerity. This practice still occurs in the Kiowa, Comanche, Apache, and other Indian communities in Oklahoma, often during public addresses at ceremonies.

While we do not know the full extent of the impact that Scott's departure from Fort Sill had for Iseeo, it is clear that both men thought highly of each other and never forgot one another. On one occasion Iseeo had come to Scott's defense to protect him from a Comanche Indian who was arrested one night after becoming intoxicated when some individuals brought whiskey into the scouts' camp at the post. The following day Scott went to Anadarko, having forgotten about the prisoner. Upon arriving he telegraphed to Fort Sill to have the prisoner released. The Comanche was soon seen pacing back and forth in front of Scott's quarters with a loaded and cocked rifle underneath his blanket. When Iseeo found out, he rode over to where the man was, pulled off his blanket to expose the rifle, and took it from him. After meting out a beating to the man, Iseeo told him to leave and warned that if he ever tried anything like it again he would kill him. Scott found out about Iseeo coming to his defense only after returning to the post (Scott 1928:166–67).

While some might view my depiction of Scott and Iseeo's relationship as overly romantic, two things suggest otherwise. First, their correspondence and visits offer clear evidence that the two deeply respected each other despite the difference in rank and considered themselves dear friends until their deaths.[9] Second, as a series of documents demonstrates, Scott did not have to do the things he did for Iseeo, such as using his personal military and political influence to ensure that subsequent officers looked after Iseeo and intervening to make sure that Iseeo maintained employment past the age of normal retirement after Scott left Fort Sill. Rarely did an Anglo military officer maintain correspondence and visits for the rest of his life with an enlisted Indian man who spoke no English. This is even clearer in that Scott went on to become chief of staff of the U.S. Army.

What evidence demonstrates this friendship? The two men were close in age, Scott born in 1853 and Iseeo in 1849. More importantly, archival correspondence demonstrates that Scott and Iseeo exchanged occasional letters from 1898 through 1919, continued to tell people about one another, and

---

9   A similar relationship appears to have developed between William P. Clark and the Northern Cheyenne Little Wolf, who became friends and planned an illustrated work on sign language (Dunlay 1982:97). Frank North also appears to have had an amicable relationship with the Pawnee Scouts he commanded from 1864 through 1877, who gave him two Pawnee names and saved his life in battle. Although North spoke Pawnee and did not require the use of sign language, he helped provide employment as scouts, supplied them with horses, arms, and ammunition, redistributed materials captured in warfare, and spoke on their behalf in Washington, D.C. From 1878 to 1885 North recruited Pawnees to work in William F. Cody's Wild West Show, providing badly needed employment and a reprieve from the poor living conditions on the reservation (Van De Logt 2010:227–28, 241–45). If not for North's early death at the age of forty-five in 1885 he probably would have continued to assist the Pawnees in governmental and economic arenas.

96 SCOTT, HIS CONSULTANTS, AND THE LEDGERS

both made efforts to seek the other out, Iseeo when visiting Washington and Scott when returning to Fort Sill for base inspections, which allowed him to see many friends. A visit from Scott was deemed important enough to be recorded in one of the Kiowa pictographic calendars. A caption in the Ananti Odlepaugh Calendar records a visit by Scott in the summer of 1911: "General Hugh Scott came to Fort Sill and a number of Kiowas went to the council."[10] Iseeo corresponded with Scott via the assistance of other post officers and interpreters. Barely a month after Scott left Fort Sill, Iseeo sent a letter to Scott in January 1898, telling of his sadness at Scott's departure and that he considered him like a "brother" and affirming his own and Ahpeahtone's feelings of friendship toward Scott. Iseeo also wrote out of concern for the governmental threats to the reservation lands and indicated that the Indians preferred that a "soldier officer" be sent as the new Indian agent when Major Frank D. Baldwin's term expired.

> Dear Captain,
> The following was written at Iseeo's request. He brought up a boy to interpret and I have taken down his words as nearly verbatim as I could; correcting errors at the same time.
>
> Beach
>
> Capt. Scott,
> I stand with you here. I was your friend. When you went away I felt bad because I was used to you. I stand with you all the time. I feel bad, because you were just like my brother all the time. Now I feel better, maybe you have hard feelings because I feel better but I and my family are in better spirits. You have been so kind to me that I felt bad when you went away, but you remember me and I feel better.
> I think I will get along. I will get along with Lieut. Beach and Lieut. Capron. They are my friends. I am glad because I have friends.
> The reason I write to you is to tell you I am getting along all right, and my family is all right.
> You told me when you went away if anything came up to tell you as quick as I could.

---

10 Ananti Odlepaugh Calendar (n.d.). While another Kiowa family maintains that this calendar may have been drawn by Tonemah then passed to Mrs. Odlepaugh (Meadows 1999:426), the entries contain clear dated references to Ananti Odlepaugh, dates of immediate family members' births and deaths, activities of Odlepaugh's father White Bear, and written notes by a grandchild naming family members described in the entries. Mrs. Odlepaugh died in 1934, as recorded in the calendar, while Tonemah died in 1953. The calendar spans 1851 to 1945. Both Tonemah and Odlepah/Odlepaugh were members of Troop L at Fort Sill under Scott, which suggests that a visit by Scott was also a significant event to other Kiowas and not just to Iseeo. Kiowa Family Record 1901; author's fieldnotes, Saddle Mountain Church Cemetery.

When you were here you were always willing to help us about our land. Lieut. Beach and Lieut. Capron will help us and tell you.

That is all.

A-pe-a-ton gave me a few words to say to you.

You were our friend. You are away, but we are hoping you are still our friend.

You are in Washington. You are in the big council house. All the Indians have hard feelings about the land.

The Commissioners want our land. We want it like this yet [as it is] for many years. We love our land. We trust you will help to make them leave our land alone. We love our land like our children. We want a soldier officer for our Agent.

When Major Baldwin goes we want another Soldier Agent.

That will be all.

(signed) I-se-o [sic][11]

The following month Scott received a letter from Ernest Stecker at Fort Sill, congratulating him on his upcoming promotion and sending regards and greetings from "Iseeo" and "all the Indian Chiefs and old men."[12] In 1920 Scott inspected the "Kiowa and Comanche Agency," during which time he undoubtedly visited Iseeo and other remaining tribal chiefs and elders. He inspected Fort Sill again in 1927, submitting a report to the chairman of the Board of Indian Commissioners, but this was after the death of Iseeo.[13] Reflecting his respect and concern for the Kiowas, Comanches, Apaches, and Iseeo, Scott continued to aid them through his extensive military and political connections after leaving Fort Sill.

When Iseeo's enlistment ended in 1897, he requested that he be enlisted as a scout. This assignment, along with some of the other members of Troop L, was extended for an additional five years. During most of this period Iseeo served as a messenger at Fort Sill, then as a counselor on Indian affairs, courier, and messenger for General Nelson A. Miles, who was department commander and sometimes visited Fort Sill in the 1890s. On one occasion Iseeo was directed by General Miles to escort a music band from Fort Sill to Cobb's Creek. En route he received additional orders to continue with the party to the Keechi Hills. On his return Iseeo suffered

---

11 Iseeo through F. H. Beach (Fort Sill, Oklahoma Territory) to Captain Hugh L. Scott, Washington, D.C., Jan. 14, 1898 (Scott n.d.b: MS 4396, Box 1).

12 Ernest Stecker (Fort Sill, Oklahoma Territory) to Hugh L. Scott, Washington, D.C., Feb. 25, 1898 (Scott n.d.b: MS 4396, Box 1).

13 Hugh L. Scott (Anadarko, Oklahoma) to Secretary of the Interior (Washington, D.C.), June 12, 1920 (Scott n.d.b: MS 4525); Hugh L. Scott (Princeton, N.J.) to Samuel A. Eliot, Chairman, Board of Indian Commissioners (Washington, D.C.), Dec. 5, 1927 (Scott n.d.b: MS 4525).

a riding injury and had to spend nearly six months in the Post Hospital at Fort Sill. By this time the concern for Indian uprisings was over. Upon recovering, Iseeo resigned his position and resumed civilian life for nearly a year. When the Spanish-American War began in 1898, Iseeo was among the first to reenlist. Because he could not speak English, however, he was kept at Fort Sill throughout the entire campaign and placed in charge of looking after the horses on the post. He continued to hold the position of scout until 1913, when all but about one hundred of the Apaches at Fort Sill were transferred to the Mescalero Indian Reservation in Arizona. Discharged due to old age, Iseeo again left the service, taking up residence with his family in the Big Bend of the Washita River near Carnegie, Oklahoma (Swett 1935:349; Nye 1937:262, 302).[14]

Iseeo never forgot Scott and was ready to help him when asked. On May 12 and 26, 1911, Ernest Stecker received two letters from Scott containing ethnographic questions on Kiowa history and the plant used for snake medicine on which he had recorded notes. Stecker is reported to have known sign language and seems to have been able to converse quite well with I-see-o, from whom he periodically gathered information for Scott. Stecker replied on May 31, having sent Scott two of the plants he desired by express parcel the day before: "I-see-o hunted two days before he found them and then found them growing within a foot of each other. He could not find any on flower but the one has a bud on it. I suppose from appearance it is too early for them to flower at this time. I-see-o asked me to call your attention to the tops of the plants, their appearance is similar to snake bones from which similarity it was named he states . . . Kiowa name of plant is Zane-na-dah or Snake Medicine."[15]

Scott recorded two incidents with Silverhorn that demonstrate not only their mutual respect for one another but Scott's sincere friendship with other Kiowas. The first involves a Kiowa calendar that Silverhorn had.

> I never heard of Hawgone's [Silverhorn's] daily calendar until after his discharge from the troop. When I drove about thirty miles to his lodge to

---

14   I have been unable to determine which relative/s this refers to. Iseeo's three sons, Pope-tsait-ke (Spotted Horse), Tsait-pau (aka Harry Tee), and Luke Tah-bone-mah (aka Luke Tee), were all allotted land in Harrison Township, Kiowa County, in Sections 11 and 14, Township 7 North, Range 16 West, near present-day Gotebo, Oklahoma.

15   Ernest Stecker, Department of the Interior, United States Indian Service, to Colonel Hugh L. Scott, Washington, D.C., May 31, 1911 (Scott n.d.b: MS 4525). Snake medicine would be Sànédàui in Kiowa. Paul Vestal and Richard Evans Schultes (1939:29) discuss the Kiowa use of *Ribes odoratum* (buffalo currant) for snakebite. Believing that snakes fear this plant and keep away from it, they sucked out the poison when a person suffered snakebite then applied parts of the plant to the wound.

ask if he would copy it for a reward, he replied, "I was a soldier with you for five years. I never asked you for anything you did not do for me. I want to make you a prairie gift of it. I do not want it." I purchased it, although he did not want any payment as I thought it too valuable a gift to take from him. In 1920 I went on an inspection tour to Oklahoma and heard he was nearly blind. I drove about the fifty miles to see him. He told me he had paid out over $600.00 to doctors in Oklahoma City for treatment without relief and I arranged with the hospital at Lawton to take him in without pay. He told me that oil had been struck on his allotment and he had eighteen thousand dollars in deposit from oil royalties and was married. All the time I knew him at Fort Sill he was a bachelor.[16]

A second incident involves a request by Silverhorn.

He came to ask one day, as a soldier, for permission to go out to his lodge, which was promptly granted him, for he was a clean, reliable, well-instructed and disciplined soldier who never was punished during his five years enlistment. He said, "Whenever I ask you for anything you always grant it. I have a bunch of horses on the other side of the mountains. I wish you would go there and take your choice of them." Of course I could not permit that but it showed his character and the relations between [us].[17]

Years after Scott had left Fort Sill he reflected on the nature of his relationship with the members of Troop L:

I was much more of a personal friend in their eyes than a commander, though they never varied in respect for the office or infringed on its dignity. I loaned them about $200.00 every month for five years when their families were in need and did not lose fifty cents of it in that time. They were loyal, faithful friends besides being positive and efficient soldiers. And those now alive are friends to this day. I have been told by the agent that the discipline and instruction imparted to them in that troop was the main reason for the advancement so patent among the Kiowa and Comanche compared to that of the Cheyenne and Arapaho just north of them and it would pay the government to maintain a troop of cavalry at every agency, thus the advancement of every tribe. Although I was ordered away from Fort Sill in 1897 I get letters from them yet and our friendship will end only with our lives.[18]

These statements are valuable in that they reflect that the Kiowas serving under Scott in Troop L, while realizing their position in a system of

---

16 Scott (n.d.b: MS 2932, Box 2, Kiowa, Tohausen Account).
17 Ibid.
18 Ibid.

rank, also demonstrated personal loyalty and interaction with their officer. Viewed in this light, this relationship more resembled the relationship of Indians to a chief than the more rigid Anglo military system of rank. While apparently never letting the two types of relationships interfere with his execution of duties, Scott not only realized but to some degree embraced their approach, as reflected in the criticisms from the officer corps regarding the Indians' attachment to officers based on personal attributes rather than solely on rank. Thomas Dunlay (1982) reports similar conditions throughout Indian scout units of this period.

Iseeo and his wife took their allotments (numbers 1863 and 1864, respectively) near Mount Sheridan. Like many Indians in the region Iseeo did not seem to have the aptitude for farming and was soon living in a state of near destitution. In 1915 he accompanied a group of Kiowas to Washington, D.C., where he called on his old friend, now Major-General Scott, chief of staff of the army. Learning of Iseeo's situation and not wanting his old friend to live in poverty, Scott brought his plight to the attention of the secretary of war, pleading that something be done for Iseeo in recognition of his earlier service. As Scott entreated the secretary of war: "It has long been the custom of the white man to employ a native against his own people, then when the war or other trouble is over, to cast him aside like a sucked lemon, with the rankest ingratitude. Look at this old Kiowa. He is down and out—broken in the service of the United States. There is no more work in him, the Army cannot use him. Yet there are Indians and whites alive today who would not be alive were it not for the fidelity of I-See-O."[19] Scott's request references Iseeo's seminal role in assisting him to prevent bloodshed between whites and Indians in several instances during the early 1890s.

The secretary of war had a private bill passed by Congress that gave Iseeo lifetime enlistment as a senior duty sergeant in the army. Iseeo was reenlisted for seven years under Army Serial Number R-1057176 at Fort Myer, Virginia, on January 29, 1915, with renewal at three-year intervals until his death. On February 1 Iseeo was given Special Order Number 17 to return to Fort Sill on February 10, to join the Fort Sill Detachment, Indian Scouts. The nature of the assignment is even clearer because Iseeo was the only member of the organization and was the last enlisted living Kiowa Indian scout (Swett 1935:350: Hollis 1977:44). On January 29, 1915, Captain Payton C. March of the Office of the Adjutant General of the Army wrote to notify the commanding officer at Fort Sill:

---

19 Swett (n.d.). See also Nye (1937:310) and Jacobs (1969:44).

Subject: Enlistment of Iseeo as Indian scout and utilization of his services.

The Secretary of War has directed that Iseeo be enlisted at Washington Barracks, D.C., as an Indian Scout, and that he be sent on Government transportation to Fort Sill, Oklahoma, for station, the Commanding Officer, Fort Sill, to utilize the services of Iseeo, after his arrival, if they are needed, but to permit him to go and come as he pleases.[20]

On February 1, 1915, Chief of Staff Scott wrote to Colonel Granger Adams at Fort Sill, informing him of the reenlistment of Iseeo and requesting special treatment for him in his new position.

I have just enlisted, by order of the Secretary of War, as a sergeant of scouts, an old Kiowa Indian named Iseeo. . . . He is 65 years old, and has been enlisted as a reward for former services rendered during the Ghost Dance excitement in '90 and '91, when, as you will remember, all the southern plains were aflame. I was able, however, to keep peace among the 8 tribes down there and bring them through without firing a shot, and in this Iseeo assisted to a very large degree. I would like to have you let him live on the reservation or out among his people, as he elects, and see that he gets pay, clothing and rations from your Quartermaster, and that when his time expires he be re-enlisted as a sergeant until he dies. He is old and mediaeval, his mind is back in the middle ages, and he has simply been stunned by civilization. I do not see how he survived this long. When the government needed him he was supremely loyal, against the wishes of his own people.[21]

As Morris Swett (1935:341–42) observed, Iseeo held a special position in the United States Army unlike that of any other serviceman, including even General Pershing. When Pershing turned sixty-four he was automatically retired due to age. Not only was Iseeo given the rank of senior duty sergeant, United States Army, on the active list for life, but he could not be reduced in rank—a privilege that no other soldier possessed. In time he became the oldest active-status soldier in the United States Army.

Iseeo provided a valuable form of service at a critical period in Kiowa and U.S. history. Were it not for his diplomacy—his ability to convey the futility of further fighting and to give whites a better understanding of Indian culture and perceptions—the transition of Indians on the southern plains to the reservation era could have been much worse than it was. For this unique role in maintaining control and peace during the potentially

---

20 Adjutant General Payton C. March to the Commanding Officer, Fort Sill, Oklahoma, Jan. 29, 1915, Special Order No. 17, Fort Myer, Virginia, Feb. 1, 1915; Gillette Griswold to Mr. O. Willard Holloway, Feb. 16, 1971, Iseeo Military Career File, Biography/Indian, FSA.

21 H. L. Scott to Col. Granger Adams, Feb. 1, 1915, Iseeo Military Career File, Biography/Indian, FSA.

volatile time of the Ghost Dance, Scott (Swett 1935:342) once declared, "I-See-O, it was you who prevented bloodshed among the Kiowas and Apaches, and it is to you that the Indian people of Oklahoma owe a great deal of thanks." As Swett (1935:341) surmised, "For it was the recognition of his efforts for peace, and not for gallantry on the battlefield, that an appreciative government had honored the veteran Indian Scout I-See-O."

In his later years (circa 1915–27) Iseeo's sole duty was to appear and collect his monthly allotment. He was noted for generously sharing his income with his friends, who would often stay with him until his funds were depleted. But Iseeo is reported never to have been in need, as numerous officers and enlisted men looked after him, reflecting how well he was thought of by his military peers (Swett 1935:352). From the perspective of some army officers, payday for Iseeo was an interesting event. When Second Lieutenant Robert P. Hollis, 1st Field Artillery, arrived at Fort Sill at the age of twenty-four, he was assigned as the assistant adjutant of the Field Artillery School. As his predecessor briefed him of his new duties, he noted the nominal, ex-officio function of commanding the post's detachment of Indian scouts. This duty consisted of drawing pay from the finance officer monthly for one Iseeo, the only member of the detachment, and paying him (Hollis 1977:41–42). Hollis (1977:42) described the ritual-like event that he experienced in January 1926, which would continue each month thereafter:

> When payday arrived I-See-O entered the office, came to my desk and saluted. Rising, I returned the salute. Then, following the ritual I had been instructed in, we shook hands. After this brief ceremony, his adult son emerged from behind him and said, "I-See-O he want draw pay," and I handed the son the $59.40 which constituted his father's pay for the month. The son beamed.
>
> I-See-O, imperturbable as always, put out his hand. We shook hands again; we exchanged salutes; I-See-O faced about and the two Indians left the office. I would not see them again until the end of the following month—light duty indeed for a commanding officer.

Hollis (1977:41), also described Iseeo's dress and demeanor on payday: "His face was deeply seamed by a long life out of doors, his expression grave and immobile. There was great dignity in his bearing. His hair hung down in two braids on his chest, each tied with green yarn. He was clad in the olive-drab, standing-collar uniform of that day, with the chevrons of a sergeant on the sleeves. His uniform was neat and conventional except that he wore moccasins instead of the regulation shoes of the period."

Around 1918 the post commander had a small cottage built for Iseeo east of the Frisco Station near Cache Creek. Although the cottage had electricity and a coal-burning kitchen range, Iseeo preferred to live as he was raised, in the traditional Kiowa manner. He soon erected a tipi beside the house to live in and did all of his cooking out of doors, although he did occasionally drop by the mess hall for a meal. Iseeo used the kitchen range as a dresser or chiffonier for storing his belongings and the cottage primarily as a storeroom (Swett 1935:352; Hollis 1977:44). A letter from Colonel Alden F. Brewster to General Scott (Swett 1935:350) described Iseeo's adjustment to his new quarters: "I-See-O is doing well. He has been living on the post. He is fixed up with a nice little house on Medicine Creek, east of the railroad. He has everything he needs and a few things he does not. For example, a range was put in the house but I notice he does all his cooking out of doors."

In May 1918 Brigadier General Edward H. Plummer took command at Fort Sill. Scott, then at Fort Dix, New Jersey, wrote to Plummer in July, describing Iseeo's service to the United States government and why he was given the rank of sergeant for life in the U.S. Army (Swett 1935:350–52). This letter speaks not only of Scott's continuing efforts to ensure Iseeo's well-being but of their ongoing correspondence:

HEADQUARTERS
OFFICE OF THE COMMANDING GENERAL
Camp Dix, New Jersey.

July 8, 1918.
Brig. General E. H. Plummer, Fort Sill, Okla.

My dear Plummer:

    Your letter of July 1st was duly received, in which you enclose me a letter from my old friend, I-See-O. I fought for those people for seven years with all my time, money, effort and influence, a fact which they all recognized, and I know that I still have many friends among them. I find that they keep in rather close touch with my comings and goings and ups and downs, and it is very grateful to know that there are so many persons, interested in one, especially after such a long absence from them. They are people that never forget those that they believe are their real friends.

    Thanking you for your letter, and with best wishes for yourself, I am

Very sincerely yours,
HUGH L. SCOTT,
Maj. General, U. S. A., Commanding.

P. S.—I-See-O writes me in his letter that he feels happy over the treatment that he gets at Fort Sill. You may not know about him, but you will

remember the time when [the] Ghost or Messiah Dance spread all over the Plains in the North and South, and culminated in the Wounded Knee fight in '90 or '91. The Southern Indians had the same dance and I was put in charge by General Merritt, in command of the department at that time, and I led through those Southern tribes without a fight. It was largely through I-See-O that I got underneath the surface of affairs. He and I went about together wherever the excitement was greatest, sometimes in the Wichita Mountains, sometimes in the Caddo country, or sometimes 150 miles up the Washita, and between us we pulled the Southern Indians through that troublesome time without firing a shot. When I left Fort Sill in '97, I left I-See-O Sergeant of the Scouts, but he got discouraged there with the treatment by some of the people of the post and resigned. He is one of the old time Indians, who are dazed by civilization and do not know how to make a living and never will. I represented his service, to the Secretary of War, although he cannot be of use, yet his services in the past have been such that any pay that he receives has been more than earned years ago. General Mann took an interest in him when he was at Fort Sill, and I am very glad to see that you are doing the same thing. I know a great deal about your services in the Navajo country and passed through various sections where they still speak of you with affection, and I am glad to see that you are taking an interest in the Kiowas and Comanches also.
—H. L. S.

A January 1919 letter from Scott to Iseeo references a recent letter in which Iseeo describes his positive treatment by the officers at Fort Sill:

My dear Friend:
Your letter of January 8th has just been received. It gives me great pleasure to know that the Army Officers at Fort Sill are kind to you. . . . I am glad to hear that you are coming along well, and hope that your wife and the other members of your family are all well.

Always your friend,
H. L. Scott
Major General, U.S.A.,
Commanding.[22]

Later that year Scott again wrote to Iseeo, referencing receiving yet another letter from him and again commending him for his earlier efforts in helping to prevent an uprising (Swett 1935:352–54):

---

22 Hugh L. Scott, Headquarters, Office of the Commanding General, Camp Dix, New Jersey, to Sergeant I-see-o, Gotebo, Oklahoma, Jan. 13, 1919, Iseeo Military Career File, Biography/Indian, 88.063.005, FSA.

HEADQUARTERS
OFFICE OF THE COMMANDING GENERAL
Camp Dix, New Jersey.

May 8, 1919.

My dear I-See-O:

I have your letter of May 1st about the death of my son, Hunter. I knew you would feel badly about it, because you used to know him when he was a little boy and he thought so much of you and the Kiowa Indians. He was out at camp with me and with you at the time of the Ghost Dance when we were trying to keep the Kiowa and Apache Indians out of trouble. You did good work at that time, as you brought things about so that there was no one killed as there was in the North among the Sioux. You and I worked well together at that time, and the Indian people of Oklahoma owe you a great deal of thanks.

If it had not been for you in those days there would have been great bloodshed among those people, as there was among the Sioux of the North, simply because they didn't have anybody who understood both sides of the Indian and white man, and who was interested enough in the Indian to lead them quietly out of the trouble that was going on there. That is where I have been most useful to my Indian friends. The government wanted to disarm the Kiowas and Caddos and take their rifles and ammunition away from them, but I stood in between them and the government and it was not done, and you and I together brought all those Oklahoma tribes through the same excitement which brought about the death of so many Sioux Indians without firing a single shot, so the white people owe much to you as do your own people.

The Navajos owe you something also, because we were enabled with Toclanny to keep quiet over in that country, and since then I have been able to do the same thing among the Navajos twice and the Piutes of Utah. It needs somebody who understands both races and is interested in both and is determined on their welfare.

I am going to leave here in a few days and I will go on the retired list of the army. I have a farm at Princeton, N.J., where I was brought up as a boy and intend to make a home for my family there. I have 263 acres. There is good rainfall in that country, and I have many thoroughbred pigs. Pigs are very high now, and I hope to do well with the farm. I am glad to know that you and yours are well and happy.

I have been appointed on the Board of Indian Commissioners. They are gentlemen who go around through the Indian country and see that the Indian is treated justly. There are ten members on the Board, and when I can get around to it I want to stop and see you. I am going to stop and see you and my other Kiowa, Comanche and Apache friends every chance I get. In the meantime, I thank you for your letter about my son. I have shown it to his wife and his mother, and they deeply appreciate the feeling that you have for him.

With best wishes for you and yours, I am

>Always your friend,
>HUGH L. SCOTT
>Major General, U.S.A.,
>Commanding.

Iseeo is reported to have treasured this letter from his old commanding officer and friend. Nye (1937:309) reports that Iseeo kept this letter in his uniform pocket, periodically asking his nephew to read it to him. Of particular interest is the reference to having Scott's son Hunter "out at camp with me and with you at the time of the Ghost Dance" on the reservations. To take his son along at such a potentially volatile time speaks to Scott's belief not only in Iseeo's character but in that of the Indian tribes of the region in general, which he believed could be successfully dealt with through peaceful diplomacy over military force.

In 1920 Scott wrote to Iseeo, again demonstrating a deep friendship also with all of Scott's family. Referencing their advancing age, Scott notes that they must see each other again as often as possible, "for we have not very much longer":

My Dear Iseeo:

I received your letter some time ago and have been trying ever since to get a flag. They are very hard to get nowadays but I have got one which arrived yesterday and it is being sent to you by parcel post. I hope it is the kind you want. We have had the hardest winter here that has occurred for thirty years. I hope you have not had it as bad where you are and that you and all my Kiowa friends got thro [through] the winter comfortably. I am thinking of going out your way sometime this spring and will hope to see you somewhere. We are getting very old now. I am 67. We are not active and strong as we used to be at Fort Sill and we must see each other as often as possible for we have not very much longer. My family all want to be remembered to you. My children often speak of you and tell their children about you.

>Sincerely your friend
>H. L. Scott[23]

---

23 H. L. Scott, Princeton, N.J., to Iseeo, Fort Sill, Oklahoma, Mar. 25, 1920, 88.063.009, Iseeo Military Career File, Biography/Indian, FSA.

Correspondence demonstrates that Scott not only kept in touch with the commanders stationed at Fort Sill but sought and received special requests from them regarding Iseeo. In 1921 Alden F. Brewster wrote from Fort Sill to Hugh Scott to point out information in paragraph 4 of Circular No. 87 from the War Department, requiring that all men enlisted prior to April 2, 1917, and having completed three years of active service, be discharged by midnight July 2, 1921:

> When you were last here you told me to let you know in case anything turned up that might effect [sic: affect?] I-see-o. . . . Knowing the interest that you take in I-see-o, I have submitted the matter to you, so that if new authority for his re-enlistment as a Sergeant is necessary, it could surely be obtained. I am afraid that if this went up in the regular way the poor old Indian would be lost in the shuffle. With regard to the old man himself, he is doing well. . . . Please get new authority (if needed) before July 1st, if possible.[24]

Scott soon remedied the problem.

On November 11, 1921, General Ernest Hinds invited the Kiowa and Comanche veterans of World War I and the surviving members of Troop L to join members of the garrison in holding an Armistice Day Celebration at an encampment at White Wolf Ford at Fort Sill. In 1927 General Scott dedicated the Parker-Iseeo American Legion Post of Indian veterans. From 1921 to the 1940s Fort Sill annually sponsored a Kiowa-Comanche Armistice Day celebration at Fort Sill.[25]

On May 9, 1922, Scott wrote to Major A.V. Arnold at Fort Sill, thanking him for news about Iseeo, while praising Iseeo and explaining both the value of his former service and his unique status in Scott's eyes:

> Your letter of the 5th has just arrived and I will enclose a letter to Iseeo as you suggest. . . . Iseeo is the only one of his class. It was thro' his fidelity largely that I was enabled to hold down eight tribes of the Southern Plains during the excitement of the Messiah Dance and carry them thro' in spite of agents and deputy marshals who seemed determined to drive them into war, without the firing of a single shot; at the time the whole of the western plains was a flutter and the battle of Wounded Knee over the same excitement in Dakota. The life and property saved then is what constitutes Iseeo's claim for consideration, which no other Indian shares

---

24 Alden F. Brewster to Major-General Hugh L. Scott. June 2, 1921, Iseeo Military Career File, Biography/Indian, FSA.
25 Gus Palmer, Sr., to Major General Harry H. Critz, Commanding General, Fort Sill, Oklahoma, June 26, 1965, Iseeo Military Career File, Biography/Indian. FSA. Photos of the event are in the Fort Sill Museum Archives.

in Oklahoma, and I could not ask for any other with any chance of success. Iseeo is in a class by himself. Thanking you for your evident interest in the old man. . . .

> Very Sincerely Yours
> H. L. Scott[26]

On June 23, 1922, Scott wrote to Major A. V. Arnold at Fort Sill to thank him for sending a photo of Iseeo that he had requested to include in a book. Although Scott had other photos of Iseeo, he described them as being of poor quality. Scott wrote: "From the photograph I judge the old man is carrying his age very well. . . . please assure him (in diplomatic parlance) of my most distinguished consideration and accept my thanks for your thoughtful kindness."[27]

In 1925 the post quartermaster provided Iseeo with a standard army canvas pyramidal tent complete with board floor. Iseeo lived in this structure while friends and family resided in the cottage provided for him by the army nearby. As Major General Robert Hollis (1977:44), then a second lieutenant at Fort Sill, recalled: "I had ridden a horse past these many times, but even after I was his commanding officer I did not feel at liberty to invade his privacy, for he had become a legend and some of the aura of an Olympian figure clung to him." Although the non-Indian troops stationed at Fort Sill tended to hold Iseeo in great respect—he was always included in the visits of dignitaries such as Generals John J. Pershing and William J. Snow and officers made time to talk to him whenever he visited the office of the post commander—many saw his continuing to live in a tipi as rather quaint and as a reflection of his inability to adapt to the modern mode of life.

Although cognizant of Iseeo's service, Colonel Wilbur S. Nye is reported to have described him as "a simple product of the stone age" (Nye 1937:310; Jacobs 1969). While probably not meant to be overtly derogatory this remark is out of context in two ways. First, by Iseeo's time the Kiowas were rarely using stone: they used iron-tipped arrows and tools and firearms. Second, in light of the Kiowas' recent encapsulation to a reservation in 1875 and the paternalistic and limiting policies of the reservation era, including status as wards of the government without United State citizenship, it is unreasonable to expect the Kiowas to have assimilated overnight

---

26 H. L. Scott, Princeton, N. J., to Major A.V. Arnold, Fort Sill, Oklahoma, May 9, 1922, Iseeo Military Career File, Biography/Indian, 88.63.13, FSA.
27 Hugh L. Scott, Princeton, N. J., to Major Arnold, Fort Sill, Oklahoma, June 23, 1922 (Scott n.d.a: Box 19).

to the standards of Anglo-American society. The decision of many older Indians who preferred to continue using tipis over wooden frame houses in the early reservation and postallotment period may, in this instance, also have been due to religious factors. In his later years Iseeo became the keeper of one of the Kiowa Ten Medicine Bundles, which had to be kept in a tipi and not a house (Nye 1937:309–10).[28] Although Iseeo had cut his hair short while serving in Troop L, as shown in photographs, he later wore it in two long braids. Like some other Indian men of the southern plains, including agency police, Iseeo now refused to cut his hair, maintaining his two long braids worn over his shoulders, and continued to wear moccasins, disliking the stiff, heavy leather shoes (Swett 1935:352).

According to James Auchiah, Iseeo was also an early peyotist, practicing this religion before 1890 until his later years. In one instance he told Major General Hollis (1977:44) that a peyote ceremony had benefited his daughter after conventional Anglo medicine had failed to improve her condition. In 1923 Iseeo was honored at a peyote meeting held in his tipi at Fort Sill and attended by commanding general Major General Ernest Hinds, Master Sergeant Morris Swett, and Captain A. R. Ginsburgh, along with James Auchiah, Delos K. Lonewolf, who served as interpreter, and Hunting Horse, who led the meeting (Stewart 1987:83).[29]

Iseeo has had an enduring influence in Kiowa ethnology. In addition to the data that he provided for Scott, Iseeo was a major influence on later Kiowa historian George Hunt. A son of Jimmy Quoetone, Hunt spent much of his youth living with his uncle Iseeo. Many a night he listened to his uncle and other noted Kiowa warriors recount Kiowa history, including the years when Iseeo lived at Fort Sill as a part of Troop L of the 7th Cavalry. Hunt was later a major source of ethnographic data collected in the 1930s by Alice Marriott, the 1935 Santa Fe Laboratory of Anthropology Kiowa Field School, and Fort Sill officer and historian Colonel Wilbur S. Nye (1937, 1962).[30]

---

28 It was not unusual for Indians to prefer tipis to wooden framed houses in the early reservation. The first ten houses for Indians on the KCA Reservation were built for tribal leaders in 1877. By 1886 only nine Kiowa families were living in houses, most of which were later abandoned or rented to non-Indians. Sixty more houses were built on the reservation in 1892 (Mooney 1898:342–43, 364; Meadows 2008:148–50).

29 Keepers of the Ten Medicine Bundles usually did not practice other religious forms such as peyotism or Christianity, so the time during which Iseeo served as a bundle keeper and whether he engaged in two religious systems simultaneously are unclear.

30 Some of the stories published by Nye (1962) were collected from Iseeo by Scott (Nye 1962:xix, 15–19, 91–93, 127–31, 155–56, 178–80, 222–26, 257–58); or obtained by Nye from Hunt, who acknowledged having learned many of them from Iseeo.

The Texas-Oklahoma Boundary Dispute

Even in his last years Iseeo demonstrated his willingness to serve when called upon. In 1924 this came in the form of seminal eyewitness testimony at the Supreme Court. Since the Louisiana Purchase of 1803 the boundary of Texas and what would later become southern Oklahoma had been contested: between Spain and the United States, between Mexico and the United States, between the Republic of Texas and the United States, and finally between Texas and what would become Oklahoma when the Medicine Lodge Treaty of 1867 created the Kiowa-Comanche and Apache Reservation, with the southern border "north of the middle of the main channel" (Vaughn-Roberson 2007). Competing claims over the jurisdiction of then Greer County led to the case of *United States v. Texas* in 1894. The Organic Act of 1890 had created the Territory of Oklahoma, and eventually Greer County would remain in what became Oklahoma (Vaughn-Roberson 2007).

In 1918 large quantities of oil began appearing along a stretch of the bed of the Red River between Texas and Oklahoma. Wells were soon drilled along the Texas side of the river and some in the actual riverbed itself. As millions of dollars' worth of oil was soon collected and the economic potential was recognized, disputes between the two states over the boundary line quickly emerged—principally regarding who owned the riverbed and the associated mineral rights. Claims of oil being pumped from under the Oklahoma side led to demands for royalty payments and claims for the wells themselves. Parties involved included the States of Texas and Oklahoma, the United States government (based on the claim that the Red River was a navigable stream and thus under federal jurisdiction), the Kiowa, Comanche, and Apache tribes, private Anglo land owners, and individual Indian allottee owners. Claims that boundaries extended across the river to the opposing bank came from both sides. Two seminal questions arose: (1) where is the south bank and (2) was the Texas-Oklahoma boundary a fixed line of demarcation or was it in a constant state of fluvial change as the course of the stream changed? The federal government contended that it controlled the riverbed and any natural resources, although the southern bank of the river was the boundary between Oklahoma and Texas (Vaughn-Roberson 2007).

With ownership unclear, a receiver was appointed to hold the money while the case went before the Supreme Court in Washington, D.C. As interested parties began sending their respective representatives and delegates, Iseeo was called to testify. He had been a young man when the boundary was established and knew about its course from his time as a scout in Troop L. Iseeo chose Guy Quoetone to accompany him to the capital to serve as his interpreter. News of the boundary dispute and their travel to Washington, D.C., spread in the media. At Union Station in St. Louis Iseeo and Quoetone were met by a large crowd. A large picture of an Indian tipi and of Iseeo in uniform with cavalry artillery boots and a drab green overcoat at Fort Sill had been erected. The picture was located at the corner of the Union Depot for use in recruitment. Recognizing the former scout, news reporters took pictures of Iseeo and Quoetone beside the display. They experienced a similar reception at Washington, D.C., where they were enthusiastically met by Indian delegates, their tribal attorney John Fane, and thousands of spectators.[31]

Iseeo and Quoetone were quickly escorted to a cab and driven to a hotel, where General Scott received them. Quoetone described their meeting and exchange, which immediately shifted to sign language:

> And we went over there and we met General Scott at the hotel. We all went in and eat [ate] dinner together. And there was [sic] other Indians that came in later on. They join[ed] us. Well, Ernest Stecker and General Scott were both working with this L Troop, Seventh Cavalry, and most of Indian didn't know how to speak English. So the Indians taught them the sign language. And they can speak to any tribe with their hands. And quick as we arrived there, General Scott commenced to make signs to Iseeo, how glad he was to see him and he said, "We gonna fight hard and win this case." He was making signs to him. It was already noon, so we walked up and went to the dining hall there. And it was a silent meeting—while everybody was eating they was [were] talking. But they didn't talk out loud, but they were just talking with their hands. They were talking about old times.[32]

Kiowa delegates included Spotted Bird, Ahpeahtone, Kiowa Bill, George Hunt, Louis Ware, and Bill Cizik, while Tennyson Berry and Frank Methvin represented the Plains Apaches and Naino, Bayho, Yellowfish, and their interpreter Wilber Pewo represented the Comanches. Quoetone reported that Iseeo testified as follows:

> And Iseeo, he said, "The man, he didn't go along with them, but the soldiers followed behind. And the surveyors marking the boundary lines went on the south bank of the Red River—across—and they made big mounds of dirt. Piled up so far apart on the south side of the river." And they said,

---

31 Guy Quoetone to Julia A. Jordan, Oklahoma, Apr. 30, 1968. Doris Duke Oral History Collection T-642:17-23.
32 Ibid.

"Now these [this] is your boundary lines. These mounds are the mark that shows it's supposed to be Texas on the south side. North of these mounds is supposed to be your land. When you're past this mound. . . . You're trespassing in Texas Territory. And if white man cross[es] these mounds, he's trespassing on your territory. . . . That's the understanding." And he said, "Now the line is between Texas and Oklahoma, those lines are the seams. Just like you sew something up. There's a seam of a cloth."[33]

Eventually the south bank was determined to be the cut bank of the Red River forming the legal boundary between Oklahoma and Texas. Photos in the Library of Congress depict Iseeo with Ahpeahtone, George Hunt, and other tribal delegates visiting Washington in 1923 to 1925, where they met and were photographed with dignitaries including General John J. Pershing, secretary of war John Wingate Weeks, and President Calvin Coolidge.

In 1923 Iseeo's wife, Pau-to-mah, died. With no one able to care for his lodge, Iseeo moved to the cottage near Quarry Hill, where his sons and nephew attended to him. In 1924 Iseeo remarried to O-tah-ty (Otahty), a Kiowa then aged sixty-six, from the Mount Scott Kiowa community.[34] On July 10, 1923, Scott wrote to General George Le R. Irwin, commanding officer at Fort Sill, thanking him for notifying him of the recent death of Iseeo's wife:

> I thank you very much for keeping me informed about his affairs and it gives me great very deep pleasure to note the interest you take in him and the kindness with which you treat him.
>
> Although he is old and crippled now, his services to the government and to the people of Oklahoma can never be too much appreciated. I feel the deepest interest in his welfare and thank you very much for your kindness to him and to me.

A copy of the letter was delivered to Iseeo on July 19, 1923.[35]

Later that month someone at Fort Sill began enforcing a regulation whereby Iseeo, due to his rank, could no longer secure accommodations from the quartermaster. A number of Iseeo's friends brought this to the attention of Oklahoma state representative Elmer Thomas, who wrote to Scott to inform him of the situation. In less than a month Scott had forwarded Thomas's letter to Commander Irwin at Fort Sill, as well as

---

33 Ibid., 22.
34 O-tah-ty (Áutájé/Áutátháijè or Salt), born 1859, was the widow of Hau-vaht, a son of Done-pi (Kiowa Family Record 1901: Fam. 274).
35 H. L. Scott to Colonel G. LeR. Irwin, Fort Sill, Oklahoma, July 10, 1923, Iseeo Military Career File, Biography/Indian, FSA.

responding to Irwin's own letter, thanking him for "taking such good care" of Iseeo.[36]

On July 4, 1924, John A. Buntin, acting as personal representative for President Calvin Coolidge, presented individual citations to the Comanche, Kiowa, Wichita, Caddo, and Apache Tribes of the Kiowa Agency for unswerving loyalty, patriotism, and military service in World War I. First Sergeant Iseeo, in uniform, received the citation for the Kiowa Tribe. The presentation was held at a tribal council that included World War I Indian Veterans and all surviving members of Troop L at Fort Sill. After Iseeo's death the citation was passed to his nephew George Hunt and then to his son Ernest Hunt, who eventually placed the citation on loan to the Fort Sill Museum.[37]

Iseeo again provided eyewitness testimony in 1926. When he was almost seventeen he had accompanied a war party against the Navajos into what is now New Mexico.[38] Along the Rio Grande they met a small Cheyenne village whose inhabitants informed them that a party of soldiers was coming to have a large council. A few days after the Kiowas returned home then camped at Medicine Lodge, an area in southern Kansas named for holding Sun Dances in the vicinity, a commission headed by Brevet Major General William B. Hazen arrived. The ensuing treaty, known as the Medicine Lodge Treaty of 1867, would place the Kiowas, Comanches, and Apaches on a reservation of the same name in the southwest portion of Indian Territory. Sergeant Morris Swett (1935:343–47) recorded Iseeo's recollections of what he saw and heard during the historic council. In 1926 the Medicine Lodge Indian Peace Council, at Medicine Lodge, Kansas, decided to erect a marker on the location of the historic council site. Iseeo, the only known survivor of the historic council, was sent for to identify the location of the event and arrived on Monday April 5. Having attended the council as a young man, he was able to show the exact location where the treaty was negotiated and signed. Since that time a historical festival including the "Indian Peace Treaty Pageant" has been held in Medicine Lodge, Kansas, in which many members of the tribes of the southern plains participate (Medicine Lodge 1994; Meadows 2008:103–104).

---

36 Elmer Thomas, Medicine Park, Oklahoma, to General Hugh L. Scott, Washington, D.C., July 12, 1923; H. L. Scott to General G. LeR. Irwin, Fort Sill, Oklahoma, Aug. 9, 1923, Iseeo Military Career File, Biography/Indian, FSA.
37 History of the Coolidge Citation to the Kiowas, as given by Guy Quoetone in 1958; copy of Citation from Calvin Coolidge to the Commanche [sic], Kiowa, Wichita, Caddo, and Apache Tribes of the Kiowa Agency, July 4, 1924, Iseeo Military Career File, Biography/Indian, FSA.
38 While Beebe (1931:356) and Swett (1935:343) state that Iseeo was fifteen, this is likely an error. His birth date (1849) and the date of the Medicine Lodge Treaty (1867) are well documented. As Iseeo reported to Scott, "I was just about eighteen years old at the time" (Swett 1935:343).

Iseeo and his wife Pau-to-mah (1851–June 23, 1923) had a large family. Together they had three sons, Pope-tsait-ke or Spotted Horse (1871–February 11, 1922), Tsait-pau or Harry Tee (1884–died after 1920), and Luke Tahbonemah (aka George Tee, 1894–September 14, 1956), and two daughters, Paugh-ti (1874–died after 1920) and Carrie To-haddle (1879–December 11, 1926).[39] Agency records show that Iseeo and Bat-chaddle were half brothers through their father Quo-haw-ty. Iseeo was also a younger brother to Tape-day-ah (Tépdéà or Standing Sweat House), who participated in a remarkable three-year journey (Nye 1962:328–29). By 1927 Iseeo had outlived two of his children (one died in December 1926) but was survived by his other three children and twenty-five grandchildren.[40] Today Iseeo has many descendants.

In February 1927 Iseeo took ill and on February 28 was unable to come to the post to draw his monthly pay. Lieutenant Hollis took Iseeo's pay to his tent, where he lay on a pallet on the north side, with his family gathered beside him. After visiting with Hollis for several minutes Iseeo acknowledged him with a relaxed facial expression and a nod. Hollis shook hands with Iseeo, gave his pay to his son, and departed. Diagnosed with pneumonia, Iseeo soon consented to be moved to the post hospital, where he died (Nye 1937:311; Hollis 1977:44–45). Military records report his death as March 11, 1927, at 1:00 A.M. due to pneumonia, with acute bronchial problems in both lobes.[41]

A funeral service was held for Iseeo on Sunday, March 13, at Harper's Mission near Fort Sill. Iseeo's commander, Lieutenant Jesmond D. Balmer, saw that Iseeo was "given the most impressive funeral ever accorded an Indian in the history of the United States."[42] The service was conducted by the Reverend J. L. Read and was translated into Kiowa by Iseeo's nephew George Hunt and into Comanche by White Parker, a son of Quanah Parker. Hunt gave a personal tribute to his uncle: "I do not tell you of I-See-O, you know him—his life is like a book. He has served his people and the American flag and had been thanked by President Coolidge for his services" (Hollis 1977:45). Hunt added: "He is like a shock of corn gathered in old age" (Nye 1937:311). The next day a traditional military-style funeral was held at the Fort Sill Post chapel with chaplain Ralph C. Deibert officiating and George Hunt translating. Attended by all the senior officers of the post and many Kiowas and individuals from neighboring

---

39 Kiowa Family Record (1901); McKenzie (1987).
40 Kiowa Family Record (1901); McKenzie (1987).
41 Iseeo Military Career File, Biography/Indian, FSA.
42 SGT I-SEE-O Enlistments and Data, Iseeo (n.d.a).

Close-up of Sergeant Iseeo, Kiowa scout, in uniform in later years.
*Photo #P11965, The Fort Sill National Historic Landmark,
Fort Sill, Oklahoma.*

Funeral of Sergeant Iseeo, March 1927, Fort Sill, Oklahoma.
Photo #P3636, The Fort Sill National Historic Landmark, Fort Sill, Oklahoma.

tribes, the service was concluded with the singing of a Kiowa song by the members of Iseeo's tribe. Large crowds waited outside, unable to squeeze into the already overcrowded chapel. The flag-draped casket was transported from the chapel to the Fort Sill Cemetery on a caisson of the 1st Field Artillery. The coffin was lowered as the post flag hung at half-mast. A bugler provided by the 23rd Infantry sounded taps, and a firing squad fired a volley over the grave. As he had requested, Iseeo was buried in his military uniform with full military honors at Chieftain Knoll in the Fort Sill Military Post Cemetery. According to a letter written by Hugh Scott (Nye 1937:311), "the funeral was more impressive than any other Indian funeral in the history of the country." According to tribal custom, after the service numerous Indians remained behind to mourn, with high-pitched keening. For many years thereafter relatives came to the grave to "cry for I-see-o" on Memorial Day (Nye 1937:311; Hollis 1977:45).

On June 7, 1931, the Friends of the Garrison and the Lawton Chapter of the Daughters of the American Revolution sponsored a ceremony at the old post chapel that included the unveiling of a bronze memorial tablet dedicated to Iseeo (Beebe 1931; Hollis 1977:45). The inscription on the tablet states (Beebe 1931:359):

> In memory of
> I-SEE-O
> Sergeant, United States Army
> The Last of the Fort Sill Indian Scouts
> Loyal to his Race
> And to the Arms of
> His Country
>
> ———
>
> Erected by
> Garrison Friends
> and by
> the Lawton Chapter,
> Daughters of the
> American Revolution

Chaplain Milton O. Beebe (1931:360) described the ceremony:

> One-half of the seating capacity of the chapel was reserved for the members of the family of I-See-O and others of the tribe (Kiowa). The tablet was unveiled by Miss Edith Rowell, who was dressed for the occasion in a beautiful doe-skin costume of the Kiowa tribe and Robert Larson, Troop No. 37, Boy Scouts of America, Fort Sill. Miss Lutie Goombi, also a member of the Kiowa tribe, interpreted the hymns, "Nearer My God To Thee," as sung by Mrs. Russell G. Barkalow, and "We Sing to God's Son," sung by the Kiowas in their native tongue, into the Indian Sign Language. Mrs. Smith, representing the Lawton Chapter, Daughters of the American Revolution, presented the tablet to Brigadier General William M. Cruikshank, who accepted it for the garrison.

Sergeant Morris Swett (1935:348) eloquently described the contributions that Iseeo made during a period of tremendous change in the southern plains and southwest Oklahoma:

> I-See-O's work was always of the quiet kind. His services have never been mentioned by heroism in the face of hostile fire, nor by the prowess of his rifle or pistol, but by the struggles that he averted and consequently the lives that he saved. He was usually the intermediary—the man who was Indian at heart, familiar with his vices and virtues, well aware of the power of the American soldier and the futility of struggle when the same ends could be obtained in a peaceful manner. It seems as though his whole

life has been dedicated to create better understanding between the white and red men. Wherever I-See-O appeared bloodshed and struggle were conspicuously absent.[43]

Due to the special circumstances involving the reenlistment of Iseeo in 1915, after the use of Indian scouts had been phased out at Fort Sill, Iseeo was the entire Fort Sill Detachment of Indian Scouts and thus the last of an era. In a 1971 letter regarding the centennial celebration of Fort Sill, retired brigadier-general Jesmond D. Balmer, who was Iseeo's lieutenant and commander while at Fort Sill, wrote: "It brought many memories of my nine years at Fort Sill. Among them was my association with I-See-O. Indeed, 'With him was buried an era.' I was his Commanding Officer and the last commander of the Fort Sill Detachment of Indian scouts. Few commanders have lost their entire command in one day."[44]

How did Iseeo's service relate to the role of Kiowa men during the reservation period (1875–1901)? With the end of warfare and confinement to the Kiowa-Comanche-Apache Reservation in 1875, the martial records of warriors from these tribes became frozen, offering younger men no future possibilities for gaining warrior status in the traditional manner. The role of the Indian male as hunter and provider for his family was also largely inhibited due to the near extermination of bison. During the reservation era service as Indian police and army scouts provided a new, and for many the only, avenue for martial service and status. Although the use of scouts accelerated with the movement of tribes to reservations, it soon dissipated. Their immediate service in rounding up holdout bands was no longer needed. Many men turned to serving as Indian police beginning in May 1878. With the formation of Troop L units in 1891, many more joined to serve in the all-Indian scout unit. Although some distinguished warriors served as scouts, an examination of Troop L and Kiowa military society membership rosters indicates that the majority were younger men with limited or no prereservation war records.[45] But the opportunity for Indian scouts to protect their peoples and remaining lands and to don martial dress (uniforms), bear arms, and engage in regular scouting and hunting activities provided important elements of martial status. Although involving a new syncretic form, service as scouts in Troop L provided the principal means of achieving martial and thus social status according to

---

43 In places Swett's article (n.d.) is a nearly verbatim but uncited copy of Beebe's 1931 article.
44 Brigadier General Retired Jesmond D. Balmer to Colonel James F. Unger, Field Artillery, Fort Sill, Oklahoma, Letter Received, Feb. 26, 1971, Iseeo Military Career File, Biography/Indian, FSA.
45 Troop L, 7th U.S. Cavalry (1929). For copies of Kiowa military society membership rosters from the 1880s, see Meadows (2010:369–88).

the Indians' traditional cultural systems during the reservation era and for many until World War I (Meadows 1999:377–81).

Dunlay (1982:201–207) has described other advantages for Indians serving as scouts, including material gain in the form of regular pay, favorable agency and government relations, and the opportunity to adjust to the changes of a tumultuous period in ways that were more culturally familiar. Nye (1937:262) made similar observations in the 1930s, noting that "they were proud of the uniform. It furnished them a means of gaining prestige, and even today the veterans of Troop L are among the most respected members of their tribes. The older Indians, the members of the passing generation, had their war exploits to talk about. But the rising generation, being forced to become farmers, had little to look forward to."[46] Another factor that may have influenced Isseo to become a scout in Troop L was that his older brother Tape-day-ah (Tépdéà), who died in 1897, had served as a scout in a small group of Kiowas in the late winter and early spring of 1875 that helped persuade other Kiowas to come to Fort Sill and surrender (Nye 1937:230).

Iseeo also holds another unique status. His lengthy service at Fort Sill between 1890 and 1927 included several enlistments as a scout and later as a regular soldier. With a total of nearly twenty-two and a half years of military service Iseeo appears to be the first Kiowa, and perhaps the first Indian of the southern plains, to have what might essentially be considered a "career" in the United States military—a road that many other Kiowas have followed to the present day. Iseeo's enlistment record from 1890 to 1927 follows.

February 10, 1890–August 10, 1890	Scout Detachment
August 10, 1890–February 9, 1891	Scout Detachment
February 10, 1891–March 31, 1891	Scout Detachment
August 26, 1891–February 25, 1892	Scout Detachment
February 25, 1892–February 25, 1897	Troop L, 7th Cav.
February 26, 1897–February 25, 1900	Scout Detachment
February 26, 1900–September 14, 1900	Scout Detachment
January 31, 1915–March 11, 1927	Sgt. Ind. Scouts/Senior Duty Sgt.[47]

---

46 In October 2000 a museum volunteer support group known as the "Descendants of Troop L, 7th U.S. Cavalry" was formed at Fort Sill. Composed primarily of members of the Kiowa, Comanche, and Apaches tribes, the group meets every second Wednesday of the month with the goals of reviving and perpetuating the history of the distinct all-Indian military unit that served with distinction at Fort Sill, Oklahoma Territory, and supporting the overall research and educational programs and objectives of the Fort Sill National Historic Landmark and Museum (Troop L, 7th U.S. Cavalry 2010).

47 Indian Scouts, Fort Sill Detachment File, p. 6, FSA.

One issue that merits clarification concerns the claim that Iseeo was the last surviving scout, which some interpret to mean that he was the last surviving member of Troop L. Iseeo retained an enlistment as a scout in the army after the deactivation of Troop L and a lifetime reenlistment as a senior duty sergeant in 1915 due to the intervention of Hugh Scott. While Iseeo was the last remaining Fort Sill Scout at his death in 1927, he was not the last living member of Troop L (Spivey n.d.). Some Troop L members such as Paul Kicking Bird, Silverhorn, and Tonemah lived into the mid-1930s to 1950s. This confusion comes largely from a lack of distinction between designations as a scout at Fort Sill and as a regular soldier in Troop L.[48] In 1942 Douglas Ripley, secretary of Robert Ripley's "Believe It Or Not," wrote to the commanding officer at Fort Sill to verify the rumor that Iseeo had served sixty years in the armed forces at Fort Sill. He was informed that it was approximately twenty-two and a half years.[49]

48 A review of Troop L membership rosters and Kiowa cemetery records shows that several other members of Troop L outlived Iseeo, such as Kiowa George Poolaw, Edgar Keahbone, E-mau-ha, and Silverhorn (Troop L, 7th U.S. Cavalry 1929).
49 Douglas Ripley to the Commanding Officer, Fort Sill Military Reservation, Nov. 4, 1943 (Scott n.d.a: Box 19).

Installation of the Parker-Iseeo Post, November 11, 1927 (Scott stands beneath flag). *Photo #1329, The Fort Sill National Historic Landmark, Fort Sill, Oklahoma.*

Iseeo's legacy continues through several locales around Fort Sill named in his honor. Tarbone Mountain in the Wichita Mountain Range, a corruption of Tahbonemah, is named for Iseeo. The mountain was earlier known as Mount Tarno and I-See-O Mountain (Morgan 1973:239). Iseeo Tank, a large water tower at Fort Sill, and I-See-O Hall, the Fort Sill Field Artillery School, are also named in honor of Iseeo. Two organizations involving Iseeo and other local Indians also developed. The Parker-Iseeo Post, named for Quanah Parker (Comanche) and Iseeo (Kiowa), was an American Legion Post made up of Comanches and Kiowas that was formed on November 11, 1927, near Fort Sill. General Hugh L. Scott officiated at the installment of the post. The post functioned briefly in the late 1920s and held Armistice Day dances. On May 9, 2001, an organization named the Descendants of Troop L, 7th U.S. Cavalry, was officially organized at Fort Sill, largely through the efforts of then Fort Sill Museum director Towana Spivey. Consisting primarily of descendants of the Kiowa, Comanche, and Fort Sill Apache members of Troop L from 1891 to 1897, and scouts for the army before and after this period, this organization serves to perpetuate the history of Troop L and as a support group for research and educational programs at Fort Sill National Historic Landmark and Museum (Spivey n.d.).

Other Consultants

Scott's other consultants were usually of three different relationships: members of Troop L, tribal political and religious leaders, and respected tribal community elders. Scott had almost daily interaction with members of Troop L, so his opportunities for collecting ethnographic materials were great. Tribal political and religious leaders (positions sometimes held simultaneously) were in frequent interaction with Scott both during visits to Fort Sill for administrative, legal, subsistence, and other reasons and during his visits to camps across the reservation. Respected tribal elders considered knowledgeable about their respective culture were queried both by Iseeo, who sometimes brought their accounts to Scott, and by Scott through visits to the camps arranged by Iseeo or others.

Kiowa
Taybodle (also spelled Ta-boodle, Taybodal, Tebodal, Tebodle, Teybodle)

Taybodle is an Anglicized pronunciation of Thépòl (Packing/Carrying A Lower Quarter/Calf Of Meat [Game]). Taybodle was born around 1809 and died in 1901. In the mid-1890s he was the eldest man in the Kiowa Tribe and was known as Êlqì (Big Man, literally, Old Man), a complimentary appellation based on age. Taybodle was a principal consultant of James Mooney for his *Calendar History* and for the ethnographic notes recorded by H. L. Scott, including accounts of White Bear's shield, the Kiowa-Comanche Peace, the Osage Massacre of the Kiowas in 1833, the Kiowa Sun Dance and religion, and other topics. The McKenzie family history places the birth of Thòkàuidè (Wrinkled Face, 1806–ca. 1899) and her brother Thépòl (1812–1901) in southeast Wyoming, in the region between the North and South Forks of the Platte River.[50]

Mooney (1898:163) noted that Taybodle was "a well grown boy when the stars fell" (about seventeen or eighteen in 1833). Scott (n.d.a: II:19, chapter 5 in this volume) refers to "Taybodle (86 years old)" in 1897, thus making him born about 1809. Taybodle reported that the massacre of the

---

50 Parker McKenzie to the author, 1993. Parker McKenzie was born in the tipi of his great-grandmother Thòkàuidè around Nov. 15, 1897, just north of Rainy Mountain in Indian Territory, southeast of present-day Gotebo, Kiowa County, Oklahoma. Although his birth date was not recorded in agency records, McKenzie chose Nov. 15 as his birthday. McKenzie translated her name as Facial Veil. To-koy-ty is listed as (Wrinkled Face) on the Kiowa Census (Kiowa Tribal Census 1881:19, 2). Based on the 1881 listing, the full name form is probably Thó-áu-káui-dè (Wrinkled Face).

Kuato Band of Kiowa occurred when his grandfather was a young man, perhaps around 1770, and that he had personally seen the single female survivor of the incident (Mooney 1898:157–58).

The 1901 Kiowa census records Taybodle's name as Ta-boodle, born in 1809, to his father Pe-ah-bo (Fâbòjè or Big Horse) and his mother Odle-po-yodle (Àulpàuóljè or Woolly Haired). Pe-ah-bo or Peahbo is alleged to have had ten wives, resulting in another of his Kiowa names, Tááuiqì (Many Wives) (Mooney 1898:233). Taybodle's sister To-kau-e-ty (Thòkàuidè) had a son in 1833 (the noted chief Big Bow) with her first husband, Big Bow, also known as Ta-ne-oh-keah (Thènéǫ̀qì or Good Eagle), who was killed in the 1840s. She later had a daughter named Peah-mah (born in 1844) with her second husband, Yeah-some (Yísàum or They Viewed Him Twice). Taybodle married A-tong-ty, a daughter of Pah-quot-ky, a Kiowa, and his Mexican wife Zeadle-ke-ah and had four daughters.[51] Taybodle was also the captive father of a young Mexican child who would be named Gúlhèì (Young Mustang Colt, b. 1839–d. 1872), who captured a red cape from a Mexican officer as a young man and was later killed in 1872. In 1958 three of his great grandchildren (Gus, George, and Dixon Palmer) gave the revived Kiowa Black Legs Society the right to wear a red cape in memory of him. A song recounting his capture of the cape is still sung in the society ceremonial (Meadows 1999, 2010).

Taybodle was an experienced warrior. He had been in one of the Kiowa camps that avoided the attack of the Osages in the summer of 1833. He participated in the 1837 fight when the Kiowas, Apaches, and Comanches exterminated forty-eight Cheyenne Bow String Society members who attempted to attack their combined village along the eastern edge of the Texas panhandle. As a young man he participated in two large Kiowa war parties that set out on foot (Mooney 1898:258–59, 271–72). Taybodle told Scott that he was the sixth generation of Kiowas to see horses and that he had participated in ten raids into Mexico to capture horses.[52] Although the full extent of his martial service is unknown, he participated in many raids and battles, including a revenge raid as late as July 1874 (Nye 1937:193), indicating that he was involved in martial activities from at least 1833 through 1874. Taybodle was a member of the Qóichẹ́gàu Society (Meadows 2010:378).

Taybodle was a healer of some renown. Although said not to be a medicine man, he possessed considerable medical knowledge. Nye

---

51 Kiowa Family Record (1901: 150, 207, 215).
52 Scott n.d.a:1:111, 2:90, chapters 4 and 5 in this volume.

(1962:105–12) records several cases in which Taybodle was sought to administer to infections, to cure snakebites, to set broken bones, and what he was most well known for, performing surgeries on various individuals, often to remove bullets from combat wounds. He was sometimes sought after the efforts of the Buffalo Medicine Men, the doctoring sodality that specialized in wounds involving bleeding, had failed and was even summoned to doctor a non-Indian bitten by a rattlesnake, which attests to his medical skill and success.

Taybodle was also associated with some of the most important religious items in the tribe. In 1839 a Kiowa named Big Black Tripe (Kone-au-beah or Kọ́áubíétjè) was wounded while escaping from a siege at Hueco Tanks, about thirty miles northeast of El Paso. Returning northeastward, the Kiowa party left him at Sun Mountain to die. As he lay atop the mountain he experienced a vision that included a Táimé figure speaking to him and telling him that he would survive. While journeying home the Kiowas encountered a Comanche party traveling southwestward, informed them of their comrade's fate, and asked them to bury the body when they found him. Upon arriving at Sun Mountain, the Comanches found Big Black Tripe alive, nursed him back to health, then turned back to take him to his home territory. As Big Black Tripe was being transported back to his home the party came upon a small crest on the rolling prairie where they encountered a small Táimé idol stuck in the ground. The image had been captured from the Crows by the Comanches and discarded. Believing that this was the Táimé he saw in his vision on top of Sun Mountain that promised to help him get home, Big Black Tripe asked the Comanches if he might have it. When they consented, he took the image. Upon returning home he was allowed to place this new Táimé beside the other two used in the Kiowa Sun Dance. This Táimé later appeared in a dream, instructing Big Black Tripe to made a wooden effigy known as the T'au (Jáu). This image consisted of a peeled two-foot-long section of chinaberry wood with a head carved like the face of the Táimé image, a feather attached to its face, a necklace of blue beads, and a skirt of skunk skin.[53] The T'au was placed beside the three Táimé during the Sun Dance, with Big Black Tripe sometimes carrying it during the ceremony (Mooney 1898:239; Nye 1962:36–45).

---

53   Parker McKenzie described a *t'au* (*jáu*, s/d; *jáugàu*, t) as a rabbit hunting stick mentioned in Kiowa mythology. Parker McKenzie to the author, Apr. 17, 1994. In 1935 HeapoBears described the jáu to La Barre (1935:135–36) as "a pointed digging stick used by women to dig up plants, throw at rabbits, etc., as used in the Bear-Woman, Seven-Sisters story."

Big Black Tripe also had a medicine wand in the form of a forked stick of seasoned chinaberry wood known as an *ápò̱jàu*. Big Black Tripe gave the T'au (Jáu) to Taybodle in 1848 and the forked medicine wand to his nephew Ko-yante or Coyante (Qàuyâ̱jè or Descending Over A Cliff). Big Black Tripe died during the great cholera epidemic of 1849.[54] Taybodle kept the T'au until he inherited one of the Ten Medicine Bundles. Because medicine keepers were not allowed to keep two different forms of medicine simultaneously, he passed the T'au on to Tay-nay-dau (Tenedooah). During the 1890s Taybodle was the head or leader of the Ten Medicine Bundle Keepers, apparently until his death. Following the 1857 Sun Dance, Ko-yante stuck the forked medicine wand in the ground at the site of the dance and left it as an offering to the Ta̱imé. When the Kiowas returned to the location the following year, they discovered that the stick had sprouted and named that year's Sun Dance, "The Year the Forked Stick Sprouted" (Mooney 1898:239; Nye 1962:36–45).

Although little information is available to shed light on his personality, Taybodle appears to have been a social individual. When the Kiowa prophet Bison Bull Emerging promised to make the bison return in 1881, Taybodle attended the encampment to witness his demonstration of power. Referencing an earlier source, Nye (1937:264) notes: "As old Tay-bodal said, 'I like to be where there is a big gathering of men smoking.' " In the winter of 1885–86 a prairie fire destroyed the tipis and much of the personal property of Taybodle and Frizzle Head, who were camped northwest of Mount Scott (Mooney 1898:354).

Taybodle died on September 15, 1901, less than two months after the reservation was allotted, and is buried in the Saddle Mountain Kiowa Cemetery. His grave marker, which reads "Tauboodle," states that he was eighty-nine years old and thus born in 1812. He is survived by many descendants through his four daughters and his adopted son. No photos of Taybodle are known.

Stumbling Bear

The name Sétèmqí̱a̱, popularly known as Stumbling Bear, more accurately denotes Bear That Is Pushing Them Down or Running Over Them. He was born in 1830 and died March 14, 1903. His father was Po-zem-ty and his mother A-yan-ty. Stumbling Bear was an officer in the Black Legs Society

---

54 Parker McKenzie to the author, Apr. 17, 1994.

and participated in the battle against Kit Carson in 1864. He is best known as a peace-oriented chief during the early 1870s who settled with a band of followers near Fort Sill, just north of Mount Scott (Kiowa Family Record 1901:39; Mooney 1898; Meadows 2010:54). Garrick Mallery (1880a:91) recorded a number of sign language signs from Stumbling Bear when he visited Washington, D.C., in June 1880. Scott's accounts name Stumbling Bear as the source of some information.

Big Bow

Zépcàuiétjè (Big Bow) was born in 1833 and died October 4, 1901. He carried the name of his father, also a noted warrior. His mother was To-kau-e-ty (Thòkàuidè), a sister of Taybodle. Big Bow is well known for going off on extended war journeys, sometimes alone. One of his noted war deeds, repelling a group of twelve Mexican soldiers with his wife, was painted on the Kiowa Battle Tipi of Dohausen or Tohausen (Jòhâusàn) (Ewers 1978:16). Big Bow was the leader of the Mountain Sheep Society. Initially resistant to surrender, he later served as a scout in guiding remaining Kiowa bands onto the reservation in 1875. Somewhat skeptical of the Sun Dance, he was involved in the early diffusion of peyotism among the Kiowas (Mooney 1898; Nye 1937; Meadows 2010:29–30, 369). Scott had frequent interaction with Big Bow, a prominent band leader in the early reservation era, including a memorable conversation during a wagon ride that he recorded.

Heidsick/Heidsicki (Hâichècì)

This is the Comanche version of his Kiowa name Càuáufìjàu (Crow [Feathered Sheathed] Lance), which was also the name of his father. He is often listed in agency records as Heid-sick and Ga-a-pia-tan. The 1895 Kiowa census (Kiowa Tribal Census 1895) and the 1901 Kiowa Family Record (1901: Fam. 65) list his birth as 1816 and his age in 1900 at eighty-four. He died on June 22, 1902. Heidsick was a prominent warrior, one of the last leaders of the Black Legs Society in the 1880s, and participated in the fight against the Cheyenne Bowstring Society in 1837. On the reservation he resided just north of the gap in the Slick Hills northeast of Mount Scott and present-day Meers, Oklahoma (Mooney 1898; Meadows 2010: 53, 374). Heidsick, who hosted ethnologist James Mooney in his camp and served as a consultant during his fieldwork in the 1890s, was one of the most informed Kiowa elders during the time when Scott also collected his information. His grandson Bert Geikaunmah and the husband of his granddaughter (Nellie Odlety), Parker McKenzie, were both accomplished Kiowa historians.

Done-pi

Dáunfài (Against The Chuck Or Shoulder Blade Area) was also known as Ágâjòjèà (Picking Up/Gathering His Feathers For Him) and Páukògái (Black Bison Bull), the Kiowa translation of a Comanche name given to him. While he died in the winter of 1892–93, the date of his birth is uncertain. Mooney (n.d.:I:51) stated that he was sixty-five when he died, placing his birth about 1828. Parker McKenzie also independently estimated his birth to be around 1828. Scott (n.d.a) placed his birth at 1817. He was a band leader and an accomplished warrior with many coups to his credit. His byname of "Quahada Tohausen" came from his frequently camping and traveling with the Quahada Comanches on the Staked Plains in pre-reservation times. He and Poor Buffalo were some of the last Kiowa chiefs to hold out, surrendering in February 1875. Donepi was a leader in the Horse Headdresses Society in the 1880s (Meadows 2010:37, 370) and the father of a large family, including Silverhorn, Kintadl, Charley Oheltoint, and Hau-vaht. He retained the pictographic calendar (*sáicùt* or winter marks) of his uncle Jòhâusàn, the last principal chief of the Kiowas, who died in 1866. In 1892 Scott obtained a version of the calendar copied on paper and recorded numerous notes on its content from Done-pi. Mooney incorporated information from this calendar in his *Calendar History of the Kiowa Indians* (Mooney 1898; Greene 1996).

Hanameahtah (Háunèmídâu or Unafraid Of Danger)

Hanameahtah was born in 1843 and died on January 11, 1914. He was a son of Jòhâusàn, the last principal chief of the Kiowas, who died in 1866. He was also known by the name of Fáibáudài (Sun Appearing). He is noted as an exceptionally brave man and accomplished warrior. His older brother, also named Jòhâusàn, was killed in combat before entrance to the reservation. He was a member of the Jáifègàu Society and was chosen by the Black Legs Society in 1885 to serve as an officer to replace Heidsick, who was becoming too old (Meadows 2010:53–54, 375). He also served as a private and later a sergeant in Troop L. Hanameahtah took his allotment east of Meers, Oklahoma, and is buried in nearby Mount Scott Indian Cemetery. He was the father of Charley Whitehorse and Amy Bear. His name was inherited by his grandson Roland Whitehorse.

Pǎutáuljè (Lean Bison Bull), popularly known as Poor Buffalo
Poor Buffalo was born in 1825 and died on May 6, 1901. He and Done-pi were some of the last chiefs to resist settlement in prereservation times, surrendering in February 1875. He bore a famous name derived from a survivor of the 1839 Hueco Tanks fight. He was one of the last leaders in the Kiowa Black Legs Society in the 1880s and was a principal figure in bringing the Ghost Dance to the Kiowas in 1890 (Mooney 1898; Meadows 2010:53–54, 374). Initially resistant to Kiowas joining Troop L at Fort Sill to serve as scouts, he later gave his approval after visiting with Scott and becoming friendly with him.

Frizzle Head or Frizzlehead (Áulpépjè or Bushy Haired)
Frizzle Head was born in 1824 and died on February 18, 1907. He was a prominent warrior and in the 1850s was involved in saving White Bear from a group of Mexican cowboys who had lassoed him and were dragging him. Frizzle Head lived between Meers and Saddle Mountain near Taybodle and was a consultant of James Mooney. He is mentioned in Scott's notes as being present at some of the sessions where Scott collected data from several of the eldest Kiowa warriors. Frizzle Head was a former leader in the Jáifègàu Society, as was his father, and remained a member in the 1880s. He was also a member of the Qóichégàu Society prior to its cessation (Meadows 2010:142, 379–80). He is buried at Saddle Mountain Cemetery. His son, who later took his name, was a principal consultant for the 1935 Santa Fe Laboratory of Anthropology Kiowa Field School.

Mobeadleky or Tom Mo-bedle-ky
(Màubílqì or Curved Down Nose Tip or High-Bridged Nose),
Also Known as Elk Tongue (Qócáuidén)
Mobeadleky was among the Kiowas who took Scott on a trip through the Wichita Mountains upon his arrival at Fort Sill in 1889. He was born in 1859 to Guo-padle-ty and Tau-guo-i-te and died on August 29, 1923. Mobeadleky was three-quarters Kiowa and one-quarter Comanche, his

Mobeadleky (Curved-Down Nose Tip/High Bridge Nose;
aka Kokoyden or Elk Tongue) and his daughter A-ke-a.
He was a member of Troop L and a scout for Lieutenant Hugh L. Scott.
Photo by H. P. Robinson, ca. 1891. *Library of Congress Photo LC-USZ62-126696.*

father being half Kiowa and half Comanche (Kiowa Family Record 1901: Fam. 236). He served on the Police Force at the Kiowa, Comanche, and Wichita Agency for twenty-seven months between 1882 and 1885 (McKenzie n.d.), was a member of Troop L at Fort Sill, and belonged to the Black Legs Society (Meadows 2010:373). He later attended Saddle Mountain Church and is buried in the Saddle Mountain Cemetery. Màubílqî's first father-in-law, who lived among the Kiowas, was reputed as an excellent sign talker. As one Kiowa (Scott n.d.a:II:164, chapter 5 in this volume) described, "The best sign talker we knew of was that old Cheyenne man, father of Mobilt's (Elk Tongue's) first wife. He lived a long time with the Kiowas. He is dead now. Whenever the Cheyennes came to visit the Kiowas they sent [for] that old man and talked to him and he told us in signs."

Paul Kicking Bird or Kickingbird

Kicking Bird (1865–July 3, 1935) was a son of Gúsáuldè (Having Horns/ The Horned One), also known as Báò (Cat). His father is reported to have been a cousin of the chief Kicking Bird who died in 1875. Paul Kicking Bird received the name of the former chief Thęnéàungópjè (Eagle Striking With Talons, popularly known as Kicking Bird) and was enrolled under a shortened form of the name as Aun-goop (Àungóp) (Kiowa Family Record 1901: Fam. 331). He served in Troop L and was an early member of the Kiowa Ohomo Society (Meadows 2010:381). Kicking Bird converted to Christianity under the Reverend J. J. Methvin and became an early member of Mount Scott Kiowa Methodist Church, where he assisted and interpreted for Methvin and later for the Reverends M. A. Clark and B. F. Gassaway (Corwin 1958:195–202). In the winter of 1894 a new church was constructed (Corwin ca. 1962:190), "located across Medicine creek, north of Mount Scott . . . built under the direction of Rev. A. E. Butterfield, who was assistant to Rev. J. J. Methvin, Methodist Missionary. Rev. Kicking Bird, a Kiowa, was made a local preacher for the new Church." This would be Mount Scott Kiowa United Methodist Church, east of Meers, Oklahoma. Kicking Bird appears in a photo with other early Comanche and Kiowa Christians (Corwin 1959:165). He married a daughter of Taybodle and had several children. Kiowas today bearing the surname of Kicking Bird are descended from Paul Kicking Bird: all of the children of the chief Kicking Bird (d. 1875) died young with no surviving offspring and all of Paul Kicking Bird's brothers (Eonety, Oyebi, and Mausape) were enrolled under their own Kiowa names, which became the surnames of their respective families. Paul Kicking Bird is buried in the Mount Scott Indian Cemetery near Meers, Oklahoma.

Paul Tsaitkopeta (Sétqópjè or Mountain Bear)

Paul Tsaitkopeta was a half Cheyenne and half Pawnee, born in 1852, and was raised among the Kiowas (Kiowa Family Record 1901: Fam. 241). His father was a Cheyenne chief known to the Kiowas as Jǫ́cáunqį̀ (Talker). His mother was a Pawnee captive who was given the Kiowa name Koy-e-ga-mah (Cûiqàmã̀ or Pawnee Woman). Paul came to live among the Kiowas when he was nine years old. He was adopted and given his Kiowa name by the Kiowa chief Woman Heart. Both were among the Kiowa prisoners at Fort Marion, Florida, from 1875 to 1878. Tsaitkopeta was a member of the Ją́ifègàu Society in the 1880s. He attended Carlisle Indian School in Pennsylvania and also served as an interpreter and consultant for James Mooney. He contracted tuberculosis in the East and suffered from its effects for the rest of his life (Mooney 1898:216). He died sometime between 1910 to 1920, as he does not appear on the 1920 census (Kiowa Tribal Census 1920).

Tchaka/Chaka (Bread/Bread Man)

Tchaka appears on the Kiowa census in 1881 as Chock-ah and in 1895 as Chock-ah, age forty-one (Kiowa Tribal Census 1881, 1895). Born in 1854, he appears to have died shortly before June 1899. He had a daughter born in 1899 but does not appear on the 1899 Kiowa census. He was married to Sa-pin, a daughter of Haun-goo-pah (Never Got Shot), and had two daughters, Mollie O-be-in (born 1881), who later married Ha-to-go (aka Little Joe), and Rose Sa-pin (born 1899) (Kiowa Tribal Census 1895, 1899; Kiowa Family Record 1901: Fam. 4, 342). According to Parker McKenzie, who worked at the Kiowa Agency from 1921 to 1958, Tchaka was half Keechi and was known as Keechi Joe. In two accounts Scott (n.d.a:I:62, II:138; chapters 4 and 5 in this volume) refers to him as a Kiowa and as one of seven male apprentices of the prophet Bison Bull Emerging in the 1890s. This is confirmed by Henry Tsoodle, Sr., another of the apprentices who listed all seven members, including "Tsa'/kai" (La Barre 1935:165). Tchaka is listed as a member of Troop L (Troop L, 7th U.S. Cavalry 1929). Along with Iseeo and Elk Tongue he helped make a feathered bonnet from the feathers of the golden eagle that Scott captured (Scott 1928:140). Parker McKenzie knew his name as Chŏc'à, and this name was later passed to Joe Big Bow. This is not a Kiowa name but the Kiowa pronunciation of a name from another language. First it does not resemble the Kiowa words for bread, *ébáu* and *égáu*. Second, a foreign origin is indicated by the apostrophe in the second syllable, denoting the absence of the (y) sound in syllables beginning with the consonants *c*, *k*, or *q* followed by the vowel *a*. McKenzie believed that it might be the early Kiowa pronunciation of "Joe," which would correlate with both individuals bearing that English name. Kiowa has no (j) sound, so the letter *j* is used in the McKenzie orthography to denote the soft or unaspirated (*t*) sound.[55] The association with "Bread" or "Bread Man" is unclear, possibly indicating another name of Keechi or some other origin.

Mud/Discharge From The Nose

Scott (n.d.a:I:16, chapter 4 in this volume) mentions the "oldest living Kiowa woman, Discharge From The Nose" and in other places states that the oldest living Kiowa woman is Domat's great-grandmother "Mud," which in name form would be Chén. This is probably the same woman, but he appears to confuse two similar but variant sounds of the letter *s* in Kiowa, in "Nose Mucus" (Sén) and "Mud" (Chén). In the McKenzie orthography these variants are expressed by the consonants *s* and *c*. This individual is most likely Sin-ah-quo (ca. 1809–99) (Kiowa Tribal Census 1881: no. 185), given as "Snotty." In the 1895 census she is listed as Sin-nah-quoa, eighty-six years old (Kiowa Tribal Census 1895: no. 883). Parker McKenzie knew the name as Séncùtjè or Séncùtà (Running Nose Mucus).[56] Domat was a member of Troop L who died around 1892.

Comanche
Quanah Parker

Quanah Parker (ca. 1852–February 23, 1911) was the son of the Comanche leader Peta Nocona and Cynthia Ann Parker, a white woman captured on May 19, 1836, during the raid on Parker's Fort in Texas.[57] Quanah became

---

55 Kiowa Tribal Census (1881, 1895, 1899); Kiowa Family Record (1901: Fam. 4, 342); Parker McKenzie to the author, Oct. 12, 1998.
56 Parker McKenzie to the author, Oct. 4, 1993; Sain-ah-quo (Séncùtjè) (Kiowa Family Record 1901: Fam. 312) was the mother of Peat-mah and Po-e-to-mah, the wives of Hunting Horse. Hunting Horse and Po-e-to-mah later served as consultants for Wilber S. Nye, Alice Marriott, and the 1935 Santa Fe Laboratory of Anthropology Kiowa Field School.
57 My thanks to Dr. Tom Kavanagh for contributing data for the biographical sketches of Scott's Comanche consultants. Tom Kavanagh, personal communication to the author, June 15 and 17, 2010.

an active warrior in the last years of the prereservation era and an emerging but low-ranking leader of the Quahada Comanches, who were among the last Comanches to surrender. When a friend was killed by Tonkawas scouting for an American troop detachment from Fort Griffin, Texas, Quanah solicited a pipe among the Kiowas, Comanches, and Cheyennes to lead a revenge raid but was prevailed upon by higher-ranking leaders, who proposed that the bison hunters who were severely impacting the Comanches' livelihood be punished first. The result was the attack on Adobe Walls in the Texas Panhandle on June 27, 1874. During the fight Quanah had his horse shot out from under him from a lengthy distance and soon after received a deep bruise to his right shoulder from a deflected bullet. Although he rarely discussed his war exploits with whites, he was likely active in the engagements with troops and raids against Texas settlements that constituted the Red River War of 1874–75. Quanah and other messengers arrived at Fort Sill on May 13, 1875. When the main body of Quahadas surrendered on June 2, 1875, Eschiti remained the recognized leader. Due to Randall MacKenzie's admiration and respect for the Quahadas, those Comanches brought in under J. J. Sturm received better treatment than other bands, were allowed to retain more horses, and were not placed in the guardhouse or icehouse with other Comanche prisoners (Hagan 1993:3–15).

Quanah Parker's political influence truly emerged in the reservation period (1875–1901). Scott had frequent contact with Quanah on various political issues during his tenure at Fort Sill, especially concerning the activities of the Jerome Commission and allotment. During a meeting in Washington, D.C., Quanah threatened to kill Scott over differing views on allotment. Part of Quanah's status came from his unique mixed heritage and continued interest in his mother, which drew the attention of army officers and gave him a lasting notoriety, his political acumen in negotiating grazing and reservation politics, success as a rancher, and leadership in the peyote religion (which became the Native American Church in 1917). His public performances as a Comanche warrior and leader (Hagan 1993:3–15) also brought notoriety. Several historical and biographical works on Quanah Parker are available. With seven wives Parker is survived by a large number of descendants, many of whom participate in the Quanah Parker Descendants Organization. In describing his collecting of ethnographic material Scott noted: "These tales were . . . told directly to the writer in the sign language of the Plains with the exception of Quanah Parker, who talked partially in signs, partly in Comanche, and partly in broken English."[58]

---

58 Untitled four-page account in "Notes on Kiowa History and Culture and Relations with Other Tribes" (Scott n.d.b: MS 2932, Box 2).

White Wolf (Esarosavit or Isatosavit)

White Wolf was the leader of a local Yapainʉʉ band in the prereservation and reservation era. When his brother was killed at Adobe Walls he adopted his nephew, later known as Howard White Wolf, who was a principal consultant for the 1933 Santa Fe Laboratory of Anthropology Comanche Field School (Kavanagh 2008). White Wolf married a sister of Tabenanaka (Kavanagh 2008:292). He resided just north of Fort Sill near a hill that bears his name and would have had frequent contact with Scott. A descendants' group holds an annual dance at his allotment, known today as the Esa Rosa (White Wolf) Dance Grounds. Scott recorded in his ledger: "White Wolf. Died September 29, 1897, [of] heart disease" (Scott n.d.a:I:188, chapter 4 in this volume).

Tabenanaka

The name "Tabenanaka" is based on Comanche *tabe* "sun" and *nanaca* "noise." Lila Robinson and James Armagost (1990:174) give the name as "Hears the Sunrise" or "Voice of the Sunrise." On his tombstone his name is given as "Sound Of The Sun." Tabenanaka was an active warrior and a Yapainʉʉ subleader. His sister was married to White Wolf (Kavanagh 2008:118–19, 292). Tabenanaka was a signer of the Little Arkansas Treaty in 1865 (Kavanagh 1996:402–403). Kavanagh (2008:293) states that Tabenanaka and White Wolf were leaders of separate Yapainʉʉ local bands both before and during the reservation period. While it is known that Tabenanaka, White Wolf, Tabenanaka's distant relative Cheevers, and Cheevers's uncle Esananaka competed for the role as Yapainʉʉ principal chief after the death of Paruasumuno in 1872, the historical role of White Wolf was minimal. Tabenanaka was highly resistant to settlement but eventually took a "small ranch" four miles north of Fort Sill. Scott recorded information on Comanche men's societies from him. On April 28, 1893, Tabenanaka died of heart failure while running to catch a train in Anadarko. He is buried in the Otipoby Cemetery in Comanche County, Oklahoma (Nye 1937:253, 1962:246–47).

Tahpony

Tahpony (ca. 1833–99) was a Yapainʉʉ Comanche who lived on West Cache Creek, near present-day Lawton, Oklahoma. On October 29, 1897, Scott visited him at his lodge below the Comanche School house at the spring belonging to the Daley family on the Henrietta Road. Although censuses report his birth between 1844 and 1859 (Kavanagh 2008:226), Tahpony reported his age at this time to Scott as sixty-four and thus was born around 1833. His name has been translated as "Walks In Place" or "Marks Time." He was listed as the leader of a small local Yapainʉʉ band in 1879. In 1890 this band contained eleven people. Tahpony died in the measles epidemic of 1899 and was buried on his residence, now within the city limits of Lawton, Oklahoma. When the city of Lawton developed, Tahpony was exhumed and reinterred elsewhere. He was a brother to Permansu (aka Comanche Jack). Kavanagh (2008:226–28) provides three accounts of a story about Tahpony.

Cabaya or Cavayo

Cabaya/Cavayo (*caballo* is Spanish for "horse") was a member of Tahpony's Yapainʉʉ band around 1890. He was born about 1860 and died in 1918. He is buried at Deyo Mission Cemetery, where his tombstone reads "Cavvay 1918." Scott recorded a number of accounts on Comanche origins, men's societies, social organization, sign language, and other topics from Cabaya. In June 1912 Robert Lowie interviewed Cabaya on Comanche men's societies and dances (Kavanagh 2008:489).

Comanche George

This individual appears to be George Maddox, who is the only Comanche named George listed in the Troop L Roster. Scott makes several references to "Maddox" and his family throughout his ledgers. George Maddox or Pesuwiyeckwit (translated in censuses as "Independent") was an early peyote man and a member of the band of Pertooavoniquo (Goes To See His Son) after 1883. Maddox's identification is confirmed in a second roster of Troop L under corporals, "George Maddox, Pur-su-su-wite-yerqueth, I Do As I Please."[59]

Big Cow

Scott mentions Big Cow as a scout at Fort Sill at the time he arrived (1889) and as accompanying him on several trips. This may have been

---

59 Troop L, 7th U.S. Cavalry (1929), A.G. 062.14, Troop L, 7th Cavalry, (1-2-29) ORD, War Department, Adjutant General's Office, Jan. 9, 1929, copy, Fort Sill Museum Archive, Fort Sill, Oklahoma.

Sohe (Hairy), born in 1851, who was the leader of a small Yapainuu band around 1890. Although his sons Mike Poafpibitty (b. 1882) and Donald Pesevonete (b. 1884) had the surname "Big Cow," they were too young to have served in Troop L. Big Cow may have been a nickname.

Plains Apaches
Gie-san

Isseo reports Gie-san (Little Child) as the oldest Kiowa-Apache man in the 1890s, "much older than White Man." He visited Gie-san at his camp on Sweet Water Creek (now called Sugar Creek, near Sedan, southwest of present-day Mountain View in Kiowa County, Oklahoma), just below the Rainy Mountain Road. It is likely that Gie-san was sought out due to his advanced age and thus his knowledge of Apache origins and culture.

Anglo-Americans
Ben Clark

Ben Clark was an Anglo scout and post interpreter for the 7th Cavalry at Fort Reno and was married to a Cheyenne woman (Hyde 1968:293n12). Scott (1928:176) described Clark, who was fluent in both Cheyenne and sign language, as "the most accomplished white sign talker I ever met." Scott visited Clark several times at his home at Fort Reno to record information on sign language and accounts on the Cheyennes, which appears in volume II of his notes. Scott (1928:177–78) helped both Clark and Horace Jones (the post interpreter at Fort Sill) to retain positions at their respective military posts after they were discharged during a period of economic cutbacks.

THE SCOTT LEDGERS

Hugh Scott's ethnographic notes at Fort Sill consist of four clothbound ledgerbooks typical of the kind used by late nineteenth century clerks and traders, with numbered, ruled paper pages eight inches in width by thirteen inches in length. Based on an examination of content and syntax, the notes are direct translations of sign language handwritten in longhand English cursive script. While the notes were collected during Scott's term at Fort Sill (1889 to 1897) most entries are undated. The death dates of some individuals and other references contained in accounts indicate that some material was collected as early as 1891 to 1893. Some of the notes appear to have been collected toward the end of his time at Fort Sill, especially in the summer and fall of 1897. A date is occasionally included in some of the materials collected, usually in reference to a geographical place being described or referenced from the location where the account was being recorded.

"Capt. H. L. Scott 7th Cav. Fort Sill O.T. [Oklahoma Territory] Sign Language" is written on the cover of volume II. Oklahoma Territory was formed May 2, 1890, and Scott was not promoted to captain until January 1895, suggesting that the initial entries in volume II date no earlier than January 1895. An entry on page 3 of volume II is dated August 27, 1897, and several other accounts in this volume contain dates in the later months of the same year, perhaps indicating that much of this volume was recorded in the latter part of 1897. The cover page of volume III is dated "Nov. 1897," and several other entries are dated to the fall of 1897, just prior to Scott's transfer from Fort Sill. While he likely recorded entries over a number of years, one of the later entries in volume II (Scott n.d.a:II:182, chapter 5 in this volume) recorded from Iseeo also suggests that many of the entries were recorded in 1897.

> I think you know the sign making better than anybody. We have talked together for eight years. When I see you I understand at once just like lip talk. We have talked now all summer about these things in sign and I cannot tell you anything more. . . . I look all around for something you have not had told you before, but it is a failure. I do not see anything more. We have talked together ever since last spring, seven months, and we have talked for eight years about these things from time to time. I have asked all the old men and women what I did not know myself and now I am through.

This entry also demonstrates Iseeo's concern for ensuring that Scott was given reliable information. Iseeo continued, explaining that one elder woman he had consulted for information was no longer reliable due to the state of her advanced age and that he did not want to misinform Scott through the use of unreliable consultants. Although almost all the material appears to have been collected in Indian Territory and Oklahoma Territory, one entry related to sign language dated April 22, 1908, was made while Scott was visiting the Navajos at Smeth, Utah.

Scott's notes focus on the Indians of the southern plains, with the majority of data on the Kiowas and lesser amounts on the Comanches, Plains Apaches, Cheyennes, Arapahos, Wichitas, Caddos, Tonkawas, Poncas, Crows, and Navajos. Volume I consists of 266 pages, with 13 blank pages.

Scott Ledger, vol. I, page 1: "Buffalo Bull Medicine."
Courtesy of Fort Sill National Historic Landmark and Museum Archive and Wade Popp.

Volume II contains 192 pages, with 9 blank pages. Volume III contains 25 pages of ethnographic material. The ethnographic data recorded in the three volumes total 483 handwritten pages with 22 blank pages, leaving 461 pages of actual data. Approximately 326 of 461 pages (70.71 percent) focus on the Kiowas. The remaining 135 pages consist of data on other tribes and alphabetical entries on signs. These materials constitute the following subjects (followed by the number of pages for each).

Kiowas	326
Sign Language Signs	48
Comanches	31
Kiowa-Apaches	17
Witchitas	11
Misc. Intertribal Data	9
Cheyennes	6
Ponkas	5
Arapahos	3
Crows	2
Tonkawas	2
Navajos	1
Total	461

Volumes I, II, and the first twenty-seven pages of volume III consist primarily of ethnographic notes with some reference data, usually along the margins of the pages. These materials represent chapters 4, 5, and 6 of this work. The remainder of volume III and volume IV of Scott's notes consist primarily of drafts of essays that Scott was writing, reference data, and notes of comparisons with numerous early western explorers, military officers, and anthropological publications by ethnographers such as Alfred Kroeber, Robert Lowie, Clark Wissler, and George B. Grinnell. The date written on the cover of volume III is November 1897, so parts of this volume and much of volume IV are likely notes that Scott made while temporarily assigned to the Bureau of American Ethnology in late 1897, where he was reading many of the ethnological and historical publications on the western United States until called away for military service in the Spanish-American War early in 1898.

The small amount of information recorded from the Comanches raises the question of why more data were not collected by Scott. Ample evidence shows that the Comanches knew and used sign language, with documented instances dating from 1805 to as recently as the mid-1980s (Kavanagh 1996:165, 181, 348, 2008:274–75, 293; Taylor

1996:276–77).⁶⁰ Living at Fort Sill, Scott was physically closer to the Comanches than to the Kiowa and Apache communities, the Comanche population was slightly larger than the Kiowa population, and several Comanches served in Troop L. One of Scott's entries, however, sheds light on the disproportionate collection of information and relates to both qualitative differences in the use of sign language by the Comanches and Scott's research focus.

> The Comanche are the poorest sign talkers on the Southern Plains. This is due partly to their careless nature and partly to the fact that their language is considered easy to acquire and partly to their former force and dominance. They were the most numerous of all the southern tribes and if anyone had business with a Comanche he had to speak his language or he would not bother with him. The consequence was that Comanche was spoken largely by all the other tribes including the Southern Cheyenne and Arapaho, among whom I have seen many who understood Comanche, although they would rather use the sign language. . . . While I have lived long among them, could understand the subject of conversation, and frequently checked up [on] interpreters who failed to give my real meaning, I was always so occupied with the sign language, always searching for new signs and new meanings that I made no study of the Comanche and so far as I know there is no one who has yet done it.⁶¹

Although the Comanches clearly knew and used sign language, the prevalence of Comanche as a lingua franca in southern plains trade may have made some Comanches less reliant on sign language than neighboring groups (Goddard 2001:67). In addition, the larger number of Kiowas than Comanches in Troop L (and only one Kiowa-Apache) may also have contributed to Scott's greater interaction with Kiowas and recording data on their culture.

Content and Unique Features

Scott's ledgers contain accounts on a wide variety of cultural forms and historical events of the Kiowas, Comanches, Apaches, and neighboring tribes of the southern plains and present-day southwest Oklahoma. They include accounts of migrations, mythology, religion, warfare, law,

---

60 In a letter to President Thomas Jefferson in 1805, James Wilkinson noted that Philip Nolan had "acquired a perfect knowledge" of sign language while trading with the Comanches (Wilkinson 1805), possibly in conjunction with the Caddo-French Métis Joseph Lucas (Flores 1985:23; Kavanagh 1996:503n14).

61 Scott (n.d.b: MS 2932, Comanche). In addition to archival records, some sources in Comanche ethnography already existed (Burnet 1824, 1840, 1851; ten Kate 1885).

language, material culture, and numerous cultural practices. One significant genre is accounts of the Kiowas' origins and separation into two groups in the northern plains, often containing the expression "when the Kiowas first grew up." One account (Scott n.d.a:III:4–7, chapter 6 in this volume) specifies: "When we separated it was a little this side of the big river which has ice points sticking up on it (Missouri) near where the hot water rushes high in the air out of a hole in the ground." This was near the Yellowstone region and slightly south of the Missouri River. While this aspect is well documented elsewhere, the account provides rare evidence that the two sides continued to visit back and forth for a number of years. The southern group is said to have repeatedly invited the northern group to rejoin it until the two groups, continuing to migrate in separate directions, lost contact with one another. Published accounts reference only a dispute and separation.

Other entries describe aspects of the Kiowas' time in the northern plains (Scott n.d.a:II:163, chapter 5 in this volume).

> They did not get [many] horses until they made peace with the Comanches. They had a very few horses before. They used to fight the Comanches and sometimes get a horse but when they made peace with the Comanches they got lots [of] horses. There were five old people [five generations] died since we made peace with the Comanches. Taybodle and I are the sixth now living. We are very old and weak. I do not think we will live long. What I tell you I did not see myself. My grandfather told me. He told me the Kiowas first grew up on the other side of the rock that pushed up the children (Bear Lodge Tower in Black Hills Dakota). . . . They grew up on this side of the hot water (Geysers, Yellowstone Park). We saw Crows there and far away to the east on the River with Ice Points Sticking Up (Missouri River) we knew about the Cheyennes and Arapahoes. They were south of the Crows.[62]

Descriptions of the impacts of disease (Scott n.d.a:I:97–98, chapter 4 in this volume) are also noteworthy. One account states that a single epidemic of smallpox killed nearly two-thirds of all the Kiowas, while the description of the great cholera outbreak of 1849 states that "[i]t took off more Kiowas than any other disease." While these estimates cannot be precisely confirmed, the devastation was undoubtedly extensive. Several accounts of the same epidemic are similar and clearly indicate that it made a distinct impression on the Kiowas. "Dead Man Fainting Trance" recounts the story of an individual who had a near-death experience and saw his relatives

---

62 The reference to being of Taybodle's generation and extremely elderly suggests that this statement is likely from Heidsick or possibly Frizzle Head, the other oldest Kiowa known to have worked with Scott.

in the afterlife but was revived and lived. What is remarkable about the account is not only that other Kiowas reported similar experiences but how similar it is to the near-death experiences of people in other cultures.

Also included are many valuable firsthand accounts such as Quanah Parker's account of the Adobe Walls Fight of 1874 and data on the Kiowa Sun Dance provided by some of the eldest Kiowa tribal members, all of whom had taken part in the ceremony and been familiar with it since their youth. It is of particular interest that details of the number, origin, and extant condition of the Kiowa Ten Medicine Bundles vary from later published sources. A number of entries relate to the making of peace between several tribes of the southern plains tribes, Kiowa games (arrow game, hand game), and forms of medicine (shields, Buffalo Medicine, Antelope Medicine, Iseeo's horse medicine, and medicine for rattlesnake bites). In addition, these accounts give information on a number of unique topics, including eagle catching, paint mines, naming practices, buffalo surrounds, views on hanging and abandoning old people, the first mention of horses among the Kiowas, and Kiowa and Comanche men's societies. A number of them contain valuable ethnographic descriptions of tribal customs, especially the Red (Mescal) Bean Ceremony of the Wichitas, and references to the demographic movements of groups such as the Wichitas and Caddos.

Scott's notes also address elements of culture change as Indians adapted to significant alterations during the reservation period (1875–1901), including some of the religious revitalization movements such as attempts to "bring the bison back." In 1897 Iseeo (Scott n.d.a:III:21, chapter 6 in this volume) reported that the boy's ring game "is not played now. The children are all scattered over the country and when they are gathered in schools they play white men's games." Likewise, in discussing painted tipis, Iseeo commented (Scott n.d.a:II:28, chapter 5 in this volume): "We do not color our lodges anymore. Now we have put that custom away."

Significantly, some of Scott's accounts provide more detail and names of principal participants than found in previously published versions of the same events. Taybodle's account of the Cutthroat Massacre of 1833 contains valuable firsthand accounts, as he was in a nearby camp in which a survivor came and joined a force in pursuit of the Osages. Scott provides the only currently known account for some topics. In researching a map of the Kiowa-Comanche-Apache Reservation drawn by Black Goose, I was able to correlate the pictographic image of a bison skull beside a small tree containing offerings located along a tributary of Stinking Creek with Scott's detailed account of the "Buffalo Tree" contained in volume I (Scott n.d.a:I:172, chapter 4 in this volume; Meadows 2006:272–73).

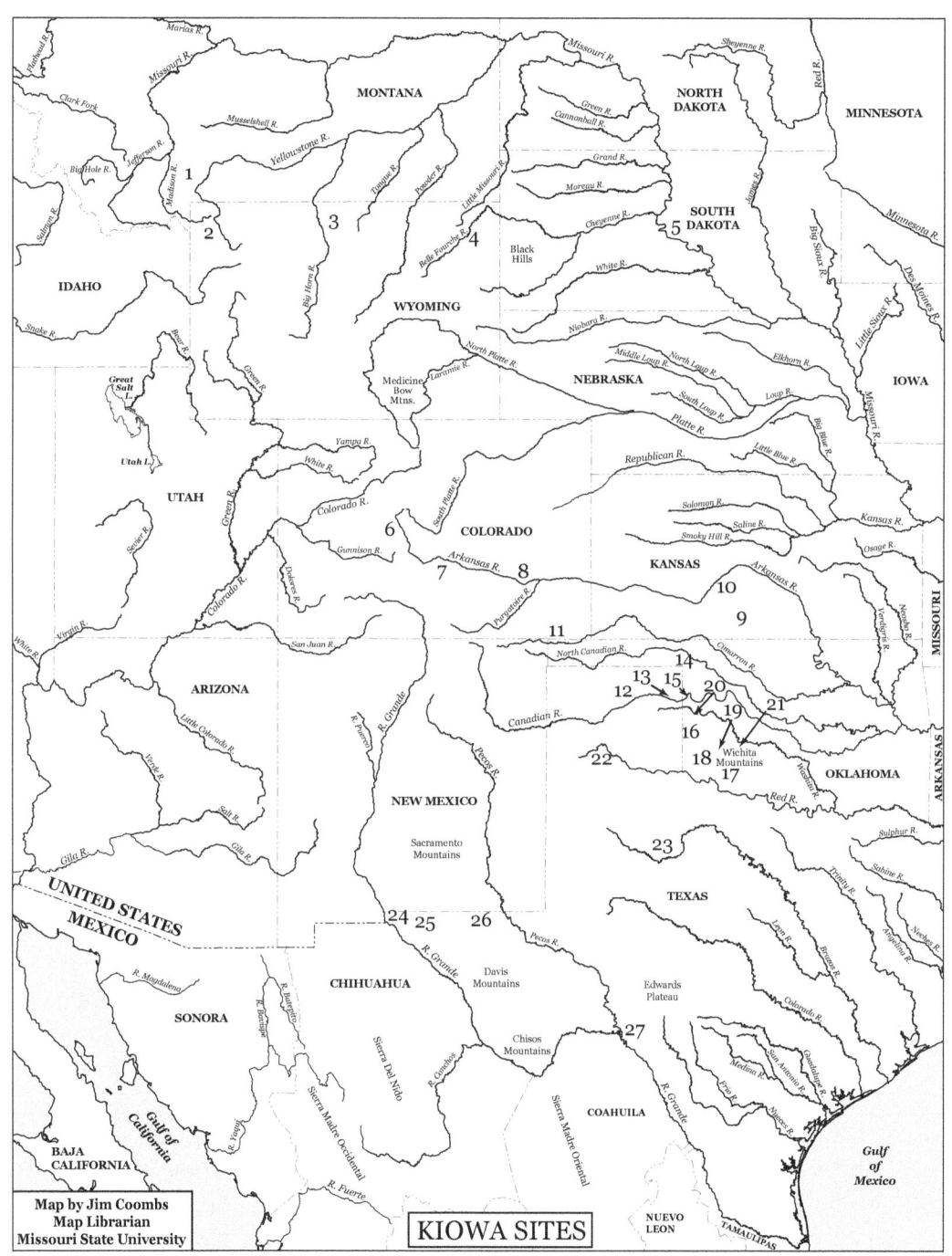

General locations of major sites mentioned in the Scott ledgers.
Copyright © 2015, University of Oklahoma Press.

Stories involving the Kiowa culture hero Scinday or Sainday (Séndé) are one of the most important and extensive components of Scott's notes. Like tales of many culture heroes in other societies, most Scinday stories focus on his attempts to get something for nothing through laziness, manipulation, deceit (most often involving food), or some culturally inappropriate action (such as marrying his daughter or his mother-in-law). Inevitably his plan backfires: Scinday ends up with nothing, providing a moral lesson (most often involving greed, stinginess, and dishonesty) for the Kiowas. In one tale called "Scinday's Laws" he is so ashamed after sleeping with his mother-in-law that he leaves earth. He does not die but now resides in the heavens above. Scinday tells the Kiowas that henceforth they cannot speak of him during the daytime but only at night. Iseeo explains that this is also possibly why the Kiowas "are afraid" of their mothers-in-law (practice mother-in-law/son-in-law avoidance).[63]

Another important genre is "obscene" or "risqué" Scinday stories that were told only among adults. There were probably limits regarding mixed company: traditional Kiowa culture dictated that storytellers not use words such as "breasts," "buttocks," or "genitalia" in front of the opposite sex and certain in-laws due to embarrassment. During my fieldwork several Kiowa elders often mentioned this "obscene" genre of Scinday stories involving sexual themes and exploits. I recorded a few such stories. Just as many Scinday stories begin "Scinday was coming along," this genre often begins "Scinday's penis was very long and he kept it wrapped around his body like a rope."[64] The stories of "Scinday and the Boy" and "Scinday and the Girl" in Scott's ledgers provide samples of this genre.

The Nature of Scott's Consultants

Although some entries are attributed to a specific individual who provided the data, such as Iseeo, Taybodle, Quanah Parker, Tahpony, or Stumbling Bear, most are not. Some entries contain clues provided by the consultant (such as their age or year of birth), indicating that many were collected from Iseeo or from him and other consultants in group settings.

Scott collected some accounts while at Fort Sill and during trips across the reservation. He also sent Iseeo on trips across the Kiowa-Apache-Comanche Reservation as well as to the Cheyenne-Arapaho Reservation and elsewhere to gather new signs and accounts. In some instances Iseeo

---

63 This story refers to the widespread Plains kinship tradition of mother-in-law/son-in-law respect avoidance.
64 Author's fieldnotes, 1989–98.

(Scott n.d.e:36) brought elders to Fort Sill to relate accounts to Scott. One of Scott's grandsons (Diker n.d.) writes in a letter: "General Scott found out about Silverhorn at Fort Sill and made it a practice to sit with him and other blanket Indians on his porch learning the fables by way of sign language." Scott also described collecting stories and ethnographic material at the camps of elder Kiowas and Comanches and Apaches, visits to the Wichita community, visits to Fort Reno, and locations on the reservation where he sat with tribal members who related stories at the locations where they occurred.[65]

Iseeo sometimes indicated that he obtained the account from another tribal member to retell to Scott. As Scott (1911:355) noted in one publication, "During this description of the Kado there were present Taybodal, Poor Buffalo, Frizzlehead, Heidsick, and Stumbling Bear, the oldest and most respected chiefs of the tribe. They had all taken part in the Kado from their youth, and had seen many dances. I-see-oh . . . , who had had daily intercourse in the sign language with the writer for nine years, was their 'spokesman.'"

In his article on the Kiowa Sun Dance, taken directly from the account recorded on pages 99–118 of volume II of his ledgers, Scott (1911:355) described the nature and the uniqueness of his data.

> The above information, as well as the following Kiowa accounts, were obtained by me during nine years spent among the wilder tribes of the present Oklahoma. They were given in the sign language of the Plains and were received directly, without the intervention of an interpreter, or the use of any spoken tongue: it is probable that the following is the first published account of an Indian ceremony described by Indians by means of the sign language alone, and may prove interesting to those who do not know of what the sign language is capable.

Scott (n.d.e:30–31) described the nature of his visits to the camps of tribal leaders, including extended trips across the reservation in the spring.

> When the grass was high enough to feed a horse in the spring, Sergeants Clancy and Chambers would pack some mules with tents, food, and bedding, and with six or seven Scouts, a cook, and a congenial companion, the restlessness of spring would be worked off exploring the country.
>
> Everywhere the places of historical interest, of battles, and happenings of the olden times, would be pointed out, and their stories told at night in the sign language of the Plains. Whenever possible, camp would be made

---

65 Although he notes that they discussed sign language together, Scott's material from Ben Clark, an Anglo who spoke English, at Fort Reno likely involved the use of spoken English.

near the lodges of some of the old Kiowa or Comanche chiefs, such as Taybodle . . . , the oldest Kiowa man living, then eighty, or of Stumbling Bear, Heidsick, Tabananica, White Wolf, Tohausen IV, Frizzle Head, Poor Buffalo, Honameatah, or Big Bow, that foremost warrior of the Kiowa, who would gather to give and receive the news of the reservation, and advice as to their tribal and personal afffairs. . . .

Their lodges would be sought after dinner, the time for storytelling, when the fatigues of the day were forgotten, and the bundles of dry twigs were gathered for throwing one at a time on the fire, to illuminate by their blaze the features on the war-path on the Texas Plains or the Arkansas, or far down in Mexico. Or again some aged historian would tell by signs of the origin and migrations of his people, as related by his forefathers, and their myths and legends, all told in the deepest silence, with out a spoken word, in the most vivid and dramatic language that exists on the earth, holding all his observers spellbound until far into the night.

The following individuals are identified in the ledgers as having provided data to Scott: Iseeo, Taybodle, Heidsick, Frizzle Head, Stumbling Bear, Big Bow, Poor Buffalo, Mobeadleky, Tchaka (Bread), Done-ty, Ziracunny, and Discharge From the Nose (Kiowa); Quanah Parker, White Wolf, Tahpony, Cavaya, Comanche George, and an unnamed elder woman (Comanche); Gie-san or Little Child (Plains Apache); a Caddo (probably Caddo Jake); and a Wichita. As described in the consultant sketches, these individuals include some of the eldest and most prominent warriors, band leaders, painted tipi owners (Ewers 1978), and military society officers living in these tribes in the last quarter of the nineteenth century, most of whom had extensive firsthand experience of prereservation Plains Indian culture. As a reflection of their reputation as respected tribal leaders and experienced and knowledgeable consultants, it is noteworthy that several of these men were also the principal consultants of James Mooney (1898:147), offering complementary accounts.

Contextual Relations

What was the context of the relationship between Scott and Iseeo as it pertained to Scott's collection of ethnographic data from Iseeo and other Indians? Perhaps the best way to examine this is by reviewing the available data regarding the hierarchical nature of their relationship, their interactions, and the general trends observed among other Indian scout units. Because Troop L at Fort Sill was formed sixteen years after the last tribes of the southern plains had ceased armed conflict and been placed on reservations, the issue of loyalty in combat was likely not paramount, as Dunlay (1982:200) describes with some white officers leading Indian scouts in earlier combat situations: "Those most closely associated with Indian scouts . . . generally testified to the seriousness with which they took their oath of enlistment and their obligations as they perceived them." The military defeat of the Kiowas and Comanches in 1874–75 and subsequent imprisonment of seventy-two southern plains prisoners for three years at Fort Marion near St. Augustine, Florida, was likely another influence on later service as Indian scouts. Under Captain Richard H. Pratt, who had already commanded Indian scouts, the Fort Marion experience may have broken their will to resist armed conflict with the U.S. Army. The use of military uniforms, drilling, guarding their fellow prisoners, and gradual freedoms led Pratt to declare the Indians to be more efficient and conscientious than the white soldiers stationed at the fort.

In terms of hierarchy, most officers selected to lead Indian scout units had extensive experience in dealing with Indians. Scott had commanded Indian scouts for several years before coming to Fort Sill and was the commanding officer of Iseeo and the other members of Troop L. Iseeo had demonstrated his character and loyalty in several situations with Scott prior to the formation of Troop L in 1891. Conversely, Scott had shown his interest in helping the Indians in issues associated with the Cherokee (Jerome) Commission and allotment.

While the majority of white officers in Indian scout units placed the benefit of the Indians to the army over helping the Indians, some such as George Crook, Edward Casey, and Hugh Scott were sincerely dedicated to helping their charges. Consequently, those field officers who consistently reported hard-working and satisfied units and who exhibited patience, sympathy, and a deep concern for the Indians' welfare were often criticized by officers in the upper echelon, who claimed such successful commands depended too much on the personality of the commanding officer. These critics complained that the personal relationship required to lead Indian scout units effectively ran counter to the army's standard of using officers as interchangeable parts and feared that Indian units would become ineffective upon the death or reassignment of its officers. Their view was also different from the Indian practice of following the man and not the rank, with Indians basing relationships on kinship and personal loyalty in contrast to the impersonal mechanical nature of armed forces in a state level of social organization (Dunlay 1982:196–97).

Scott's selection of Iseeo as first sergeant in Troop L raises an interesting question: why was he selected? As Scott (1928:169) described, "None of the Indians could read or write, and so Ernest Stecker of my Troop M was appointed first sergeant to take care of the paperwork . . . and Iseeo [was appointed] as first sergeant, who was, however, a figurehead, unable to deal with white men, never having learned any English." Iseeo's appointment may have been based on several factors, such as personal relations, appreciation or reward for his previous service, Scott's rapport with Iseeo via sign language and the potential resource that this represented, and political contexts (Iseeo's earlier service in helping to prevent several armed conflicts was well known among the Kiowas). From this perspective Scott's appointment of Iseeo could be interpreted to reflect the Indian mode of loyalty more than army criteria for officer selection.

Service as scouts also offered several benefits such as employment in a culturally attractive and acceptable form that continued a martial emphasis associated with horses and weapons, wages, a more familiar and potentially easier way to adjust to rapidly changing conditions, and more favorable terms than resistance would have produced. Scott (1928:169–70) proudly noted that none of the Indians in Troop L could read or write upon enlisting, but they were able to save enough money to build houses after leaving the army. Service as scouts also conveyed a message that the army respected and trusted Indians, that their skills as warriors were valued by the "soldier chiefs," and that "officers trusted their sense of honor to hold them to their promises" (Dunlay 1982:189).

Scott's Writing and Grammatical Style

Several patterns characterize Scott's handwriting in his ledgers. All of the data were handwritten in ink using cursive English script. Small accompanying sketches were made for some entries with the same pen and ink. For each major subject or entry Scott wrote a topic or title in the center of the page, sometimes underlined. These are listed in the table of contents for chapters 4 to 6.

Although translated into English, much of the information is recorded verbatim as it would be told in sign language. Hence the English text reflects the syntax of sign language. Entries were often recorded in present tense even though clearly telling a previous historical or distant mythological account. Thus a phrase is recorded as "eat until he was full" instead of "ate until he was full." Scott wrote in nearly complete sentences or phrases with the syntax of Plains Indians Sign Language, which typically lacks articles. Therefore articles such as "a," "an," and "the" and pronouns and verbs such as "they" and "were" are often omitted. As Scott (n.d.a:II:cover page, chapter 5 of this volume) wrote on the cover of volume II, "Many adjectives and adverbs are supplied by [the] manner of making the signs = see p. 83, shook 'violently' also 'listening intently.'" Nevertheless, the flow and content is typically clear and easy to follow.

In Scott's writing letters such as *m*, *n*, *w*, *u*, and *v* exhibit a generally similar appearance and sometimes must be distinguished by examining the preceding and following letters or through context in reading the entire word, clause, or sentence. The two sides of the letter *k* are often not connected. The horizontal cross mark on the letter *t* is frequently placed over the first or second following letter. Thus in the word "through" the cross mark on the letter *t* often appears over the letter *r* or *o*.

Scott used parentheses within sentences to include related or supplementary data, often for clarity or context. He also tended to use little punctuation in sentences and clauses, using long single handwritten hyphens instead. A sample from the following entry collected from Quanah Parker (Scott n.d.a:I:14, chapter 4 in this volume), describing preparing to lead a war party to avenge a friend killed by the Tonkawas, demonstrates Scott's writing style.

> Quanah (Smell) is the son of a white woman captured about 45 or 50 years ago by the Comanche in Texas by a Comanche man—he is the principal chief of the Comanches—1884–97 a long time ago I had a friend who was killed by the Tonkaways at Double Mountain Texas—that made me feel bad—we grew up together went on war path together—that made me feel very sorry—that man—Tonkaways kill him make my heart hot and I want to make it even that time I little big man—pretty young man but know how to fight pretty good—I wait one month I go to Noconie Comanche camp on head of Cache Creek—call in everybody.

Scott often recorded accounts several pages in length in this form. In some accounts new paragraphs are visible, with the text beginning at the start of the next line with a capital letter but not indented. While these sections are characterized by lengthy run-on sentences, the content is clear and easily edited with minimal punctuation.

In several places Scott also wrote additional information in the margins, associated with a handwritten asterisk. These are linked to a second asterisk in the text or margin from which the account continues. The spacing and context of the marginal notes suggest that they are additional data added after the initial account was recorded and were placed in the margins due to a lack of remaining available space. Some entries reference similar accounts or details contained in the work of other scholars such as "see calendar" in reference to James Mooney's (1898) *Calendar History of the Kiowa Indians* or "see Pike p. 446" in reference to Albert Pike's account of his western explorations. In a few places Scott appears to have run out of room in recording an account and references its continuation on another page in the ledger. In these instances I have moved the end of these accounts forward in the manuscript to reconnect them with their beginnings.

Scott's side notes continued into the second decade of the twentieth century, referencing works by year, volume, and page numbers of scholars such as Clark Wissler, Alfred Kroeber, Robert Lowie, George B. Grinnell, and others. The script in which these entries are written is also much smaller and finer, indicating the use of different, and perhaps improved, writing utensils than were used by Scott at Fort Sill. Some of these notes referencing earlier publications may have been added during his brief reassignment to the Bureau of American Ethnology in late 1897.

At the end of volume I Scott (n.d.a:I:220–66, chapter 4 in this volume) recorded a lengthy vocabulary of English words and phrases in alphabetical order with explanations of their associated signs. Some of these entries include descriptive explanations for their associated signs and double or triple variants for a particular sign. It is unclear why some entries in the list were left blank. Nevertheless, this is a valuable compendium. While it is not as extensive as Clark (1885) in some aspects, it offers qualitatively different data not yet recorded, including southern plains signs, additional terms (stream names, names of trees, and information on oil, petroleum, war lodge, monetary interest), and Indian names of non-Indians on the plains. In addition many entries are accompanied by important ethnographic data describing the context or origins of signs. Just as any spoken language contains the feature of productivity, making new words based on new combinations of existing elements, so does sign language. This is reflected in Scott's listing of several new sign language terms for modern items such as Jesus (Cross Man Above), interest (money's child), marshal (prisoner chief), picture (write looking glass), petroleum (fire water), and vaccinate (cut arm in back, place medicine).

Editorial Style

In editing Scott's ledgers I have chosen to keep the material as close as possible to Scott's original recording for two reasons. First, to maintain the context and intent of the data as he recorded it through sign language; and second, to preserve his style as another example of ethnographic data recorded by a late frontier-era military officer. Thus, with the exception of reconnecting divided entries (accounts continued on nonsequential pages), I have kept the material in the same order in which Scott recorded it, including material placed in parentheses.

I have limited editorial changes to eight main forms. (1) Punctuation and capital letters denoting new sentences have been inserted for clarity. (2) Capital letters (which Scott sometimes omitted) are used for proper names. (3) Roman numerals have been replaced by numbers spelled out. (4) New paragraphs have been indented in some areas. (5) Added words and spelling out of abbreviations are contained in square brackets. (6) In regard to the lists of signs in volume I (Scott n.d.a:I:220–66, chapter 4 in this volume), I have included only those items for which Scott provided definitions in sign language or associated ethnographic notes. Thus many other English words have been omitted, as their entries alone add little to the notes. (7) Where explanatory notes or references are required, I have inserted footnotes. (8) Native personal and tribal names and lexicon have been standardized except for variations in quoted material or to maintain context. Thus the account from Quanah Parker (Scott n.d.a:I:14–18, 42, chapter 4 in this volume) presented earlier appears in the following edited form:

> Quanah (Smell) is the son of a white woman captured about forty or fifty years ago by the Comanches in Texas by a Comanche man. He is the principal chief of the Comanches 1884–97.
>
> A long time ago I had a friend who was killed by the Tonkaways at Double Mountain[,] Texas. That made me feel bad. We grew up together, went on the warpath together. That made me feel very sorry, [losing] that man. Tonkaways kill him, make my heart hurt, and I want to make it even [at] that time. I [am a] little big man. Pretty young man, but [I] know how to fight good. I work one month. I go to [the] Nokonie Comanche camp on [the] head of Cache Creek, call in everybody.

Scott's Publications

Although Scott planned to organize and publish some of his data, only a small amount saw publication. He published two papers in *American Anthropologist*: "The Early History and the Names of the Arapaho" (Scott 1907) and "Notes on the Kado, or Sun Dance of the Kiowa" (Scott 1911). In July 1893 Scott delivered a paper entitled "The Sign Language of the Plains

Indians" at the International Folk-lore Congress of the World's Columbian Exposition, in Chicago, which was later published (Scott 1898). A fourth paper entitled "Notes on the Sign Language of the Plains Indians" drafted on November 5, 1915, was published in *Americanists Report* (Scott n.d.c). In one entry in his notes Scott mentions that he offered some of his accounts for publication in the magazine of the Oklahoma State Historical Society, with the provision that he could use them later in a book of his own.[66]

Scott also prepared a portion of these notes for publication in the form of two volumes with a brief introduction entitled "Tales of the South Plains" (Scott n.d.e, n.d.f). These volumes were lightly edited versions of many of the accounts recorded in volumes I and II of his Fort Sill notes. Scott (n.d.e) consists of mythological stories, of which slightly more than half focused on the Kiowa culture hero Scinday (Séndé). Scott (n.d.f) contains ethnographic accounts of cultural practices and historical accounts.

Scott had access to Silverhorn, a noted Kiowa artist and a member of Troop L for five years, to draw pictures in a target book to illustrate the stories for publication. Scott (n.d.e:iv) described the context behind Silverhorn's illustrations: "He was familiar with the tales from childhood, and drew the pictures for them off by himself somewhere in the mountains, without any direction or prompting other than a request from me, for example, to 'draw some Sinday pictures.' It was sufficient to show one of his pictures anywhere in the tribe to draw out the story. A large part of the stories are contained in the drawings themselves if one 'follows the trails.'"[67] Several of these drawings were displayed in 1993 by the Smithsonian Institution Traveling Exhibition Service's "Saynday Was Coming Along . . . Silverhorn's Drawings of the Kiowa Trickster."

Scott went back and forth with publishers trying to get the volumes published. While some liked the stories, they found the pictures below their standards, difficult to reproduce, and in some instances indelicate (regarding some of the sexual aspects of the Sainday stories). Others liked the drawings but found the stories too weak. Many of Scott's materials eventually ended up in the Library of Congress.[68]

---

66 Draft copy dated Nov. 5, 1915, and proof-sheet copy of Scott (n.d.c), titled *"Americanists Report 8025,"* pp. 87–91. Copy in the National Anthropological Archives, Smithsonian Institution, MS 1799, Washington, D. C. *Americanists Report* refers to the papers of the International Congress of Americanists. Although the 1915 congress was held in Washington, D.C., I have been unable to find Scott listed on the itinerary.
67 By "follows the trails" Scott is referring to the use of dotted lines in Silverhorn's drawings, which indicated direction and action in the stories, often connecting major elements. See Greene and Reuss (1993); Candace Green to the author, June 23, 2010.
68 Candace Greene to the author, June 23, 2010.

Scott may have intended the first part to be for children, as he wrote in the introduction (Scott n.d.e:v): "The adventures of Sinday and associated fables amused and instructed countless generations of Indian children, and my own children grew up on them in those long-ago days at Fort Sill, charmed with the evening tales that made Sinday even more a part of their lives than Brer Rabbit himself. They are of the purest essence of the American Plains, received through the medium of the ancient sign language, and are here offered as part of our heritage to all the children of America." Although the manuscript was never published, Scott did use some of Silverhorn's illustrations in his article on the Kiowa Sun Dance (Scott 1911:355).

Later Scott had Silverhorn draw another set of pictures to illustrate the materials, which ended up in the collections at the Fort Sill Museum. Years later one of Scott's grandsons came to the museum and asked for them back, telling Gillette Griswold (then museum curator) that they were on loan and were not a permanent donation. Once they were removed the museum was unable to reacquire them. The grandson and Griswold planned to have them published. Griswold produced barely revised volumes of Scott's manuscripts with a short introduction, but they were never published. Eventually he sold these to Scott's grandson, who eventually auctioned the second set of drawings and the manuscripts. The Smithsonian Institution had Candace Greene bid on the book of drawings in an attempt to procure them for the National Anthropological Archives Collection and to prevent the book from being taken apart and auctioned as individual pages, which frequently happens with Indian ledgerbooks. Charles Diker, a wealthy art collector from New York, purchased the set of drawings for $100,000 and later donated them intact to the Museum of Indian Arts and Culture in Santa Fe, New Mexico.[69]

Prior Use of Scott's Notes

The most significant use of Scott's ledgers was by Wilbur S. Nye in his book *Bad Medicine and Good: Tales of the Kiowa*, in which he published several of the briefer accounts (Nye 1962:xix, 15–19, 91–93, 127–31, 155–56, 178–80, 222–26, 257–58). Many of the accounts that Nye published were taken from Scott's second part of "Tales of the South Plains" and directly from Scott's ledgers at Fort Sill, with little or no editing, and had been obtained by Scott from Kiowas who were deceased by the time Nye was stationed at Fort Sill. But Nye used only a small portion of the entire

---

69   Ibid.

ledgers. Since Nye's publication, only small portions of Scott's notes have been used, primarily as supplemental data in larger works such as those on Kiowa mythology (Greene and Reuss 1993), military societies (Meadows 1999, 2010), and ethnogeography (Meadows 2008).

Potential Uses of Scott's Ledgers

Who will benefit from this body of data? Scott's ledgers offer a wealth of information on many aspects of traditional Plains Indian cultures and lifeways that will be useful for a wide audience, including academicians, Indians, and lay readers. For Indians of the southern plains interested in cultural preservation, revival of tribal cultural forms, and family history, this work offers a wide variety of data. This project will advance knowledge by making a set of primary archival documents accessible to several Indian tribes of Oklahoma as well as to academic scholars and lay readers.

In particular the notes provide numerous lengthy accounts translated from sign language that offer a rich body of texts for future study by linguists interested in comparative sign language.[70] Although most of the data in Scott's notes reference a way of life that is increasingly divergent from that of contemporary Indian cultures of the southern plains, many of these cultural forms persist in adapted or syncretic forms, such as religion (Kracht 1989), military society and social dances (Lassiter 1998; Meadows 1999, 2010), naming ceremonies, mythology (Greene and Reuss 1993), ethnogeography (Schnell 1994, 2000; Meadows 2006, 2008), ethnonymy (Meadows 2013), and the use of tipis for special events (Greene 1996; Meadows 2010).

As with any source, Scott's notes are one individual's recording of data from many other individuals and must be used with caution. The ideal use of these notes is through careful comparison with archival and published sources combined with contemporary ethnographic fieldwork in Indian communities. Major sources of ethnographic material on the tribes of the southern plains include works by scholars such as James Mooney, Alice Marriott, and the 1935 Santa Fe Laboratory of Anthropology Field School (Kiowa); William Bittle (Plains Apache); Karl Schmidt (Wichita); and James Mooney and George Dorsey (Cheyenne). Other archival sources such as the Kiowa Indian Agency Records and the Doris Duke Indian Oral History Interviews contain material on numerous tribes. Major ethnographic publications focusing on nineteenth-century Indian cultures of the southern

---

70 Linguists who want to use the Scott material to reconstruct the signs used in these texts should review the original accounts at Fort Sill, as some punctuation has been added in this work to make the texts more readable.

plains include works by Thomas Kavanagh (1996, 2001, 2008) on the Comanches; Gilbert McAllister (1937), William Meadows (1999), and Kay Parker Schweinfurth (2002) on the Plains Apaches; and George B. Grinnell (1923) and John Moore (1987, 1996) on the Southern Cheyennes. In addition, contemporary ethnographic fieldwork in these communities remains vital for documenting cultural survivals of older traditions and discovering new sources of data. In many instances I have found Scott's data to be highly accurate in comparison with these other sources.

This research follows a major principal and goal of ethnohistory: the editing and publication of primary documents for educational and scholarly growth. While some of the material in Scott's ledgers is well known and has been documented independently by other scholars, the vast majority of the material has remained unpublished. A significant body of supplementary material, some overlapping and some completely original, is located at the National Anthropological Archives. This work presents all of the primary ethnographic material collected by Scott relating to the tribes of the southern plains that remains at Fort Sill, including the information contained in his ledgers and his manuscript drafts (Scott n.d.e, n.d.f), which allows Scott's materials to reach fruition by more fully contributing to future studies of southern plains Indians and sign language.

Being allowed to enter another culture for prolonged ethnographic fieldwork is both an honor and a privilege. It is also a trust regarding what is shared with you. I have tried to pass on a sense of respect and trust to my students in regard to the responsibility of others opening up and sharing their lives with you. For myself, perhaps the most touching aspect in Scott's notes is a statement that he made in a writing entitled "Tales of the Kiowa" (Scott n.d.b:36) concerning the sense of responsibility that he felt in having this knowledge shared with him. "Most of these old friends are now dead; their country was opened for settlement by white people about 1900 . . . they are gone, but their memories and their stories are a sacred trust to me to be cherished and preserved for those that come after us, their children and mine."

I hope that this work will be not only a valued reference work but an example of a unique body of data collected through cross-cultural friendship and primarily through an inaudible means: Plains Indian Sign Language, a form of communication that has been well recorded but is no longer fully extant in the southern plains.

Much of what Iseeo and members of several Indian cultures of the southern plains conveyed in silence through sign language to Hugh Lennox Scott can now be given a voice and heard by all.

PART II

The Scott Ledgers at Fort Sill

CHAPTER 4

Volume I
Indian Sign Language Notes

CAPTAIN H. L. SCOTT, 7TH CAV.

[1]
BUFFALO BULL MEDICINE

A long time ago when the Kiowa[s] lived up north, the Pawnees attacked a Kiowa village and carried off a Kiowa woman to the Pawnee town on the Republican River. After a while the man that had her got tired of guarding her and said to her, "Now I am tired of guarding you, I turn you loose" and in a few nights she escaped (sign = lost run away) toward the Kiowa village. As she was traveling on foot one day on the open prairie looking for her people, she saw a fierce thundercloud coming toward her, and she looked about for some place in which to hide. There was no timber that she could see or even [a] cut bank to get behind. Finally she saw something on the prairie at a distance and ran toward it and found that it was an old carcass of a buffalo bull covered with dry hide. She crept into the carcass and the rain and lightning and thunder raged around her but left her harmless [unharmed] and soon she went to sleep inside of the buffalo bull, and the buffalo bull said to her, "You arrived here poor and naked. I am going to help you. You are going to reach home safely; you are going to attain old age. I am going to help you." And she did reach home safely. She was married to a man and one day she said to him, "You are a man and I am only a woman, but I am going to help you. You get the skin of a buffalo bull's neck and make a round shield of it. [2] Peg it down all around and clean off the meat from it. Pour hot water on it and clean off the hair. Turn it over and over before the fire. Trim it off neatly around the edges. Put eagle wing feathers around the outside. Get the buffalo bull's tail and fasten it to it and whenever you go to war the bull will help you." And he was helped that way.

I have myself seen a man up north who was shot through the body from side to side, not Big Bow, another man who has since died. He sent for the Buffalo Medicine Man, [who] gave him the pipe (i.e., made him his agent in this enterprise) and the bull helped him, and he got well. I saw a man who was shot through the knee joint and had the bone broken. It was gangrened and had a very bad color. The medicine man did not put anything on it, he only blew on it and sucked it and the man got well, the bull helped him. When the medicine man had sucked the black, bad swelling blood and spit it out it no longer smelt badly. It was sweet like sugar, the bull helped him and he got well.[1]

[3]
What Makes the Wind Blow
All Kiowas say there is a wind person somewhere N. S. E. or W. or maybe above. He has big ears that bend backward like the horns of a mountain sheep and he wags them backwards and forwards. Sometimes the wind is strong sometimes gentle according to the way he wags them. I myself think he is above (compare Kroeber's tale #44 *Gros Ventre*, Vol. 1, p. 188).

Wolf Helped a Man [Version A]
(see [Vol.] II, [p.] 76)
A long time ago a very young single man lived in the same lodge [tipi] with his married older brother. They were in a big Kiowa village. One day the older said to his wife and brother. "Let us take down the lodge and move out by ourselves for a while. I am hungry and I know where there are some antelope and deer and we will come back to the village afterwards." They took down the lodge early the next morning, packed up, and moved to a stream where there were deer and antelope. Early the next morning the elder went out to hunt and killed a deer, brought it in, and threw [it] down in front of the lodge, and he did this every day. And

---

1 This is the story of the Kiowa woman later known Páuchòhį̀ (Old Lady Bison Bull), who received power from a bison bull and passed it on through her husband to their male descendants. These men became the doctoring society known as the Páuìyoi (Descendants or Offspring of the Bison Bull) that specialized in treating injuries involving bleeding. In English the group is often called the Buffalo Doctors.

one day while he was out the young man was sitting off on the point of a hill and the woman longed for him and said to herself, "I will call him in. He is not married. I want him." So she called him and he came down from the hill into the lodge and sat down and the woman said, "I want you" and they sat silent for a long time. [4] After a while he said, "No, you are my brother's wife. I love my brother, that would be a bad thing," and the woman became frightened and said to herself, "If he tells his brother about this, his brother will kill me." So she said to the young man, "Do not tell anybody what I said to you and I will be thankful to you" and he said, "I will not tell." But everyday he looked sad as if something was rankling in his heart and the woman saw it and felt uneasy and thought, "He is going to tell his brother who will kill me." So while the men were back out she dug a deep hole [inside the tipi] and covered it with [a] robe and when she saw him coming in by himself she called out to him pleasantly, laughing and joking, "What is the matter? Come in," and when he entered she pushed him over on the bed and pulled the robe out from under him and he fell down into the hole, which was so deep she could hardly hear him call. Then she covered the hole over with wood, thick pieces of wood, and put a robe over it, and while she was doing this he called out that if she would let him out he would do what she wanted but she was afraid of him and covered the hole over so that no one could hear him call. [5] After a while the older brother come [came] in and asked after his brother and the woman said, "He went out early and he may not yet come back." The sun went down and came up again and the young man did not come back and at noontime the man said, "I think he has gone back to the Kiowa village. Take down the lodge and we will move there too." When they reached the village he asked everybody about his brother and no one knew anything about him and after looking for him for a long time he gave up and said maybe the bears have eaten him up.

After a while a wolf came and dug a hole in the pit where the young man was and he crawled out of the wolf's hole and was saved. The wolf took pity on him—that is the reason the old scouts carried a wolf's skin on the left arm. When they went scouting the wolf helps them and makes them swift of foot like the wolf and stealthy.[2]

---

2   This is a partial account of the origin of the name Lone Wolf (Cûifà gàui), which the young man later received, after living with wolves and being rescued by the Kiowas. According to Mooney's fieldnotes, the well-known chief Lone Wolf who died in 1879 was the fourth person to bear this name, suggesting that the event occurred long before in the northwestern plains. Mooney (n.d.: MS 2531:I:68, I:6:pt. 2:205, 246; MS 2538); Boyd (1983:198–202).

Pipe Stems

Pipe Stems are made from "tough" wood that has poles hanging from it in a bunch. = Ash. It is cut to the proper size and trimmed. The pith is punched out with a wire now but in the old time before we saw wire it was done with a stick. Then a mouthpiece is made and the other end fitted to the bowl. It is a tough wood and will not break. It is strong.

[6]

Buffalo Tail Shield Medicine

When the Buffalo Tail Shield men make medicine, they do it by sucking and blowing the wound. Once I saw them when Zebile was shot in Texas.[3] He was chasing a white man clutching at him, both on horseback. The white man fired his pistol back at Zebile, he was bending forward. The bullet struck him in the right eye, went out of his neck on the right side down through his shoulder and out his back. The others rushed to help him. He staggered on his horse and nearly fell off, but the others took him off gently. They tried to give him some water, but the water came out of the hole in his neck and he could not swallow it. They made medicine over him but his belly was puffed out by blood (internal hemorrhage), and he could not swallow. Taybodle looked on and said, "I am going to tell you something wise, press the heel of your hand over the hole in his neck and he can drink." They did it and made the man drink until he vomited the mixed blood and water four times, and the fourth time the water he vomited was clear, and then they knew he would get well, and the blood swelling went down. The bull helped him and he recovered.

When the Bull Tail Medicine is made, a lodge is pitched on the prairie by itself, away from the village.[4] The men who have the Bull Tail Shields go inside with the sick man. The sick or wounded man is then blown or sucked then [by] the [7] medicine men who all have buffalo robes on all rush out and roll on the ground like buffalo wallowing, run around the lodge four times, then go inside and blow him again.

[Scott n.d.b: MS 2932, Box 2, adds:] "There is a bull society in many different tribes. The members practice medicine by imitating the acts of a buffalo bull and the bull helps their patient. They lie down and roll and grunt just like a buffalo bull." "The cult seems to take care of the wounded rather than those ill of a disease." He describes the medicine as "bull tail shield medicine."

---

3   This is Zêbàèl or Zêbàèlqì (Big Arrows), born in 1842 (Kiowa Family Record 1901:102 Za-bile).
4   This account concerns the Buffalo Doctors. See note 1 above.

Names of Months, Kiowa

Taybodle

Red men all have the same custom to have seven cold and seven hot months. The names of the seven cold months are:

1st "Half hot and half cold" some antelope drop horns.

2nd "Trees red" as the moon gets larger and larger, the trees get redder and redder, and at the last [of the] month the leaves all fall down. When we lived on the Arkansas [River] it was quite cold then.

3 "Nights very cold"

4 "Heavy snow"

5 Sweat house

6 Birds go north

7 Half cold and half warm.

Hot Months

1 "Little warm"

2 "Grass 2" long

3 "Little hot"

4 "All hot"

5 Very hot

6 Little hot last half not very hot

7 Last half cool

August 13, 1897, all hot month.[5]

[Tribal Names]

Kiowa Apaches are called "Kau-pa-to" = Whetstone Men by the Kiowas. Comanches are called Ki-ah-qoo = Fighting Men by the Kiowas because we used to kill them and find they carried wolf skin head caps [hides] to scout with. The Comanches call the Pawnees Qui-tar-a. They call the Wichitas To-can-a.[6] [8]

---

5 Compare with the list of Kiowa names for the months of the year in Mooney (1898:366–69).

6 These Kiowa names are Qâufàdàu (Knife Whetters), sometimes known as Qâufàjòp to the Kiowa-Apaches, and Câigù to the Comanches (Meadows 2013). Elderly Comanches report this derogatory name (Qui-tar-a) for the Pawnees as Qui-ta-rai (Anal Entrances) and To-can-a as (Dark Lodges/Houses) (author's fieldnotes, Comanche, 1994). Apache elder Alfred Chalepah (1910–2007) also reported the sign language designation of Knife Whetter and the Apache name Bay-cah-yeh. Alfred Chalepah to the author, Apr. 29, 1992.

Looking for Buffalo

In old times the buffalo would go sometimes off to a long distance and leave the people hungry in the Kiowa village. Then the chief who had everybody would get on his horse and ride around among the lodges and call out, "I want men to go out at sunrise to hunt for the buffalo." Everybody hears him, then he rides to his lodge, dismounts, and goes in. Then after a while somebody who heard him call out gets up and goes to his lodge and tells him, "I will go look for buffalo before sunrise tomorrow" and the chief says, "Thank you. Thank you" to each one. Next morning while the people are having breakfast the chief mounts his horse and harangues the village, calling out the names of the men who went to hunt for the buffalo before sunrise. Then they all pack up and travel on and after several days' travel they see two men standing on the point of a hill. One mounted. The other stands still while the mounted man rides up and down past him in a straight line backward and forth about fifty yards to the right and fifty to the left of the man. Then he dismounts and the other man takes off his robe and throws it out from the corners a number of times and all the people know that they have found lots of buffalo not grazing in [a] small herd but covering the country and [9] everybody is glad.

Holding the Buffalo (see [p.] 82)

Iseeo

One day the Kiowas were holding the buffalo at the "End of the Mountains" (South Fork Red River beyond Comanche Springs) and were moving camp. Satanta (White Bear) was the leader of the soldiers. The soldiers were out in front and stopped on a hill looking at the buffalo grazing out in front and Satanta said, "Our horses are panting, let us dismount here." The village went into camp behind us. I was with the soldiers, fifty-seven Rattle Band [Jáifégàu Society members] of us, just like your troop of cavalry. Satanta was captain and we saw three men way out to the right going to run buffalo, everybody saw them. Satanta said, "Four or five come with me" and we went down to where the three men were getting ready to run buffalo. Satanta said, "Hold on. Wait, we are holding the buffalo." Two of the men were mad and would not answer. Satanta said, "What's the matter, [are] you mad? I am going to give you some wise talk. You pick it up and hold fast to it. You can go back to camp." Then one of the angry men who was Kicking Bird's brother-in-law and was a good chief said, "My sister, Kicking Bird's wife, is very sick. Coming along the road today she was played out [exhausted], so I am mad." Satanta said, "You poor weak little man, you go back, we are holding the buffalo." Then that chief struck Satanta's horse across the face with his quirt [10] and two of them bolted forward. The third man whose heart failed him remained behind. Satanta pulled back his horse and told me to bring the soldiers and pretty soon we all came back to Satanta and we all started after the two mad [angry] men. When we got on top of a ridge we could see the two men charge a band of buffalo and shoot their revolvers into the air to frighten them and when the band had scattered they did the same things to another bunch and then another. We all charged after these men. Satanta came behind because his horse was played out. One of the mad men stopped when we got near him and a soldier shot his horse through the head and it dropped dead in its tracks without turning on its side and the man stepped off. The soldiers took his things from him and pretty soon the other man rode up and each of the soldiers shot an arrow into his horse and killed him. Satanta took their arrows and broke them across the sole of his foot, broke their bows, and slit their robes into ribbons with the knife. "You are mad, are you? You talk mad to me and I will cut you this same way." Both of them kept still, Satanta all the time giving them wise talk. After the soldiers had slit up their saddles and bridles and everything [11] they had, Satanta said, "Every soldier whip them" and the soldiers hit the two men across the face and over the shoulders with their quirts until Satanta said to the two men, "Now I leave you here on foot. No soldier can take you behind him."[7] It was very hot and it was a long way to water. One man said, "I didn't do it." Kicking Bird's brother said, "Kicking Bird told us to do it."

Satanta said, "Where is Kicking Bird, I will go and see him" and we all went back to the creek where they were pulling up the lodges and Satanta asked for Kicking Bird. Pretty soon somebody said, "Kicking Bird has not come into camp yet. His wife is sick. He stopped back on the road but will come in later." Then we watched a long time for Kicking Bird but did not see him. After a long time we saw two men coming into camp with their faces covered. Pretty soon a man came into camp and said, "Kicking Bird is mad and is going to whip Satanta." He [Kicking Bird] said, "All right, all right, good. [12] You go ahead. You whipped my brother in law. I will see who can do the most crazy thing" (i.e., who can do the worst).

---

7   This account is a good example of the laws associated with closed or policed bison hunts, the repercussions involved, and how effectively a body of men of that size could monitor the preparations to hunt a herd.

Satanta said, "All right, all right, you go ahead. You begin the trouble. You go ahead and whip [me]." Kicking Bird stayed back on the trail with his wife and we watch for him to come into the village every day. After a while Satanta call[ed] all the soldiers to council and said, "Tomorrow we will go and make peace with Kicking Bird. Everybody saddle up and bring something he has that is valuable." And next day they brought valuable things, four horses, a white mule, two saddles and bridles, a gun, and blankets, a big pile of valuable things, and made packs on the horses, covered the horses all over, and went back to see Kicking Bird. And Kicking Bird was setting [sitting] under a shade and said, "What are you coming here for, to fight?" And Satanta said, "We have come to make you presents (we want to make peace)," and they gave Kicking Bird the presents and he said, "All right, I began the trouble. I do not feel my heart stabbed anymore. I shake hands with everybody."

Sometimes when we were holding the buffalo the soldiers would notice a man tying up four or five horses in front of his lodge and they would go and turn the horses loose and drive them away because they knew he was going after buffalo. But if he had [13] only one horse tied up they let him alone for he might be going about anything else but if he had four or five horses he wanted them to carry in the meat and robes so they would turn them loose and drive them off.

Tay-bodle—Tsait-an-te's Shield = Sun Shield

Tsait-an-te's [White Bear's] shield had red cloth strips on one side and yellow on the other. It had a sun in the center and two rings around it just as you see rings around the moon. There was a crane's head tied to it. When he went to war with the shield he wore in his hair the longest wing feather of a crane. When he was invited to smoke and the pipe had gone around once and the pipe had been put down and another man came to smoke, they called out, "No, Black Horse is here. He is afraid." That was his road, when he went to war he had a buckskin shirt painted red on one side and yellow on the other. When he went into camp he kept the shield on a tripod about two hundred yards from his lodge and above it on a pole there was a crane's wing tied to it waving loose in the wind. Black Horse made it and gave it to Tsait-an-te. Black Horse made it before I was born. When I grew big enough to know things I knew that one. Black Horse made six. That is the only one left now. Black Horse was an old man and was killed by the Satickee (Saux and Foxes) he gave it to Tsait-an-te who gave it [continued from 18] to his son when he went to prison and he gave it to you when he died. That shield has been in fights with every kind of red man and many times to Mexico. I know of one time now, Tsait-an-te had it with him near the city of Durango in Mexico and the Mexicans came out to fight us with ropes. A man roped Tsait-an-te (see [p.] 42) [continued from 42] tied the rope to the horn of his saddle and jerked Tsait-an-te off his horse and was running off with him. Tsait-an-te [was] bounding along first on one side and then on the other. Frizzle Head, whom you know, ran up with his spear to kill the Mexican who got scared, dropped his rope and Tsait-an-te was saved. His back, his sides, and legs were skinned from the dragging and he was very stiff for a long time. He had a shield on him at the time. I was along once when he killed a Mexican with a spear in Old Mexico, again when he killed a Sateavo [Saukeahbo—Sauk and Fox?] on the other side of the Arkansas, a Pawnee up near Fort Lynn on the Arkansas, and I know that Stumbling Bear and one man who is now dead saw him kill a Ute with a spear at night. I know of these fights that he had the shield in. That shield has a strong road. Black Horse made it and gave it to Tsait-an-te. It was made before I was born but I have known it always. It has been in more than a hundred fights. Neither Black Horse or Tsait-an-te ever stayed at home long, they fought with every tribe and with Mexicans and white men. All Kiowas know that shield. It is called a "Sun" shield, and is the only "Sun" shield.[8]

[14]

Adobe Walls Fight
Quanah Parker, told in English, Signs, and Comanche
(Quanah (Smell) is the son of a white woman captured about forty or fifty years ago by the Comanches in Texas by a Comanche man. He is the principal chief of the Comanches 1884–97.)

A long time ago I had a friend who was killed by the Tonkaways at Double Mountain[,] Texas. That made me feel bad. We grew up together, went on the warpath together. That made me feel very sorry, [losing] that man. Tonkaways kill[ed] him, make [made] my heart hurt, and I want[ed] to make it even [at] that time. I [am a] little big man. Pretty young man, but

---

8   This account involves Sétthái̱dé (White Bear), Chê̱kǫ́gái (Black Horse), and Áulpépjè (Bushy Haired, often called Frizzle Head). White Bear's shield is in the collection of the P. B. Hearst Museum in Berkeley, California. It is currently on an annually renewed loan to the Fort Sill Museum, Fort Sill, Oklahoma, where it is on display in the "Warrior's Journey" Exhibit Gallery. Towana Spivey to the author, July 7, 2011. See also Scott (1928:165).

[side note extending from 14 to 17]
* There were two stores, a blacksmith shop and a salon starting out along Adobe Creek to supply buffalo hunters. Stores were branches of Meyers Co. and Rath Co. from Dodge City, Kansas. One was made of sod and not yet completed. They were all above the adobe walls, which were still standing, said to have been built by Col. Bent and St. Vrain. The saddler and his brother were killed outside at their wagon. Billy Tylor [was] inside. Fight occurred June 27, 1874. Billy Dickson has a ranch there now. A little store and adobe walls were built by a white man named Red Neck in 1845 (see calendar), he traded there two years and went back to the Arkansas. Long afterwards [a] white man named Tomi (Necklace) traded there in a lodge, [until finally he] untied his wagon and went away. Post Office. He was [came] afterwards and [served as] a scout for General Miles in 74 [1874] Expedition, and after at Fort Elliot, Texas. There were twenty-seven white men in the fight. Only three [were] killed, as above. Watson the driver at [Fort] Sill was in his wagon four hundred yards from store and was waked up by his employee who thought he heard wolves. They saw the Indians coming and barely got into the store one hundred yards ahead of the Indians. Nine Indians and seventeen horses were killed just outside. After [the] hunters left, Indians came and gathered up bones of dead Indians and put them

[I] know how to fight good. I work one month. I go to [the] Nokonie Comanche camp on [the] head of Cache Creek, call in everybody. I tell him about my friend, [Tonkaways] kill him [in] Texas. I fill [the] pipe. I tell that man, "You want to smoke." He take[s the] pipe and smoke[s] it. I give it to another man. He say[s], "I [do] not want to smoke." If he smoke[s the] pipe he [must] go on [the] warpath. He [will] not hang back. God [will] kill him [if] he [is] afraid.

I go [to] see [the] Kiowas on Elk Creek and [the] Quahadas. Then I go to [the] Cheyenne camp up on Washita near Fort Elliott where [the] Washita forks with round hill between, lots [of] Comanches there. Otter Belt, He Bear, Tabenanaka, and Old Man White Wolf there, a big village, camps in different places. And they ask me, "When you go [on the] warpath" and I say, "Maybe tomorrow, maybe next day, only before, dance all night [15] Big Horse Dance here, Little Horse Dance over there, Fox Quirt Dance over there, and I hear somebody [say], "Quanah. Old men want to see you over here" and I see old man Otter Belt and White Wolf and lots [of] old men. And they said, "You [are a] pretty good fight[er], Quanah, but you [do] not know everything. We think you [should] take [the] pipe first against White buffalo hunters. You kill [a] white man, make your heart feel good. After that you come back, take all [the] young men, go to [the] Texas warpath." Then I say to Otter Belt and He Bear, "You take [the] pipe yourself. After that I [will] take all [the] young men and go [on the] warpath [in] Texas" and they say all right. Esati make [made] big talk that time. "God tell [told] me we [are] going [to] kill lots [of] white men. I stop the bullets in [the] gun.

Bullets [do] not penetrate shirts. We kill them just like [an] old woman. God told me [the] truth." Before that pretty good medicine. He sit [sat] down away, [and] listen[ed]. God told to him, "Maybe so fifty miles over there [at] Little Creek. I see white soldiers. We go kill them." Pretty soon time, this time he [will] listen [to] what God tell[s] him.

Well, pretty soon we move near Fort Elliot. Got no fort [there at] that time. I pick up seven men, go back for white men's horses on Canadian [River] (Adobe Walls). Old Man White Wolf go [went] with them. They [were] gone all night. Next day a man watching from [a] little hill call[ed] out, "Here they come" and we ran out and see [saw a] scout circle four times [16] to the right and we know [knew] they find [found] horses. Then women and everybody make [a] long line in front of the village, Old Man Black Beard in the middle. Then seven scouts come up in single file in front [of] Old Man Black Beard. He say[s], "Tell the truth, what did you see?" And [the] first scout say[s], "I [will] tell you true, I see [saw a] farm of five log houses. I see [saw] horses moving around" and all seven scouts say the same thing. Black Beard say[s], "All right, pretty soon we [will] kill a white man. Everybody saddle up, take your war bonnets and shields." Then we start out about eleven a.m., stop about four p.m., put saddles and blankets in trees and hobble extra ponies. Make medicine, paint faces, put on war bonnets then travel in [a] column form until [we] cross [the] Canadian [River at] sundown. Keep along until pretty near a Red Hill near

wrapped in blankets on trees on [the] South side of the Canadian along adobe wall. These blankets were afterwards taken by soldiers under Major Compton. Ben Clarke says thirty Cheyennes were killed. Adobe walls were built by white people many years before 1853, see Beckworth's trip in 53 [1853] up [the] Canadian from Fort Smith with Capt. Gunnison. The traders name in Kiowa was Tomi = bone necklace or hairpipe first seen there by Kiowas had beads, woman's shawls, hairpipe, etc. George Bent told Ben Clarke his father built them. [The] later Adobe Walls was built in 1845 by a white man named "Red Neck," who traded there two years, then abandoned the place and went back to the Arkansas.[9] (See Tohausen calendar.) Also oldest living Kiowa woman, "Discharge From The Nose" (1897 Nov.).[10] Probably built by order of Bent as George Bent says, but Kearny's and Doniphan's expedition during [the] Mexican war probably prevented "Red Neck" from returning with goods as they must have cleaned out Bent's Fort of goods. Red Neck had no trouble there and went back to the Arkansas of his own accord. "Tomi" was a later trader who traded from a wagon aside [from] when sold out and went to Arkansas and did not return. For Bents Fort, see Coms. [Commissioner] "Pike" (p. 446).

---

9   Several non-Indians were known by the Kiowa name Red Neck (Qólgúljè) in the second half of the 1800s.
10 The Kiowa name Discharge From The Nose would be Séncùtjè (Running Nose Mucus).

a little creek where houses were. We walk all the time, hear trot [the sound of a trotting horse] a long way off and then get pretty near, somebody want[s] to go to sleep. He Bear say[s], "Dismount and hold [the] lariats in hand. [When] I call you, mount again." Some go to sleep. Some smoke tobacco and talk until He Bear and Tabenanaka call, when we mount again and go on until little light. Pretty soon we make a time. The chief try [tries] to hold young men back [who] go too fast. No good [to] go too fast. Pretty soon they call out, "All right, go ahead." We charge down on horses. He cried charge. Threw up the dust [17] high. I saw men and horses roll over and over. Some men ahead wanted to catch the horses. They drove off the horses. I was in [the] middle and got in [the] house with them Comanches, and poked holes this [way] to shoot. We killed two white men in [a] wagon. The white men killed six Comanches, four Cheyennes, and some Arapahoes. The white men had big guns that kill a mile away. That [was a] pretty hard fight—from sunrise until twelve o'clock. Then we go back. I had on [the] war bonnet. I gave you long time ago. That time I got shot in the side. My first wife's father had his leg broken with a bullet. The Cheyennes [were] pretty mad at Esati. What [is] the matter [with] you[r] medicine? You [have] "pole cat medicine" (a term of derision). One of the Comanches killed was a yellow nigger painted up like other Comanche. He left a nigger soldier company. Everybody knew that. Pretty soon all go back, get saddles and bridles, and go back to [the] village. Then I take all young men, [and] go [on the] warpath to Texas.

QUANAH

Comanches have different ways [of] making telegraphs. If we see [an] enemy, we travel around to the right four times in a ring. If we see buffalo we tie [the] horse and walk backward and forward from him in [a] straight line. Sometimes [we] ride [the] horse backward and forward. Sometimes [a] war party splits where we leave [18] ponies hidden and one party has some men killed and gets back to ponies before [the] other one. We leave a bone at the water hole and paint signs on it just like [the designs on the] dead men's shields, [when the] other party comes back they know the names of killed men. Sometimes [a] village move[s] away and some men away hunting come back and find two sticks tied this way [and] they know the village [has] gone that way, maybe [the] upper stick is bent [and] we go that way one sleep then the other way and we find it.[11]

---

11 For information on turning trees and other Comanche trail markers, see Gelo (2000).

Sometimes a Comanche man dreams and a big bear comes and tells him there to do this way [do something a certain way or style]. You paint your face this way, your body other way. I help you—(i.e., he sees [a] bear in his dream then he make[s] medicine that way). A dead Comanche goes to the sunset.

[COMANCHE SOLDIER BANDS]

The Comanches have five soldier bands. 1) Big Horse, 2) Little Horse, 3) Black Leggins, 4) Fox Whip, 5) Crow.

OATH

When a Comanche is sworn to tell the truth the blade of his knife is painted red, held up to the sun, and drawn between his lips, maybe first [it is] put in the ashes. [remainder of 18 moved to connect with end of 13]

[19]

LEADERS

A leader's road is a hard road. Some men are good leaders of war parties. Everybody knew [knows] who they are. Sometimes he meets a man and tells him he is going on a warpath and wants him to go along. Then another and another and after a while he calls a council and says he is going on a warpath against the Pawnees and fills and pipe and offers it to a man to smoke. If the man smokes the pipe he says yes he will go on [the] warpath with him. One night they go into a big lodge, women talk, they sit down in a circle, sing on a drum, one man beating on a lodge pole with a stick for a little while, not long. Then they take a hard hide, man and women holding all around it, drumming and singing until the middle of the night and then stop. This is done the night before they start out.[12] A war party usually goes out at the full of the moon [so] as to have the moon to travel by. This depends partly on the distance to which they are going. They want moonlight when they get there so as to see to find horses, etc., at night. If near a mountain they climb up and remain hidden in the timber looking about during the day and come down at night. They usually attack at daylight if they are in sufficient force to make a bold attack.

---

12   The Kiowas call this type of gathering and singing *gúdáugà* (literally, Stirring Up [to Emotions] Songs). This genre of songs later evolved into the '49 songs sung at all-night social parties, usually held late at night along desolate unpopulated county roads following powwows. Mooney (1898:403) offers another possible meaning.

When the leader starts out, he mounts his horse and holds his pipe with [the] stem down in his left hand with his reins. He never ties it on his saddle but carries it in that way until he gets back home and then puts it down. [20] When they get tired they stop near the top of a hill so someone can see over [the surroundings] and all can smoke. If they go to fight he puts his pipe in his quiver and takes it out and carries it as before after the fight. He always travels first. He goes to the first camp first and when he camps he looks back at the others one after the other. When they have all arrived he holds a council and says, "Back in the village. I decided to go to war. Everybody knows it, woman and children. Now I see you here I feel glad, a big war party. We are going to war. I want three lieutenants (all are called pipe men or leaders but only the real leader, a captain, actually carries the pipe)." No one speaks out but they talk about it among themselves. Then the leader says just as if he was scolding them, that man there is a good man and that one and that one. Then one [of the] men designated says he will go with the leader and the leaders says, "Aho. Aho. Thank you. Thank you." Then another and another say the same thing and the leader says, "Thank you" to each one. They follow right behind the captain in single file and are just like your lieutenants. Their roads are the strongest of all in a fight. The leader rides alone in front of the enemy up and down before the young men to encourage them and hold them. If a man's horse is killed the leader gets him up behind him and out of the fight. If the man is killed and the enemy approaching the [21] body the leader takes it across his horse and saves it from the enemy or if all the young men retreat the leaders stay back and shoot off the pursuers. The leader's road is the strongest of all. He is ashamed to get scared. He will die first. He does not have commands for advancing, retreating, [or] firing like while soldiers, he just calls out "take courage, do not be frightened" or "charge" (Ah Ko) and encourages the rest.[13] He never abuses anybody. He would be ashamed to do it. He loves his men, all of them, and they love him. If he should be killed the young men all charge to bring away his body because the enemy will strike and cut it if they get it and the people back in the village hear that and everybody will be ashamed. Everybody is that way, white men too. I have often seen it. They charge to recover a body so the other side cannot take it. If it is a mean man they do not all try so hard and maybe let the enemy get it but everybody tries to recover the leader's body.

---

13 Ah ko (Àkô) is a Kiowa speech particle usually initiating an expression, meaning "and now" in English (McKenzie 1991).

A long time ago a party of five went to Mexico on the warpath. One night they saw a fire and crept up and saw a lot of mules and a Mexican walking around and around on guard over the mules. The leader said, "Get ready. Take charge when he comes around again. We will rush and shoot him with arrows." When he came around again they charged and shot him but he called out and gave the alarm and upon [22] that a great many people charged and shot at us and we ran away. The leader fell down but it was night and we did not see it. After a while he called out, "I am shot. My die night has come. Tell about it when you get home." We called back, "Where are you wounded?" And he answered, "My leg is broken." Then we heard them catch him. Then bang, bang, bang for a long time, and after a while we saw them make a big fire. The next morning as we were hidden in the bluffs we saw that it was a large force of Mexican soldiers and after they had packed up and moved away out of sight over a hill we went back and found a large pool of blood. That was where he was when they caught him. That other was where they shot him to pieces. And that fireplace was where they burned him up. Not even a little bit of him was found. He was all burned up and we went back to the village ashamed. Everybody is afraid of that (losing the leader).[14]

SATANTA'S MEDICINE ARROW

Santanta (White Bear) had a medicine big arrow. It was a foot longer than that lance (regular size) and was feathered like a small arrow. That was his medicine.[15]

[23]

HOW TO FIND A VILLAGE

[Iseeo]
I was at the Medicine Lodge council (Timber Mountain) 1867. I had been on the warpath against the Navajo[s] and met a small village of Cheyennes who told us the soldiers were coming with beeves, sugar, coffee, etc., and were going to have a big council. I went and heard it. There were many soldiers there. The council was an immense one, "a great many rows." The soldier's chief said, "Here are two propositions. You can live on the

---

14 While much has been made of scalping and the mutilation of bodies by Indians, this is an equally powerful example of how Anglos also sometimes performed comparable actions against Indians.
15 This refers to the well-known *zébàut* (fletched arrow) of White Bear.

Arkansas [River] and fight or move down to the Wichita Mountains and I will help you. But you must remember one thing and hold fast to, that is you must stop going on the warpath. Which one will you take?" And all the chiefs chose to move down here. The following fall, Tohausen (? dead) was holding the pipe (Honameatah's father) and we went to war in Chihuahua on the other side of the big river (Rio Grande).[16] There were nine of us all riding mules. That was a long way to go and a horse soon gets tired so we rode mules. The Kiowa camp was on the Canadian River at the Antelope Hills. We went past the head of Red River (Big Sandy River) up on to the Staked Plains (High Flat Country) and we were two days without water twice. We traveled for a month. We did not go fast on account of the mules and sometimes when we struck a good camp we remained in it four or five days until the mules got rested, until finally we reached an Apache camp (Mescaleros) and remained there for some time. Then we went on the warpath across the Rio Grande until we came near [24] some high mountains when the leader said, "Hobble the mules and turn them loose here. Put your saddles and robes on this tree and two men take packs of dried meat on your backs, everybody take a rope and a bridle and tie ten pairs [of] moccasin[s] to your waist by this way. We are getting close to the white man's horses (left hand)." If we go on the right hand it will be a long journey. We will go up on that mountain tonight and the next morning at daylight we could see all around. There were streams running out of the mountains, many white men's horses, and the valley outside of the foothills was covered with cattle. We slept up there all day and that night we went to look for horses. We were not trying to kill a man only looking for horses. As we traveled along we saw a light and crept up to it. It was a white man's house and we could hear the children talking. Tohausen said, "You stay here until I come back. I am going to look for horses." After a long time he came back and said there were no horses there. Then we went on looking for horses but did not find any and pretty soon Tohausen said we must go up on a mountain it is pretty near daylight so we went up on a mountain, tired out. We kept going on that way for ten nights. When the white men's horses are thick they keep the horses hidden and they are hard to find. On the tenth night we found some horses and were saved. We started back traveling on the horses and [25] one day we killed a calf. We had had nothing to eat for two days and everybody was hungry. We made a fire in a small creek bed

---

16 This raid must have been in the fall of 1866, as Tohausen (Jòhâusàn) died in the winter of 1866–67.

and were turning the meat before the flames. Everybody [was] hungry and watching the meat when someone looked up and said, "Here come some Mexicans." Then there were four Mexicans coming who had not seen us yet. We threw the meat and the fire out into the creek and Tohausen said to hide well in the brush and not to kill these men unless they find us. If they find us kill them all and [do] not let one get away for we are here in the midst of these houses and if one gets away and gives the alarm the Mexicans will surround us and kill us all. The Mexicans stopped as near to us as that bear (tame) is (fifty yards). We had a Mexican captive with us who understood their conversation. They were laughing and joking. We kept hidden until they rode off in a different direction without seeing us and we were saved. We rode on until we got the mules and saddles and traveled back until we met a big Mescalero and Quahada Comanche camp where we stayed for our mules were played out and our moccasins worn out. Here we met another Kiowa war party who told us the Kiowa village had moved to the forks of Wolf and Beaver Creeks (Fort Supply since) when they started south.

One day our leader said, "I am going on warpath into Mexico again. What are [26] you going to do? Say out plainly what you[r] heart is. I am going back to look for more horses." I and two other men said, "We are going back to the Kiowa village." So we started back across the Staked Plains. When we came to the head of Red River my mule played out so I couldn't do anything with him. His ears lopped down and I abandoned (put away) [turned it loose] it and came on foot. The mules of the other two men were there and only able to travel slowly. One day their ears looped down and the others said to me you go on in [on] foot to the next creek and see if you see any signs. I went on then to the Salt Fork. At the place the Kiowas often went to get salt at a salt spring where I looked for tracks. I saw some old horse tracks and I said these were made by a war party. I next went over to Walnut Creek (N.F. Red) [North Fork of the Red River] beyond the end of the mountains and looked for tracks but did not find any. Then I waited for the other two men and we slept there that night. Next day, when the morning star was rising I got up and the other men said, "You go over toward the Washita and look for tracks on little creek this side and we go on slower and will join you there." I went over on little creek and looked back but nobody came. I went to sleep and look again next morning [but] nobody came. Maybe they passed by in the night or maybe they have lost their mules. I will go over on Washita.

[27] Then I went over [to a] divide on to the head of a little creek that runs into the Washita where you and I got into the Cheyenne village after

dark that night (1890 Mad Wolf Village). Then I saw some people. They had no lodges but had horses and I couldn't tell what people they were so I crept down the bed of the stream until I could hear them talk and they were talking Kiowa. Then I spoke to them and they were astonished to see me and said you left a long time ago on the warpath and now you have come back (astonishment). I said, "Where is the Kiowa village?" And they replied, "You walk on foot down the river and you will get there before the sun goes done." And they packed their horses and all formed a larger village and my own lodge was with them and that was when I first heard that the Cheyennes had been wiped out on Washita (Black Kettle's Band) by white soldiers (Nov. 27, 1868). Then the grass was a foot high (about June, 1869). Two days after, the other two men got in and they said their mules had been lost for one day and I [was a] pretty fast walker.

Arapahoes call the Kiowas "Wicha-pa-ha-to." [It] means Island Mountain, refers to the Sioux first meeting Kiowa[s] in the Black Hills of South Dakota, like an island on the prairie.[17]

[28]

Buffalo Bull Skulls and Taime [T<u>a</u>imé]

A skull of an old bull is always put in the medicine lodge opposite of the door—it was painted half red on left side and black on right (side). We do not know why except that it came to us from the Crows long, long time ago—a Crow chief gave it to an Arapahoe and he helped his Kiowa friend with it. Everybody knows that—the bull helped the old people.

The skull is used in front of (rock hot house or slap body house) sweat houses also.[18] I think because the bull helps us. But do not know only that it came down to us from the old people. There were three Taime Medicines. Two of these were captured by the Utes when "Heap Of Bears" was killed [around July 10, 1868]. They were little ones and were often carried slung under the arm on the war path. The Utes took them in the fight which took place at the Canadian River salt springs where you get good salt. You can look up there and see the big mountains. The present Taime was the

[side note, 28] Major Keyes, formerly 3rd Cav., promised to get one of these Taime which he saw some years ago in the store of Maxwell the trader of Maxwell's Grant, New Mexico, where it had been left by the Utes, and give it to me.

---

17 This is a rare reference explaining the basis of the Arapaho name Island People/Men for the Kiowas. Levy (2001:924).
18 The Kiowa names for the sweat lodge are *sálcúgàu* (literally, heat striking house) or "slap body house" (referring to striking oneself with grass swatches to enhance sweating) and *tépfábôfè* (domed structure), sometimes given as *tépgàu* (emerging), which is an archaic name that preceded the later name. Parker McKenzie to the author, Sept. 25, 1994.

principal one, strongest medicine, the other two came behind. Together all were dressed alike and were held by three different men. If a man died his son or his brother took it. Since Taimeday died [1894] his sister has it. It was never known before that a woman should have it, but it does not make any difference because we are not allowed to have the Medicine Dance. If we were to have a dance Lucius's [Aitsan's] father "Loco" used to be with the Medicine and he can make* [29] the dance. A person having Arapahoe blood has always had it.[19]

The Ten Medicines are much older. They grew up with the Kiowas. After that they got the Taime from the Crows. "Taime" means "Mosquito." I do not know why they give it that name.[20] The Cheyennes have four medicine arrows for a Taime. That is what keeps the smallpox away, the arrows are unrolled and carried around among the people and that is what does it. The medicine takes pity on them.

TAIME [TÁIMÉ]

Taybodle = Calf Of A Leg Of A Bull

When we lived up north long ago and carried our property on dogs the Kiowas had no Sun Medicine. And one time they went to trade with the Crows. An old Arapahoe and his wife went with them who were very poor and weak. After they had finished trading they went back (?) but the old Arapahoe and his wife were too poor, weak to go back so he was left with the Crows. And after a while the Crow chief noticed them and said to them, "You are very poor and weak. I am going to take pity on you. I give you a horse and he got four in this way and he and his wife lived with the Crows. And one day the Crow chief looked at him and said, "I see you there poor and weak. I am going to give you some medicine" and he gave [30] him the Taime and after some years, the Kiowas came again to trade

---

19 The full name appears to be Táimédédè (Standing Táimé). Táimédè's (One Who Is Táimé) sister (cousin) was Emaa (Émàà or Being Provided With Food or Food Giver), who married Botone. Màucîn (Mokin, 1849–1933), the father of Lucius Aitsan, was a Mexican captive, the son of two unknown Mexicans (Kiowa Family Record 1901: Fam. 255).

20 In Kiowa, Time, Time', Taime, and Taime' are properly Táimé. The statement that it means 'mosquito' is unclear. The adverb *táimél* denotes in a lonely, lonesome, and desolate fashion (McKenzie 1991). Kiowa linguist Parker McKenzie (1897–1999) translated the name as meaning "Alone" or "Lonesome" in reference to its solitary position. He remembers seeing it kept outside on the west side of the keeper's tipi during his childhood, like all medicine bundles. The following expressions demonstrate a similar interpretation: *Gà táimé* (It is alone/lonesome); *Yá táimé* (I am alone/lonesome). Parker McKenzie to the author, Nov. 24, 1995. The Kiowa terms for mosquito are *áulhái* (s/d) and *áulháimáu* (t), which was preceded by the now archaic term *áulháimé*. The first syllable denotes hair; no two-syllable compounds with the syllables *hai-me* or *hai-mau* are contained in McKenzie (1991). All ethnographic sources that I have seen and all Kiowas that I have interviewed have always given the pronunciation of Táimé for the bundle.

and this time the Old Arapahoe went back with them and made the Sun Dance with them until he died and some of his relatives took it up. When I was growing up, "Tonanti [aka] Long Foot" had it. He was old when I saw him and he grew older and older as I grew up and up until his ribs came together and he died old. He died at the Sand Hills (Water Dust or Powder) on Elk Creek the winter after this fort was finished 1869 or '70. He got it when he was a young man and died a very old man. He made a great many dances. The next man who took it up was "Plenty Stars" (Plenty Stars' other name was "Got No Moccasins"), he made two dances omitted the 3rd, made the 4th, and died the next fall—a fever killed him. His own brother "Plenty Bears" then took it. He was nephew of that Plenty Bears who was killed before by the Utes [1868] on the north side of the Canadian River where the salt spring is at the mouth of the little creek. He had it four years and made four dances and then [got] sick, died of a fever. After him "Taimeday-day" = Standing Taime, his own brother, took it and he made three good dances. The fourth arrived but the soldiers stopped it (spring of 1890 H.L.S.). Now a woman has it. Tonanti's daughter her name is Ee-mah-añ= Gives Food. Looka—Lucius Aitsan's father, knows how to make the Sun Dance. I have heard that four men got it while they were young and died old men with their ribs caved in and Tonanti was the fifth whom I saw. They must have had it for seventy years each.[21]

[31]

Dead Man Fainting Trance

A long time ago Tabaharty's (Sweat Lodge) name [was] Doy-hart-y (Walks On A Cloud), feints was [he fainted] in the Kiowa camp, which was in the cattle trail crossing of the Washita River (Lodge Pole River) at that time.[22]

---

21 For the names of the Táimé Keepers, see Mooney (1898).
22 The name Tabaharty (Sweat Lodge) would be Tépèdáujè. The name Doy-hart-y/Doy-hau-ty (Walks On A Cloud) appears to be Dáuhájè (One Who Is Power/Medicine). Dáuhájè is listed as Do-hah (Kiowa Tribal Census 1880:254). In the last paragraph of "Dead Man's Medicine" (Scott n.d.a:I:43–44, chapter 4 in this volume) the translation "medicine man" is given for Doy-hau-ty, which is more accurate. Doy-hau-ty was better known as Mamanti, a noted war party leader and medicine man possessing owl power. Parker McKenzie's grandfather Que-ton (Wéjàn), who accompanied Mamanti on several war parties reported that his full name was Cáumâmájè (Goose Flying Overhead), in shortened form Mâmájè, Parker McKenzie to the author, Apr. 7, 1991, and July 30, 1991. Mooney (n.d. MS 2531:6:125) lists "Mam-an-on-de, Crying Above, (mam) above, (an-on-de) honking or squawking like goose in air," which would correlate with the popular translation "Screaming On High." The association of Doy-hau-ty with the translation "Walks On A Cloud" appears to be the mixing of his two names: *pán* (sky or cloud, firmament) is not present, although the syllable *mâm* denotes "above." The story entitled "Dead Man's Medicine" supports this identification by discussing Mamanti's role as a prisoner at Fort Marion and his disdain and eventual curse of Kicking Bird for singling him out to be sent to prison. See note 31, this chapter, and the associated story.

He had a fever and died at sundown. He was dead all over except his heart, which had a slight movement so he was not rolled up [wrapped for burial]. He remained dead until sundown the next day when he recovered and opened his eyes and looked around and in a week he was sitting up. He did not say anything about it for a year and one day while we were camped on N.F. [North Fork] Red River near the cow road he sent for his friends to come to his lodge to council and I went with the others and he said, "A year ago I was very sick of a fever and got much emaciation. I died of a fever and my heart went up above. I saw the dead man's road and traveled on it. It is a wide road and where I followed it to the top of a smooth ridge I saw some steams on the other side. I saw a big village below on a stream with timber on it. The lodges were like the grass in number. A number of people were running about in the village and out on one side the horses were grazing wide in immense numbers. Someone called and in Kiowa and they looked up and saw me and came to meet me in large numbers. I saw my father, mother, brothers, and sisters and relatives dead long ago. They took me into the village. [32] They said, "We left you a boy down there and now you are so big. We put away poverty and sickness down there."

They had horses and everything that we have. I looked around the inside of the lodges and the things lying on the ground were just like the things we have. This country is behind. Those people (above) live good. I am homesick for that up there. I do not want to live here. I want to go back. Sometime after that the Kiowas were made prisoners and moved to Fort Sill and were put in prison [1874–75] and that day he said, "Call in my friends" and we go [went] in and sit [sat] down and he said, "My friends, I am sick, not strong sick, but I do not live good here. I had a bad journey in here. About 9 o'clock tomorrow I am going to die. I want to go back along where I told you about before. I am not strong sick but I am going back tomorrow." The next morning he said, "Call my friends quickly," and we went in and looked at him. He did not appear to be very ill. He said, "I am going above this morning," and he got up and pulled a blanket over his head as if he was going to sleep. We talked about it together for a long time. He did not make any movement. After a while one man went and pulled the blanket off of his face to look at him and he had been true dead for a long time. His name was "Walk On The Clouds." [33] The Cheyennes and Arapahoes all knew him. He said the first time that the dead people took him into their lodge his long ago dead relatives [were there] and that everybody crowded in to see him and to talk to him. Some of the people he knew before and some he did not. They all stared at him and the latter said, "He died down below." After a while he got frightened and started to go out of the lodge, but they all said, "Hold up, wait, do not go," and "Sit down." But he bolted out of the lodge and his eyes opened and his live relations were all around him and then he stood and said to himself, "I have been with dead people and I got away. If one stays a little while only in the dead man's lodge chair he will recover from his sickness and get well. But if he stays with them a long time then he is true dead and will not recover. I have heard the old people tell about people who died up north, when we lived there and who came back and said the same things and I think they must be true. Since we surrendered I have heard the white medicine men collect the Kiowas on medicine day (Sunday) and preach to them saying these things are true, we all live bad down here. Red men and white men, our relatives and friends who are dead live good up there. When we die we will meet (see) them up there. I think it is true.

[34]

Man Having Medicine

I have known three men to have medicine. I have heard of others but these three I have known well. Isa-ti = "White Eagle," the Comanche, you know him.[23] He is a Quahada Comanche. The Kiowas were camped on Elk Creek. Quanah had a nephew killed in Texas by the white people. He was a good looking young man and Quanah was going about giving the pipe, and one day we heard that he was coming to the Kiowas. One day we saw somebody coming over the prairie crying and we said, "There he is. Quanah is bringing a pipe" (always a custom to cry in these cases for the person un-avenged). And he came into the village and said, "Where is a chief's lodge," and I showed him where my uncle's lodge was. He went to the left of the door all around the outside of the lodge and into the lodge and sat down opposite the door. Pretty soon my uncle came out and called all his young men. They came in, sat down, and I was there and Quanah said, "My nephew was killed by the white people. His body is lying in the ground in Texas. I want to retaliate or get even. I am looking for you. I big want you. I give you this pipe to smoke" and all heard him, all the young men watching to see if the chief smoked the pipe. If he was afraid of the pipe they would not smoke it. If he was not afraid they would. All who wanted to go to war smoked it with him and the chief said, "I am not afraid of that pipe he's holding. Wait until all the old men

---

23 Isati is enrolled as White Eagle on reservation censuses. The name Isa-ti (Rear End Of A Wolf) may have been bestowed on him in mockery of his failed power in the Adobe Walls fight of June 27, 1874. For a semantic discussion of this name, see Kavanagh (2008:9n8).

have heard [35] about it and if they say all right, I will smoke that pipe." Quanah said, "All right. I [will] talk to [the] old men" and they [were] all afraid of that pipe. There was a big camp of Cheyennes higher up the creek and he went up there and a large number of them smoked that pipe and went over to the North Fork [Red River]. About six or seven foolish Kiowas went with them to attack the white man's house on the Canadian River above the Antelope Hills (Adobe Walls) now the headquarters [of the] Laurel Hansford Cattle Co. J. M. Abrams manages [the] brand = turkey track [image of three-toed turkey track].

Isa-ti had a strong medicine and he told them all, "Go ahead, those white men cannot. I will stop their guns and then you can charge and wipe them out." They went up close early in the morning before light and charged the white men and killed two of them. The white men got into their fort, buffalo hunting white men who had big heavy buffalo guns and large cartridges that would kill a man a mile away and they began to shoot and killed so many Indians they all ran off. The Cheyenne chief was very angry and was going to kill Isa-ti but he had run away (hidden out of way) secretly, could not be found. He made a false medicine.

A Kiowa man [named] "Lives A Long Time" had a medicine to bring the buffalo.[24] The white men kept killing them off until there were [36] only a very few left and I kept hearing for several years that a medicine was going to be made to make the buffalo bones, the carcasses, rise up. "Lives A Long Time" was going to do it right after the Sun Dance was over. We had the Sun Dance on Walnut Creek (N.F. of Red River) and after it was over we all said to Lives A Long Time, "When are you going to make the buffalo," and he said, "Send me a young man before daylight tomorrow and he will come back with meat at noon time, and next day before light [sunrise] a young man went out to look for the buffalo and everybody waited to see his horse loaded when he came back at noon with buffalo meat. Noon came, he did not come back. Night came, he came not back.

---

24 Lived A Long Time's name (Jáudèką́u) is more accurately translated as "Kept/Retained His Name A Long Time." He then took the name Páutépjè (Bison Bull Emerging/Coming Out). The translation of "Lived A Long Time" appears to have an inferential rather than actual basis (Retained His Name A Long Time, thus lived a long time) that may be based on another individual or incident as he was still a relatively young man at this time. The name is composed from the roots for "prolonged" (jáudè) and "name" (ką́ugà). Several of Alice Marriott's consultants also gave the translation of Retained His Name A Long Time. He was also less well known as Cáulą̂umàu (Bison Maker) for his prophecy and ritual attempt to make the bison return. Frank Given to Alice Marriott, Apr. 13, 1922, July 16, 1936; Mrs. Lone Wolf to Alice Marriott, "Buffalo Returning Ceremony," V-77-83, July 24, 1936, AMP. See also chapter 5, notes 32 and 37.

Tomorrow morning came and then sundown and he came back without any meat and Lives A Long Time was very much ashamed and quit talking about making the buffalo.

Stands In The Middle, a Kiowa man you know, had a medicine, just like Isa-ti's.[25] He was going to stop the soldier's guns from shooting. I met him one day and he said, "I want your son. I give medicine to thirty young men. You got a good looking many men [several sons?]. I give him medicine. Everybody get a war bonnet and buckskin shirt and leggings and we wipe out the soldiers." I say, "Hold up, I [will] think about that and afterwards I tell you." I think that [is] pretty dangerous to kill white soldiers. I say to my son, "Do not take that medicine, it is dangerous." [37] Pretty soon I meet Stands In The Middle and tell him I [will] not give my son and he say[s], "Why not," and I say, "It [is] dangerous" and he quit talking to me and my son.[26] Pretty soon he put his medicine lodge in the head of Elk Creek and a great many Kiowas go over there. I live at Stumbling Bear's N. [North] of Mount Scott and I have [a] son and nephew at [the] Kiowa School at Anadarko, and I was afraid of that medicine and would go and see those boys. So I go up to Anadarko and see a great many Kiowas taking their children out of school and going off to be with Stands In The Middle on Elk Creek. The white man teacher and other white men didn't know anything about that medicine. Pretty soon I see Sun Boy and he say[s], "What [do] you think about that medicine," and I say, "I am afraid of that medicine and I am going to stay with white people around the school house," and Sun Boy say[s] he think just the same. After a while we hear [he is] going to wipe out the white soldiers right after [the] beef killing [beef distribution] and only my two boys [were] left in school so we tell the teacher, "We take these boys and go home to Yamparika Creek" and say, "If Kiowas fight we come back." The Kiowas going by the Elk Creek make [made] a big dust. There were so many of them and I and Sun Boy go [went] to Stumbling Bear's camp. Then we hear about agent "Red Neck," Capt. [J.] Lee Hall (an old Texas Ranger) he been their agent one year. He go up the [38] Washita with soldiers (Capt. Dodd 3 Cav. 2I [3rd Cavalry, 2nd Infantry]) and camped beyond mouth of Rainy Mountain Creek. Next day he send [sent] for Sun Boy to go to the camp and in twenty-four hours he came back and said, "We are saved, it is all over without a fight." Red

---

25 Stands In The Middle would be Váuigàdédè. He is better known by a shortened form of the name, Váuigài (In The Middle).
26 In The Middle's movement occurred in the summer of 1888, so this probably refers to Iseeo's oldest son, Spotted Horse (born in 1871, who would have been sixteen or seventeen years old at that time), and coincides with Iseeo's mention that he has two sons in school.

Neck sent for Stands In The Middle to come to his camp and Bolaute and Koh-mar-ty (Big Head) and said they must go to the agency and stay [as] their prisoners for a month and Standing [Stands] In The Middle's heart was behind and they went.[27] If the agent had not prevailed and Standing In The Middle weakened they would have charged the soldiers but now we are all saved and the Kiowa[s] have separated and everything quieted down and I felt glad of it. That was another man [that] made a false medicine. I have heard of the old people telling of others but these are the only ones, and that [the] Arapahos that brought the Ghost Dance down here that you know, and the only ones I have seen [are] the Arapaho Sitting Bull, Isati, and Standing In The Middle, did like setting fire to the dry grass, [they] set a big fire to the grass.

Crier or Haranguer

Crier. When the Kiowa camp was altogether it was controlled by two men. The chief who held everybody decided which way to move. Sometimes one day's move, sometimes four days moved and he said to some old man, "You stay with me and harangue the camp so the people will know what to do."[28]

[39]

Eagle Catching

If a man wanted an eagle the best way was to catch him. That was the strong way. It was thought bad to shoot it. You know very well the eagle is the wisest of all birds. A long time ago the Kiowas had no guns and it was very good if a man got an eagle. If he caught it good luck will happen to him (i.e., something good [he would] attain).

He would go out on the prairie away from the lodge and dig a deep hole. Deep enough to be two feet over my head as I am sitting here (on a low chair) not as wide as this room but about six feet in diameter. He threw all the dirt into a hide or a blanket and disposed of it a good distance away from the hole. He cut some saplings as thick as my waist and placed them side by side so as to cover the hole, not peaked like a roof, but laid them flat. He then went to a distance and cut some sod, laid it over the sticks, and left a hole to go into the pit, then fixed it over smooth so that if you

---

27 Bolaute or Bob Poolant (Fólą́jè/Crawling or Approaching Snake) was a Kiowa man killed in September 1891. See Nye (1937:275–76). Koh-mar-ty (Cómą̀jè or Friendship Tree) is the namesake of the Komalty family born in 1851 (Kiowa Family Record 1901: Fam. 124, Ko-mah-ty).
28 The Kiowa term for camp crier is ôéljòqì (literally, Big Voiced–Speaking-Man).

looked at it you would not know that there was a pit there after it was all made good. He then hunted for a coyote and killed it and opened it and struck a stick through its meat as thick as my waist and as long as my arm, laid it across the hole, and pegged it by a rope to the bottom of the pit.

Before the dawn next morning, he went out and got into the pit and fixed over the [40] top and sat down. The eagle has a custom every day at daylight of ranging about hungry looking for something to eat and when he sees it, he lights on it with both feet. He is not long about it, but does it swiftly. The man looked through between the sticks. The eagle stands quietly looking all around until he is satisfied and then begins to peck at the wolf meat. After he has eaten awhile the man puts up his hands and catches the eagle by both legs, jerks him down into the pit, kills him by breaking his neck and throws him to the floor. Some days a man will catch one, sometimes three or four. He never catches many. He keeps on day after day however until he gets six or seven to make a war bonnet, in that way he gets a war bonnet quickly. If he shoots eagle they are so wise that it takes a long time to get enough to make a war bonnet.

The eagle must be jerked down quickly and his neck broken as in that way he dies all over just as if he was scared to death. But if you make ineffectual jerks to get him down or only catch one leg he will do something dangerous. I knew a Kiowa man who sat two days in a hole. On the third day he saw an eagle light on his wolf and reached up and pulled him down, but he only got one leg. The eagle was quiet at first but soon recovered from his fright and stuck his talon thorough the flesh of the man's wrist and it wouldn't let go but held on, the blood gushed [41] out of the artery and they fought each other like two men in the hole until after a long time, the man killed the eagle. When the man got home, his arm was swollen as big [a]round as the calf of his leg. This happened at the head of the Arkansas River where there are high mountains. There are a great many eagles there. That is the way to get a good war bonnet. It is bad to shoot them.

We do not want bald headed eagles for anything. We use almost all the feathers of the war eagle [golden eagle].[29] The tail feathers [are used] for war bonnets and fans. The wing feathers for lances and shields and to feather arrows with. There are several fluffy feathers under the tail that are highly prized as ornaments for the hair or in war bonnets. A (poor in spirit) man did not have a war bonnet. Only those with strong hearts, chiefs, that has been the custom always from the very old times.

---

29 Many similar accounts attesting to a general disdain for the bald eagle are found in the literature.

The Kiowas learned to wear single feathers from the Sioux. A large party of them once came to the Kiowa village with some Cheyenne[s] and they all had eagle feathers in their hair, and danced with the Kiowas and gave them the dance with feathers, just as you saw Sitting Bull the Arapaho give the feather to the Kiowas and Wichitas and the Messiah Dance. We call that dance you saw the Cheyenne[s] [42] dancing. The Sioux dance ever since (Omaha or Grass Dance of the Sioux). That was on the head of the Washita River when I was a boy like that boy (10 years old). I am forty-five years old now.[30]

[43]

Dead Man's Medicine

Doy-har-ty [Doyharty] (Walks On A Cloud) had the dead man's medicine.[31] He died once and saw the dead people's village and came back and did wonderful things. That I knew about myself. One day we were on the warpath in Texas and camped on a little creek and we heard an owl say "Whoo, whoo, whoo." Doy-har-ty listened to it and said, "Give me a pipe. That owl is smoke hungry." And they gave him a pipe, which he pointed (stem) to the owl and said, "You wanted to smoke now smoke." Pretty soon the owl said, "Whoo whoo whoo" again and Doyharty listened to him and said, "If you meet four white men tomorrow do not try to kill them, you will fail and they will get away from you. But if you meet some soldiers attack them and it will make you paint your face [in victory] and you will get a mare, and a bay stallion, an old horse with gray on his back. Give me that mare, I want it." And about ten o'clock the next morning they saw four white men. The young men could not be held back from charging them but they plunged into the woods and escaped from seventeen of us. And Doyharty said, "Didn't I tell you last night?" We went on after a while and got dismounted for a rest. About one o'clock somebody said, "Here comes a lot of soldiers" and we attacked them and killed two. Iseeo struck one with a lance and got two horses, one mare and one [44] bay

---

30 This account seems to refer to the Omaha Dance (popularly known as the War Dance), which the Kiowas received from the Cheyennes. Iseeo was born in 1849 and was forty-five years of age at the time of this account, so it would have been recorded about 1894. Iseeo reports it to have occurred when he was around ten years old, thus ca. 1859. Other sources including elder accounts and membership lists date it to 1884, however, which suggests an earlier performance (by the Sioux) of a dance prior to a formal exchange from the Cheyennes around 1884. In addition, the Lakotas received the Omaha Dance around 1865, which predates this event, further indicating some other form of dance. See Meadows (2010:260–65).

31 This account refers to Doy-har-ty (Dáuhájè or One Who Is Power/Medicine), better known as Mâmä́jè. See note 22 and associated story above.

stallion, and Doyharty said, "The man to get the stallion and ride it would count first coup" and Tohausen [aka Done-pi] got it and counted first coup.

Doy-har-ty was one of the prisoners sent to Florida about 1874. He and Paul [Tsaitkopeta] were on their way to Caddo on the R.R. [railroad] with others when Doy-har-ty said his heart felt sore towards Kicking Bird because he had given in his name [reported him] as a bad man who was all the time going on a warpath and would not listen, and he said he died on the 7th day [after] he bewitched him.[32]

Another time the Kiowas were camped on Rainy Mountain Creek and Doy-hau-ty (Medicine Man in Kiowa) said, "I dream [dreamed] last night that something dangerous came to catch us. I see [saw a] big fish with [a] big mouth try to bite us and he call[ed] a council and tell [told] them about it, "You had better send two young men up Walnut Creek near the end of the mountains and let them see what is dangerous over there." And they pick[ed] out me and another young man to go over there and next morning we start[ed] and sleep [slept] on Walnut Creek and did not see anything. Then we go [went] on the end of the mountains and saw soldiers coming and we went back and [45] told about it. I know that myself.

Docto's Medicine

Docto had bewitch medicine. He told me about it himself. He started out to steal horses with six others and one very hot day they camped on the head of Red River near the mouth of the canyon where there was a large deep pool with turtles on it. They drove the horses down to the pool and he saw the turtles, a great many in the water, and thought he would bathe himself. And it made him lazy [relaxed] and he was lying in the shallow water eating roots of the rushes and went to sleep. He found himself in the back part of a lodge and there were monster fishes on each side of the door with huge mouths facing each other. The door was a big turtle. Around the lodge were medicine men of under-water frogs and snakes and turtles, etc., and the Sun order[ed] them each to give him a piece of his medicine what he wanted, just as if General [Nelson] Miles give [gave] me a paper to the soldiers to give me what they wanted. One give [gave] me a shirt, another a blanket or a pair of shoes, just that way they gave Docto a piece of medicine, what they wanted, and they gave him bewitch or medicine arrow shooting also to make bewitch fail, to cure sickness and to have success and [46] women, and all kinds of medicine, and he have it.

---

32 The Kiowa prisoners left Fort Sill on April 28, 1875. Kicking Bird died on May 3, 1875 (Hoig 2000:242). Mamanti died on July 29, 1875, at Fort Marion.

He said he [did] not bewitch anybody. He deny [denied] it, but everybody say[s] he was a bad man, he kill[ed] people. They say that Tabenanaka and Cheevers were killed that way. They died but they were not sick, they were bewitched. When he went to cure sick people he would sit by his bed and sing with a rattle. The sick man liked to hear that, it make [made] him feel good. And Docto gave him something; I do not know [what], different things he had. One for stomach and one for other sickness and [he] slapped him gently with a bunch of eagle feathers, five or six in a bunch, not a dozen, sometimes [he] suck[ed] the place that hurt or scratch it with flint knife and suck[ed] out the blood and spit it out, the blood and sickness together. Sometimes he sing [sang] and dance[d] a little while. Sometimes he blow[blew] on it and the man gets [got] well and he pay [paid] him for it. His medicine was a rough tailed turtle with back and tail [having] rough points on it like on the tail of that stuffed alligator there. That turtle he keep [kept] him.[33]

[47]

Going to the Medicine

Big Young Man

Big Young Man once gave a horse to the medicine. He tied it to the outside of the Medicine Lodge (Taime) and left it there when he moved away. That is not the usual custom. When we gave things to the Medicine we gave them to that old man the Medicine Keeper so he would not be poor. Big Young Man thought it would be better to do otherwise, that the Medicine hear[d] him better, and he left the horse, a spotted horse there to die. Once he ran away with a woman and never came back. We think this woman is with the Utes and that was what we talked about at the last council to ask the Com [Comanches?] to find her and bring her back home. And then we hear[d] what happened to Big Young Man. Once he held [solicited] the pipe for old men to go to Mexico on warpath [but] he [was] not a good leader, always have had bad luck. One day he called up the old men, thirteen of them, and say [said] he must cut a piece of each man's tongue and give it to the sun. And he made them sit down and he cut off

---

33 Docto (Dóctó) is the Kiowa pronunciation of the English "doctor." His other Kiowa name was Tónàuqàut (Rough Tailed/Snapping Turtle). He was a noted shaman who was known both to heal people and to use sorcery on people to make them sick. For an account of his activities and his death and burial at Rainy Mountain Cemetery in 1894, see Nye (1962:267–75). Snapping Turtle is reported to have been a brother of Gotebo. Delores Toyebo Harragarra to the author, Mar. 6, 2010. After his death another Kiowa man (b. 1871, d. Nov. 3, 1911) who served in Troop L bore the name Tónàuqàut (To-nah-cot: Kiowa Family Record 1901: Fam. 311). He is buried at Saddle Mountain Cemetery, where his grave marker indicates his service in Troop L.

a piece of each man's tongue and gave it to the sun. He dream [dreamed] about it and they believe[d] him. Whenever a piece of flesh is given to the sun the man goes upon some high place and prays there. He cuts off the flesh and holds it up to the sun and prays. Then when he is through he leave[s] [48] [a] piece of flesh on a dried buffalo chip.[34]

Catching Wild Horses

A long time ago there used to be big bands of wild horses about here, and a great many up in the Canadian [River Valley] and on the head of Red River. They looked black at a distance, no white ones. Whenever we saw spotted ones we said that horse has escaped from somebody. The horses were very wise, very cautious, and always kept a look out. When we wanted to catch them, we got up early in the morning, a large party of us and found the bunch of horses grazing. Then we made a very large circle, six miles across and gradually contracted it, drawing near each other until the horses would see one and start to run. They would run against the wind until they smell[ed] somebody then they would show itself [themselves] in front. The horses [were] running around in this way at full speed until they were tired out, the circle closing on them until at last the horses would break through somewhere, but being tired, they were soon run down and caught. Some of them were very fine horses. (* NOTE: Kobi = Wild Horse in Comanche. Sign = prairie horse.)

[49]

[side note] See brief on Wichitas-Choctaw claims by Philip Walker of Washington, 501 "D" St. N.W.

Wichitas

A long time ago the Wichitas, Pawnees, Tawaconies, Keecheis, [and] Wacos all lived together near the Arkansas River. We do not know where they came from. First we think northwest of there but they were all together then and they separated. We do not know why. It was not on account of any quarrel, they just separated. The Pawnees went north and the Wichitas south. The Tawaconies and Keecheis went southeast of here and the Toyeash [Taovayas] west of here until they struck [reached] these mountains. We did not see any other tribe here when we came and we have lived always about these mountains.

Old Niastor over there was born at the base of Mount Scott. We had a village on North Fork Red River, [and one] where Fort Sill now stands

---

34 Big Young Man is Jõgúlêl in Kiowa. He was killed in 1861 (Mooney 1898:310).

[this is referring to two sites, one on the North Fork Red River, and one on the east side of the Fort Sill base] on Red River near the mouth of Cache Creek, on Rush Creek, and all around here. I do not know why we left these places but it was a custom we had whenever things we planted did not grow well, we moved somewhere else.

The Pawnees have always been our friends. When we go there they give us horses and when they come to see us we give them horses. We never had any medicine dance like the Kiowas or Cheyennes. We had a dance with a red bean [mescal bean]. We used to get that bean in Mexico. Two men would stand up with rattles and a [50] bow in their hand. [On] one end on the ground they would eat four of these beans and fall down drunk and the sun would help them to see some medicine. We used the mescal bean a very long time ago by chewing one of those and spitting the juice in our hands and rubbing it over our arms and breasts when we went to war. But we put that away a long time ago and do not use mescal at all now.[35]

All the way traveling down after separating from the Pawnees, the Wichitas had dirt lodges like the Pawnees until we got to those mountains [Wichita Mountains]. Then we put them away and used grass lodges. We had hoes made of the shoulder blade of the buffalo. We had no iron kettles. We made them out of earth [pottery]. We had corn, pumpkins, [and] watermelons smaller than the white man's, but very sweet. We had tobacco* and Punkins [pumpkins], the Sun gave us the seed and put it in the ground and it grew up for the support of our life. It happened this way a very long time ago. There was a rain and hail storm and the Sun sent the seeds down with the hail stones and they grew up and we have some of the seeds yet that we have planted ever since. I will go and get some and give them to you. "Ishtick, we gave you corn first. We have not got any old tobacco seeds now anymore." [Ishtick, a name?] [51] The pumpkins were snake colored (i.e., color of a rattlesnake).

We used to travel on foot and pack our property on dogs whenever we moved and one time on the North Fork Red River near the mouth of

* Breckenridge and Bradbury 1811—Bradbury Liverpool, 1817—Makes had corn, beans, melons, squash, and tobacco. Rustica Nicotiana. Gray botany p. 377. Wild tobacco, annual, found in old fields from New York westward and southward. A relic of cultivation by the Indians of unknown nativity, leaves ovate petioles, tube of dull greenish yellow, corolla cylindrical 2/3 longer than the calyx, the lobes rounded. See Catlin for Wichita's tobacco gardens on Missouri River, also Beckworth for Crows and Snakes [Shoshones]. See also Marcy *Thirty Years of Army Life on the Border.*

---

35 The mescal bean is *Sophora secundiflora*. James Howard (1957:84–85) and George Dorsey (1904:16–20) discuss the Wichita Deer Dance, which centered on the mescal bean, and the Wichitas' role in diffusing the dance to northern tribes.

Elk Creek where the buffalo were very thick and we made a surround on foot and when we got near the buffalo we saw two strange things with them. They were horses and a man shot one and wounded it with an arrow and then they caught it. Everybody came to see it. It was such a wonderful thing. It was a stallion and not long after we saw men from the south with horses and we found out how to use them. We used to try and ride them the same way but when we tried to round up the buffalo we fell off.

We have the same belief about dead men as have the Kiowas [and] Comanches. We call a ghost a whirlwind. We do not call an owl a ghost. We are afraid of the white owl [snowy owl?], not of the other. The white owl says, "You are no good. You are very weak. You will die soon" and we are afraid of it. When we hear it we do not answer back and if there is anyone sick when he calls, the sick person soon dies.

We call ourselves "Kitti-ki-dish" which means "Tattooed around the Eyes." We call the Pawnees "A-wa-hay" which means a grasshopper, a big grasshopper. [52]

Chee-kee—"Good" in Delaware, also Willette.

Caddo—Hahut.

Wichita = Ot-sta.

Pawnee—Durahey [Dwahay?].

We have a Scinday like the Kiowas, a very deceitful man. We call him ([in] Wichita) Scan-to-ka.

Delaware Scinday = A-te-lo-ha-kan.

Caddo = Carri-o-kan.

Cheyenne = Hota-hay-yin, which means Sioux. [see Vol.] II, p. 35.

Arko, Comanche = Nun Kiwash [Kiawash].

[The following appear to be names for tribal medicine bundles.]

Nix-hant = Gros Ventres Prairie. [See] Anthropological Papers, Museum of Natural History, Vol. 1, p. 68, etc.

Arapaho = Ba-taa-ni-ti-ha. Flowing Hair of Ten Meds [Medicines?].

Kiowa-Apache = Sinti-Saa-ma. Flowing Hair of Ten Medicines.[36]

When we lived at Mount Scott a Wichita young man climbed up on top of the mountain and stayed there three days and nights without eating or drinking anything and while he was lying on his back looking up at the stars one of the stars came down close to him and said to him, "I am going

---

36 These two entries seem to be names for the Ten Medicines.

to take pity on you. You go down to your village early tomorrow morning. Paint yourself and dress yourself in your best clothes and about eleven o'clock an Osage war party will attack your village and you will whip them off" and so it was. The Osages attacked the Wichita village but they were ready for them and killed a whole lot of Osages. The star helped him.

Mount Scott and out at the west end of the Mountains where the end is there is another little mountain close by on top of [a] small point called Rock Mountain just off [the] extreme end of these mountains, and there is another medicine place for the Wichitas. If a man stays there four days and nights without eating or drinking, while they are asleep a ghost will come and touch them and take them where they will see some medicine.

One young man I know was waked up that way one night and the ghost took him out on the plain below where the spotted tailed eagles had a council and the ghost told the eagles to have mercy (pity) on him and to give him some medicine that would help him and [53] they gave him some medicine and after a while the Osages came on the warpath and every time they shot at him they missed him.

Four generations of Kitti-ki-dish lived in this country about these mountains (Wichita [Mountains]), were born here, grew up, their breasts collapsed and they died (of old age) that I never saw [before the consultant's time]. They are very old about one hundred years for each generation.

Toyeash = A Trader. To-we-ash = Is a Mexican name for the Kitti-ki-dish. Wichita is an Osage name for the Kitti-ki-dish.

Near the Fort Sill village there used to be some spring that had something like wagon grease come out of it (petroleum or asphalt). We put the earth off of it and took some out. It was sticky and we chewed it like gum. It smells good, makes a horse run fast, and if you put it on his nose he will not be afraid of the buffalo. When the Kitti-ki-dish separated from the Pawnees the Tawaconies and Keecheis and Wacos went south through the timber east of here and they knew of the hot springs of Arkansas. The Kitti-ki-dish kept out on the prairie on their march south.

We used to make forts to put the women and children in when attacked by the Osages. They were just about like that hole [in the] side of fort on east side of Sugar Creek in 1859 village of Kitti-ki-dish on north side of Washita River.

[54] First there was a large center pole selected and in old times it was chopped with

[side note] They had spoken at different times in the past of their village on North Fork of Red River as being their old place. They were there in 1834 (Catlin) but had occupied it previous to this time and had abandoned it and were back there for at least the second time in 1834.

stone axes and sometimes burned down. It had five or six branches coming out together to form supports for the roof [image of upright tree trunk with the bases of several lower branches extending from top]. Then there were palisades [palisade poles] split in two. They were a foot in thickness, planted in a circle for the outside about three or four feet deep and the circle about thirty-five feet in diameter. The door of this one was to the east and had an extension about ten-foot long. It was not closed during an attack but was guarded by men from the inside. The circular part had postholes about three feet above ground so a man could kneel down inside and shoot through them. The roof was made of logs, thick enough to resist bullets, resting in the different crotches of the center pole and tied at the other ends in circular palisades by elm strings [woven elm bark cords]. There was an opening in the roof to get light. This was not in the center but out to one side between two of the roof supports and the whole [structure] was covered with dirt like a Pawnee's house. We used to have one in every village.

The elm tree was called "bark string" tree by us because we got string by stripping its bark to tie our roofs on our forts and to tie our grass lodges and our fences. We used [to] have hoes made from the shoulder blade of a buffalo. The women used them to dig our corn fields. The way it was done was by each family to have its own field fenced in and [55] the woman dug up a circular space about two feet in diameter and planted seven kernels of corn in it. Then another space was dug of the same size about three feet or four feet away and planted and so on. They hoed it a little after it came up but the whole village left not long after the planting to look for buffalo and did not come back until the melons were ripe. They remained until the pumpkins [were] ripe (1st September) and then cut these into strips, platted them into a mat about six feet long and two feet wide, dried these, rolled them up and put them away.[37] (See Long p. 447 [in pencil]. See same page of description of women on their way to their fields, Pawnee women.)

Our custom was to dig a hole about three feet across the top, taking out the sod very carefully, and after going down three feet, commence to enlarging the cavity until it was eight feet in diameter and was just deep enough for me to stand on the bottom and see out on every side. The earth was taken out very carefully, put on hides, and thrown away off somewhere by the women in little piles. When it [was] ready, it was

---

37 One of the Kiowas' names for the Wichitas is Évą́udàu (Pumpkin Braiders), referencing this practice (Meadows 2013:21).

left a little while to dry out. Then a hide was put on the bottom and grass was spread over that and dried meat, pumpkins, melons, and corn was put in there, covered over with grass, and dirt was packed in the hole for the depth of three feet. The sod put back, carefully smoothed off, and no one could tell there was a hole [56] anywhere about. When these things had been done we moved away off somewhere to hunt for the buffalo and sometimes did not come back until the middle of winter sometimes until spring and we would dig up our caches and find the melons still good to eat even if it was the next spring after planting.

When the Osages would come down on the warpath during our absence they would look for those caches so they could rob them but if they were carefully made they could not find them. Sometimes we put them under the floor of our lodge's shades or other place where the grass had all been worn off. This was the best way to keep from showing. We used to take our corn and melons and pumpkins to trade with the Comanches and Kiowas and sometimes they came to visit us to trade horses.

We call ourselves Kitti-ki-dish = Men Who Are Tattooed around the Eyes.

Hitti-wa = True or so.

Hatta-wa-kan = He said so.

Kiddi = No.

Wa-a = Yes.

Toyeah = A trader.

Ta-wee-ash = Spanish name for Wichitas.

Wichita is the Osage name for the Kiddi-kidish. When the Tawaconies and Wacos came back to the Washita from Texas (1859) we lived at the mouth of Sugar Creek (sugar maples near head), the Kiddi-ki-dish on the left bank near mouth, high plateau near edge, fort [earthen lodge?] is just over the edge toward Sugar Creek. The Tawaconies [57] and Wacos were on the right bank scattered in grass houses for a long distance down Sugar Creek and around the turn on the Washita there were no trees on the Washita there. These have grown up since the corn fields were on both sides of Sugar Creek and the graves were out on the flat on the Washita above the village, west side Sugar Creek. The Keecheis were on [the] south side of the Washita up close to the Keechei Hills on Delaware Creek. The Wichitas got frightened when the Tonkaways were killed (1862) and ran away north to the Arkansas River and did not come back until the Civil War was over.

We used to tattoo our faces in old times but we have abandoned that now. We tattooed along the lower edge of the jaw, around eyes on the eyelid, down the bridge of the nose, some with circles on the cheekbones, a line down center of chin from lip to point. Also some had marks on each cheek like this ^^^^^ from mouth to ear. The women had some of those marks also; concentric rings around [the] bust from near the nipple to the body. They wore nothing on their body but a skirt leaving the upper part bare. Tawaconies, Wacos, Keecheis, and Kiddikidish all did it. It was not done until the person got of age. The children did not tattoo themselves. It was done with an awl and charcoal was rubbed into the spot. Mt. Sheridan in the Wichita Mountains [is] called Turned-Up Nose by the Kiowas and Bull's Face by the Wichitas. It resembles a buffalo bull's face seen from the northeast.

[side note] Comanches call the Wichitas Tocana = Dark Houses/Lodges. Topa—black, Kanica—lodge. To-goo'a is Kiowa for Wichita. To = tattooed, goo'a = in rings. Tattooed in Rings—'Co [Qóp] = Mountains [Wichita Mountains].[38]

[58]

Kiowa Bands

Iseeo

Kiowas have no idea of totems on clans in the usual term but they have three bands: 1) Kiowa Proper 2) Elk 3) Shield. [A fourth was the] 4) Biter (made like biting corn off the cob). These last are lost, separated long, long ago and they do not know where they live but it is said that Ahpeahtone saw some of them on his trip north to look for the Messiah. The Kiowa[s] proper are the largest in numbers, Shields 2, and Elk 3. These bands intermarry and it is preferred to cross the bands as it is said to cross the blood, which suggests the idea that these bands were originally not amalgamated tribes or remnants of tribes which Iseeo does not know about, but will ask "Calf Of Leg Of Buffalo Bull" or Taybodle who is the oldest Kiowa and who knows about those things. Kiowas do not allow marriage between first cousins. The children are fools and people would be ashamed to marry their first cousin.[39]

38   Although they are also known as Tattooed Eyes, the most common Kiowa name for the Wichitas is Thǒcútgàu (Tattooed Faces), with the middle syllable denoting marks, writing, painting, and tattooing and not rings (Meadows 2013:25).

39   This appears to be an incomplete list of bands. Most lists of Kiowa bands include seven groups: five Kiowa bands, the Kútjàus who were exterminated in the northern plains, and the Naishan-Dene (Kiowa-Apache Tribe) as a seventh component at the Sun Dance. The Biters are recognized in the bands of the late nineteenth century. While there may be some relationship to the Kiowa who separated and went north, the band continued in the southern plains during the 1800s (Mooney 1898:228–29).

Spotted Horse Sun Dance

That horse stolen by the Navajos was the fastest horse of all Kiowa horses. He had [a] black head, [a] small black spot in front of [his] throat, round black spots on [his] back lip about three inches [in] diameter and a moon around his tail, and he was stolen by the Navajos together with a whole bunch of horses belonging to another man named "Red Mud" at the time of the Taime Dance [Sun Dance] on [the] Washita River south of the antelope hills.[40]

[59]

Sun, Moon, and Morning Star

The morning star is called the "Big Star." It, with the sun and moon, are strong. If you pray to them they may keep you. The North Star does not move, others move. It is called Pawnee Star because the Pawnee towns are right under that star.

The Pleiades are called the "Rising Women" and when they are on the Meridian in winter it is the middle of the night. When they almost set, it will soon be morning. There is a circle of stars July 10 '97 [July 10, 1897] about 9 p.m. tonight in the west, high up. The handle of the dipper is a part of it and another star in the center, which is called the "Old Star" because it is like an old man with a fire in the center of a council. Has no knowledge of the dipper.[41]

The Milky Way is called the "Backbone of the Stars." Figure in the moon is said to be a man (Scinday) with side toward us, stirring something in a pot with a spoon, with a parfleche sack behind him.

Meteors are thought to be pieces broken from another star. Stars all flee before dawn. The dawn lifts up like a curtain to indicate the light that comes before the rising of the sun. The red flaring rays (i.e., sunburst) also has a sign [picture of hands together side by side, back side up, fingers extended] with both hands. The dipper is called the Jack Rabbit by the Kiowa[s], the Handle is his arched back and the pointers are the tips of his ears. The Cheyennes say that it is a buffalo bull and the pointers are two Cheyennes [60] standing in front ready to shoot him. Two stars that come up [illegible, now bright?] with a twinkling movement like the motion of a duck's wing, we call the Duck.

(see [p.] 173)

---

40 This fits Mooney's (1898:319–20) description of the 1867 "Sun Dance When Black Ear Was Stolen."
41 This is an important observation, as many younger Kiowas today associate the Big Dipper with the Star Girl's/Devil's Tower Story. Older Kiowas and older sources state that the seven children became the Pleiades, however, not the Big Dipper. See Meadows (2008:290–91) for a list of Kiowa astrological place-names.

Ledger image of the Rabbit (Big Dipper) constellation (vol. I, p. 59). Courtesy of Fort Sill National Historic Landmark and Museum Archive and Wade Popp.

THE PLEIADES—6 BOYS AND A GIRL

Six boys and a girl were playing and the boys had a bearskin scaring each other. There were some holes that they hid in. The boys were going to put the skin on the girl but she was afraid it would turn her into a real bear if that should be done. The boys insisted on putting it on her and she said, "If I am turned into a real bear you must run away or I will kill you and you will be safe if you get into a dog's hole" (dug by dogs to escape heat and flies). They put it on her after a while and she became a real bear and chased them. They ran away and jumped up on a rock, which raised [upward] as she jumped to seize them, higher and higher until it pushed them up to the sky where they now are.

The Milky Way is called "Backbone of the Stars." Its appearance was caused by a race between a wild horse and an antelope and its dusty look was from the dust raised by their feet.

[61]

CUSTOMS—HANGING

To hang me would be bad. It would be killing me. It would be bad to kill me. I do not know whether I would go up (heavenward) or not if I was hung. I do not know anything about that. In old times many people did not die that way, only now and then one. I do not know even one man who did it himself. When a woman wants to die she does it with a rope. I have often heard the old men talking about suicide and I find out the trick in that way. A long time age we used to range the prairies to the west (pointing to head of Red River). A man had a relative, a son, or a nephew and refused to give him a horse or anything he owned. The nephew's heart would be on the ground or if a man had a horse and his son or his nephew would secretly take the horse and ride him until he was wet all over and the man should see the horse in that condition and should scold the boy, then the boy's heart would be on the ground. He would not say anything but would go off on the warpath looking for a fight and would die there. That was a man's way of committing suicide in old times. Now they do not have that way [i.e., no longer any warfare].

A woman had her way also in old times. If her father scolded her badly she would say to herself, "My father scolded me badly. I am going to die." And she would take a rope secretly into the woods saying nothing to her father and would hang herself and so die quickly. That is a strong way, and [62] a few do it. I myself have never seen but one do it. Four or five years after we surrendered [1874–75, thus ca. 1879–80] a Kiowa Apache woman did that way. I have heard of other cases when we lived up on the Arkansas, but I have known of a number of men who died quickly on the warpath because their hearts were stabbed (i.e., felt badly). They would go away off on the warpath without mentioning the matter to their father and when the fight day arrived they would say to the others with them, "Today I want to die. My father held back his horse. My heart is on the ground. I want to die." And he would in the fight die and the others would carry the heart back to the village and everybody would hear of it. I know that a man and a woman have different customs.

It is said by some that men who have been hanged do not go to the same village of the dead that other dead people go to. Nobody knows where it is.

Kiowa Hair Customs

In old times Kiowa men often used to cut their hair off on one side, square over one ear to show their earrings. Comanches and Apaches sometimes did it also (sign to cut is made with back of hand up and not down as in "Kiowa" and little finger edge is squared against head above top of ear). The other side was braided long and nice. They usually had their ear on the cut side pierced or slit in a lot of places and a big bunch of earrings hung far down. If sign was made over right ear the hair was cut on that

198   THE SCOTT LEDGERS AT FORT SILL

side and vice verse. Some men parted the hair over each temple and brought forward from the top of the head—slicked and stiff ended with glue, smoothed out as wide as my [63] three fingers, the ends cut off very square with a sharp knife and made to stick straight over the nose like a visor (see Cabbias picture) [Cabaya's photograph] the rest of the hair was braided long on both sides. I saw those two ways when I was a boy, before I grew up.[42] I saw no more worn like a visor or cut on one side. Comanches and Apaches did not use the visor sign. Comanches, Kiowa[s], and Kiowa-Apaches have [their] hair braided nowadays, above [the] ears. Cheyennes below, as the loose hair covers [their] ears.

Glue Making

To make glue, take the skins off the jowls of a buffalo bull. Make a fire and put the hide before the fire, turning it over and over until the hair is burned off, like a scorched pigskin. Keep turning it until the skin is hard but not burned. Cut it off then into strips an inch wide. Then put it in a pot with water and cook it for two or three days and it will be strong glue, which is used most for gluing feathers or arrows. If you put it on gently (dipping points of thumb and fore finger in glue and sticking gently) the feathers will not come off in rain. If you put it on roughly it will fail.

Wichitas and Iseeo

[Iseeo]
When I was the size of that little girl (ten years) [thus ca. 1859] we were on the head of the Red River and some Wichitas came there trading. I was afraid of them. They looked very strange. Their faces were tattooed down the ridge of their noses down [the] lower edge of their jaws, above that on lower cheeks ^^^^^^^^, [and] center of chins to the mouth, around their eyelids on [the] point of [their] cheekbones in circles. And the women were naked to the waist although it was the middle of winter. They only had on a skirt coming to the knees and their breasts were tattooed in concentric rings beginning near the nipple and ending where the bust springs from the body. The hair of the men was clipped on the sides and stuck up straight on top of the head. They were very strange. I did not see them again for a long time it was at their cornfields on the Arkansas.

---

42 Both of these hairstyles can be seen in various nineteenth-century images of Kiowas, including drawings by George Catlin, Kiowa ledger art, and photographs (Mooney 1898:175, 195).

Then again when they were at Sugar Creek, 1865, and they were different, the women had shirts on. The men had their hair long and braided like a Kiowa and they had stopped tattooing themselves. I have not seen one of them tattooed now for a very long time and then it was old people. They have not tattooed themselves since they came back from the Arkansas. My wife is half Wichita and we lived with the Wichitas when the Kiowas were captured and imprisoned [1875]. I was not imprisoned. Her brothers died then we moved down here with [the] Kiowas again.

[64]
Accidental Killing
You yourself know when Tonacho killed Bayelah's son by accident (prairie killed). He had a pistol in his hand which went off accidentally (prairie fired) and killed the boy without his meaning to do it. Bayelah and his relatives went to kill Tonacho and quarreled with his relatives. The chiefs intervened and separated the two sides and then counseled as to what was best to be done. The chiefs said this is not a case of fight[ing] or [a] secret killing. It was a prairie killing (or an accident). If Tonacho wants to live he must make it even with Bayelah. Tonacho put up five horses, a mule, some cows, and money. I do not know how much, and the chiefs said to Bayelah, "What are you going to do? He wants to make it even and give you these. This was not a fight killing, it was an accident." Bayelah took the things. Tonacho is alive yet and Bayelah's heart was glad.

If one man catches his wife with another man he will try and kill him or to whip him. If the man says all right go ahead and whip [me] or refuses to fight, everybody is afraid to do him an injury. He is on a good road and does not want to fight. Everybody is afraid of him. Tonacho and Bayelah were three years together in "L" Troop, 7th Cavalry, and got on well together.[43]

[65]
Judges/Oaths
When a man does a crazy thing to another man sometimes he complains to one of the Ten Medicine men. The medicine man goes to him and says,

---
43 This account involves Tónàuqàut (Rough Tailed/Snapping Turtle) and Ba-lah-kah (Bêlắc'á), also known as Vǎusótgúl (Red Thunder), who was born in 1849 (Kiowa Family Record 1901: Fam. 324). This individual was in Troop L, which indicates that he was the later Snapping Turtle (1871–Nov. 3, 1911), who is buried at Saddle Mountain Cemetery, and not the earlier Snapping Turtle, the noted shaman, who died in 1894 (Nye 1962:267–75). This account is interesting in its use of the term "prairie" to mean accidental or not intentional. Other examples of this usage occur throughout Scott's notes.

"Did you do that?" If he tells a lie to the Ten Medicines he will not live good. Something dangerous will happen to him and the medicine man decides whether he did it or not. The medicine knows it. The medicine man acts the part of a judge. Usually the man who does the crazy thing when asked by the judge, "Did you do that," he is afraid to tell a lie and says, "Yes, I did that." Then the judge says, "That is all right, you will attain old age. You did not tell a lie" and the man says, "I will make it even with a horse" and then it is all over. I do not know what the Comanches do. I do not want to tell you anything that is not true and I only tell you what I know about. The Cheyennes have four medicine arrows they keep rolled up [in a bundle], Sacred Arrows, and they use them just as we do the Ten Medicines about knowing. We did not know any way of administering an oath in old times but we know the white man's way now.[44]

The Ten Medicines are used sometimes in a sweat house. No women go [in] with it. The sweat house is made good. The medicine man goes in with others and prays to it [the bundle] and it prays for you to the Sun, "Let me live long and in plenty [with plenty]. Let my children grow up." In some sweat houses the men [66] do not make it so good [perhaps in those not involving bundle use]. The women like sweat houses. Each sex bathes by itself. When two men are quarreling one of the Ten Medicine men sees it and separates the combatants. No one talks back to him or strikes him. All are afraid. When he separates them they quiet down. [I] do not know of any other ceremonies before going to war, etc. The Ten Medicine men are afraid of bears. Other Kiowas are not. Some of them eat bears.[45]

[MISCELLANEOUS: SWEAT HOUSES/TATTOOS]

We use sweat houses usually to sweat clean and because it makes you sleep good after it.[46]

---

44 Regarding pledges to tell the truth, several plains tribes had traditions of swearing to the sun, kissing or biting a knife (Cheyenne, Arapaho) (Scott n.d.a:II:15, chapter 5 in this volume), shooting an arrow, and thrusting a lance through or counting coup on dried bison chips (Plains Apache, Cheyenne, Crow) (Grinnell 1956:53–55, 88; Marquis 1962:91; Meadows 1999:207). See Jack Doyeto's account concerning the Kiowa use of bison chips in "History of the Following Story, a Year after the Battle with the Ute Indians" (Scott n.d.b: MS 2932, Box 2); and Kavanagh (2008:540) concerning Comanche oaths.
45 This statement suggests that the now ubiquitous Kiowa respect-avoidance taboo for the bear once applied only to the Ten Medicine Keepers.
46 This is another useful observation in that many Kiowas today state that sweat lodges are only for sacred activities. Iseeo's statement indicates that they also have secular uses. Part of the problem in classifying the use of sweat lodges relates to the differences between Western societies, which often sharply divide or separate the sacred and secular, and Indian societies, which often blend the two in a wider range of cultural activities.

Kiowa young women saw older ones tattooed on [the] forehead between the eyes with a ring and thought it looked pretty and wanted it done to themselves.

[Kiowa Mourning Customs]

When a woman has a son killed, a good-looking man, she does not wash her face or fix her hair or wear good clothes for a year. She mourns all the time for her son. When a war party is successful and has got even, the man who killed the enemy paints her face black. After that she puts sorrow away from her and she dresses up again.

Mobil's [Mobeadleky's, aka Elk Tongue's] wife had a brother on the warpath after Utes. Word came back that he had been killed and she cut off [the] first joint of [her] little finger. After a while he came back. It was a lie. She cut off the first joint of her other little finger for her first husband "Kicking Bird." After that they do not cut off anymore. Comanches do not cut their little fingers. [The] oldest Kiowa woman has two little fingers and [a] third on [her] left hand cut off.

[Defensive Earthworks]

Sometimes when expecting a fight we used to dig holes in the ground on [the] edge of [a] cut bank on [the] bend of a creek. Sometimes we took old wood and made a small corral. We call it a "shield prevent." We have places to shoot through (see Long p. 478).[47]

[Sun Dance Bison Hunters]

[67] That Point of Ridge Sun Dance was held in [the] point, [the] bend just below Poor Buffalo's place on the Washita about 30 years ago. Taybodle killed the buffalo for a long series of years and was succeeded when he got old by Tohausen (Honnameatah's brother), and [then] by Honameatah. Taybodle killed that buffalo I think.[48]

[Seasonal Changes, Miscellaneous Signs]

Some above person [God or Creator] make [made] the earth ground old

---

47 The Kiowa word for these defensive earthworks is *kíájôi*, which seems to imply "shield-house."
48 This correlates with the location of the 1865 Peninsula Sun Dance (Mooney 1898:317). The name is Háunèmídâu (Unafraid Of Danger).

(when leaves are off the trees). They call it earth old and is made good every spring. No person alive on the earth can make it good, that was understood.

Honey is signed "tree sugar."

Make rain = rain, wind, blow (sign).

[TEN MEDICINE BUNDLES—WATER TABOO/RAIN MEDICINE]

A long time ago a Ten Medicine man put some water in his mouth and blew it on one of the Ten Medicines about sundown. In the middle of the night the rain came and it rained for seven days very hard and all the streams were full to overflowing. It was dreadful, and they stopped right there and have never blown water on the medicines since. A Comanche is said to have the power to make it rain. He is Maddox's brother-in-law. I do not know how he does it. His name in Comanche = Doa-bony (Sees His Child). I have seen a man drive off a thunderstorm with a buffalo robe, throwing the robe out just as if he said, "You go that way."

[BISON HUNTING]

When a party of Kiowas charged the buffalo and they killed a great many they would lie on the ground in many places. [68] If they were killed by arrows there was no trouble for each one recognized his own arrows at once. On the space between the feathers and the notch he painted all his arrows and his private mark and everybody recognized it. When five arrows were used it was sometimes difficult but each man would tell where he shot his buffalo. If there was a dispute between two men, both of whom shot the buffalo, the man who shot it in the vital place took it.

[TIPI MAKING]

Lodges were made by women in summer, a new one every year. They were [became] rotten from frequent rains. They were ready in the fall and by the middle of next summer [needed replacing]. Lodges required from twelve to fifteen skins to make a cover, eighteen skins was a big lodge, twenty-two or three poles inside and two outside. The buffalo were killed in summer, cows, because the hair was easier to get off. Just about this time of year (middle of July). The robes [were] all pegged out first, then fleshed and left in the sun for several days. Then the brains of five or six buffalo (with some grease and livers) were put in a pot and boiled a long time, until you can [could] take them in your hand and squeeze the material out of them that makes the water all white. They are diluted and all squeezed out and the water all made white. Then six or seven hard hairless robes are taken and a piece of blanket is used as a sponge and a hide is sponged off. You must watch it all the time and stop sponging when it is all white and the robe is put in the sun to dry. The others are all done in the same way and next morning they are soaked in the creek for two days [69] until they are all flexible. Then two upright [poles] and a cross pole are put up with the hide stretched on that and afterwards hauled over the cross piece and softened by breaking the fibre [fiber]. The hair is removed by holding it and [pulling] the grain when the hide is hard.

Deer and antelope are tanned the same way, but the hair is taken off by soaking the skin in water for a couple of days then taking off [the] hair and grain while soft with a rib of a pony. It is always smoked afterwards if [it is] to be used for clothing.

[side note] The brains of one buffalo are sufficient to tan its hide. [A] lodge would load three ponies, cover and poles, four [ponies for] a very large one.

Making Rain

Kee-ar-by's, Bootale's father, used to make it rain.[49] He prayed while the sky was clear and there was no sign of rain and pretty soon you could see little clouds that got larger and larger then you could hear it thunder and in a little while it rained. We do not know how he did it, it was his medicine. He has long been dead. "Squrrel" [Squirrel], a Caddo, will make it rain if you give him $50.00, and a Comanche man is strong that way, Maddox's father-in-law.

[70] Scalping

A long time ago we lived on the Arkansas and I know of that, a person alive without a scalp. A party of Comanches were out four days looking for buffalo and were attacked by some Osages. They fought for a long time and the Comanches were being thinned out and an Osage man drove a knife into the throat of a Comanche woman and she died and was scalped. The Comanches were all killed except one man who ran away

---

49 Boat-tah-le (Bóttàlyì or Stomach Boy) was born in 1845 (Kiowa Family Record 1901: Fam. 191). His father was Ke-ah-ve (Kį́fài or Against A Shield).

and escaped. The Osage[s], fearing more Comanche[s] should come, ran away also without cutting of the heads according to [their] custom. The Comanche man went to his village where the lodges were as thick as trees in a forest and gave the alarm. A great many Comanches and Kiowas who were camped with them saddled up and went out (redup.) [were rounded up?]. I was a boy in that camp and pretty soon we heard that a Comanche woman had died and had been scalped but had risen up and they were bringing her into the camp. Everybody turned out to see her and there she was without a scalp. It looked very badly. She did not die. I have seen her since and whenever people would see her they said, "The Osages did that." In the time I was growing up she wore a black cloth over her head just as Pahsita's wife does. (Comanche wife of Pahsita = Hairless)

[71] I knew about a Ute man without a scalp. We were on the warpath against the Utes (he was shot but not good shot, i.e., wounded). He was captured. He died and was scalped. The Kiowas left him there and went home. That man's friends that evening missed him and saddled up and spread out looking for him. They saw a man at a distance coming walking toward them over a smooth ridge. They all galloped up to him and found him to be that man walking home without a scalp. They got scared, packed up, and went back to the Big Mountain and took the Ute man to the soldier's house where the white doctor made medicine over him. This happened when the grass was an inch high. When the trees got red another Kiowa war party went up that way and attacked a Ute camp, the women and children plunged into the creek and hid in the brush. The Kiowas surrounded the camp and on going into a lodge saw a Ute lying there without a scalp. He was very thin, weak, and emaciated and a Kiowa man stabbed him with a knife and they all came home and told about it and after consultation it was agreed that that was the Ute that had been scalped in the spring about three years ago. Big Bow (a very noted Kiowa chief) made a visit to the Utes and asked about that and it was true. I never knew that to happen to a Kiowa or Cheyenne. That Comanche woman was ashamed and wore a black cloth over her head and would not let anybody see it.

([Marcel] Giraud and Rees—scalped [?] houses) Scalp locks are braided that way to hold [a] feather and ornaments by young men. Old men often put that custom away.[50]

---

50 The Kiowa name for the scalp lock is *câivàudàu* (s) and *câivàun* (d/t), literally, "fight braid."

[72]
Property Rights—Kiowas

On death the property of a man goes to his oldest son. If one of the younger children wants a horse or something like that he always gets it. A woman always owns her own property and takes it with her on divorce. She always makes the lodge and it belongs to her.

Counting Coups

All southern Indians even Comanches do this at a dance. Some strong man [will] get up during an interval and says, "I am going to tell you something good," and they call out "Good, good, what is it?" He replies, "At a big fight up the Canadian. I struck the body of a Ute and took his gun and war bonnet." Then somebody strikes the drum and people call out "How, how." "I struck the body of an Osage at another big fight on the Arkansas," drum, exclamation. "I struck the body of a Navajo on the Rio Grande." Drum. "How, how. Good, good." The baddest [worst] thing is to strike the body of your enemy before he is dead in the heat of battle. To pull up an Elk Soldier arrow or a crooked lance or to ride down with a war-bonnet [with] everybody firing at you alone are [is] about equal to it, to get a war-bonnet and do those other things you will attain the chief's road right away. A good many people [73] get killed that way. When you hear the volley and see him riding alone into the smoke and dressed with his war bonnet on, you say that man is not afraid to die.[51]

Marrying [a] Younger Sister

If a man has a daughter married to another man he observes his son-in-law's conduct. If he is [a] good worker, never gets angry, does not draw back from work, then if he has a younger daughter he may give her to his son-in-law to marry as a prairie gift. If his son-in-law draws from work, is cross to his wife, and does not work well, then he holds his daughter and does not allow her to marry him. If a married man dies and has a brother without a wife, his brother observes the widow and may marry her, not soon, but maybe after a year or so if he wants to.

---

51 Reciting war deeds or coups is called *qóitąujétjàu* by the Kiowas.

[74]
Thunder and Lightning

L = "Lightning." Two people prayed to the T [Thunder] or Shooting Bird when they saw the storm cloud approaching. "Hold up, stop, wait. Stop coming this way. Do not shoot down here and kill somebody. Shoot upwards into the clouds." They had no medicine to stop it. One thing I saw once, a man was struck by lightning and died and they put him in cold water and kept him there a long time. All of a sudden he jerked one leg then the other and after a while an arm and caught his nurse by the hair. Then they took him out and he recovered. It was old chief Lone Wolf of the Kiowas and [I] knew one other man too.

T [Thunder] was called Big Throat Man ever since. I was a boy and have heard that more. Whenever I saw rain blowing this way and heard loud voices coming out of it, it sounded like a man with a big throat like a man's voice as loud as the sound of the discharge of the Revelle [reveille] gun over the guardhouse just like a shot and that is what the sign name is for it. I have seen persons killed by lightning. They were dead just as if they had been shot. I have heard the old men discussing it and two sides were maintained. One said we are blind people. We do not know that it up there above, maybe somebody up there shot him with a gun. The other side maintained [75] that it arose from the content of two clouds but we do not really know anything about it except we hear the noise, see the flash, and the man lies dead. A long time ago near the head of the Canadian a Kiowa man saw far up in the sky an immense bird. It had the appearance of an immense eagle with a big throat, wings about fifty feet across (tip to tip) it was soaring in the air with its head turned to one side and its eyes were shut, every time it opened its eyes a bolt of lightning darted out of each eye and set fire to the grass. Bolts came from the wings also. This was very long ago. I did not see it but one of the long ago men saw it and told the people. Since then it is called the Thunder Bird or Shooting Bird.

[76]
Burials

If a Kiowa dies in a lodge (i.e., from sickness), he is buried in a deep good grave in the ground with his head to the west. Women and children the same way, and if a man is killed in battle, that is all right, that is good. Everybody wants to attain the position of a chief. Every man has a die [death] road given [to] them long ago. Some will die of sickness and some will get killed. We do not know how it will be, but it is all right to be killed in battle, it is not bad. Kiowas, Comanches, and Kiowa-Apaches have the same burial customs. The Cheyennes and Arapahoes bury alike, but different from the Kiowa[s]. They put their dead bodies up in trees. The Caddos bury in a small crib like a log house to fit the body with a flat roof. The Wichitas bury in a house made of logs in this shape. Caddos and Wichitas have confirmed this.

Abandoning Old People

I have never seen an old person abandoned and have only heard of one in our history (Kiowas). An old man had no family or relatives of any kind, and he got so old and weak he could not travel. The buffalo were many days travel away and the old man said, "I am tired out and cannot travel anymore. I am too old, leave me here, it is too far for me," and they left him there alone, abandoned him on [the] Staked Plains beyond [the] head of Red River [in Texas]. He had no relatives to look after him and it was too far. All the others are treated very well. You saw how that old woman "Mud," Domat's great-grandmother, was treated. She was one hundred years old, foolish, when she died two years ago (died in 1895). She couldn't walk or do anything for herself, but they took good care of her until she died. Her breast collapsed, she died of old age.

[77]

Holding Camp

When the Kiowas did not make a Sun Dance in the summer as happened sometimes they usually separated into bands, and went into different parts of the country, unless they secretly heard that somebody was going to attack them. Then the camp was held together. A long time ago this happened. I did not see it, I heard about it from the old people. Tohausen was the chief and held everybody. It was the summer after the Osage cut the heads off the Kiowas [1833, and thus 1834] and they were afraid of Cheyennes and Osages. The camp was on Walnut Creek, beyond the end of the mountains. Tohausen gave the pipe to the Black Leggins band of soldiers [military society] and they were holding the camp. Some soldiers counted the lodges every day. One day they moved the camp and at sundown they counted the lodges and one was missing. The soldiers caught up their horses, saddled up, and went back to the old camp, and looked at the trails the next morning and found the trail of one lodge going off by itself to the Southwest, in the direction of the Quahada Comanche camp on the head of the S.F. [South Fork of the] Red River. They followed it all day and until noon the next day and then they saw them on a ridge in front, caught up with them, and found there was one man with several [78] women and children. The soldiers asked the man where he was going and he said he wanted to go to the Quahada camp at the edge of the Staked Plains, and they said no, Tohausen decided before that they must hold the camp and he must go back. He said, "No, I am going to the Comanches." So the soldiers shot his horse and whipped him and killed all his horses, put women and children and man on foot, and drove them back to camp. It is dangerous to run away from a big camp. They held them during the summer and turned them loose in the fall when the danger of big war parties was over.[52]

Tohausen

Iseeo

Tohausen was the biggest chief the Kiowas ever had. He controlled everybody, the Cheyennes, Arapahoes, Kiowa[s], Comanches, and Apaches.[53] He was a wise chief, never got angry at anybody, always pleasant to the women and children. He was my father's uncle and I knew him well. He died of old age on Cimarron [Bison Bull] River near where it crosses [the] Kansas line. He was [of a] very old age and he loved the white people. He had been to Washington and never forgot what they told him there. He died the spring of the year of the Timbered Mountain Treaty [later winter-spring 1867], when the grass was three inches high. One time before the Osages cut the heads off the Kiowas; Tohausen was a [79] young man and was down in Chihuahua with a big band of young men driving horses north. One day they were attacked by Mexican soldiers and all but fifteen of them abandoned the horses and ran off. Tohausen remained behind with the others all chiefs. They got down in a place that had high walls of stone on both sides. It was at the head of a stream at the very head of which there was a cave with a spring in it. The soldiers surrounded them at once and killed two horses and one man. The others got back in the

---

52 This is probably the incident in which a man named Peah-bo (Fâbòjè or Large Mustang) aka Tááuiqî (Many Wives) attempted to leave when a closed camp rule had been declared and was punished by the policing society. He was the father of Taybodal and is known for having ten wives, some say concurrently.

53 While Dohausen/Tohausen (Jòhâusàn) was a very influential leader and the last tribal chief of the Kiowas in prereservation times, this statement provided by a relative is exaggerated, as neighboring tribes were clearly not under his rule.

cave so they could not see them but the soldiers shut up the mouth of the cave and had them in a pocket with a cave in the upper and [image of an elongated u-shaped opening to the left with a *c* marked in the bottom of the right end denoting the cave] with straight walls and no timber. The next day the horses and the men swelled up and smelt very badly and they had nothing to swallow but water. Every now and then during the day the soldiers would fire a valley at the mouth of the cave and they would put wood on the edges of the walls during the day and make fires with it at night to see the mouth of the cave by. One day they could hear wagons coming and a Mexican called down to them they were near several forts and more soldiers were coming. Tohausen said, "Try hard, men, and we will all get out of here" and encouraged [80] [the] others. They were all chiefs and he knew them well. On the 9th day they had become emaciated and weak and the Mexicans began to throw rocks down on them and were going to cover over the mouth of the cave with stones and let them starve to death. Tohausen said, "I have decided to try and bolt out, escape, which one of you will go first? If some of us lie dead on the prairie that is all right, two or three will get away and carry the news to the Kiowa village, how we died fighting. Which one will go first?" No one answered him for a long time then he said, "Nobody says he will go first so I will go first myself, but I was going to go last." Then one man said he would go first so they waited until dark and one at a time crept to the end of the wall at the mouth and were within a few feet of the soldiers. Tohausen had made them all cut strings from their leggings to tie their bows to their wrists so they would not lose them if they should fall down in the rush. He then told them to go ahead and they made a bolt right into the midst of the soldiers, some of whom could not fire on account of their friends, and the Kiowas got most of them through the middle of the soldiers in the darkness and stopped in a ravine close by. When Tohausen counted them he found three missing. They heard the soldiers galloping by looking for them and they kept quiet for a while then made off in a diagonal [81] direction and escaped.[54] Tohausen was Honameatah's (Charging Man) father. He was a big chief. Every chief the Kiowas have had since were behind, Big Bow, Satanta, Satanke, Stumbling Bear, Lone Wolf, all of them behind. He was a rare [special?] man like Honameahtah.

---

54 This incident is the siege at Hueco Tanks, northeast of present-day El Paso, Texas, which occurred in 1839 (Meadows 2008:68–79). The event is well documented: it happened after and not before the Osage attack at Cutthroat Mountain (1833), as referenced in the account.

Ledger image of Hueco Tanks Fight (vol. I, p. 80).
Courtesy of Fort Sill National Historic Landmark
and Museum Archive and Wade Popp.

Names

[Paul Tsaitkopeta]
Woman's Heart the Kiowa chief adopted me and one day while he was asleep he saw two lines of men in front of him facing each other at a short distance apart with one man in the space between. The two ranks were getting ready to fight each other. Both sides wanted the man in the middle because whichever side he took would win, that one which beat the other. And Woman's Heart went to see who it was and it was I and he called "Tsait-compt" or Mountain Bear because the bear is so strong that the side he takes will win. His medicine told him that would be a good name for me.[55]

Omens

On the warpath if the leader dreams, or one of the Ten Medicine keepers if he is with them sees a fire in his sleep they turn back and go home because there will be bad luck. That fire will burn you. Or if he sees a river very full that will be bad luck and we turn back. That river will drown you. If he sees an eagle lying dead and goes up and gets some feathers then you will strike your enemy and you will paint your face black [in victory].

---

55 Paul Tsaitkopeta or Sétqópjè (Mountain Bear), born in 1852, was half Cheyenne and half Pawnee and was raised among the Kiowas (Kiowa Family Record 1901: Fam. 241).

Hueco Tanks, cave at the rear right of the canyon.
Author's photo.

[82]
Guarding/Holding the Buffalo
When the Kiowas were all in a large village, they guarded/held the buffalo. This was because if they did not do it men would sneak off before light in different directions and drive the buffalo far away from the village, and they would be played out looking for them. This is done by the soldiers. If they see anybody going to chase the buffalo they stop him. Then when the right time comes all go out, the soldiers [a military society] in front, until they get near where the buffalo are grazing when they make a long line. The soldiers scattered along the front, holding it [the line] back and restraining their impatience until all are ready, when the principal man gives the signal and they charge the buffalo. Everybody kills the buffalo that way and you get enough to eat.[56]

---

56 Regarding the policing of closed hunts, one of the Kiowa bynames for the military societies, known as Yàpfàhêgàu (Temporary Police/Guards), was *qíthádàu* "men stoppers" (Meadows 1999:71).

They cut up the meat, enough to last usually for ten or twelve days or more. By that time, the buffalo have recovered from their fright and are back near the village again, and they do it again. If they use guns or pistols it frightens all the buffalo for a long way around. They hear it and they leave, and all the old men advised them to use only bows and arrows. In that way the buffalo would be back around the camp in two days. Small camps did not hold buffalo. When they were holding buffalo the soldiers would whip anybody who went out alone to shoot deer or anything else. A buffalo, when scared, will usually run about three miles then walk for about four more and then his fright is quelled and he eats grass. The elk and the big bear [83] do not get tired and stop, they are strong. They keep going. The bear goes over mountain after mountain before he stops.

Surrounds, Driving Buffalo into Corrals, Etc.

In old times when we had no horses, we used to get up early and get together men, women, and children and make a big surround. When we saw buffalo grazing we went away around it [them] on foot and gradually closed in the buffalo running around and around inside of the enclosure without trying to bolt through until they were tired out and stood still, panting, when the men shot and killed them with arrows. Sometimes they drove them over high bluffs by surrounding them and broke their legs, and then killed them at the foot of the bluffs with arrows, and sometimes they made a corral of logs at the base of the bluff. They had wings made like a funnel to get the buffalo to the edge of the bluff. The wings were made of logs like a man, big thick logs.

They used to put on wolf skins and creep up on their hands and knees on the leeward side until they got within good range and shoot the buffalo with arrows. I have seen a Comanche kill antelope this way. He had an antelope hide with horns on his head. The [antelope] skin was tied by the hind legs around his wrist and he would creep toward the antelope. He had his arms striped with white paint and his legs too. When the antelope look at him, they think he is another coming toward them, and look down to graze. He [84] stops every little while and puts down his head as if grazing until he gets near enough to shoot. The Mescalero Apaches like that way. There are a great many antelope on the Staked Plains' flat country and the antelope can see a man coming a long way off. Sometimes the Kiowas had corrals made of trees near where a point of a hill juts against a round cut back in a creek and swings out from the door of that. This was not done often, only when the antelope were seen in the right place. A man would watch the place and when he saw the antelope grazing in the right place he would tell them in the village and the people would surround and drive them in.

Ponkas

There used to be some men the old men knew in the north. They platted their hair on either side like a Kiowa but the hair on top of their heads was cut so it hung over their foreheads in a bushy bang. The old men told us about them and one time they came to the Kiowa camp (about 1883) when we were making a Sun Dance on Washita [River] above Cloud Chief. They helped us make it, they had been moved down northeast of here, and I hear they have gone north again. Yes, I think that is their name, Ponka, but I will not be sure. Their sign name is "Bushy Bang Men." Our old people knew them up north.[57]

[85]

Mescal [Peyote]

Mescal is good for a man with weak lungs and for other sickness. We do not give a weak man much, only four or five [buttons]. They are chewed soft, rolled into a ball, and swallowed. We give him more if he is strong, six or twelve. He lies down on the bed and pretty soon he feels it all over like whiskey or beer. You feel nervous at first but in half an hour that passes away. Sometimes it does not agree with you and you must vomit, but you must try to hold it down. But sometimes you cannot keep it. Some men eat forty or fifty in one night. I eat twelve. I do not want to get too much. Quanah once eat [ate] one hundred. He did not know about mescal. He heard of it. He heard of it [and] he counted one hundred in the lodge in front of him and said to the mescal, "I hear[d] about you. Make you make me see some medicine. I [will] eat one hundred. If you do not help me and make me see some medicine I do [will] not eat your flesh anymore." He gave them to the others to chew soft for him and to pray for him and he eat [ate] one hundred and he saw a man standing in front of him dressed

---

57 The Kiowa name for the Poncas is Áultǫ́àulkàuiqìhǎgàu. The Kiowas knew them in the far north and during their movement to Oklahoma and subsequent return to the north, so this account appears to refer to the Nez Perces, whom the Kiowas called Áulqáujôigàu, some of whom were relocated to Oklahoma in 1877 and visited the Kiowa Sun Dance in 1883. The Kiowas named it the Nez Perce Sun Dance. The Nez Perces were returned to the Colville Reservation in Idaho in 1885 (Mooney 1898:351; Walker 1998:434–35; Meadows 2013).

in buckskin, yellow buckskin, with a feather in his hair very pretty. And he looked at the man and saw that it was himself and he heard the mescal say, "Look at him, Quanah. I [will] make him chief. He [is] not afraid of me, I [will] make [86] him lead the people." He [was] not [a] chief [at] that time only [a] poor weak man and now he is chief of [the] Comanches.

Sometime next day after you eat too much mescal you [do] not [get] any headache. You [are] lazy, you want to sleep and after that you feel good everywhere. We put sage around the lodge and not any blanket to sit on, that is the mescal custom and everywhere there is medicine we use sage. That is the old custom. We do not know why. We use it with the Taime and with Ten Medicines and everywhere we make medicine. We make a worn shaped place in the lodge and put a wakoare in the middle, the father wakoare [father peyote button] to look at it. We pray to it and it hear us. We say to it, "God made you for my like [liking] just like meat to eat for our life and mescal hear[s] us. He speak to the Great God for us and the Comanches to the Sun. We say the Great God made for you our life. We do not know him. We cannot see where he is. Maybe you know him and ask him to give you more power for our life." We tell him, "You tell God to give us good life, let out children grow up and live good. Let us die of old age. We pray for the Secretary (Interior), for President, for Genr. [General?], for Congress, anybody who work and decide about this country. We say give them good thought, kind hearts, and true things to help us."

[87] We pray for General [Nelson] Miles. We pray for you every day because you help us. We say that to the mescal, "Tell that to the Great God" and the mescal hear us.

Heidsick got the mescal road from the Esaquitas (Mescalero Apaches) when we make [made] peace with them when he was a young man. The Esaquitas had it long ago but they fight us and we not know that road. Kiowas [did] not have that before. Heidsick is 70 years old now.[58]

If I eat it, it makes me feel light. I eat it because I have consumption [tuberculosis] and it keeps me alive. It makes me feel light and I walk a long way good. That is what makes Quanah so smart like a white man. He eat [ate] this medicine and it make [made] him very strong [and] wise.

Sunboy's son went crazy and is dead because he made fun of the mescal. He make [made] fun of it—to tell [he told a] lie to the Great God. You must think of what you want true and not otherwise, to [of] what you ask

---

58 The Kiowa Family Record (1901: Fam. 65) reports Heidsick as eighty-four years of age and born in 1816. His age as reported here appears to be off by several years, as Scott did not arrive at Fort Sill until 1889.

for the Great God know[s] what is in your heart. You must believe it. If a man have [has] consumption only one year it cures him, if he have [has] it more [longer] it cannot cure him. It makes [him] feel light not heavy. It makes him feel new a long way distance fast.

[88] We chew the mescal a little at a time and soften it and when it gets soft it is easy to chew. We spit out the juice like tobacco but it does not hurt to swallow it. We hold it out to the mescal four times and then swallow it, rubbing it down in the breast stomach. We get four first and when we want anymore we tell the leader, "I want two" or eight or how many you want and the leader talks to the mescal and it hear[s] us just like your church. Nobody talk[s] in church but the preacher. A young man stays in front of the room and keeps a small fire in it to make a light so we can see and in the middle of the night he tells him to bring in the water and puts it at the entrance of the room and stays there himself. And the leader takes a handful of cedar, throws it on the fire, and says, "Father, you give us this tree 'cedar,' you love it. Every other tree dies and grass but this tree does not die. In winter you keep it always green, it does not drop off its leaves in the fall. I think you love it. You give it a good road and that water by which we live the whole world uses water. I want you to send down your spirit into that water and when we drink it to wash us pure." The same things are done at sunrise only a woman takes the place of the young man and the leader says, "That woman by whom we live. If there is no woman there will be no more people living on the earth. I [89] want you to take care of that woman."

There are usually about eighteen men in the lodge. Some of them are dressed very well and many have a fan or a bunch of eagle feathers to look through at the mescal. In a case (Aug. 1897) seen there was a handkerchief spread near the mescal outside the moon [moon-shaped earthen alter] on which were placed two prayer books gotten from some missionaries. On top of the prayer books was a whistle made from the wing-bone of an eagle, which was used in bringing in the water. Besides the prayer books was a silver watch in the buckskin case, which was consulted from time to time by the leader. This and the prayer books were very modern innovations. When the water was brought in, the leader Elk Tongue put two eagle feathers across the water pail, blew his whistle, and prayed for a reason. Then he put the tops of the feathers in the water, taking them out with a flick which threw the surplus water against the sides of the lodge above the men,* then fanned himself first, then his acolyte ("Caddo") then the rest of the assemblage, sprinkling a little of the water on each of

> * He touched the four (cardinal points) different sides of the pail inside of the water with tips of feathers and then the bottom before he flicked the water.

them and then drank [some].[59] Then his acolyte on his right did the same. Then the many leaders left and it come [came] all around to the acolyte again and there was a recess at intervals during the singing and drumming. (See p. 114.)

[continued from 114] The leader made a prayer, pulling his hands out palm to the front and pointing upward then bringing it down extended and touching the earth. Sometimes one of the learned men did this who were qualified to be leaders at other mescal ceremonies. Sometimes the man who tended the fire would put his hands out over the fire toward the mescal and would take a cigarette and hand it to some of the older men who then smoked it for a while and handed it to the leader who finished it and threw the stump into the fire. (This was a special feature first by the fire tender in the middle of the night, then by a well-dressed girl who was brought in just before sunrise to bring in the water.)

Every now and then the fire tender took a small broom and brushed the light ashes off the moon and outside [around the crescent]. All around the fireplace and outside the room were kept very neat and clean. No one was allowed to go out of the lodge without permission of the leaders who always gave permission, but compelled each person who came in to go all around the fireplace from left to right before going out. The utmost ceremony, reverential attitude, and absolute decorum were observed by all. The women were present during the evening.

[90]

Many Scalps Medicines or Ten Medicines

The Ten Medicines or Many Scalps Medicines are very old, as old as the Kiowa tribe, and when they disappear not only will the Kiowas come to an end, but the whole world.[60] There used to be only nine for [a] long time but Tsait-ape "Afraid Of Bears" used to work for the nine medicine keepers and give them a blanket or something good he had.[61] Different

---

59 "Caddo" most likely refers to Caddo Mausape, born in 1868 (Kiowa Family Record 1901: Fam. 192). Màusép (Pierced Noses) is the Kiowa name for the Caddos. Mausape was full Kiowa, however, so the name likely is based on something other than descent.
60 Áulbéáuihyằ (Many Scalps or One of Many Scalps) is one Kiowa name for the Ten Medicine Bundles.
61 This statement is significant, because Kiowas have maintained for many decades that there have always been ten bundles. For another example of the increase in the number of tribal bundles, see McAllister (1965).

medicines he worked for and after a long time, the keepers said, "Tsait-ape is a good man, he is kind to us and now we going to help him, How [are] we going to do it? We are not medicine men; we [are] only men. Suppose we pray for him and afterwards it is not so, it does not come out as we ask. What are we going to do?"

And after a long council it was decided that each of the nine should give him a scalp and a piece of his medicine and their ritual and they did it. He had it, and there was [were] ten medicines, and his son Tsait-ape has it now.[62] Tsait-ape got to be a medicine man, a doctor. These others do not understand that, they are more like preachers to pray for people, not to cure them. At first there were eight, then the boy split and made nine of them. Tsait-ape's was made. That made ten. Now Poor Buffalo and Kohmar-ty's are burned up in fires when their tipis burned up, and we have only eight. If you want to use sweat house medicine, you know how, you have seen it. You make a sweat house, a good one. Cover it over and put a buffalo bull's [91]skull on a mound in front of it, looking into the door, the door facing the east. Then you go to the man's lodge who keeps it and there it is tied on the lodge pole opposite the door [on the west side], and you say, "Grandmother (Taidlee) help me. I come for you, Grandmother, I make a house for you, and take you there. I want you to have mercy on me and give me a good life."[63] Whenever any kind of medicine is made, the door is always to the east and we always go in and around by the left [south] of the door. We do not go in the cold wind [north] side, the sun goes that side (left), our hearts are on that side and when you go out we keep on around, we do not turn back. At the back of the lodge you put a row of dried buffalo chips on top [of] some with sage and lay a filled pipe along on these chips and you take it [the bundle] down to the sweat house and you carry it four times around to the left and stand in front and push it toward the house, as if approaching the house, and then you go in and

---

62 This refers to the father of Sit-a-pah-ta (Sétáfètjàui or Afraid Of The Bear, 1844–1923) the later leader of the Kiowa Ghost Dance. His father is listed as Ko-le-ah-ty (Qólyìjè or Shell Gorget) (Kiowa Family Record 1901: Fam. 223), and on the Kiowa Tribal Census (1881) as Koodle-ye-hay (Shell Breast Plate).

63 There has long been a debate over whether one of the names for the Ten Medicine Bundles is Tàlyîdàui (Paternal Grandmother Medicine) or Tàlyìdàui (Boy Medicine). Collectively they are known as Tàlyópcàu (Paternal Grandmothers). Statements by Kintadl, Jack Doyeto, and others in the 1935 Santa Fe Anthropological Field School Notes indicate that paternal grandmothers is correct. Parker McKenzie also related how as a youth Frank Given, a bundle keeper whose allotment was beside theirs, frequently ate meals with his family. Before the meals he led the prayers with the address of "Tàlyîdàui" (Paternal Grandmother) in Kiowa. Parker McKenzie to the author, 1991–98.

put it down on the west side and the keeper must come, he cannot refuse you. He comes and lights a pipe. He is like a leader or a priest. He lights a pipe and holds it toward the Ten Medicines and says, "Smoke it first. It is your house. It was made for you." Then to the (earth) mother, to the "cold wind," to the "warm wind," then to "Sun," and hands it to the man who made the house. The house maker works for the keeper so he prays for him. He will not refuse to go. He prays for him. Before going to war, some young men who were ambitious worked for the Ten Medicines so they would help them, keep them from being killed, enable them to strike their enemy first, to attain a chieftainship. That is what all of them are hungry for and they made sweat houses often before they went to war, also when they came back.

The keepers are like priests, not doctors. They pray for him, that young man. They do not ever get angry or say bad things; they are [92] peaceable men. They never whip their wives. They do not do anything bad so their Medicine is more apt to listen to them, and the keeper says, "Now you listen. Now you hear me. These young men are going on [the] warpath. Make their enemies weak. I want you to help them get black paint." Just before an attack a man chooses which one of the Ten Medicines he wants back at home and says to it, "Now today, you help me. If I kill my enemy and take a scalp, I give it to you now. You help me today." And when he gets back he has already given it to the Medicine, it belongs to it. We do not bead the scalp for that. Sometimes [we] cut it in four, sometimes in three pieces. A white man's scalp is usually thrown away, it is not good, the hair is too short. A white woman's is sometimes used when the hair is good. When the Medicine gets too many scalps they are taken up to the top of a mountain and given to the sun. Then they are thrown away carefully (i.e., tied on a tree and left there). We want Indian scalps with long hair; Utes, Pawnee[s], or Navajo[s]. No one ever strikes the Medicine Keepers. The Medicine does not like that. He does not talk bad to anybody, if he does it, he will not live long. Something will happen to him. If he gets angry at anybody he swallows it. Care must be taken not to let fire drop on him. He is afraid of bears, that is his medicine custom.[64]

Sometimes if a man wishes to worship [93] he gets some cloth or enough calico for a dress or something good that he wants to give to the Medicine and he enters as before and says to it, "Grandmother, I want you to take care of my life, my everyday life. I want you to bless me, to

---

64 This suggests that the Kiowa taboo concerning bears was related to the Ten Medicine Bundles and in turn to their keepers. At what date it became a relatively pan-Kiowa taboo is unclear.

make my children grow up strong. I want you to give them good life," and he puts the present on the Medicine. If the present is a horse, a stick is put on the Medicine, and the keeper takes it up and puts his hand on the ground, rubs his hand over the present and over himself, and puts his hand on the ground, rubs his hand over the present and over himself, and puts it back, and those things belong to the medicine keeper. That horse belongs to the keeper. Nobody touches him until after the keeper touches him and then anybody can ride him. That is our custom.

Sometimes a man says to the keeper, "I am going on the warpath. If I come back safe I make for you a house" and they usually give presents when the sweat house is made to the keeper, and he prays for them. When a man dreams about a sweat house, when he wakes he says, "All right I will make it for you," because they believe about it.

When the Ten Medicine Keeper goes to war they take out of the medicine bundle some medicine that is worn around their necks and under [the] arm by a string, like red beans. Hey take it off every time before they drink and afterwards put it on again. When they return from war it is put back in the [94] bundle. The Ten Medicines are all alike, they have scalps with them. They have rings for the ring game (and possibly/probably a mountain sheep horn) and some other things I do not know about. The Medicine Keeper himself does not know what is inside.*

[side note] Originally there were mountain sheep horn spoons with each medicine used to dip water to put on the hot stones, but they have been lost with possibly one exception. Domat is said to have one. Koh-mar-ty [Komarty] maybe was very anxious to buy mine.[65]

When we take a scalp we say we give it to the Medicine. We give it to our Grandmother, we worship it. It is kept tied on a lodge pole opposite the door [west side] in a clean lodge. If you make a sweat house all right you go into the keeper's lodge and get his Medicine and put it down in the sweat house. He must come and pray for you. Anybody can go in if there is room, just like your church, and after it is over the keeper takes it home.

[side note: It] goes over the shoulder and neck and [is] held in [the] right hand.

We do not let white men know about that Many Scalps Medicine. We have been made Indians by the power above. We have red skins and long

---

65 Scott is known to have commissioned ten horn spoons made from big horn sheep that he gave to the Ten Medicine Keepers. Towana Spivey, personal communication to the author, Mar. 7, 2010. Kiowa bundle keepers have also stated this to me independently. Parsons (1929:110) reports that a consultant (probably Mark Keahbone) stated: "General Scott, before he went to the Spanish American war, gave some capes to tsaidetali." I believe that Parsons misheard "capes" for "cups."

black hair. He made us that way, and you white man with different customs. He gave them to us. We are different. He did not make any mistakes in his work. He made us wear a blanket and buckskin clothes, he knew what he wanted and when the white man makes us cut our hair, wear his clothes, and change our customs, he (the above power) does not like it. It changes his work. It makes him [95] angry, by making a white man where he wants an Indian. That is the reason we keep very secret about the Many Scalps Medicines because they are our life. If these are all lost, then that will be the end of the world, and if white people hear about it maybe they will take it away from us. The above power gave them to us for our life, we live by it.

Before going to war the man makes a good sweat house and the keeper prays for them. He says, "Now listen, Grandmother, these men are going on the warpath, make their enemies weak. I want you to help them to get black paint."[66] Sometimes a man does something crazy and the Medicine Keeper asks him about it, and he stretches his hand towards the Medicine (wherever it may be) and says, "Look at me, Grandmother, I [did] not tell [a] lie, I [did] not do that," and everybody believes him. If he tells [a] lie to the Medicine he will not live long, he will die soon.

The Cheyennes have four Medicine Arrows they use in that way. The man touches them. These arrows are very old, they have stone heads, two of red stone and two of black, and were captured once by the Pawnees. Every two or three years they make the Medicine Arrows, about the time of the Sun Dance. I have been in the Cheyenne village while it was done, [96] they were all collected for the Sun Dance, and they were camped just as the Kiowas camp for their Taime. Every two or three years the feathers and sinew wrappings of these arrows are worn out and must be renewed in the "Arrow Making." Only this is done, the same heads and shafts have been used since the Cheyennes originated. They grew up with them.

The arrow makers go into a lodge at night, sing arrow songs, feather [re-fletch] the arrows, and come out the next morning and ride around the lodges with the bundle containing the arrows on the arm and the ceremony is over. When a man who keeps the arrow dies, his son takes them. If he has no son, then his brother, the man who keeps them, is like the keepers of Ten Medicines. He never gets angry, never does anything bad, always has a good road. Young Whirlwind's son keeps them now. Little Man [is] his name.

I know the Medicine arrows prevent smallpox. When I was about ten years old [ca. 1859 if referring to Iseeo], Cheyennes, Arapahoes, Kiowas,

---

66 Black paint represented successfully obtaining vengeance.

Comanches, and Apaches were living about the headwaters of the Arkansas near a soldier fort and one day a Kiowa war party went over the mountains to the southwest, looking for Utes. They reached some Mexican settlement over there and saw lots of people dead of the smallpox and they returned home. [97] After they came home, a man had a sudden pain in the back as if he had been shot there, fell down, and died in about three days. That was the beginning. The Kiowas, Comanches, and Apaches were together south of the Arkansas. A few who had been vaccinated at the fort (eight or ten) did not get sick. I took the disease but some medicine took pity on me. I did not have it badly, most everyone else had it.

They got frightened and scattered. The smallpox came when it was a little cold and lasted until the redbirds came out and then stopped, and when we came together that spring for the Sun Dance there were only one third of the Kiowas left, that had been there before they died. While it lasted everyday and every night also the Comanches and Apaches they died everywhere, and were left where they were.

The Cheyennes and Arapahoes kept together north of the Arkansas. They heard that we had the smallpox and sent word to us not to come to their camp, and their "Leggins Soldiers" were ordered to keep all Kiowas away from camp.[67] The Medicine Arrow Keeper rode around the camp four times every day with the arrows and they did not get the smallpox. We met the Cheyennes and Arapahoes the next spring and the Medicine Arrows had kept the smallpox away from them all Kiowas and Cheyenne[s].

[98]
CHOLERA

[probably Iseeo]
[I] know that. When my father was a boy the smallpox came and killed a great many Kiowas and since then the "Cramps" [cholera] all over killed more than any. A man would lie just as you and I are now, well all over, and the cramps would come on him and he would die like a beef shot in the head. I do not know when it occurred. It is marked on your calendar. It took off more Kiowas than any other disease.

The Kiowas were making a Sun Dance and were about to scatter the next day. The first man died about 9 o'clock that night. The next about 10 o'clock and so then they crowded about them in astonishment that they should die so suddenly. Maybe [he was] bewitched. Well one moment when the cramps would strike them and dead the next. Forty or fifty

---

67 This probably refers to one of the Cheyenne military societies.

would die in a single day. No attempt was made to bury them. Many bodies were lying on creeks. They died on the march and were abandoned where they died. It lasted for half a month and then stopped. Only a very few of the Kiowas remained after it. I think Taybodle saw it. I have often heard him tell about it.[68]

[99]

Origin [of] Bear Lodge Tower

Before the Kiowas came south, they were camped on a stream in the far north. There were a great many bears about there. Lots of them and one day the children were playing about at some distance from the lodges and were chased by some bears. The children ran toward the village but the bears being about to overtake them, they jumped up on a low rock lying there about three feet high and ten feet square at [its] base. And a boy prayed to the rock and said, "Rock take pity on us," and the rock began to rise, elongate upward, and when the bears jumped at it they broke their claws and fell back. The rock rising [rose] higher and higher until it got to be very high and the children were far out of the reach of the bears. The bear marks of their claws are there yet, just like the side of the Medicine Bluffs [near Fort Sill]. We have never heard how the children got down again. No Kiowa who is alive has ever seen that rock, but the old men have told about it. It is very far in the north where the Kiowas used to live. It is a single rock with scratched sides rising up straight. There is no other rock like it in the whole country. It is very high and the sides scratched by the bears.[69] There are no trees on it, but there is grass on top. This is undoubtedly the (continued on [p.] 103) [103] Mato Ti of the Sioux. Mato a grizzly bear—tipi a lodge = Bear's Lodge. This was renamed "The Bear Lodge" by Capt. G K Warren, Corps Engineers, on the maps of his survey of the Black Hills of Dakota in 1855.

* Reynolds 1859—p. 32. Far in the distance, up the valley of the Shayenne, the exp [expedition] also noted the singular peak of Bear Lodge rising like an enormous tower and from its resemblance to an Indian Lodge suggesting the origin of its title.

Kiowas call the Bear lodge = Tso-aa = Stone Wood—when they came to look they found the bear's claws all around there turned into stone.

---

68 This probably refers to the great cholera epidemic of 1849.
69 The Kiowa name of Devil's Tower is Xòâi (variously translated as Rock Tree, Rock That Grew Upward, and Up a Rock). For Kiowa accounts of the origin of Devil's Tower, see Mooney (1898:160, 428); Boyd (1983:87–93); and Meadows (2008:269, 2010:321–23). See Scott (n.d.a:I:103, chapter 4 in this volume), which lists Stone Wood (Tree).

Years afterwards [in 1876] Col. R I [Richard Irving] Dodge 11th Infantry changed its name without warrant to "Devil's Tower" but the name "Bear Lodge" is much the more ancient and effitable [effable?]. The rock is a laccolith of columnias phonolite and is most remarkable. The Belle Fourche River runs at the base and it is masked by the Bear Lodge Mountains on one side, the Little Missouri Buttes on the other, and can only be seen from up and down the valley of the Belle Fourche River which is called "Bear Lodge" Creek by the Sioux as far as the entrance of its tributary, the "Red Water." I myself have seen the top of the Bear Lodge from the top of the short Pine Hills, ninety miles away, looking up the main valley of the Belle Fourche River and across the Little Missouri divide.

Dodge also stated [in] his work on the exploration of the Black Hills [in] 1876 that the name for the detached mountain on the east side of the Black Hills, "Bear Butte," was a misnomer, that it should be called "Bare Butte being devoid of vegetation," but this is true only of the rock slides as there are stunted pines on every side of it. [104] The peak was named first by the Sioux "Matopaha," which means Grizzly Bear Butte, and was so laid down by Warren before Dodge ever saw that country. This is one of the Medicine Places. Little Chief's band of Northern Cheyennes was camped there in the summer of 1878 with the 7th Cavalry on their way to the Indian Territory and the celebrated Ben Clark "Red Neck" came there under orders from General Sheridan to go down with them as guide and interpreters. These Indians then started that. There was a big medicine in the Main Butte that dead Cheyennes entered, the smaller Butte and then into the larger one, where there was a council of medicine men always going on. That if a man wanted help he climbed to the top of Bear Butte and remained there four days and nights without eating, drinking, or sleeping. The medicine would have mercy on him and would keep [i.e., help] him to have success on the warpath, strike his enemy first and bring back horses. That if he ate or drank or slept, the medicine would not help him. There were many evidences of the presence of persons about the Butte such as peculiar piles of stone on [105] top in which the Indians had sat pieces of calico and red flannel tied to the trees (low scrubby pines) and the way up there were a number of trees that had flat stones placed in the forks and the tree had grown around the stones leaving only the ends sticking out.[70]

---

70   Scott (n.d.b: MS 2932, Box 2, Kiowa, Origin of the Bear Lodge Tower) also gives the translation "Tree Rock" for the name Tso-aa. He also notes that "seven little girls were playing about": "This is one of the most important medicine places of the Cheyenne and Sioux. The Kiowa do not speak of it—in fact I have never heard a Kiowa mention it."

I was told by a Blackfoot Sioux Indian at Standing Rock in 1879 that he had made a vigil on that butte thirty years before and had put a stone in the forks of a tree on his way up to commemorate the occasion and that that was a custom of his people. When the Cheyennes were camped at Bear Butte an (1873—July) eclipse of the sun was expected and the Indians were told to look out for it on a certain day and when it came to pass they were greatly astonished.

The Kiowas at Fort Sill were told to expect an eclipse of the sun in July 1897 and when a partial eclipse took place they could not understand how the white man could find it out beforehand.

The "Deer's ears" were called "Antelope Horn Hills" by the Sioux because they were arranged like the A's [antelope's] horns with prongs. The tops of these were sacred places.

[100]
Angry Lone Wolf, Stumbling Bear, and Kicking Bird
When one man gets very angry at another he sometime says, "I give you to the sun" because long ago we worshipped the sun and sometimes gave whatever they wanted to give to the sun, maybe a blanket, a buckskin, or a piece of their flesh to the sun and never took it back again.* They did not use it anymore and I think, "I give you to the sun. You never come back anymore." Sometimes they would say, "You are a poor weak little fellow" which means you are not able to fight me.

One day when they were good men Lone Wolf (Wolf = Qouy, One = Parkoe) was riding with his cousin "Stumbling Bear," "Settin Gea," and another man and Lone Wolf was making fun of Stumbling Bear and laughing at him. Lone Wolf said to Stumbling Bear, "You are a poor little fellow," and Stumbling Bear said, "What do you mean, do you want to be hit across the nose?" And Lone Wolf said, "Who will save you if you hit me across the nose? Who will keep you alive?" Stumbling Bear said, "What do you mean? I will save myself. I do not need anyone to save me." Lone Wolf said, "I do not see anybody here to save you." Stumbling Bear said, "Lone Wolf, look at me. I am going to strike you across the nose." He had his wooden handled quirt by the lash and when Lone Wolf held up his head to him and said, "All right, strike me across the nose." [101] And he struck him across the nose with the wooden handle. Lone Wolf put up both hands to his face and the blood spurted out and he fell off his horse on the ground rolling with pain. Stumbling Bear thought he would try and kill him when he got over the pain but he laughed at him all the more. He had been joking all the time and they all made more fun of Stumbling Bear.

While quarreling and one man gets angry the other man says to him, "Are you mad?" and he replies, "Yes, I am mad." That means he is ready to fight. Another insult is, "You are no good" (i.e., you are a trifling worthless fellow) or "You are no good. You are not fit to live on the ground" or "to go about alive." Stone Calf = his right [actual] name is "Mountain Calf" was the Cheyenne chief, now dead. When I was a boy I first heard that the buffalo calves that lived on the mountains were the best. The old man said so and I found it to be true myself. I have seen these mountains all covered with buffalo even the very tops and when you killed a calf up there it was very fat while the calves killed down below on the plains were lean. This man was named for looking [102] for those calves all the time. That was his road (see also Gros Ventres Prairie).

Buffalo Holes

When Little Chief's Band of Northern Cheyennes [were] on their way back to the Indian Territory in the summer of 1878, they were under escort of the 7th Cavalry from Fort Buford at the mouth of the Yellowstone (Dec. 1877), wintered at Fort Abraham Lincoln with the 7th Cavalry, and were escorted by them to Bear Battle in the Black Hills, then to Sidney, Nebraska. Ben Clark was with them as guide and interpreter. While at Bear Butte the Cheyennes told me that in old times there had been a hole in the mountains near Harney's Peak where the buffalo had gone into the ground after being chased too much and when they recovered they would arrive out of that hole again and spread over the country. [But] that they would never do so anymore because there were too many white men there digging gold and that there was a similar hole somewhere south of the Arkansas River.

The buffalo had left the Black Hills prior to 1874. Custer saw none or recent signs of any and [buffalo] did not return to its neighborhood until the Northern Pacific [Railroad] split the Yellowstone herd about 1880, where they were abundant about thirty miles northeast of Bear Butte in the Moreau [Moreau River Valley], Little Mission.

N.B. They left the neighborhood of Old Fort Rice in 1867 except [for] an occasional straggling bull.

Medicine Butte

[side note] This butte is on the north side of the Canadian and can be seen from the top of the Antelope Hills. It looms up high above the other like a mountain with cut side, is up the river. It is called Medicine Butte (Tohausen's Tipi).

There is a high pointed butte up on the [106] Canadian [River] that has a strong medicine.

I knew an old man by the name of "Lean Old Man" who died when I was young. He was very sick. He went up and slept on that butte and the medicine said to him, "Look at me. I see you lying there poor and sick. This is my medicine house. I live here. Get up and go down to your lodge. I am going to take pity on you. You will attain old age." When I saw him he was very old. He could not stand up. His chest was squeezed together [collapsed] and he died old. When a man is young the muscles on his ribs are strong as well as those on his breast and back and the joints are strong but when he grows old they get weak and when he is very old they do not hold his ribs on each side apart. And when they come together he dies. Ribs squeezed together, collapse, dies old.[71]

Crane's Friend

One time Jackson's worker, a tall man with a hooked nose, told me that he has seen cranes migrating and one time he saw something fall from a crane into some grass nearby. He and another man saw it and went to look for it, found it in the grass. It was a bird without wings. He was a little afraid of it, put it in a piece of muslin, rolled it up, and tied it tight. And when he got back to camp he called everybody in to see something wonderful. When they all got there he unrolled the muslin and there was nothing there. He was afraid when he picked it up and did not examine it very closely. Its wings were flexible, soft, with no long feathers. Its body was about three inches in diameter and round. I myself have seen cranes migrating circling overhead and heard loud voices and little voices as if they had their young on their backs.

[side note] Stumbling Bear says that "Lives on Crane's Back" is around 3" or 4" [inches] in diameter, is bluish in color, short bill down on its back and has no feathers.

---

71 This butte is known as Mount Rochester in the 1884 Indian Territory Map. The Kiowas called it Dáujóhâu (Medicine Bluff Concavity). The Antelope Hills are located in northwest Roger Mills County, Oklahoma. Lean Old Man would be Táulqàptàu. See Meadows (2008:48, 265).

[107]
SCOUT (WOLF)

[probably Iseeo]

We make different signs for scout. One sign is for "quiver on left arm (like body) looking." Another is "Wolf Looking." A long time ago a scout had on a wolf's skin, well tanned with head on, and put it over his head to scout and look over hills with and that is why [we] make [the] wolf sign sometimes. Sometimes we say, "Quiver on left arm man looking." Formerly we had no horses and we went on [the] warpath on foot and then when the scouts comeback [came back] (they always went two together) they would stand on a hill opposite one another with faces towards each other bent over, a bow in the hands of each of them, one end of the bow on the ground. They would stand this way for a while. Then they would straighten up again then bend over again and those of the main party behind watching would say, "They have never seen a man" and then the scouts would go back and report. That was before I was born. I never saw it (45 years old).

Sign—arrow and hold quiver on left arm against body like a baby. In old times we had no guns or horses and when young men who could run fast were send [sent] out in front, their quivers were brought around in front and held against the body with [the] left arm like [a] baby in arms so they could run better. They run badly with [a] quiver on [their] back. Whenever anybody saw them carrying [a] quiver that way they knew [108] they were scouts. Wolf signs with a quiver on [the] arm is [were] sometimes made.

A long time ago a scout had on a wolf hide well tanned with head and legs and he put it on over his on head to scout and look over hills with and that is why we make the sign sometimes for scout—"wolf looking." Scouts always went at least two together. [109 blank]

[110]
GETTING HORSES

In old times the Kiowas traveled on foot and packed their property on dogs, big dogs. But they were unsatisfied with them and one day they met to council what they should do and prayed to the sun for help. The sun replied that they must show him what was wanted so they made an animal like an elk of mud and covered it with an elk skin. The medicine man stood it there and said, "Look at that" and they all looked on in wonderment. The people were different from us. Those medicine men were helped by the sun father. He gave them different roads, one road to make the deer, one to make the antelope, one to make the trees and everything. Even the little things like that fly were made that way.

The medicine man told the mud elk to move out once and its fetlock joints moved but its knees and shoulders were stiff. Everybody [was] looking on astonished. Then he told it a second time to move forward and its shoulders and hips were still stiff. Then he told it to move forward a third time and it moved a little bit forward, but was blind, having no eyes, and the fourth time it had eyes but it could not see the ground, it must look up always. Then he got tired and said, "Let us turn it loose on the prairie" and the others said, "No. That will not do. The above father [God] told us [111] to make it and it will not do to turn it loose on the prairie, that would be dangerous."

Then one man said, "Let us turn it loose, up to the Father." And they said, "All right. This experiment of making horses has failed, let us turn it loose to the Father" and they turned it loose upwards, saw it rise and rise and rise and rise out of sight in a cloud. After that the Kiowa[s] grew up without horses because that medicine horse failed. They packed dogs and went on foot for a long time until after they grew up as a people when one day a Kiowa met a Comanche man on the war path, for they used to fight the Comanches, and this time the Comanche was on a horse and the Kiowa did not understand it and he talked to the Comanche about it. Afterwards, they separated without fighting and when the Kiowa man got home to his village, he told about that horse and the whole village moved south until they got near the Comanche village. Then they put aside their women and children, and moved down, nearer the Comanche village and made peace with them, and they gave them some horses and they bought others until they had quite a no. [number] and they went back north, got their women and children and went to their own country beyond the Platte River and the mares had colts, and soon they had a great many horses. Taybodle is the sixth generation to see horses.[72]

---

72 Taybodal (Thépòl or Packing/Carrying A Calf Of Meat [Of A Bison]) was born around 1812 and died in 1901. If he was the sixth generation of Kiowas to see horses, then this would place their acquisition of horses in the late 1600s to early 1700s. The English pronunciation of the name mistakenly uses a *b* for a (p) sound and places the first letter of the second syllable in the first syllable (thus Tay-bodal), but the correct pronunciation is name is Thép-òl.

[112]

The First and Only Time Peace Was Made between the Kiowas and Pawnees

Before the Kiowas surrendered they used always to fight the Pawnees and steal horses from them and the Pawnee[s] did the same from the Kiowas from time immemorial.

About the year the soldiers first came to Fort Sill [1869] the Kiowa[s]' village was at the same place you and I found the Cheyenne chief White Shield's village on the Washita when we were looking for Messiah dances. One day a single Pawnee came to the village (I did not see him but I heard about him) in the middle of summer and said if the Kiowas are willing a great many of my people will come down and make peace with you and he went back saying he would return when the trees are red with a great many of his people and in the fall he heard that a great many Pawnees were on their way on foot to make peace with the Kiowas. One day a Wichita chief came to the village and said, "The Pawnees are not far away. What are you going to do, make peace or fight? Tell me now [are] some of the Pawnees are afraid?" And the chiefs told him they wanted not one thing (i.e., to make peace) and the Wichita chief went back to the Pawnees. He had a horse but the Pawnees were on foot, and the Kiowa chief called a big council and said, "We have always fought the Pawnees but now we are going to make peace with [113] them." Then nobody must do anything foolish, everybody must put foolishness out to one side and make the peace strong. About 3 p.m. the crier said the Pawnees are close by and to bring in the horses and go out to meet them and they went out to meet them and lined up in two long rows three hundred yards long, the Kiowas on one side and Pawnees on the other.

[side note, 112] Comanches call the Pawnees Qui-tar-a = big fundament. Kiowas call the Pawnees Wolf Men.[73]

Kicking Bird had a black spotted horse with a good saddle, bridle, and lariat on it. A fine gentle horse and Kicking Bird rode him into the middle and called out, "Where is the Pawnee chief" and when he stepped forward Kicking Bird dismounted and put his horse lariat in his hands and said, "I make you a prairie gift. I want to make a strong peace." Then the Kiowas rushed to give horses to the Pawnees. It was just like a charge, give, give, give until every man had five, six, or seven horses each. Then they were taken into the village and feasted everywhere.

---

73 One Kiowa name for the Pawnees is Cûiqàgàu (Wolf People).

That night the Pawnee[s] gave a dance just as those Cheyenne[s] did you know of and the Pawnees remained a long time with the Kiowas before going home. That was the first time we ever made peace with the Pawnees (1868 or 69) and it has lasted ever since. I saw that with these eyes and I did [114] not see anything done with a pipe except at the dance that night. The Pawnees gave the Kiowas some pipes as the Cheyenne chief gave you one that night.

[115]

Kom-au-dy's Shield

Kom-au-dy means "Black Stomach." He lived a long time ago. He went on the warpath in Mexico and was wounded and they thought that he was going to die. The flies [got in] his wound and he had screw worms and they left him by a little stream to die. The screw worms were in his wound and it smelt badly for a long distance and while he was waiting to die the ravens and buzzards came to eat him but they did not hurt him and at night he saw the moon above him. At first he would crawl down to the water on his hands and knees to drink but after a while he got too weak and was waiting to die, and one night he heard a wolf call on the mountain, "Oo-oo-oo" and after a while he heard it again, nearer, until it came sniffing around him like a dog. But it did not hurt him and as he looked up at the moon he thought about his home and his children. He was homesick and he dream the moon said to him, "You are going to get well and see your people, you are not going to die." And one day he heard a whistle up on the mountain and he kept getting weaker and weaker and when he heard the whistle he saw the Taime on top of the mountain and he looked at him and said you are not going [116] to die, I am going to help you, you [will] not die. And soon after it rained and cooled his fever and washed off his body clean, and washed out the worms from his wound and the raven ate the worms and he felt better but he was too weak to move. And one day a Comanche war party came to camp on that creek and he heard somebody there and thought they were Mexicans come to kill him and he heard them talk Comanche but was too weak to move or speak, but a Comanche young man smelt something dead and went to look for it and he saw a raven fly up and went there and found Kom-au-dy. And they took him and washed him, fixed his hair and gave him food and water and turned back and

[side note, 115] * Kom-au-dy died the summer before (they made silver ornaments for hair dance 1866) he died in '65 [1865] he was about 70 years old and died of a fever on Medicine Lodge Creek, Kansas.

took him home to the Kiowa camp and he got well and he made a shield that way. I saw a raven's head on it and a Sun Dance eagle bone whistle and a moon was painted on it. That was Big Bow's shield afterwards and when he lost his talk [became mute following a stroke] he thought that shield did not care of him and he sold it to Dr. Glennan [Brigadier General James D. Glennan; U.S. Army Medical Corps], who has it.[74] Big Bow has been leader on warpath more than one hundred times, nobody can beat him.

[117]

Comanche Bands

(Cabaya)
We have five principal bands among our people. I am Yapparika (Yapa-inuu). We call all Comanches "Neum" = liver. Comanche is a Mexican word. We do not know what it means. 1. Penethethka = Honey Eaters 2. Noconie = Always traveling 3. Tanimmi = Liver Eaters 4. Yapparikas = Root Eaters 5. Quahada or Antelope. The Quahadas have been called also Cochetetheka = Buffalo Eaters and Qua-hay-hi-ki + Backshade. There are also a few people we call Tichakenah = to Sew as a Moccasin Sole, they are on Cache Creek with Puhkanick.

We also have Titch-ta-noy-ya-ka Bad Travelers, the same as the Noconies which means to travel in a circle. The Coche-tuh-ka Buffalo Eaters are part of the Yappa[s]. Penetuhkas are sometimes called Tuh-ka-puh = Nothing to Eat or Beggars. There used to be a band called Ah-ah-homes. We don't know about it now.[75]

A long time ago we lived beyond the Platte River. We grew up there northwest of the head of the Platte [River] beyond the mountains at the head of the Platte northwest where there is a big river and very large trees. That is what the old men have always told me. I have always listened to the old men since I was a boy and now I know something myself. There are no more very old men alive now. There must be some of our people up there now. I hear that Ahpiatim [Ahpeahtone or Wooden Lance, a Kiowa] saw people who talk our language when he was looking for Jesus. We

---

74 This is a segment of the Hueco Tanks Fight. Komaudy was left at a spring near Guadalupe Peak in present-day Culbertson County, Texas. For a full account of the incident, see Meadows (2008:68–79). Big Bow suffered a stroke and became unable to speak a few years before his death. Consequently he was called Jóhę́qì (Speechless One) during these last years. Parker McKenzie to the author, Dec. 12, 1992, and Feb. 13, 1993. Big Bow was the brother of McKenzie's maternal grandmother Thòkàuidè.
75 For correlations of Comanche bands and social organization, see Kavanagh (1996, 2001).

are two separated bands, Northern and Southern Comanches just as the Northern and Southern Cheyennes are two bands of the same people.[76] We used [118] to be together up there but one day two chiefs got to quarreling, one said to the Yapparika chief, "You are poor, weak, and few" and the Yapparika chief said, "No, you are." And they bandied words backwards and forward until they got real angry and their bands took part in the quarrel and began to fight and they fought each other all that day and the next. The Yapparikas were smaller in number than the others and were surrounded and their horses were driven off and they themselves compelled to fortify [build a fortification]. A number were killed on both sides and then the Yapparikas were turned loose and allowed to go. The Yapparikas said to each other, "Our friends have treated us badly let us separate from them" and they came down this way on foot. Up there they were all together but when they had gotten down here the Penetethkas wanted a warmer climate and kept on south to "Mountain with Plenty Timber" south of here in Texas. The other Comanches drew back from them and lived here, all around here. They did not part in anger they just separated, looking for a warmer climate. Afterwards the Quahadas liked to live on the Staked Plains at the head of Red River so they went there. The others [119] lived wherever they felt like it, sometimes up on the Arkansas, sometimes down on the Canadian, Washita, or Red River sometimes about these mountains. When the Comanches first came down here they did not know the people here but after a long time we knew that they were Wichitas and Caddos. We call those people we left northwest of the Platte "Pay-beah." I do not know what it means.

The Penetecas were so named because they used to hunt around the trees down south for tree sugar (honey). They did it often and we called them honey eaters. The Noconies were so called because they never rested in one place but were always on the move, restless people. The Quahadas were named that last because they lived on the Staked Plains where the antelope were most numerous. They were called buffalo eaters before that and also Qua-hay-hi-ki, Back Shade, because there were no trees on the plains and there was nothing to shade them except when a man wanted to shade his face he turned his back to the sun. When we left the Northern Comanches we all came away together. The Yapparikas were named up north. There was a root that we [120] used to dig up. It was a white root we liked to eat about three or four inches long. There are none

---

76   The Comanches separated from the Shoshones, so this is clearly a reference to the Shoshones.

like it in this country. When people saw the ground dug up they said the root eaters did it, "Yappa rikas" [Root Eaters] and that is the way we got the name. The Comanche sign was given us by the Cheyennes without doubt. They made the sign language and gave the names to the Kiowas, Comanches, Apaches, and Arapahoes in signs and we do not know what they mean except that the sign for the Cheyennes we know because they used turkey feathers on their arrows. When we used to fight and found a Cheyenne arrow we saw it had turkey feathers and knew that it belonged to the Cheyennes, so we called them Tsien-avo = striped feather.

Origin of Comanches

There was a man, his wife, four sons, and a daughter. One son [was] larger than the others, who were of different sizes. One day the father scolded the oldest boy and he went off with the others and said to them, "My father has scolded me badly. Let us go away from him. I think it would be good to be stars. They appeared quiet. There is no trouble up there. I think they live good up there. Let us be stars." And they all became stars. They are these stars we see together in the east and the Comanches grew up from the father. After the Comanches got to be numerous they used to live on roots and rabbits and turtles, turnips, and were always hunger. An old woman had the buffalo in a corral made of trees and whenever they asked her for some meat she killed an old bull and gave the meat to them. After a long time Kiwash told them she was not treating them well. That they must all come to a council and they would discuss what we would do for their interests. And during the council Kiwash told [121] [a] young man to go down to the creek to where the old woman's son went for water and Kiwash told him that when he got there he would turn into a water animal and the boy would catch him and take him home, that when he did so the old woman would try and kill him but the boy would keep him safe and after four days had elapsed he should go to a mountain. Kiwash pointed out and yell with big throat and [his] shout would stampede the buffalo and they would break out of the corral and the Neum would follow and kill them and that was the way the buffalo got all over the country. Kiwash did it. Kiwash made them everything they had. He made all Comanche customs. He made a bow and arrows and said, "Look at those things you make others like them." And this is the way we got bows and arrows. Kiwash did it. And that is the way we got the skin lodge. Kiwash gave it to us just that way and he told us every year on July and August to kill the buffalo and gets lots of skins to make lodge covers and he gave us the stone to dress the hides with. Kiwash did it.

When we first grew up we had no horses. We packed our things on dogs when we moved, big dogs, and one times we went to war in Mexico and saw horses there and we began to bring them back from the Mexicans and they increased until we had a great many. We were at war with everybody at first. When we first separated from the Northern Comanches [Shoshones] and came to this country we found the Wichitas and Caddos here before us and we occupied the country with them ever since. We have a Scinday he is call[ed] "Nim Kiwash" which means a crafty man, a deceitful man. Kiwash is not here now. I do not know where he is. The one who made us all must have him corralled somewhere under guard. We do not know where.

We call the North Star "the star that does not move." We call the Dipper "The Jack Rabbit." The morning star is called the Big Star. Kiwash told us to worship it.

We call the prairie dog owl "poco" because he cries, "Po-co, po-co." We call a ghost "Pway-ti-ya" = long dead. We only see dead people in dreams. We call a whirlwind a ghost, no other. Where a Comanche dies his spirit goes fast on a broad road to the west. If he goes east he will get lost, there is no trail that way. But if he follows that trail he will not get lost. We bury in the ground different ways but most put the head toward the west. Kiwash told us about those things. He arranged them. Before that when a man died he ran around on the earth but one day Kiwash told them to come to him and he said, "Look at me. I am going to throw this stone into the water. You will not see that stone anymore. That is the way it is going to be with dead people. You will not see them anymore."

[122]

COMANCHE STORY: HOW KIWASH DECEIVED THE WHITE MAN
[probably Cabaya]
Kiwash = deceitful man.

One time the Neum saw some white people traveling. They did not know who they were and were afraid to go near them but Kiwash showed them how. He went first. He built a fire near where the white men were going to pass and when the ground was very hot he put the fire out and took away the ashes. And after he had put another kettle of hot water on the hot ground, the water began to boil. Pretty soon the white men came along and saw the kettle and said, "What makes that water boil without a fire?" And Kiwash said, "That is the way it is. That is a medicine kettle. I put water in it and meat and it boils itself." Then the white man wanted to buy the kettle but Kiwash said, "No, I love that kettle. I am very lazy and do not like to go after wood." And the white man said, "I will give you a horse for that kettle" and Kiwash said, "No, I want to keep it." And the white man said, "I will give you two horses for that kettle." Kiwash thought for a long time and finally said, "Good" and the white man gave him two horses and kept the kettle and went on. That day at dinnertime he put some water and meat in the kettle and waited a long time for it to boil but it would not boil. Then he became angry and broke it. Kiwash deceived him. He beat him.

[The] Comanche word "Naddy-kuh-yun-nap" means something that never truly happened or a fable. Kiwash stories are fables.[77]

[123]
Old Lone Wolf Killing Buffalo
The best man I ever heard of to kill buffalo was Old Chief Lone Wolf of the Kiowas.[78] One man would sometimes kill three buffalo in one run. Lone Wolf would kill seven or eight or nine or ten with arrows. When he was in the middle of a herd he would shoot a buffalo on each side of him with the bow. That is pretty hard to kill a buffalo on the right side. He would kill a deer, which was standing on the ground with an arrow at one hundred yards. All Kiowas know what a bowman he was. Nobody was like him. And I have seen him chasing antelope and shoot with an arrow an antelope and kill it, both running at fifty yards. He was very skillful. See Gabriel Renville of Dakota & [with] Henry Rifle & [shot] sixteen buffalo at one run. When you charge the buffalo you look at the humps and when you see a cow with a wide hump you charge and turn her (wide hump = sign for fat) that will be the fat one. You can see her some distance away.

White Buffalo
The white buffalo is a medicine buffalo. I have seen two hides of young one. I never saw an old one. Their hair is more like a yellow. When you find them they are always surrounded by black buffalo in a big herd to hide them. They are always [124] very fat. A man who has never struck

---

77 Due to the reference to Kiwash in the end of the previous story and this story's focus on Kiwash, this account is also likely from Cabaya.
78 This is the Lone Wolf who died in 1879, after returning from Fort Marion Prison in 1878.

his enemy first cannot shoot a white buffalo. He [the man who kills a white buffalo] must count a coup before he shoots it and if he misses he must count another, etc., count a coup every time before he shoots first as in killing the buffalo before the Sun Dance and if he cannot do it he must let somebody else do it who can count plenty of coups. The man who skins both white buffalo and Time [Taime] buffalo must first tell where he scalped his enemy before he cuts the skin. The meat of the white buffalo is not eaten but is left there. It is given to the Sun.

[from 98]
Origin of Ten Medicines, Also of Kiowa People

Before the Kiowa[s] grew up (as a people) there used to be other people living on the ground, strong people.[79] They had strong medicine [125] and wonderful things. Scinday lived in those days too. "Scinday" means "The Deceitful Man." I do not know what became of those people. One day the children (eight girls) were playing about near the village and they saw a porcupine (the porcupine does not exist south of the Arkansas [River]) on a tree and the prettiest girl said, "I want that" and she climbed up to take hold of the porcupine but when she reached out her hand for it was just out of her reach. So she climbed up a little more and the porcupine was still out of her reach. And this kept on until the tree, which had grown by little jerks had pushed up to the sky and the girl was taken up there by Sun or by Thunder. I do not know which. I think it was Sun and she married Sun and had a little boy. Her husband used to go out every day and hunt for meat and he told her just to eat all the berries she wanted and all the plants and roots, but not to touch the "tan" (this grows on North Canadian). It is a root, good to eat, having bark easy to get off. White inside, top grows this way because the buffalo like it.[80] They had buffalo up there just as we had, and one day the woman thought, "Why did my husband warn me not to touch that? I want to learn." And one day while

---

79 Scott provides another version of this story (n.d.b: MS 2932, Box 2, Kiowa Origins) with the words "the porcupine who was the son of the Sun"; they married and had a son. She pried up the tán plant with her root stick (digging stick). This version does not name any of the crops in the garden. Regarding the Underwater Monster, Scott writes, "He is 'Big Mouth' (a river monster) they call him 'Zem-a-coon-y.'" This is Zémáutqṳné (s/d), Zémáutqṳnóp (t). The name literally translates as "teeth-held-rolled over and over" in reference to how it kills its prey. Big Mouth appears to be his name in sign language. The creature is popularly called Underwater Monster.
80 This is the tán plant, also known in Kiowa as tháiqáudálègàu (s) and tháiqáudálè (d/t, literally, white-round-edible). Scott identifies the tán plant as the pomme blanche (n.d.b: MS 2932, Box 2, Kiowa Origins).

her husband was away she pulled one of the plants up by the root [126] and in so doing made a round hole in the sky through which she could see down to the earth where her people were and which looked so beautiful. She could see the streams and the forest and the grass and the buffalo and she longed to get back to her people and she covered the hole back again.

When her husband got back she told him whenever he killed a buffalo he must bring her back the sinews on his back (every buffalo has two) and he always did so and she began to make (twist) a rope without her husband's knowledge. She made it out of sinew and one day she went out and let the rope down through the hole to measure how far it went toward the earth but it was not long enough and she took it back and worked at it until when she let it down again it just touched the earth. Then she stuck her turnip stick into the ground near the hole, tied the rope to it, tied herself to the other end, and tied her boy just above her and let herself down through the hole but she had not calculated in loss of enough rope by tying and she could not touch the ground but swung backward and forward in the air.

When the man came home he saw the lodge was deserted, no woman there. No fire built, no supper cooked, so he looked out over the prairie and saw the turnip stick standing up and went to see what it was. When he got there he saw the [127] hole and the rope and then he understood and was very angry. He looked down at the woman still swinging and said, "She always was a fool." And he made a stone round and flat and grooved at the edges like a pulley wheel. He had a strong medicine and he made the stone run down the rope and (medicine) told it to jump over the boy and the stone jumped over the boy and struck the woman on the head and killed her and the rope broke and she and the boy fell to the ground.

The boy was quite small and still suckled [nursed] his mother (and slept beside her), who soon became putrid. Every day he played around her going farther every day until one day he saw a lodge, which belonged to an old woman and he walked around the lodge but was afraid to go in like a wild horse. He was wise (cautious). Finally he went in and found something to eat in the pot. That day the old woman (she was an Old Spider Woman who had a garden [of] corn, pumpkins, melons, [and] tobacco somewhere, and she went everyday to take care of it) came home and saw the little tracks and thought, "Who is that[?] It is not good for me to be alone. I will catch that person. I wonder whether it is a boy or a girl? How shall I find out? The tracks do not tell." So she made a ball such as girls bounce on one foot. Also a bow and arrow and left them there when she went [the] next day to work in her garden.[81] When this boy came he took the bow and arrow and played around with it, shooting but he did not disturb the ball and when the [128] Spider Woman found two arrows displaced she knew it was a boy. Every morning when she went to work she left cooked corn in the dish and every night [when] she came home the boy had eaten it.

One day she hid herself near the door on the inside of the lodge wrapped up in a roll of rawhide and the boy came along, stopping every few feet to listen. He listened at the door but hearing no one he looked in. He did not see anybody but he felt scared like a wild horse and drew back outside again. But he did not see or hear anything and finally came in and sat down to eat the cooked corn left for him. Then the Old Spider Woman jumped up and caught him. He began to cry and bite, scratch, and kick but she held him, fed him, talking kindly to him, took him to bed, and next day put him in the hood of her robe and carried him with her to her garden. He cried all the time and she hushed him until finally his fear and crying quieted down (was allayed) and he remained with her.

One day he said to her, "Grandmother, make me a wheel and stick" (Goom-ah). And she said she had no hide to make the wheel with but after a while she cut a piece of skin from her thigh, cut it in strips, and made the wheel and gave it to him, but told him to throw the wheel on the ground only and not in the air. [129] He played with it every day with great satisfaction until he thought, "Why did Grandmother tell me not to throw it in the air? I think I will throw it up and find out." So he threw it up in the air and the wind caught it and brought it back. It struck him in the forehead and split him in two in the middle and there were two boys just alike standing opposite one another in great astonishment.[82] And one said, "Is that you, Brother?" And the other replied, "Yes, I am your brother." And the Old Spider Woman heard them talk and called out, "Who is there" and [the] boy said, "Grandmother, come and see Brother." She came out and saw two boys and said, "You threw that wheel up into the air. You are a naughty boy." But she was glad there were two of them. And she said, "Boys, you play wheel game with each other but do not throw it with the wind."

The boys played together for a long time and one day they said, "Why did Grandmother tell us not to throw it with the wind? Let us try it and

---

81   Although a garden associated with the Spider Woman appears in this story, there is no indication that the Kiowas ever practiced any form of horticulture or agriculture.
82   This is the origin of the Záidètàlyì (Half or Split Boys), the Kiowa culture heroes.

find out." And they threw it with the wind following after and the wheel ran faster and faster until the boys were very tired and stopped watching it and the wheel began to go slower and to wobble from side to side. Then thinking they could catch it they ran again and the wheel went faster and faster [130] keeping out of their reach until they were tired out. They saw it roll over a smooth ridge and when they reached the top they saw it roll down to a lodge standing there and up to the smoke hole where it stuck. They went down to the lodge and saw skulls of people lying around on the ground and thighbones and they said, "This man is a dangerous man." And the man in the lodge heard them and called out asking what they wanted and they said they wanted their wheel on the smoke hole. And he told them to come in and he would get their wheel. So they went inside and sat opposite to the man and his wife. They noticed bags tied to each lodge pole graduated in size and the man told his wife to open one of the bags. She did so and it liberated a terrible smoke which filled the lodge and one boy said, "Brother, I am choking." And the other boy said, "Hold your hand just above your eyes" and when he had done it he found that the smoke did not go below his hand. The man and his wife were rolled in their robes. After a while the man said, "Take a look and see how they stand it" and when she looked at them they jerked their hands down so she would not see how they were stopping the smoke. She told her husband that it did not [131] seem to hurt them any and he told her to open another bag and still a bigger smoke came out which nearly strangled the man and his wife but which did not injure the boys. And so it went on until all the bags were opened but two and the man said to his wife, "Those boys are dangerous. Do not open any more bags. They will kill us. Let them go out and give them their wheel and let them go." And she gave them their wheel and when they got home it was very late and the old woman said, "Where have you been, boys?" And they told her about the wheel and she cried out, "You so foolish boys. That is a very dangerous man." But they laughed and said he was a very weak man. They could beat him very easily.

They asked their Grandmother one day, "Grandmother, where can we get arrow wood." And she said, "There is a very dangerous man over there in the river who has arrow wood, but you cannot get it. He will kill you. He is very dangerous. Do not go near him, he is a big river monster." (Zema coon = which has a mouth and tail, and legs like an alligator, horns, and hair like a buffalo.)[83] But they said, "No, no. He will not kill us. We will get the arrow wood." So they went over to the river and saw the arrow

---

83 This is Zémáutqū̱né, the Kiowa underwater monster.

wood (rushes) growing in the river, swaying with the wind [132] and when they went to get it the underwater monster opened his mouth wide to catch them but they had sharpened the stick which their Grandmother had given them to play the wheel game and they drove it down his open throat until it pierced his heart and he died and they got the arrow wood (plant ?) and took a bundle of it home and when she saw it the Grandmother called out, "Oh my, so foolish boys. You will be killed if you do that" and they laughed again and said, "No, we killed the underwater man." So they had the arrow plant but they had no feathers or any sinew so they said, "Grandmother, do you know where we can get sinew?" And the Old Spider Woman said, "Yes, I know where there is sinew. The Bull has got it on his neck, but he is very dangerous. He is standing out there on the high prairie and he will kill you if you go near him. He has a baldheaded eagle standing on the one horn to watch one way and a black tipped tail eagle [Golden Eagle] standing on the other horn to watch the other way, and when he sleeps they watch for him. And when they see anyone coming they wake him up and he kills them. He is very dangerous do not go near him." But they laughed at her and went off to find Bull and up on the high prairie they looked over a ridge and [133] the hill lying down on his left side, with an eagle on either horn watching in every direction and the boys turned themselves into mice and ran through the long grass (one foot high) secretly until they got just below the eagles and taking the sharp stick the Old Spider Woman gave them to play the wheel game they drove it into the Bull's heart just behind his fore-shoulder and killed him and they caught the eagles and pulled out their long feathers and took the sinew off the Bull's neck and carried them to the old woman who cried, "Oh you so foolish boys. That Bull is very dangerous. He will kill you." But they said, "No, Grandmother he is very weak. We have killed the Bull" and the old woman was very much astonished.

They wanted bows to shoot the arrows and said, "Grandmother, what is the best wood for bows?" She said, "I know all the different woods in this country. They are all behind. There is a big elk over there with big horns that is best for bows. When you shoot [an] elk horn bow you do not miss, you shoot good. He is very dangerous. He lives on the high prairie. If anybody goes near him he horns [gores] them and stamps on them until they are dead. You must not go near him. I have been telling you wise things for a long time but your ears are shut. You are crazy boys. You must not go near that elk." They said, "No, Grandmother, we are only going out to play." They deceived her. She said, "I scold you about that because I love you. I do not want to see you killed." [134] They deceived her. They went out and played for a long time. Then the older [brother] said, "We will go and get those elk horns" and went out west on the prairie, peeped over a hill, and saw the elk lying down out there. The older said, "Brother, sit down. I am going to take a mole's road and burrow underground so he cannot see me and when you see him fall come over there. Do not look at me now." Brother drew back carefully below the hill and sat down for a long time and when he looked around the elder was not there. He went up again and watched the elk until he saw him jump up suddenly, walk a few steps swaying from side to side, and then he fell dead. Brother ran over there and met the elder and they cut off the elk horns and were carrying them home and said, "Grandmother will scold us when we get home." They were very late and Grandmother called out to them, "Where have you been?" They said, "We have been playing about and got away too far." Then they went on and threw down the horns and said to Grandmother, "Look at that. We killed elk and took his horns. He is not dangerous. He is very weak. We killed him." And Grandmother called out in dismay, "Oh you crazy children. I told you not to go there" but they laughed at her. Then they made the bows and arrows and killed meat, different kinds of meat. They grew up to be tall and good-looking and one day they meet Scinday and he asked them where they came from. They told him their mother came down from above on a sinew rope and was killed and they were split from one [boy]. Scinday said, "I live over in that (west) direction, let us [135] travel together over there. I know all that country, all the rivers." And Scinday said, "There are some medicine women over there, six of them." And they went over there and Boy and Brother married each a Medicine Woman and Scinday married four of them and from those all Indian (red men) have descended; Cheyennes, Arapahoes, Sioux, Pawnees, Kiowas, Comanches, Wichitas, all.

There was no sun in those days and Scinday got the sun and put it in the sky for everybody's light. And the Red Men began to grow up, lots of them, and one time Scinday called them all together to a big council and told them to come up one at a time. He rubbed some medicine in the palm of his hand, like rubbing tobacco, and spit in it, and put his fingers on it and when a man came up he rubbed his finger on his lips and poked his finger in his ears, bored his ears so he could hear, and then they told him to speak. And when he spoke to suit him he put them aside and did the same to another man, making them to speak and understand different languages. Before that they used only the sign language, but now they spoke different languages—Cheyenne, Pawnee, Sioux, Wichita, Kiowa, Comanche, and Apache, all different. Then he made that fight road you know about and the Kiowas and Kiowa Apaches fought all other tribes together. They did not have two Scindays, they had but one. They grew up together near those big mountains in the cold country, north beyond where the tall rock [Bear Lodge Tower] is. Then when they made peace with the Comanches they came down here, the Apaches with them, and they found the Wichitas and Caddos down here and all lived in this country in peace and fought the Pawnees, Osages, and Utahs [Utes]. After a long the Kiowas and Caddos peace was broken, I do not know why, but now they are all at peace together. That is what all the old people tell.

[side note] Afterwards the Cheyennes and Arapahoes came down from the north and we fought them for a long time until we made that peace you know about.

[136]
Star Woman's Tree River—Salt Fork of Red River

In old times the old Kiowa women had a road (custom). They make [made] seven sticks of cottonwood (Sun Dance Tree) and placed them in the ground in a cluster in the shape of a horseshoe with its heel [opening] to the east this way.

When an old woman had a brother or sister whose little girl was frequently ill she become [became] uneasy about it and she got seven other little girls and sat them down in the back part of her lodge and gave them each a cottonwood stick about four feet long and thick as my wrist with a bunch of yellow flowers tied at the end with a buffalo string. That flower grows on the Washita [River] but none of it [is] about here. Then she takes [took] a girl at the end of the row and leads [led] her around by her left. The others all following [followed] in single file, clasping hands out the door and around by her right to the back of her lodge where they all stand in [the] horseshoe facing the east. Then she prayed to the seven sisters who were raised up on the rock and saved from the bear (Bear Lodge) and are now stars ([see p.] 173) and said, "Look at these little girls. Take pity on them and help them to live good on the ground. They shall have no sickness. Let them have a good woman's road. Let them attain old age like me and that other sick one let them all move about good on the ground." Then the sticks are placed strong (solid) in the holes prepared for them before by driving in a big peg and taking it out and then they go back the same way on the opposite side [137] of the lodge to the door where the ceremony is ended and all disperse. One time this ceremony was performed long before I was born. Some old women did it and the following summer a man camped near them going on the warpath and saw the seven sticks had grown up into seven good trees with leaves on them and ever since the Kiowas have called that stream the Star Woman Tree River.

All Kiowas, Comanches, and Apaches know about that wonderful thing. This occurred once with some ash sticks put down by the Sun dancers. These sticks were given to them by Kom-au-dy and they stuck them in the ground by the cedar screen in the Sun Dance Lodge and left them there in the dance on the Salt Fork of the Arkansas 20 miles south of the Kansas line (no. 2) and west of the Meridian. The dance was called "Strong Wood" or Ash Sun Dance in consequence. Kom-au-dy died many years ago.[84]

[138]

Scinday Stories

A long time ago Scinday lived. He was a crafty man, a deceitful man, a wise man. He was a tall man and went naked with his penis wrapped three or four times around his waist and hanging down at the side like a sash. That was a very long time ago when the Kiowas first come out of the ground and some people who lived over east had the sun, and the Kiowas and all the animals lived in the dark. There was no light there and they had [a] council to see what we [could] do, how we can get [the] sun, and Scinday said, "We cannot try it. They will laugh at us and how can we get it? We cannot steal it. They will not let us. We must find some way to get it. And these people who had the sun used it to play a game with. It was a ring about four inches in diameter and they have [rings] like it in the Ten Medicines. They play the game with two sides in a place smoothed off for about thirty yards. Only two men play at a time. We call it Goom-ah—Arrow Notch Game." One man of each side has a spear and they throw the ring and both race after it and throw their spears and try to put [throw them] through it. They measure from the ring, certain marks on the spear which one beats [wins]. Then [when] they get tired and two other men take their places and [139] they make big bets on it. And they played Arrow Notch Game with the sun for a wheel and it was light all around them.

---

84 The Salt Fork of the Red River is called Jámátáunàváu (Star Girl's Tree River) by the Kiowas. This event and location resemble the 1857 Sun Dance (Mooney 1898:301). Komaudy was the individual wounded in the escape from Hueco Tanks in 1839. See "Ko-mau-dy's Shield" (Scott n.d.a:1:115–16, chapter 4 in this volume) and Meadows (2008:68–79).

Scinday said to the animals, "Pick out the fox (or wolf) and the jack rabbit, the prairie chicken and the magpie and you must do as I say. You fox, go there and try and get it, and jack rabbit hide this side, and then prairie chicken and then magpie." And the fox went where they were playing and they said, "What [did] you come looking for? You are [a] stronger fellow. We do not want you, you go away." And fox said, "What [are] you afraid of? I am only [a] poor, weak little fellow. I watch the game; I am so interested in the game. What, [are] you afraid of me?" And finally they all allowed him to remain [and] see the game, and as the players went back and forth the fox was so interested he went back and forth awhile watching them and after a while they forgot about him. And when they went back in his direction he seized the sun, put it on his back and ran off. The men were much astonished, but gave chase after him until he was tired and they began to gain on him and he called out, "Where are you, jack rabbit? I cannot see you" for he was hidden in the grass and the jack rabbit said, "Here I am" and he gave [140] the sun to jack rabbit who put it on his back and ran off with it. Fox ran off to one side and they were so intent on catching jack rabbit that they did not notice him but chased jack rabbit until he was tired and were about to catch him when he gave it to prairie chicken, who put it on his back and flew off with it, giving it to magpie who flew up in the air where the men could not follow. And when the people saw it getting light they cried out with fox, "It is getting light. It is getting light." And pretty soon magpie came and gave the sun to Scinday, who took it in his hand just as the men came up, panting for breath, and demanded the return of the sun. But Scinday threw it up in the sky and said, "You [will] not get their [the?] sun. You [are] selfish people. You want to keep it for yourselves. Now this sun [is] for everybody. You [will] not get this sun." And Scinday made it to go around in the heavens and come up every morning and go down in the evening for everybody.

Turkey

Scinday left his wife and children in the lodge one day and went out to hunt for something to eat and he saw a turkey and called out, "Is that you, Turkey?" And Turkey did not answer but kept very still thinking he might be taken for a black stump. Scinday said again, "Is that you, Turkey?" But turkey stood [141] still and Scinday said, "Oh, I made a mistake. That is a black stump" and began to walk around carelessly [and] whistle. Turkey kept perfectly still until Scinday got very near and by a sudden movement [Scinday] grabbed him by the neck and he said, "Is that you, Turkey?"

and Turkey began to kick thinking he was going to be choked to death. But Scinday said, "You [should] not be afraid, Turkey. I [do] not want to kill you, Turkey. I am too far from home. I want to send you to my wife and go on farther myself. Will you go?" And Turkey said, "Yes, I will go." And Scinday said, "You go and tell my wife to kill you and cook you and I will be back at noon and eat you. Will you go?" And he said, "Yes, I will go" and he went back to the lodge [and] stood there. The woman said, "What are you looking for here, Turkey?" and Turkey said, "Your man told me to come and tell you to strike your youngest child on the head and cook him and he will be here at noon to eat him" and then ran off. The woman began to cry out. She was afraid not to do what her husband said, so she killed the child and cooked it. And at noon her man came back and saw how she was sad but said only, "Has Turkey been here and tell [told] you?" and she said, "Yes." He said, "I am glad. I will go eat," and he called the children to come to dinner [142] and they ate white meat like turkey meat and pretty soon he said, "Where is my youngest child? Why doesn't he come to dinner" and his wife said, "You are eating him" and he cry [cried] and [exclaimed], "Oh" and the turkey beat him.

[side note] Compare *The Northern Shoshone* — R. H. Lowie American Museum, Vol. 11, 1909, p. 278, quite like Shoshone coyote = Scinday.

[142]
How Scinday Deceived the White Man

One day Scinday saw something strange coming toward him and when he got near he saw that it was a man and he looked at him in astonishment. It had on a hat [and] was setting [sitting] on a mule. It had a gun and spurs and a mustache and had a white skin and he said, "I never saw anything like that before" and the white man looked at him with big eyes, both of them astonished. And the W.M. [white man] said, "Who are you?" And he said, "I am Scinday." And he said, "Are you Scinday?" And he said, "Yes, I am Scinday" and the White Man said, "I hear of you as [a] very deceitful man. I want you to deceive me something so I know about you." And Scinday said, "I cannot deceive you. I am only [a] poor, weak, man. I cannot deceive you." And White Man said, "Yes, you deceive me something." And he said, "No, I cannot deceive you. I left my medicine at home. I cannot deceive you." And White Man said, "Yes, you deceive me. You go home and get your medicine." And he said, "No, I cannot. I cannot walk that far, that's too far" [143] and White Man said, "Yes, you go and get your medicine and I will be here." And Scinday said, "If you will lend me your mule I will ride home and get my medicine." And the

White Man said, "All right, you ride my mule" and dismounted and gave him the mule. But the mule was afraid of him, neighed and snorted at him. And Scinday said, "What is the matter [with] this mule? You lend me your hat. He was afraid of me." And he went up and took the mule by the bridle and pinched the mule's lip and it snorted and shrunk from him again. And Scinday said, "He sees my legs are naked and different from yours. Lend me your trousers and spurs and he will not be afraid of me." And he put on the White Man's trousers and spurs and pinched the mule secretly again and he shrunk from him in fear. And the man [Scinday] said, "You lend me your gun and whip and he was not afraid." And he lent him his gun and whip and then the mule was not afraid of him and he got on him and rode a little way and he laugh[ed] at the White Man, "I not need any medicine to deceive you. I have got everything you have." And the White Man began to cry and call him back, "Come back and give me my things," but Scinday left him naked, sitting on the ground crying.

Scinday, the Prairie Dogs, and the Coyote

One day Scinday came to a prairie dog village and saw a good many fat prairie dogs sitting around their holes [144] just like at a dance and he went among them but they all ran off. He had a stick in his hand and he called them all back and said, "I want you to dance. Everybody dance and I will beat on the ground with this stick just like [a] drum." And the dogs began to dance and flip their tails in time with the drum and put up their little paws in front and dance and everybody have a good time. And Scinday began to sing and drum and he said, "Everybody dance and shut your eyes until my song is ended" and they shut their eyes and he kept drumming and singing, keeping time to the drum.[85]

> Saa to, Saa to, to-in ba-a-to-ti
> Prairie Dogs, Prairie Dogs, tail jerk it
>
> Saa to, Saa to, to-in ba-a-to-ti
> Prairie Dogs, Prairie Dogs, tail jerk it
>
> Oye yan po-lo-si
> This time I am heavy or tired
>
> Oye yan po-lo-si
> This time I am heavy or tired

---

85 For the Kiowa Prairie Dog Song, see Meadows (2010:20–21).

And when he saw all their eyes were shut he began striking them on the head in time to the music and the song until he had killed nearly all of them. But one crazy little fellow who would not do as he was bidden opened his eyes and saw him killing the others [and] cried out and ran away. Scinday ran after striking at him with the stick but the prairie dog dodged him very often and finally got into a hole and Scinday was very mad because he was a fat little dog but he said, "I let you go. You stay here and raise [a] family. I let you go." And the dog was saved.[86]

[side note, 144] The Apaches and Comanches have a similar story. The Comanches sing "Yuh-ha-hay-na-ha-ho, "Dance hard, dance hard and you will never be sick." He told them they would die if they opened their eyes before the song was over.

[145] Scinday took all the dead dogs and dug a hole, put grass on the bottom of it and laid the prairie dogs in rows on the grass after they had been skinned and cleaned, covered them over nicely with grass and leaves, and then with dirt, and built a fire over it. That is the way we used to cook turtle, big water turtle. There was a tree close by with a fork in it not far from the ground and Scinday sat in the fork looking at the fire and thinking about his dinner and he sat back so proud and sang some [illegible word] songs and after a while he saw a wolf coming on three legs and he said, "What do you want here?" And wolf said, "I am very hungry and lame, and I want to eat the bones you throw away." And Scinday said, "I [do] not want you here. You go away. I will not give you any bones. You go hunt for yourself. I am a man, I hunt for myself. You try hard and hunt for yourself." And Wolf said, "No, I am too lame" and he showed his leg that had matter on it. "I am too lame. I [will] not disturb you. I [will] eat only bones you throw away." And Scinday sat on the fork so proud and singing and he said, "I [will] run you a race," and Wolf said, "No. I [will] not beat you, you are too fast," and [then] he said, "Yes. I [will] run you a race around in a circle and I [will] share some meat with you." And Wolf said, "No. I am too poor and weak. You are too fast." And Scinday said, "Tie a stone on each of my ankles and [146] we're even."

[side note, 145] Compare Wissler and Duvall *Blackfoot Mythology*, American Museum Natural History Anthropological Papers, Vol. II, 1908, p. 28. Old Man said to the Coyote, "You get out of here or I will cut up my genitals and beat you over the head" (Note: Old Man's genitals are also spoken of as a lariat). The rainbows are often spoken of as such using either term apparently at random—genitals were used as a rope. Grinnell, pp. 157–58; McGlean, *Journal of American Folklore*, Vol. I (II), p. 297.

---

86   See Meadows (2010:20–21) for a complete translation of this song.

By that time the fire had died down but it was too hot to open and the Wolf said, "You tie a stone to each ankle and all be matched even" and Scinday tied them on and they began to run. And the Wolf ran on three legs holding his paw up but kept just a little ahead. They ran over a smooth ridge, the Wolf gaining a little and when he got out of sight of Scinday he ran fast, letting down his lame leg (which was only fixed with pine gum to deceive Scinday) and looking over his shoulder until Scinday came up in sight when he held up his paw again. Then they turned back to go toward the oven and they went over four ridges. Each time the Wolf deceived him about the lame leg until when they crossed the last ridge he was away ahead and when Scinday came over the rise he saw the Wolf running as fast as he could toward the prairie dog oven when he cried out, "Wait. Wait." But the Wolf ran faster and Scinday cut the stones off his ankles but the wolf was away ahead and got to the oven and eat [ate] up all the prairie dogs and stuck their bones in the oven and covered them over nicely with the dirt. And Scinday came along panting and hungry and saw the oven undisturbed. He was glad and began to dig up the prairie dogs for his dinner but he found only the bones.

[147]
THE WOLF AND THE ROCK
One day a wolf was walking about and crept up on a high rock and looked over the prairie and saw everything so pleasant and all the green trees and grass and the streams and he felt so happy to walk around and he [was] so fast when anything chase[d] him. He run [ran] right away from it and he looked down between his feet at the rock and said, "Rock, you [are] very poor, you stay here all the time. You [will] not catch me. I run fast." And he make a fun [made fun] of the rock and pretty soon he felt the rock turning over more and more until he had to jump off and the rock rolled after him faster and faster. He ran into the woods to hide but the rock knocked the trees down like grass and he ran out and over a ridge where he thought the rock could run against the bank but it jumped right up over the bank. And he saw a panther coming and called out to it, "Save me, save me," and the panther jumped up against it and caught it in his paws and it rolled over on him, [and] mashed him flat. And the wolf was nearly tired out when he met a nighthawk, one of those striped birds that dive down suddenly in the air, "foom," and that blow [rush of air] it made diving stopped the rock and the wolf got away.

(Compare *The Northern Shoshone*, R. H. Lowie American Museum of Natural History, Vol. II, 1909, p. 268.)

[148]
How the Crow Came to Be Black

A long time ago the crow used to be pure white, like a pigeon, but he was a tall tale [often told false tales]. He always told the animals, "Run, run. That man is after you to kill you. Run away, run." And the Kiowas were kept hungry by that bad crow and they went away and told Scinday about it and he said, "All right, I['ll] catch him," and he went and laid down on the prairie and turned himself into a dead elk with an opening made in his ribs. Pretty soon the crow saw him and flew down and stood at a distance. He is a very smart bird, very wise, and he [was] afraid of it and after a while he called out, "Caw, I know you, Scinday" and came around and pecked him hard on the bridge of his nose and hurt him very much. "I know you, Scinday" [he called out], but Scinday did not move, but it hurt him very much and after a while the crow was satisfied that is a dead elk and lit on his side where the opening was and began to peck at him. The crow's toes were down in the hole in his ribs and suddenly he closed down his foreleg and shut the ribs together; and caught the crow and took him to the Kiowa camp and called out to come [and] look at him, the crow that did these mean things. And he called them to decide how they will punish him for his mean things and they built a big fire there and some were for roasting him, some for killing him in different [149] ways. But an old woman (Spider Woman) said, "Give me that crow. I will tie him a prisoner" and she tied him with a spider's web that the others did not see and the crow did not feel. And she let the crow loose and as he flew up he laughed at them and said, "I will treat you worse than before." And the people were very angry at the old woman for letting the crow loose and said, "Kill that old woman." But the crow had gotten up very high and the old woman began to pull him back, hand over hand on the spider's web, and the crow called out, "Let me go. I did not mean that. I was only joking." But they pulled him down and threw him into the fire and he was burned black and hopped out and has been black ever since.[87]

Another version is the Spider Woman took him home and tied him out the smoke opening of her lodge and kept him there to punish him and he got smoked black. *The Geography of the Heavens*, E. H. Burritt, Cinn. [Cincinnati] W. B. Smith and Co. 1867, p. 79.

History: The crow it is said was once of the purest white, but was changed for tale bearing [telling false tales] to its present color, a fit punishment for such a fault.

---

87 This story and the last one were told in reference to the characters (a crow, a wolf, and so forth) rather than about Crow or Wolf, so the words are not capitalized.

"The raven once in snowy plumes was dressed.
White as the whitest dove; unsullied breast.
Fair as the guardian of the Capitol.
Soft as a swan; a large and lovely fowl.
His tongue his prating tongue had changed him quite.
To sooty blackness from the purest white."

[150]

Antelope

In the old times the antelope used to have teeth like a dog and chase men and eat them and they were so swift they caught anything. They were dangerous. They bite [bit] anybody those first time[s] and the Kiowas were all afraid of them and they said to Scinday, "What [are] we going [to] do, they eat us?" And Scinday said, "All right, we [we'll] fix them" and he made a trench near where the antelope were accustomed to graze, a miry place (lake) where the wild horses and buffalo go in and could not get out, buried down to their bodies, and Scinday made like that. And one day the antelope were there and the people showed themselves on the other side of the miry place and when the antelope saw them they ran at them and got mired down. And when Scinday saw that he went down and filed their teeth off even like a buffalo's teeth and fixed them so they cannot bite any more.

Bonee

A man and his wife and daughter lived in their lodge apart from the Kiowa camp and were very hungry. One day they heard something strike the door of their lodge and fall to the ground. The man told his wife to see what it was and she looked and saw a young antelope lying there dead. She [151] looked all around to find out who had thrown it there but could not see anybody and she took it in and they eat [ate] it up. The next day they heard something strike the door again and the woman saw a middle-sized antelope lying there but no one was visible in the neighborhood and they took it into the lodge and eat it up. Next day a large antelope [appeared], and [the] following day a "bull antelope." Then an elk [appeared] four times under [the] same circumstances. Last one a bull elk. Then buffalo four times, last one a bull buffalo, and she saw a very short man disappear into the brush and she saw a wren who told her that that was Bonee (Bonee is strong, is dangerous, it is the noise made by an approaching hail storm or cyclone).[88] Bonee had given them that meat because he wanted to marry their daughter and if they did not want her to marry him they must all run away, not wait for anything or Bonee would kill them. But first they must bury a stone mallet used to crack marrow bones under the door place of the lodge and then run.

Pretty soon Bonee came, he was a short thickset man and came into their lodge, but there was no one there so he looked for tracks, smelling around until he found where they had started out and was about to follow when he heard a baby cry in the lodge and turned back and searched the lodge and didn't see anything and started off again. [152] Again he heard the baby cry in the lodge and went back and searched the lodge more carefully but found nothing again. He started out and heard the baby cry again. This time he went back and swallowed everything in the lodge and started out again. Again the baby cried and he went back and swallowed the lodge and swallowed everything he could find as big as a pin this time (fourth). He got away on the trail. The daughter being young and swift got away ahead of [her] father and mother and Bonee overtook the father and swallowed him, then the mother and swallowed her, and pursued the trail until he was in sight of the daughter. The daughter ran over a ridge out of sight of Bonee and saw an old man sitting there making a bow and she ran up to him. He said, "What [is the] matter [with] you?" She said, "Bonee is chasing me, have pity on me" and the old man's hair had been allowed to grow in front ever since he was a boy and it was tied over his forehead in a big bunch as was the custom of some of the tribes of the far north whose names we do not know. And he took her and tied her in that bundle of hair on his forehead. Pretty soon Bonee came and said, "Did you see a girl?" and [the] old man said, "No." Bonee said, "Yes, you did. Her tracks came right here." Old [153] Man said, "No, you go away. You bother me. I cannot make my bow. Go away." And Bonee kept on bothering him until the old man struck Bonee over the head with his

---

88 Scott uses two spellings for this name: Bonee and Bone. I have chosen the first for standardization. This is Bôhį̀ (Real or Original Bo/Very Strong), whose name may refer to the words bôgàu (bow) and hį̀ (real or original), hence Original or Very Strong Bow. Kiowa elders described Bo as a short, stocky, extremely strong man. Mooney (1898:411) reports Bo as a mythic dwarf of great strength. In 1935 Mary Buffalo reported to Weston La Barre (1935:120): "Dwarfs are small, but human beings; they live in the rocky mountains; they could crush a person's arm or leg, if they grabbed at it. They kill people also by throwing rocks at them. They make a sound [bo!] = the sound a bull makes, according to Kiowa notions. These dwarfs really lived long ago; Mary had heard an old woman talking about them." A brother of Taybodle had this name in the mid-1800s and composed a song about Young Mustang (Gúlhèi̇̀) that is now sung in the Kiowa Black Legs ceremonials (Meadows 2010:51).

bow and killed him. Then he said to the girl, "Where are you going?" and she said, "I have no place to go." And he said, "I will marry you and take you to my lodge, but I have got an old woman wife there and if she asks you to go swimming with her you go and swim six times but do not go seven times. It is dangerous." And he took her home to his lodge.

The next day he went out to hunt and the old woman asked the young one to go swimming and they went to where there was a deep pool at the foot of a large rock that had a cedar tree on it and tied a rope to the tree to hold on by and they swam out holding by the rope alternately six times. And the older woman tried to get her to go the 7th but she would not. They did this for six days in succession and on the 6th day they were playing together in the water, wrestling, when the younger one threw the older one down in the water and drowned her. There were lots of skulls there and bones where the older woman had drowned other people before. Pretty soon her husband came home and asked after his old woman and (see p. 155) said, "Where is my old woman?" And the younger wife said, "I drowned her" and the old man was very much astonished and said, "You drown[ed] her?" "Yes, I drown[ed] her." And the old man said, "Her brother is very dangerous. He will kill you. He is 'Sun.' He will kill you. Now if a man comes here while I am out don't you look at him, he will kill you if you look at him. Do not look at him."

[The] next day he went out to hunt and a man came and told her to look at him, but she did not look at him. He told her four times and got tired and went away. The next day he came again and said, "What [is the] matter [with] you, woman. Now you look at me." And she [did] not look at him four times and he went away. [The] next day he came again and said, "You [do] not look at me. Today, woman, I [will] kill you" ([repeated] four times). As she [did] not look at him, he went away. [The] next day (fourth) he said, "You [are a] pretty strong heart woman. You [will] not look at me. I [will] not allow anybody look at me, but you [are a] strong heart woman. I [will] let you look at me, and [if] you [do] not look at me today you [will] not see me anymore. I [will] not come back." And she [did] not look at him and he went out but she began to think, "I wonder what he looks like. He is not coming back again. I wonder what he looks like" and she [156] took her awl and bore [bored] a tiny hole through the lodge cover to see what he was like and he called out, "I know. You look[ed] at me, you [are] not [a] strong heart woman" and he came back. It was Sun and he see [saw] her look through the hole and he killed her.

[154]
Arrows

Cheyenne arrows always have a black or dark blue band of paint around the shaft near the notch and have turkey feathers. They never have other feathers except the little boys who may use others.

    Cheyenne and Arapahoe [see figure]
    Cheyenne and Arapahoe
    Kiowa and Comanche
    Kiowa, Comanche, and Apache both [sides]
    Kiowa, Comanche, and Apache

Osage [arrows have] no fluting, they have thick arrows and a very thick notch for the fingers to grasp and a long feather. The head is straighter across behind. Caddo arrows have no fluting, its [their] head is beveled off behind. [A] Pawnee does not wet the sinew wrapping about the end of the feather. He ties it on with dried sinew. Otherwise, it is like the Wichita arrow.

    ([p.] 156 continued)

Scinday and the Boy Who Killed the Eagle

A long time ago there was a boy in the Kiowa village whose father and mother were both dead. And he lived with his grandmother who was very poor. They lived poorly and had a small lodge. The chief who had the village had two daughters. The older was the prettier and this chief came out one day and harangued the camp, saying that the man who shot an arrow up and killed a young eagle that was high up in a nest on a tree close by should marry his daughter. Everybody wanted her but she wouldn't listen to any one [and] said, "No. No. Go away" whenever any young man made love to [approached?] her. The boy heard the chief and said, "Grandmother, I am going to make some arrows" and his grandmother laughed at him [and] said, "You. You are nothing but a boy, a poor, weak, boy. You are unkept and frizzle-headed. Big men are trying to kill that bird. You are only a poor, weak, little boy." [157]

Then the boy started to make some arrows and everyday he saw the best men of the village shooting at the eagle and their arrows turned in the air and came down long before they got as high as the nest. He made four arrows and a bow. The bow made from the rib of a buffalo, very strong, and when all were finished he hid them under his arms with his robe around him and approached the group firing at the eagle. Scinday

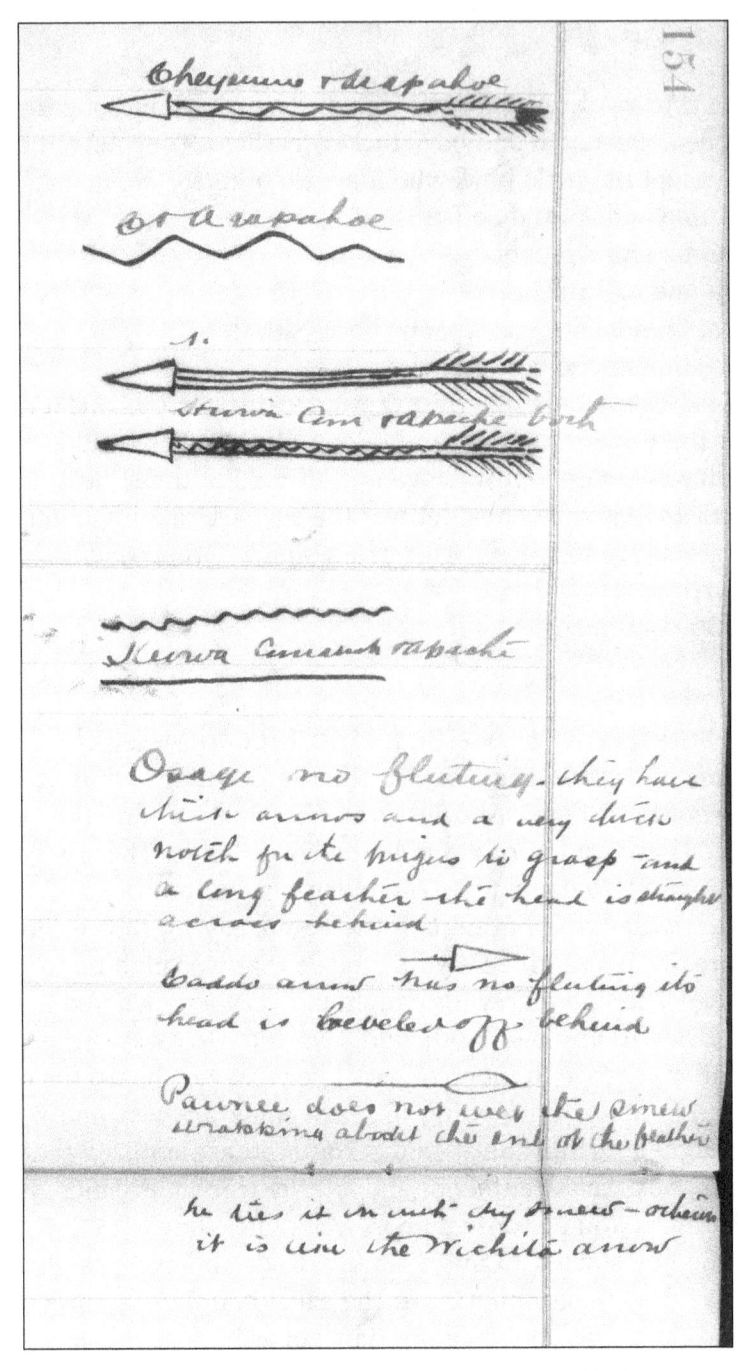

Ledger image of arrow styles (vol. I, p. 154).
Courtesy of Fort Sill National Historic Landmark and Museum Archive and Wade Popp.

was there shooting but had failed to get anywhere near the bird and he made fun of the boy, "Hello, Boy. What [are] you looking for? You going to shoot [the] eagle?" And [the] boy said, "Yes, I am going to shoot [the] eagle" and everybody laughed at the idea. Then he made one shot which fell short of the nest but way above where any of the others had gone, and they all cried out in wonder at the boy. His second shot touched the nest but did not penetrate. His third [shot] penetrated the edge of the nest and went through without touching the bird. The fourth penetrated the nest and the bird and knocked it out of the nest. When it fell to the ground they called the chief to come and look at it and Scinday took his own arrow and put it in the bird and claimed the girl when her father came. But the bystanders [158] all declared that the boy had done it. Scinday insisted that he had done it and the chief, being unable to decide, gave the elder, prettier girl to Scinday and the younger to the boy.

That day the boy said to his wife, "You watch the point of that hill. I am going to come up over it just at sundown. If you see a fine-looking young man coming that will be I" and he went to his Grandmother's lodge and said, "Grandmother, get me a big kettle," and she went out and borrowed the biggest kettle she could find, filled it full of water, and put it on the fire and made it boil. And Boy said, "Go out, Grandmother, but stand where you can hear me call" and he got into the boiling kettle and came out a handsome young man. Some medicine took pity on him and made him a handsome young man and he called his grandmother who put aside the door and looked in and was struck with amazement. Then he told her to go out again and she went out and this time he thought of what a good man needed, leggings, shirt, war bonnet, and pulled them out one after another. Then he pulled out everything a good man needed, shield, bow and quiver, arrows, etc., [159] put them on, and called his grandmother who was delighted that he was a poor boy no longer. Then he went down secretly in the place where the paint juts out at [the] bend of the river and just before the sun went down he raised [came up over] the hill. His wife was watching for him and she called out for everybody to come out and look at the fine young man coming. Scinday was mad and would not come out. He sulked in the lodge lying on the bed on his side. When everybody was through admiring him, the boy came into the lodge to put his things on the bed on his side and the elder sister fell in love with him. Scinday would not say a word from envy and jealousy and pretty soon his wife scolded him and told him he was no good and she left him and went over with the boy who married them both, and he beat Scinday.

Scinday and the Beavers

One day Scinday was very hungry and came to a stream full of beavers and he wanted to deceive them so he could eat them. So he said to them, "What are you poor beavers looking here for? There is very little water in this pond and you have no trees left to eat. You live poor. I saw a stream with [160] water right over that smooth ridge. There is a great deal of timber there and if you move there you will be always full of wood."

The Beaver Chief said, "What do you have that club for?" Scinday said, "That ought not to scare you. I always carry it." After a council among themselves the beaver agreed to move if he would show them the way. They gave him the pipe and they started off to the new place, making a column almost one hundred yards long with Scinday in front. When they got to the top of the divide the chief beaver said, "I do not see any stream over there" and there was nothing there but a high prairie and the beaver got scared and started back. But Scinday hit him on the head with his club and killed him and struck at the others, killing them in their flight back to their creek until he had killed all but one which reached the creek and got away. Then Scinday made a hole and lined it with grass and put the beavers on it covering them with grass and big rocks, then with earth and out on top a big fire. [The] next morning he took off the fire and let the pit cool and eat [ate] beavers until he was full up to his eyes. [161]

Scinday and the Bald Headed Eagle

One day Scinday was watching a bald headed eagle (white headed) and he was diving into the water sometimes where there was an open space in the ice. The eagle had a whistle and every now and then he whistled, dived, and caught something good to eat. Sometimes it was a beaver, sometimes it was a fish, a big fish. Then Scinday went to him and asked the eagle to have mercy on him and give him some of his medicine so he could do that also and get something good to eat when he was hungry. At first the eagle would not listen to him but after Scinday pushed him a while, he got tired and gave in and said, "All right I give you this whistle. You take it, paint your head and arms and legs white with white clay and then you can dive and catch things. Shut your eyes and dive four times, not anymore." So Scinday did as he was told by the bald headed eagle. He painted himself, put on the whistle, and went down to the creek and when he saw a beaver under water he blew his whistle, shut his eyes, and dived for him but he struck his head against the ice. The blood flew out and he was knocked insensible but when he came to he caught the whistle and threw it away, very angry at the bald eagle and his bad medicine.

[162]
When the Osages Cut Off the Kiowa[s]' Heads
Taybodle
Before the Osages cut the heads off the Kiowas the big village was on Mirey Creek.[89] The buffalo were far away so they moved first right to Eagle Heart's and next to Apache Creek where Carrither's Mission now is and the young men went up to the Keechei [Keechi] Hills looking for buffalo.[90] They were not plentiful then only here and there one and the young men found one killed that day and a broken Osage arrow lying by it. This was near the Keechei Hills. They picked it up and examined it and recognized it. It was an Osage arrow and they took it back to the village at once and the old men ordered the horses brought in as soon as they saw it and they watched until morning.

Early the next morning they divided up into three parties my father [Taybodle's father] took me with one party south of Mt. Scott to Quanah's, another party went in behind Saddle Mountain (between it and the mountains) through the Cuthead Pass and camped at the Cuthead Spring (Jackson Spring now).[91] Tohausen went back with a 3rd party to the then camp at Rainy Mountain [at the mountain and not the mouth of the creek]. None of these parties had many men with them, only women and children, old men and a few good men. The others were all on the warpath against the Utes.

Before daylight the next morning, a man camped near the Cuthead Spring; a man got uneasy about his horses and went out to look for them. They were back near the camp, back toward the pass. The man saw some people coming who chased and fired at him. He was a fast runner and ran back and called out "The Osages are coming." Some women were moving about camp and heard him and gave the alarm. Some ran away and escaped. Some got on top of a little rocky hill nearby, most of them

---

[89] Chènvǎu (Mirey or Boggy Creek) is the Kiowa name for the lower portion of Rainy Mountain Creek, so named for its deep channel and muddy nature, which joins the Washita River just east of present-day Mountain View, Oklahoma.

[90] Eagle Heart's camp was located on Cache Creek eleven miles south of Carnegie, in Caddo County, Oklahoma. Eagle Heart Bridge is in the vicinity. The Keechi Hills are just south of Anadarko in southeastern Caddo County.

[91] Quanah Parker was not yet born in 1833, so this refers to where he would later camp on the reservation. The spring and site of the attack are located on the Jack Hailey Ranch, section 7, T4N, R15W, Cooperton Quadrangle, Comanche County, Oklahoma.

women and children. The Osages surrounded [163] them and killed them all but their women and one boy.[92]

When they come down the valley from the pass shooting and making a noise the horses stampeded to the west and they did not get any of them. Some [of] Tohausen's people heard the shooting and came over and found the village destroyed and the people lying on the ground with their heads cut off and missing.[93] Five chiefs were killed and a great many women and children. They followed the trail for the Osages had taken back through the pass but were too few to take it up and accomplish anything. They found the missing heads where the Osages had left their robes and baggage before making the charge at the bottom of the little rocky hill. To the left of the pass going west they had left the heads in a circle there, gotten their robes, and gone back through the pass afoot and camped somewhere near Stumbling Bear's (who lives on creek running into Medicine Bluff at the foot of Mt. Scott). They were all very tired and laid down in a circle around their prisoners. A rain was coming up during the night and one of the women woke up and sat up and saw that all the Osages were asleep. She got up carefully and stepped gently over the Osages and escaped in the darkness. She followed the party I belonged to past Quanahs and they had gone past Navajo Mountain and one day they saw someone coming on foot far out on the prairie and knew it was an escaped person. She was brought into my father's lodge. [164] I was old enough then to round up a buffalo calf. There was no Sun Dance that year and it was in the middle of the summer. A message was sent for the woman's husband who was with Tohausen. She told us what had happened and when her husband came he put her on his horse behind him and went back to Tohausen's camp. The Kiowas all went to a small stream running into the Arkansas. There were a lot of Comanches there and a man who had been wounded by the Osages died there. The Comanches were all angry when they heard about [the Osages'] cutting the Kiowas' heads off. And a Comanche chief named "Big Wolf" gave the pipe to the Comanches, Kiowas, Apaches, and Wichitas and a big war party was collecting as they moved south and camped on the head of Elk Creek. From there they sent a few scouts to look for the Osages. They found the Osage village moving beyond the North Canadian and came back and reported. Then the big village moved to the Washita below the mouth of Stinking

---

92 This is the small hill that was just south of the encampment.
93 According to U.S. Geological Survey 7.5 topographic maps the Cut Throat Massacre Site is 11.9 miles from Rainy Mountain.

Creek where they camped and sent eight Wichitas on foot to look for the Osage[s]' village again. They came back in ten days and reported that the Osages were on Beaver Creek east of [Fort] Reno. Then a big crowd of them saddled up, went over on the South Canadian and discussed there a plan of action. The Osage village was not far away. Four men on fast long distance horses were selected. They were selected to go over and draw the Osages into an ambush [165] because the Osage village was too large for us to attack. Ten men started over, three of whom went together, two Comanche[s] and one Kiowa. As they neared the Osage village they found a freshly killed buffalo in a little creek running into the North Canadian and a gun was lying beside it so they hid there behind a cutbank in the creek. They said to each other, "That man will come back for his gun and we will kill him." When he came to look for his gun they charged him. The first Comanche about to spear him had his horse put his foot in a hole and both fell to the ground. The second Comanche struck his spear into the Osage, knocked him off his horse, and the Kiowa struck him and took his scalp. The Osages all saw it and mounted up and followed the scouts. The Kiowa and Comanche warparty were waiting for them and when they came up charged them on horseback. They fought each other until both sides were tired out and separated, each going home. They killed and scalped that first man and so retaliated for cutting off the Kiowa heads. They got even. Only that one man was killed on either side.

Not long after that a Comanche war party went east looking for Caddos. They crossed south of Fort Sill over on to the Beaver and saw up near the Little Washita some people coming at a distance. They were not Caddos. [166] They could see that but could not tell who they were, a big crowd of them. They watched them for some time and saw that they had a white flag. Then three men in fast long-distance horses were sent to see who they were with another white flag. They met and the scouts came back and reported that they were white men, that they had a pipe from their great chief to make peace with these Indians, and they were now looking for the Kiowas. They had a Kiowa woman with them and ten Osages.

The Comanche war party turned back with them south of the mountains and went to the Wichita village on the North Fork Red River (Walnut Creek). The Kiowas then were camped at the mouth of Mirey Creek on the Washita. A Comanche brought them word that white soldiers were at the Wichita village and waited to see them. The Kiowas then moved to Elk Creek and Tohausen with some of his principal men went over to the Wichita village. They saw white soldiers but were afraid to go near them.

The soldiers were camped in the timber to the west of the village. After a while a Comanche came out and told them to come in, that it was all right. The soldiers were not looking for war. They did not come to fight. Then they went in and next the white soldiers. The soldiers called a council at which [167] Tohausen and his people were present and the soldiers told Tohausen, "Our father gave me a pipe. You and the Osages have been fighting each other. It is bad to fight each other now, cut it off. I want you to make peace. That is what I am moving about for. I have got here a Kiowa woman. I give her back to you. I am not looking for any money. I give her to you as a prairie gift. I want you to make peace with the Osages." The woman was one of those stolen at the Cuthead Pass by the Osages, the rope tied around the lodge poles at smoke hole. Her name was Wum-pan-to-da. The council said that, "It was bad to kill each other all the time. We will not put your words aside. We will take them up and make peace." Then the soldiers moved the men to the Washita at the mouth of Rainy Mountain Creek and off down the Washita and Tohausen, as he had agreed, followed them over with a party of men and women. They went with the soldiers somewhere northeast where there was a big white man's village and someone who could talk signs and there the white man's chief gave them beef, sugar, and coffee. They had never seen spotted cattle and sugar coffee before and were surprised at them and they saw a wagon for the first time. The chief asked them how long they wished to stay there and they replied "four days." They camped [168] off by themselves. Someone was sick in the white man's village and the Kiowas camped at a distance. When only one day was left the white man chief sent for them to come to a big council where there was a shade built like this one. When they got there they were astonished. There were big piles of presents there, blankets and guns on each pile for the men, and woman's things in the piles for women. There was a big pile for each person, women and all, a great many different things for each person and the white chief said, "I am going to do something wise. I am going to give these things to you as a prairie gift. I am going to give each man a medal and then stop and tomorrow you can go home." And the white chief ordered that they be given a medal of hard white money to each man and they had them. Then the chief took them out of a box, chief's medals. He ordered it and next day then they started, went home afoot driving all their horses loaded down with presents to the Kiowa camp which had moved to where "Cloud Chief" is now on the Washita at the mouth of the Cavalry Creek and everybody was astonished at the presents they brought back.

They traveled [and] moved about that winter and next spring moved to the Red Hills and they heard that a party of Osages were coming to [169] make peace with them. They met them at the Caddo Springs north of Darlington, the Osage village was north of that place on a creek that headed up toward Caddo Springs (probably Kingfisher Creek). The Osages took their men to their village and the Osage chief said to Tohausen over there on the mountains we got two of your medicines, one big and one little Taime. Do you want them? And he said, "Yes, I want them." And the Osage chief took the big one out of a box and they recognized it and the O [Osage] chief said the other one was on another creek where an Osage had it, and they went over there and an Osage young man told the Osage what the chief had said and he replied, "All right good." He had not heard before that the chief had given the medicines to the Kiowas but the medicines now belonged to the Kiowas and he would give them and they were recovered. And Tohausen took them each to the Red Hills where they made a Sun Dance right away. After that they moved down to where Fort Sill is now and a great many Comanches and Wichitas moved there and camped where the Post Garden is now. The Lodges covered the whole country down past the quarry and over where they kill the beef (Red Store) and Heidsick made a Calumet Dance right where the flagpole is now. Heidsick was [170] younger than I am but not as strong as I am now.

Peace Made with Cheyennes and Arapahoes*

When we lived north in the country of the Wood Rock [Devil's Tower], in very old times before I was born, we used to fight the Cheyennes and Arapahoes. We used to go to visit the Crows, and when a small party went the Cheyennes saw them, they would kill them all. That is the way it used to be until I was grown. I remember a fight with the Cheyennes on Wolf Creek. It was over a big extent of country between the Wolf and Beaver, just above where the soldiers afterwards built the fort (Fort Supply). There were twenty-one Kiowas killed, I do not know how many Cheyennes, I saw ten myself. It covered a large country and I did not see them all. I was married and a good man at the time of the fight.

[side note, 170] * Note we call the Apaches (Kiowa) Kau-pa-to = whetstone men in our language. We say they each talk dif[ferent] languages. He says woman buy horse in Kiowa. We call Comanches "Fight Men," because we used to fight them. We call Pawnee[s] = Wolf Men because they used to have wolf skins on their heads while scouting.

When I was still young, two Arapahoes came to the Kiowa camp, which was on the head of the Red River, looking for the Kiowas to make peace that was some time after the Osages cut off the Kiowas' heads. We fought the Cheyennes and Arapahoes at that time. The two Arapahoes made peace and went back to their people who were with the Cheyennes and told them that they made a good peace. The next spring, two Cheyennes came to Kiowa peace looking and we made peace with them. It was the custom always to give good pipe when they came looking for peace that way. We made a Sun Dance [171] twice that year. The Cheyennes helped us to make one, the second one. That is the only time we ever made peace with the Cheyennes and Arapahoes. (This was probably in the year 1841: see Tohausen's Calendar.)

Cut Off Heads Pass: Sitting under Sain-to's (Horse Looker) [Tsa-toke or Hunting Horse] shade on Spring Creek and looking behind Saddle Mountain toward the Cut Off Head Mountains, the pass looks as below (Aug. 9, 1897).

The heads were found in a circle to the left of the pass at the foot of a little rocky hill on the west side of the range. The pass is a pony trail, and [a] fine view can be had from its summit west and S. [south], [the] flat beyond the spring is covered with mesquite trees, thousands of them. There is a cottonwood tree blazed just below the spring said to have been blazed about at the time of the fight to commemorate the event, but [the] tree looks too young for that, it is a very old blaze nevertheless.

Medicine Bluffs

When the Kiowas first saw Medicine Bluffs they were astonished at seeing a mountain split in two and half of it gone. We called it Medicine Split in Two Mountain. There was nothing like it anywhere we went. I never heard that the Kiowas slept for medicine dreams on it, but I know that the Comanches did and the point of Mount Sheridan. The Strong Spring was a medicine place [172]. Also there is such a deep hole in the spring down through the rock there must be a strong medicine there (Zoo-dle-toon) Vomit Springs or Sulphur Spring on Stinking Creek which heads at Saddle Mountain. This spring is at a high hill near [the] crossing of upper [Fort] Elliot and Fort Sill trail is another Medicine place where we first knew of it. If a man's stomach were very sick and he drank some of its water it mixed around in his stomach for some time and then he would vomit both the water and the sickness. The buckeye nut, which grows on a little bush on the Washita, was used that way also. The nut was pounded up into a powder and swallowed and acted like a vomit water.

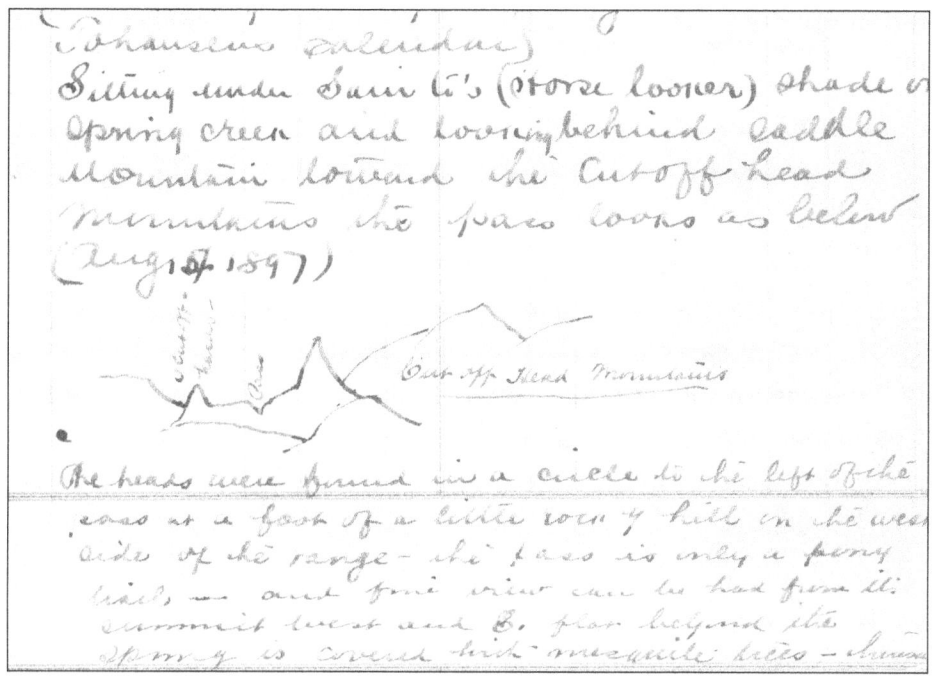

Ledger image of Cutthroat Mountain (vol. I, p. 171).
Courtesy of Fort Sill National Historic Landmark and Museum Archive and Wade Popp.

Buffalo Tree

Out on the big flat east of Vomit Creek and east of Man Who Stands In The Middle is a place where you and I camped the time you were coming back from killing those turkeys there in a tree.[94] That is a Buffalo Tree. One year the Sun Dance was made below Poor Buffalo's on the Washita in the big bend opposite to high painted bluff and they set out to kill the buffalo for the Sun Dance and they killed the buffalo here. And some time afterwards a woman had a dream in which she saw a buffalo who told her to come out on the flat and when she saw some bones there they would be his. And when she woke up she went there where the dream told [173] her and there was a mesquite tree grazing among the bones of

---

94 Based on the name, this individual is probably Vàuigài.

the Sun Dance buffalo. That is the buffalo's spirit and the Kiowa[s] make presents to it sometimes.[95]

BEAR LODGE AND PLEIADES (SEE PP. 60–99)
Taybodle
Before the Kiowa[s] grew up there were other people who lived up north before the Kiowas. They were all medicine people the before or first people. They all had strong medicine. I do not know what became of those people. I think Scinday was one of those people.

One time up there there were eight children playing bear together, chasing each other.[96] First one was bear and chased the others until tired and then another took it up and bit one who said, "No. I do not want to be the bear. I will be a real bear if I do." But they insisted until she was tired and gave in to them. But first she told them, "If I am a real bear you must get in a dog house (made for a bitch with puppies) or I will eat you." Then she became a bear and chased them but the children ran into a doghouse and she could not get them. The doghouse was too small and uncomfortable for them all so when the bear went away the seven little girls came out and started off but the bear found it out and came after them again. She was gaining on them when they met a medicine man who asked them why they were running and they told him a bear was after them. So he gave them stone sharp points which they threw them down and when the bear came she got them in her feet and stopped to take them out and lost a great deal of time in doing it. The [174] girls gained on her for a while but looking backwards for her they saw her come up over the hill gaining on them. Then they met another Medicine man who gave them the manifold of a buffalo which when they threw it down behind them caused the earth to form deep canyons and so delay the bear climbing over them. They kept looking backward and again saw the bear come over the hill and they met another Medicine man who gave them the stomach of the buffalo, which they threw behind them and turned the country into deep

---

95 Because the Kiowas took only the hide from the bison bull sacrificed to obtain its hide for the Sun Dance center pole, its carcass would not have been butchered (though probably scavenged by animals) and would have remained in a fairly confined area. A picture of this tree with offerings is contained in the map of Black Goose (Meadows 2008:194–95, 199–200).

96 This game is called Sétyáiàum (Bear Play). It is similar in some aspects to the game of tag. In some forms it involved one person who was bear and protected a cache of "plums" made of mud in a cluster. The others tried to steal a plum from the nest without being tagged ("bitten" by the bear and thus becoming the bear). The object was not to become the bear (Meadows 2010:321–23).

hollows. And the fourth time she came up on them a medicine man made a river rise and an alligator took them across but the bear swam across and gained on them again. Finally the children saw a small rock and jumped on it and called to the rock to take pity on them and the rock began to raise them up higher and higher out of the reach of the bear who jumped at them again and again and broke off its claws which were found around the rock turned into stone. But the seven sisters were raised up and up to the clouds where they now are the seven stars in a cluster.

Kiowa Bands

Taybodle

The Kiowa[s] have 6 bands: 1. Real Kiowa, 2. Elk Men, 3. Big Shield Men because they used to carry big shields, 4. Bite Men, 5. Black Men, darker than Real Kiowas, 6. Scinday's Son Men.

Four [the fourth] were [175] call[ed] "Biter Men" because a part of the Kiowas liked the Biters [Arikaras] and stayed with them a good deal and so got the name. These bands are not affiliated bands or remnants of other peoples but they are all Kiowas related to each other and grown up together from the first. Specify identically the same language and in fact one people. We call the Cheyennes "Sarco." We do not know what it means. We call the Sioux "Codle Pache," which means "Necklace People." The Comanches call the Cheyennes Tsee-en-mavo "Turkey Feather" or spotted stripped feather because they used the turkey feathers on their arrows.[97]

When we gathered together for a Sun Dance we always camped in one way, in a circle with the opening toward the east, the different bands by themselves.

Long ago these bands usually went in different parts of the country. I used to hear the Elk Men are over there, and the Biter[s] are in another place, etc., the men and women of the same band often marry and all bands intermarry. My mother was a Shield. My father was a true Kiowa and I am a true Kiowa.[98] The bands are all intermixed—they marry themselves [within the same band] also.

Tsatante [White Bear] was [176] an Elk. Poor Buffalo [is] a true Kiowa. Tohausen was a Shield Man, Koh-mar-ty is a Scinday.

---

97 One of two interpretations of the sign language sign for the Cheyennes is based on the use of striped turkey wing feathers for arrow fletching (Clark 1885:98). These Kiowa names are Sáqàutjàu (Northern Biters) for the Cheyennes and Qólpàgàu (Necklace People) for the Sioux (Meadows 2013).
98 This suggests a patrilineal tendency in recognizing descent.

> When we gathered together for a sundance we always camped in one way — in a circle with the opening toward the East — the different bands by themselves
>
> ✓1 Ímo sumas
> ✓2 Elk
> ✓3 Sindiap
> ✓4 Black men
> ✓5 Shield Big
> ✓6 Biters
> ✓7 Kiowa Apaches
>
> Long ago these bands usually went in different parts of the country — I used to hear the Elk men are over there — and the Biters are in another place Etc — the men and women of

Ledger image of Kiowa Sun Dance encampment, image A (vol. I, p. 175).
Courtesy of Fort Sill National Historic Landmark and Museum Archive and Wade Popp.

Calumet Dance

[Iseeo]

The Calumet pipe is called in the sign language "child wave feather pipe." The stem is used without the bowl. It is decorated with red horsehair and eagle tail feathers. The Cheyennes and all red people have this dance I have heard. I saw the Wichitas do it once. My wife is half Wichita and I lived with them for a while. Lone Wolf, a Pawnee chief, made a Calumet Dance. The Pawnees came down and we heard that they had a calumet looking for the Wichitas and one night a crier rode through the camp and said they will be here tomorrow.[99] When they arrived they had a council of all Wichita chiefs and the Pawnees were a little on one side by themselves and the Wichita chiefs argued by themselves as to which one loved his child the best (most?). Finally one chief was selected and

---

[99] Quaker missionary Thomas Battey (1875:130–34) witnessed a Calumet Ceremony between the Pawnees and Kiowas from March 3 to 15, 1873, when peace was made between the two. The Kiowa name of the Calumet Dance is Í àumcùngà (Child-Making Dance). See Meadows (2010:254–56, 262–64).

his name given to the Pawnees who said, "Aho. Aho. [Thank you. Thank you.] Good. Good. What is the name of another man who loves his child?" And another was selected and the Pawnees said, "Thank you. We will dance tonight. We will not sleep at all and tomorrow before the sun is up we will seize and capture the child."

I did not know [177] about that dance and I wanted to see it. It was a wonderful dance I heard and when I heard a drum that night I went over there and saw the Wichitas' men and women standing around in a circle. They had a wide lodge (i.e., opened out), and within the circle was a fire to make a light and two Pawnees were dancing. Each Pawnee had a calumet in his left hand and a rattle in his right. They had [no] clothing on but their breechclouts, they were equipped alike. The other Pawnees were looking on with the Wichitas. Their dance is a hard one, just as hard as the dance of the Chiricahua Apaches here, the Esaquitas. They start together forward with long steps like the Apaches. Then they sit down and wave the calumet and shake their rattles. I cannot do it as they did. Then they get up, pass and repass back to each other going under the calumet, which is raised for the purpose like a wing of a bird, the drum going all the time. Then they squat down and wave [the] calumet again, swaying their bodies to the time of the drum and the singing. Then they sit down in their place and put their calumets in two forked sticks a little in front and to the side of each one. [visualize a pole laid horizontal supported by two upright forked poles]

The space has been cleaned off for twenty feet in diameter and made smooth for the dance and a fire is kept at the other end (see <p.>180). [178] In front and at right angles to the two calumets are eight or ten pipes with bowls filled ready for smoking and placed so the bowls are upright. When they get up to dance they start forward together, take up the calumets from the racks, waving it, and dance their peculiar steps, rushing past each other and under their wings raised to permit it, then when these [men] are tired the calumets are replaced on the racks and they sit down and eight or ten Pawnee men take the pipes, light them, and present the mouth pieces (first to two dancers) to the Wichita and Pawnee men standing about as spectators, and so on, all night.

The next morning they already knew where the chiefs lived and when it began to get light before the sun came up the Pawnees crept secretly to the chief's lodge as if they were making an attack and rushed in and seized the child, brought it out in their arms, and put it on a man's back who held his arms in front and two Pawnee men held his legs behind.

They then seize[d] the other child in the same way and go [went] back to the dance ground, first the men with the children, then the drum and crowd of singers, then the two dancers with [the] calumet, and when they get back each of the children are seated on a pile of fine blankets a foot or more thick in front of the dancers and the Pawnee chief tells his people to bring out ([continued on p.] 180)

[179]
Night Arrangement with about Four Wide Lodges
Day Arrangement
The lodges are folded up at daylight and taken away and a shade is put up overhead of the dancers and drummers of a hide lodge cover.

[180] [continued from 178] anything they have that is valuable, [or] good, [is brought out] and make [placed in] piles, and they bring out blankets, guns, shirts, leggings, [and] anything valuable they may have and make one row of piles near each boy. And they put a post in the ground near the fire with a buffalo robe wrapped around it (represents a man, just like a man standing) and the father of one of the boys dressed up men with [a] shield, war-bonnet, etc., just as if he was going to war and mounted on a horse rides up as if he was angry, strikes his spear into the post, then rides up to the drum, [and] counts his coup, which goes "Poww." When he is through he dismounts, gives his horse to a dancer, and goes out and does it again until he is tired and the father of the other boy does the same. They do not touch the piles of things.

Afterwards the relatives of each boy in their respective side do the same, they strike the post, go up to the drum, count their coups, and [he] goes back to some pile that he places on his own side. The Pawnees all watch him and know their own piles and when he takes up a pile to the Po [Pawnees] who own it, goes there and the Wichitas give him the horse which is put in with the other horses on that side. When the piles are almost exhausted they are replenished by the Pawnees and so on until all the Pawnee valuables are exhausted. Then the dancers get up and dance until they are tired out and sit down. [181] Then the Pawnee chief says to them, "You have made a good dance. I see you are very tried. I want you to go to that herd of ponies and take your choice of those horses" and the two calumet men say, "Aho, aho" (Thank you, thank you). Then the calumet men each give a calumet with its proper bowl attached to each of the boys who are presented each with the pile of blankets he sat on during the ceremony and the ceremony is over.

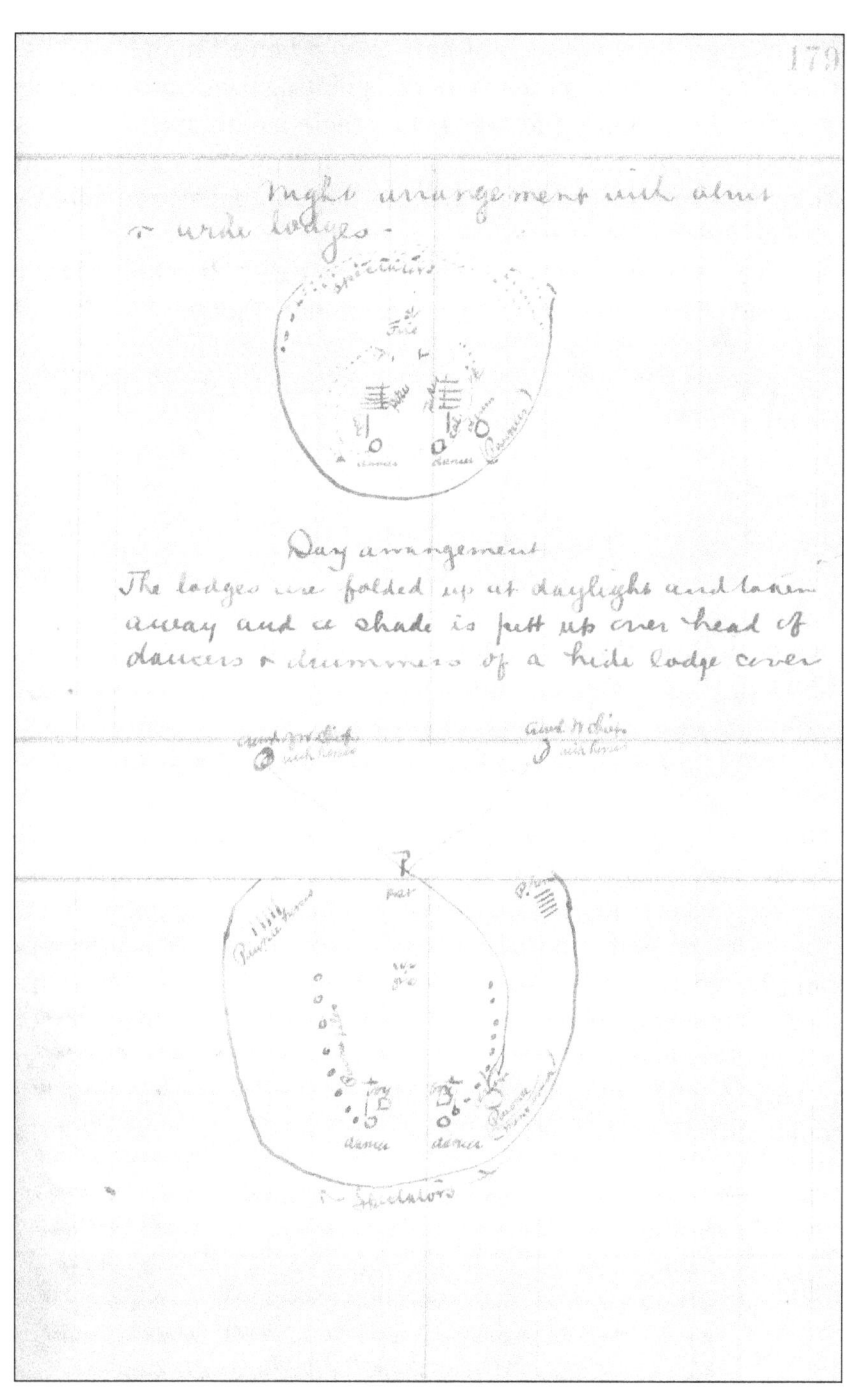

Ledger image of Calumet Ceremony, night and day arrangements. (vol. I, p. 179). *Courtesy of Fort Sill National Historic Landmark and Museum Archive and Wade Popp.*

The calumets have a bunch of hair from a horse's mane colored red, fastened near the mouth piece in a bunch pointing backward, and another about the middle pointing forward with eagle feathers below. The stem above both are preudent [similar in position?] to the way the calumet looks, very [much] like the new Catlin's picture, page [probably Catlin Vol. 1:plate 98].

Some far away northeast timber men we call "Ollar-ho." They have shaved heads like the Osages.[100] They come down looking for Kiowas to Zebile's where he lives now.[101] They gave him the calumet and after a few years he gave it to the Comanche chief Atta-Kanick [Attockanie] who has it now. It was done where he lives now north of that pass back of Quanah. There was only one calumet I think but I do not know for I didn't see it, but when the Pawnees made it there were two. I know because I saw them. Qua Kanico made it one or two years before I came with the soldiers here.

[182] I came a few days after you did, February 1889. Zebile kept it about two years and gave it to Atta-Kanick. One time the Kiowas were camped at the end of the mountains and the Wichitas came looking for the Kiowas. They had two calumets and they gave them to Hawgone's [Silverhorn's] father, Tohausen. Qua-ha-da Tohausen and to my uncle "Rises From The Water." It was fourteen years ago. [today's date] August 19, 1897.[102]

Another was made many years before I was born by Heidsick who you know. It was long before the soldiers made this post, Fort Sill. He made it right where the flagpole is now standing on this parade (center). The Kiowa lodges were all down Cache Creek to the rock quarry and all around [the] cemetery now to Quinette's Store to the creek. An immense number of Comanches were camped almost where the sub-agency of the Comanches is now. The Wichitas had come over from their village on the North Fork Red River at the Wichita Mountains (it was before they lived here) and gave the calumet to Heidsicki, who was a boy then.[103] I do not

---

100 This may refer to the Quapaws, whom the Kiowas call Àláhògàu.
101 This refers to Zabile (Zêbàèl or Big Arrows), who took his allotment along Stinking Creek just west of Carnegie, Oklahoma. That may have been the area referred to.
102 Silverhorn's father was Done-pi (Dáunfài or Against The Chuck Or Shoulder Blade Area). His byname of "Quahada Tohausen" comes from his residing near the Quahada Comanches on the Staked Plains in prereservation times. "Rises From The Water" may refer to Tǫ́cài (Arose From The Water) or Tǫ́càbáudài (Appeared From The Water).
103 As Heidsick was born in 1816 (Kiowa Family Record 1901: Fam. 65), this ceremony would probably have been held in the 1820s. Hâichècì is the Comanche version of his Kiowa name Càuáufìtạu (Crow [Feathered Sheathed] Lance), which is often listed in agency records as Ga-a-pia-tan.

know about another boy with him, I forgot. Long ago the Arapahoes gave it to the Kiowas on Stone Creek west of here.[104] I do not know where and the Osages gave it to my brother Iseeo, whose name I have taken (who was killed by the Sik-kee-vo, Sauks and Foxes in 1854) before I was born, but it was after the peace with the Osages. [183] All those different tribes make the calumet dance in exactly the same way as I have told you about the Pawnees and the wide tipi was made, just like that picture in Catlin's book p. [blank].[105] The wide tipis sometimes have four lodge skins. Lodges opened out so as to make a big place. All tribes do it sometimes. It is expressed this way "Some red tribe has a child wave feathers pipe and they come looking for a Kiowa chief, they make a dance (wave), and give the calumet to the children."

Crazy People and Mad Wolves

I have often heard of mad wolves biting people. The only case I know about is Son-kia-do-te [Sankadota, a Kiowa man] who lives at Mount Scott. A Comanche who had wolf medicine knows, [he] made medicine and cured him, San-kia-do-te.

I used to know a crazy Kiowa older than I am. He played with the children while he was a grown man. He used to whip the children while he was not angry, laughing all the time. He did not do anything dangerous. The time the Kiowas ran off from Anadarko (? 1874) he was with them at the head of Red River. It was the middle of winter and very cold with deep snow. The soldiers were following them about. [184] One day there was an alarm and the Kiowas mounted in a hurry and abandoned the crazy man and they never saw him again. We do not know whether the soldiers killed him or the cold. Sun Boy's son was crazy. He was not angry crazy, he just walked about silent, then he got thinner and thinner until he died.*

* The results of an investigation made by the Commissioner of Indian Affairs in 1897 show that there are but sixty-eight insane Indians in the United States. Some of these are idiots [mentally challenged]. Horace P. Jones tells me that eleven rattlesnake bites were reported to him among the Comanches in one year with no deaths.

---

104 This is probably modern-day Sugar Creek, near Sedan in Kiowa County, Oklahoma, which was also known earlier by the Kiowa name of Xòdômvằu (Pebble Creek) for the prevalence of sizable stones that lined its course.
105 For images of calumets, see plates 55 and 98 in Catlin (1841).

Comanches Cure Snakebites
(Iseeo Brought the Root)

This is the root the Comanches used to cure rattlesnake bites. All Kiowas and Comanches know it. It is chewed up like mescal and put on the wound and it will not swell up after a bite. I know that has cured bites made by rattlesnakes. Most Comanches carry some of the dried roots about with them. See Whipple Report (1853, Ex. Doc. No. 90, 33rd Congress, 2nd Session—I).

Vincente says that when he was a captive among the Comanches he was bitten by a rattlesnake. The Indians scarified the wounded foot with a flint, rubbed it with a weed, bruised the snake and told him to take hold of it. He was afraid to do so but they told him he would die if he did not. He then grasped it anvalsiou [?] and then coiled it around the wound. He was cured of course and his foot now bears the scar.

Capt. John Pope 1853, Botany, p. 163, *a cerates paniculate anantherix paniculatus Natt.* [Found in] sandy soil, [along] headwaters of the Colorado (Texas), April. This is the snake medicine of the Comanche Indian. Pah-sila = Hairless, Comanche, Sept. 11, 1897. Yes, I know that root. See p. 217 [below].

[217] (from p. 184). It is called by Comanches Quassy no von nat see = Medicine = Snake Medicine. Four men knew about that. Black Horse, the lame man below Quanah's, saw it first in a mescal dream and helped Quanah with it. Sarriet-tethka = Dog Eater, also means Arapaho, who died E. [early = young?] and is buried in the soldier graveyard, [he] knew it. And I am the fourth. I was going to Navajo one day with Quanah and he dismounted and dug up this root and when I asked him why he did it he said it cured snakebite.[106] It grows on the side of a hill and has a white flower. You get it in July. You cannot find it now. The stem is gone. When you want to go out on the side hill and when you see it, dismount, go around to the east of it and keep on around until you face the sun. You say to it, "I am [have] come for you. I want you to take pity on me. I am going to carry you always. I want you to cure the snakebite for me." Talk to it that way and it will keep [help] you. Then you take out your knife and dig a big hole around it and when large enough take out the bulb leaving the long thin part in the ground. Then cut off the stem and plant it again, cover it carefully. It will grow next spring. It will be bad to throw it away. If you get bitten, chew up and swallow a piece of the root as big

---

106 This may refer to Navajo Mountain, northwest of Quanah's encampment, in present-day Jackson County, Oklahoma.

as this [1 centimeter diameter]. Then take a larger piece and chew it up and spit it in the two tooth marks and some on your hands and rub it all over the swelling. If it has only swollen a little, take two fingers, spit some of the chewed root on them, and draw two rings around [the] upper part of [the] swelling. If the bite is old and there has been a big swelling do the same with four fingers and the swelling will go down. It may go thus, three fingers [in] depth, but when it gets to the fourth finger it will go back and recede (see p. 211 [below]).

[185]

CADDOS

[probably from Caddo Jake]
Pronounced Nashi-dosh. See Parkman's LaSalle, p. 281. Caddo Jake born [in] Louisiana, part (1/4) French blood.

Caddo Tribe. The Caddos were composed of the following bands. Hainai = Meaning unknown. Anadarko = A big black and yellow wasp, 1-1/2 inch long. Caddo = Adarko = Sharp Caddo. Na-co-a-doches = Northern, the same white people call Nachez. Nache-doshy = Paw Paw Indians. Ya-ta-chi = Unknown. Haish = Yellow Men, lighter in color than other Caddos. Ha-da-i = Thicket Men. Apa-lash [Appalachicolas] used to live sometimes with the Caddos but are somewhere on the Gulf now. Gulf [of Mexico] is called "Big Water."

The Caddos used to live under ground. I don't know how they got out but they came out of the ground on the north side of Red River near its mouth. They remained around the hole until they were counted and the way it was done was for each man to take up some dirt on the point of his arrow and come up and throw it in a pile and when they were through counting them the pile was a mountain.

The first thing they found to eat was a weed that is good to eat when it is young but is hard when it grows up (Lambs Quarters). Afterwards we got deer and bear and fish and a water lily root, blackberries, persimmons, and Indian potatoes. We have some of those potatoes here on Sugar Creek. They grow wild [and], taste just like sweet potatoes, and are red, blue, and yellow inside. They are very large in Louisiana. We also eat a plant called Chicos (means peeling), which is a plant like green brier with a root about six to eight inches in diameter. We slice it, mash it in a corn mortar, wash and strain it through a cloth, and when dry it makes a flour from which we baked a bread that is better than [186] white man's bread. The root grows around Tuskahoma [Oklahoma] in the Choctaw nation but not around here. The bread we called "Chicos Bread." We used the roots like potatoes sometimes. We lived in grass houses like the Wichitas near where we came out of the ground. We Caddos came out first (from the ground), afterwards other tribes, all Indians came out of that hole, Muscogees, Seminoles, Shawnees, all kinds of Indians. Some went east looking for something to eat. Some west, some north, some south, and after they had separated they got different languages. At first they spoke the same language. Once we got settled we got corn and beans of different kinds like the white man's beans. One kind, a flat white bean, and we raised melons [and] persimmons. We did not know anything about tobacco.

We got smallpox and a great many Caddos died. Then smallpox came again and we moved away to the south side of Red River (we call it Red River also), near its mouth and made a town. It was called Anadarko. West of there were Anadarkos who lived in it (but [now there is only] one Anadarko left. I saw him today August 10, 1897. Harry Shirly, son of old Bill Shirly [William Shirley] the interpreter). After a while two families settled close to us (not French) from the north then more came. Then they killed two Caddos then drove off some of their horses and the Caddos had no peace there and moved away to Texas near Hueco [Waco] but lower down [the] Brazos [River] without hurting any white man. Then we were uneasy about white people and moved to Fort Belknap on Clear Fork [of the] Brazos and there we were driven out of there and came here. You know about our coming here in '59 [1859] with Horace P. Jones. I do not know where we can go now unless it will be [187] to Mexico. We used to travel east sometimes trading with other Indians and we talked a sign language with those people, something like the men we use here now but different in some things. All these tribes talked sign language. We did not fight those people. We fought Comanches, Kiowas, and Osages, not Wichitas. We often came out on the Plains as far as Comanche Peak looking for buffalo. It is [so] named because the Comanches used to climb it when searching for a look and "Caddo" means a little bird with yellow tips to its wings that lives about here in the brush, lots of them together. Jake is a Nachi-dosh, so is Bob Dunlop. Red bean is called Day-kin-o. The Caddo[s] had a great many signs [sign language signs] in their old home, now woman, horse, deer, bear, Osage. I cannot think of any more now. We learned these other signs after we moved out on the prairie.

Persimmons

Persimmon is called Na-say-kay by the Comanches. Kiowa, Ko-pa-a-lo (Osage Man Fruit).[107] That is also the name for dates [the fruit]. In the sign language it is called "Osage Man's Fruit." A long time ago the Kiowas lived on the Arkansas and did not understand the persimmon well and the Osages came out that way. They understood the persimmon. They had something blue that was like a long plug of tobacco, flat and blue. When we bit off a piece [it was] like biting off a [188] chew of tobacco. When we tasted it, we understood it was dried persimmon. The Osage women gather them off the ground, take out the seeds, press them into a flat cake like a long plug of tobacco and dry them and they are very good to eat. They are sweet. If you eat persimmons in the summer they will choke you [from their bitterness]. You must wait until fall and they fall to the ground [ripe]. The Comanche women do it now sometimes, press them into wide sheets. Also the Kiowa women [do this], when they find enough persimmons, but they are not thick here like they are in the Osage Country.

Old Man Esa Rosa—White Wolf. Died September 29, 1897, heart disease.

[189] Quanah Parker died of pneumonia [and was] buried at Post Oak Cemetery west of his house. Thomas Clancey died in Manila May 30, 1911, of injuries from falling out of a window. [It was] a great sorrow for the Scott Family. He was our sergeant Troop [L], 7th Cavalry at the time of his death. He was with me and [Ernest] Stecker nine years at Sill. He came to me in Cuba (four years) when I was ordered to Puerto Rico as Chief of Staff and got transferred there. I was ordered back from Santiago de Cuba and never went to Puerto Rico. Clancey got his discharge and a swell position at the Palace at Havana until the intervention ended in Washington. I got him a position as clerk for the Inspector General at San Antonio, Texas. I saw him next at Jolo, P.I. [Philippine Islands] in about 1905 for the last time. I asked Secretary of Indians Garfield then to appoint Stecker Agent at Anadarko, which he did. Francis Leupp, Commissioner of Indian Affairs, said, "Do you know what you have done? You have defeated Dr. Hugh Scott of Oklahoma City for the position of Agent at Anadarko. I had never heard of Dr. Hugh Scott before."

---

107 Osage fruit would be Qáupàlåugàu in Kiowa.

[190]
Tree Signs (see p. 200 also)

Iseeo (Kiowa)

Birch = strip bark tree.

Chokecherry = berry pounded in left hand with bottom of closed right fist. Grows along a ridge in places.

Pine = chewing gum tree, because the pine gum is boiled and used as a chewing gum.

Greasewood = cactus bush, on account of thorns.

Oak = acorn tree.

Willow = tree growing along water. Signs are water, tree growing, down left arm.

Spruce = lodge pole tree. Kiowas say spruce makes best lodge poles of all varieties of wood.

Cedar = smell tree.

Elm = two kinds. One low growing on prairie by itself wide, white and red shade = buffalo tree, because buffalo used to congregate under their shade. Other variety grows in the woods and is called "Saddle tree" because the old time people used this elm to make saddles.

Cottonwood = "Sun Dance Tree" because it is always used for center pole and to make the medicine lodge.

Ash = tough tree, because its wood is tough.

Walnut = cut nose tree, because the weathered nut separates into two halves with two small holes in each half, which brings to mind the nostrils of a woman who has been caught in infidelity and her nose cut off.

Pecan = end of thumb (size) and fat, because it is a very oily nut.

Hackberry = small berry tree.

Bois d'Arc = yellow bow wood.

[191]
Navajos, April 22, 1908, at Smeth, Utah

Navajos are not sign talkers in the meaning of that term as applied to the Plains tribes. But in [on the] above date they made the following signs used as gestures to accompany their spoken language, viz. grass, equality, go.

"Clar" the Navajo judge made the sign for "growing up from childhood," also "to go," also a "far" and a "near" sign with identical meaning as shown by his spoken language, also a "calm down" and "all gone."

Dr. John of Shiprock, N.M., said the Navajos lived under ground long ago. The water rose and they came out of a hole near the La Plata Mountains (Utah ?, Col. ?). "Clar" used the term in spoken language to Kill by a Lily "for nothing" (i.e., murder him).

Navajos were called Navajos by the early Spanish who said it meant "Grandes Sementerias." See papers of the Archaeological Inst. of America. American Series III. Final Report of Investigations, Part I. A. F. Bandolier, Cambridge 1890.

[192]

SOLDIER BANDS—KIOWA

The Kiowa boys all belong to one band, which is called the "Rabbit Band." The old women all belong to the "Old Woman Band." Young women and girls are not organized.

Soldiers

1. Elk Horse, All have whistles   Capt. Dahawsen
2. Black Leggins   Taybodle
3. Goat   Tahbonemah Capt.[108]
4. Horse Eaters?
5. Rattle
1. Rattle foot—Tsait'ant'e
2. Rattle horse—Old Lone Wolf
3. Goat—Big Bow
4. Black Leggins—Poor Buffalo
5. Elk Horse—Tsait'anke

1. Elk   Captain = men who had the soldiers
2. Shield   Elk Tongue—all are now given up.
3. Biter
4. Kiowas

---

108 The placement and temporal context of these three names are unclear but imply that they are leaders of the first three societies listed in the left column. While Dohausen was the Qóichégàu or Dog Society leader up to 1866, Taybodle was also a member of that society when it ceased to meet around 1887. By the time this account was collected (ca. 1897) all of the Kiowa men's societies were defunct, as reflected in Elk Tongue's subsequent statement. Similar statements were made by E-mau-tah (Émàuthâầ or Arising Crying, born 1860) (Kiowa Family Record 1901: Fam. 34), also known as Frizzle Head II (Áulpépjè II), in 1935 (Meadows 1999, 2010:447).

Each company of soldier bands has four officers just like you, a Capt. and three lieutenants. When we go on the warpath two officers march in front and two behind.

Elk Horse
    Rattle   Satanta Capt.
    Goat   Big Bow Capt.
    Black Leggins   Heidsick Capt.
    Scout Horses   Satanke Capt.

6th: This used to be in existence in old times and was called Goy-e-tain (meaning unknown). These different soldier bands have dances and songs different from each other. If Elk Horse soldier is about to meet the enemy, he sings one of the soldier songs. One interpretation is, "If we should fight a battle, I will not leave the field alive." If a Rattle soldier, he might sing, "If my enemies kill me somewhere, do not cry for me I will not know it." If a Goat soldier, he might sing, "The band [193] (i.e., the spirit goat band in the other world) wants me I will go now." Another song is, "Everybody must die, but the sun and the earth remain eternal. Everything else dies, all else is mortal."

The Black Leg soldiers paint their legs black below their knees when they go dance. One of them has a crooked lance. The Rattle soldiers have two arrows and two red squaw cloth sashes. When Satank was taken away from here and killed in the flat below here by the soldiers, he was singing his soldier song because he knew he was going to die.

The women's band of soldiers is called the "Old Woman's Band." A woman joins it when she gets married. They have songs of their own and a dance. They dance around in a circle to the left, without holding hands. The men look [watch] but do not dance with them.

There are five soldier bands for the men. The Elk skin soldiers wear a sash of elk skin over their shoulders. Only ten of them wear these sashes, which are painted black with a hole at the end of the long streamer, which is usually rolled up and carried under the arm. When he wants to make an example to keep the young men from retreating in a fight, he unrolls the streamer and shoots an arrow into the hole pinning it to the ground and he is like a horse tied to a peg. He can only go around the arrow until he is killed or some have [a] friend [who] at the risk of his life pulls up the arrow and liberates him. These are both very brave deeds. That elk skin have had the hardest road, the Black Leggins next, and the other bands behind. In the Black Leggins Band there are eight men with lances, four with crooked lances and four with straight ones wrapped with beaver skin, the custom being in reverse [retreat], to stick the lance into the ground, dismount, turn their horses loose, and remain fighting around their lances until they are killed or rescued by a friend, pulling the lance up and take them away behind them on their ponies. Everybody charges back to their assistance to rescue theses from the enemy. This is a good way to attain a chief's road. The Rabbit band of foot soldiers are foot soldiers only during the Sun Dance ceremony. We used to have a great many other soldier bands when we had more men, but when we got fewer in number, we put those ceremonies aside when they Sun Dance, until we only had five left. Now we have but throw all away.[109]

MEN'S NAMES/PLACES

[194]

Isee-o = Plenty Camps

Bolant = Bo, a snake; lant, to travel = traveling snake

Satanta = White Bear

Satanke = Sitting Bear

Sitting Bull

Black Coyote

Black Wolf

Horse Comes Last

Horse Road

Horse Guard

White Horse (Kiowa)

Black Horse (Comanche)

Quanah = Smell

Ahpiatun = Wooden Lance

Walks In The Clouds

White Wolf

---

109 This is one of the few instances that notes the presence of other previously existing societies. For the most extensive works on Kiowa military societies, see Meadows (1999, 2010).

Big Crow

Hanameatah = Charging Man

Tabahenty = Sweat House

Lone Wolf

Tieh = Morning Star

Black Goose

Running Antelope

Lone Bear

Lame Bull

White Bull

One Ridge Bear

Red Elk

Whistling Elk

Touch The Clouds

Stone Calf = Mountain Calf

Satanta = Satanke

Tohausen = Little Mtn.

Taybodle = _____

Agent Hayward = Red Beard

Agent Day = Big Belly

Agent Stall = Red Neck

Darlington—False Teeth, 1st agent for Cheyennes and Arapahoes and who have a sign of their name for all their agents = False Teeth called Ca yay yay = by the Arapahoes

Major Woodsen called "Scar Over His Eye"

Cpt. Scott called by the Comanches = Molaytayquap = Sign Talker

By Kiowas—Wide Trousers. By other plains tribes "Metal Eyes"—called metal eyes first by Kiowas until death of namesake

Tah-bone-mah = grandson when name was changed to prevent the reoccurrence of the sorrow of relatives on hearing name of the dead

American Horse = Tall Horse

Cpt. Bonnerite = Bald Head

Agent Hayward = Red Beard

Col. William Bent = Eagle Nosed White Man Married To Cheyenne Wife—(Kiowas) Roman Nose [195]

Col. William Bent's fort on the Arkansas = Stone House

Thomas Fitzpatrick = Bad Hand (Snakes [Shoshones]) Bad = Brown Hand

Capt. [Wm. Philo] Clark = Wa po sta ona—White Hat (Sioux)

William Sublette = Cut Face (Snakes); Left Hand (Cheyennes) Beckworth

Gen Wm. Clark = Red Haired Chief = Beckw [see *Beckworth*] (184)

Gen'l Sheridan (Southern Indians) Little Man with Big Stomach, at Sill

Gen'l Custer = Yellow Sash (short)—had one on in '68 campaign, Fair Long Hair

Gen'l Custer = Long Hair Among Sioux

Gen'l Miles = Bear Coat. North and South

James Beckworth = (Crows) "Medicine Calf" Beck; White Handled Knife (Snakes); Cheyennes "The Crow"

Horace Jones = Comanches; Co-cha-no-toa = Buffalo Calf; No-no Ba? Co-cha-paraivo, Buffalo Chief—that is more romantic

William Tulleck of Fullocks Fork (Crows) The Crane

Gen'l McKenzie = Cutfinger, Kiowa and Comanche [name]

Gen'l Harney = "White Bear" [see] *Sioux*, Renolds (p. 148)

Gen'l Crook = Grey Fox Three Stars

Amos Chapman = No Walker

Billy Dickson = Long Hair

Philip McCuster = Mac [MacKenzie expedition?]

(wild) Stillwell ["cat" marked out before "(wild)," Wildcat?].

Jack Stillwell = Jack

Fort Sill = Soldier House at the Mountains

Fort Peck = Red Haired Man's House (Sioux)

Fort Keogh = Bear Coat's House—Red Cloud

Sitting Bull = Sitting Bull

Crazy Horse = [no entry]

Spotted Tail = [no entry]

Tini Pete = String Beard

Long Neck = a white man who talked good Kiowa on the Arkansas when we lived there and who came back to us here three years ago

Agent Hayward = Red Beard

Col. Wynkoop = Red Neck

Red Neck (1845): The man who came down from Arkansas River with Adobe Walls and went back after two years trading and abandoned the house

Dr. Clark = EL = Nock a toa = "Ears Child" (on face in front of right ear) from (execesemes) [eczema on face near right ear]

Fort Reno = Cheyenne soldier house on Wolf Creek

Fort Supply = Cheyenne soldier house on Wolf Creek

Fort Elliot [no entry]

Fort Sill = Soldier house at the mountains or Kiowa or Comanche soldier house—preferably "Mountain Soldier House" (see p. 207)

[196]
Descriptions of Signs That May Be Forgotten
Fog = rain smoke, points of fingers down in front.

Smoke = something like a rain cloud, jagged ends down made by arms at full length in front hands at right angles to arms, fingers spread out, and downward like a curtain in front of face with jagged points. It hangs down before you like a curtain.

Jealous = push outward with both hands, one at a time, giving idea of effort to elbows, one at a time. Just like Quanah, Big Looking Glass, Comanches, each wants to be a chief, anything that two men are trying hard to attain, to make a chief's road or both want a woman [and] each tries to push the other off to one side. All Kiowas, Cheyennes, Arapahoes, [Comanches], and Apaches understand that sign.

Horse race = horse contest.

To bet = to meet equally. Number one left forefinger, number two right forefinger, opposed. Make often to show progress of making bets until race or other matter is arranged and all property put up.

To bet horses = make sign with right and left hands opposed in front of face of horses facing each other, standing still, in front of speaker, fingers down.

To get even = make sign for buy or swap, bringing the fingers upward with emphasis. As soon as forefingers are crossed. Suppose you killed my son and I met you. I say a long time ago you kill[ed] my son. Now I kill you. X [forefingers crossed]. I get even, just that way like swap or if a man steals something from me and I find out without his knowing it. I think that man is a fool. He steal [stole] that from me. He got [a] good horse today. I take it. I get even. X [forefingers crossed]. If one man who has a lot of relatives is killed on [the] warpath, a good-looking man, his relatives' hearts cry. It rankles in their hearts and they go about unhappy for a long time. Everybody knows about it. After a while the chiefs take pity on the relatives and all get together and go to [197] see them and say, "We [are] going to take pity on you. We are going to send [a] warparty down to get even. X [forefingers crossed]."

Accidental Killing = prairie killing. I will tell you about a case you know of yourself. Tonacho killed Baylaka's son.

Murder = secret killing or quarrel killing. They also recognize accident and killed in war or battle or fight killing or warpath killing or mad killing = killed in wrath.

Point of a hill jutting against round cut bank on a creek. To-hau-sen = Little Bluff = [image].[110]

Shadow = with a man, with a dog, etc. For a man's shadow, a dog's shadow. When you are a baby and your mother holds you, it comes. It is with you all day. It lies down with you at night. You see it by the light of the fire. It grows up with you. That is the reason it has that name. Also make shade along with left hand down low and point to shadow it makes with right.

Soft = catch point of right forefinger loose and flexible with tips of left thumb and forefinger so as to flex it loosely. This means soft like dough or flexible like a rope.

---

110 A protruding bluff face, often with an undercut face or recess is known as a *jòhâu*. Several Kiowa oral and calendar sources reference this feature in both personal and place-names, often giving the translation "bluff." But a protruding bluff point, typically with an undercut, is a more accurate description of the geographic form. *Qā́ugáu* is a bank, bluff, or cliff.

Slow = bad legs behind, like a mule.

Quiver = motion over left shoulder like grandfather. [198] with sash down in front from left to right.

Polecat [Skunk] = stripe over head or flirting tail with bad smell.

Scalp = swipe down right side of head.

Otter = water swimmer and, if misunderstood, sign for wrapping hair braid also.

Thin = little greasy.

Aurora = strong cold rising above horizon, tips of fingers spread out above [entry crossed out with pen marks in original]

Sundogs = strong cold standing, two of the fingers crept and bobtailed. [entry crossed out with pen marks in original].

Leaf = tree with left hand bursting towards right.

Snow and Hail = white rain for hail, cold white hard lump of proper sign.

Gall = Kiowa name for gall = standing spoon, for standing make the same sign as for man.

Spoon = scoop up from left to right.

Scout = several signs. One, hold quiver in left arm like buy. Second, wolf looking, or wolf skin held in left arm like baby.

Soap = rub palm of left hand with half closed right.

Gray Fox = quirt handle or loop which the wrist is put through to support. A long time ago whenever a man saw one of those he wanted it for his quirt loop and so they called it that. [199]

Box Elder = Kiowa Tree because its pith smells like a Kiowa.

Snake Medicine is a plant that grows near Fort Sill.

Red Flower Wood = red bud. The Judas tree.

Ghost = spirit or owl's ears or round eyes or whirlwind. Sometimes you see something misty: look at it for a while and then look away somewhere else and you see the same thing over there and then you recognize it. It was the spirit or ghost of that Kiowa you know that died over there. Kiowas [are] not afraid of ghosts. Also "feather leggin" is a ghost. Whirlwind gives facial paralysis by twisting your face.[111]

---

111 Kiowas traditionally attribute facial paralysis or "twisting" (Bell's Palsy) to encounters with spirits of the dead (via owls or the sudden appearance of ghosts) and whirlwinds. They call this *pópqûngà* and in euphemism *chòicúngà*.

Poison Vine = vine scratch.

Spirit = the escaping breath spirit as efftatus–life source. See dictionary.

Dogwood Tree = arrow wood.

Bear Kidney Tree = kidneys in fat. Has large bean pod in which seeds lie like beans.

Green = black. Trees are said to be black when in full leaf as they look black in the prairie at a distance.

Cedar = smell tree.

Platte River = Fat or Greasy [River].

Cattail = water plant blind, because the fruit will make you blind if it gets in your eyes.

Sage Wood or Plant = white plant. A patch of it looks white from a distance. It is used with the Sun Dance or Time [Táimé] ceremonies because it came down with the Time from the Crow Indians.

Crow = sign is same as in north. Kiowa name is Kaw-gia = Crow. Gia = man. See [illegible].[112]

[200]

Sioux Gahe' wichasta = Crow man.

Plum Tree = end of thumb, size of plum, tree.

Grapevine = pull berries and winding over tree.

Mesquite = bean tree, showing long mesquite bean pods of which bead is made.

Osage Orange = bow wood. Another bowwood is better called "side hill" tree. It grows on the edge of the Staked Plains on head [of] Red River. Wood is brown in color and is most elastic of all woods for bows.

Pomme Blanche = Kiowa sign same as for heart.

Peach Tree = end of fingers in a bunch, size of peach.

Apple Tree = fist tree.

Bark of a Tree = stripping bark.

Hackberry [Tree] = rough bark tree.

Elm Tree = Buffalo tree, because the buffalo when they were plentiful used to stand in its shade and scratch themselves against its bark.

---

112 This appears to be a shortened form. The Kiowa name for the Crows is Càuáuqàgàu (Crow Men/People).

286   THE SCOTT LEDGERS AT FORT SILL

Cattail = Blind Plant. It grows in the water and old men say that if you get the pus in your eyes it will make you blind.

Walnut Tree = Cut nose tree.

Willow = Sweat house tree. Sweat houses are usually made of them.

Skunkberry Tree = Buffalo robe paint tree. The Kiowas used to paint their robes with red ink [paint] made from the berries.

Devil's Catchers = Are sometimes called antelope's horns, sometimes buffalo's horns. Seeds are eaten.[113]

Cactus = Prickly spines.

Liver = [no entry].

Frog = first and second fingers jumping into the water.

Beads = roll points of thumb and first finger [of] left hand pointed upwards as if turning hole in the bead to insert needle—just with right hand, as move fingers and points down. [201]]

Rays = See sunburst. Rays extending above horizon (right hand extended forward with fingers and thumb extended) widely expanded, sharply to the front. On the morning when the sun comes up the rays come through holes in lodge like a rope as it flares above the horizon before the sun comes up and after it goes down. A Comanche would not recognize that sign because he does not know the sign language but all Kiowas, Kiowa Apaches, Cheyennes, Arapahoes, Caddos, Wichitas, Pawnees, and Osages understand that when they see it.[114]

Box Elder Tree = Kiowa smell tree because the bush smells like a Kiowa Indian.

Lightning = bolt downward and zigzag flash.

Thunder = shooting down (after slapping hands with both hands).

Aurora = Springing of grass, on opening out of leaves, toward the north. Plenty soon spring will come.

Milky Way = Backbone of the stars.

Backbone = Hump. Both closed fists as in kill, back of right to right, left to left, left on top in front of body, slowly move apart a little. See stripe down back.

---

113 This plant is called *thàuigų́dólêgàu* (s), *thàuigų́dólê* (d/t) in Kiowa and Devil's Claw in English (*Proboscidea louisianica Martyniaceae*). Parker McKenzie to the author, Nov. 25, 1994, and July 26, 1996.
114 The context of this statement is unclear, as the Comanches clearly knew and used sign language.

Stretch = Haul apart. [202]

Meat = Kind, as buffalo eat, antelope eat, and speaking of meat on a hide they say, "Eat is cut off" (i.e., meat cut off).

Medicine Ties on a Pole = Two poles coming down from top, inside, tied on.

Strong (has three signs) = Brave, muscular, way ahead (superlative).

Different = Divergent as roads, another. Another in right, then in left.

Pawnee = Is called "wolf" [Wolf?, people] because we used to kill then and often find [found] that they had wolves' skins to put over their heads to scout with. The Navajos do that too.

Future = Beyond, on the other side.

Picket a Horse = Drive peg, tie.

Grasshopper = Sun fighter. If you look up toward the sun you can see sometimes the battle going on, mixing up among each other when in battle. Red tail, grass eater.

Eclipse = Sun dies.

Brains = Orifice and tan [referring to tanning hides].

Bat = Naked wings.

Ash Tree = Called Lance Wood because the lance handles are made of it. Sometimes tough tree also. Tent pins are made of it.

Horse Road = Pony trail.

Martinia = 1) antelope horns, or 2) buffalo horns = Seeds are eaten raw. White man calls them Devil [Devil's Catchers].

Basket = wooden, platted, kettle.

Crow = Black bird.

Blackbird with Yellow = Yellow, throat, and head.

[203]
Birds[, Snakes, and Plants]

Goose = Calling Bird, sometimes black stripes at throat.

Crane = Bird That Carries Its Child on Its Back. Sometimes as they pass over you hear them call and you can hear the cry of the young one also.

Blackbird with yellow throat = Spring Bird.

Cow Black Bird = Horse Bird, stands on horse's backbone.

Hawk = Bird That Strikes with Talons. Kiowas distinguish the "Red tailed, the striped, and swallow tailed hawks." The swallow tailed has some medicine. I have seen Heidsick go to war with a swallow tail on his head and another tied to his pony's tail.

Chicken = Imitate his turning up and then down on each side in flight.

Turkey = Striped wing bird and neck moving through grass. In old times it was called "Fast Trotter."

Quail = Little Turkey.

Sickle Bill Curlew = Long Curved Bill.

Grass Plover = Bird That Cries in Summer, from its plaintive note and time of southern migration.

Red Bird = Red Bird.

Night Hawk = Horse Lie, no reason known.

Red Headed Woodpecker = Red Head.

Flicker = Red Spotted Bird.

Bull Bat = Horse Lie.

Whippoorwill = Is called Big Throat. Does not sleep at night.

A big bird with black head = Sand Bird.

Road Runner = Rock Bird.

Scissor Bird [Scissortail Flycatcher] = Long Tail.

[204]

Buzzard = Stretch Out Blanket Bird. From habit of stretching out wings while at rest just like a man holding out the corners of a blanket.

Dove = Bird Comanche Make. No reason [why] known. Wichita = Fast Bird.

Prairie Dog Owl = Strong Water's Brother-in-Law or Prairie Dog's Brother-in-Law. He lives in same hole.

Birds' nest = Birds (X) Lodge.

Five kinds of eagles. No. 1 with large dark tips to feather of tail, rest white. Best of all. No. 2 Next best, spotted black and white on tail feathers. No. 3 Next in value = striped feathers in tail. No. 4 Next, spotted breast and tail. No. 5 Bald Eagle with white tail. Nobody wants the bald eagle.

Duck = Flies Up from Water.

Bird's Egg = Bird's Child, indicates sure of egg.

War or Golden eagles have sometimes one, sometimes two eggs. If there are two it is bad luck to take them both out of the nest. See my sickness on cattle trail and drowning of Ft. Sill soldier—told you so, [referring to the warning that] Elk Tongue, Domot, [and] Comanche George [gave him against disturbing the nest, see chapter 3 in this volume].

Lark = Bird That Talks All Different Languages. He says, "Woman, boy, horse" in Kiowa. The owl says Ee-ta-bee-ta-quoo—"Big Fire, big fire" in Kiowa.[115]

"Lives on Crane's Back" = (Kiowa), is about four inches in diameter round, is blue, has short bill, down on its back, and has no feathers. Kiowa have scared the crane, seen it fall off and caught it.

[205] Persimmon = Osage Man's Fruit.

Rushes = Water Plant.

Adder = Short Body and Big Flat Headed Snake.

Bull Snake = Rattles with Throat (i.e., like a rattlesnake hisses with rattles).

Rattlesnake = Rattle.

Water Lily = Water Plant with Broad Flat Leaves or Nostril Plant.

Magpie = Black and White Bird. They eat meat they steal it. None about Fort Sill, plenty in far north.

Wild Gourd = Vine on the Ground. Gourd size of fish called Stick Plant by Kiowas. This is the only thing cultivated by Spider Woman. Kiowas never cultivated anything. It was Spider Woman's Medicine Road. Red women never cultivated this plant, only Spider Woman. Mosquito hawk that found the buffalo [in Kiowa mythology].

[206 blank]

[207]

Names: Men and Places (see p. 195)

"Kiowa" Mountains are mountains near the head of the Missouri River. All the old Kiowas knew about [them] in the country of the geysers of Yellowstone Park.

---

115 The first word is this expression is *étjè* (large, big), followed by *fí* (fire).

Wichita Mountains, [the] main chain are called simply "The Mountains." They have a separate name for the northwest point of them, "Cut Off Head Mountains" referring to the cutting off the heads of the Kiowas by the Osages in 1832 [1833]. Separate names for Mount Scott and Mount Sheridan, for several peaks in southwest corner where the elk used to be very abundant = Elk Mountains. For the mountains about cattle trail on North Fork [of Red River] = Wichita Mountains from the former two villages of the Wichitas. There, [an] old, old village [was] abandoned once and the site reoccupied and again abandoned about 1850. End of the Mountains where mountains run out up the North Fork Red River near Comanche Springs, Texas.

[People] at Bent's Fort

Information obtained by Dr. [George B.] Grinnell from George Bent [in] 1908.

Tom La Forgie = Lame Man.

L. [Lt.] Maxwell = Big Nostrils (when Colonel Bent was away).

Murray (Irish) = Flat Nose.

Hatcher = Freckly Hand.

Tom Boggs = White Horse.

John Smith = Gray Thunder.

Kit Carson = Little Chief.

Charles Davis = Wolf.

Murray [=] Always In Charge.

Father DeSmet among the Blackfeet (p. 157), Long Tooth, McClintock (p. 166), usually called "Black Gown" as he was a Jesuit (p. 159). When he left to go back to the Flatheads he sent two other Black Robes, Short Man and Scar Face (p. 158). Because Motokis would not go to his class ceremony and went instead to hunt although warned by him, a bear killed him. DeSmet claimed it was because he would not heed [the] warning and the Bear Claws Worn People—Buffalo Chips and Snake Robes became his followers.

[208]

SIGNALS (SEE ALSO P. 8)
Kiowa

(Mobeadleky)
Buffalo = backwards and forward on top of ridge in plain view. Enemy = same, hidden below crest from the enemy. Yes, I had seen signals made by smoke. Sometimes large boys go out with a war party to learn. When they reach the place to hobble the animals and leave them and go on foot from there. The pipe man calls the boys up and gives them a wise talk and tells them that the white soldiers are moving about and they must look out for them and must watch the animals and if the white soldiers get too near they must drive off the animals and set fire to the prairie and while they are far away they will look backward and if they see a smoke there from a distance they will avoid that place lest they should be captured by the soldiers while returning to their horses. Another thing I have seen often, when a war party had been out against the Utes and had killed a man. While several days journey away from the village they built a fire with a big smoke and the women who looked every day towards the Ute country said, "They are coming back. They have killed a man." No fire was built unless they were successful and no Kiowa man had been killed.

Stumbling Bear
When the scouts found buffalo, plenty buffalo, and the village was moving in near in view of them, they would ride backward [209] and forward in sight of the village. If they are with a war party and see a man they ride in a circle. Sometimes they throw the blanket up in the air holding [on] to two corners, three or four times, which means they see buffalo.

When a war party (defeated) comes in sight of the village and we see them wave a blanket all around horizontally that means all [some] on our side have been killed. When we are returning from the warpath and want to find our village and do not know where it is we burn grass (see Custer's book p. 218 *My Life on the Plains*).

When a man is away from his village and it moves a stick is left in some prominent place to show him how to go straight. If it is a straight stick will be far away. If crooked they will not be far away. When a separation is made with view of meeting at [the] same spot and one man is killed belonging to the party that gets there first and goes away again, they paint the figures of the dead man's shield on a piece of blanket or skin and put blood on it. Then when you come there you know that man that had that shield is already dead. One time we came there and put a bear on my head and a sun on Sun Boy's head and they knew we had been there (see Long p. 478).

[210]
Paint Mines
Red paint at Stumbling Bear's house on Yamparika Creek = Timber Pass Creek. Red paint [is found] near [the] canyon of the Arkansas this side. We used to put it in big parfleches and carry it about with us. It was used a great deal in the medicine lodge. There is red paint at "Big Red's" place north of Mount Sheridan.

A yellow paint mine [is located] near the head of Apache Creek, south of Carrither's Mission.[116] A black paint mine [is located] near Double Mountain, Texas. Sometimes a man prayed to the paint medicine and gives it a present and it is tied on a tree nearby. We used to use white paint by digging it out of the ground and the women would put it in a kettle with water and boil it. After that they would spread the buffalo hide lodge cover out on the ground and swab that white paint on it and leave it to dry there. When it was put up it was white as your shirt. All southern Indians did that. There are many places to get white paint. There is a place in the middle of the road that goes to Mount Scott, just as you pass over the ridge where you can see Cheevers' house it is right in the middle of the road. There is another near Quanah's, another near [the] mouth of Rainy Mountain Creek, and all over the Plains of the Canadian and Cimarron [Rivers], [211] but there are but few red paint places.

[Rattlesnake Bite]
One time Poa-dee-a's brother was looking for his horses back of his lodge on the Blue Beaver [Creek]. There was a rattlesnake under a rock that bit him in the ankle as he stepped over the rock. He went to see what it was under there that bit him and saw that it was a rattlesnake. He called to his wife to bring a horse. He was very sick at his stomach and vomited. They got him home and sent for Quanah to come and told him they would give him a two-year-old horse and a beef. He came and reached there about 4:00 p.m. and spit some of that root on the leg, which was

---
116 Carrither's Mission was west of present-day Apache, in southern Caddo County, Oklahoma. I know of one Kiowa woman who collects yellow clay for paint from Palo Duro Canyon south of Amarillo, Texas.

very much swollen as he had been bitten in the morning. His heart was slow. He couldn't sit still, he was very ill. He eat some of that root and swallowed it. Quanah rubbed some in the bite and all over the swelling. Chew the root, spit it on his hands and rubbed it over the swelling. It did not swell any more and began to go down. He slept that night and next day said he was almost well. The swelling had gone down except a place as big as my fist about the bite. All Comanches know about that. Not long after it was put on he said he was water hungry. Then in a little while he said he was sleep hungry and went to sleep.

One time my horse was bitten on the foreleg while I was in camp coming down from Anadarko and I had a piece in my pocket. I made him swallow a small piece and rubbed and spit on the wound and swelling. He had been hobbled and was very lame from the bite. I chewed the root, spit it into the wound and spit and bubbled the swelling. In about two hours I went to look at him he was nearly well. I hitched him up and in a little while his lameness disappeared. I know that good. That root is chief, just as you are a chief (with shoulder sign __ it __chief).

I have got another medicine in this bag to cure earache. You smell it and it goes up through your nose, makes your head big, and the ache will go out your ears. I have another root at home like the snake medicine. I have cured tarantula bites. I cured Arko (Captain [of Indian] Police) and he offered me $10.00 to show him the root but I didn't want to let him know. I cured another Comanche at Anadarko. He vomited and was tired down when I got there. He had been bitten under the arm while asleep. He gave me two good horses and I cured him. I will come down in a few days and take you out and find the plant so you will know it yourself. I will give you a piece of this snake root I always carry in my pocket also and we will go out and find that root too. I have got another medicine Pore-to (a leaf) to cure cold and that is all the medicine I know.

[212]
Four Winds
Kiowas call the north wind the cold wind, east the right in front wind because their lodges always face the east and [the] east wind blows into the front of the lodges. West wind is called the sundown wind. South [wind] is called Apache Wind, reason unknown. Have no names for winds from other directions.

[213] Kiowa Mountains are near where the Gros Ventres live. They are very tall mountains. Sheep Mountain South Dakota = (Same) Sioux. Sheep Mountain Montana = (Same) Assine [Assiniboine].

Names of Mountains

Big Horn Mountains = Crow Mountains.

Wichita Mountains = same.

No Water Mountains at head of Otter Creek.

Cut Off Heads Mountains = Where Osages cut off heads [of] Kiowa[s].

Red Hills on Canadian [River] above Reno.

Big Mountain = Mount Scott.

Turned Up Point of Nose Mountain = Mount Sheridan.

Black Hills Dakota = Black Hills.

Bear Butte = Grizzly Bear Butte.

Bear Lodge Tower = Bear Lodge.

Double Mountain, Texas = same.

Mount Scott = Big Mountain.

Saddle "Bull Mountain" Montana Crow, same.

End of Mountains on N.F. Red River.

Staked Plains = High Wide Flat Country—Edge of south plains.

Antelope Horn Hills = The Deer's Ear, Dakota.

Antelope Hills on Canadian—same name.

Medicine Tohausen = Is on the upper Canadian River on the north side, has a very strong medicine.[117]

Mount Scott = Highest Mountain.

Mount Sheridan = Bull's Face Mountain.

Medicine Bluff = Split Mountain.

Quarry Hill from which stone for quarters at Fort Sill was taken = Hill Where Three Pawnees Slept.

Old Wichita village on present side of Fort Sill = Split Mountain Village, after Medicine Bluffs.

Old village on North Fork Red River also Mountains there = Kitti-ki-dish.

Buttes at the head of land and Sugar Creek = Barking Dogs.

---

117 This is Mount Rochester (Dá̄ujóhâu or Medicine Bluff Concavity) in Texas (Meadows 2008:265). For listings of many of these locations by their Kiowa and popular name, legal geographical location, and cultural affiliation, see Meadows (2008).

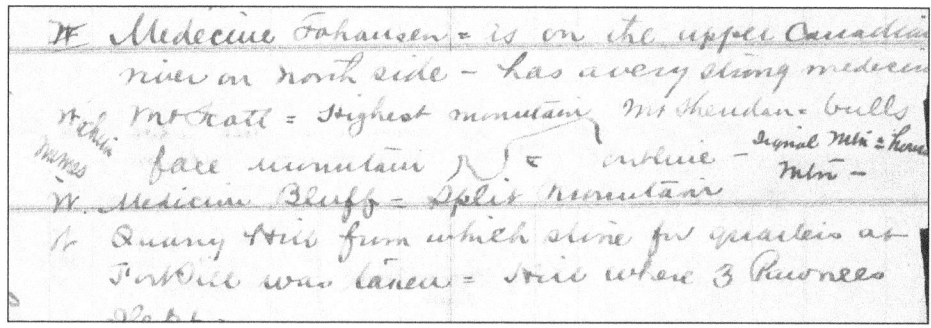

Ledger image of Mount Sheridan (Bull's Face Mountain) (vol. I, p. 213). *Courtesy of Fort Sill National Historic Landmark and Museum Archive and Wade Popp.*

High Hill on north side of Washita opposite Anadarko = Osage Hill—used to be a lookout for Osage War parties when Wichita[s] lived on North Fork Red River.

Keechi Hills = same name. [Where the] Keechi[s] lived when Wichitas moved to Washita River in 1859.

Wolf Mountains (Crow) = Rosebud Mountains (Sioux name).

Larnil Peak = Goose Mountains.

Wichita Prairie = Prairie at mouth of Sugar Creek.

Saddle Mountain = same name.

Osage Hill = just opposite North [of] Anadarko on the north side highest hill where Osage war parties used to lookout for Kiowas.

[214]

Names of Rivers

Rio Grande = Big River.

Palo Duro = Bull River.

Pecos = Comanche, Sands River; Kiowa, Little Rio Grande.

Pease River = Prairie Dog River.

Red = Big Sands.

Washita = Lodge Pole Creek.

Beaver Ck. [Creek], Tex. = Mirey Creek.

N. F. [North Fork] Red River = Walnut Creek.

Canadian = Red River.

N. F. Canadian = Wolf Creek, it is found by Wolf and Beaver.

Elk Creek = Fat Creek or Pecan Creek.

Otter Creek = Soldier Creek—Old Camp Radziminski was on it before the war [Civil War].

Cache Creek = Soldier Creek.

Brazos (Comanches and Kiowas) = Wood Arrowhead River.

Deep Red = [entry marked through].

Yamparika Creek = Timber Pass.

West Cache = Quanah Creek, old name Thick Timber Sugar Creek.

Noconie = Owl Creek.

Sulphur Creek = Vomit Creek—if you drink the sulfur water from spring you will vomit.

Rainy Mountain = Rainy Hill.

Rainy Mountain Creek = Mirey Creek.

Elk Fork [Red River] is called Salt Spring Creek.

Salt Fork Red River = Star Woman Wood Creek, whole river has this name.

Cobb Creek = Sugar Creek.

Sugar Creek = Sugar Creek.

Cimarron = [Bison] Bull River.

Salt Fork Arkansas = Salt Fork.

Medicine Lodge Creek Kansas = Timber Hill Creek.

Arkansas = Flint River.

Kansas = [no entry].

Republican = Chief River Cheyenne (see Long p. 440).

Wolf = Wolf [River].

Solomon = Turkey River (Cheyenne).

Smoky Hill = Grove River (Cheyenne).

N. Platte = Shell on Neck, also main Platte.

S. Platte = Fort River.

White River = Sioux Nasiisita = Two Morning East R.

Niobrara = Wind Changing [?] = rapid.

Missouri = Big River.

Bad River = Walepaha Saucha.

Cheyenne = Wakpala Washtay Good River.

[Illegible] = Inyan Wakka [creek?].

[215]
Missouri River is called by the Kiowas = Hard Stick Down River = which means the roughness due to broken ice cakes stick[ing] down or up or "Rough Ice River."

Pryor's Gap = Pryor's Fork = Arrow River (Crow) Mapora Agie. So named from arrow dents in rocks in the gap.

Grand River = Ree River. Chay-shoka-wakpala (Sioux).

Little Missouri = Thick Timber (Antelope—Cheyenne).

Belle Fourche (Upper) = Bear's Lodge Creek. Mato ti wakpala satu mini aha (Sioux Belle Fourche (Lower) = Red Water.

Box Elder = Hole in the Rock Creek. Inyan Okoloka; Chakady-tachesi-Son-yin-yan-its-ska (Sioux).

Power Tongue Rosebud = [no entry].

Little Big Horn = [no entry].

Big Horn = Es-ski-ska-wakpala (Sioux); Ets-pot-acis (Crow).

Clark's Fork Yellowstone = Stinking/Spoiled Buffalo Lingering.

Piney = [no entry].

Yellowstone = Elk River (Crow) Echida cashi agie.

Crazy (Lewd) Woman Creek = Weah witko wakpala (Sioux).

Clear Creek= Lodge Pole creek. Toshu Wakpala.

Milk River = Little River. Wakpala Chigalo.

[WICHITA STREAM NAMES]

Pond Creek, north of Washita River = The Water You Get Water Lily Roots to Eat.

Red River = Red River Caddos call it Red River also.

Wichita name for Washita River = River that runs around pointed bluffs in a crooked manner.

Cache Creek = Kitti-ki-dish = Wichita Creek.

Comanche Springs = Sparkling Springs. Saw them spurt like a geyser long ago.

North Fork Red River = White River; South Fork [Red River] Sand River.

Medicine Bluff Creek = Split in Two Mountain Creek.

North Fork Canadian River = Lots [of] Spider Ribs Creek. Spiders abundant there [illegible].

Arkansas River = White River, Flint River.

Quanah's on West Cache Creek = Sand Creek.

Blue Beaver (seven miles from Ft. Sill) = Good Arrow Wood Creek.

Big Spring, Northeast Saddle Mountain runs northwest into Stinking Creek = Whetstone Spring. Known by that name to Kiowas as Big Spring.

Rush Springs = same name.

Where Osages Cut Off Kiowa Heads Spring = Prairie Spring. This was owned by a spirit Wichita.

Elm Fork Red River = Fork or Place Where the River Forks.

Elk Creek = Pecan Creek or Fat Creek.

Stinking Creek = heads [starts] at Saddle Mountain, has a sulfur spring on it and is called "Vomit Creek" because the water will make you vomit if you drink it.

Tonkaway Creek = Maneater's Creek (see p. 258).

[258]
(names of Rivers [continued] from [p.] 214)

Republican called Iron Creek by the Kiowas.

Smoky Hill called Black Wood by the Kiowas.

Salt Fork Arkansas called Timber Mountain by the Kiowas.

[Note: preceding three lines crossed out in original.]

Kiowa spoken word for Arkansas River means Iron Arrowpoint. Cheyenne name is Flint River.[118]

Kiowa name for Palo Duro = Sun Dance Creek.

Cheyenne—Republican River = Chief River

Cheyenne—Soloman River = Turkey River.

Cheyenne—Smoky Hill River = Clumps of Cottonwood or Grove River.

Cheyenne and Kiowa—Pawnee Fork = Where "Red Arm" Was Killed [River?].

Cheyenne—Arickaree Fork = Ree [Arikara] River.

Cheyenne and Kiowa—Adobe Walls = Mud House on Canadian [River].

Cheyenne and Kiowa—Bent's Fort = Stone House on Arkansas [River].

Staked Plains = high flat prairie country.

Kiowa and Comanche—Pease River = Cedar River.

Cheyenne and Kiowa—Big Wichita = Blue Cedar [River].

Cheyenne and Kiowa—Little Wichita = Boggy [River].

Ponds. North Swan Lake = Where You Get Water Lily Roots to Eat.

Pond Creek = Water Lily Roots Creek, also Dr. Sturm's Creek.

Yellowhouse Spring = Yellowhouse [illegible word], Springs at the Head of the Brazos.

Sunwater Springs = [no entry].

Brazos = Arrowpoint River. Found stone arrowpoints there.

Laramie River = Goose River (Cheyenne).

Nueces = Pecan River.

Colorado of Texas = Blue or Clear Water [River] (Comanche).

San Saba = Rock Creek.

Salt Fork Red River = Star Woman's Tree Fork (Kiowa—medicine from quantity of weed they use as perfumes). Weed or Perfume Weed River—Comanche.

---

118 The Kiowa name for the Arkansas River is Sésèváu (Arrowhead River). It does not specify flint (qâuiqò, s/d/t: flint chips) or iron (hā́u), but is understood by older Kiowas originally to have implied flint points. Parker McKenzie was told by his grandfather Que-ton (b. 1844) that during his time Kiowas did not make stone projectile points but often collected them from campsites along the Arkansas River to use. Parker McKenzie to the author, Mar. 18 and Mar. 26, 1994.

Standing Rock = [no entry].

Forks of Washita from Gageby Creek = [no entry].

Chandler's Creek = Kobi (Comanche) [name] or Wild Horse Creek from a Kiowa chief of that name killed just above the Anadarko Road by Caddos just after "One Armed Man's" Sun Dance on the Arkansas—1862 Calendar.

Blue Beaver = Persimmon Creek. Persimmon groves near head.

Chandler's Spring = Big Spring (Kiowa and Comanche).

Comanche Springs = same Kiowa and Comanche. mn's [means] Wife Springs, where the man was killed for interfering with another.

[259]
Deep Springs = [no entry].

Walnut Creek, Kansas = One Armed Man's Creek (Ashley ?).

Tongue River means the tongue of some ruminating animal.

Heart River same. See Sioux names, Ta Chari Tongue and Ta Chanta Heart, in which Ta means a ruminating animal as the elk or buffalo.

[216]
Deaf and Dumb [Mute] People

I have known three Kiowas, one man and two women, born dumb [mute]. One Comanche boy who lives with George Ross, his wife's son, all were good sign talkers. Patterson's sister was one of the Kiowas. A man who has learned to talk and after is struck dumb = talk lost. If born deaf and dumb = born mouth shut. I knew Ida Lonewolf's mother for three years in soldier camp at Fort Sill and I saw her August 14, 1897, living in old Capt. Black Beaver's house at Anadarko. She talked very rapidly, understood some very intricate questions asked her, but lacked the dignity and grace seen by men accomplished in the sign language. She had just been divorced from a Mexican who had treated her very badly and her whole conversation was devoted to showing her pride and delight in her daughter Ida, the things she had given her, etc.[119]

---

119 Patterson would be William Patterson. He was enrolled under the Kiowa name Chard-ley-ah (Kiowa Family Record 1901: Fam. 339). I have been unable to determine who his sister was. Ida Wansey Lonewolf's mother was Pong-quodle (Fógùljè or Red Beads), born 1843 (Kiowa Family Record 1901: Fam. 168).

Hairpipe or Bone Necklace

The first hairpipe necklaces I ever saw was [were] while I was young and lived in the Arkansas River country. White men brought them to trade. The Kiowas did not have them before that. They were first bought from To-mi = (Bone Necklace) Hairpipe = White Man, who traded out of a wagon at Adobe Walls on the Canadian [River] and went away north. That was his name, "Bone Necklace White Man." He had beads, women's shawls to give, and everything Indians needed. He was the first man we saw with them. "Red Neck" built the Adobe Walls (Adobe Walls, Texas) 1845 and went back to the Arkansas. ([p.] 217 [connected to 184]).[120]

[218]

Expressions

To give a pipe = a mission.[121]

To have or hold the pipe = to be a leader.

To make a buffalo calf = to humble.

To rub a person's nose in the dirt = humble.

To get even/To retaliate = When a gun "prairie shoots" it goes off by accident.

A prairie gift = a mad killing = an accidental killing = a prairie killing.

Wild Horse = Prairie Horse.

A quarrel killing = when one man murders another in a quarrel.

A fight killing = when a man is killed in battle.

A warpath killing = same as above.

Make it rain = ran wind bring.

Rain pass by = [same as above?].

A great many rows at a council = [no entry].

I have had enough of your abuse.

To see money = [no entry].

To see anything = [no entry].

---

120 Bone breastplates, necklaces, and chokers were called *tǫ́sèqòlpà* (literally, bone-neck-tied about) by the Kiowas. Bone Necklace White Man would be Tǫ́séqòlpàthǎukàui or possibly in shortened form Qólpáthǎukàui.

121 This seems to be a list of expressions for which Scott was collecting the sign language terms, some of which he did not record.

To lend = [no entry].

To borrow = [no entry].

To go slow = little while go.

To return in a little while = little while go.

To allow to rest = put down for a little while.

Do either you please = [no entry].

To make a mistake, also not to consider.

To contemplate = [no entry].

Crier = Big Throat Man.

To bring black paint = to triumph over your enemies.

To paint your face black = same.

To believe without foundation = to think prairie.

What is the matter with you, sick [?] [=] Answer, "I do not know" may be rendered "Sick for nothing."

Accident or done without intention = do it for nothing, also "lost do it."

What do you come for? [=] Reply maybe, "For nothing (p. 219) come" (i.e., I do not want anything).

To do a thing intentionally = I do it because I want to.

To go straight in front = face go.

None of your business = stop, that is my work not yours.

Not my family = ? done to me for nothing.

To disobey me = to break my talk.

What did you come for = Looking for come.

Bewitch = medicine secret arrow shoot.

Interpreter = knows or hears Sioux or Cheyenne, etc.

Abuse = throw lies.

Many come out to meet us = [no entry].

Whole country covered with buffalo grazing, a herd.

Surround and stare at me = [no entry].

Like the forest trees in number or like the grass = [no entry].

Big village = two watermelon and lodge poles like a forest.

Honey = tree sugar.

When = How many days remain.

Remain = To have left to recover, to be saved.

War pony = fast pony or very good horse.

Sign = Touch the pen.

History/Long Time Ago talk = tradition or old men talk.

To have the Kiowas = to be chief or control them.

To beat anyone at a game, a horse race, etc.

A gratuitous lie = prairie lie. Used by Taybodle, August 1897.

To kill a man on our side = kill toward us.

To die of old age = breast squeezed together, to die old.

Talk lost = to have tongue paralyzed; if born deaf and dumb [mute] = born with mouth shut.

To step gently over = Osage Cuthead story.

Stands in the Middle = [no entry].

A group standing about = Give to each other.

Large man = thick arm.

Dug Prairie = red dig.

To move forward like soldiers in line = col 4rd [column forward?].

To pull up and stand = [no entry].

Bring it here = Take it away.

Look at me = [no entry].

Grow flat on the ground = [no entry].

Lip talk = spoken words.

Hand Talk = sign language.

To be homesick = tipi long for (see p. 239).

[220]
Signs "A"

All the time = everyday.

Agent = father, all.

Agent [of the] Cheyenne and Arapahoe = False Teeth.

Arise = stand up.

Abuse = [no entry].

Arapahoe = [illegible; see Clark 1885:38–39].

Ash Tree = Strong or Tough Tree, used in making tent pins.

Awe = [no entry].

To arrive—in sense of happen or occur or with idea of time = [no entry].

Assassination = Murder.

Attain = [no entry].

Attack = charge.

[Afraid of Horses, Lakota] Ta shunkakan kokipa = His Horses Are Afraid.

Ah-pia-ton = Wooden Lance, Kiowa chief.

Alive = [no entry].

Afraid = [no entry].

Afraid of each other = [no entry].

All among the lodge (serpentine motion) = [no entry].

Another = [no entry].

Ashamed of (two signs). 1) cover face with blanket; 2) [no entry].

Abandoned = Put out to one side.

Antelope (bull antelope) = [no entry].

Astonished = [illegible; see Clark 1885:54]

Allay = quiet down.

All together = collection.

Crow = black bird.

American Horse [Lakota] = Tall Horse.

Absent = got none.

Adobe Walls = Mud Brick House on Canadian [River].

After a while = a while, bigger.

At intervals = (longer or shorter intervals) up left arm.

All gone =1) wiped out, 2) wiping pattern back and forth.

Arrive = came to, one with whole hands, two with both forefingers.

Armbands (metal) = [no entry].

Arapahoe (northern and southern) = [no entry].

Asphalt = black chew (i.e., black gum).

Ant = little with slim waist and neck.

Alone = one.

Accompany = with and forward motion.

[221]
Another = something else.

Agree = yes.

Angry = close fist with thumb up—you are no good. With thumb between first and second fingers is Caddo sign for woman. Kiowas are ashamed of that. They never use it.

Awhile = little time.

Allotting land = country, cut up.

Absent = got none.

[222]
Signs "B"

Band = large number.

Bunch = signify of what.

Bunched = crowded together, as buffalo.

Brains = interior of skull.

Bet = to meet (index fingers coming together side by side).

Barracks = soldier house = fort.

Best = way ahead, good.

Broad = big, also wide.

Bent's Fort on the Arkansas = Stone Fort.

Baptize = water sprinkle on head [Tah-oot 12-1897].[122]

High Bluff = rocky or smooth, high, a point bluff or Tohausen.[123]

---

122 This probably refers to Methodists, whom the Kiowas called Áultą́dóp (Hair Wetters) in reference to their style of sprinkling water on the head during baptism. Parker McKenzie to the author, Oct. 24, 1994.
123 See note 110 above.

[223]

Become = take up a road (as Zemaucunny's son took up a white man's road for a little while). "Elk's Horn Big Mouth [aka Zemaucunny] is a mythical water monster, part fish and part animal, who lives under water. He is chief of all water things, geese, ducks, water snakes, frogs, turtles, etc. He has horns like an elk, red hair like a buffalo calf, and an alligator or gar fish's mouth."

[224]
Signs "C"

Custom = have a road.

Imdaughtah, Kiowa, had a Crow grandfather captive. Ahpeahton had a Sioux grandfather.

Cottonwood Tree = Sun Dance tree.

Chief = top chief, or way ahead chief.

Captive = to serve, or, to make a prisoner.

Chase = as buffalo = two, one coming, other following.

Crier = big throat, call out load.

Count = enumerating.

Cook = eat, make fire.

Country = wide land.

Cholera = cramps.

Choke = throat grip or stop.

Cave = hole in a rock.

[225]
Camp = lodge set down.

Choose = take up.

Coffee = black water or ground fine black.

Chew = chew with jaw and grind (made near right cheek).

Cannon = big gun.

Come along = finger coming.

Congress = chiefs, strong, far east or big council.

Clouds press down = sorrowful.

China Man = yellow man with queue.[124]

[226]

Signs "D"

Dances, go to war = soldier [dance?].

Disturb = heart on different sides.

Different = divergent (as roads), also another on right or left.

Dotage = old crazy.

Die of old age = old die.

Deposit money = put money down on.

Door = lodge poles stop.

Do something to him = ? make toward person.

Disobey = break talk or decision.

Dispatch = paper.

Decreasing = getting less and less by wiping out.

Deceive = under ground make.

Dream = sleep see.

Do it = make it.

Deep = far down, under surface.

Discouraged = heart wiped out.

Disobey = do not take up your talk or put your talk to one side.

Do = make.

Do different things = make in various directions.

Deaf and dumb = mute. Talk lost = person who has become dumb by paralysis or other cause.

[227]

Dakotas (Western Titowan and Eastern) = pierced nose.

    Hunkpapa = Throw Dirt in your Face.

---

124 Parker McKenzie related how as a boy he was fascinated with a Chinese laundryman near Mountain View, Oklahoma, who wore his hair in a long queue.

> Minneconjou = Plant by the Water.
>
> Brule = Sie-chan-gu = Burned Thighs.
>
> Sans Arcs or Itaxiptcha = No Bows.
>
> Two Kettle = Oo-hen-opa = Two Kettles.
>
> Blackfoot Sioux = Blackfoot.

Dangerous = strong.

Dotage = old crazy.

Dandy = face painted, well dressed, push.

To do or effect by magic power = medicine do it; by judicial power = soldier do it.

[228]
Signs "E"

Escape = lost run off.

Elm Tree = buffalo tree.

Emaciated = ribs showing.

Empasses = two strong signs and striking hands.

Eclipse = sun dies.

Everyday = all day.

Every = all.

Exterminate = wipe out (Black[en] out ?).

Enlist = touch soldier pen; also to make soldier.

Expect = look out for, watch for, listen for.

East = sun rise side.

Enemy = fight man.

Escape = lost go.

Exchange = swap fingers, pass close by.

[229 blank]

[230]
Signs "F"

Frog of a horse's foot = antelope hand or antelope tracks hand.

Fog = water smoke.

Flute = wood with key fingers.

Flash = lightning fire from the eyes (as does the thunderbird).

Finished (two signs) = 1) to draw apart as at the end of a battle, 2) to cut off.

Find = see.

Fort = soldier house, also shield house.

Filled = covered over level.

Fall to the ground = earth or country fall forward.

Fewer and fewer or less and less = palms of both hands wiping out more and more until there is but little left.

Fan = as eagle tail fan.

Future = other side of beyond.

Frog = water jump.

Father = parent man.

Farm = corn rowed.

To farm = to plow.

[231]
Flag of truce = white flag.

Flag = 1) waving right hand, 2) water plant, two feet high.

First = way ahead.

Frequently (left arm, right forefingers) = time to time

To Fall in love with = to want.

[232]
Signs "G"

Glue (two signs) = 1) to glue feathers on arrow; 2) to stick with tips of thumb and fingers.

Get up = arise.

Graze = two signs; to park and to nip grass.

Grasshopper = grass eater.

Games = awl game, basket, shinney, hands, ball on toe, wheel game, wrestling, throwing arrows. Make a hole and catch point (Cheyenne game with bones strung on a string with holes in them and a point to the string to stick into the holes in the bones).[125] Monte—cards. For basket game—simulate taking the edge of the basket with fingers and thumb, thumb down, back of hand up and juggle the basket so as to jostle the dice.

Glad = heart open or heart good.

Ghost = 1) owl, also 2) small whirlwind.

Gros Ventres = Big Stomach (Cheyenne, used by Kiowa[s]).

Gone = got none with fingers and second with wiping palms.

Goose = big bird that goes south in the fall overhead with white throat.

A Great Deal = 1) heap, 2) round like watermelon.

Gentle = 1) heart good, as a horse with a good heart.

[233 blank]

[234]
Signs "H"

Have left = recover.

High = tall.

Hold back = guard.

Happen = to arrive at the point.

Honey = tree sugar.

Horse (two signs) = one Plains Indian sign, one Caddo.

Wild Horse = prairie horse.

Half breed = Paul Tsaitcompte is half Pawnee, half Cheyenne, was adopted by Woman's Heart, Kiowa chief, and is a Kiowa to all intents.

Herd = 1) to hold, 2) to park.

History = long time ago, talk.

Heavy = hands cannot hold up.

---

125 This is a form of the game commonly called "cup and pin" in English.

Head of a stream (two signs) = 1) stream wipe out, 2) point of finger touching palm of hand.

Happy = good heart; hands, palm up moved in front of heart from side to side.

Hand talk = sign language.

Headache = pulsating of temporal arteries.

[235]

Hear one side only = hear talk in one ear.

Handsome = good looking.

Hunt = look for.

To Hollow out (as a wooden bowl) = scoop out.

Hush = wait, listen.

[236]
Signs "I"

Ice = water cold hard.

Covered with Ice = closed over by bringing flat horizontal hands toward each other and touching little forefingers.

Iseeo [name] = Heap Round Fire Places.

Incite = make a fire.

Infantry Soldiers = walk soldiers; Cavalry Soldiers = horse soldiers.

Invite = take by the wrist.

Intermixed = both hands.

In fun = joke do it.

Oh I am so sorry = dismay = rubbing palms of hands.

Indian = red man.

Inside of a thing = (like deep).

Insist = push hard.

Interest = money's child.

Itaxiptcha Sioux = No Bows.

Interpreter = hears or knows Kiowa, Comanche, etc.

[237 missing]

[238]

Signs "J"

Join = "with" sign.

[More] Expressions (see [also] p. 239)

To treat me well = good to me make.

To treat him badly = bad to him make.

[239]
(expressions [continued], see [also] p. 218)

Looking for nothing = prairie looking. [An] Arapahoe at Darlington used this, August 1897.

To have a road/trail = to have a custom or a way.

To give me a road = to give an office.

To punish = to give one a hard road.

Pray = poor talk give [i.e., humble, pitiful talk].

Massacre = rub out or kill all.

To abuse = to throw lies at me.

To talk sharply to anyone = talk with right hand vehemently.

Oh my, I am so sorry = dismay.

Plurality of names = different name; name, name, name, have, have, have.

To trust blindly = hold on with both hands, head bent and eyes shut.

To be saved by the skin of one's teeth = a very little recover.

To take care of = to hold it good.

What is your name? = name have?

How old are you? = winters, have, how many, you?

To hear one side only = hear talk in one ear.

To hear both sides = hear talk in both ears.

Watch, mark, and remember = see, see, take hold, take hold.

Suppress = put a blanket over one's head.

To sit in a circle in lodge = lodge, go in, circle with fists in opposition.

None around here = all around, got none.

To have a road = a custom.

To make another/different road = new road or another road, make.

To disobey my order = road, mine, break.

[240]
Signs "K"

Keep = hold fast to.

Kill a Great Many (as buffalo) = not wipe out, but "kill, kill, kill, kill" with each hand alternately in front.

Konza [Kansa or Kaw Indians] = use word and sign, shaved head.

Kiowa = is made by the old people (Taybodle) by pivot elbow against ribs and use whole forearm.

Know more and more = widen one's vision.

Sitting with knees crossed X = touch knees with each hand and cross forefingers.

Kettle = eat round.

Kill Each Other = [kill?] alternately each hand.

[241 blank]

[242]
Signs "L"

Lend = little while give.

Lizard = good man, as Kiowas call it.

Leader = man that holds pipe.

Lipan [Apache] = Wood Apache; Comanche [name] Ho Tavso (Wood Apache).

Lone = one.

Lone Wolf [name] = One Wolf.

Lodge hide = lodge cover.

Buffalo Lying Dead All Around = lying prone, lying probe, first right, then left, then right, etc., all in front of body.

Lean = emaciated.

Live = move about.

Leave = put aside.

Lip Talk = spoken words.

[Lodge, wide] Wide lodge = for dancing purposes it is spread out.

Lean, emaciated (i.e., in training), fit to run a race = down left arm with right hand, belly smoothed off.

Lewd woman = crazy woman.

Lazy = no work man, soon tired.

Light = open.

Lark (2 signs) = 1) "yellow breast" and 2) spring bird. It talks different languages and says woman, shield, arrow in Kiowa, and scolds like a man when he is angry. It scolds the boys when they shoot and miss it with an arrow.

[243]
Lodge pole trail = lodge pole claw [marks].

Light = not heavy.

Loud = big throat, also call out loud with emphasis; or big, listen.

Live = move about; either one finger for one person or all for many persons.

Load a gun = put in cartridge according to model of gun (Winchester, Sharps, Springfield).

To leave, as to abandon = put aside.

[244]
Signs "M"

Mirey = muddy.

Mulberry Tree = "Robe Paint" [tree], from the red fruit or paint made from mulberries to paint robes with.

Mistake = wisdom, miss mark.

Multitude = like the grass in number.

Maybe = doubt.

Mistake = to miss the point, also lie sign is often made.

Milky Way = star's backbone.

Mesquite = 1) thorn tree, 2) bean tree.

Mix up (as in battle) = intermingle.

Have mercy on me = two hands up to the sun, also help me.

Measles = red eruption on right arm.

Menses = blood born.

Mouse = night jumping, little thing, with naked tail.

Milk = cow milk.

Message = talk or writing.

Massacre = rub out.

Mirage = hot shake.

Mean = stingy = money or meat (or any) wisdom has; afraid he will run out—he loves money.

Mother = parent woman.

Monkey = long tailed white man.

Full Moon = big moon.

Migration of Birds = birds pass over head.

Minneconjou Sioux = Plant by the Water.

Mandan = Tattooed on Chins.

Metal = hard.

Marshall = prisoner chief (modern).

Miss (as a target) = go astray.

Mean = stingy, all guards, loves money.

Marrow = bone fat.

Meat = eat. Antelope meat = antelope eat, etc. To retrieve the meat from a hide = scrape the ear.

[246]

SIGNS "N"

Near = since.

Nez Perce = See Caddo.

Next = after or another.

Nothing = got none.

Negation = No (two signs) 1) forefinger emphatic, 2) no good sign of anger—thumb upward.

[247]

Seasons

   1st   Comes winter or cold.   New moon.
   2.   Middle of winter.   Full moon.
   3.   End of winter.
   4.   Grass starts up.
   5.   Leaves come out.
   6.   Summer.
   7.   Middle of summer.
   8.   Little cold = Cool.
   9.   Leaves red.
   10.   A little cold.

Ages of Buffalo

Red calf = under six months.

Black calf = over six months, when first hair is shed and black winter coat is on.

1 year = straight horns.

2 years = little bull, one tooth [in] lip in front.

3 years = two teeth [in] lip in front.

4 years = tall bull.

Little Cow = two years.

7 years = middle bull [and] cow same.

8 years = old bull.

Time

Now = today.

Twelve o'clock = middle of the day.

[248]
Signs "O"

Otter = water animal wrap hair.

Osage = (Wusazhe [Osage] word) and shave head.

Owl says "lots fire" in Kiowa.

Obey = talk take up; sometimes "talk hear."

Oil = greasy water, also melted beef tallow.

Office = road, to give a road is to give an office.

Once in a while = at intervals.

Open = as a fruit.

On the other side of = as a forest or a stream.

To Open one's heart = and take out heart or liver.

Onion = smell bulb.

Only = one.

Overwhelm = as white men close in when overwhelm a reservation [after a land run?].

Older = bigger.

Oh my = an exclamation of dismay.

Open wide (as throwing doors wide open).

[249 blank]

[250]
Signs "P"

Pecan = fat nut tree.

Prairie dog (two signs) = 1) strong water, 2) flirt of tail, always from right to left and upward with forefinger in time to the jerks of dogs in cry.

Pine Tree = lodge pole tree.

Panther = long-tailed cat.

Porcupine = cactus hair.

Pumpkin = shape when braided.

Paper = [illegible].

Pueblo = hair tied behind man.

Pierce = penetrate.

Prairie High = tableland, as Staked Plains.

Dry Paint = red dig.

Paint sign is same as red sign.

Picture = write looking glass.

Present = offer pipe for a person to smoke.

Possum = shave tail.

To Pack = roll up and put in place.

Pray = poor talk give.

Ponka Indian = man with a bang.

Plainly = openly.

Persimmon = Osage man's fruit.

Punish = give one a strong hand road.

Pulverize = dust ground, like tobacco.

Poor = weak and despised.

[251]
Pawnee = Wolf Man.

Prairie fire = grass fire.

Petroleum = fire water.

Peace—to make = clasped hands.

To Break Peace = clasp hands, break in same place hands were clasped.

Playing About = joke intermixing.

Parfleche = hard hide.

Place = country.

Prairie (two signs); 1) country, 2) for nothing.

Practice = [no entry].

Plate = [no entry].

[?] Paa-kui [or] Pankui, in Kiowa = Goose or bird that passes over head going south in the fall's neck.[126]

---

126 The spelling and etymology of this term are unclear. I could not find a matching term beginning with the letter *p* in McKenzie's list of Kiowa birds (1977).

Pregnant = child big belly.

Pluck up courage = heart pull up mad.

Peak = point forefingers one hand up.

One Pound = one weight.

Pretty good = a little good.

Played out = tired.

Play = laugh make.

Property = things lying around, circumference of lodge.[127]

The President = top chief or also Father.

Priest = black robe.

Prairie dog (Crow) has = prairie (both hands in front) hole (left forefinger and churn in circle—right hand coming out showing head and barking).

[252]
Signs "Q"
Quanah Parker = first chief, Comanches.

Questions (two signs); 1) all kinds, 2) question who are you.

Quarry = rock dig.

[253]
Indian Names of Each Tribe
Kiowas call the Comanches = Kee-u-gu = Fight Men or Enemies.

Kiowas call the Wichitas = To-goo-a = Tattooed in Circles, to = tattooed, goo-a = in circles.

Kiowas call the Caddos = [no entry].

Kiowas call the Kiowa Apaches = [no entry].

Kiowas call the Arapahoes = Ai-ya-toh, meaning not Kiowa. O-say-pin-hay = untied moccasins.

Kiowas call the Cheyennes = Sarco (unknown) also A-goo-a = striped turkey wing feathers on arrows.

Kiowas call the Sioux = Odle-pan-kay = Necklace People.

---

127 This is an interesting reference in that it suggests the concept of private property concentrated about a person's lodge.

Kiowas call the Utahs = Ea-tah-gu = Looking for Buffalo.

Kiowas call the Shoshones = Shoshone same as Comanche word.

Kiowas call the Gros Ventres = Bot-ki-er-ko = Big Bellies.

Kiowas call the Osages = Koh-pa-tuh = Shaved Heads.

Kiowas call the Pawnees = Qui-y-a-qui-er-cu = Wolf Men.

Kiowas call the Navajos = Navajos [Abajos].

Kiowas call the Tonkaways = Gee-a-him-pee-a-guh = Man Eaters.

Kiowas call the Crows = Go-ooh-gia-cuh = Crow Bird Men.

Kiowas call the Biters [Arikaras] = Kau-tuh = Bite Man [Men].

Kiowas call the Kiowas = Koom-pah-bee (old name) = Big Lodge Smoke Flaps; Kiowa is other name (unknown meaning and origin).

Comanches call the Kiowa Apaches = Tah-see = Whetstone Men.

Comanches call the Arapahoes = Sarriet-tuh-ka = Dog Eaters.

Comanches call the Mescalero and Chiricahua Apaches = Essa-qui-tas = Gray Rumps.

Comanches call the Pawnees = Qui-tara = Big Fundaments.

Comanches call the Wichitas = To-cana = Dark Houses, referring to grass lodges.

Comanches call the Kiowas = Big Smoke Flaps (of lodges).

Comanches call the Caddos = [no entry].

Comanches call the Sioux = [no entry].

Comanches call the Cheyennes = Tsee-en-navo = Striped or Turkey Feather [Arrows].

Comanches call the Osage[s] = [no entry].

Comanches call the Shoshone[s] = Lots [of] Grass Men, also Po-hoi = Sage.

Comanches call the Tonkaways = Nimme-tuh-ka = Comanche Eaters.

Comanches call the Comanches = Neum = men or people.

Comanches call the Kutenays = Mountain People.

Comanches call the Stoneys = Assiniboines.

[254]

Signs "R"

Recover = have left.

Rainbow = rain arc it makes the rain stop, made of different colors. A long time ago a wise man said it makes the rain stop and ever since then it does. (Right forefinger extended right side, left forefinger extended left side meeting in middle, both descend in arc to the side.)

Refuse = draw back.

Remember = hold finger.

Real = true.

Recognize = soon know.

Remain over = have left.

Rushes = water grass.

Reach = attain to or arrive at—point.

Rotten (as a tree) = old and dead (as a piece of buckskin) = tore open.

Head of river = water rubbed out.

Recognize = soon know, also see and know.

Roast = warm before the fire.

Rotten Tree = old tree or wood, or old buckskin = rotten.

Rank of officers, colonel = bird on shoulder, etc.

Rawhide = hard hide.

[255 blank]

[256]

Signs "S"

Some = now and then one.

Shadow = with.

Man's shadow = with a man.

Dog's shadow = with a dog.

Sinew = roll threads on thigh.

Succeed = fail not.

Sweat lodge = 1) hot house or house hot, or 2) slap body and shoulders, from slapping body with sage or bundle of willows to make the perspiration flow.

Soon = hurry up.

Squirrel = lives on tree and jumps over on another tree.

Star (two signs) = 1) X, 2) twinkle.

Go Straight in front = forehead or face go.

Scalp = hair round.

So = true.

Sign = touch the pen.

Since [=] nearer, this side of.

[257]
Spunky = 1) hurry up mad, 2) [name of] band of Northern Arapahoes.

Sand = powder or water powder.

Adobe Walls = mud house.

Bent's Fort = stone house.

Sign language = hand talk.

Suck = hole, lips, take out.

Silent = hand over mouth.

Silence = all calmed down.

Sapoul = Mountain Owl.

Skillful = brave and strong.

Semacoun = Big Mouth, has hair like a red calf [mythological creature].

South = warm side.

Strange = strong.

Shingle = roof shingle.

Sun Dance pole = whistle, forked pole.

Starved/Starving = hungry, tired.

Show = unfold—spread out to view.

Stingy with Money = guards money and loves money.

Sell = buy.

Salt = sugar.

Sundance buffalo = whistle bull.

Sunday = Medicine Day.

Stiff = not soft, strong.

Sawdust = wood dust.

Sorry = heart on the ground.

Something else—see another.

Safe make = to save.

Since = this side.

[258–59] [connected to end of 214]

[260]

Signs "T"

Tall = high.

Tired = putting down travois pole.

Tay-bodle = Calf Of A Leg Of Buffalo.

Town = lots of houses.

Tough = strong right arm.

Together = with.

Tonkaway = Man Eater.

Thank you = bless you.

Taboo = afraid or afraid road.

Thirsty = water hungry or water tired.

To take care of = to have it good.

Then = in that case.

Thin = grease little.

Tame (as deer) = foolish.

Trembling = shaking right hand.

[261 blank]

[262]
Signs "U-V-W-X-Y-Z"

Uneasy (two signs) = 1) heart flutters up, and 2) heart is on different sides of breast alternately.

Unkapahpa Sioux = End of Circle.

Understand [two signs] = 1) know, 2) circle around eyes.

Understand strongly = good know.

Unarmed = poor (i.e. without anything, stripped).

Utter = milk dugs.

To Warm oneself = fire, hands, turn palms toward blaze.

Well = good.

Which one = different ones?

Wake up oneself = eyes open.

To Wake up someone else = shake arm.

Wild (as game) = wise.

Wisest man = wisdom, ahead man.

Weak = poor.

Waves = water rush.

Waving of rushes = rush agitate.

Waterlily = man nose holes plant = nostril plant. If you cut root across, it will show like nostrils.

West = sun down side.

Whisper = hide talk.

Water up strong = very high water.

Watch over = look down, watch.

Watch backtrack = trail, look over shoulder.

Wide = see big and broad.

Well (health) = good.

Wash = put water on head.

Wonderful (two signs); 1) mouth __ [illegible word], 2) striking hands [see also Clark 1885:408].

Wichita Indian = tattoo circles on cheek, sometimes has sign for Grass Lodge People. Pawnee has similar house only covered with earth (sign = digging dust).

Warrior = good man.

War lodge = "shield house" because you fight from behind the breastworks as our forefathers did.

Wild Horse = prairie horse.

Withers = backbone.

Watch = time piece.

[263]
Which one = V = first and second fingers of right hand, left forefinger [points] first to one and then [the] other.

Visit, come to = come looking for you.

Vaccinate = cut arm in back, place medicine.

Valuable = good sign is used (see Calumet dance, p. 180).

Village = a large number of lodges.

An immense Village = lodge poles like a forest.

Vain = to peek before a looking glass.

Yet = now.

[264]
MODERN SIGNS

Interest = money's child.

Cheyenne agent = [no entry].

Steel Trap = [no entry].

Coffee, Milk = [no entry].

Wringer = [no entry].

Shoe = white man's moccasins.

Matches = [no entry].

Lock = [no entry].

Weigh = [no entry].

One Pound = [no entry].

One Mile, How Many Miles = [no entry].

Sunday = Medicine Day.

4th of July = Big Medicine Day.

Roman Catholic = santaguarse.

1908 Jesus = (+) Cross Man Above.[128]

God = Father Above.

1919 German Kaiser (Blackfeet [name]) = Mustache Points.

Iseeo (June 6, 19_ _) [illegible numbers]
Telephone = wire talk.

Flying machine = Soar man.

Machine Gun = many shots, imitate motion of while shooting a gun.

Automobile = make turn handle.[129]

[265 blank]

[266]
Thrust = push.

---

128 The Kiowas called Catholics Jáisáugàu (Cross People). According to Saingko and George Hunt (La Barre 1935:182) this referred to their wearing of crosses as necklaces. A byname for the Catholics was Tàucu̱dàu (Kneelers or Squatters) in reference to the practice of genuflection. Baptists were called O̱bópgàu (Immersers/Dunkers) from their style of baptism. Parker McKenzie to the author, Oct. 24, 1994.

129 These entries demonstrate that Scott continued to collect data on sign language after he left Fort Sill in early 1898.

CHAPTER 5

Volume II
Sign Language

CAPT. H. L. SCOTT, 7TH CAV., FORT SILL, O.T.

[WRITTEN ON COVER PAGE] FEATS OF ARMS—MANY ADJECTIVES and adverbs are supplied by manner of making the signs = see p. 83 shook "violently" also "listening intently."

Comanche separation [from] the Shoshones up north, p. 160. Tapony.

1
COMANCHE MONTHS
Cabaya
The Comanches say they have seven cold months and seven warm. Seven Cold. 1. Little cold moon or cool moon. 2. Cold moon. 3. Cold moon. 4. Coldest moon. 5. Buf. [Buffalo] shed hair month. 6. Snow month—not cold, snow today, gone tomorrow. 7. Half warm half cold. Seven Warm. 1. After deer drop horns. 2. All deer horns are dropped and trees are red, last half leaves fall. 3. Ten days cold. 4. Everyday rain. 5. Sweat house. 6. Birds go north grass an inch high. 7. Grass all up.

COMANCHE SOLDIER BANDS
Cabaya
The Comanches have soldier bands who are common to all the Comanches and when they went to war a man took a pipe around to the different bands. It didn't take long to go from the Yapparikas to the Peneteckas

in Texas and from there to the Quahadas at the head of Red River. Then when we came together the soldiers had their own dance each company might have men from every Comanche band in it.

    Black Leggins
    Rattle [Little Horse]
    Rattle [Big Horse]
    Walk Around
    War Club
    War Bonnet

Six soldiers [soldier societies] in all. The Bull Dance can be borrowed by any of the Kiowas the same.

[2]

[Quanah Parker]

Quanah gave the name of the soldier bands as follows. 1. Black Leggins, 2. Big Horse, 3. Little Horse, 4. Fox Whip, 5. Crow. The Bull Dance is used by any soldier band, also among the Kiowas the Bull Dance is used in the same way.[1]

[3]

Arapahos, August 27, 1897

The name the Southern Arapahos have for the whole Arapaho tribe is "Hen-nan-na-i-ye'-na," whose meaning is not known. The Southern Arapahoes call the northern Red Eye Indians, also Sage Brush Indians. The northern Arapahoes call the southern "Southern Indians." We have a medicine pipe we call the "flat pipe." Whenever a man smokes that pipe he has got to tell the truth. We use it in the Sun Dance, the sweat house, and whenever we want to worship. "The Bear" has it now. He lives at Fort Washakie. It has always been in the north and was never kept south. We have never seen it. The old men had some rocks that represented it but the last old man is dead now and his wife has them. Her name [is] "Old Sun" and she lives at Watonga. (That flat pipe was given [to] us by the Father where we grew up, when the Arapahoes were first made. That word Arapaho is a white man's word.) We know the two signs for Arapaho and suppose the sign for the Northern Arapahoes is because that one is the

---

1 For the most comprehensive account on Comanche warrior societies, see Meadows (1999). The Bull Dance probably refers to the Páucùngà (Bison Bull Dance), now usually called in English Buffalo Dance, which the Kiowas attribute to the Comanches. See Meadows (1999:281–82, 2010:130) and Kavanagh (2008).

parent tribe and that sign means parents. We also make the sign for "Big Belly" for the Gros Ventres of Milk River who are our people.

We originated above there beyond the Missouri River and we got separated by the breaking up of the ice on the Missouri River. That is the way we left some of our people up there. Since we came south of the Black Hills we separated because the Northern Arapahoes preferred to stay north and we preferred to come south. We did not do [4] it on account of any quarrel or unpleasantness we just came south on account of there were more horses and a milder climate and those other ones preferred to remain in the north. They are our people. We used often to visit them and they us. We have lived since usually with the Southern Cheyennes. Our Sun Dance is like theirs but it is held separately. We have a cottonwood lodgepole and have a buffalo robe on the pole.

We have two divisions called. 1. Ugly Face Men 2. Funny Men. These got their names, the first from having suffered from the smallpox. Their faces were pitted and they had ugly holes in their face. The last because they were a smaller people and looked funny [because] they were so small. We had soldier bands graduated according to age.[2] The lowest or youngest were called 1. "Fox" Band. 2. "Star" Band. 3. "Tomahawk" Band. 4. "Drum" Band. 5. "Crazy" Band. 6. Dog Soldiers. 7. Buffaloes. 8. Old Men. When a Fox boy got too old he went into the Star Band, etc. They have different songs and different dances for each band. It is the same way with the Northern Arapahoes. If a Star Boy was about to go into battle and die, he [5] would want people to know to which band he belonged and would sing a "Star" song. There are no words to those songs. We used to have a great many medicine places. Any place where there is a high hill or mountain is a place where one can be blessed by the above person. We worshipped the earth also but nothing below it. The very oldest people also said the first people had a last rib of a buffalo for a bow and for arrows used rushes with leaves from an elm tree for heads. This shape was copied afterwards in the flinthead and then they got to using feathers.

The Northern Arapahoes have two divisions as we have that usually camp in different places. One is the Spunky Men. They get angry easily and got angry every little while at the other band, which was called the "Antelope" because they were never in the one place like the antelope. Spunky = hurry up mad. "Left Hand" is now chief of the southern Arapahoes and lives on North Canadian [River] above [Fort] Reno. When Cheyennes and

---

2   This refers to the Arapahos' system of age-graded military societies.

[side note, 5] * See Whipple's Report, p. 30, for Comanches with same custom. "Before allowing them (Comanches) to depart we gave them a pipe and tobacco to smoke. They performed the operation in a singular manner. The two first puffs with much ceremony and nothing between were sent toward the sun. The next in similar manner were blown down to the ground. Having told us that up on the other side of the Canadian there were large numbers of their tribes. They suddenly forgot all other Spanish and by signs desired to know that they could not understand a thing we said to them." See also Kiowas and Adobe Walls history—Mexican Trader (Scott n.d.a:I:14–17, chapter 4 in this volume).

Arapahoes go to smoke they say, "Sun make it first, then earth, then ENSWX" [east, north, south, west, central point]. Some only say "Sun and Earth smoke." The old Arapahoes said that dead people go upward. Sometimes the dead (see 17) [17] turn into owls. Sometimes when there is a sick person in a lodge and a whirlwind strikes the lodge the sick person dies and his spirit goes out with the whirlwind. When we see a whirlwind coming down the road we get out of the way. If it is a dead man's spirit, if you do not get out of the way, it will take my life.

The Southern Cheyennes believe that the possum is another dead man. We call the possum "Shave Tail." We call the crane "Tall Bird." We have heard that it carries another bird on its back but we never saw it. A sign was then made to an Arapaho who came in asking him what he was looking for and he replied that he was not looking for anything, "Prairie looking."

[6]

Cheyennes

Ben Clark, August, 16, 1897
What you have told me about the Medicine arrows is true. They were kept done up in a bundle of red cloth. They are kept now by "Little Man" which means the "runt" of the family, at the Cantonment. It is true that they have flint heads, two red and two black. "Medicine Arrow" had them when I first knew the Cheyennes in 1865–56. [Major Edward W.] Wyncoop used to be their agent and was called "Red Neck." I looked somewhat like him and it was thought that I was his brother and they gave me the same name "Red Neck." Those arrows were gotten eight generations ago of old men. Little Chief told me this in 1879, you would naturally think that they got them somewhere about 1600. (Look at Henry's journal by Elliot Cines, La Venendres Brothers also.)

Medicine Arrow carried the arrows for the whole tribe and used to make trips to the north every few years to give the Northern Cheyennes the benefit of the Medicine.

The Cheyennes call the Arapahoes "Istanivva" which means "Nose Men." The Cheyennes call themselves Tsis-ta'as, the Men or the People. They do not know the word Cheyenne.

The Arapahoes call the Cheyennes "Tusishin" (meaning unknown). Cheyennes call the Sioux Ko-he-mor (unknown). They call the Assiniboines Ho-he-istan, which means "Stone Boilers." The Cheyennes and Arapahoes call the Pawnees Wolf Men. The Medicine Lodge or Sun Dance Lodge is called "Cottonwood" Lodge [7] and the dancers are called "Cottonwood Lodge Men." In the spoken tongue the Cottonwood is called the "real tree."[3] Ash is = mo-to.

Pawnee Fork [of the Arkansas] is called Ash Creek.

Missouri River = alligator or similar monster river.

Musselshell = same.

Osage Orange = Yellow wood.

Walnut = Black wood, the nut with a hole in it.

Elm = Ground tree.

Sometimes [we] made bows from the mulberry [tree].

Smoky Hill River = "Has Clumps of Cottonwood in It" (Grove River).

Republican = Chief River.

Solomon = Turkey River.

Red River = Forsyth's Fight—Had fight with Rees there long ago, long before the Forsyth Fight.

Medicine Lodge Creek, where the council was, is called Medicine Lodge also "Where the overcoats were issued."

North Platte = Shell in Neck River for North Platte and main Platte to Mo. [Missouri] River.

South Platte is called "Vit-tan-e'-o-ha" from an edible rush which is found toward its upper waters. This species of rush is called "vit-tan-o-se" or greasy plant. The edible part is white and is the lower part that is in the water. Make the sign of fat or greasy.[4]

N. F. [North Fork] Canadian is Wolf River to its junction with main Canadian although Beaver [River] is larger stream.

---

3   Grinnell (1923:2:19) gives a different Cheyenne name for the cottonwood, *mohk wi hio mohk tut tuts* (robe painters), for the use of its buds mixed with blood or paint to decorate robes. The Kiowa name for the cottonwood tree is *ā́hį̀* (real or original tree).

4   The Kiowa name for the South Platte is Jónvā́u (Fat/Greasy River). This name for the South Platte River is significant. Other sources that translate its name as "Greasy River" often attribute the name to the thick herds of bison along its course (Clark 1885:424; Mooney 1898:400; Grinnell 1906:17; Meadows 2008:52, 244, 278). But Vestal and Schultes (1939:12) record the Kiowa name of *don-pä* or fat plant (*jón-ā́*) for *Equisetum arvense* (field horsetail). The Kiowas and many plains tribes ate the bulbous base. On the basis of the Kiowa names of other plants and edibles, however, the name *jón-ę́* (fat-edible) is more likely.

Red River is "Bitter Water."

Rio Grande "White Man's River."

The mouth of the Pecos [River] is Forks of White Man's River. I do not know [the] name of [the] Pecos.

The Northern Cheyennes called the Southern "Ha-e-va'-tan" or Hairy Men [8] they say because after they came south they were more careless in the use of the tweezers on the face and body. Northern Cheyennes were called "O-mis-is," the Southerns say because they were big eaters. The circumstances under which they originated and when these names commenced I have been unable to find out. The Northern Cheyennes have the same bands of soldiers as the Southern and have the same names for them, and when they are together, join in their dances and ceremonies the same as members of different camps or lodges of secret societies might do when they meet.[5] The "Dog Soldiers," at least of the Cheyennes, are not renegades. It is simply one of the soldiers' organizations of the Cheyenne tribe. A branch of them is with the Northern Cheyennes.

Way back in the sixties [1860s] the Dog Soldiers were the most numerous and the band had more prestige especially up to the decade of Roman Nose (sign) who led the Cheyennes in the Forsyth Fight on the Arickaree Fork in 1868 and who was killed there.[6] Roman Nose was a Dog Soldier leader. He had been wounded in many fights but had been so successful that he was considered invincible until he died from the wound he received from the Forsyth Battle [9] (He died sitting up and believing he would recover.) The Dog Soldiers band being so much stronger in numbers and so powerful in council the tribe was practically ruled by them for a long time so that while other leaders may have preferred peace it usually went the Dog Soldiers' way, which may have started the renegade idea because the Dog Soldiers would sometimes precipitate a war by their hostile (strong) acts and finally draw the rest of the bands in. I knew them personally at the height of their power and I knew that they were Cheyennes and not renegades. They might have had a captive or so among them as all other bands have but they were not renegades. The Cheyennes all say that they did use turkey feathers on their arrows. It was their custom as you say.

The farthest back the Cheyennes know of they were in a big cave in the north beyond any place they have since lived in. They came out in a

---

5   Beyond the similarity in Northern and Southern Cheyenne military societies, this suggests the intertribal participation of societies of similar origins or style. I have discussed this phenomenon as "chapter organizations" (Meadows 1999:55–57, 363).

6   This was the Battle of Beecher Island of September 1868, near present-day Wray, Colorado.

place where there were many stones and wandered about subsisting on rabbits which they killed with sticks and made robes of their skins. As they say they came down a big river traveling eastward and kept down the river until the lighting struck a dead tree and they got fire from that and preserved it as they traveled [10] down this river eastward (probably the Saskatchewan—[per] Clark) until they saw a large body of water they could not see across (do not know whether it was fresh or salt [water]) and there they [saw] signs of Indians. Before that they thought that they were the only ones in existence. While camped in this neighborhood (probably Lake Manitoba—[per] Scott), they experienced quite a famine. Game was scarce. It was a very cold winter and snow was on the ground.

An old widow woman lived on the side toward the creek and one time she heard the voice of a child calling to her from the willows, "Grandmother, Grandmother." She called the boy into her lodge and he said he was hungry and although it was a famine she had a small store hidden away for an emergency. She fed him with it, the last she had. The boy remained with her and one day he told her to roll a hoop (Gom-ah) across the floor and she rolled it and he threw a forked stick through it and instead of a hoop it was a buffalo cow and they had all the meat they wanted. He grew up to be a fine young man and his name was Mock-sois (an endearing term given to boys). He showed them [how] to make bows and arrows and one time [11] when they were famishing for food he told them to go over a hill and see what they would find and they found the buffalo. When he grew up they called him Sweet Root.[7] Then they came south to Devil's Lake, Dakota. The first in advance came there and camped and heard strange noises and saw ___ fat ____ [illegible] and one of them shot and wounded a deer and the deer swam out in the water and was dragged down by some kind of a monster whose head they saw come up and drag it down and it never came up so they called it "Medicine Lake."[8]

The principal enemies in those days were the Assiniboines, Hohe'-is-than they were called, Stone Boilers in [the] Cheyenne tongue because they seemed to prefer their meat cooked in a hide or earthen vessel by throwing red hot stones in it making the water boil. The Sioux used to fight the Assiniboines at first also. The Gros Ventres (sign is made for Big Bellies). The Cheyennes had wars with Assiniboines until one time the Assiniboines [used] guns, which the Cheyennes had never seen and were badly frightened and whipped. After this defeat one of the Cheyennes went off out into the

---

7   Although Scott gave no Cheyenne pronunciation of the name, this appears to be the Cheyenne culture hero Sweet Medicine (Motse'?eo'eve) (Moore et al. 2001:873).
8   Medicine Lake is often believed to be Devil's Lake, North Dakota.

hills by himself. He was mourning for the dead killed in that fight. He was willing to sacrifice himself for [12] his people but did not have any definite idea as to how he should proceed. He was suddenly confronted by an old man in the dress of an Indian who could talk Cheyenne who asked him why he was in mourning and he replied that he was crying for his people. The old man said, "Stop crying. Go with me and I will take pity on you." He pushed a stone aside (somewhere in the Devil Lake country but out in the hills somewhere) and they went into a cave. There they saw all kinds of implements hanging that [were] all made by Indians; shields, bows and arrows, spears, war clubs, etc. The old man told him to select anything he wanted to have and he selected a bundle of four arrows tied up together.[9] Then the old man told him what kind of a ceremony they should have with these arrows and what to do with them from time to time when the feathers got old and he said then, "Go back to your people and when you have fights hereafter, if you obey my instructions the Cheyennes will be successful." The next time they fought the Assiniboines they whipped them and captured their guns which were the first guns they ever had. Their wars with the Assiniboines caused them to move toward the [13] Missouri River and [they] met the Rees. The Mandans were above and the Cheyennes planted and raised corn there. They did no farming until they met the Rees, yet they say the Rees stole the corn from them, which is not consistent.

The Sioux came from the east and fought them. The Cheyennes crossed the Missouri River in advance and then they went to the Black Hills where they met the Arapahoes and they have been friends ever since. They call the Rees [Arikaras] "Corn Planters." They only speak of corn while on the Missouri River. They call the North Cheyenne River "Dug Paint" River. The Mandans were above and they went to farming with the Rees. They did no farming until they met the Rees. They call the Rees O-nun-nee and the Mandans Mun-nun-nee, almost the same name for the Rees. They say that the Crows were their old enemies while in the Black Hills. They had frequent troubles with the Sioux then but not real fighting. They fought the Blackfeet ([and they] call them also Blackfeet), [then] they made peace with the Sioux. All made common cause against the Crows. They met the Kiowas on the Arkansas after they had come south. Living old Cheyennes now know of old people whose fathers had never been south of the Republican River. The Southern Cheyennes and Arapahoes from the northern [country], they simply migrated to [14] get horses. They had heard that there were wild horses in the south and they came down and

---

9   This account refers to the four Cheyenne Sacred Arrows.

met the Kiowas and traded with them. Those who had remained in the north had intermarried with the Sioux and preferred to live with them and they began to consider the Arkansas the dividing line. They began to separate one hundred years [ca. 1790s] ago but became distinct seventy-five years ago [ca. 1815–20]. Since 1865–66 the separation has become more and more strengthened by the influence of white immigration, etc.

The Cheyennes first saw horses when they met the Arapahoes with them in the Black Hills. The Arapahoes told them the Shoshones had horses, also they met the Arapahoes first on the west side of the Black Hills. The Arapahoes came from the north where the Gros Ventres of the Prairie are now. They were separated from the Gros Ventres first by the breaking of the ice in the Missouri River. The Gros Ventres remained north of the river and the Arapahoes came south to the Black Hills. They met the Comanches in the far south. In 1866 I heard of a fight they had with the Kiowas thirty years before. It [was] twenty-five miles up Wolf Creek from Camp Supply. Little Raven was chief of the Arapahoes. They whipped the Kiowas and made peace soon afterwards.[10]

[15]
Palo Duro Rock—Cheyenne Oath
Above Camp Supply a creek runs into Palo Duro, which runs into Beaver about three miles above the mouth on [the] west side, comes into Beaver from the south side (good water). There is a stone a mile from the Palo Duro. It is about seven feet high, three feet one way and five feet the other, and slopes into the ground inward. It is blackish and probably meteoric and has blow holes in it. I first saw it in 1870. It had beads placed in the holes by Cheyennes and Arapahoes. Some of the beads were of a style not sold by traders. In my time the Cheyennes and Arapahoes made offerings there. Yes, the Cheyennes say they did use turkey feathers on their arrows.[11]

They have a story also about seven stars (Pleiades). A party of children were playing by throwing a sort of arrow tipped with buffalo horn and with feathers behind, and while they were playing a bear rushed out at them and chased them. They all ran up a steep hill that had its opposite face vertical. There were six girls and a boy and when they saw they could go no farther and the bear was gaining on them the boy shot his arrows

---

10 This would refer to the lengthy 1838 Wolf Creek Battle between the Cheyennes and Arapahos who attacked a joint Kiowa, Apache, Comanche camp, which concluded in a draw. Peace between the two sides was made in 1840. See Mooney (1898:275–76); and Grinnell (1956:45–69).

11 This appears to be slightly southeast of Hardesty in Texas County, Oklahoma, near where Chiquita Creek joins Palo Duro Creek (before Palo Duro Creek meets the Beaver River).

up to the sky and it [the arrows] went out of sight and a lariat was let down immediately and took them up into the sky where they are now.

When Cheyennes and Arapahoes used to swear a man to tell the truth or do something true they made him [16] kiss a knife. That was [the] most common oath. They thought he would die by a knife if he told a lie. Now they all understand the white man's way of holding up the right hand to God. [18 blank]

[19]
What Old Kiowas Say about the Crows
[Iseeo]

Crows are called Black Birds. The old Kiowas used to see them, Crow men, far in the north on the Missouri River which we call "Ice Sticking Upon" [River]. Sign is "hard stick down." The stick down is made like "hatchet" sticking under water. When the ice breaks up into little mountains [it is] just like stone mountains, like the limestone ledges at Stumbling Bear's [camp]. In other words, it is "Rough Ice River." The old, old Kiowas used to visit the Crows and see them when the ice broke up. The Crows were wonderful people. They knew when the ice would break up and used to line the cut bank of the river looking for it. The buffalo used to be on the Great Plains on the other side and the Crows were unable to cross it. The river was so wide except on the ice and the buffalo used to cross on the ice. And when the spring warmth came that river was worst and the buffalo used to fall in, in great numbers and got drowned and when the river broke the buffalo used to come floating down, just a little of its hide reaching above water. Then a Crow with a stick about three feet long and a rope tied at his waist would run over the cakes of floating ice, jumping from one to another until he reached the buffalo, and tied the rope to the horn and use the forked stick to push the cakes out of the way to make room for the buffalo and to drag it to the shore and his relatives lining the [20] bank would throw it onto the shore. And he would go after another. Lots of men would be doing it at a time. Sometimes a man would get caught between the cakes and it would break him in the middle [crush or cut him]. It was very dangerous and the buffalo would be all swollen up, the meat spoiled, but that was what these old Crows wanted. When they had good meat that did not smell they used to tie a rope to it and put it in the water and in three days or so come and look at it. If it didn't smell bad they would put it back. In seven days it would smell bad and everybody liked it. Those old Kiowa men lived long before Taybodle (86 years old) [thus born ca. 1809]. He came way after these men. They told about it and we hear of it. Those Crows were wonderful. A great many of them died in that way. It was very dangerous. The Kiowas did not do that way they only saw it when they visited the Crows. These old Crows did not have parfleche [rawhide] on the soles of their moccasins. They were made like a Caddo's, all flexible so they would not slip.[12] If they slipped and went down between two cakes they would cut him in two like a knife. He would not be saved. Lots of them have died that way, every now and then one.

[Scott adds this note to the account in n.d.b: MS 2932, Box 2]
Iseeo evidently confuses the Hidatsas with the Crows who separated from the Hidatsas in prehistoric times, but what was told by those old Kiowas who were accustomed to visit the village tribes of the Missouri [River] at the time they lived themselves about the Black Hills of Dakota is remarkable and much of it is verified by our own records. The Kiowas were south of the Arkansas by 1682, see Mooney, Letter of LaSalle.

[21]
Medicine Lake (see Vol. II, p. 151)
Far away in the north is a medicine lake where there are many rushes and cattails. The old Kiowas and Apaches tell about, it was a wonderful lake. We do not know exactly where it is but the old people knew of it and saw it when we lived in the far north. The Apaches used to try and sleep on the bank of it to see some medicine but after a little while they would get frightened and run away. There was something very mysterious there. The water would be in a turmoil and they would run away and it would fail. It was a very large lake and had sand on its banks. The young men I mean would try and sleep in the bank so they would see some medicine but they always got frightened and ran away and it would fail.

One time there was a poor young Apache man, poor and naked, and he said, "I live poor. My relatives are all dead. I am the only one of my family left. I am going to sleep on the bank of the Medicine Lake." So he told the other men, "I want to sleep on the bank of the Medicine Lake. Maybe something will come out and kill me. If it does all right, I will die." And he asked them where best to sleep and they showed him a smooth place there and he got them to tie him down with ropes to pegs, his legs and arms, and they left him there pegged out. This was done in the morning and about noon he saw the water begin to move and there was a great turmoil and he got scared and tried to break away but the pegs held him

---

12 This refers to a soft soled, one-piece style of moccasin as opposed to the two-piece (rawhide soled, soft leather upper) style common to the groups on the western plains.

and he could not run away and he began to cry and call to the Medicine to take pity on him and after a while the commotion ceased, and he quieted down but about [22] three o'clock in the afternoon he saw a man poke his head over a smooth hill and look at him. And he saw it was a Pawnee man watching him and he said, "That Pawnee is on the warpath looking for Kiowas and Apaches. He is going to kill me." And he cried again to the Medicine to have mercy on him. Then the Pawnee drew back and pretty soon there were two of them. Then they drew back and after a long time three heads came up and watched him. He cried for somebody to save him for a long time until finally he saw three ravens fly up from there and he found they were ravens, not Pawnees.

When it was nearly sun down the commotion in the water began again and he was frightened again. After a while a big wave from the lake passed over him and when it receded it took him down into the water where there was a water monster like an alligator (Ze'ma couny in Kiowa). He had a single black lodge there and the Apache man was taken into his lodge and seated there. And Ze'ma couny said, "I heard you cry and I saw you there poor and naked. I am going to help you. This is my house. It is my medicine house. I have a very strong medicine. I am going to call my children in and when they come in and sit down I will tell them each to give you some little of their medicine. I am not going to kill you. I am going to have pity on you and turn you loose." And his children came in and sat down and he said, "Look at this [23] Apache man. He is poor and naked. I want you each to give him some of your little medicine."

And the first one said, "Look at me. I have got a pipe and chief's clothes with hair down the legs and arms (scalp fringes). Do you want these?" And he said, "Yes, I want them." And he said, "All right, I will give them to you. When you go back you will soon attain a chief's road." And the second said to him, "Look at me" and he showed him a man's scalp with blood dripping from it. "Do you want this road?" and he said, "Yes, I want it."

And number three said, "Look at me. Do you want this road?" and he opened his chest so the heart and other organs could be plainly seen and he said, "Yes, I want that road." And he said, "All right. When you get back to your people, whenever anyone is sick you can open his chest, see where the sickness is, take it out, and throw it away and close his chest up and he will be well." And the fourth man said, "I will give you my road too. Whenever you go to war and anybody is shot—say this [is] the body—if you take that man and plunge him into the water and take him out in a little while his wound will be healed."

Then the Medicine Father said to him, "I will give you some of my medicine and I will give you this black lodge and now you can go to your people, but wait. I will send by you more of [24] my children and when they go away you can go with them." And he waited. When he was first tied out to the pegs on the beach, the next morning his friends came to look for him but he was not there and they thought maybe a Pawnee has killed him or possibly a bear. But there were no tracks they could find there so they had to give it up and stopped looking. And when the other two children of the Medicine Father came in he saw they were cranes and the Medicine Father told him to shut his eyes and to take hold of a wing of each of them, of their wings, and said, "I am very fond of you. I sit here and will keep a watch on you afar off and your people. I live here in the water. I will not die. You are just like one of my own children. You will attain old age. You will not die. When you do not live well there, I will bring you back here and you will never go out anymore." Then the cranes took him away with his eyes shut and after a while a crane told him to open his eyes and when he did they were standing on the ground on the prairie at some distance from the lake. Then they told him to shut them and when they told him to open them they were flying around in circles very high in the air. And he saw the streams and the timber far below them and far away in the distance were some white lodges that belonged to the Apaches. [25]

The whole Apache village was watching an arrow game and there was one man there lying on his back looking up at the clouds and suddenly he saw some cranes circling above him and with them something that was not a bird coming nearer and nearer. And pretty soon everybody was looking and wondering at the strange object up there and the cranes circled lower and lower until they lit on the prairie at some distance from the people and they saw there was a man with the cranes and when they went toward him the cranes flew away and left the Apache man they thought the bears had eaten earlier who had been away four days. And he had his big medicine lodge put up and he lived with the Apaches a long time. Whenever he went to war with any people the Apaches whipped them and none of the people died for when they were taken sick the Apache man opened their chests, took out the sickness, and threw it away, and when he closed the chest the person was well. He got many scalps and soon reached the chief's road [became a chief]. He had all the Apaches. They belonged to him. He was a big chief.

One time some white people with guns came to that camp and the white man said to the chief, "I hear you know some medicine. I know a little white man's medicine. Let us see who can beat [win]." and the Apache chief said, "No, I don't know but a little medicine. You are a white man

[26] and will soon beat me." But the white man insisted on it and finally he agreed. The white man [was] to begin and the Apache was to do the same things that the white man did. There was an immense crowd there just like 4th July and they made a great many bets on both sides. Then the white man had a lodge cover brought and spread it out on the ground he took a gun by the barrel (midway) and struck the stock on the ground four times and on the fourth time a little harder than before, when the gun fell all in pieces. Then he threw the lodge cover over it, then off again, and the gun was lying there whole.

The Apache man did the same thing and duplicated every one of his feats until he had no more so it was declared that neither beat [the other] and it was a draw. Then the Apache man said, "You duplicate some of my tricks and if you cannot do them I will beat you." The white man objected at first but finally consented. (The Apache man put a gun about one hundred yards away and stomped his foot four times and at [the] fourth time the gun was discharged. This is [was] a mistake. This was the white man's second trick, which was duplicated by the Apache.)

The Apache man saw a white boy running around. He seized him and went under the lodge cover and when he come out he had [27] swallowed the boy and he went about with a big belly. The boy's father begged him to give him his boy but the Apache only laughed at him. Finally he said, "I have got a good horse I will give you if you will give me back my boy" and he said, "All right. I want a horse. All right." And he went back under the lodge cover and called to them to pull it off and when they did so the boy ran out unharmed. The white man could not do that.

Then the Apache man made some medicine. He ran around the circle, around and around and then jumped into some deep water close by. He was down there a long while and when he came up he had a big fish about five feet long in his arms flapping its tail and he threw it down and told the white man to get another like it, but he gave it up and the Apache man beat him.

The Apache lived long with his people. He was married and had a child running about and one day in the fall he was in his lodge and heard some birds called as they were going over on their way south, cranes migrating, and they circled over his lodge calling. He said to his wife, "Keep quiet. Listen to what the cranes are saying." And he listened for a while and told her the birds had told him the time had come. The Medicine Father wanted him under water. [28] He had long wanted to go back and now the time had come and the father would take him. They would all go together (the family). The woman told the other men about it secretly and they came into his lodge to try and hold him back. But he said, "No, my father sent the birds to tell me to go back. I have often longed to go back. It is not bad, it is good."* And then they surrounded his lodge with little wickiups to prevent him and guarded his lodge for several nights. But they got tired and one night were fast asleep. When they awoke next morning the lodge was gone. They looked for tracks circling around and around but could not find any. Then some men councilled and one man said, "Let us go to the bank of the Medicine Lake where he was staked out" and when they went there they found the travois trail going into the water. And then they knew and gave up the search. He had gone back to his father under water.

[side note, 28] * The father gave me medicine to cure different diseases but he did not give me anyway to cure smallpox and crane says "smallpox" is coming. I cannot cure smallpox and my Medicine Father has told me to go back. That is all right, that is not bad. I am going back to live there.

All during the time I was growing up, I used to see a black lodge in the Apache camp and the old men told me that descendants of that man had it.[13] We do not color our lodges anymore. Now we have put that custom away. [29]

The old, old Kiowas and Apaches saw that Medicine Lake when they lived in the far north before they came south. All Kiowas and Apaches know about it. There is only one place like it.

It is believed that this legend refers to "Devils Lake" in North Dakota. This lake may be Lake DeSmet near [the] Powder River. The Cheyennes have a legend about it and the Sioux all know about it. The Issiton [Sisseton], Wapeton Sioux, and Cuthead bands have told me that big water monsters lived in it and that buffalo had been pulled down by them in modern times while attempting to swim across. They say also that the trail of a large snake or water monster was seen going from Devil's Lake, or as the Sioux call it Minne Wakan or Medicine Lake, to Stump Lake, the first lake east from its eastern extremity.

As late as 1882, only one Sioux ever had the courage to sail in the boats at Fort Totten on that lake. They were afraid of the medicine. Charley Ironheart was a carpenter there and an educated Indian, probably the first ever to go out on the lake (about 81) [1881]. The Gros Ventres came from under its surface and left many of their people at the bottom of that lake.

[30]

Thunder

One time Thunder had a wife and Quail fell in love with her and he went to her and told her he wanted her but she said, "No, you are too ugly and

---

13 The context of this statement implies that a Kiowa is relating the story about the Plains Apaches to Scott.

your legs are too big and I don't want you. Go away." And Quail went away ashamed and he told all the birds that Thunder's wife had made him ashamed. All the birds wanted her so each one painted and dressed himself up the best way he could in order to please her. The Lark painted himself yellow on the breast where everybody could see it and the others in different ways and went one at a time to see Thunder's wife.

Turkey shone himself up and met her first and said, "I have come to see you. I want you." And she said, "No, your neck looks ugly and I do not want you. Go away, Turkey" and Turkey went away ashamed also. Then came Eagle next. He had on a fine war-bonnet but she said, "Go away, you ugly hook nose. I do not want you." Last of all came Crow dressed "so pretty" with white clay on his head and red around his eye and she liked him and said, "Yes, I like you. You are the best looking man I ever saw" and they ran away together and as they traveled along she said to Crow, "I do not know [31] [if] we are going to be saved. Thunder is angry. I do not know who will save us." And pretty soon they heard Thunder coming and I saw a big cloud with lightning flashing, all of it blowing right toward them and Crow got some buffalo chips and they sat on the chips and Thunder shot down at them and each time he shot at them Crow jumped up, flapped his wings, and called "Caw, caw" and Thunder shot [at] them four times and missed them each time. And then he got tired and let them go. Then Crow turned around to the cold side (north) and called, "Caw, caw" and the cold wind come [came] and Thunder sat down with snow all over him and an icicle on his nose and they punished him and Crow his wife take [took Thunder's wife] away from him.

Cold belongs to Crow. Summer rains and hail belong to Thunder. Thunder is afraid of cold, does not like cold. It does not Thunder in the winter.[14] Crow loves cold and snow, is perfectly happy flying about in it. It belongs to him, it is his.

[32]

Scinday and Coon

One day long ago the buffalo were coming down to water in single file and a big bull at the head saw a coon on the bank and he said, "Coon, what are you standing there for?" And Coon said, "I want to go across

---

14 On the southern plains it is rare for thunder to occur during winter, although I have occasionally heard it happen. The first thunder of the year, usually in early March, is important as a symbolic marker of spring. Several southern plains tribes hold ceremonies soon after the first thunder of the year, such as the Kiowa Ohomah Lodge bustle cedaring ceremony and the Kiowa Gourd Clan's visit to the Táimé and Ten Medicine Bundles.

but it is too deep. I am afraid." Then Bull said, "You can get on my back. I'll take you across." Coon said, "No. I am afraid I will get drowned." Bull said, "You can hold on to my horns," but he said, "No. I might let go and be drowned." Bull said, "You can hold on to my tail," but Coon said, "No. No, I am afraid." Then the Bull said, "How then do you expect me to help you. What can I do" and Coon said, "I will creep inside of you (anus) so I will not be drowned." And Bull said, "All right" and Coon crept into Bull and Bull swam across the river and when he got across he called out, "Now you can get out," but Coon began to bite and tear his insides. Bull bucked and plunged but Coon tore at his inside until he fell over dead. Then Coon called his wife and children and they came and cut up the meat and took it up to the top of a tree that leaned out over the water and put it up high on the branches to dry. After a while Scinday, who was always hungry, came along with his wife and children naked and [33] looking for something to eat and upon looking into the water, saw the reflection of the Coon up in the tree and the meat and he called out, "Coon. You have got lots of meat," and the Coon and shadow nodded its head as the wind blew among the branches. Scinday said, "How can I get some?" Coon nodded his head again and Scinday say, "All right, I'll come" and he dived head first into the water to get some meat and he struck his head on a rock which knocked him senseless and his wife called out, "Oh, oh. My old man is drowned" and she caught him by the foot and pulled him out of the water all covered with blood, and she stretched him out on his back and when he came to he was looking up in the air and saw the real coon sitting up in the real tree and the meat on the boughs, and he called out, "Maybe you have killed me. I think you had better give me meat" and Coon said, "All right. I'll give you meat." And he took a piece of backbone and hit him with it and hurt him and he cried out, "That is not meat, give me meat," and Coon threw another piece of bone and killed a boy, and then another boy and the woman (i.e., knocked them senseless). Scinday [was] such a hungry fellow.

[side note] Compare *The Northern Shoshone*, R. H. Lowie, American Museum of Natural History, Vol. 11, 1919, p. 268, has several analogies.

Cheyennes have a Scinday. They call him "Hota-hay-you," which means "Story." They call him that. Scinday = means foxy smart, deceitful.[15]

---

15 Séndé (literally One Who Is Nose Mucus, also known as Sainday and Scinday) is the Kiowa culture hero who speaks the Kiowa language in his own way and is endowed with supernatural power that enables him to transform himself into various animate or inanimate beings. His name comes from his always having a runny nose (McKenzie 1991). As a Kiowa name, Tricky or Deceitful One would be Xándè.

[34]

Sapoul

Sapoul = owl, and sign is made for the owl's ears. Sapoul the monster = Mountain Owl. [Kiowa] Apaches call Tsen-tsin = Skull Owl.[16]

This story is not about Scinday. It is just an old story about "Sapoul" that means a monkey that used to eat men. They tell about it to scare children. He eats men and children. He walks around in the day time and hunts for men and children. He eats naughty children and the women say, "Now you stop crying. Sapoul [will] hear you. He [will] eat you." Sapoul had hair all over and was very strong, like a red buffalo calf. He could catch anybody. He had a big bag and carried it around on his back and when he killed a man he put the body in the bag and slung it up on his back. He had a stone fixed like a mallet the old women used to have to crack bones and he killed men with that mallet.

[side note, 34] (Compare *Blackfoot Mythology*, Wissler and Duvall, American Museum, Vol. 11, p. 138. Tale No. 1 miscellaneous, called the Lost Children. Water Bull carried them across from a cannibal woman. His lice had a bad taste. Grinnell p. 50. *Gros Ventre*, Kroeber p. 102. *Arapaho*, Dorsey and Kroeber p. 293).

One time the Kiowas camped somewhere and they say that time the Kiowas, the whole tribe, had one chief and the chief, whatever he says, they do it. They never break [ignore] his word. One day the children saw the chief defecating in the woods and when he went away they went to look at the chips and they saw that part was white and part black, more like paint. And these boys and girls were surprised and made fun of it and said, "It was spotted like a horse" and the chief heard them laughing at him and he got very angry because they made fun of him. They were out some distance from the camp and he hurried back and gave the order to move camp quickly, right away [35] and if any man went back to look for his children he would kill him. And so they took down the lodges and packed up and he watched them all the time. Then they moved away and were all gone.

The children did not know about this moving and late in the afternoon they came back and the first one looked over a hill and said, "The village is gone." And the second came up and said, "The village is gone" and each girl and boy as they came up said the same thing and they did not know what to do. And one girl carried her little brother on her back and these children then took up the trail of the village but the chief ordered

---

16 Kiowas distinguish between single and dual versus triplural terms for owl, *sàupól* (s/d) and *sàupótjáu* (t), usually in reference to any species of the owl family, but usually used for the great horned owl. Qópsáupól (Mountain Owl) is the mythological mountain ogre of children's tales. Other species of owl have their own specific terms.

that the village must move every day and the children could not catch up. One day while they were following the trail of the village they saw a man coming, very tall, coming like a buffalo, and it was "Sapoul." And Sapoul caught them, all these boys and girls, and he had them prisoners and took them home with him. He lived in a rock and every day he killed a boy or a girl and cooked and ate them, every day one, and the children did not know what to do. The girl who carried her brother on her back was last. He had eaten all the others just like a chicken or a bird and that day a bird, a very small bird, his name was [36] "Wren," came and told that girl something. Everyday Sapoul said to her, "You go out and get some wood and make fire," and every time she went she put her brother on her back and Sapoul always had a rope to pull her back away and that day Wren said, "You untie that rope and I will hold it and you run away from him," and Wren held the rope and the girl ran away with her brother.

Pretty soon Sapoul called out, "Hurry up, bring wood" and the bird made some excuse and Sapoul thought the girl was still there but she was not. It was Wren, and Sapoul cry [cried], "Hurry up." By and by he got angry and went out there and found the girl had gone and the bird flew away. Sapoul looked for her track and smelled along like a dog after a deer and after a while the girl looking back saw Sapoul coming. She came to the bank of a river, very wide and deep, and stood there crying, looking back at Sapoul, when "Zemacouny," a water monster like an alligator, part fish part something else with horns and hair all over it, came up out of the water and said, "What is the matter, girl?" And she said, "Sapoul, he chase [he's chasing] me. I cannot cross this river, it is too deep" and Zemacouny said, [37] "All right, come here. Come, I [will] carry you on my head." Zemacouny he said so, "But first I want you to look for my fleas and eat them and I carry you over." And the girl began to look in his hair on his head and she found a frog and she said, "I find [found] a frog, Zemacouny" and he said, "Yes, that is one of my fleas" and the girl eat [ate] the frog and Zemacouny said, "What is it like, the taste, this my fleas?" And she answered some nice kind [of] sweet fruit. It taste[s] like that. And he said, "All right" and she found three more frogs and every time he asked her what they taste[d] like, and she told him different kinds of sweet fruit and Zemacouny said, "Very good." And Sapoul came very near now and Zemacouny put the girl and her brother on his back and said, "Sit on my neck and hold on my horns," and he carried her over and Sapoul cried out not to take her over but Zemacouny did not listen to him but put the girl on the other side and she ran off.

Sapoul then called out to come and take him over also and Zemacouny answered, "All right" and Sapoul cried out, "Hurry up. Hurry up." But Zemacouny went very slowly and Sapoul was going to get on his back but Zemacouny said, "First you hunt for my fleas and eat them. You eat four and I [will] carry you over." Then Sapoul [38] found a frog and eat [ate] it and Zemacouny said, "What does it taste like?" And Sapoul replied that it was "bitter and no good" and Sapoul ate four and when Zemacouny asked what they tasted like, Sapoul was mad because he was so slow and he told him that the frogs tasted like everything bad he could think of. And Zemacouny said, "Get on my neck now" and Sapoul got on his neck and Zemacouny carried him over to the middle of the river where he sunk down and Sapoul was drowned and that girl and her brother were saved, but all the other children were killed and eaten by Sapoul.

Scinday's Laws

Scinday, they tell about it, made the earth. He put [the] sun [in the sky], he make [made] buffalo, he make [made] everything, Scinday. And they thought the White Man had Scinday. He was very wise and clean. Kiowa Scinday was very dirty and wicked, yet had power to do everything. Scinday went to heaven, he said, "I go up now. Don't you tell about me in the day time, only in night." He did not die, he did something shameful and he said, "I cannot live on the ground. I go up now." Scinday, he laid [lay] with his mother-in-law and he was ashamed. That is Scinday's law and any Indian custom that is Scinday's law. I think that is why [we are] afraid of [our] mother-in-law, Scinday said so.[17]

[39]
How the Ant Came to Have Such a Slim Midwaist

One time Scinday make [made] laws. He said, "I think it [is the] best thing we have no sickness. We not [won't] die, anybody not die [nobody will die]." And the people said, "No. If we [do] not die we [will] cover the whole world and there will be nothing to eat. We had better die." That was Ant that said so and every creature listen[ed] to him and took up his talk and Scinday said, "All right, we [will] fix it that way." By and

---

17 According to tradition Scinday/Séndé stories are only to be told at nighttime and only in the winter under penalty of a number of repercussions, such as getting a prolonged "itch." The association between Sainday having had relations with his mother-in-law (resulting in his leaving this world) and the historically documented mother-in-law and son-in-law respect-avoidance relationship is a rare explanation for the presence of this relationship.

by one of Ant's boys died and Ant cry [cried] and mourn[ed] for him and Ant [was] so mad at himself. He said, "I wish I could cut my neck" and he squeeze[d] (hold) his neck this way and he hold [held] his waist this way and Ant became almost his waist and neck cut. That is [the] reason Ant [is] so small here they say. Ant went to Scinday and said, "Scinday. You see we are not going to die. I want you to give my body back" but Scinday said, "No. We already fix[ed] that. You break [broke] my talk. I cannot change it. That already been fix[ed]."

Scinday and [the] Pawnee

One time Scinday had a daughter, a very pretty girl, and this daughter was not married. She was very pretty and he said to his wife, "Now my old woman, you do what I tell you. I don't think I [will] live long. I got [have gotten] very sick now, pretty soon I [will] die. I know I [will] not get well." Scinday said so and this old woman very sorry to hear her husband and he said, "My dear old lady. My love lady. I love my daughter. I am not [40] afraid to die. I am afraid about my daughter. When I die no one will take care of her and [the] Kiowas I don't think treat her right. Now I want you to listen to me. If I die, if any Pawnee man comes to visit the Kiowas here, you give him to marry my daughter." He said to her, Scinday to his old woman, "And now when I die I don't want you [to] bury me. If I die I want you put me in [a] tree, don't you put me in [the] ground. Do what I say to you and when you put me in tree, after four days, you come and see me. If you come and see me there, I [will] not be there. I [will] be buffalo bones. If you see buffalo bones, that [will] be me." He said so, Scinday. Pretty soon, Scinday was very sick and died. The old woman told what Scinday said and they took him now on [a] tree. They [did] not put him in [the] ground. And after four days that old woman went [to] look at him and found buffalo bones and that old woman say [said], "Oh. That is [the] way he told me. He is [a] buffalo now." She believe[d] that.

[side note, 39] Compare the *Northern Shoshone*, R. H. Lowie, American Museum, Vol. 11, 1909, p. 249. Coyote (= Scinday) marries his daughter.

After that the Kiowa[s] travel[ed] about and one day that old woman hear[d] about one Pawnee Indian come to camp and this old woman say [said], "Oh. That is the man my old man tell me [told me to] invite him. I must do what he say[s]." And she went to the Pawnee and [the] Pawnee was sitting there. His hair was dressed like [a] Pawnee and the other people asked her what she wanted and she say [said], "My old man say [said if] any Pawnee man come[s], my daughter [will] marry him" and they told [the] Pawnee [41] and [the] Pawnee say [said], "Ach Dur-va-hay" = ("good" in the Pawnee tongue) and the girl could not refuse to marry him because her father said so and she married him. One morning he slept very late (Scinday had scars on his legs, deep ones, and old woman knew that) and had [a] blanket across his legs and they stick [stuck] out under [the] blanket and the old woman know [knew] Scinday's scars. She see [saw] them and said, "Oh my. This is Scinday. This [is] not [a] Pawnee" and she took a big stick and struck his legs as hard as she could and said, "Get up, my son-in-law. Get up," she said, that old woman. And Scinday caught his legs and cried with the pain and talked Pawnee talk, not real Pawnee but in high tone like Pawnee to deceive her. And she hit him again and said, "You [are] not Pawnee but Scinday" she said, and that is the way they found out that was Scinday. And he was ashamed about marrying his daughter, he [was] so deceitful [a] man. He was [a] funny man, Scinday.

Scinday and the Fight Tree

One time Scinday killed some bears. One time I told you he cooked prairie dogs. That way he made them and he put them that way and he cooked them. There was a tree there whose forks were low down and he sat in the forks while the bears were cooking. He watched the oven and by and by he opened the oven to cool. It was too hot to eat and he sat on the forks of the tree and was very happy. And while he sat there a coyote came up, attracted by the [42] smell of the meat. And Scinday said, "What [did] you come looking for here? I don't want you here. Go away," he said, just like he did that prairie dog time [that time with the prairie dogs]. And Coyote said, "What[']s the] matter [with] you? I [will] not eat your meat. Maybe you throw away bones. I eat them." Scinday was sitting in the fork of the tree holding a limb in each hand, kicking up his heels singing happy like a boy and he said to Tree, "Now tree bee-mo-taa tight me," he said to that tree, and Tree tighted [held] him.[18] "Now," he said, "Loose me, Tree" and Tree loosed him. Then he said, "Bee-mo-taa" tight [squeeze] me several times while Wolf [Coyote?] was watch[ing] him and again he said, "Tight me a little harder" and he said, "Loose me now" and Tree [did] not loose him and he struggled with Tree but it [did] not loose him. Then Wolf ate all the dinner and Scinday cry [cried] and beg[ged] Tree to loose him, but Tree [did] not loose him until Wolf eat [ate] up all the dinner and run [ran] away. Then Tree loose[d] him and he [was] so mad he beat Tree with [a] stick and cry [cried] and what he work[ed] for hard,

---

18   This appears to be the command *Bé máuntââ*.

Wolf he eat [ate] it. If he do [did] not do some foolish thing, sit on tree and play like [a] boy, or if he invite[d] him, Wolf, and share[d] with him something and treat[ed] him polite, he [would] not lose it, dinner, and somebody else [would] get it. [43] They say that after they tell that story. He deceived those bears some way when he kill[ed] them. But I [do] not know about it. He work[ed] hard for them.

(Compare Gros Ventres Village, Kroeber Vol. 1, p. 68—almost identical, the mouse carries it across.)

SCINDAY AND THE GIRL

One time the children were all swimming in the river and Scinday sat on the bank watching them. There was a girl sitting opposite to him across the river and she sat with her knees apart toward him and she was watching the children swim. Scinday put his penis down under the water to copulate with the girl across the creek but she jumped up and cried out and drew the attention of everybody. They asked, "What is the matter with that girl?" And Scinday, who was on the opposite side, said, "Im-pos-tun-a-say-boh. She got hurt with a sharp stick cut by the beavers." But Scinday did it himself.[19]

[side note, 43] Dorsey and Kroeber, p. 36, tale 2. Penem trans flumen witter.

SCINDAY AND THE BOY

Scinday's penis was very long and he kept it wrapped around his body like a rope. And one day he met a boy. He was "Wren." And Scinday say, "Boy, I exchange with you" and they exchanged and that time the boys and girls were playing they were married to each other. And they saw Scinday's penis. It was small, they were not afraid of him and he use[d]

[side note, 43] Compare *Blackfoot Mythology*, Wissler and Duvall, American Museum, Vol. 11, p. 34, exchanged genitals with a bird. Dorsey and Kroeber p. 73.[20]

---

19 In the expression "Im-pos-tun-a-say-boh," the first word is the pronoun *ém* (you), followed by *fó* (s/d) (beaver).
20 Parker McKenzie related one story in which Sainday was in love with Thélé (Thélé s/d; Thélélóp t), a mythical miniature bird about two centimeters in size that was considered to be the most beautiful thing in the world. Sainday, extremely smitten with her, wants to have sexual relations but is too large as an adult human. Sainday finally pledges that he would do anything if he could shrink his genitals so small that he could have sex with her. Upon having his genitals shrunken, he approaches her and makes his affections known. Thélé rebukes him and will have nothing to do with him. Jilted, Sainday is thus distraught, stuck forever with his microscopic genitals that he cannot change back. Parker McKenzie to the author, Sept. 5, 1993. Thélé is reported to be the smallest of birds, probably the smallest of the hummingbird species (McKenzie 1977).

it. But [the] boy got angry. Scinday's penis was too heavy for him. He dragged it on the ground and beat it with a stick. I do not know how [44] he took it back, Scinday.

Scinday and Hashmeats/
Why Cat Has No Nose and [a] Short Tail

Once there were seven different kinds of hashmeats. First, just meat hashed and made into a ball. Second, a ball of marrow butter. Third, [a] ball of meat mixed with a black berry that grows in the far north in summer; the Sioux eat the stem. "Ay-ha-hy" we call it. Fourth, Kan-sim-gea, a red berry that grows in the far north on bushes mixed with meat.[21] Fifth, three other balls of meat [making a total of seven] mixed with different kinds of berries with Indian names which I forgot and these fruits were mashed with meat into round balls and were about ten inches in diameter. One day these seven kinds [of] hashmeat went on the warpath and Hash Meat held the pipe and those fruits were behind him and that marrow butter next [to] him, and Blackberry third, and Kan-sim-gea fourth, and then the others and Scinday saw them coming rolling like balls, one after the other. We do not know what tribe they were looking for and Scinday saw them. He was [a] very hungry fellow and all these fruits taste good and Scinday did not want to show himself for fear these fruits all run away, so he watched them over a ridge just like [an] antelope. Then Scinday ran around so as to get over a ridge just in their course and laid sprawled out on his [45] back, naked like a dead man and when they came over the ridge they saw him and Hashmeat said, "What is that?" And they looked at him and said, "That is a man. Poor fellow, he is alive, he is not dead." And they ask[ed] him, "What's [the] matter with you? You sick?" But Scinday only groaned. They say [said], "What tribe are you?" And Scinday deceive[d] them. "We['ve] been on [the] warpath a long time with my friends and we [are] all very hungry. One my friends over here and the other over there just like me [are] starved, and I am [the] last man, and I am weak and cannot walk anymore for [I am] hungry. We have had nothing to eat," he said.

Then that chief meat took pity on him and told his people, "This man we save[d] him because he was hungry. We give him each one bite so he will be save[d]." And he said, "You bite me now, one bite." And Scinday

---

21   "Ay-ha-hy" may be something akin to *éhàuhì̧*: from *éhàu* (eaten, ingested bread) and the syllable *hì̧* (real or original). The syllable *é* can also refer to any edible form. "Kansemga" appears to be *qáunsèmgà*, from *qáungá* (any superficial caky matter) and *sémqì* (pemmican: pounded dried meat often mixed with tallow and sugared).

opened his mouth wide and took a bite, and next one gave him a bite and so on and they say [said], "I suppose you feel better now. You can go." And Scinday said, "Yes, I feel better now, a little" and they went on and Scinday called to them, "If you go over there you will find one of my friends lying there. Maybe he is dead. If you[']ll be kind enough maybe you[']ll save him." Then Scinday got up as soon as they got out of sight and ran away around and got in front of them as before and [46] when they got there they saw another man right there. And they said there is another poor man and they each gave him a bite as before and when they started off he said to them, "There is another man just like me over there, we die for hungry [we're dying of hunger]." This happened four times and the fifth time when they saw him sprawled out on the ground they looked in his mouth which was wide open and saw the skin of a fruit sticking to his teeth and they recognized him and all ran away.

Scinday jumped up and ran after them and chased them to a pond into which they jumped like frogs where it was too deep for Scinday to get them and Scinday cried, "Why [did] I not catch them when I had them? I [am] such a foolish fellow" and he pondered as he sat on the bank, how he should get them. Pretty soon he said, "Oh yes. I know." So he got a lot of wood and built a fire and heated a great many stones red hot and threw them into the pond until the water began to boil and the oil to come to the surface and Scinday sat there happy, singing to himself, "Now I[']ll catch them" beating time on his hands before his mouth and by and by he said, "How I going to get that grease, it is too hot. I have no spoon. How am I going to eat it?"

[47]Just then a wild cat came up. That time cats had fine long noses like [a] fox and very pretty long tails. And Scinday said, "What for you here, Cat? I don't want you here, go away, Cat." And Cat said, "I am only walk[ing] about" and he said, "Go away, Cat." And Cat started to go but Scinday said, "Hold up, Cat. I want to go find a buffalo horn I saw up on the prairie to make [a] spoon. You watch this grease and when I come back maybe I[']ll share you something" and he ran off to get the buffalo horn and while he was away Cat put his paws in the grease and licked them until there was nothing left but water and ran off.

[side note] Compare Wissler and Duvall, *Blackfoot Mythology*, Vol. 11, Anthropological Papers, American Museum of Natural History, p. 26. Lynx stole Old Man's squirrels, cooked in an oven dug in the ground while he slept. Old man caught him asleep, broke off part of his tail, threw it away, stretched his body on [a] hook, punched his face flat on a rock, etc. (Note—see a Crow tale, Field Museum Columbian Publications No. 82, p. 285; Grinnell p. 155; *Arapaho*, Dorsey and Kroeber p. 60 footnote; *Gros Ventre*, Kroeber p. 71; Dakota Contributions to Names entry, Vol. IX, p. 114, Riggs; Jones, *Fox Texts* p. 289; Russell, *Cree Myths* p. 213.)

When Scinday came back Cat had run away and he said, "Oh my. I got no dinner" and he followed the Cat's tracks very angry. And Cat was so full of grease he went to sleep close by and Scinday found him asleep under a bush and he pushed on his nose and flattened out his face so ugly and cut off his tail and Cat did not know it. And when he woke up he went to drink and wash his face in the water and ran away scared. And that is why he[has] got no nose and [a] short tail, and those spots are grease spots.

[48]
How the Kiowas and Comanches Made Peace
Taybodle
We call the Comanches Ki-a-gu fight men because we used to fight them.[22] A long time ago when we lived in the place we grew up, somewhere in the far north in the cold country where the tall rock is, where we used to pack our things on dogs, when we had no horses. We used to fight the Utes and Comanches and one time seven or eight Kiowas went on the warpath looking for Utes and reached some Mexican settlements to the west of the headwaters of the Arkansas River (? Taos). The Kiowas were at peace with the Mexicans and so were the Comanches. There were some Comanches camped near but the Mexicans kept it secret from the Kiowas for some days. Then they told them, "We are glad you came here. There were some Comanches here looking for you to make peace. They have not gone yet, their village is nearby. The Comanche chief says he has been fighting the Kiowas for a long time and now he is tired and wants to make peace. What do you think about it? Will you go over to his village with me?" And the Kiowa chief, whose name was "Sleeping Wolf," said, "No, you bring the Comanches over here and we will talk." And the Mexican said, "All right" and went and told the Comanches who came over and talked in the Mexican house.

The name of the Comanche chief was [49] the man who Carries Firewood On His Back. He said to the Kiowas, "We have been fighting each other a long time and now I am tired. I am a chief and back in the Comanche village is another chief who controls all the Comanches. We have counseled over this before and decided to make peace with the Kiowas. It is good that you have come. What do you think about it? I want to know your name?" He said, "My name is Sleeping Wolf. I am like you, a warpath chief. I will go back to the Kiowa village and ask them what they think but you and I will make peace right now. We will give each other something

---

22 The Kiowas call the Comanches Câigù (Fight/Enemy People).

little (presents) we have and go home. In the spring I will meet you here at the Mexican house and we will make it strong." And the Comanche said, "Come back to my village and go home from there" (somewhere on [the] headwaters of Red River) but the Kiowa said, "No, I do not know that country. I will go north from here and then northeast and will come back here when the grass is an inch high and go to your village with this Mexican." And they gave each other some of the little things they had with them (made presents to each other) and separated, going home to their villages. When the Kiowa got home he told the principal chief about it and he said, "All right. You first decided to make peace over there. All right, I am glad of it" (see p. 55).[23] [55, continued from 49] "We will all do it" and all Kiowas agreed to make peace.

The next spring, Sleeping Wolf said to a Comanche captive who was in the Kiowa village, "I am going to make peace with the Comanches and [I] want you to go with me. You hear both Kiowa and Comanche (i.e., understand). They may kill me but you are a Comanche, you will be saved." And he said, "All right I will go." Then Sleeping Wolf called a big council and said, "Tomorrow I am going with this Comanche as I agreed upon over there (i.e., Mexican house). I am going alone" but they said, "No, no, [the] Cheyennes [will] kill you alone. We will go with you, a big crowd." He said, "All right," and they started for the Mexican house afoot, for they had no horses then. They began soon to get footsore and to turn back for different reasons. It was so far to travel and before they got to the Mexican house, only Sleeping Wolf and the Comanche [captive] were left.

When they got to the Mexican house, the Mexican recognized him and said, "All right, in three or four days I will have some mules loaded and go and trade with [the] Comanches and you will go with us." He thought the Comanche man was a Kiowa, and Sleeping Wolf said to the Comanche, "You hear (i.e., understand) Comanche, they think we are both Kiowas. Keep it secret, if they talk about killing us in Comanche, you tell me about it. [56] They may kill me but you are a Comanche, you will be saved." The Comanche said, "All right, if they kill you they will kill me too. I have grown up with Kiowas. I have not been treated badly up there. I have lived good with Kiowas. If they kill you, they must kill me too."

Then they started out, the Mexican chief going ahead, and they found the Comanche village on the Staked Plains at the head of Red River, and

---

23 Sleeping Wolf or Wolf Lying Down (Cûiqą́ujè) was the name of the Kiowa leader. John (1985) places the Kiowa-Comanche peace in 1806. Based on other data Kavanagh (1996:146–48) places it possibly in the 1820s and says that the leader was Black Prairie Dog instead of Afraid Of Water. See also Mooney (1898:162–64).

the Mexican[s] came to meet them and said, "The village is close by, a big village. Dress yourself up and paint your faces," and they did it and when they got on top of the ridge, they saw an immense village. The horses covered the country and the lodge poles were in number like trees of the forest. A man who was herding horses saw them and came and said to the Mexican, "Who are these two red men with you?" And the Mexican replied, "These are two Kiowa men" and he went back and told the Comanches. The Mexican held back his horse and stopped on the ridge, and they saw a great commotion in the village, a great dust where they were driving in the horses, and after a while a big band of Comanches came charging out to meet them and "Carries Firewood On His Back" came out and saw Sleeping Wolf and recognized him and dismounted and shook hands with [57] him and they all moved down like soldiers to Carries [Firewood On His Back's] lodge and took the two Kiowas in. The Comanche captive listened to them talk and told Sleeping Wolf in Kiowa, "It is good talk. Nobody say [said] kill us." Then a big council was called and all chiefs but the head chief came in to the lodge. Everybody looked at the two Kiowas and talked about them and Sleeping Wolf asked the Comanche captive what they were saying and he replied, "They are talking about nothing bad yet. If they kill you, I will kill three or four and then they will kill me. If they kill you, I do not want to be saved. If they treat us both well then I will be saved."

Then Carries Firewood On His Back sent a message asking the head chief, Comanche head chief's name was Pah-tuy-y-yah = Afraid Of Water, to come but he replied, "No, whatever you do I agree to."[24] But Carries Firewood On His Back said [replied], "No, you are the head chief. You have the decision. You come to the council." And the head chief said, "I am too fat. The heat makes me pant. I want to lie down and rest." But he had his horse brought and went over there and went into the lodge on his hands and knees. He was so very fat (his belly was out to the full extent of your arms). He sat down and they asked him to look around carefully and say which men there were Kiowas and which were Comanches and after looking carefully [58] around he said, "I do not know. We will not talk long about this. I am fat and tired and want to go and lie down. These Kiowas look just like us. They have the same colored skin that we have. If you want to make peace, hurry up and make it. I want to go and lie down." Then he went home.

---

24 The Kiowa name of the Comanche leader Afraid Of Water is Tǫ́fêtjàui.

Carries Firewood On His Back said to the other chiefs, "I saw those Kiowas coming here on foot. Their feet are tired. Has anybody got a horse to give them?" and they gave them many horses. The Comanche captive then called out in Comanche, "Where are my relations?" Everybody was surprised at him and soon recognized him and his relatives came and took him away to their lodges and when he came back he said that they had given him many horses. Next morning a crier went through the camp inviting everybody to a "Bull" dance and Carries Firewood On His Back said to Sleeping Wolf, "You are a Kiowa chief and I am a Comanche chief. We will both go to the Bull Dance and count our coups.[25] If you have killed a Comanche anywhere and struck his body tell it out plainly. Do not be afraid and if I have killed a Kiowa I will [59] do the same." And he said, "Yes" and two horses were brought and the two chiefs went to the Bull Dance. In the "Bull" dance the chiefs are mounted on horses and the others are on foot in line. They move up in line a little way like the advance of a warparty, then stop, and dance. The chiefs are mounted on one flank and while they [the line] are moving forward a chief rides alone down the front [of the line] everybody shooting at him and when they all stop he counts his coup (i.e., tells where he has struck his enemy) and when the Kiowa began he called out, "I see you over there. I struck your relative with a spear at such a place and killed him" and all the Comanches called out, "How, how. That is true" and all applauded him. Then the Comanche chief did the same until he had no more to tell about but the Kiowa was not nearly through yet and everybody was astonished at that man and said he was a very brave man.

Next day the women and children all came to look at such a brave and the Comanches gave him many horses. And Carries [Firewood On His Back] asked him how long he intended to stay in the Comanche camp and he said, "Four days. I left in the spring and they told me this year they would have the Sun Dance in the middle of [60] summer so I could see it and I told them I would be there. They will be looking for me. I told them that if I did not go there before the trees got red then they have killed me. I see you chiefs here. I am going to tell you something brave. I want to see if some of you will go back to the Kiowa camp with me." A party of chiefs said they would go back with him and they went back driving

---

25 While coups were frequently recited at military society dances and even during some naming ceremonies and giveaways, the association with the Comanche Bull Dance and the description of its choreography in imitating the advance of a war party is noteworthy, as the Kiowas obtained the dance from the Comanches.

a large band of horses. And after a long journey north they found where the Sun Dance had been left three or four days before so they took up the trail and when they got near the Kiowa camp they left their horses and the Comanche captive was sent in ahead. He met a Kiowa who asked him where Sleeping Wolf was and he told him, "He is coming back there with a great many Comanches." And as soon as they got the news the Kiowas all came out to meet them on foot and escorted them into their village. The Kiowa head chief called out, "I see you there all good looking men. I want the Kiowas to give you something they have a little good. We are very poor and have no horses but we will give you what we have got." And they gave the Comanches what they most wanted. The switches [were] glued to their hair and [covered with] dug paint, lots of it, and the Kiowa [61] chief asked them how long they intended to remain with the Kiowas and they said "three days" and he replied, "All right. We will make free gifts today and tomorrow and then we will stop giving and then trade after that." And the Comanche chief said, "I want a party to go back to the Comanche camp with me" and Sleeping Wolf said, "All right, I will take back a big party." And they went back with the Comanches and carried rolls of switches and sacks of "dug paint" that the Comanches desired most. They found the Comanches east of where they were before and they made free gifts for three days and then stopped and began to trade. Mares were brought first until they had a great many and the Comanches said to them, "I see you there poor and on foot. I want you to put away your 'dog horses' (i.e., packing of dogs [travois dogs]). If you will move down here we will break up your dog horse road and give you a horse road. We have a good country down here. You move south and live in it and we will fight other tribes together." And the Kiowas and Apaches moved south and lived with the Comanches, good friends ever since in this country. The old time Kiowa[s] [62] used to keep the hair [that] the women and others cut off while mourning and glue it on their own hair with glue and made their hair very long. The Comanches wanted those hair switches and dug paint more than anything else.[26]

---

26 Men in several plains tribes extended their hair by attaching swatches of hair with glue and or clay to their own hair. The Crows were especially noted for this practice. In another account of this story [Scott n.d.b: MS 2932, Box 2, "Taybodle Tells—How the Kiowa Made Peace with the Comanche"] Scott reports the Mexican's house as southwest of the head of the Arkansas River and lists the location of the Comanches' village at the "Headwaters of the Red River of Nachitoches" (in the western region of the Staked Plains of Texas). He describes the lodge poles in number "likes blades of grass" instead of like trees of the forest. When he is told not to travel alone because he would be killed, the Cheyennes are not specified in this version, only that "they will kill you."

[Scott n.d.b: MS 2932, Box 2, "Taybodle Tells—How the Kiowas Made Peace with the Comanches" concludes:] "Note 1. This must have been some time prior to 1682 when LaSalle wrote a letter from Illinois saying they were then south of the Pawnee[s]. Note 2. The old Kiowas used to keep the hair the women and others cut off while mourning and glue it on their own hair with glue, making their hair very long. The Comanches wanted those switches and dug paint more than anything else. 'Dug paint' is paint made out of the dift [different] colored oxides of iron dug out of the ground and made into a ball with buffalo fat in contradistinction to the paint bought from the white trader, which [is] much inferior. They use only the 'dug paint' in their medicine ceremonies."

[Scott n.d.b: MS 2932, Box 2, "Kiowa Peace with the Comanches," concludes:] There is reason to believe that the Kiowas and Kiowa Apaches were south of the Arkansas River before 1695 and it is probable that this peace has lasted for more than two hundred years.

H. L. Scott
Major General US. Army Retired.

This story was received from Taybodle, the oldest living Kiowa, over eighty years of age in 1897. It was told to me in the sign language of the Plains without a single vocal sound and shows what the sign language is capable of. Iseeo, Poor Buffalo, Heidsicki, and other old Kiowa[s] since dead were present, agreeing in the story.

[50]

Giving Names

When we name a baby sometimes we take it to an old man and say to him, "Give this child a name" and in old times they used to pay him for doing it. Heidsick named his daughter "Different Tribes." He meant that he had killed so many different tribes, one Osage, one Pawnee, one Navajo, one Ute.[27] He had struck the bodies of many different tribes. Big Bow called his oldest son "Good Road" and his second son "Travels Alone" and he meant that he found out himself different countries, nobody guide[d] him, and "Good Road" because he had lead himself [and] his people on the warpath many times and killed his enemy, and brought his people back to safety.[28] Stumbling Bear named a woman Killed In Front because her father was killed that way in the front of battle.[29] When my boy was a

---

27 Her name was Jéáudé (Different Tribes/All Tribes).
28 These names are Hǫ̀àunthą́gài (Good Trail/Road) and Ą́ugàutóyài (Lone Traveler or Travels Alone).
29 This name may be Thàumbą́hóljè.

baby, he had no name and we took him to the old Time [Táimé] Keeper "Long Foot" and the woman carried the baby and a bunch of strips of ermine to give to the old man to name the child. And I said, "Now Old Man Long Foot I want you to give my boy a name and we will give you these ermine," for he was like a priest of [the] Time [Bundle] and the boy would prosper, be a useful man, a good luck man. And this old man name[d] him "Standing In Front," meaning [when] they open[ed] [51] the Time [Táimé] Medicine, they stood it up in front, everybody looking at it. That is a medicine name.³⁰ We have a name for the Ten Medicines "Plenty Medicine Scalps."³¹ Everybody soon understood that. Maybe the Comanches would not understand (see [p.] 78).

[continued from 78] "Bull Comes Out Of A Lodge"'s name all the time he was growing up [was] "Lives A Long Time."³² But when he was going to make the buffalo rise he said to all, "I want now another name—"Bull Comes Out Of A Lodge" and they said all right you know about it and they gave him that name. That is the medicine custom.

My name was first Tahbonemoh—Sees Big (Morning Star). Komaudy was my father's near brother and when I was little I was very sick and dying. I had no name then and was about four years old. Komaudy said, "That is my child, he's very sick. I will call him Tahbonmah and maybe he will get well." We all used to have a way and must have it now to get up early and look out the door to the east and if we see the morning star it will soon be day. When I enlisted first for a soldier, I took my brother's name Iseeo "Plenty Of Round Fireplaces" which you see when the village was moved away. My brother was a very big chief. He was mortally wounded north of the Arkansas in 1854 by the Satse-vo = Sauks + Foxes. Komaudy died the summer before the Sun Dance was made where (everybody had German Silver Headdresses 1866) [thus the summer of 1865].

What Shield Keepers Are Afraid Of

That old man,* Oh-so-to, Tonanti, Long Foot, gave them Taime [Táimé] Shields and told them what to be afraid of. He died about 1870, very old. He had the Taime since he was a young man, made [the] first dance when [the] Taime was gotten from the Osages [1834]. The Taime Shield keepers

---

30 This name may be Thàumdédè.
31 This name for the Ten Medicine Bundles is Áulbéáuihyà (Many Scalps or Having Many Scalps).
32 This is Jáudèkáu (Kept/Retained His Name A Long Time), later known as Páutépjè (Bison Bull Coming Out/Emerging).

are afraid to look at themselves in a glass. If they do, their eyesight will be ruined. They must not eat buffalo hearts or touch a bearskin, or have anything to do with a bear. They must not smoke with their moccasins on or kill or eat any kind of rabbit or kill or touch a skunk.

[side note, 51] * On-so-teen—Long or Big Foot in Kiowa. Tonanti was his other name. It is in the Arapaho language and we do not know what it means.[33]

Bird shield keepers must not touch birds, nor throw feathers in the fire, nor put a knife in the fire in a tipi. If you cook something for them, and the knife touches the fire, they will not eat what you cook for them. They must not eat heart of any kind, must not cook a heart in his kettle, nor his wife and children eat a heart, nor any kind of bird, because he keeps a bird shield. Satanta had a crane shield. Every shield keeper is afraid of something. The Cheyennes [are] the same way and the Comanches worse yet. The buffalo shield [52] keeper is afraid of raw liver or anything raw from the inside [of an animal]. He is afraid of putting a buffalo horn in the fire in his tipi. He is afraid to have a pipe stem above, [he] always takes it below your hand. He may be afraid of other things too.

[53]

Holding the Buffalo

One time Kicking Bird was chief of all Kiowas and the camp was near the Salt Fork by Red River, and Kicking Bird said to three men, "You go and get some beef." And they went out and that time the soldiers were holding the buffalo [a Kiowa military society was enforcing the no hunt rule].[34] If all get ready to look for the buffalo together, that is good, everybody gets beef. But if two [or only a few] men only go they drive off the buffalo too far.

Kicking Bird said, "I am chief, and if I send these men to get beef it is all right, I am chief." Three of these men went, Kicking Bird sent them, but the soldiers whipped them and killed their fine horses. Kicking Bird did not say anything because the soldiers did it, these men broke the law. If they do not fight back and after a while, the soldiers do not hear any angry words about it, they pay them. They give them horses, blankets,

---

33　The name is Àunsṓcį́nyíjè (Long Foot) or in short form Àunsṓjè (Foot). He was the Táimé Keeper who died ca. 1871.
34　This account likely reflects the bias of the consultant, who was perhaps associated with the peace-oriented bands that followed Kicking Bird in the early 1870s. After the death of Tohausen in 1866 no single Kiowa leader was recognized as tribal chief by all Kiowas. While Kicking Bird and Stumbling Bear were associated with several peace-oriented bands, Lone Wolf, White Bear, Big Bow, and others were associated with other bands seeking to retain their independence.

arrows. That is their custom, these Kiowas, but if they fight back or get angry, they do not pay them, that is our custom.³⁵

Electing Chiefs

Soldiers choose their own leaders. In old times if a leader had bad luck he was whipped when he got home, but that made leaders scarce. The soldiers only choose soldier chiefs. If you go on the warpath and strike your enemy they (people) ask who did it? [54] And they say Capt. Scott struck the Pawnee[s], Capt. Scott struck the Osage[s]. Who did it? Capt. Scott did it. And everybody hear[s] of you, everybody respect[s] you. The women all want you, and other tribes all hear about you, and when you say something everybody listen[s]. Then you are a chief, nobody take[s] that chief [status] away from you. Just like a doctor, he learn[s] something and nobody take[s] that away from him until he die[s].

Kicking Bird was not a warrior, the white men made him chief, just like Ah-piaton [Ahpeahtone]. You made him chief yourself, you gave him power, you knew about that. All Kiowas know that you made him chief. Quanah was made by white men, but there are other chiefs the white men did not make. These others are not chiefs, war chiefs maybe. Hanameahtah is a chief, he has struck his enemy many times. All Kiowas and Apaches know Hanameatah is a brave man, he is a real chief.³⁶

[62 continued]
"Lives A Long Time's" Medicine Road (see [Vol.] 1, [p.] 71)
When "Bull Comes Out Of The Lodge" or his other name "Lives A Long Time" was going to make the buffalo rise up he chose seven men to help. Tchaka (Bread Man) was one, Emo-tah was another you know.³⁷ You have

---

35 This is a classic example of a "policed hunt" where a military society escorted all the hunters in a camp out to attack a herd jointly to maximize the quantity of meat available, thereby allowing a large encampment to remain together longer. This was common as bands formed a larger composite camp en route to the Sun Dance.
36 This statement refers to Scott's role in helping get Ahpeahtone appointed as Kiowa chief during the reservation era and to the government's role in the appointment of both Ahpeahtone and Quanah Parker as chiefs rather than being chosen by the people. See also Scott (1928:157–58) and Hagan (1976). Hanameahtah (1843–1913) was a son of the noted chief Tohausen (who died in 1866) and the father of Charley Whitehorse and Amy Bear.
37 This is Jáudèkạu (Kept/Retained His Name A Long Time), later known as Pạutépjè (Bison Bull Coming Out/Emerging). See note 32 above, this chapter. Emotah would refer to E-mau-tah (Kiowa Family Record 1901: Fam. 34) or Èmáutháạ̀ (Arising Crying), the son of Frizzle Head, and born in 1860; not to be confused with Sétèmmâuạ̀ (Bear That Repeatedly Arises And Lies Down), enrolled as E-mau-ah (Kiowa Family Record 1901: Fam. 350, 1861–1917), who served in Troop L.

seen Tchaka's scars. They commence at [the] knuckle of [the] second joint of [the] second finger of [his] right hand, go up his wrist and arm, across his heart, and down to the same place on left hand so wide [two lines approximately 1 centimeter apart]. The medicine man passed an awl through the skin, first on the knuckle, then cut the skin, rolling up the strip on it until it was very long like a string, and after he cut it all he gave it to the Sun. He left it up on a mountain on a buffalo chip. Emotah's was very much the same only a little different.

"Bull Comes Out" had a bull cut that way out of the skin of his back below the shoulder blades. It was a foot long, just like a picture. It was not painted it was cut. That was his medicine road. That medicine was a big lie. In very old times I did not hear much about medicine making. The Taime and the Plenty Scalps Medicines [Ten Medicines] were enough. Now lately we hear about medicine making all the time and they are all big lies.[38] "Stands In The Middle" and that Arapaho "Sitting Bull" you saw who brought the Ghost Dance, they are all lies. Big lies. I don't want them.

[63]
Where Ten Medicines Came from First
Scinday lived a long time ago. He lived with those medicine people who lived in the ground before the Kiowas.[39] There were no Kiowas then but medicine people who were not like us. They had strong medicine. That was before Boy came down. There were a great many of these Medicine People then. After the boys [the Split Boys] were living one time they met Scinday and he said, "Where did you come from?" And the Boy said, "I came down from up above there with my mother who was killed.[40] This is my brother, he was 'split off,'" and Scinday said, "Oh yes. That is good. All right" (nodding his head), and Scinday and [the] two boys each made a girl and when they got larger they married them and from them came the Kiowa people growing larger in numbers all the time. Each of the other tribes have a Scinday. [Each tribe had] one of those before medicine people who was [the] father of the tribe, just as Scinday was of the Kiowas. Apaches, Comanches, Cheyennes, Arapahoes all had

---
38 Iseeo is referring to the many revitalization and millenarian movements led by prophets that arose during the late 1800s in response to the rapid changes in Plains Indian culture.
39 This places Scinday under the ground before his and later the Kiowas' emergence onto the surface.
40 This places Scinday living on the earth simultaneously with the Split Boys (Záidètàlyì) and suggests that the medicine bundles also entail protection in warfare similar to the Cheyenne Sacred Arrows and other types of plains tribal-level religious bundles (McAllister 1965).

their Scinday with a different spoken language for each tribe. After the Kiowas began to get numerous, Scinday and the two boys and the Bear Woman (see the Bear Lodge story) got to be very old and the Boy said to the Kiowas, "We are getting very old and will soon die. When we die you must not throw us away [or] abandon us on the prairie anywhere, or up in a tree, but dig a hole and put us in it good. There is Bear Woman. She knows all kind of sickness. When we die you must cut a piece out of us somewhere and [64] keep it. It will help you. Where you lose those the end of the Kiowas and of this world will come. You must make a sweat house for them. You must put them in the sweat house, going around four times before you enter. Put it down on some sage in the back part of the sweat house, put some buffalo chips there and a pipe. And when you go to war we will help you.[41] You must fight all other tribes. We will die, [our] breast collapses [when] old, now. But our spirits will make a trail through the air to where the sun sets. When you go to war we will watch you. We will not be gone, absent, we will watch for you, and when you come to die you must follow that trail to the sunset. It will be a broad trail. If you follow it you will not be lost."

Scinday said, "Do not hurry me. I will take my pack and my stick I always use and go out on the prairie and never come back. You will not see me here anymore." And one time the Kiowas found them dead. Scinday had gone out on the prairie to the eastward and never came back in the east. Shortly afterward they saw the moon rise for the first time, Scinday made the seven hot moons and seven cold ones, and they saw Scinday standing in it, leaning with his left hand on the tripod which supports a kettle over a fire, stirring the contents with his old stick and his pack lying on the ground behind him, just as you can see him now at the full moon. And they cut the scalps from each of the boys, took a round piece of skin off the chest of the boy that came down, a foot in diameter, took a big toe from each of the boys, each of the Bear Woman's ears, her right forepaw and the first foreclaw of the left foot, and those are now the nine first medicines. Many Scalps Medicines. You know about Tsait-a-pay's medicine, they [65] manufactured that one long afterwards [the others].

      Boy scalp
      Brother's scalp
      Skin of Boy's chest
      Boy's big toe

---

41 This would be Fàitàlyí (Sun Boy, the son of the Sun). Later a Kiowa chief known as Sun Boy, who died in the winter of 1888–89, held this name.

Brother's big toe
   Bear Woman's right ear
   Bear Woman's left ear
   Bear Woman's right forepaw
   Bear Woman's first claw of the left forepaw
Made by the other Medicine Keepers for Tsait-a-pay in modern times. These are each carried rolled up in something and put in a parfleche.[42]

I know that Ehota's is wrapped in something and put first in a turtle's shell. Eueanah's is wrapped in the skin of the breast of an eagle with the feathers on it. Sok-kone's is wrapped in a spotted fawn's skin.[43] The scalps are tied to the inside of the parfleches. If the string that holds them gets old, rotten, and breaks, and the scalp falls on the ground, it is not put back [on] again. I do not know why. But it is taken up and left on the top of a mountain.[44] With each one [bundle] is a straight pipe. I do not know whether it is red or black. The straight pipe that lies on the buffalo head in the Sun Dance pointing east I have seen. Everybody, even the children see that. It is a black pipe, straight one. Its bowl does not turn up. But these pipes no one ever sees. The Medicine Keepers never see them themselves.[45] Those things that were cut off the Boys and the Bear Woman are wrapped in those bundles, those very things, and [they] have never been opened since the Kiowas grew up. It would be very dangerous to open them.[46]

[66]
   RENEWING [THE] PARFLECHES OF [THE] TEN MEDICINES
Nobody ever sees them. In the same parfleche there are roots, dug paints, and medicines that were gotten by the Kiowas in the far, far north in the country where that rock is [Devil's Tower]. One medicine there is a strong one. If the Pawnees came [come] down looking for horses and drive off

---

42 This is a rare account indicating that there were originally only nine medicine bundles and that they include parts of both the Split Boys (Záidètàlyî) and Bear Woman (Sétálmá or Bear That Chases), the Kiowa girl who turned into a bear in the Devil's Tower Story.
43 These keepers are Harry Ahote (Cáujâuéhótjàui or He Kills Buffalo, popularly called Buffalo Killer, often used in abbreviated form of A-hote or Éhótjàui); Eonah, sometimes spelled E-one-ah (Éàunhâfàui or Trailing The Enemy); and Moses Tsokone (Xókǫ́ or Black Stone).
44 In 1956 or 1957 the bundles were last cleaned at the home of Henry Tsoodle, Jr., south of Mountain View, Oklahoma. Harry Domebo was asked to assist the bundle keepers at this meeting. During this meeting the scalps were removed from all of the bundles, taken out, and buried. Harry Domebo to the author, June 22 and June 28, 1993. The bundles have reportedly not been opened since.
45 Red pipes are typically of catlinite, while black pipes are of black steatite.
46 Bear Woman refers to Sétálmá (Bear That Chases). When the bundles were "sweated" and repaired, new wrapping, ties, and so forth, were placed around them. These repairs were done inside a dark sweat lodge, taking great care not to see the contents of the bundles.

a bunch and next morning the Kiowas find it out, they follow the trail until they were [are] tired and one of the Ten Medicine Keepers takes some of their medicine in his mouth and spits it into the tracks of the Pawnee horses. It puts a rope on them to drag them back by and pretty soon they get tired and go into camp and we overtake them, run off the horses, and kill the men. It holds them back and we overtake them, run off the horses, and kill the men. It holds them back and we beat them.[47] There are other things in these parfleches I do not know about.

In very old times those Ten Medicines used to be carried everywhere to war slung around the Keeper's neck, but since those times they have been kept in parfleches and left at home. When the parfleches get old and rotten new ones are made about the time of the Sun Dance when all Kiowas are collected for [the] Sun Dance. One time Taybodle told one [me] they were going to take pity on me and give one a road. I was a young man then. It was not a hard road, it was a good one. They were going to make me "a child." I said, "All right. It would be good for me, make me live long." I said, "All right, good." Next morning early at daylight there was a big lodge out by itself on the prairie and a man came to invite me. I went after him and saw the Ten Medicine Keepers and their wives in front. They were in single file, first the ten keepers and then the [67] ten wives behind them all in single file. They told me not to drink anything until the ceremony was over, which might not be until the following morning.

They went first around the outside of the lodge and then in. I remained outside to warn people away. If anybody came near I told them to go away. That was my road [duty] and they would turn around and go away. When they went into the lodge I listened and could not hear a sound, not even a movement of a man's feet when he got tired or a restless motion of his arms. It got very hot at noon and I was very water hungry. About afternoon they told me to bring in some firewood and they told me to come in, go around by the left, and put down the wood. They were all perfectly silent with their heads down except one woman who was making the parfleches. The other women sat by themselves and the men by themselves. The medicines were all tied to the lodge poles except the one the woman was working at. When the parfleches were all made, the old and new ones were handed to a man who covered them and himself all over with a buffalo robe and transferred the contents from the old to the new under the robe where no one could see him do it. This is his road. No other Medicine Keeper could do that. It is that woman's road to make these parfleches. No other woman

---

47   This is another reference to the use of bundles' power in warfare activities.

can do it. It is my road to stand there and warn people off. The person is called the "Medicine Keeper's" Child. They are the parents and I will keep that road until I [68] die. They said the Medicines would help us, make us attain old age, and live good on the ground. I think that it true for I am alive yet. I live very good on the ground.

(Compare Kroeber tale 27, *Gros Ventres*, Vol. 1, p. 105.)

BEAR WOMAN'S ROAD

Bear Woman's road at first was a very dangerous one. She made everybody poor. She killed them whenever she met them. All the medicine men were afraid of her. When they met her they did not escape. She killed them. One time Scinday called them all to a big council. The little things, spiders, etc., the birds, the deer, etc., and all, and told them, "I am going to make a law. Your crazy roads must be abandoned. Cut them off now. And you, Bear Woman, let your anger quiet down. When you all separate, go live where you want to, but put away these crazy roads." And Bear Woman's heart quieted down and she lived many winters with the Kiowas. She helped them until she got so old she laid [lay] down and couldn't get up and she told the Kiowas when she died to cut some pieces from her and keep them. That is where some of the Ten Medicines come from—Bear Woman.[48]

[69]

HOW THE KIOWAS GOT THEIR COUNTRY [VERSION A]

When Scinday met the [Split] Boys they made the girls and married them that was the beginning of the Kiowa tribes. They had children and they got more and more numerous and one time they made laws for the Kiowa people, laws for everything. How they should marry, dress, and wear their hair, all laws were made by Scinday and the [Split] Boys, red man's laws. And one time Scinday collected all Indians, Kiowas and all other tribes, on the bank of a lake in the far north and he told them to send him, each tribe, its bravest man. And when they collected together he told them, "I want the bravest man to jump into that lake." They could not see the water on account of a slight rise in the ground but it was stuck full of spear points and knives. "The tribe of the bravest man can live in this country and the others will have to move off in different directions and this tribe must fight all the others. I am going to give them a warpath road." And he called the first man to him and said, "Try hard now. Go ahead." And he ran up the

---

48 See note 46 above regarding Bear Woman.

slope to jump into the lake but saw the spear points sticking out of the water. His heart was wiped out [became afraid] and he turned back. So [it was] with the next one, and then another and another until the Kiowa man was the only one left. And Scinday said, "You are the only one left now. Try hard. Try hard and [70] you will be chief of your tribe. If the Kiowas are not brave enough I won't make any warpath road at all." And the Kiowa man called to the others, "Scinday. I am going to die. I am not afraid to die" and he ran up the hill calling "Rah-ah. Rah-ah. Rah-ah" and dived into the water and when he struck the spear points they divided before him. All rushed up to see and then they found out they were nothing but rushes. When he came up Scinday said, "You are the bravest man and this shall be the Kiowa country, the other tribes shall move off in every direction and you shall live in the middle and fight them all." And he showed them how to fight everybody.[49] That was where we grew up in the far north, where the Star Woman's Rock is. I told you about [it] (Bear Lodge).

(Compare Kroeber Vol. 1, Anthrop. "Amer. Mus. Nat. His.," Vol. 1, p. 46, etc., good, p. 48.)

Cyclones

One day Scinday and the boys made a horse. There were no horses then in this country and they made a horse of mud and put an elk skin on it but it would not go. It started up in the air and could not see the ground. They told it to move but it did not listen. It moved a little bit but stopped and stood still. They told it to move (from both sides) but it failed and Boy said it is a failure. It will not do to turn it loose on the prairie. We must send it up and they took it and threw it up in [71] the air and watched it going up and up until it entered the clouds and was lost to view. It is up there now. Often when a storm is coming up we can see a horse's head among the clouds and we say, "There he is. That is the horse made by Scinday and the [Split] Boys. That is a very dangerous horse. He makes it hail and twist trees off and makes them fly like birds."

One time a Kiowa war-party was coming back from the Ute country. "Plenty Stars" was the leader and Stumbling Bear and Old Lone Wolf who is dead was with them.[50] I was with them too. We were right where the bodies

---

49 Folklore and religion often serve to explain the presence of cultural traits or practices in a society's cosmology. By situating the Kiowas on a "warpath road" this account validates their claims to a particular geographical area and a warrior ethos. See Nabokov and Loendorf (2004:67, 71–75) for another version of this story.

50 Plenty Stars was Jáisáuáuidè (Many Crosses, literally, Many Morning Stars). He was also known as Jòhéjè and Náfèwàt, the Kiowa and Comanche names for "No Moccasins."

were lying, Cheyennes. The summer after the Cheyennes were rubbed out on the Washita, Black Kettle's band.[51] We saw a big block cloud coming and the leaders said, "Dismount, it is going to rain hard" and we dismounted and made some shelter. Pretty soon we heard a roar coming that sound like the buffalo at a distance during the rutting season (August) and we all looked to see what it was. There was a big black cloud that extended down to the ground. It was a little red in the middle. Bolts of lightning came down through the center and set the prairie grass on fire. It tore up big trees and sent them flying through the air like a twig. It was coming straight at us and all [the] Kiowas were afraid. It made their hair stick up straight (electric ?) [electricity]. When it got near they wanted to mount [up] and run away but the old men said, "No try hard. Try hard. [72] Brace up, brace up." We understood this. That is the horse the medicine men made doing that. Get out all the pipes and light them and they lit them, seven or eight of them, and pointed the stems to the clouds and said, "Smoke it. Smoke it" and begged it to go around and pass by without hurting them. "Do not come here, pass around" they prayed to it, and it heard them. It understood the Kiowas, they talked to it and it passed around and went off. We were saved as by a hair. Then we went to see its trail. It [had] broken off big trees and pulled up some by the roots that were 3 feet in diameter and made them fly through the air like birds. It had cut the forest on the Washita [River] like a trail through the trees. Even the weeds it tore up and when it struck a big rock it shattered it into many pieces. It was the Medicine horse that did that we call it "Man-ca-yee"—"manca" means a sleeve. "Yee" I do not know. The Kiowas were saved that time by the skin of their teeth.[52]

---

51 This would be in 1869 at the site of the Battle of the Washita, near present-day Cheyenne, Rodger Mills County, Oklahoma.

52 This account is clearly referring to a tornado, which are common in this region of the plains. In Kiowa mythological accounts Chêgùl (Red Horse), from the making of a horse from clay, is the name of the tornado, used only in the singular form. Parsons (1929:15–16, 43–44) provides a version of the Red Horse story and the Kiowa origins of cyclones in the story of "Sendeh Courts Deer Woman and Whirlwind Woman" (M̃ to'wikyamayi/Máutóiqàmáyì or Máutóigàmáyì is Whirlwind Woman). Red Horse and Whirlwind Woman are two different characters in Kiowa mythology. If Scott's reference to May-ca-yee as denoting "sleeve" is accurate then the root word máunkáu (sleeve) applies, as in the Kiowa woman's name Màunkàugúl (Red Sleeve [Dress]). This would suggest that May-ca-yee is Máun-káu-ì for cyclone, which literally denotes "Little Sleeve," from the root word for sleeve and the terminal suffix ì, a contraction of íyòi (offspring of child of). If accurate, this name is based on the analogy of a sleeve with the formation of a tornado. The disyllables máu-kói, which is both a verb (having stirred) and an imperative verb (stir), and máu-tói, an imperative verb (cause to whirl, spin, rotate, etc.), are related (McKenzie 1991). Comparing the orthography and tonal qualities recorded by Harrington (1928:116, 120, 212) in the Kiowa terms for cyclone and whirlwind with other vocabulary, he includes the equivalents of máu-tói-gà for whirlwind and máun-káu-ì for cyclone, which supports Scott's listing of May-ca-yee with "sleeve" and suggests that there were two similar Kiowa names for tornadoes in addition to Red Horse.

CHEYENNE MASSACRE (1837)

A long time before I was born the Kiowas were camped near where the Soldier house was (Fort Elliot, Texas) near the head of the Washita [River] on a creek we call "Where We Rubbed Out the Cheyennes." A Kiowa man was sitting on top of a little mountain looking to see if buffalo would come that way. He sat here for a long time but did [73] not see anything and began to straighten his arrows. Then he looked again and saw nothing and got tired and went to go back to the village he could see at a distance. He got part of the way home when he discovered two heads over a hill watching him. He thought that they were Kiowas trying to kill a deer and went toward them. When he got pretty close he saw they were not Kiowas and stopped to look at them better. They called out to him in signs [asked in sign language], "Who are you?" And he said, "I am a Kiowa. Who are you?" They said, "We are Cheyenne scouts looking for Kiowas." And he said, "Where is your party?" And they said they were back on the east creek and he said, "Did you come to fight" and they said, "Yes, we came to fight," and fired an arrow at him. He drew his arrows and fired back until he got an arrow through his right forearm and then he rode to the village as fast as he could and gave the alarm. All [the] Kiowas turned out to find out what had happened and when they saw the arrow they recognized that it was a Cheyenne arrow and the horses were driven in and they mounted and went out to attack the Cheyennes. When they got to the creek they saw the Cheyennes were afoot and followed their trail and rising [over] a hill they [74] saw the Cheyennes had dug a deep hole for a fort and were ready for them. There were a great many Cheyennes there and the Kiowas waited until the stragglers had gotten up when they surrounded the Cheyennes and began to fight. The Cheyennes killed two Kiowas when they got mad and closed in on them, shooting into their hole until they killed them all—rubbed them out.

Tohausen's calendar makes this to have happened in 1835.[53]

HOW THE KIOWAS CROSSED THE SALT FORK RED RIVER (ELM FORK) AT HIGH WATER

I went on a war party to Texas once. White Horse was leader. We got down on the head of the Brazos and saw the trails of a great many soldiers going

---

53 The Kiowas call this creek Sáqàutjàuáàutàundèvàu (Creek Where the Cheyennes Were Annihilated). Multiple accounts suggest that it was in the vicinity of Beckham County, Oklahoma. Most sources place it in 1837. The Wolf Creek fight occurred the following year (1838). Peace between the Kiowa-Comanche-Apaches and the Cheyenne-Arapahos was made in 1840. See Mooney (1898:271–72) and Meadows (2008:80).

in different directions. We held a council to see what we would do. The country was full of soldiers. If we went on down to Texas and came back our horses would be tired out and the soldiers would catch us quickly. We could not escape. After a while White Horse decided we would go on until we saw some soldiers and then turn back. So we went on south. Our scouts were ahead and came back and said they saw some white men, five of them, and we charged them [75] and got their riding animals and pack mule. They got into the brush and escaped. Then we turned back as fast as we could go, for if they told the soldiers they would be right after us.

We got down where Navajo is, now south of Navajo, on Star Woman's Tree Creek when we saw one of our scouts motioning with his shield to come on quickly. We were driving the loose stock along slowly. When we saw that we hurried them on and when we got there he pointed out the other scout and told us he saw a soldier trail down there. We went down to see it, it was a very big trail of soldiers and a big pack trail was with them and when we saw a pony trail also we knew those were Tonkaway scouts and they had passed there that morning. We saddled all our fast horses and White Horse sent me [and] another man to look up that trail and I saw their camp. It was a very big camp with white tents and men walking about intermixed. There were two sentinels out looking, one mounted and the other dismounted, but they did not see us and we went back and told them about it. It was a very flat country there and [we] were afraid if the soldiers saw us we couldn't hide. So we hurried off north.

When we got to Salt (Elm) Fork, oh my, the river was full and very wide. We looked back to see if the soldiers were coming. [76] It was [a] very dangerous place, soldiers on one side and a deep and wide river on the other. We did not know how we were going to be saved. We began to gather bushes, platted them together, and made different sized rings with them, spread out some canvas shelters we had with us, divided up into squads of four to eight each shelter, put these rings inside, put our saddles, guns, blankets, and other property on top, turned over the corners and tied them with lariats putting round stones in the canvas to tie to, then tied two other lariats to the bundle with another canvas outside, daubed it all over with mud on the outside, and lowered it down and put it in the water. Two men swam before [ahead] dragging it with lariats in their teeth and others swan behind holding it up and we swam across that way first. Then we saw the others coming after us and we went back and drove over all the horses and we were saved. We waited there watching to see if the soldiers would come until sundown and when we saw they had not gotten our trail we came on slowly back.

[side note] See Long's Expedition to Red River 1849 p. 429.

I do not know anything about bull boats and never saw or heard of one. We used to use a lodge cover before we got canvas. A hide lodge cover is very good.[54]

[77]

Sitting Down Rock (see Palo Duro Rock p. 15)

One day when I was with my father and a number of Kiowas on Sun Dance Creek (Palo Duro) we went up a small creek that runs into Sun Dance Creek near its mouth (proper name San Francisco Creek) called Sitting Down Rock Creek and we saw a crowd of Kiowas standing in a group and went over there and they were standing about the Sitting Down Rock. All about it were pieces of cloth, beads, and other things and I asked my father what those were and he told me that when people prayed to that rock they put those things down and left them there. And when I saw that rock I recognized it for the one I had heard about before. All Kiowas, Comanches, Cheyennes, and Arapahoes know that rock. It is not a tall rock, not any taller than you are. It has a brownish color and looks like a buffalo standing there from a distance but when you get close you see it is a rock. It is the only one around there. There are no other rocks anywhere in sight. If you pray to it, it may take pity on you. I do not know. It is on the south side of the creek and as far (out from this creek) as from here to the Caddo crossing from the Creek = (one mile) and on the flat.[55] [78] [connected to 50]

[79]

Kit Carson Fight

Kiowas fight with Utes and white soldiers and lose their lodges. A great many years ago, 1864, the Kiowas were camped on the Canadian River at the Red Hills. There was [were] two hills with that same name, one low down the Canadian. This one is above Adobe Walls. Even now it is called Red Bluff and it was the middle of winter.

Some of the lodges were strung along a little creek but the main body were at a distance and under the Red Bluff. One night a man did not feel easy about his horses and went to look at them and saw somebody coming to attack us up the river. He called out, "Wake up, the Utes are coming to attack us." Everybody ran out, a good many without moccasins or leggings

---

54 Parker McKenzie's grandfather Que-ton was on this raid. He told Parker that the Kiowas used makeshift rafts of frames of tree saplings covered with bison hides and canvases to transport clothing and weapons across swollen streams. Parker McKenzie to the author, 1991–94.
55 For the vicinity of this creek, see Meadows (2008:281). See also p. 335 of this volume.

[on] and began to fight. The women and children ran off on foot down the river. We got out horses and had a big fight, driving each other back and forth. Finally they drove us off and we abandoned our lodges and they burned them up with everything inside them. They made us poor. Half our lodges were below, we saved them and all the horses and went down the Canadian and over to [the] forks of Wolf and Beaver [Creeks] where we spent the rest of the winter. We helped (shared) each other with lodges, our relatives to some gave little tipis and some we took in lodges with us and we bought some lodges from [80] the Comanches with horses. After the fight was over, we found two old people burned up in the lodges, an old Kiowa man and an old Kiowa woman. A good Comanche chief was killed and two Apaches and a good Kiowa man. A Ute and two soldiers were killed also (1864).[56]

KIOWAS AND CHEYENNES FIGHT (1837)
[probably Iseeo]
That picture in the calendar means that in 1837 after that fight with the Cheyennes in their fort, not one escaped. The Cheyennes did not know what had become of them. They watched for them to come home until it got to be the middle of winter and they were tired [of] watching for them and next spring [1838] they found out the Kiowas had rubbed them out. They collected a big war party to look for Kiowas to retaliate. The Kiowas were gathered together for a Medicine Dance Time, at the forks of Wolf and Beaver [Rivers], about one days march (fifteen miles) up from the junction. They attacked us right in our camp, and we drove them out and we fought backward and forward for three days. I did not see it. I was born afterwards. I heard about it. I heard that they lost about one hundred men on each side. They fought for three days and they were tired out and separated. The Cheyennes went to their camp away up north somewhere.[57]

[81]
COMES OVER A RIDGE'S OWL MEDICINE
I have told you so much now everything is wiped out, and I do not see what to tell you. When I went home last night I talked to my wife about it and told her try hard and think of something I have not told him, but

---

56 The fight occurred on Nov. 25, 1864, a short distance above Adobe Walls, along present-day Kit Carson Creek in Hutchinson County, Texas (Mooney 1898:316).
57 This fight occurred in the summer of 1838. For lengthier accounts of this fight, see Mooney (1898:273), Grinnell (1956:45–69), and Powell (1981:51–66).

she failed. I thought about it after I went to bed and found a little. I do not know whether I told you before or not, if I have tell me.

I once saw a man who knew an owl (ghost) well. No, it was not Eapah's brother or Dohauty (Walks On Clouds) [but] something more wonderful than either.[58] I have often seen men making medicines. I looked on and said to myself that is true I think not [i.e., I do not think it is true]. That was my way about thinking about making medicines but this one I saw with my own eyes. Many Kiowas are alive now who were there and know about it. The man who knew the Owl Medicine was "Pea-goo-ah," Ridge—Come over [or] "Comes Over A Ridge." He knew an owl well. We used to live on the Arkansas. One time we did something bad at Fort Larned. We had a fight there, ran away scared, and moved our village south of the (beyond) Cheyenne Red Hill on the Canadian and camped south of it.[59] While we were on the Arkansas "Tape-day-a" had gone [on a] warpath to Mexico with four other men and did not come back. We thought they had not been killed down there but that they would go back to the Arkansas not knowing about that fight and the soldiers would kill them. We waited and watched for them for a long time but they did not [82] return and we got tired [of] watching. Then I heard about "Comes Over The [A] Ridge." He knew an owl. I had heard of him before but did not believe it. Now I would see it and find out. I had heard that he sometimes made medicine, not often, only once in five years. He told them to put a lodge out by itself, fix it good, and that night we were all invited there. A great many Kiowas, women, etc., went to see it and I went with them. I saw a big lodge with its door to the east, its smoke flaps were closed tight, and there was a little tipi such as the little girls play with inside at the back part with its door to the east also. It was made of antelope skin.

"Comes Over The [A] Ridge" said for half of us to come inside, the other half to lie flat down in a row on the north side, not to be on the south side. He was afraid of the south side. After a while the fire went out. The smoke hole was closed and it was very dark. "Comes Over The [A] Ridge" said to some above person, "Now tonight one thing the Kiowas must want," he said to it. "I want the same," he said. "Our children long time on warpath come back not. One owl who knows all about it come down. One owl who won't lie send down," he said. "That is what all Kiowas big want," he said. Then he sang four songs in a low tone. I have forgotten those songs but he

---

58   Eapah is Ìvâugài (Baby/Infant). See Mooney (1898:340–41).
59   This was on the north side of the Canadian River between Adobe Walls and Mustang Creek in the Texas panhandle (Mooney 1898:314).

said he would sing four other songs and wanted everybody to sing with him. When these four songs were over everything was very still he called out. [83] He called out very loud, "Hooo Hooo Hooo Hooo" four times and then it came. The smoke flaps shook violently although there was no wind outside. Then it came down and went into the little tipi, which shook very hard and soon we heard something go, "tap tap tap tap tap, etc." on the inside. Everybody [was] listening intently and soon it spoke in good Kiowa. That was wonderful. It understood Kiowa just like a Kiowa man. It said, "I used to live on this ground. I have been dead a long time. My name is 'Yen-go-nee' (Big Bow's big son has the same name now). When I died I took the dead man's trail. This country is behind you, do not live well. Here that country is far ahead. I know before what you most want. Tomorrow morning, not noon but before (ten or eleven), you will feel glad. These men are not dead. I have seen them. Tomorrow you will see their faces." Then all was quiet until it spoke again. "I have come a long way. I am a little tired. I am smoke hungry." A filled pipe had been placed before by the little tipi and Comes Over The [A] Ridge lighted it and presented the stem. We could hear the pipe being smoked and could see the fire in the bowl and when the pipe was smoked it was put down again. It spoke again and said, "Thank you. I feel glad now as you will tomorrow when you see your children. Thank you, thank you. I am going back now." Then it was [84] still until the tipi began to shake again. Then it went up through the smoke hole although there was no wind and it was all over. I went home to go to bed. It was very wonderful but I would wait and see what happened tomorrow and then I would know.

Next morning a man was out looking up his horses and saw five men coming and went to see who they were. When he met them he recognized Tape-day-a and the other four men. He rode in fast and called out loud, "The men who went on the warpath and did not return are coming." Everybody ran out to greet them and it was truly Tape-day-a and we all said, "Comes Over The [A] Ridge knows medicine good."[60]

There are many Kiowas alive now and know about that. I saw it and know about it myself. It happened in the fall. The Flower Sun Dance was made the summer before on Timber Mountain Creek (Medicine Lodge Creek). Then in the fall the Owl Medicine was made and the Utes and

---

60 Pea-goo-ah or Comes Over A Ridge would be Pígùá (Approaching Hills/Ridges). This is a textbook example of divination, the use of magic for obtaining useful information. Divination is frequently used in locating lost objects or people. The Apache medicine man Daveko performed a similar feat, predicting the return of a party of Kiowas out searching for bison for the Sun Dance ceremony in 1881 (McAllister 1970:53–54).

soldiers attacked us in the middle of the next winter on the Canadian [River] at Red Hill.[61]

After the Flower Sun Dance we moved down to the Arkansas at Fort Dodge/Larned (named by us after a Comanche who was killed there long before in an attack we made in a wagon train there). His name was "Shirt with Red Sleeve" or Red Sleeves. (Ben Clark [stated], Red Sleeve the Comanche man killed at the __ [illegible] = Pawnee Fork of the Arkansas.)[62] [85] We did something bad. We had a fight and ran off south of the Canadian.

When "Comes Over The [A] Ridge" [Pea-goo-ah] died his son Tape-day-a took up that owl medicine and one time he made it the same way. The owl came into the little tipi but it did not speak and after tapping for a while on the lodge cover it went out through the smoke hole and never came back and the medicine failed. It did not understand Kiowa.

BULL MEDICINE (SEE VOL. I, P. 146)

A long time ago the Pawnees captured a Kiowa woman and guarded her every night until they reached the Pawnee town north of the Platte River, when he turned her loose. She went about for some days thinking up a plan to escape and finally one night she ran away and got to the Platte which was very wide and deep. She had no way of crossing and thought, "If I try to cross I will drown. If I go back to the Pawnees they will kill me" and she walked up and down crying. Finally she found an old log about two feet in diameter which she pushed into the water and rolling her clothing up she tied them to the log and pushed off and finally reached the other side. She then started south across the prairies living on roots, berries, mice, and [86] anything else she could find, going on and on until on crossing a high table land she saw a black storm approaching. She looked about for some timber to hide in or a cut bank but there was nothing. The storm was a very dangerous one. It was very black and big hail stones dropping made a load roar. She ran from it crying with fear when suddenly she saw an old buffalo bull carcass that had the dry hide left on its ribs. She crept

---

61 This would be the Ragweed Sun Dance of 1864. The attack by soldiers and Ute Scouts under Kit Carson was in the winter of 1864–65 (Mooney 1898:313–17).

62 This fight was in 1847, near where the Santa Fe Trail crossed the Pawnee Fork of the Arkansas and below where Fort Larned was later built in 1859 (Mooney 1898:286). The Kiowa names for the stream are Ákòvàu (Dark Timber River) and Màunkàugúldévàu (Red Sleeve's Creek) (Meadows 2008:273, 279). According to Scott (n.d.a:II:7, chapter 5 in this volume), the Cheyennes called the Pawnee Fork of the Arkansas River "Ash Creek."

into it and the hide kept the hailstones and rain off her. She went to sleep in there and the storm passed on and while she was asleep the bull talked to her. "What are you doing in my carcass? Do you want something?" he said. "I came to get away from the hail. I escaped from Pawnees. I am looking for Kiowas but I think I will die this side. I am very thin," she said.

The Bull said, "No I am going to take pity on you. You (are) not going to die. You are going to attain old age. You are going to find the Kiowas. I am going to help you. You will be saved." And after a while she woke up and said, "Oh my. I have been talking to a Bull." She got up and went and on and in a few days she found the Kiowa village. She said nothing about the Bull for a long time but she used to see him every once in a while. He talked to her and gave her a medicine road and after a while she married a young [87] Kiowa man. Her name was "Bull Woman." That was her medicine name. His name was "Big Leg" (Calf). And one day she said to him, "I am going to show you some medicine. Sometimes you go on the warpath and a man is shot through the body and is not killed at once and you get there he will recover. I am full of red, blue, white, and black paint. If I vomit that into a wound it will get well. I am a woman and you are a man. I am going to teach you something. I have not got the warpath road but you go on (the) warpath and the bull will help you."

And she showed him the medicine. It is a good medicine. I have seen it. One time we went on warpath to Texas. She told him to get a shield, take off the hair, make it good, and cut it round and get a bull's tail, and do what I say to you whenever a man is shot through the body you can save him.

It is good medicine I have seen it. A long time ago we went on the warpath to Texas and had a fight among the white man's houses and a Kiowa man was shot sideways through the stomach. There were two men who knew the Bull Medicine. Their bellies were full of paint and they vomited some into the wound and he got up and got onto his horse and they made off looking backwards and expecting soldiers to follow them. They had to go very slowly. Every little while [88] the man fainted and the medicine men would vomit some paint into the wound and the man would come to and go on. The fight was early in the morning and they had only gotten as far as the "Big Mountain" (Mt. Scott in the Wichita range) twelve miles when the sun went down. They kept on that way all night and the man got better and better until the hole in his side had closed over and he got back to the Kiowa village but he had not been there long before a crazy horse bucked and threw him off on the ground and his stomach bust open and he died.

Sometimes I have seen them suck the white matter out of the wound and swallow it. I was surprised at that, it smells so badly, but they said, "No, it is not bad. That is what makes the paint inside of us." When they make medicine in the village a good lodge is taken and put up outside and the men go and get the patient and stand him on his feet. He is weak and staggering. They run around him and butt into him knocking him back and forth. They run around the lodge inside and then out in single file with their robes turned the hairside out with a bull's tail in their hands (each) and roll on the ground and bellow like a bull. They do everything exactly like a bull and the bull helps them. This [is] done at sunrise and sunset twice every day, and the man gets better and better until he finally recovers. This medicine is good only for wounds, gunshot or arrow or spear wounds, not for anything else. There used to [89] be a good many of them. Big Leg made a good many Bull Medicine shields and gave them to different men. There are some of them alive now, "Little Robe," "Birds Who Travel Back and Forth On A Ridge," "Stands In The Middle." That is all I think of now.[63]

War Trails

When we went to war against the Navajos, we used to travel across the Staked Plains. That is a very dangerous country. Sometimes we went three days without finding water. Before we started out, our leader told us to get buffalo stomachs and fill them full of water. Everybody had one. Those leaders were wonderful men, they traveled right across that flat country and went straight to water they had seen before. Big Bow is a wonderful leader. He knows the country in every direction. He has led war parties everywhere. Sometimes the water was dried up, that made us poor. Sometimes men would go crazy for water hungry, and they would be strung out all along the road. Then when the leader would reach water, he would drink himself and carry some back to those who were dying along the road and save them. Those yellow house springs are far away from any other water. When the troops used to chase us we went there and they would be without water so long they would have to [90] turn back without finding us.

There used to be in old times but one trail to Mexico. We called it the Old Men's Trail. It went down through the Sunwater Springs. We called

---

63 This is the origin story of the Buffalo Bull Medicine. The men forming this sodality of doctors were all initially descendants of the woman who received the medicine and her husband. These doctors were known as Páuìyoi (Offspring/Descendants of the Bison Bull).

the [spring] Sunwater because they were in a horseshoe-shaped gulch with its opening to the east, where the sun looked into it when it first came up.[64] When Taybodle began to grow up, they found other trails where they could get water and go to different places in Mexico and the Navajo country who lived on the Pecos River. The Lipans and the Mescaleros lived on the Pecos [River] also. The old trail was the only one that was plainly marked. It was like the trail you saw over the North Fork of Red River when we were there with Lieutenant Quay, watching the cattle trail, only there were more bones on it. The Mexican soldiers used to chase us sometimes and the horses we drove up from Mexico use[d] to give out and die along the road. Taybodle drove horses from Mexico ten times, big bunches of them, larger than from here to the adjutant's office (probably 1,000 horses) (see *Pope's* Report). The other trails were not worn that way. The leaders knew them and did not need to have them marked. They knew always where to find water. (See Mooney Pai-ton = Sun Spring.)

[91 blank]

[92]
Told by an Old Quahada Comanche Woman
When my grandmother was alive she told me that seven Comanches went north to [on the] warpath to find (looking for) the Kiowas. We used to fight the Kiowas then. The chief's brother-in-law was with them as second chief. They traveled north very far beyond the Platte River and when they got near the Kiowa village they went into camp and sent two wolfmen [scouts] to find the village.

The Kiowas were then having a Sun Dance and when the two Comanches heard the drum, they came back and reported the whereabouts of the village. Then the chief said, "We will wait until night and run off their horses. We are not enough of us to fight them." But his brother-in-law said, "No, let us go right now in daytime and maybe we can kill a Kiowa, take his scalp home, and have a good dance." But the chief said, "No, there are too many of them. If they see us in the daytime they will kill us all." But his brother-in-law insisted upon attacking them at once until the chief consented and then he said, "All right we go down now, but you must stay with me and not run away when they attack us." And he said, "I am not a coward to run away." Then they left a boy with saddles and extra horses. They mounted

---

64 This is probably Sun Spring, one and a half day's journey southwest of Double Mountain in Texas. See Mooney (1898:417).

up and went near the village and saw two Kiowa horseguards who retreated before them and alarmed the village and the Kiowas mounted and came out. The Comanches all ran away except the chief who dismounted and went [93] into the brush. The Kiowas surrounded him and whenever a Kiowa got near enough he killed him with an arrow, and he fought them this way until dark and after dark sometime he crept out the bed of a creek, and escaped. He went at once to where they had left the boy and found the boy crying, and he had heard nothing of the others who had run away.

The chief said, "Stop crying, boy. We will go down near the village. They nearly killed me today. I am going to get some of their horses." So they moved down near the village and he left the boy in a good place with the extra horses. Then he prayed to the father, "Father, look down on me. Take pity on me and make it rain. Then those dancers will go to sleep and I caught some of their horses." After a while a cloud came over the moon and it began to rain and he put his blanket over his head and went into the Kiowa camp to look for horses. The Kiowas, fearful lest the Comanches should steal their horses, had driven them into the village and tied them at the doors of the lodges, and had guards riding around them all night. He walked right among the horses and right up among the spectators and watched the Sun Dance until it rained harder and everybody went home except the dancers, inside of the Sun Dance lodge.

While he was watching the dance, he heard something groan up at the place where they tie the buffalo. He [94] (looked) up but could see nothing. Soon after, he heard it groan again, then he said, "I will see what that is," and he put his quiver, etc., down. So he climbed up to the roof of the Sun Dance lodge and started to climb up to the center when he heard the drum stop. Then he waited silently until the drum started up again, when he went up until he reached the top. Then he put out his hand and felt around until he discovered it was a person. When he spoke to him in Comanche and said, "Who are you, friend?" He replied in Comanche and said, "How do you do, friend" and said, "I ran away with the others. Today I got into the brush and they caught me when my arrows gave out and they have a present of me to the sun." He said, "Where are you?" "I am tied in the forks of the cottonwood pole on top of a buffalo skin." The chief then took his knife and cut the lashings and told him to come with him but he had been tied too long. His arms and legs could not be used. So the chief unlimbered his arms sufficiently to hold on to him, and he put him on his back and crept quietly down the roof, stopping every time the drum stopped inside until they reached the ground.

It was thundering and raining very hard, and the Kiowas had gone home to bed, and he carried the Comanche out of camp. He said to him, "I am very thirsty, it was very hot on top of that cottonwood pole and I have had no water today. I am very thirsty." Then the chief put him down and went back to the camp and [95] hunted for water until he found two buffalo stomachs hanging up under an arbor. They used to carry water in the stomachs of buffalo in those days, and he took one and brought it to his friend. It was full when he brought it and his friend wanted to drink it all, but the chief took it away from him, only letting him have a little at a time until he had drank half of the water. Then the chief threw it away, and took him up on his back again until he got back to where he had left the boy and the boy said, "What are you bringing here?" And the chief said, "That is our friend who was caught by the Kiowas and given to the sun." And he put him down and said, "I am going back for some horses" and he went back and got three fine horses that were tied in front of a lodge, took a saddle off a saddle rack, then brought them to where the others were waiting, and put the Comanche man up on one, got behind him for he could not hold himself on or guide his horse, and they traveled all night south toward the Platte River, the boy driving the loose stock. Next morning, the Comanche man said, "I feel better now and can ride alone, you get on another horse." And they came on south.

Next morning after they left, the Sun Dance man was holding his hands up praying to the sun and looked up and saw the Comanche man was not on [96] the forks of the pole where he had been put and he gave the alarm. The Kiowas came rushing in and one man said, "I have lost three horses and a saddle." And they said, "Those Comanche men are very dangerous people." They looked about until they found the trail and followed it a long way, but they never caught up with them. The man who had been given to the sun was a Comanche chief and his sister was the prettiest girl among the Comanches. When those men who had run away got back, they told it that the other two men had been killed and would never come back and the girl and their parents cut off their hair (Comanches do not cut off fingers), gashed their arms, faces, and breasts and thighs, and gave away all their property. And one day the girl and her mother were mourning up on a little hill outside the village and saw two men coming. A horse guard went to see who they were. He recognized them before he reached them, turned about, galloped up to the mourners and called out, "They are coming. They are coming." And they ran down from the hill and met them. They threw their arms around them and after they had embraced them, the mother danced and sang for joy. The news soon spread about the village. The second chief took his friend [97] to his lodge and all the Comanches came to see them. The first chief's brother-in-law came to see him and held out his hand, but the chief put his hand away and said, "No. I have got no brother-in-law now. Go away. I do not want you." And the second chief then said the man (first chief) is my brother. I am going to give my sister to him for a wife and he gave him to her.

Indian Women

When you are in a crowd at a dance and wish to establish an understanding with a Kiowa woman secretly, you take hold of her hand and press on the back of it a number of times with your thumb. If she does not want you she will pull her hand away roughly. But if she lets you continue it will signify her consent.[65] The other way is to go down where the women go for water and stand there. When she comes she may ask, "What are you standing here for?" And you say, "I am waiting to talk to you." And when she comes up to you whisper to her and make *anauguuueu* with her. The Cheyenne women are very strange. A Cheyenne man will not take hold of her like a Kiowa woman. He catches her roughly and tries to throw her down right before everybody. They are not ashamed. It is like a quarrel. They wrestle and if he throws her down and gets his hands on her bare skin, she is his. He turns her loose [98] then. But after a day or so he meets with her and she is his for a while. If he touches her dress and not the bare skin of her it is a failure. If he touches her bare skin it is just like counting a coup, she does not escape. The Cheyenne women are wise women. They do not have one dress, they sometimes have three on. They take a horse rope, tie it around their waist with both ends hanging down, then she [each woman] gathers up one of the dresses and wraps it around her thigh, wrapping the rope in half hitches around and around until it is down to her ankles. The other thigh is fixed the same way and a man cannot get at her to touch her bare skin (and she often puts big logs around the inside of her lodge to prevent the men from pulling up the pins). The Cheyenne men are very rough. They will often try to touch her as she is standing over the fire cooking and sometimes will creep into her lodge while she is asleep and cut her rope. If he succeeds in cutting it before she makes out a cry, and touches her bare skin, she does not

---

65   One Kiowa woman told me of an instance of this custom involving her grandparents around the 1960s.

escape. She will not allow you take hold of her gently like a Kiowa or a Comanche woman. You can only touch her skin when the rope is off.

A Kiowa or a Comanche woman would not allow you to touch her bare skin at all. You can take hold of her hand gently; if she doesn't want you she will pull away. If she consents you will soon know it.

Porcupine

There are no porcupines in this country. There are none on the Arkansas [River] or among the mountains at the head of the Arkansas. They see them on the Platte [River] and some distance this side they see them.

[99]

Kiowa Medicine Dance

During the winter the Kiowas used to be divided up and camp in different parts of the country where they would get plenty of game, good grass for the horses, good fire wood, and plenty of shelter from the cold and away from their enemies. In the middle of the winter the man who kept the Taime [Táimé] or medicine would consider about having a medicine dance the following spring. If they have a Sun Dance it will ward off sickness among the people.[66] He would be living somewhere with only a few lodges. Then he would call in the people and tell them what he had determined upon and told them to send messengers to the other villages and tell them that in the spring he would hold a Sun Dance when the grass was __ [ten?] inches high, that they must stop all foolish or crazy work like going to war, and everybody must come in to where the Medicine Keeper is.[67] Nobody [can] stay away. Then they all move in to the place appointed by the Medicine Keeper and he asks if everybody has come and they say, "Yes, all the lodges are here" and he says, "Then we will make a Sun Dance." And he says, "Bring me a gentle horse before sunrise" and he gets on the horse. And the first thing he says, "You must stop all the quarreling and everything foolish. I forbid it." He has the medicine [100] in a sack tied on his back by a string around his neck and some chief

---

66 Scott later published this account of the Kiowa Sun Dance (Scott 1911). The Kiowas used the terms Sun Dance (Qáujó), Táimé Bundle (Táimé), and Táimé Keeper (Táiméqì) or Sun Dance Man (Qáujóqì).
67 Scott's later publication based on this account (Scott 1911:355–56) says "when the grass would be a foot high."

harangues the village, "Do not go out to look for your horses, stay in your lodges. The medicine keeper says so." Then the Medicine Keeper rides around the village on the prairie at a distance. Everybody looks at him and watches him. He goes all the way around the village to the place he started from. Then he goes home and dismounts. All Kiowas know him. He forbids quarreling and crazy work. If any man thinks of doing that he is afraid of the Taime Keeper.

Two young men were sent out just like scouts to look for a tree where there is plenty of good timber and a wide stream. They look for it carefully and do not do it in a hurry. They do it wisely and all move over there and camp. If they do not find the tree they come back and the chief harangues the camp, "Have patience and we will soon find it." They search during the early morning because they cannot drink anything while looking for it. They are afraid of drinking. If they drink water then there will be a great deal of rain and spoil the dance. They are afraid to wash themselves and throw out the water also. When they find the tree they come back and [101] tell the Medicine Keeper, "We have found the tree." During this time the Medicine Keeper does not do any work. When he wants anything done he tells the people and it does not fail everybody is afraid of him during the time of different kinds of work. They drink no water, everybody is afraid of the Medicine Keeper. When the work is done then they drink. When the Medicine Keeper announces that they have found the tree then all the lodges move over there. They call in the soldiers [military societies]. They have five bands of soldiers just like the companies of the regular army.

The mounted soldiers move out in front and after a little drill on the prairie, they move out. Then come the lodges with the women and children—the 5 Co [Fifth Company] on foot remains in camp (Rattle Foot Soldiers).[68] First come 4 Cos [companies of] mounted soldiers, then the lodges of the women and children. The Medicine Keeper is ahead of all. He has the Sun Dance Medicine on his back. He looks back at the soldiers coming. They come up and dismount. There are ten or twenty old men with the Medicine Keeper. The soldiers all sing and drill as they come along. When they dismount the Medicine Keeper smokes one pipe of tobacco. Then they all mount and start out singing and drilling. They go on for about a mile. When they halt again the Medicine Keeper smokes another pipe full of tobacco. This [102] is done four times in all and when the fourth pipe has been smoked everybody knows where the tree is and

---

68   This is the old Jáifègàu (Unafraid of Death or Skunkberry) Society, from which the Kiowas revived the Gourd Dance in 1957 (Meadows 2010).

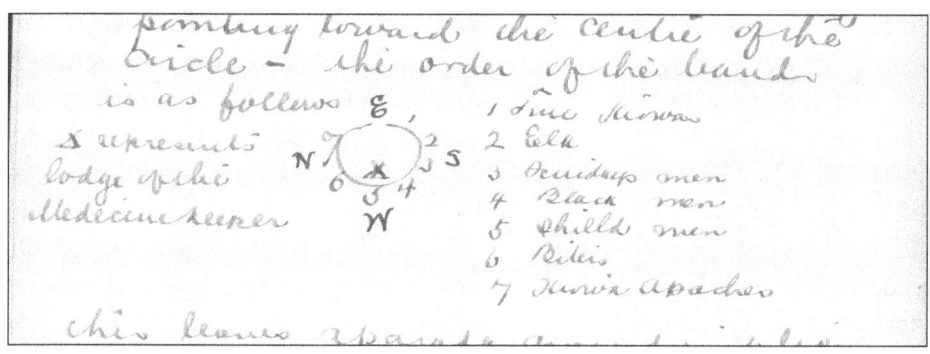

Ledger image of Kiowa Sun Dance encampment, image B (vol. II, p. 102). *Courtesy of Fort Sill National Historic Landmark and Museum Archive and Wade Popp.*

all gallop to it to put up their lodges. Each one selects his own place to camp. The women follow with the lodges, which are pitched by bands in a circle incomplete with the opening to the eastward. The doors of the lodges pointing toward the center of the circle—the order of the bands is as follows: 1. Taime Keeper 2. Elk 3. Scinday Men 4. Black Men 5. Shield Men 6. Biters 7. Kiowa Apaches. This leaves a parade ground just like the soldier's parade ground where the flag pole is—The Medicine Keeper camps inside the parade opposite the opening.

The foot soldiers who remained in the old camp have two horses. They remain there until the village reaches its camping ground. They send out two mounted scouts. They look for the village just as scouts do on the warpath. After a while we see them rising [going up] a hill returning and they report its location. Then they move out as did the others making four halts and they move in a good line. When the main village reached camp they built a big lodge and cook[ed] food so the foot soldiers will [would] have something when they got in. They go to the big lodge and everybody drinks water and eats [103] until sundown.

Next morning before sunrise a man goes to look for a buffalo bull, no cow—a bull. Two men saddle up, go to the Sun Dance Keeper's lodge and say wake up we are going to look for the buffalo. He has a little piece of medicine 1-1/2 in [inches] in length made of a piece of wood or root that came from the far north and it is lent to the man to kill buffalo. Other people never have it and do not know what it is. The Medicine Keeper says to them, "Go out on the prairie and find a little bunch of buffalo. Have two arrows in your hand, not four. Bite off a little piece of that wood, chew it up, and spit it on the arrows." Then he stops talking and the men go out the right side of the village. The killing of the buffalo is done by a man who holds the office. Nobody else can do it. Honameatah has it now. Tohausen his brother used to have it. They find a small bunch of bulls and the buffalo killer starts out. The other stays back and watches him. He first counts his coup before he can shoot. He does not shoot with two arrows unless the first one fails. He shoots him right behind the fore shoulder. He chases the bull so that when he falls his face will be to the east and he falls dead on his belly, not on his side. He dies with [104] [his] face toward the east and on his belly. That is the wonderful thing. He does it himself everybody knows it. He is shot in such a way that blood does not come out of his mouth. In past times when this has occurred great sickness has come to the Kiowas and that is what they are afraid of, also if he falls on his side. They generally kill the buffalo quite early in the morning. When he falls with his head toward the east the other man comes up, walks around him, and says, "Yes he is dead." They picket their horses toward the south and gather a big bundle of sage and bring it to the buffalo. They put some dried buffalo chips about fifteen feet from the buffalo and spread sage on it.

Then they go to his head. They have a very sharp knife. A buffalo bull has a very sharp skin, it is a two-year-old bull. The skin around his neck is the thickest. Before the buffalo killer cuts the skin he must count a coup, often where he struck his enemy. He makes an incision over the right hip bone. He does not saw the hide but rips it, from the incision up to the shoulders and to the butt of the ear and corner of the mouth without taking the knife out from under the skin. Then he goes around the buffalo to the left hip and rips up the hide as he did on the right side without getting in front of the buffalo at all. Then he goes back, cuts off the bone of the [105] tail, and rolls up the skin of the back until he gets to the horns and gets the skin of the face all the way to the corners of the mouth and across the nose. Then they lift it up and move backwards keeping the head towards the east and they spread it out on the sage. They do not drink any water but clean the meat from the inside of the hide good. Then the man who killed the buffalo brings up the horses and covers the saddle with sage. The horse is held with his face to the east. The skin is unrolled about three feet, the head outside their feet on the saddle. The man goes around the horse's tail to the right side, gets on the saddle behind the buffalo skin and makes a prayer to the sun. "May the women and children live good, the buffalo cover the earth, may sickness be put away." Then he don't [doesn't] turn to the right, he turns always to the left and goes to camp. He trots fast in the mean time. The people in camp are watching for him. When he gets near camp he goes slower. The first man who sees him calls out, "There he is, coming bringing the Sun Dance Bull." Then he arrives at the end of the enclosure and stops there four times.

The biggest chief of the Kiowas is in his lodge dressed with [a] shirt with scalps down his arms and scalps down his leggings, everybody watching him. He goes up to the horse of the man bringing the buffalo skin. [106] The horse is still facing the keeper's lodge in the enclosure. He unfastens the hide, going around always by the tail. He gathers the hide and the sage and puts the hide down on the sage as the Medicine Keeper does. Then the women and children all bring presents and throw them down there and make a prayer to the sun. They all have the same prayer, "Let us all attain to the way of old person[']s road [old age]" and then they all scatter to their lodges. Maybe a long time before a big sweat house had been made inside the enclosure in front of the Medicine Keeper's Lodge. It is well covered with robes. After the prayers are all over and then people separate, fire is brought and they put hot stones in the sweat house lodge. Then they bring two chiefs, the man who had the scalps on [his] shirt and leggings and one other. They come with their backs to the east one behind the other and take hold of the robe with the right hand. The first one takes the robe so the head laps over the right arm and takes it into the sweat lodge, carries it around by the south side and lays it flat with its head to the east. Then the Medicine Keeper with a few others go inside. They close the door and throw water on the stones, then they open the door for awhile. This is done seven times. Then they stop and come out and two men go in [and] carry the robe out around [107] by the north side, stopping four times. Then they go in the door turning to the south and lay the hide on the sage prepared for it in the Medicine Keeper's lodge, and everything is over for that day, the second day's ceremony of the dance.

The next day about eight or nine o'clock they have a (joke fight) Sham Battle. That day they cut the cottonwood tree, a woman cuts it whose office it is to do it always as long as she lives. They cut the tree and bring it in stopping four times on the way. When they get there in the enclosure of lodges they dig a hole [and] put the cottonwood tree in the hole. It is a forked tree. Then they make a row of smaller forked trees all around in a circle of about forty-two yards in diameter with a gate toward the east and the hide is brought in to the first tree.

[side note, 107] * (After the sides are finished being walled the old women soldiers go out and fill their robes full of sand, bring it in, and cover the floor of the medicine lodge with clean sand all over and dance on it for good luck. Early next morning the sand is piled in a cone around the foot of the middle pole and a flat stone is put in the doorway. Whenever a dancer goes out of the lodge he puts his foot on that stone.)

On the first day they move into the village.
On the second day they look for buffalo.
On the third day Sham Battle and bring in tree.
On the fourth day bring in the seventeen minor poles.
On the fifth day they put on the roof of slanting poles.
On the sixth day they put on the sides of branches* and the medicine lodge is finished.

No water is brought inside the lodge and at sundown on the sixth day the dancers go into the Medicine Lodge for four days they have no water for four days or nights. On sundown on the fourth day they all stop and go out. Next day the village breaks up and separates in different directions and they [108] leave the Medicine Lodge standing there. When they put up the middle pole first a man climbs up the pole and a rope is thrown over the crotch and the two chiefs bring the robe and tie it to the rope and many men pull it up to the crotch and tie it so its face will be to the east not in the crotch but across the =y= (picture) [fork]. When the Sun Dance is over the hide is left there and anybody who comes by and sees it says, "Yes, there it is. That is the Sun Dance hide left there."

When they have a Sham Battle on the third day, everybody knows about it. They have breakfast, bring in the horses, and the soldiers saddle up and mount, all prepared as for war. They tie up the ponies' tails they have, [and bring] guns, some spears with eagle feathers, and shields and war bonnets. They all collect together a short distance from the village. The four bands [military societies] together come galloping through the gate. The foot soldiers [other military society] are already in the middle of the enclosure.[69] The four horse troops come in by the left, go all around the enclosure and out the gate again, turn to the left around the outside of the enclosure until they reach the gate again and go in repeating this four times. Then they ride out and stop on the prairie. Then the foot soldiers go to the tree they are going to put the buffalo hide and make a shield house around the tree. All have their guns and go out of the fort and form a line toward the horse soldiers. Then they are [109] charged by the horse soldiers both firing at each other for fun, they have no bullets in the guns.[70]

---

69 For the military society associations of this event as described by Kiowa elders in 1935, see Meadows (1999:73).
70 The Sham Battle is called Ácàijàu or Ácàijàugà (Timber Fight). It often involved each side pelting the other with mud balls stuck on the end of saplings that were propelled by slinging them off of the end of the poles. This was called Chénqáádàu (Mud Stick Flinging) (Meadows 1999:73).

When the horse soldiers charge they send the dust high in the air and the foot soldiers retire into the shield house. The horse soldiers surround them and fire and shoot into the lodge. They strike the foot soldiers with sticks and spears. So much dust and smoke is made that it blinds you like a real fight. When the foot soldiers get tried they dash out of the shield lodge and that ends the fight. Then they cut down the tree. It is cut by a woman whose regular office it is to chop the tree. All the time I was growing up the same woman cut the tree. She got old and died and another woman took it up. She was a good woman. Her children grew up good like these children. She was afraid of anything foolish, afraid to do anything wrong. They fell the tree in any direction, cut the limbs all off the tree, just leave [leaving] the two strong forks. There are a lot of soldiers there. They put sticks under the tree and carry it. All that can get room put sticks under it and carry it to the hole that has already been dug for it by a band of woman soldiers, all women—the women put all the uprights around the outside of the lodge. Only one man is with them, a chief. He puts in the center pole that is his office and when the [110] pole is put up and the hide is tied to it they stop for that day—(third [day]).

[side note, 109] A mounted soldier sees a woman he likes and if she wants him he asks her to ride behind him. Sometimes she says yes and gets up behind him. He has a rope attached to the tree tied to the pommel of his saddle, lots of them drag the tree, singing, to where it is to be planted. Same way with outside y trees [forked lodge wall poles].

[110 continued] On the fourth day the other forked poles are brought in and put up. On the fifth [day] the outer walls are made of branches and the roof is finished by sundown of the sixth day and they go into the Medicine Lodge at sundown on the sixth day.

On the morning of the sixth day they herd (?) a lot of buffalo. They take a number of robes with the heads and hair on them, the men and boys and one woman with them, always the same woman. They put these robes on and go out without arms [weapons] like children. They all go out on the prairie and have a sham fight, butting and kicking each other.[71] After that they make them assemble, boys with calf robes on assemble on the plain near the lodges just like a herd of buffalo, some lying down and some standing, a great many, just like a big buffalo herd.

One man well dressed appears with a necklace, a quiver and a bow and arrows in his left hand, and a fire brand in his right, moves along [with] all the people watching him. The buffalo in the flat do not see this man. He goes towards the buffalo and into the medicine lodge. There are

---

71 The Kick Fight is called Àunmáijàu or Àunmáijàugà (Foot Upward Fight) (Meadows 1999:76).

[side note, 110] A man with a st [straight] pipe stoops down with back to the Taime' Keeper who stands in door of [the] Medicine Lodge. When the buffalo jump up he points the pipe at them and draws it back (thus drawing the buffalo). This is done four times, each time going back towards the door until the fourth time when he goes inside and stands at [the] West end. The buffalo are drawn by him, run around outside the medicine lodge four times, then enter, run around [the] center pole four times, and then lie down. This man is called "The Man Who Brings The Buffalo" and the man with the lighted brand is called "The Man Who Drives The Buffalo."

lots of men in there. He sits down with them and say[s], "Look at the buffalo out there." He talks with the Medicine Keeper then goes out and runs over towards the buffalo,

[111] with the fire band in his right hand on the windward side. They smell the smoke and all jump up and look at him. By that time he is opposite the enclosure. They all run away from him just like buffalo. The people in the village all look at them and say, "They are just like buffalo." They dash around the enclosure four times outside [the] Medicine Lodge, inside and into the Medicine Lodge and after running around the center pole four times, all lie down like buffalo. Ten men with robes on came into the lodge and sit down and the whole village comes and stares at the buffalo. Three men come in each holding a straight pipe in their hands. These pipes are straight [stemmed], they have a wooden stem and they are made of black stone like that black pipe that you have that belonged to Tohausen. These pipes are kept by the Medicine Keeper with the medicine and he lends them to the three men. They are very old pipes and belonged always to the Taime'. The three men hold these pipes with the mouth piece presented. One stands still and the other two go out and pull the robes off the faces, looking for the man who has counted the most coups. They pull the robe off a man's face, look at him, and say, "No, that is not the man" and keeps on until he [they] finds him. Then they call out his name to the third man standing who comes, [112] touches him with the pipe, and calls out his name as loud as he can as "Big Bow is a fat buffalo" and puts a short stick on his hump which he has and everybody claps their hands. This is done four times, one each for the four biggest chiefs who have struck their enemies the greatest number of times. Then all go out and the sun goes down.

That night the men who are to dance without water go into the Medicine Lodge. These men are to dance four days and nights without anything to eat or drink. The Medicine Keeper dances with them. If a man cannot hold out he goes home and gets something to eat or drink but does not come back. A great many begin the first day but by the next night they begin to leave. Then they fall off in number until the morning of the fourth day, only a few are left, five or six, all weak with hunger and thirst. I did that once. I was there with them dancing. It was pretty good at night when it was cool but it was very hot in the middle of the day. We almost died from the heat and want of water. On the morning of the fourth day the Medicine Keeper encouraged us and said, "Try hard, try hard. This is the last day. I have the same road that you have. I want you to help me now through to the end. Then you can eat and drink" (at sundown). Toward evening he sent some women to bring in some tubs of water. I looked at that water and longed for it, water hungry.

Nearly sundown he took up [113] the Medicine (Taime') and put it in a sack. He took the same piece of wood that was used by the man who killed the buffalo, powdered a little piece of it, and put it in the tubs of water brought by the women. He said, "Our father the sun is looking down at you now. He sees you poor and weak. He is going to help you live a long time. You are going to see your children grow up good and you are going to have many of them." Then we drank the water in the tubs and we left the Medicine Lodge. And the next day the village broke up.

When a man goes into the Medicine Lodge he has a whistle made from the wing bone of an eagle and some sage in his hand. I do not know why he has the sage, it came to us from the Crows who gave the Taime'. Every kind of medicine has sage with it. I think Scinday said so. We do not cut anybody in the Kiowa Medicine Dance. We are afraid to do that, we are afraid to see blood then. The Cheyennes and the Arapahoes and Sioux cut the dancers but we are afraid of the blood. We do not let the buffalo get shot through the lungs because he would belch blood, which would be dangerous. We would have trouble happen to us if he belched blood. We are afraid of it.

Before we go into the Medicine Lodge the Keeper with seven or eight [114] other men (any who wish it among the dancers) go into his tipi, take the Taime' out of its sack, fix it up, put its feather in its head and tie it on a pole about six feet long. Then they come out, the keeper in front, the others behind as far from here to the flagpole from behind the Medicine Lodge, the keeper carrying the Taime' with stuff in both hands in front of him. They stop behind the Medicine Lodge then go around by the left, stop near the door singing all the time, then around to the right side of the lodge, stop again, and then four times around the lodge and then inside of it. (It is empty when they go in, and [he] places the Taime' in its place in the middle and in front of [the] cedar screen. In old times the little Taime' used to be planted in the same way, one on each side and all facing the east, but the Utes got those little ones.)[72] They are then followed by the dancers and the singers with a big drum just like that little drum you have but about three feet in diameter. Ten persons can drum at it at one time. Then the spectators come in around the door and there is a fire built a little to one side of the door. The only use of the fire is to tighten the drum when it gets slack, by heating it. When they all get in they begin to dance in rows all with their backs to the east and facing the Taime'. They stand in one place bending their knees in time to the drum and blowing their whistle at the Taime'. Behind the Taime' is a cedar screen running across the lodge from north to south leaving doors at each end, the butts of the [115] cedars being out from the wall and the tops resting against the wall (inclining above the cedars are hung the seven or eight Taime' Shields against the wall).

In the middle of the night the dancing stops. The singers [and] spectators go home to bed and the dancers and Taime' Keeper go to sleep. Before the sun rises next morning the singers come in and there are four men who are chosen by the keeper for four years each to assist him to whom he tells the Sun Dance road. These four men have each a fan made from Crow (Raven tail) feathers in this shape. When not in use they are kept near the Taime' against the butts of the cedar trees on the ground. These four men go around among the dancers who rush around the lodge (inside) intermixed. They move these fans through, among the dancers, searching for the man they want. When they find him they wave it at him horizontally, which makes him jump up in the air. Then it is swung specially in front him, which makes him turn around and fall down as if he was drunk. This is done three times every day, at dawn, at noon, and before sundown. It confers long life and health on the persons it is done to. This is explained at first by the keeper when they enter the lodge and each time before it is done the keeper bites off some of the medicine stick, the same he lent the man who went for the buffalo bull. [116] He chews this up and goes around the lodge spitting it upon the dancers. This is good for them. He explains to them that he has no medicine himself but the Taime' sees them. It has the medicine. He himself is only a priest.

After the running about and killing [of] the four men the singers go home to breakfast. The dancers do not eat or drink. About nine o'clock the singers come back. The dance begins again and lasts until dinner time. A man gets up and dances when he feels like it and then sits down

---

72   For an account of the Utes' capture of these two Táimé Bundles in 1868, see Mooney (1898:322–25).

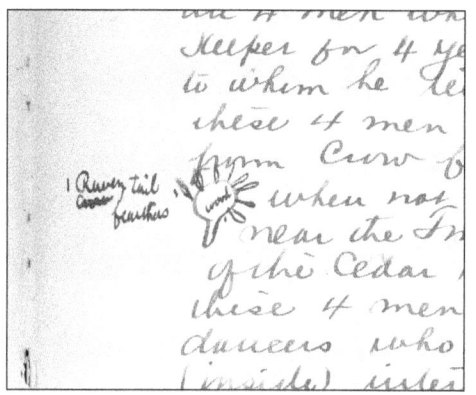

Ledger image of Kiowa Sun Dance fan (vol. II, p. 115). *Courtesy of Fort Sill National Historic Landmark and Museum Archive and Wade Popp.*

around the wall or behind the cedars. Just before the Taime' Keeper spits on them they all get up and dance at once, then he spits on them. They run about and four other men are killed then the singers go to dinner and come back at about four o'clock. Then they dance again and the running about and killing four men is done just about sundown and the singers and spectators go to supper and the dancers rest until after supper when the singers come back and the dancing is resumed until the middle of the night. This is done every day for four days. Just before sundown [on] the fourth day the keeper takes the Taime' rolls up its feather, and puts it in its sack. He has two sacks, one for the Taime' and the things that belong to it and another for his rabbit-skin cap. They are made of parfleches just like these parfleches you have only [117] they have a moon painted on them. When the Taime' is put away then the water is brought in three pails as I told you before. Some of the medicine wood is spit into the pails and the dancers drink it a very little at a time. If they drink as much as they want it will kill them. They are only allowed a little at a time until they have got enough. Then the dance is over and next day the village breaks up and scatters in every direction and war-parties are made up to fight all kinds of people; to go against the Mexicans, the Utes, the Pawnees, or the Texans.

The Taime' Keeper dances with the others and does not eat or drink or go out of the lodge for the four days. He is painted yellow all over [and] has a buckskin skirt made of two deer skins painted yellow. He has sage tied around his wrists and holds cedar in his hand. He has an eagle bone whistle around his neck and a sun painted black in the middle of his breast and another in the middle of his back—a jack-rabbit skin cap with a fluffy eagle feather (from underneath the tail) in his head.

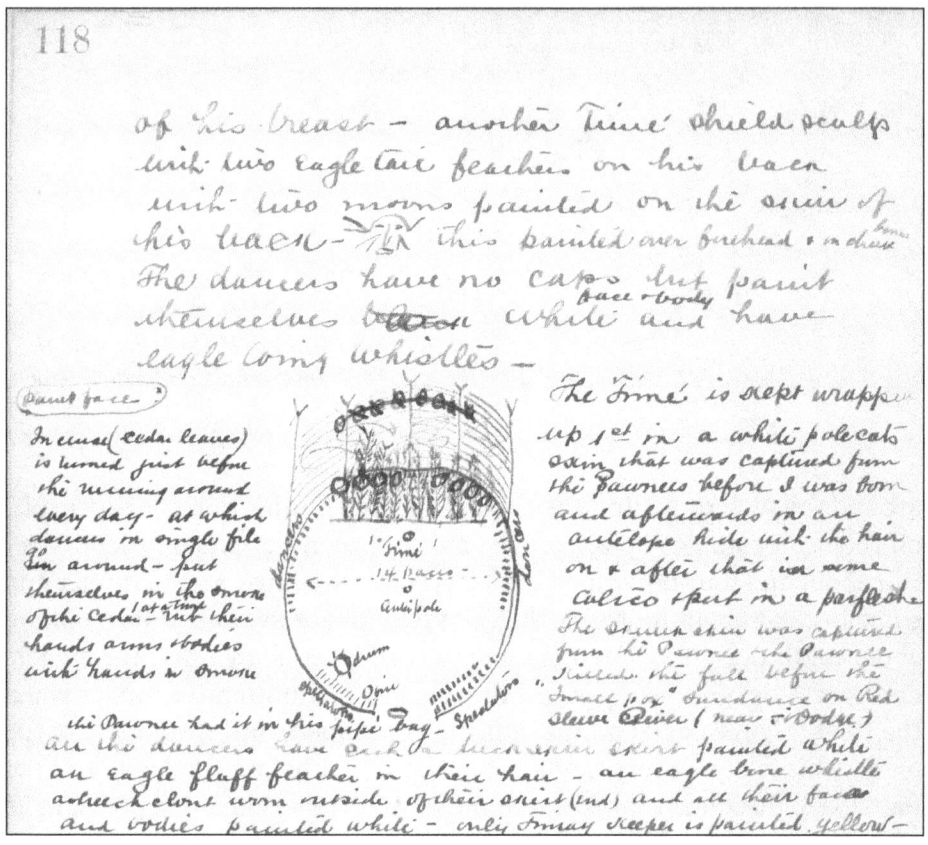

Ledger image of Kiowa Sun Dance face paint and lodge interior (vol. II, p. 118). *Courtesy of Fort Sill National Historic Landmark and Museum Archive and Wade Popp.*

The four assistants have a white skirt of buckskin each, a wreath cap made of sage with a fluffy eagle feather, sage tied around [his] wrists and ankles, cedar in his hand, a scalp from one of the Taime' shields on his breast with two eagle tail feathers in front on his breast with two moons painted blue on the skin [118] of his breast, another Taime' shield scalp with two eagle tail feather on his back with two moons painted on the skin of his back (illustration), this painted over forehead and on cheek bone. The dancers have no caps but paint themselves face and body white and have eagle bone whistles.

Paint-Face Incense (cedar leaves) is burned just before the running around every day, at which dancers in single file go around, put themselves in the smoke of the cedar one at a time, [and] rub their hands, arms & bodies with hands in smoke.

The Taime' is kept wrapped up, first in a white polecat skin that was captured from the Pawnees before I was born and afterwards in an antelope hide with the hair on and after that in some calico, and put in a parfleche. The skunk skin was captured from the Pawnees and the Pawnee [was] killed the fall before the "Smallpox" Sun Dance on Red Sleeve River (near Ft. Dodge). The Pawnees had it in a pipebag. All the dancers have each a buckskin skirt painted white, an eagle fluff feather in their hair, an eagle bone whistle, a breech clout worn outside of their skirt (end), and all their face and bodies painted white. Only [the] Taime' Keeper is painted yellow. A bull's skull has the eyes stuffed with plugs made by doubling a bunch of flags and tying them about six inches from [the] right making a puff at the end. One half of the horn and skull (left) is painted black to represent the black paint brought home after scalps are taken. The right half is red to represent the attainment of old age, horn and all. Near the altar is a woman's turnip stick sharpened and stuck in the ground. The stick is of ash and is dressed like a man. Its head is somewhat smaller than your fist and has a fluffy eagle feathers hanging on it. Its breast has eagle fluff feathers hanging down like Taime'. This stick was added to the outfit by Komauday and has no strong medicine. It is not Kiowa what it represents.

Medicine Dance is held in the spring when the horses are fat. We watch the sage and when it is about eighteen inches high then it is the time. Before the Utes captured the two little Sun Dance medicines, they were all three kept by one man until On-so-ti took pity upon Koh-marty (who was killed up north—this Koh-marty [was an] uncle [of On-so-ti?]) and gave him one of the little ones—and kept the other little one and big one himself.

[119]
How Wild Horse (Kiowa) Was Killed
It is a very dangerous thing to disobey the Medicine Keeper (Taime). One time the Kiowas were going to make a Sun Dance on the Arkansas near the house of one of the armed white men (see calendar 1867) and the Kiowa chief said he was going to war. The Ten Medicine Keepers told him not to go, the Taime Keeper has forbidden any war parties until after the Sun Dance, but he insisted. Then the Taime Keeper talked to him but he would not listen and all the Medicine Keepers held a council about it and

decided to turn him loose. They asked him again what he was going to do and he said he was going to war against the Caddos and they said, "All right, go. We will not prevent you. We turn you loose. Go ahead, go." And as the village was moving to the Sun Dance Tree they say him and six or seven of his men moving over the hill on the warpath and never saw him again. He never came back. He was wiped out. We heard all about it afterwards. They were going south of the Washita [River] and camped near [where] Eagle Heart's place is now. Next morning they packed up and got to Apache Creek and saw a man coming on horseback alone. They hid there and watched him coming until [he was] near enough and rushed out and surrounded him and saw he was a Caddo. Some wanted to kill him right away and run off so his people would not chase and catch them but others wanted [120] not to kill him at once but to find out where his camp was. So they asked him and he said it was on Chandler's Creek.

They asked him how many people were there and he said he was the only man. His wife and family were there guarding a big branch of horses. He deceived them awfully. Some wanted to kill him now but Kobi (Wild Horse) (a Comanche name) said, "No, we will make him take us to his camp and then we will kill him and take the women and horses." And they told him they would go to [the] camp with him and he said, "All right" and turned back with them. He deceived them.

As they got near Chandler's Creek a Kiowa young man went up on a hill above the Anadarko Crossing on the north side and saw the valley was full of Caddo lodges and some white soldier lodges there too, and lots of horses. He gave the alarm but it was too late. The Caddos saw them and the Kiowas waited for them near some oak trees on the north side near the road. The Caddo chief came there and told them to get down and eat but they were afraid to dismount. Somebody went to tell the white captain but he was not there and the soldiers rushed over there. The Kiowas saw them coming and dashed into the timber on the creek. Three of them escaped but Kobi and the rest were surrounded in the timber and wiped out. The three survivors came home and told about it. It is very bad not to listen to the Taime Keeper.[73] All Kiowas know that. The Kiowas and Comanches call that creek (Chandler Creek) Kobi or Wild Horse Creek.[74]

---

73 For a similar example of a group of warriors flaunting the directives of a religious leader prior to the completion of a religious ceremony and their subsequent demise in combat, see Grinnell (1956:45–48) concerning the Cheyenne Bowstring Society in 1837.

74 Chandler Creek, which the Kiowas call Éqúvàu (Planting or Crops Planted Creek), is just north of Porter Hill, now forming Lake Ellsworth, in Comanche County, Oklahoma. The name of the creek would be Cóbèvàu or Cóbèjèvàu (Cóbè's Creek, literally, Wild Horse's Creek). Cóbè is the Kiowa pronunciation of a Comanche name, Kobi or Kobe (Wild Horse).

[121]
Scinday and the Ghost (Whirlwind)

Scinday was going along and saw a woman sitting on the top of a very high cut bluff over a creek. She was sitting on the very edge with her legs hanging over and swinging. He called up and asked if she was married. She said, "No. I am not married." He said, "I want you to marry me." She said, "No. I do not want to marry you." "Why won't you marry me, " he said. "I never stay long in one place. I do not want to stay here and marry you," she said. Scinday said, "I am ahead of you in moving about. I never stay in one place." Then she said, "All right, come up here." And he went up and sat down by her. She told him to take [a] tight hold of her sleeve and he took [a] tight hold of it. And she blew right off the high bluff with him. She was a whirlwind and they blew whirling into a thicket of thorns which scratched Scinday all over his head, ribs, and legs and threw him down hard. When he got up he was very angry and scolded her. She said, "Come along" but he was mad and told her to go away by herself.

Scinday, the Bear, and the Tight Tree

Scinday was going to look for some red plums he knew of before in a plum thicket. When he got there, there were no plums. They were all gone. He looked around for tracks and found the bears had eaten them. He was hungry and the plums were all gone and he got very angry. He followed the bear's trail abusing him, "You have eaten all the plums. You are no good. Your feet smell badly. You have eaten all the plums." He looked ahead and saw some red plums hanging and went to get some, still scolding the bear. The bear was [122] lying hidden under the plum thicket and heard him coming, scolding, and it made him angry. He kept hidden until Scinday reached out his hand for some plums and then he raised up and caught him in his arms and held him and growled in his face, [and] showed his teeth. Scinday was much frightened. He began to laugh and said, "I didn't see you, my friend." The bear said, "I heard you scolding me." He said, "That was only a joke. You and I are good friends. That was [in] fun" and after a while the bear let him go reluctantly and after eating the plums they walked off together.

Scinday made a hole in the ground, covered it over with brush and dirt, and put some rocks at the door and made a fire on top. He said to the bear, "I am going inside. I can beat you staying in there. You put the rocks so as to close the door. When I call out, 'My eyes are going to pop out' you pull the rocks away and I'll come out. I can stand the heat longer than you can." And he went into the hole and the bear closed the door with rocks. Scinday stayed in for a long time then he called out, "My eyes are popping out." Then the bear pulled the rocks away and Scinday came out and the bear went in. He stayed in there for a long time and finally called out, "My eyes are popping out." But Scinday threw more rocks on the door and hauled wood and made the fire larger. The bear cried and asked him to let him out but Scinday told him to "let his eyes pop out" and loaded down the roof and door heavier and made the fire larger. After a while the bear stopped crying and was dead and was being cooked in the oven.

[123]
When the bear was well cooked Scinday took him out, pulled some leaves and grass and spread it out on the ground, laid the bear on it to cool, and sat in the forks of a tree watching it cooling and singing very happy. While he sat there he told the tree to hug him and the tree hugged him. Then he told it to loosen him and it loosened and while he was fooling [around] there a wolf came up and Scinday said, "What are you looking for here, wolf? Go away. I don't want you, wolf." And the wolf said, "I came solely looking for bones you throw away and maybe when you are through you [will] give me a little piece." Scinday said, "No, I don't want you. Go away, wolf." Then the wolf told the tree to hug him until he had eaten the bear and the forks of the tree closed on Scinday and held him and the wolf eat [ate] up all the meat and gnawed the bones. Scinday cried about his dinner and said, "Wolf, leave a little piece for me." But Wolf said, "I won't leave you anything" and he cleaned the bones and then ran away. After a while the tree loosed him, Scinday, and he got down very angry and got a stick and whipped the tree.

Scinday, Sapoodle, and the "Cheet" Bird

Scinday was looking for something to eat in the brush and met Sapoodle right close by. He was very much scared. He was afraid of Sapoodle. He said to Sapoodle, "Do you eat children?" He said, "Yes, I eat children." Scinday said, "I eat men" and then they began to wrestle. Sapoodle caught him, put him in his bag, slung it on his back, and started home to eat him. Scinday was very much frightened. After a while (see [p.] 132) [continued from 132] he said to Sapoodle (only his head was out of the bag), "What are you afraid of?" Sapoodle said, "I am not afraid of anything." Scinday was very much dismayed. After a while he said, "Are you not a little afraid of

SIGN LANGUAGE 397

something?" Sapoodle said, "Yes, I am afraid of the 'Cheet bird.' " Scinday laughed to himself. After a while, he made the whistle of the bird, "Cheet, cheet" (a sparrow that lives in the brush). Sapoodle started and listened behind him, but did not hear it again and thought he was mistaken. After a while Scinday did it again. This time he [Sapoodle] heard it good and plunged into and through the brush in fear. Scinday got his arms out of the bag and warded off the branches from his face as Sapoodle rushed through the trees and when he looked ahead he saw a leaning tree and threw his arms around it. As [continued from 133] they passed under he held on tight with both arms, which tore him loose from the bag. He said, "Cheet, cheet," again, and Sapoodle kept on running and Scinday was saved.

[124]
TATTOOING
[probably Iseeo]
When I was a boy we used to see the Osages on the Arkansas [River]. We were at peace with them then. First we made peace and afterwards I was born. I used to see the chiefs tattooed around the neck with a ring of points, the points upward then lower down, another ring [of] points downward that came down on the chest. Only chiefs had that, before a man killed his enemy he could not have that. I used to see them frequently and most all chiefs had it. The Kiowa-Apache women sometimes tattooed a ring or a cross over the nose and between the eyes. You have seen some of them. Only a few did it. In the old times, they did not do it very many, only now and then one. They take a bunch of cactus thorns and bind them into a sort of a brush (like a shaving brush). Then they tap on the skin gently with the points until the blood comes freely and put powdered charcoal [in]. They draw pictures where they want them. After that a scab forms on the sore place and when that peels off, you will see the picture just like a brand on a horse. It never comes off until they die. The Tawaconies, Wacos, Keechis, and Wichitas tattooed the way I told you before. Those are the only people we knew of who tattooed themselves. I never saw a Comanche woman do that.

[125]
DEATH OF TSAIT-AN-KE (SITTING BEAR)
When this post was first built and the Kiowas were brought in here, Tsait-au-te (White Bear), Tsait-an-ke (Sitting Bear) and Big Tree were prisoners under those barracks over there (south end of west post) over there in the

> around the neck – each a ring of points the points upward their lower down another ring points downward that came down on the chest
>
> only chiefs had that, before a man slewed his enemy he could not have that – I used to see them frequently and most all chiefs had it – The Kiowa [Apache?] women sometimes tattoed a ring [or a cross] over the nose & between the eyes – you have seen some of them – only a few did it – in old times they did not do it very many – only now & then one. they take a bunch of cactus thorns and

Ledger image of Wichita tattoos (vol. II, p. 124).
Courtesy of Fort Sill National Historic Landmark and Museum Archive and Wade Popp.

basement. Tsait-an-ke (Sitting Bear) was an old man. He had been a strong fighter but his son was dead and it made him very sorry. He wanted to die and he told Tsait-au-te and Big Tree, "You two are going to be saved and get back to our people. I am not going to be saved. My son is dead. I do not want to live anymore. When you get home tell the Kiowas how I died." They would talk to him and tell him to "try hard" but he said, "No I am not going to live any longer" and he would not eat anything trying to starve himself. One day the soldiers told them to come out and get in some wagons. They were going to prison in Texas. Tsait-an-ke told the others to get in one wagon. He wanted to be in one wagon by himself. He did not intend to go beyond a line of trees south of Fort Sill (a mile and a half). He was not going to live but they were going to be saved, and someday get back to their people and must remember and tell them how he died.

As the wagons went down the hill leading from the plateau the post is on he began to sing his soldier song but the soldiers did not know what he was doing. When they got near a little slough on (below the corral) the

Texas Road and he tried to stab a soldier and they shot him. He fell out of the wagon with his hands tied and was taken up to the hospital where he soon died. Tsait-an-ke's son had been killed some years before in Texas on a little stream coming into the Brazos from the south. He went down the next year got his bones, packed them on the horse, and brought them to the Kiowa village. He had two lodges, one for his son's bones and one for himself. His son's lodge was always pitched. A good bed was put up in it with the best blankets he could find and his son's bones were kept in the bed rolled up good. Whenever he went anywhere his son's lodge was taken down [and] packed on his best horse. It had a good saddle and bridle and the bones were packed on top of the lodge cover. That was done all the time until after the soldiers killed Tsait-an-ke here on the flat. Then his bones were carried somewhere and abandoned.[75]

[125]
KOMAUDY'S SHIELD IS CALLED SUN DANCE SHIELD
Komaudy means "Black Stomach." When I was a boy he was a very old man and he died at the Sun Dance where we made German silver head-dresses (1865) [1866].[76] When he was a young man he went to war with Tohausen in Mexico. That time Tohausen was corralled by soldiers in a rock.[77] They were driving horses north out of Mexico when they looked back one day and saw the soldiers coming after them about three miles back. Tohausen said, "The soldiers are not near let us drive the horses on fast and they can't catch us." But the others said, "No, today we will have a good fight." They insisted on it until Tohausen drew back and let them do it. They bunched the horses and went back near a little creek and waited for the soldiers to come and charged them but the soldiers defeated them. Some of them ran away and got home safe. Tohausen with some chiefs ran down into the bed of the creek. Komaudy was with him. He had been shot in the side. They followed the bottom of the very crooked creek with high banks up to the very head where they got into a cave with a spring in it at the very head of the creek. The cave made a turn inside so the soldiers could not see to hit him when they fired into the cave.

---

75 Alice Marriott recorded a detailed account of this incident in 1935. Piatonma and George Hunt to Alice Marriott, July, 22, 1935 (AMP). See also Meadows (2010:52–53).
76 His full name was Kǫ́áubı́étjè (Big Black Tripe). Komaudy (Kǫ́áujè) is a shortened form of the name.
77 This is the Hueco Tanks Fight that occurred in 1839, approximately thirty miles northeast of present-day El Paso, Texas. Compare with Mooney (1898:302–305) and Meadows (2008:68–79) for other details relating to Black Tripe's experiences. See also Scott (n.d.a:1:78–81).

Komaudy fainted in there and was put on the ground around the corner. One man and a horse were killed and laid outside the mouth of the cave. It was very hot and they even swelled up and caused a very offensive odor. They were shut up in there for nine days. A Mexican who could talk Comanche called in to them, "What kind [127] of men are you?" and Tohausen called back, "We are Kiowa men." And the Mexican said, "Try hard now, try hard, the soldiers are not going to turn you loose. They are going to wipe you out. The captain has ordered it." That night they built fires along the top of the banks (there was no timber on the creek) so they could watch the mouth of the cave and every now and then they would shoot a volley into the mouth of the cave. And on the second night the Mexican called out in Comanche, "Another big lot of soldiers are coming" and they could hear their wagons come into camp. Tohausen thought every night and every day how to get out but he failed, the soldiers had them so closely surrounded.

They had nothing to swallow but water from the spring. If it had not been for that water they would all have died from water hungry. Finally on the ninth day Tohausen said, "I am tired out. I am emaciated. If we stay in here we will die hungry tired out. It will be better to die in a fight. Maybe one man will escape and tell our people how we died. I will go out last, who will go out first?" He asked everyone but one. He urged them, "You are chiefs, big chiefs. You have got hearts of your own. Who will go out first?" But they all said, "No, it is too dangerous." At last, the last one who was a very small chief said, "I will go and die first." He was Komaudy's brother. They looked at Komaudy. He was very thin and weak. And his brother said, "You come with me and we will die together."

Tohausen told them to cut a string from [128] their leggings and tie their bows to their wrists so they would not lose them if they fell down in the darkness and to get ready. And after dark they crept around a corner that was a little dark and got just at the mouth of the canyon within a few feet of some soldiers they could hear talking. The first man whispered, "Are you all ready" and dashed out followed by Komaudy and the rest and ran through the soldiers shooting and stabbing, followed last by Tohausen [in] the most dangerous place. They got down into another gulch in the darkness and heard the soldiers going off another way in pursuit of some of the rest of the band. Tohausen said, "Who is here?" and there were five or six and Komaudy. He put his bow down from the top of the bank to help Komaudy up. There was another man there wounded at the bottom.[78] They asked him, "Where are you wounded?" He said, "My leg's broken."

---

78 Based on Mooney's account this would be Dagoi, who had to be left behind and was soon thereafter killed by the soldiers.

They said, "We will have to leave you. If you were shot in the body we could take you but not with a broken leg." And he said, "All right, leave me. I cannot travel. Tell the people how I died here." Komaudy could not walk and his brother carried him on his back every night and they hid away during the daytime until they got far away from the soldiers. Every now and then Komaudy would die (faint) and his brother would put him down. They would all stop and look at him and after a while he would open his eyes and his brother [129] would pick him up and go on. One day while they were resting his brother said, "I will go on to the next creek and hunt and kill something to eat. You bring Komaudy along slowly." And he went on and killed a deer and watched for them to come. (Komaudy died over there and they watched him a long time waiting for him to come to but he did not). And they said, "He is true dead now." They had nothing to roll him up in but they laid him out and put stones around his body and came on after his brother. As his brother sat waiting for them, he counted them coming and one was missing and when they got close he saw Komaudy was not there and he said, "Where is Komaudy?" And they told him he was really dead but he said, "No, that is a lie. I am going back after him." But they caught and held him and said, "No, he is truly dead. We watched him a long time. He is dead." And they held him until he agreed to go on with them and they got home safe.

Komaudy come [came] to after a while and looked around for his brother but they had all gone. Then he saw the rocks and knew they had left him for dead. He was nothing but skin and bone. He looked black like a dead person. His wound was full of screw worms and was very offensive. He had only strength enough to crawl down on his hands to the water about six feet and back to the [130] bank again. He had nothing to eat and was dying all the time. At night he saw the moonrise and go over his head and he could hear a wolf come nearer and nearer and walk about smelling him. He kept awake watching the wolf and said, "Now he is going to kill me. I am too weak to fight him and he will kill me." But the wolf smelt him for a while and laid down near him like a dog and next day went away but came back every night and slept near him like a dog. In the day time the ravens came and sat on him and looked at him and picked the screw worms out of his wound and one night in his dream he saw the Taime Medicine on a mountain whistling to him and it told him he would get well and see his lodge again.

He laid there for a long time getting weaker and weaker and one evening at dusk he saw the wolf jump up and smell the wind and run back and forth in a very excited way and then run off. And he heard footsteps of horses and thought they were Mexicans who would kill him if they found him. After a while a man on a horse came near who saw him lying there in the dusk and shaded his eyes to see him better. The man smelt his wound and felt him with his lance and called out to the others in Comanche, "There is a man here. A dead man." And they all came to look at him. He was all bones. His hair was matted into a [131] bump and he was black like a dead man, his stomach all caved in. He spoke to them in Comanche and told them who he was, that he had been abandoned as dead. They said they knew who he was and gave him something to eat, washed him all over, and fixed his hair (his wound had all healed up, he had no wound only starved and weakened) and the Comanche chief said, "We were going to war but if we leave this man he will die. We will turn back and take him home." They fed him every day and washed him until he got a little better. They took grass and wound it and made a thick ring of it and put it up on their pack horse and put Komaudy lying down on his side doubled up in the ring and led the horse until they got to the Kiowa village. They put Komaudy on the ground and begun [began] to cook their supper and a Kiowa man came up and saw Komaudy and said, "What is that?" The Comanche chief said, "This is a man. A Kiowa man we found." And he looked at him closely and knew it was Komaudy and ran off to tell his relations. He had a great many relations and they came and took him into his lodge and the Comanches with him and told them rest here tonight and do not go away tomorrow. And they counciled what they should do and agreed that they would each give the Comanches a horse tomorrow and each would bring something valuable he had and give it to the [132] Comanches and they made them full of presents. After Komaudy got well he got to be a big medicine man. He said, "I know some shield road medicine" and he made some shields. That shield Dr. Gleeman had was one, they had a Taime and that bird, a moon on them. Taybodle had it and lent it to Iseeo who was killed by Sa-kee-bo [Sauk] (in 1854). Big Bow had it afterwards.

Komaudy knew a great many different kinds of medicine. The little things showed him while he was lying on the ground. The wolf and the ravens taught him some medicine too. He died very old in 1865.

[133]

Scinday's Race with Sapoodle

Scinday met Sapoodle another time and he was very much scared. He was afraid Sapoodle would eat him. He opened his breast and took out his heart and liver and put them on the ground and said to Sapoodle, "Can you do that?" Sapoodle said, "Yes, I can do that" and he put his heart and liver on the ground near Scinday's. Scinday said, "I can beat you running. If I do, I [will] take your heart and liver, all right?" Sapoodle said, "Where are we going to run?" And Scinday pointed out where they would turn around to come back. Then they began to run and Sapoodle ran a little faster than Scinday and Scinday suddenly sat down and said, "Oh, I must pull a thorn out of my foot" and hopped along on one foot. And Sapoodle ran on towards the turning point. Scinday was deceiving him. Sapoodle ran over a little rise out of sight then Scinday turned back and ran and got his heart and liver and Sapoodle's heart and liver and ran away with them. He was saved.

Scinday and the Flatulent Root
(Compare Kroeber Tale No. 7, *Gros Ventre*, Vol. 1, p. 68)

Scinday and the Elk's Head

Scinday was looking for something to eat and heard a Sun Dance whistle and went to see what did it. He came to a big bleached elk's head with horns on it and heard the noise of the whistle and dancing in the brain cavity. The mice were having a Sun Dance [134] and he poked his head in there to see them. They told him to go away, that was their medicine dance. But he would not listen, he insisted on staying there and watching the dance. His head was inside, his body was out, and his back bent looking in. After a while he got tired and went to take his head out but he couldn't do it. His head was caught back of his ears. He was fast [stuck] and he had to go about with this old bleached elk's skull with heavy horns. He could not see very well and fell in the river which was very high and the current swept him off. There were some people below on the bank of the river and they saw a bleached elk's skull coming down. It raised up a little in the water and called to them to catch it and they were surprised. They threw a rope over the horns and drew it in. They were astounded as the elk's skull said, "Split open my skull" but they were afraid to split open his skull. But he insisted on it, "Split open my skull [and] you save me" and they split open his skull and it was Scinday. They saved him.

[side note] Compare *Blackfoot Mythology*, Wissler and Duvall, Anthropological Papers, American Museum of Natural History, Vol. 11, 1908, p. 32, Tale no. 16; *Arapaho*, Dorsey and Kroeber, pp. 107–11; *Gros Ventres*, Kroeber, p. 68; *Arikara*, Dorsey, p. 137.

Scinday and the White Eagle's Medicine

Scinday came near a high, rocky, split bluff and a creek near its base, like Medicine Bluff, very high, [and] the water very deep. He saw a white eagle sitting on top. He could look down into the water and see the fish and the beavers down below. The ice was about a foot thick and covered with water. Scinday watched him. Every now and then he blew a Sun Dance whistle, plunged down from the bluff into the water, and brought up a beaver, took it to the top of the bluff and eat [ate] it. Scinday climbed up to [135] him and asked him to show him some medicine so he could get something to eat that way. White Eagle told him to go away, he did not want him. But Scinday insisted until White Eagle got tired and told him to take the whistle. He must look down into the water, see a beaver, whistle the medicine whistle, shut his eyes tight, and plunge down into the water, catch the beaver, and bring it up. He might do that three times, but the fourth time was dangerous. Then he flew away. Scinday put the whistle around his neck, looked down and saw a beaver, shut his eyes, whistled, plunged and brought up a beaver. Scinday said, "That is pretty (a little) good." Then he did that three times and brought up a beaver each time and thought, "Pretty soon I'll make an oven and cook lot [of] beavers and eat until I have enough." Then he thought, "What made White Eagle tell me not to do it four times. I think he told me a lie. I will get another beaver." Then he shut his eyes, whistled the medicine whistle, and plunged downward and struck the ice with his head and killed him (made him faint). After a while, as he was lying on his back, he came to and saw the eagle soaring above him in the air. He took his whistle and broke it and threw scoldings at the eagle for his bad medicine.

[The] Blind Man and His Wife

A long time ago a man went blind. He and his wife and little girl were in their lodge in the Kiowa village, which went off and left them. Their food got scarcer and scarcer and finally gave out [136] and the woman went out and hunted for berries and pomme blanches and gave her husband only a little. He was blind and could not see what she got and could not hunt for himself. After their food was all gone they had nothing but water and it began to snow. It snowed all day and all night and next morning the woman opened the door to get some wood and she saw the buffalo were feeding all around, close to the lodge. She told her husband who took his bow and arrows and fired at the nearest one. His wife scolded him and told him he was no good, he had missed it. But he had truly hit it behind the fore shoulder and it had run off a little way and died. He fired at another but he missed that one and she scolded him again and he went back to his bed. His wife then told him she was going out after berries and roots and would be gone a long time. She stole his knife and whetstone from him and went out with her daughter and cut up the buffalo. It was a fat one. She eat [ate] all she wanted to and put the rest up to dry and went home and gave her husband some berries. She didn't let him know they had any meat. This went on for some days and he began to think, "What makes the woman [137] go out every day and stay? I think I smell something fat." He caught his little girl and kissed her, saying he was going to die from hunger and while he kissed her he smelled her mouth and fingers and smelt fat on them. Then he got up and went out to see if some medicine would not have pity on him and get his eyes well and get him something to eat. As he went along he heard an owl, stopped to listen to it, and the owl called to him, "I see you here hungry, and poor, and blind. I am going to make you see." And he put some medicine in his eyes and asked him if he could see and he said, "No." Then he put in some more and asked him if he could see. He said, "Yes, I can see a little way" and the next time he put medicine in his eyes he could see away off. Then the owl told him, "Your wife is deceiving you, she has plenty to eat but she keeps it from you." Then he went home. His wife and child were not there. He sat down on his bed as usual [and] pulled the blanket over his head. He was very angry. When his wife came home near sundown she came in and saw him lying [there] covered with his blanket. He asked her if she had found anything to eat. She told him no, then he jumped up and pulled out both her eyes and threw them away. A long time [138] ago women, women were fools and they have not put that road away yet.

[side note, 136] Compare Rev'd Als. Morice, *Notes on the Western Dene*. Trans Canadian Institute, Vol. IV, 1892, p. 171. Similar, Carrier narrative, the man was cured of blindness by a loon. He gave the loon his shell necklace as a present and threw some dentalium shells at him. This is the cause of [the] ring around the loon's neck (white) and the white spots we now see on his wings.

Killing Herders near Fort Sill

Tchaka
While sitting on a high hill back of Loco's Village with Iseeo and Tchaka, October 15, 1897, all looking over the landscape, Tchaka said, "Do you

see that road?" (Heyl's Hole Road north of Medicine Bluff Creek).[79] A long time ago there was no road there. That road was made after. Behind the point of that mountain that runs off to Tabenanaka's house (now Pu-Kawick's) there was a large Kiowa war party hidden behind the point of that mountain. It was two years after the white soldiers came to Fort Sill.[80] It was a big war party, over two hundred. We were both with it [Iseeo and Tchaka]. The Kiowa village was away on the head of Red River. We came down north of the mountains and our plan was to send ten men in to the post. Iseeo was one of the ten. They were to kill someone there and run off toward Signal Mountain (House Mountain) when about two troops of cavalry would chase them and about that time the soldiers would be tired (four miles). The rest of the party would attack and kill them all. Before daylight the main body came down where you see that road now, crossed at Heyl's Hole crossing, and found a white man herding cattle there. It was not yet daylight but you could see a little. The white man ran off and hid in the grass and the whole war party surrounded the place and after a while someone shot him and Big Tree was the first man to strike [139] his body. He was killed right where you see that horse in that cornfield (Chatto's). They all fired a shot into him. The ten men scouts had gone down Medicine Bluff Creek and hid in the timber where that little ravine runs in where White Wolf Road crossed Bluff Creek at the east end of the bluffs and on the north side. It was not yet light and we heard some firing over from the other party. We thought they had a fight and we went right over there. We found them waiting in the pass north of Signal Mountain. The herder was already dead. The soldiers came out soon and took our trail but soon turned back and we went back north of the mountains.

Another time Tchaka was with a war party who killed a herder among those mesquite trees over there, on [the] right of White Wolf Road going from past [beyond or behind the road?] and close to Tabenanaka's Mountain. Smoke, who used to be a soldier at Sill, afterwards killed him and struck his body first.[81] Another man was killed near Dullard's place south of the post on Cache Creek. White Horse was the leader then. Killed A Mountain was leader the other two times and he has been dead a long time now.[82] One time Lone Wolf's son was killed in Texas near the Rio

---

79 Loco's village most likely refers to the camp of Luka Mokin (aka Mokeen) or Màucîn (the Kiowa pronunciation of Joachin) and the father of Lucius Aitsan, who resided in the Saddle Mountain area.
80 Soldiers began building Fort Sill in the spring of 1869 (Mooney 1898:188), so this account suggests that it occurred in about 1871.
81 This is probably Smoky (Áiséjè), born 1857 (Kiowa Family Record 1901: Fam. 96).
82 This may refer to a man named Qópfàhóljè (Killed Them At The Mountain) (Mooney n.d.:7:26, 11:62, 116), who was killed by Thènézélbé (Fierce/Dangerous Eagle) in 1870.

Grande on a little creek this side. The next year he [Lone Wolf] told the agent he was going to get his bones and retaliate by killing a white man. The agent (Bald Head [Laurie Tatum]) said all right go ahead and he went with a war party but did not succeed [140] in killing a white man but he took a big lot of soldiers' horses and drove them off.[83] I saw them come in. The village was on the east branch of Elk Creek. The horses were very thin and played out. They abandoned a number [that] played out on the road. They were not much good. They were divided up here and there.

Did you hide them anywhere? Mr. Jones [Mr. Horace P. Jones, Post Interpreter] said, he looked for them in the Kiowa villages when they came in for rations and could not find them anywhere. We rode stolen horses around here to the issue and everywhere. We didn't hide anything. We were very foolish in these days, all the time fighting and going on the warpath. Capt. Dodge 9th Cav. [no additional information]

BUFFALO COW WOMAN
(Compare [with] *Gros Ventres,* Woman Married Buffalo Tale #24, Vol. 1, p. 100.)

Tchaka told me two stories today for you and when I heard them I recognized that I knew parts of them before. A long time ago there was a good-looking young Kiowa man. It was after the Kiowas had grown partly up. There were a great many Kiowas then and Scinday was with them. There was a good-looking Kiowa man and he had a flute. He lived in the Kiowa village and when he wanted to court a young Kiowa woman he went on the prairie outside the village and played on the flute in the middle of the night and when the girl heard the flute she would get up and come out to where he was. The village moved and he came along behind, the last one and came to a creek that had been fouled up by the [141] buffalo. He stood there looking at the creek which smelt badly, like the buffalo, and noticed a buffalo cow lying dead there. It had been dead a long time. Its head was on the bank and its body in the sand. It had a very fine hide on it. He looked at it again and said, "If I had a bull's road I would marry you." And the cow heard him. He didn't know it but she heard what he said. Then he went on after the village.

Several years after that he went one night on the prairie outside of the village to play his flute in the middle of the night, as he played on his flute

---

83 Lone Wolf's son Tàu̯ágài (Sitting Astride/In The Saddle) and his brother's son (cousin to the other decedent) Cûîîtèndè (Young or Baby Wolf Heart) were killed in late 1873. A revenge party set out in the spring of 1874 to avenge the loss (Mooney 1898:337–38).

he saw someone coming toward him and spoke to him. It was a woman. He asked her what she wanted and she told him she wanted him. He looked at her and saw that she was a very handsome woman. He did not know her. She was just like a very handsome Kiowa woman but he had never seen her before. She said, "Look at me. Do you know me?" He said, "No, I do not know you." She said, "I am not a woman. I am a buffalo cow. One day you saw me lying dead and you said you had a bull's road and would marry me." He was very much astonished. He said, "All right. I told you I would marry you, I will do it." And he took her off to his lodge. They kept it secret for a long [142] time. She went away before daylight and came back sometimes after dark and nobody knew about it. One night she told him she was tired, "Let us both run away and live in some other country. Let us elope." And he said, "All right" and they eloped. He disappeared and the Kiowas did not know what had become of him. They thought he had been killed somewhere. They lived together for sometimes and had a boy born to them and she said, "My father is a bull. He is a chief bull. I want to take my boy to see him. Are you afraid? Is your heart weak and poor, or is it strong?" He said, "My heart is strong. I will go with you." Then they took down their lodge and went to look for where the buffalo were thick and after a while found them.

The buffalo were moving about inside of a herd, throwing up the dust. It was so thick you couldn't see inside the herd. She told the man to sit down and hold the child and she would go and find her father and would come back. She was behind him and told him not to look until he could no longer hear her footsteps. Then he heard her going off farther and farther. He did not look that way until after he could no longer hear her for some time. Then he turned and looked and saw a buffalo cow go down into the creek. She was gone a long time and when he saw a buffalo cow coming towards him and come [143] down into the creek. He turned away his head and soon heard footsteps coming behind him and there she was, a woman. She said she had found her father after a long search and he said to bring her husband and child to him. He didn't like red men, buffalo were afraid of red men, they killed them. But if his child was married to one, good and strong, all right. But if they were not married strong he would kill him. When he came he would have to pick his wife and child out of a lot of buffalo. If he picked them he would be saved. If he failed he would not be saved. The bull would kill him. His wife talked to him and told him not to be afraid. And he told her to put some mud on her horns and to have one side of her hump licked so the hair would lie down flat and the boy told him told him he would wag his right ear when his father looked at him and would have mud spots down his back bone.

Then they started toward the herd and all the buffalo stared at him separating to let him pass. He met a big angry bull and was very much frightened. The bull twitched his tail in anger. His horns were wide and sharp. The hair hung down from his face and his eyes were terrible. He twitched his tail and charged at him to hook him. He stood still and looked at the bull who stopped right close to him [144] without hurting him. Then he said, "You are not afraid. You must come and recognize your wife and child then you will be safe." All the two-year-old cows were together. All the bulls and calves were put away to one side, only two-year-old cows, many of them and all alike. He went around looking for one with mud on her horns. The bull called out, "You must hurry up. You have not got long to look." Then he looked and saw one with mud on her horn and all around he didn't see any other. "I must be careful," he said, "or I will not be saved" and he looked very carefully and saw the hair on her hump had been licked and plastered down flat and when the bull called to him again to hurry, he said, "I see her now" and pointed her out. And the bull said, "That is your wife. That is all right. Find your son and you will be saved."

There were a great many calves there, hundreds of them, and he went around looking for his son. The calves were all alike. The bull called out to him to hurry. He saw a calf wagging his right ear and looking closer saw mud spots down his back and he pointed him out. And the bull said, "That is your son. You are saved." But Scinday came and said, "We are going to have a race, all buffalo race. You must race with them. Run around that far hill and turn and [145] come back here." They thought when he went down into one of the creek-beds the buffalo [would] all pile in and would kill him. They got all the bulls in line and while they were getting ready, his son, the calf, came up secretly and gave him a buffalo chip and a bull's tail. He told him that if he would pinch and powder some of the hair of the tail he would fly along like a bird above the buffalo and they could not hurt him. If he pinched and powdered some of the chip he would fly over the creeks like a bird when the buffalo plunged in. He would be on the other side. Scinday and Bull were talking there and said, "He is dead now. They have trampled him to death. He cannot be saved." But when they got pretty near the Kiowa man was ahead and came in first. The bull was going to have him do something else, but Scinday said, "We['ll] turn him loose" and they turned him loose and he was saved.

Breaking a Chief's Bad Road

There used to be a Kiowa chief who had a bad road. He was dangerous and everybody knew it. He had a road that when he saw some fat meat hanging up, he sent his wife over there. She would say her husband sent her for that fat meat and they would give it to her because he would get angry and kill somebody. He [146] had killed [a] lot of people because he was angry at them. There were two old people in the village, a man and his wife. They were very poor and when they hunted buffalo they used to give the old people some meat. But after a while they forbid [forbade] them meat. One day they ran buffalo and the old man told the old woman to go and see if they would give her something when they cut up the buffalo, but they refused her and she waited until they were gone, saw where one had been wounded and gone [went] away without anybody knowing it. She followed the blood spots. It dropped down into the creek bed for a long way and came to a big clot of blood, which she took up. The buffalo had belched it out of [their] lungs. She had followed it so far she was tired and let it go and went home having picked up a liver on her way back. She put them in a pot to boil and was talking to the old man when they heard a child cry in the pot and when they went to examine it they saw a small baby in the pot. They pulled it off the fire and took care of the baby. It knew a great deal when it was a month old, more at two months, and at six months it knew everything and was running around and it called the old people Grandfather and Grandmother.

One day he saw the people going out to kill buffalo [147] nearby and he said he would go out and get some meat. He followed them out and went about picking the hair off the lumps of the fat buffalo and when he got through he had a back load of hump meat, very fat. He carried it back and threw it down outside and they asked him if he got any meat and he said, "Grandmother, you will find some fat humps out where I came out of the creek" and the old woman cut them and hung them up to dry.

Next day that Chief saw the fat meat hanging up and told his wife to go and get it. She stood outside and called into the lodge, "My husband chief sent me to ask you for that fat meat and bring it home." The old man said, "Yes, take it." He was very much scared but the boy said, "No, he can not have it." The old people told him to give the meat to him, he was very strong and very dangerous. But the boy said, "No, he has a bad road. He is not strong. If he comes here I will kill him." But the old people told him to let the meat go, yet he would not listen. The woman went back and told her husband they refused her the meat. This made him very angry at those two poor people and he came over and said, "Who refused their fat meat?" and the old man, very much [148] frightened, said the boy had refused it, he had not done it, the boy had done it, and the chief said he was going to kill them all and take the meat. The boy said, "You are a chief. You have got a bad road. I carried that fat meat a long distance on my back. It is my meat. I refuse it to you. You are a chief. You can get plenty of meat of your own." But the chief was very angry and started to get something to kill them with but the boy took his Gomah spear and threw it at him and killed that chief—he broke his bad road.[84]

Scinday and Porcupine

Scinday killed a buffalo and cut it up and laid the meat out and went off to get his children so they could get something to eat. When they came back there was no meat there. They looked for tracks and found a porcupine's tracks which led down to the river. They followed it down and when they got there they looked in the water [and] saw the porcupine on [at] a fire cooking the meat. Scinday was very angry and dove down in the water to kill the porcupine but he struck his head against a rock at the bottom and the blood bubbled up from his head, [and] the children squint[ed] and said, "He is killing the porcupine, see the blood?" After a long time Scinday came up and was lying on his back in the [149] water and saw the real porcupine in the tree cooking the meat and he asked him please to save him some meat, but the porcupine refused.[85]

Why the Kiowas Do Not Have Tails

A long time ago before Kiowas grew up Scinday lived. He had a tail like a buffalo. He was naked and moved a long looking for something to eat. He saw a wolf eating plums and he watched him and went down and asked the wolf to give him some of his medicine so he could do as the wolf did. The wolf dug a small hole in the ice in a pond, [and] put in the end of his tail, which caused plums or persimmons or blackberries to appear, and Scinday asked him to give him some of his medicine so he could get something to eat in the same way. But Wolf said, "No. I don't want you.

---

84 The Kiowa name for the game called Gomah is Cáumáuqàudàl (Aiming/Circle Wheel). Parker McKenzie to the author, Sept. 25, 1994.
85 Séndé/Scinday is often fooled by a reflection. Some aspects of this story resemble those in the Medicine Eagle story above.

Go away." But Scinday insisted until the Wolf was tired and told him to dig a small hole in the ice, put the tip of his tail in it, and he would find something to eat there and not to do it more than three times, and Wolf went away. Scinday dug a small hole, put the tip of his tail in it, looked around, and found it full of persimmons. Then he eat [ate] these and did the same thing a little farther on and found the hole full of plums, and again and he found the hole full of blackberries, ate all them, [150] sat there, and thought about it. "Why did wolf tell me not to do it four times. I am still hungry. I will dig a big hole in the ice this time and get enough to eat." Then he dug a big hole, put his tail clear down in it and the ice froze his tail in so he couldn't get it out. He pulled and pulled at it crying with pain but it was stuck fast and after a while he cut it off and left it there, the blood running from it. That is the reason the Kiowas have no tails.

SCINDAY AND SAPOODLE
([FOR] ANOTHER VERSION; SEE P. 132)

Scinday was coming along and met Sapoodle suddenly. He was secretly afraid of him and said he would kill him. He said, "I will deceive him" and asked Sapoodle if he was looking for men to eat. Sapoodle said, "Yes, I am looking for men to eat." Scinday said, "I am looking for men to eat also. I know where there is a camp of them over there, fat ones. If you want to go and attack them I will be [the] leader." Sapoodle said, "Yes, we will charge them." Scinday said first, "We must leave our hearts here so we will not be frightened" and he opened his breast and put his heart on the ground and Sapoodle put his beside it. Then they ran toward the village. As they ran along Scinday said, "I am going to deceive him." He sat down crying. He had [151] a thorn in his foot and held his foot in his hand until Sapoodle ran over the next hill. Then Scinday jumped up, ran back, and got his heart and drove a sharp stick through Sapoodle's heart, which killed him.

KIOWA APACHES

[Gie-san (Little Child)]

Kiowa Apaches call themselves Na-ish-shan = Whetstone [People]. (Apache) (Medicine Lake see p. 121). The oldest Apache is Gie-san = "Little Child." His hair is white. He is very old like Taybodle. He and "White Man" are the only old Apaches left. He is much older than White Man. I found him on Sweet Water Creek, just below the Rainy Mountain

Road.⁸⁶ I went there [and] he said, "What are you looking for?" I said, "My friend, the soldier chief gave me a pipe. I am looking for you. You are an old Apache man. You know where the Apaches first grew up and what Scinday you had with you." He said, "Hold up, wait." He thought a long time and then said, "Yes, I did not see the Apaches grow up. I was born this side. I saw my grandfather, a very old man. What he told me I know. He told me that the Apaches and Kiowas grew up together. They did not have two Scindays they had the same one. We call him 'Kiowa Man.' He could hear (understand) Kiowa in one ear and Apache in the other. He ordered both to grow up together. They did not fight each other. They decided to fight other tribes together that I know. My [152] grandfather told me about it. He told me about the Apache man going into the lake."⁸⁸ "I did not see that myself. My grandfather who was a very old man, older than I am now, he told me about it when I got to be old enough to understand that water had a strong medicine. It had no water flowing out of it. It was a lake. On the north side there was a cut, rocky, bluff. Also on the south side the water came up to the edge of the bluff but not on the east and west sides. That country up north where the Kiowas and Apaches used to live was all medicine country."

"When the Apaches first saw that lake, they were surprised. They knew there was a strong medicine [that] lived in it. The water was very deep and was never still. It moved back and forth all the time. They knew a strong medicine lived in it. They wanted some of that medicine but when a young man went to sleep there the water would move and he never remained there until night. He would be frightened and run away and it would fail. A young Apache man wanted that medicine. He was at a council and told them, "I have got a strong heart. I am going to try and get some of that medicine. Before, the Apache men have run away frightened. My heart is strong, if that medicine hurts me I am going to come back. If it does not do anything dangerous to me I will stay. I am going to sleep then if

[side note] Comanches call the Kiowa Apaches Tah-see (Whetstone), the Mescaleros and Chiricahuas Essa-quita (Gray Rumps). Kiowas call [the] Apaches Taw-goo-a (Lazy Men).⁸⁷

([side note, 151] The Apaches call this man The Man Who Went Into The Water.)

---

86 This is probably Sugar Creek, an eastern tributary of Rainy Mountain Creek in Kiowa County, Oklahoma, known earlier by the Kiowa name of Xòdômvàu (Pebble Creek) for the many sizable stones that line its course (Meadows 2008:286).
87 The Kiowas call the Mescaleros Ésècwìjàgàu (White Buttocks) and the Kiowa-Apaches Tàugûi (Sitting on the Outside) (Meadows 2013).
88 This is Medicine Lake.

I get very much frightened, if my heart beats me [153] I will come back. If it does not, I will stay four days. If I do not come back in the morning of the fifth day, come and look for me."

Then he went and laid down on the west side on some sand near the lake, looking towards the east, and while he looked a wave came toward him and went back leaving Big Mouth standing there looking at him like a man (Big Mouth has horns like an elk, a long fish tail, a very big mouth like your stuffed alligator, and has hair on it like a buffalo calf, red).[89] They looked at each other close. The Apache man was much frightened. He said to himself, "Try hard. Try hard. (Bee-pay-tee bee pay te)."[90] After looking at him a while Big Mouth—(Zerma couny) went back with another wave and disappeared. The Apache man looked around all the time frightened. After [a] while he saw a big bull elk coming out of the water looking for him and the elk saw him. He was angry, his mane stood up, and he lowered his head to hook him but the Apache man did not run. He said, "Try hard. Try hard" and when the bull elk had lowered his head to charge him several times without scarring [scaring] him away he went back into the water and disappeared. Next came a buffalo bull, a strong one, not very old but about four years old, with horns a little curved and very sharp. He stood there throwing up the dust with his horns but when he did not frighten the Apache man away he went back again into the water and disappeared.

About 4 o'clock he saw a big snake [154] coming looking for him. Its head was up, moving from side to side looking for him. Its body was about three feet thick and it had a rattle about two feet long. It coiled itself when it saw him and raised its head right over him to strike him. He was more frightened then than ever but he looked at it without stirring. The snake gradually lowered its head, finally turned back, and went into the water. Then the sun went down but he could not sleep. He was so scared always looking about for something until the middle of the night when he saw a big wave coming and out of it came "Big Mouth." He stood there close to him like a man. A long time he [they] stood there looking at each other and then he spoke to him. "I am looking for you. You have beat[en] me. I tried to frighten you but it failed. Before other men came here looking for some medicine. I did not want them. They got frightened and ran away. I did not want them. I want you. Do you want to go into the water with me?" And the Apache man said, "Yes. I am not afraid." And they went down to the

---

89 This creature is the Apache equivalent of the Kiowa Zémáutqū̱né (s/d), Zémáutqū̱nóp (t), popularly called an underwater monster.
90 In Kiowa this expression is *bé fêjè, bé fêjè* (try hard, try hard!).

water together. Big Mouth told him to take hold of his hand and shut his eyes and they went into the water. When Big Mouth told him, he opened his eyes and found it to be just like this country, streams, and trees, and grass. Big Mouth said, "That big lodge is mine. Will you go in with me?" He said, "Yes, I'll go in with you." There were a good many other lodges there. Big Mouth said, "I am the chief. All these other people are mine." [155] A big water turtle was the door of Big Mouth's lodge. It had points on its tail. It was on its back with its feet moving in the air. They went into Big Mouth's lodge and he told the Elk to call in all the people. When they came in the Apache saw they were water people, frogs, snakes, beaver, muskrats, otter, turtles, all kinds of water people. And Big Mouth asked him what he wanted. He said, "I am water hungry, tired, and meat hungry tired."

[side note] When they first entered the father asked what he wanted to eat and he said, "I want water lily roots" and they brought him some. Then the cranes brought in fruits and berries of different kinds. The next time the father asked him he said, "I want some buffalo meat."

Big Mouth told the cranes, two cranes often stayed near the door, big white cranes, to bring in some water. They brought it in and the Apache drank it up. Then they brought in a tripod, a kettle, and put some meat on to boil. And while it was boiling they put some balls of sweet grass mixed with fat in a circle around the fire and set fire to them. The smoke filed the lodge and all the water people got up and danced and put their hands in the smoke and rubbed themselves with it. Then they cut off a piece of meat and gave it to each man with fat with it and gave a piece to the Apache man (first water lily roots, fruits craving). And after they had eaten Big Mouth said, "This is my friend. I want you all to give him some of your medicine and when you have done that I will give him some of my medicine." First one of the medicine people got up and they heard somebody coming crying. They were children dead one day and he asked the Apache man, "Do you want the road to make children dead one day alive?" And he said yes. "Then I give it to you. So on to people dead four days."

Another man got up and a sick person came. He was very thin and sick. He opened his chest, took out all of his organs, sucked out the sickness one after another, and threw them into the fire, [and] closed the man's chest up again. He got up, [156] stretched himself, and said he felt better. Then they all gave him different roads of medicine, all kinds of medicine, and the medicine father said, "Do you want to go back now?" He said, "Yes, I want to go back." And the medicine father told the cranes to go with him. They told him to shut his eyes and when they told him to open them again he was on the prairie. Then he mounted straddle of a crane's back and they all went up high in the air. He could see the rivers below him and the trees and far away he could see the Apache village.

The people were all out watching them playing the wheel game. One man looked up and saw the cranes circling high in the air. He looked for some time and saw something very strange. He called out to all to look. The cranes came lower and lower until they lit at some distance on the prairie and they saw it was a man who beckoned to them. They were afraid of him but he called out in Apache for one man to come. The man came near and stopped close enough to recognize him. He told him he could not go into camp until he had had a sweat bath = (heat house). After that he had a bath and shook hands with everybody. He got a chief's road soon. He knew all kinds of medicine. When a man was sick, he opened his chest, took the sickness out, and threw it in the fire, closed up his chest and he was well. He lived a long [157] time with the Apaches and nobody died for good. If he was only dead four days he was brought to the Apache man who saved him. The Apaches got very numerous while he lived. Nobody died for good. He saved them. When a man was shot through the body he closed it up and saved him. He was sitting smoking with some men and heard the cranes passing over. He said, "Hold up, listen. The cranes are talking to me." He listened a long times until the crane had passed over and told them his father Big Mouth had sent for him. He had given him all kinds of medicine except smallpox. He forgot that and smallpox was coming. He did not want to die. He wanted to go back under the lake where he would live with Big Mouth and never die. Everybody heard that and they were very much scared. They held him. They guarded him all night but fell asleep before light the next morning. When they waked up the lodge and the Apache man, wife, and child and all their property were gone. They circled to find the trail but could not find any. They discussed the matter a long time and one man said, "Look where he slept on the back of the lake." They went there and saw where the lodge poles had gone down into the lake and he was gone.

These Apaches still cook meat that way when anybody's sick. A few men go into a lodge and cook meat. They put balls of sweet grass mixed with fat around the fire in a circle, set fire to them, and dance around the fire putting their hands into the smoke of the sweet grass and [158] rub their faces and arms and bodies and pray to the Apache man who is under the water up north in that Medicine Lake. They ask him to make that sick person well, to give them a long life, to make their children grow up strong. They frequently do this yet, maybe in spring, in summer, and fall and winter. Not every day, now and then [they] do it.

Antelope Medicine
[probably Zemacouny]
Antelope Medicine was made first by "Poor Boy," afterwards it came down to Bone Earring that way.[91]

Long ago while I was a young woman there was a man named "Bone Earring" who knew how to make antelope medicine. When the buffalo were far away and everyone was hungry he made it. He made it when the lodges were plenty, not when they were few. He had two eagle tail feathers one with a black tip and the other with a stripped tip. He fixed them each on a stick with a bunch of little bird's feathers (flicker's tail) tied also to the stick. Bone Earring asked the people if they wanted antelope and they would say yes. They were all hungry and the buffalo were far away.

Then a big lodge was pitched off by itself and at sundown a lot of men went into it. Bone Earring sat down on the west side and stuck the two sticks in the ground in front of him and they would all sing. Women [sat] back of the men near the lodge cover. They sang until the middle [159] of the night when one man would go out and call out for all the women to come.

They would surround the lodge until daylight drumming on the lodge cover outside with little sticks. At sunrise Bone Earring would take up the sticks, one in each hand, cross his arms, and the men on his right and left would each take one of the sticks in his left hand and go out of the door around both sides of the fire, [the] right man around by [the] right [side] of the fire; left man by the left of it. They would separate at the door going around the lodge by opposite ways, pass each other at the back of the lodge and go in the door again and give the sticks to Bone Earring, and it was over.

Then Bone Earring would take the sticks, one in each hand, and go far out on the prairie on foot. The people would eat breakfast, drive in the horses, saddle up, and follow him out to where he would be setting on the top of a hill, no antelope in sight. When they were all collected he picked out two men, chiefs, fast runners, who stripped off their clothing and stood one on each side of him. The others, men, women, and children, all mounted would go make a big circle, as large as from here to

---

91   The name Bone Earring would be Thàuátèm. The word for bone, *tǫ́sègàu*, is usually given in the alternative form *témgù*.

the mountain with a horse on top of it (six miles in diameter). When the circle was made the fast runners would each take a stick and run around outside the circle going in different directions as fast as they could go until they were played out. Then they would each give them sticks to a [160] mounted man who would continue on around at full speed until his horse played out. Then another man would take it and so on until they got back to Bone Earring again. Then they would begin to close in toward Bone Earring. When the circle contracted to about two miles you could see the antelope running around and around inside whether there had been antelope in the country before or not. The medicine made them there. The circle would then be contracted to half a mile. The antelope would be very tired running around but none would attempt to break through. Whenever they came near the line a man would wave his blanket at them and they would run back. They would then contract the circle to about 300 yards and you could see the antelope milling about, jumping and piling on top of each other in their fight.

Then all the women on foot made a circle around the antelope, each woman with a rope and the mounted men [forming] another circle behind the women and they would watch and see when the antelope were very tired. At [the] command of the medicine man they would close in close to the antelope, which were piled on top of each other. The woman would rush into the mass, catch an antelope, and put her rope around its neck and look around until she saw her man and give [gave] him the rope. And he would drag the antelope out, knock it in the head, and kill it. And she would then dive in among the antelope and catch another. Each woman would get six or seven, then [161] they would have enough and let the rest go. That was a very old medicine that Bone Earring had. Somebody gave it to Poorboy when the Kiowas were growing up. They did that until the Kiowas were taken into Ft. Sill as prisoners.

[side note] Old Kiowa woman named "Zemacouny." She stated when asked if the old Kiowas had ever been an agricultural people that they had not. When Spider Woman's garden was mentioned she replied that Spider Woman cultivated the wild gourd, worthless for any purpose. Compare the *Assiniboines*, R. H. Lowie, American Museum Vol. IV, 1904, p. 155.

[Scott n.d.b: MS 2932, Box 2, Kiowa Origins, adds:] An old Kiowa woman named "Zemacouny" was asked if the Kiowas had ever been an agricultural people—did she know any story that would show they ever planted anywhere. She replied that all she had ever heard was about the old Spider Woman who planted a garden and the only thing she cultivated was the wild gourd found on the prairies of Indian Territory but is worthless for any purpose. This has been confirmed by Taybodle, Poor Buffalo, Heidsick, and other old Kiowas, who all insist that they and the Kiowa Apaches have always been nomadic hunters and never planted anything anywhere until their settlement on this reservation.

Buffalo Surround on Foot

My grandfather told me about that, surrounding buffalo on foot. I never saw it myself. My grandfather told me about it. I was born two summers after the stars fell [1833, thus 1835].[92] I did not see them fall, I was born this side. What my grandfather told me I will tell you. He was a very old man when he died a long time ago. I am next oldest Kiowa to Taybodle. He was about sixteen years old when the stars fell, he saw them fall. I didn't. When the buffalo were thick [and] we could not kill all we wanted, then we would drive them over a high cliff. We would send out and find where a high point would jut out with a stream on three sides of it, and the buffalo thick on this side, but the wind blowing towards us. Then we would separate in two long lines which would have the ends near the bluff. We would creep along out of sight of the buffalo and do it secretly. When the time came the people farthest from the buffalo would stand up and show themselves. The buffalo would raise up and look at them and run the other way; somebody getting in front shaking their robes at them until they ran out on the point and plunged over the [162] bluff, those behind pushing those in front over. And when the Kiowas came up and looked over it was wonderful, the buffalo were all piled up under the bluff, some with backs, front, or hind legs broken, or necks broken and they would be full of meat.

They did not have any medicine for that, they did it "prairie" or with nothing. After the Kiowas got horses they put that away and surrounded them on horseback and chased and shot them with arrows. My grandfather told me about that, it was while we lived far north that we did that. We had dogs to pack them. We did not have many lodges then. Every man that had two wives did not have a lodge, it was too heavy. Lots of people lived in one lodge. It was as big as this one (good-sized, about twenty poles). Each man would have eight or less dogs. The poles were as big as these but these were made of a different kind of wood up north, not so heavy as these cedar ones. They were good poles made of spruce, the same kind of wood the white man build their houses [of] (not a pine tree in Oklahoma).

It would take four big dogs to carry the poles and the lodge cover was folded up and put on the travois behind the dog. When a child was too

---

92   This indicates that the consultant was born in 1835, but his or her identity is unclear.

young to walk it was put behind a dog on a travois and the parfleche sacks were put behind the other dogs. They did not carry much meat (dried) because the buffalo were plenty then and it was too heavy. They moved a little way and then camped. They did not go very far and camped a long time before they moved [163] again. They did not get [many] horses until they made peace with the Comanches. They had a very few horses before. They used to fight the Comanches and sometimes get a horse but when they made peace with the Comanches they got lots [of] horses. There were five old people [five generations] died since we made peace with the Comanches. Taybodle and I are the sixth now living. We are very old and weak. I do not think we will live long. What I tell you I did not see myself. My grandfather told me. He told me the Kiowas first grew up on the other side of the rock that pushed up the children (Bear Lodge Tower in Black Hills of Dakota).

The only other wonderful things I have heard about in that country is the Medicine Lake where the Apache man saw the medicine and north of the tall rock there is a place we saw hot water shoot up high. When the Kiowas saw it at a distance they did not know what it was. But when they got close they knew it was water. It was a very dangerous place. They grew up on this side of the hot water (Geysers, Yellowstone Park). We saw Crows there and far away to the east on the River with Ice Points Sticking Up (Missouri River) we knew about the Cheyennes and Arapahoes. They were south of the Crows. We fought the Comanches then, driving them south until we made peace with them, and we fought the Cheyennes and Arapahoes, they followed us coming south and we made peace with them in this country since I can remember myself.

We did not see any Sioux [164] up there. We heard about them in the far east. We did not know the Sioux until we made peace with the Cheyennes. Then when we both visited the Cheyenne[s] on the Arkansas we saw them. They looked just like the Cheyennes. We never saw them before that. The* only Indians we saw up there were Crows, Cheyennes, [and] Arapahoes that we fought, and the [Plains] Apaches helped us fight them. We were friendly to the Crows sometimes. When we live[d] up there and fought the Cheyennes we had different languages and then [the] Cheyennes made the sign language and we used that all the time I was growing up. The Cheyennes know that better than any other tribes, they made [it]. We do not see that now like we used to see it. Women and everybody knew it

* Kiowa Indians have mentioned Shoshones, Biters [Arikaras], and men who wore their hair tied in a club over the forehead.

then. The best sign talker we knew of was that old Cheyenne man, father of Mobilt's (Elk Tongue's) first wife. He lived a long time with the Kiowas. He is dead now. Whenever the Cheyennes came to visit the Kiowas they sent [for] that old man and talked to him and he told us in signs. It was just like talking with lips. Just like talking to you.

[165]
COMANCHE SEPARATION FROM SHOSHONES
Tahpony
Tahpony is a Yapparika Comanche who lives on West Cache Creek. He was seen at his lodge below Comanche School house at the spring belonging [to] Daleys on the Henrietta Road, Oct. 29, 1897. Emmett Cape interrupted the conversation. Tahpony is sixty-four years old and was born around the mountains (Wichita Mountains). He says the Comanches originated near the Arkansas River. Our father made the earth, the sun, the moon, the stars, afterwards the grass and then put the Comanches on the ground. He placed them somewhere near the Arkansas River. One time they held a council of their chiefs who got to disputing as to which one present was the bravest. Not being able to decide they began to fight over it with knives. After that was over some of the Comanches came south and some were left up there. We called them all "Neum" = people or folks, those that were left had two names, Pohoi = "Sage" and Shoshone = "Grass." Some of them are up north now. The Penetechsias [Penetekas] lived in middle Texas down about the Brazos. The Noconies west of the Cross Timbers near [the] head of the Trinity in North Texas and the Cocheteth-kas [Kotsetekas] = east of the Staked Plains and around the [Wichita] Mountains. The Quahadas [lived] on the Staked Plains proper. The Yapparikas [lived] from Red River to the Arkansas [River].

Those were considered their [166] countries but they often visited each other. Tichaneuas were in the Yapparikas country.[93] When the Comanches first came down here they came down on foot. They had neither horses or dogs. They packed their property on their backs. God gave them the buffalo but they stole horses from the Mexicans after they got down here. They were the first to inhabit this country. They saw the Wichitas and Kiowas afterwards. A Yapparika chief named Pah-tuy-y-ya "Afraid Of Water" arranged a peace with the Kiowa chief "Lying Down Wolf" and

---

93 For the most in-depth discussion of Comanche political divisions, see Kavanagh (1996).

after that the Kiowas moved down here and lived with us. Five generations of old men have died since we came to this country and I am the 6th (I am sixty-four years old). There are few of us left. Here and there are [continued after next paragraph].

[The following paragraph was recorded but crossed out in the ledger.]

(Pah-tuy-y-ya was of the 4th generation from the time we came down here that I have any account of. He was killed by the Cheyennes on Wolf Creek (North Fork of Canadian) on a little creek that runs into it from the south, near some high white sand hills East of Cantonment. His son's name was "Titch Tenapi" = "Worthless Man." Pah-tuy-y was a young man when he made peace with the Kiowas and he was old when he was killed.)

[continued from above] Kiowas and Comanches were in that camp together on Wolf Creek and knew an old man who was present [in] 1834 and saw the soldiers come to the Comanche camp. He had a name given to him by the Mexicans, it was Olla which is the same as [167] a bucket. He saw them. I did not see them myself. I was a baby in arms. He has told me about it. The Comanches were all gathered here, all bands represented except the Quahadas, half of each band. There was a big camp right here where we are sitting now. It stretched from near the Red Stone to below Daley's place right here on [the] West side of Cache Creek. It was a big camp.

They had a custom if anybody had a relative killed, he would tell the people when they assembled, the chiefs, and they would decide about retaliating on some together tribe. They were assembled here then for that and some men saw some people coming to fight from the east. Everybody put on their war-bonnets, shields and bows and quivers, and went out to fight them. At a distance away, they saw the people had a white flag displayed. The Comanches had heard before that when the white people were not looking to fight they had a white flag. Two white men came out alone ahead and two Comanches and a Mexican captive named Pa-ha-bib = Bather—he was a Wee-ya (awl) Tenapi (man) brave and daring, sharp like an owl. The two met the others and made peace with them and the soldiers came down and camped with the Comanches on this creek. We do not know exactly where, but we knew they camped with us here somewhere on this side of the (Cache) creek. The meeting took place [168] near the asphalt Spring east of Cache Creek and east of Dr. Clark's place now. We do not know where they went from here. We know where the cattle trail crosses the North Fork Red River. Those Mountains are called "Where the Nokoni Lodges Were Burned." They were burned there by white soldiers the same year they wiped out "Black Kettle's" band of Cheyennes (1868). Before that we called those Mountains where the Wichitas (Tocana "Dark House People") were burned. The Wichitas (Tocana) used to live there a long time ago and moved to where Fort Sill is now. They abandoned the other place. While there [were] still a few there the Osages killed some of them and cut off their heads and burned some of their grass lodges. And afterwards the Comanches burned what was left. The Comanches were always friends of the Wichitas and always fought with the Osages. We did not burn them together. First the Osages burned some. The Wichitas had abandoned them before to go to Fort Sill, and we burned a few they had left unburned.

[169]
KIOWA-COMANCHE-CHEYENNE-ARAPAHO FIGHT ON WOLF CREEK
([SEE] 1837 CHART [KIOWA CALENDAR])
Old Kiowa Woman's Tale
When I was a young woman the Kiowas and Comanches were over near the forks of Wolf Creek (junction of Wolf and Beaver, afterwards Fort Supply) about eight miles up Wolf Creek. They were moving looking for the Sun Dance tree (the Comanches were making [a] Sun Dance with Kiowas) going north and the Cheyennes and Arapahoes were moving south. The Kiowas and Comanches camped on Wolf Creek and the Cheyennes and Arapahoes camped on Beaver a few miles apart and they did not know of each other's proximity. Next morning a Kiowa man went out to look for a buffalo bull, a lone buffalo bull to eat, and rising [at the top of] a hill saw a great many lodges on the Beaver. He thought they belonged to the Cheyennes. He turned around, galloped back to the Kiowa village, and called out that there were a great many lodges over on Beaver Creek. They all collected to hear about it but no one believed him. They abused him, telling he was crazy and made a lie, and next morning half the Kiowas went out to hunt buffalo because they did not believe him. About noon that day the Cheyenne[s] attacked the village. They had a big fight and killed a great many on either side. The Kiowas began to get scared. The women and children were all put to digging a big hole.

[170]
   They dug it about five feet deep and all the women and children and what Kiowa men were left got into it. Then the Cheyennes got mad and charged up on them and the Cheyenne head chief was killed close to the

hole. Then the Cheyennes drew back, let the Kiowas go, and went home. There were about an equal number killed on both sides a great many were dead. The Sun Dance was made sometime afterwards it was called "Mourning Sun Dance" because so many were crying for their friends and relatives who had been killed in that fight (see chart 1837 [Kiowa calendar]).[94]

One year after that the Kiowas got even up on "Iron Creek"—so called because the stone lying on the ground looked like the iron in that grate [pointing at nearby grate] (Republican River).[95] A Kiowa war-party went north to find the Cheyennes and a Cheyenne war-party came south to find Kiowas. The Kiowas saw them first and wiped them all out, killed every one of the Cheyennes and got even. Soon after that we made peace that has lasted ever since. Long before another peace had been made but it was somehow broken. Those were the only times we made peace with the Cheyennes. This time the Cheyennes had a Kiowa woman captive. A Cheyenne man who had her brought to the Kiowa camp, he was not afraid. They came right into the village and he made a peace.

[171]

Pawnees Attack Ten Medicine Keeper and Two Other Lodges

A little while after the Kiowas grew up there was a big Kiowa village. The buffalo were far away and all were very hungry and the children were all crying for something to eat. They had nothing but deer and antelope to eat. One of the Ten Medicine Keepers decided to call a council. He said, "I will take two lodges and go out this side and a few lodges go out that side. If I find meat, I will send in and the village can move over there." But it must not go moving about separated because the Pawnees would catch them. This was the Pawnees' trail and they would kill them if they caught them in small numbers, and the village must keep together.

Next day he moved out with two other lodges and his own with all the women and children. The men of the other lodges went out ahead, scouting. That afternoon he went into camp on a little creek and watched for the scouts to come in. The children were all crying with "hungry tired." They watched until after dark when they heard footsteps approaching. The two men came in without any meat and sat down. After a while they

---

94 This refers to the well-known Wolf Creek Fight of 1838.
95 This fight would have occurred in 1839, as the Wolf Creek Fight occurred in 1838 and the Kiowa-Comanche-Apaches made peace with the Cheyenne-Arapahos in 1840. This is a rare instance of the mention of an earlier peace with the Cheyennes.

asked them, did you see any meat? They said they came over a hill and saw some buffalo and felt very glad but while they watched them moving they saw a big party of men they took to be Pawnees attack the buffalo and kill a [172] great many and cut some up. They left and came home. They said you are leader. I want you to consider, try hard and consider. The Pawnees have not taken all that meat. They have abandoned some of it. We can go back tonight and bring some meat. These children are all hungry tired. Try hard and consider. Early tomorrow morning we can go back to the village. He said all right go and get some meat and they went back. They heard their footsteps again and this time it was the two men standing in front of the door. They threw down the meat and the women put it in to cook. While they were waiting for it they heard footsteps. Someone came up to the door, raised it, looked [at] it, shut the door again, and walked off. They looked at each other very much afraid. It was a Pawnee. They thought they eat [ate] their meat then began to fortify their lodge by putting raw hide buffalo hides all around the inside as high as a man's waist and digging a hole in the bottom of the lodge. Just at dawn, the Pawnees attacked them. The Kiowas cut some little holes in the lodge cover and shot through them. The Medicine Keeper told his wife to sit down by the fire. He gave her a small stick and told her that whenever a Pawnee arrow came through the lodge and fell in the fire she must rake it out with the stick and preserve it. The Pawnees shot a great many arrows through the lodge and fought them a long time. Then one Kiowa man went out of the lodge, ran all the way [173] around and into the door again. Then the other did the same thing but was shot through the body by an arrow. He came in staggering and fell down on the ground and the blood poured out of his mouth. The Medicine Keeper said he was not a Medicine Man but he had heard some little medicine. He pulled out the arrow but the head stuck in his backbone. The Medicine Keeper had a dead and stuffed grass plover (bird that moans in summer). He offered it four times toward the wounded man and the fourth time he shoved it at him hard and the bird put its bill in the wound and after some time working it in the wound drew out the arrow head. They were all standing about amazed. Then he took some yellow dug paint, powdered, threw it in the wound, and when they brushed it off the wound had closed over.

The man stretched his arms out, first one and then the other, and when he got up he was well. The Pawnees after a while charged the lodge and then head chief was shot dead at the door. He had a war bonnet on. When the Pawnees saw this they gave it up and went away. They could hear them mourning as they went. Then the women gathered up the Pawnee arrows into several bundles, put them on their backs, and when they had scalped the Pawnee chief and taken his war bonnet they started for the Kiowa Village. They were saved from the Pawnees.

[174]

Poor Boy

Poor Boy lived with the Kiowas.[96] He had no relatives but an old poor grandmother. They had nothing but a very small tipi. They went about from the lodge to lodge and when anybody had something to eat they went there and eat with them. They did not have anything to eat of their own. They were very poor and weak. When the village moved, the poor boy would follow behind the village and very often had to sleep out by himself hungry on the prairie. A long time before some medicine had taken pity on them and had helped them. He knew some medicine secretly. He sat in the little tipi with his grandmother. They heard a crier coming through the camp. It was a big village. The crier said, "The buffalo are far away. If anybody knows any Antelope Medicine, make it. Everybody is hungry tired." Poor Boy said, "Grandmother, go out and bring that man in here." Grandmother said, "What for?" He said, "I know some medicine." She said, "You are a crazy boy. You are making a lie." He said, "No. Go and bring that man in here." She said, "No, you are a poor, weak, crazy boy. That man is strong and dangerous. You are a crazy boy." But the boy insisted until she consented and went and told the crier the boy wanted to see him. He was amazed, but went into the lodge. He looked at the boy who sat there. His hair was all matted. He had on a calf robe. They were very poor and dirty. The man laughed at him but the boy told him to have a big lodge pitched [175] the next day. To have a kettle, two eagle feathers with back tips, and a flicker tail feather fixed and two choke cherry sticks, and after sundown he would make the medicine.

The man went out and told the people who all knew the Poor Boy. Half said he is a crazy liar. The others said, "Hold up and wait. Maybe some medicine has taken pity on him and given him some medicine. Let him make the medicine and then we will know." Next afternoon they pitched a big lodge and that night he went into the lodge. The feathers and choke cherry sticks were there. They asked him if it was all night. He said, "Yes it is all right." He tied the eagle feathers to the end of the sticks and a bunch

---

96   In Kiowa the name Poor Boy would be Kʼáuàuntàlyì.

of flicker tail feathers hanging down from each and struck the sticks into the ground in front of him. He put some water into the kettle and put it on the fire. He sang for a while then stirred the water with one of the sticks and put it back and handed the kettle to the few people who came in to see him make the medicine. They were amazed, it was full of antelope hair. Everybody saw it and then someone went out and harangued the village. "Poor Boy has got some medicine. He brought antelope hair into a kettle by stirring it with a stick." Those who had gone to bed got up and all crowded into and about the lodge. They saw Poor Boy stir the water with the other stick and afterwards he handed the kettle around and they saw [176] it had antelope droppings. They took some out in their hands and smelt it. Yes, it is real antelope droppings. They were all amazed. He told them to sing and drum on the side of the lodge. They drummed and sang there until daylight. He had a man sitting on each side of him.

For the balance of this story see the "Antelope Medicine" (p. 158) which is exactly like [this account]. Poor Boy made it first just after the Kiowas first grew up and it has been handed down to "Bone Earring" who made it. When the old woman was growing up that was the origin of that medicine road.

Wolf Helped a Man [Version B]

See [Vol.] I, p. 3. Story [is] the same as I, p. 3 except: There was a big, white medicine wolf and when the wolves came to eat the scraps left in the camp they heard something down in the pit. They dug a hole in the covering, tore it all off, and then they looked down and saw a man. He was very weak and thin. The medicine wolf asked him what he wanted. He said, "I want to get out." The big white medicine wolf put down his tail and the man caught hold of it and pulled him[self] out. The wolf said, "What do you want?" He said, "I want something to eat. The inside of a buffalo (eaten raw). I have no knife or fire to cook anything. I want some of the inside of a buffalo." The medicine wolf told the others to scatter and look near where deer had been killed and maybe someone had forgotten a knife.

They all scatter[ed] looking for a [177] knife but they all came back without it except one who came in last with a knife in his teeth and threw it down. The medicine wolf sent them out again and told them to look in an old Kiowa camp where the fires were still burning there and to bring back a firebrand. Then they scattered looking in every direction and one brought back a firebrand in his mouth. Then they all charged an old buffalo bull, a scabby bull running around and around biting at his heels until they had worn him out and killed him and the young man was saved. When he had eaten enough the medicine wolf said, "I want you for my son. Will you go with the wolves?" He said, "Yes, I will go with you." He said, "You can go around in the daytime but at night you must have wolves' hair and run about with the wolves." He said all right and he lived with the wolves for two years. After that he said to Father (the medicine wolf), "I want to see my brother." He said all right, "Hau" [Yes]. His brother had a custom of going out of his lodge every night and crying for his lost brother. About that time he heard the wolves crying about. He listened to them and heard one cry [that] was different from the others. It was that way every night. This [one] cried like a Kiowa. He went back to his lodge and told his friends, "I think that wolf is my brother I lost while I was hunting antelope. Tomorrow we will all listen and when we hear him we will charge and catch him."

He took [178] his rope and went out with his friends and when he heard that wolf they charged him and the man caught him with his rope and took him home. Next morning it was his brother tied there and he asked him where he had been. Then he told him all about his wife and her husband listened and said, "Yes, she killed you. Now do you want to marry her?" He said. "No." "She killed you. What do you want to do with her?" He said, "I will ask my medicine father." He went away out on the prairie to do so and when the wolves came he asked his father, "Do you want to eat a woman" and they said, "Yes." He went back and told his brother to throw her to the wolves and they threw her out and the wolves piled on top and tore her to pieces.[97]

Tonkaways

(Comes Pipe, p. 705 note 12, also 785)

The Kiowas called the Tonkaways Gee-a-him-pee-a-guh = Man Eater.[98] The Comanches called them "Numme-tay-ka" = Eats Comanches. The sign is the same = "man eater." They used to eat people, not many men, but just one man, when they killed someone they would eat one. They would medicine do it [ritually consume]. The sun told them to do it, to medicine eat him. They would sit around in a circle and eat him all up. No other

---

97 This is another version of the story associated with the origin of the name Lone Wolf. See also Scott (n.d.a:I:4–5, chapter 5 in this work).
98 The Kiowa name for the Tonkawas is Qá̱hífi̱gàu (Man Eaters).

people used to eat men that we knew of. We used to know a Kiowa man called "Heart Eater" who eat [ate] a piece off a man's heart. When the Kiowas surrounded some men and they [end of account]

[179 blank]

[180]

Mirage

Mirage is heat trembling. You do not see it in winter, only in summer. If you come up over a hill and look far out on the plain you see a pond of white water. You stop, and look, and consider, "That is real water I think," [and] pause. It is "heat trembling." Sometimes you see trees around the pond and there is nothing left but grass. It is all gone, nothing.

Kiowa Mountains [and Tribal Names]

Iseeo

On the other side of where the Kiowas grew up, there different tribes lived. We knew the Shoshones to the west. We call them by the same name that the Comanches do, "Shoshone" which means "Grass-Lots Grass." We knew the Crows, we called them Go-soh-gia-cuh, "Crowbird," also the Crow Men. We know the Pawnees, we called them Guigyako, Wolf Men. We knew the Utes who lived this side, "Ea-tah-ga = Looking for Buffalo." We knew Cheyennes and Arapahoes, the Kiowa Apaches. The "Biters" [Arikaras] whom we called 'Kau-tuh = "Bite Men." We knew a people who tied their hair up in a bunch on their foreheads. We do not know their names now. And the farthest north, beyond the Crows we knew the "Bo-at-kier-ko" or "Big Bellies." They lived just this side of the Kiowa Mountain, it was a large mountain. We did not know the Mexicans, the Tonkaways, Wichitas, Osages, Caddos, Choctaws, or even the Sioux until after we came down here. We did not know the Sioux until we saw them in the Cheyenne and Arapaho camps after we [181] made peace with the C and A [Cheyennes and Arapahoes]. We never fought the Sioux, the Apaches, or the Wichitas. We have fought all other tribes we know anything about.[99]

---

99 The Kiowa names for these tribes are Sónjǒdàu (Grass House People) for the Shoshones, Càuáuqàgàu (Crow People) for the Crows, Cûiqàgàu (Wolf People) for the Pawnees, Ījàgàu (Looking for Game [Bison]) for the Utes, Qàutàgàu (Biters) for the Arikaras, and Bótqàgàu (Stomach People) for the Gros Ventres (Meadows 2013). The statement that the Kiowas never fought the Lakotas seems inaccurate, as the Lakotas drove the Kiowas from the Black Hills region in the 1700s.

Cheyennes, the Makers of Names
([Sign Language] Sign[s])

You have asked me about all those sign names. We do not know about those names, we think the Cheyennes made them. Those Cheyennes are very skillful in talking signs. When I was a boy I used to see my father talking signs to the old Cheyenne men whenever their villages met. The old Cheyenne men came into my father's lodge. I looked at them with amazement. I looked at them conversing. I took some and held on to it. Took some more and held on to it, did not let it go, and when I grew up I understood it. It was wonderful, just like lip talk. They talked slowly, if you talk fast, every now and then you lose something. That is a mistake. If you talk slowly, then you do not lose anything.

You know the various red people talk differently. All these southern tribes talk signs just alike, but the Caddos. When we made peace with the Caddos I saw them make this sign for a horse (Caddo sign). I was amazed. I asked what it meant. They said it was a horse (prairie sign). They made another sign for deer jumping high. They made other signs, I do not remember. All these other southern tribes made their signs alike but they had also a great many different names for things in their lip talking. But almost all their sign names were the same, understood by all Kiowas. [182] Comanches, Apaches, Cheyennes, and Arapahoes, all the time I was growing up I heard the Cheyennes made those names (sign) and we do not know why they made them. They talked slowly and when you saw them talk you understood them at once. It was just like lip talking. It was very wonderful. Those were the old Cheyennes. They do not understand it so well now, those Cheyennes who come down here. You know them. White Shield had to have an interpreter.

I think you know the sign making better than anybody. We have talked together for eight years. When I see you I understand at once just like lip talk. We have talked now all summer about these things in sign and I cannot tell you anything more. I ask all Kiowas that come to visit me. I have told that oldest Kiowa woman, "Try hard, try hard, and tell me something to tell my friend." She goes along on the trail for a long way and then she gets off, does not arrive at, come to the point, and says she is foolish, she cannot arrive at the point. I think every night when I go to bed. I look all around for something you have not had told you before, but it is a failure. I do not see anything more. We have talked together ever since last spring, seven months, and we have talked for eight years about these things from time to time. I have asked all the old men and women what I did not know myself and now I am through. I have asked that old woman everything, but what she says now she does not know good [perhaps forgetting with old age] and she is afraid to tell a lie, and I have turned her loose, let her go, and do not talk to her anymore. It is no use. You have there written down all she knows good. When my daughter's child is born she will go back home, she understands childbirth well.

[183]

[SIGN LANGUAGE] PHRASES

That is good (I) think not = I do not think that is good.

Consider = true (I) think not = Looking on the question I do not think it is true, or maybe upon reflection I do not think it is true.

What is your name? Name or speak have? You?

Newly made = old not or little while this side made, or born, or ground up.

What are you looking for or what did you come for = Arrive here looking? You.

I have not come for anything = prairie come looking = or nothing came or nothing looking.

What do you want? = Want? You = nothing = or prairie want = Ru. p. 162.

I have no opinion = Think not or know not.

Was that Comanche killed in a fight or by accident? = Comanche fight kill? Or prairie kill?

Was it done secretly or openly = Secretly kill make? Openly kill make?

Where are you going tomorrow = Tomorrow go? (different directions)? You?

Are you ill? = Sick? You.

Yes, I have a fever today—I think I will be well tomorrow = Yes today hot sick me, tomorrow?

Have you got a fever (hot sick) = Hot sick (fever)? You.

Yes, I have a bad fever = Yes, fever (towards myself) strong.

I did not see it well = good see not me.

Which is the older, you or your brother ? = Your brother big?

Exhausted from hunger, thirst sickness, etc. = hungry tired, etc. = water hungry tired = sick tired.

Two other men = Another man two.

To wise make a thing = Is to make it by one's own intelligence as, against "medicine doing" it.

To go to sleep on some elevated point = Medicine sleep.

Sound asleep = Strong asleep.

To save some one = Recover make them.

All night good = Assent, yes good.

A spark flew out of the __ [illegible] fire = Fire little piece __ [illegible] and

Take up a road = become—as Zemacouny's son took up a man's road for a while.

[184]

I do not hear / see well = Good hear/see not—me.

Did you find the horse = Horse see? You answer.

See it or see it not = No, I do not think so = True I think not.

To leave one poor = Poor abandon.

Let go for a while = Little while let go/turn loose.

What he orders as others do not (otherwise) = [no entry].

They go out (naked = poor) = Poor go out of lodge.

You have all the ordering/Whatever you think then do it = All decisions you have = whatever think you = then do it.

First Quanah said, "Ahpiatone [Ahpeahtone], I want to know what you think ([regarding] Wyandotte land sale)" = First—said Quanah now today Ahpiatone think hear I want.

The Kiowas have many different opinions. I have brought them to one = All Kiowas talk divergent (both hands), carry horses, drive some, I corral (or prevent) drive into one road.

I have been hearing it or accustomed to hear it = Hear, hear, hear, hear.

All Kiowas are "drawing back" from the agents talk (i.e., they refuse his proposition or they not take up his talk or they do not join with him).

I am looking for wisdom = Wisdom the ground looks over.

[185–91 blank]

[192]
First Mention of Horses
(LaSalle of the *Discovery of the Great West* by Francis Parkman pp. 390, 417–19.) LaSalle saw horses in the village of the Cenis on the Trinity River of Texas in 1689, "numerous horses" which they had gotten from their allies the Comanches (Penethethkas). LaSalle had no horses himself (p. 369) but bought some. He used signs with the prairie Indians (p. 399). The Cenis used grass houses. Their faces were tattooed like the Wichitas, Tawacanies, and Wacos. Their women went naked above their waists with their breasts tattooed as no other Indian women yet heard of had a custom of doing. (See brief for Wichitas by Philip Naener p. 138, Pawnees had horses in 1682 in Nebraska.) Cabeza de Vaca saw horses, died on the gulf [in] 1527–35. Coronado does not mention any [horses] except those he had, 1541.

[193 blank]

[194]
The Sign Language
[Because this two-page account is illegible in several sections, it is omitted here. For lengthier accounts on the sign language by Scott, which contain the section originally contained here, see Scott (n.d.c, n.d.d).]

[202]
Adequacy of the Sign Language
The question is often asked if the sign language is adequate to convey intelligence in a precise and definite manner. Every language, even the richest and most complete, is a weak and imperfect instrument to convey our thoughts. We are never able to fully express our meaning in all its parts; language is symbolic and gives only an outline, a mere hint of our concept.

The forms even of the richest known languages embody and bring to distinct consciousness only a small part of the infinity of relations which subsist among the objects of thought and which the mind implicitly recognizes even when it does not direct attention to them by expression (L & G of LW [no explanation given] p. 106).

We leave much to suggestion and to the imagination. We understand far more than we hear; the hearer must find in the outlines and by a sympathetic intention mentally complete the figure of language. Even the most precise seldom means the same to different persons as proved by the constant labor of our courts in determining the true intent of our wills, our laws, and other civil instruments, upon which thought has been expected to give them clarity. "We look at each other as through a glass darkly."[100] And if this is true of our people, the fear of all the ages of experiences and stored up wealth of expression born of the necessity of our speech to express the precise relations of mathematics and other sciences, how much more must this be true of a primitive people ignorant of science, whose cognitions are frequently vague and indefinite and their language lower in the linguistic scale. [In this context?] the sign language was born [203] of the necessity of primitive man's intercommunication in his habitat and answered his purposes in his time, fully as well as our language meets ours.

I have often speculated as to the effect produced in my use and comprehension of the sign language from a previous training and education in English and as a member of a civilized community; or upon the Indians due to his ease of his vocal utterance that these must react favorably. There seems to be no reason to doubt, but I have not been able to measure it. The Indian often seems more ready in catching the meaning of allusions either because of the possession of a quicker mind or a better knowledge of the circumstances surrounding his life but possibly from a combination of both.

[204]

Synonyms

The higher languages (i.e., those that have a more advanced, higher position in the linguistic scale) have many synonyms; words whose general meaning is the same but which at the same time have shades of difference. These shades evoke a richness of means of expression of a language but their value is apparent only to those comparatively few in any community, gifted by a true discrimination in the choice of words to fit them exactly to their meanings. As primitive man however is by no means so discriminating and would see little difference in the shades of meaning conveyed to us by the words—fear, fright, apprehension, panic, timidity, fearfulness, [and] terror, except in their comparative degrees; more or less fearful, all those meanings could be comprehended under the sign "fear" or "afraid," made by drawing back the two vertical forefingers at the same time bending the first joints forward to represent two men drawing back down a ridge and woman head to the left in alarm and bending down in concealment from the sight of an enemy discovered on the opposite side of the ridge. Each one of these words has its own associations and would have its appropriate place when it alone should be used, but there are few of us who would notice the difference between them and in rendering the meaning of the sign back into English that one can be selected which best agrees with the context.

---

100 See 1 Corinthians 13 of the Bible for the origin of this statement.

CHAPTER 6

Volume III
Sign Language
and Stories and Fables

CAPT. H. L. SCOTT, 7TH CAVALRY, FORT SILL,
O. T., NOV. 1897

[1]
KIOWA PEACE WITH CADDOS

When the old Kiowa woman (Snot) was a girl the Kiowas used to see the Caddos hunting for deer down Red River. They ranged with the Comanches down Red River to the timbered country (Gainesville and Denison, Texas) on both sides and up north as high as east of Fort Reno, all around these mountains [Wichita Mountains]. After that they moved out toward the head of Red River where I was born (Mulberry Creek). After ranging there they lived for a while in the Canadian country, then on the head of the Arkansas, then lower down the Arkansas, then down here again.

I used to hear the old men talk of the "Medicine Bluffs" long before I saw them. They talked of the "Mountains" (Wichita Range) and the time they had the Bluff Sundance [Sun Dance] below Poor Buffalo's. We moved to Eagle Heart's place and that was the first time we saw these mountains and the Medicine Bluffs but I knew all about them before, the old men told about them. They said there were a great many wild horses and elk all about these mountains and east, northeast, and southeast of here to the timbered country. They ranged away down Red River below the mouth of the Beaver. They met the Caddos but never saw any town [village]. They met them while hunting for deer and were friendly to them. While the old woman saw [2] a great many men had German silver rings in their noses when she was a girl.¹ After that every time she saw them there were fewer and fewer until when the Kiowas were brought in here to prison. Only one old Caddo had a ring in his nose (1874).

When the Kiowas stopped living east of them they fell out with the Caddos. I do not know why, and after I grew up the Caddos killed a Kiowa chief on Wolf Creek above Fort Reno the year the Sun Dance was made in a grove surrounded by trees. The next spring the Kiowas coming on the warpath saw a Caddo and his wife on the Washita just below where the Arapaho village was (I showed you the place, once when we were coming down from the place the Cheyennes were wiped out; east side below big bend and above Cloud Chief) and killed them both and got even.² After that, while we lived on the Arkansas about Fort Dodge we heard some Kiowas had made peace down here with the Caddos. I do not know how it was but soon after some Caddos and Wichitas came up to live on the Arkansas and we did not fight with them. I saw some of them still with rings in their noses of German silver and through that is the reason for their sign name as I had heard before. Peace was made the summer of the Smallpox Sun Dance [1862]. After that "Kobi" [Wild Horse, the Kiowa not the Comanche of the same name] was killed on Chandler's Creek (fifteen miles from Fort Sill). Those Caddos had Tonkaways and white soldiers with them that did not break the [3] peace. Some of the Caddos lived on the Arkansas and some in this country.

How the Kiowas Got Their Country [Version B]

The Kiowas who were lost in the far north. All living Kiowas did not see them. It was very long ago in the far north where it is very cold. Where the Kiowa Mountains are on the other side [of] the hot water goes high in the air out of holes in the ground [Yellowstone area]. The mass of mountains is round and the geysers in the middle of the mountains which are surrounded by prairie. They were in the country where the Kiowas first grew up.

---

1   Based on the date of this account, this jewelry may have been another grade of silver: German silver (an alloy of copper, nickel, and zinc) did not become common among plains groups until the 1860s.
2   These events resemble the killing of Bird Appearing (Thę̄nébáudài or Appearing Bird/Eagle) in 1860, which was not on Wolf Creek. The Timber Circle Sun Dance was 1858. Likewise the revenge raid for Bird Appearing in 1861 took place farther down the Washita River near the head of Sugar Creek on the Wichita-Caddo Reservation (present-day Caddo County, Oklahoma), where only a man is recorded as being killed (Mooney 1898:305–308). Thus these may represent two separate instances or variations and inconsistencies in the accounts of the same event.

All red men, different kinds of red men were there. Scinday was with them and they were all gathered for a big council, the birds, the antelope, the spiders and all the little things. They made a big council, not sitting down but standing in a big circle. They made laws. That old woman [Mud] did not see this, her great-great-great-grandfather told about these things and she heard them from her father the same way. Scinday said, "We have been making laws. There is now one left. When we make it we will separate and go live where you want to in every direction." Then Scinday chose one man from each tribe, one Kiowa and one from each tribe. There was a geyser hole close by. It threw hot water high in the air every day. Scinday said, [4] "There is one thing left. I am going to make a fight road. Whichever man is not afraid to jump into that hole his tribe shall live in the middle and the tribes of the men who are afraid will be pushed outside and be afraid of the one in the middle. Everybody try hard now." That is all he said. All looked on intently. First a man ran up to the edge of the hole. He looked in and saw knives and spears sticking up in it. His heart was rubbed out. He became frightened, turned around, and came back and was put out on one side. This happened to one after the other until there was only one man left, the Kiowa man. He ran up and jumped into the hole but the knives and spears were nothing but rushes and cattails that bent with him and gave away without hurting him. He beat them all and the Kiowas kept that country in the middle and had to fight all tribes on the outside. That was their country and they traveled about in it with the Apaches who were their brothers.[3]

Antelope Udder (Milk Bag) Heart On the Ground Move Away People

Iseeo

After the Kiowas grew up (as a people), in that cold wind country, there were two chiefs who had all the Kiowas. They ordered everything. What one ordered the other went with him. His talk was not put aside [ignored, not listened to] by the other. That was their road (custom). When the grass came up and the time when the antelope had their young arrived, a big village had collected [5] and was moving on foot. They had no horses then. Some men had killed a doe antelope and were skinning and cutting it up. Its kids were hidden somewhere in the grass. One of those two

---

3   For other versions of this same story, see Parsons (1929:15), Nabokov and Loendorf (2004:67, 71–75), obtained from Sherman Chaddlesone (Kiowa), and Meadows (2008:117, 316).

chiefs came up and said, "I want those antelope milk bags" (udder). They said, "All right, we give them to you. After a while the other of those two chiefs came (arrived) up and said the same thing, "I want this antelope's milk bags." The chief who had arrived first was still standing there and heard it. The men were a little disturbed about it. They said our friend who came first and said he wanted those milk bags first. The second chief said, "I want one very much. Let the man who came first take one and I will take the other." The first chief said, "No. I came first. They are both mine. We have been together for a long time making laws. Us [we] two, we both want the same milk bags (udders) and you put aside what I say. I spoke first. Why do you want to put aside my talk?"

The men stood there watching them and were frightened about it. They said to them, "Stop quarreling. One of you take one bag and the other the other." But they would not listen. They insisted each on talking all. Then the chief who came first took it all and went away while the second chief watched him do it and then went off to his lodge. His heart was on the ground (sorry). He had a great many relatives. He sent for them to come to his lodge and told them the truth. For a long time my friend and I worked together. We have always taken up each other's talk, we never put it aside. [6] Today moving along some men killed a doe antelope. My friend came up and said he wanted the milk bags. I came after and said I wanted the same milk bags. My friend put my talk aside. Today that is why I invited my relations to come here. My heart is on the ground, away off this side. My relations altogether move I want. My friend has treated me badly. My heart is big on the ground.

The first chief heard about this talk. He went into the lodge and said, "What is this bad talk I hear?" [The] second chief said, "Moving along today you made me big ashamed, you treated me badly. I want to move away off this side." [The] first chief said, "Hold on, wait. Let us talk about it." [The] second chief said, "No. I do not want to talk about it. I am ashamed. If I go away off I can put that shame away, stop talking about it." Then [the] first chief saw it had failed and went out.

The next morning [the] second chief moved away with his relatives, a little big number of them (comparison little-big). They separated and never came back. They lived on the cold wind side. We used to visit back and forth for many years. We sent messengers to them to come back and live with us but these failed. They moved farther north and we moved farther south. The distance between us got greater and greater. We asked them to come back but it failed. Then we let them loose, the visits stopped. We did not hear anything more of them. Then they were lost. That was very long ago when we lived in the Cold Country.

Since then we have heard of Sioux and Cheyennes and Crows in that country, but we do not hear of any Kiowas up there. We do not know [7] whether they are alive now or have all been wiped out but we listen to hear of our relatives up there (north). We call them "Antelope Milk Drags Heart on the Ground Move Off People."[4] That is their name. Whether sickness wiped them out, whether they were all killed, or whether they still live in the far north we do not know. When we separated it was a little this side of the big river which has ice points (rough broken ice frozen) sticking up on it (Missouri) near where the hot water rushes high in the air out of a hole in the ground [Yellowstone region]. Since then we do not know whether they crossed the big river and went north or what became of them.

[Scott n.d.b: MS 2932, Box 2, Separation of the Kiowas, pp. 5–7 adds:] It has been said in this case, and that of the separation of the Crows over a buffalo paunch, [these separations] were very trivial reasons for such drastic action but there is more here than meets the eye at the first glance in both of these cases. I see in the refusal a loss of prestige and power. It was a custom of the early times to give a chief what he asked for and it was a great affront to him to be refused. Moreover what seems to us to be a small thing in itself to cause such consequences was in all probability a culmination of a long series of difficulties, the last straw in fact that broke the camel's back. But in this point the account is silent.

Omaha (Long [expedition] 1819, [in] Thwaites edition, Vol. 14, p. 300) concerning the custom of according game to chiefs, "Formerly when the chiefs possessed more power than they now (1820) do. One of them would advance towards a carcass which struck his fancy and the rightful owner would relinquish it to him without a word, but they now (1820) seldom put the generosity of the people to the test." American [Bureau of] Ethnology Annual Report 27, p. 273, again, "Should a chief or a son of a chief appear on the scene when butchering was in progress he would be allowed the choice of any portion of the animal." It will be seen then that in this case of separation as well as in that of the Crows the slight put upon the chief by the refusal was the cause of offense and not the mere loss of the meat, a much smaller matter.

The roots of the vocal tongues of the tribes of the north and northwest have been compared by philologists without finding this "lost tribe."

---

4   This Kiowa name for this group is Àuzáthàuhyòp, sometimes given as Àuzáthàuhòp (Disgruntled/Angered on Account of the Udders People).

440 THE SCOTT LEDGERS AT FORT SILL

There has lately been a report of a language of a pueblo of the Rio Grande that has some resemblance to the Kiowa but these resemblances are not sufficient for me to believe in a common ancestor and I must hold with those Kiowas who believe that they have all been "wiped out" in the far north.

Horse Medicine

[Iseeo]

The medicine you saw tied up in the back of my lodge belongs to me. My father gave it to me. His name was "Moving About With Lodges." He died an old man two years after the Medicine Lodge Treaty [in 1867, thus 1869]. I saw it tied up on the lodge pole in the back of his lodge while I was growing up and asked about it and my father told me it is a horse medicine. If you have that your horses will not be all gone. It is a root inside of that sack. I do not know what kind of root it is for I have not seen the top of the plant only the root. You give a little piece of the root to the horse. Not often, but once in a long while. My father told me he gave a piece to his horse when he wanted to chase wild horses. Then his horse ran a long distance without getting tired (tired horse, attain or slack, fail, not). He did not fail to reach (attain to) or overtake the wild [8] horse (question does it truly do that?). I have only used it twice, once before I came here [to Fort Sill] (in 1889) and as a scout. The soldier chief at Fort Reno was going to horse race on (Big Medicine Day) 4th July. The Kiowas were invited to go up and lead their horses. I looked at my horse. He is a far runner I think. Then I made him, got him into condition, and [with] eight days left went to the Cheyenne Soldier House and [with] four days left arrived there. There were a great many Cheyennes and Arapahoes there, Caddos and Wichitas, and Kiowas. And on 4th July they had races. The soldier chiefs put down a great deal of money. The Cheyennes wanted to race against my horse but their course was a little one. I wanted to run three miles but they would only run 600 yards and I refused. They insisted on it but I drew back. After the soldier's races the Cheyennes said they would race two miles and bet each horse against the other, the winner to take them back. I said, "All right." I had given my horse a little piece of that root early in the morning before coming there. We had the race and my horse was ahead. I took their horse home with me [won their horse].

I did not make that medicine again until last summer on 4th July here (1897) when the soldier chiefs made the race. I was looking for money. I trained [Ernest] Stecker's horse and gave him a piece of that root to swallow and he beat them. I saw [earned] $8.00. I keep it hidden about that medicine, do not tell the Kiowas about that. They do not know it. I want to beat them racing horses. That is twice I know it. It was good. It was very good [9] my father said for catching wild horses. He never failed to catch them. He said not to use it often, only once in a long while and to give [it] to a good horse, not to a poor one when you use it.

How Scinday Broke His Legs and Mended Them

Scinday was a wonderful man. He knew all kinds of medicine. He had a Roman nose [high-bridged nose]. I have always heard that Scinday came walking on the prairie and saw a canyon of a little stream. He stood on one edge and looked down below into the water and thought, "I will jump across to the other wall of the canyon." He jumped and fell to the bottom of the canyon and broke both his legs. He sat there a long time and was very hungry. He searched out and chose a stick which he used to take the marrow out of his bones and eat it until he had enough. Then he poked the stick down in the marrow cavity to stiffen the bones when broken. Then he got up and walked home. He was a wonderful man and knew all kinds of medicine. Whenever anybody died he did something to him and he recovered.

How Scinday Deceived Panther

Scinday was a very deceitful man. He had children and was accustomed to send them out to hunt for deer and antelope to eat, but they failed. They only brought back plums and berries. Scinday was hungry tired and he scolded [10] them for not bringing back deer and antelope but it was no use.

Scinday met Panther. Panther was fat. His children went out to hunt for deer or antelope and brought them home to eat. They did not fail. Scinday looked at Panther, "I will deceive him," he said. He said to Panther, "My children are [the] best children. I send them out for deer or antelope to eat. They do not fail (every day we have plenty to eat). They bring me all the time something good to eat." Panther said, "My children are that way, the same, I have got best children. They always bring me deer or antelope to eat. They do not fail." Scinday said, "My children are best children." He was deceiving him. He said, "You lend me your children. I will lend you mine. We will exchange." Panther said, "All right, good. We will exchange." They exchanged and next day sent each other's children out to hunt for deer or antelope.

Panther looked out of his hole and saw Scinday's boy coming. He examined him coming. He said, "That is not a deer that he has got. What is it?" When the boy came he had nothing but berries to eat. Panther said, "What is that?" The boy said, "Those are berries. That is all I could find." Panther said, "Take them away. I do not want berries." He was very angry and scolded the boy. Scinday saw Panther's child coming, bringing a deer and laughed secretly. He eat [ate] until he was full. He deceived Panther, he beat him. He was very happy.

[11]

How Scinday's Lodge Burned Up

Scinday coming walking on [the] prairie met Flicker (golden-winged woodpecker, sign name = red spotted breast), who invited him to go to his lodge, a hole in an old and rotten tree. Scinday went with him. When they arrived there Flicker said, "What do you want to eat? Do you like fat?" Scinday said, "Yes, I like everything" (all eat roads I have). There were young flickers playing about and the father caught one, pulled out a tail feather, and let him go. He put the oil that was in the feather into the pot and cooked it. Scinday ate it until he was full up to his eyes. He was satisfied and felt happy. He said, "Will you come looking for my lodge tomorrow[?]" and Flicker said, "Yes, tomorrow I will come looking for your lodge."

Next day (tomorrow) he came. Scinday asked him what he wanted to eat. He said, "I only want one thing. I want some white worms from an old rotten log." "All right, good," said Scinday, "I will get them." He took an arrow and thrust it into his boy's thigh to draw blood so the screw worms would come in it. (Flicker laughed secretly, he knew he was deceiving him.) The blood rushed out of the boy so fast he died. While they were sitting in the lodge a spark flew out of the fire and ignited behind the bed. Flicker was the (only) one who saw it. He laughed secretly and watched it get bigger and bigger until it got a little big, then he told them. They all looked at it but it was burning strong, it was a big fire. The lodge burned up and all the property (i.e., the things lying about the lodge). Flicker laughed at him. He lost his boy, his lodge, and property because he made a lie to deceive Flicker.

[12]
[SCINDAY AND THE BISON HUNT]
Scinday was very hungry. He hunted a long time for something to eat but failed to find it. He was hungry [and] tired. He sat down and considered for a long time then he said, "Yes, I see wisdom." He got two rattles and climbed up on the side of a high bluff (cut) and sang and shook his rattles. He medicine sang to bring the buffalo. When he had sung and rattled for a long time he heard the trampling of feet and redoubled his efforts (he tried harder) and the buffalo came jumping over the bluff one after another. He saw them fall to the bottom piling on top of each other. Their legs, backs, and necks [were] broken until he saw enough, then he stopped. (Eat heap attained.) He had enough to eat. He went to his lodge and told his wife and they cut up the meat and put it up to dry (hung it up to dry) on scaffolds. That night they went (strong) sound asleep and the wolves came around, a great many of them, and pulled the meat all down and ate it up. Then they ate up the hide lodge cover as high as they could reach while they were strong asleep. Scinday's wife wake [woke] up in the middle of the night and saw the lodge was gone. She woke up Scinday and told him. He said, "Hold up. Wait. Go to sleep, soon the moon will be big and it will be light." She said, "No. The lodge is all gone." He said, "Wait, [until the] moon [is] big." Then they went to sleep and slept sound until the sun rose. When they waked up the lodge cover and all the meat was gone and they cried about it.

[13]
[SCINDAY AND THE ANTELOPE KID]
In the spring an antelope kid was lying in the grass. Scinday coming along found it and caught it. He said, "It is weak. I will take off my quiver, put it around its neck, and lead it home." He did that but when he had put the quiver around it the kid tore away and ran off. Scinday chased it around and around but failed to catch it. He kept after it. He did not let it go. He followed it for three years while the antelope was growing up larger. The rain and snow fell on the quiver and the sun made it hot and it got old and broke [rotted] so it fell to the ground. Scinday picked it up: "Oh my." The arrows were all gone and the skin was rotten. [The] only thing left was the bow. Scinday was very angry at antelope. He said, "You are no good."

[ZEMACOUNY AND THE KIOWA GIRL]

The Kiowa girls and boys were playing on the ice. The boys were dragging the girls who sat on buffalo skulls with ropes attached to them. One girl sat looking on, sitting down by the side of the stream. She had nobody to drag her. She was a very good looking young Kiowa girl. A handsome young man came along and saw her. It was Zemacouny, Big Mouth's son. He has taken up a man's road [transformed] for a while. He was very handsome. He fell in love with her (wanted her). The young people play that way still. They have not put that away [14] yet (now).

The young man said, "Will you play on the ice with me?" She assented and they played on the ice for a long time. Then he asked her to marry him and she said, "Yes, I will marry you." He was a very good looking young man. After a while he said, "We will take up another road now. You shut your eyes until I tell you to open them." He was deceiving her. She shut her eyes and he dragged her into the hole in the ice. When he told her to open them they were standing in front of a lodge, Big Mouth's lodge at the bottom of the lake. There was a horny tailed turtle as a door. They went into the lodge. Father and mother Big Mouth were there. They went to bed there. When the Kiowa girl waked up next morning her man was gone and Big Mouth's son was there with her. He had taken up Big Mouth's road again [transformed] and she began to cry. She cried all the time and wanted to go back to the Kiowa village.

Big Mouth said to his son, "What made you bring that woman here? You are crazy. Look at her poor [and] crying." His son said, "I love her. I have married her." Then father Big Mouth said, "All right. Take her out to her relation's lodge and live with her." Then he called two geese and told them to go up out of the water and fly about and find the Kiowa village. They flew up out over the prairie until they saw the Kiowa village and came back and told the father it was close by. Then he gave his [15] son two mules and two horses and told him not to pack [meat] on those horses, they were afraid of it, to pack the mules and ride the horses. Then they started for the Kiowa camp. On the way they killed a buffalo, cut up the meat, and loaded the mules, but a great deal of meat was left over. Then he said, "I will load the horses. We cannot throw this meat away. We will pack [the] horses." She said, "No. The father said not to pack meat on the horses, they are afraid of it." He insisted on it. He took some meat to load them and told her to lead them up. But when he did that the mules and horses both flew away. They were geese. They flew up fast and left them there poor. This astonished them very much. They said, "Oh my, they have gone." Then he told his wife to go back to the Kiowa camp and he would go back after the horses, and they separated, going different ways. When he got back his father said, "You are a crazy boy. I told you before not to pack meat on those horses, that is their afraid road." Then he gave him others and he went back and rode up to the Kiowa village with the horses and mules, his wife coming out of the lodge.

Scinday Kills Deer Woman

Scinday came [along] on the prairie and saw deer woman near her lodge holding a robe. He was very hungry and wanted to kill and eat her. He went up to her and said "You are very foolish. You are holding a robe close to this cut bank. Pawnees all the time came this way. Some Pawnee will creep up behind this bank and shoot you with an [16] arrow." She said, "No. I do not think so" (true I think not). Scinday looked at her, she was fat. He was very hungry. He went away leaving her holding the robe. He got behind the cut bank and crept close to her secretly and shot her in the side with an arrow. She ran to the lodge and Scinday, keeping hidden, ran off to where he left his quiver and went to meet her from the opposite direction unarmed (poor). He said, "What is the matter?" She said, "You told the truth, some crazy man shot me with an arrow." "Oh my, I am so sorry," he said. "I told you before, some Pawnee would hide and shoot you and now it has happened. I am so sorry. I will make some medicine for you." Then they went into the lodge and Scinday prayed to the Sun. He sang and shook his rattle. He was deceiving her. He held his hands up to the Sun and said, "Deer Woman, die before sunrise." She heard him and said, "What is that I hear you say? You are praying wrong. I heard you say, 'Deer Woman, die before sunrise.'" [Then Scinday said,] "Oh my, you make [you're making a] big mistake. Stop. That is foolish talk. I am trying hard for you. I am praying good." Then she died before sunrise. He deceived her.

Then Scinday said to her husband, "Deer do not have a good bury road. I will take her and bury her good." "All right, good," the Deer said, and Scinday took the body up on his back and went out into the thick [17] woods to bury her and then he got away, off in the thick woods. He threw her down, built a fire, cut her up, and roasted the meat turning it before the fire. When it was cooked he ate it until he was full up to his eyes. Then he felt happy.

How Scinday Became Blind

Scinday came walking on the prairie and saw a sparrow (Hawgone [Silverhorn] made a mistake in the picture) playing alone. He was taking out his eyes and throwing them up in a tree. Then he brought them back (medicine brought them back), fixed them in his head. Scinday saw this, "Oh. My. I big want that," he said, "Give me some medicine so I can do that." At first sparrow was playing and did not hear him. Scinday spoke louder and sparrow said, "You are crazy, go away" but Scinday insisted, "Take pity on me and give me some of that medicine." After a long time sparrow got tired and agreed (consented) to give it to him.

[side note, 17] Similar tales [are found] in many other tribes: *Blackfoot Mythology*, Wissler and Duvall Anthropological Papers, Museum of Natural History, Vol. II, 1908, p. 29, tale no. 13; see Grinnell, *Lodge Tales*, p. 153; G. A. Dorsey and A. L. Kroeber, *Arapaho Tales*, Traditions of the Arapaho, Field Columbia Museum, Pub. 81, 1903.

Then Scinday took out his eyes and threw them up in the tree and brought them back and put them in his head. Sparrow said, "You must not do that often, only once in a long while play that way." Scinday did it again several times. He said, "Sparrow is crazy to talk that way." Then he did it again but this time he could not draw them back. They remained up in the tree and he stood there blind and mourning. Sparrow laughed at him and went away, left him poor (poor abandoned him). [18] Black white bird (magpie) eats meat. He steals it. There are none near these (Wichita) mountains but there are a great many in the far north when the Kiowas first grew up.

Scinday Let Out the Buffalo

When the Kiowas first grew up there were no buffalo and all Kiowas were hungry. They now and then got deer or antelope and sometimes lived (ate) on plums or berries and roots. There was one man who lived far away by himself with his wife and little daughter. He was fat and whenever he came walking to the Kiowas came the wind [that] blew the smell of fat to the Kiowas. They smelled it and said to one another, "That is fat." Scinday said he has got the buffalo guarded. When he comes to see the ring game we will watch where he goes and follow him.

Magpie came to see the ring game. As he came they smelt the fat blowing from him. Scinday laughed secretly. When the game was over he took a bird road [transformed into a bird] and sailed away up in the air and the Kiowas watched him flying up into a cloud and he disappear[ed] from view. Scinday picked out the jack rabbit to watch him next day on account of his big eyes and after the game. He sailed away up in the clouds. Jack Rabbit failed. Next day he picked out Owl on account of his big eyes. Magpie walked over the ridge like a man but when he got over, [he] sailed up again into the clouds until Owl lost [sight of] him. It failed. [19] Then the last day of the game Scinday gave the pipe to Mosquito Hawk (Koi-kon-ope [in the] Kiowa language), and when Magpie sailed up he went up likewise, followed him up high and saw him go down behind a mountain and came back and told Scinday.[5] He said, "All right, good. His lodge is over there behind the mountain. We will take down our lodge and move over there." Next morning they took down their lodges and moved over there behind the mountain and went into camp near Magpie. The rest of this is just like Mobeadleky's tale.

(Kiowa name for mosquito hawk = 'Koi-kon-ope)

Ring or Spear Game

This is a game for men. They used to play it when the Kiowas were first growing up. The whole village becomes absorbed in it, half on one side and half on the other. They meet [make] big piles, throw down until these piles are high[er] than your head; blankets, robes, saddles, bows and arrows, everything. They provide two piles of sticks (to be used as counters) three feet high each, big piles. They have a ring about three inches in diameter and two spears of wood five feet long which have squaw cloth (of different colors) streamers at ends behind them and fringe tied around the body near the end. The ring is made of a piece of hard hide wrapped first with sinew and next with buckskin thongs. A court fifty yards long is cleared (smoothed) off and all [of] the village turns out to see it. Sides are chosen and the game is begun by two young men, one from each side. The ring is thrown alternately, first by one man and next by the other. It is sent rolling down the course followed by the [20] two young men running after it and trying to throw their spears through the ring. If the ring stops and falls over on either spear that side takes two hundred sticks from the other. If it falls on the rear streamer they take six hundred sticks. If it falls on the fringe they take ten sticks. This is also the case if the spear falls on the ring. If the point of the spear enters the ring that side takes two hundred sticks. If it is thrown through the

---

5   This term was not in McKenzie (1977: list of Kiowa birds). It appears to be *káuiqáunhól* (dragonfly), which mosquito hawk could be a byname for.

ring far enough to touch the squaw cloth they take six hundred sticks. They play from early in the morning sometimes until sundown and go on with it [the] next day. It takes a long time for either side to beat [win]. Sometimes three or four days, sometimes one side gets tired first then the other one soon beats it. After the first two players are tired [from] running two more take their places until one side gets tired or loses all its sticks or the sun goes down. This game was made by the Kiowas first. It has long been dead. It is not played now. It is a man's game. The Kiowas call it 'Kau-lah or Ring Game or Goom-ah = Spear Game. The sign for it is "ring throw" game. I played the game often when I was a young man.[6]

[21]

Boys' Ring Game

The boys have a game with the same name. It is called " 'Kau-lah" = Ring Game.[7] The spears are about three feet long, some with a toggle at the end and some with a split fork Y. The ring is from eight to twelve inches in diameter and has an inner ring of rawhide. There are a number of these rings and the game is played with many boys on a side who are stationary, and the rings are passing and re-passing each other continually. They throw the spear through the ring if possible and when any boy on one side throws his spear through the small inner ring as it comes to him his side charges the other and whips them with stick[s]. They run away to escape it. It is just like a fight, a play fight. Then they begin again. There are no bets made, it is a child's game "Spider Woman" gave "Boy." She made the ring by cutting some hide off her own thigh. This game is taken up in the fall, played all winter, and thrown away in the spring. I played it when I was a boy. It is not played now. The children are all scattered over the country and when they are gathered in schools they play white men's games.

The sign name for this is the same. The ring is the one the Boy split himself in half with before the Kiowas grew up.

[22]

Arrow Game

The boys also play an arrow game. They put a ring about thirty feet away lying flat in the ground. One boy stands at the base endeavoring to throw

---

6 The Kiowa name for the game called Gomah is Cáumáuqàudàl (Aiming/Circle Wheel). Parker McKenzie to the author, Sept. 25, 1994. See note 7 below for 'Kau-lah.

7 'Kau-lah or ring game appears to be Qáulâu, possible from qáudál (ring or wheel) and áugà (any form of game or gambling). A similar possible basis of the name may refer to the compound câulà (a verb meaning "turning this way or that way in route").

his arrows so they will land inside the ring. When he has thrown all his arrows the other boy picks them up, goes to the base, and throws them again. The boy that lands the most arrows inside the ring takes them all.

Moccasin Game [Hand Game]

The young men have a game for winter nights. It is played inside of a lodge. They choose sides and each side has a leader. They make bets on it. They have a certain number of counters which are divided in half between the two sides. One leader has a bean or a pebble in his hand. He crosses his hands at the wrists and moves them back and forth in time to different songs to deceive the opposite side. He sometimes pretends to pass the pebble on to other members of his side. The attention of the other side is distracted by the motion of the hands in unison. They hop up and down [bounce in place] as they are sitting on the ground. Suddenly a member on the opposite side who thinks he knows where the pebble is claps his hands and extends the right with the thumb extended (fingers closed) [23] to the right or left according as he desires him to open the right or left hand. If the pebble is in that hand his side gets the pebble and takes a stick from the other side that lost the pebble. This goes on from side to side until all the sticks are won and lost. Expert leaders have many ways of deceiving the other side and are well known and sought after on important occasions.

This is called by Kiowas Doo-au = Moccasin Game.[8] The sign for it is crossing wrists alternately right in front, then left, as is done in the game to distract the attention of opponents. This game is played by all the southern tribes.

[Another] Arrow Game

There is another arrow game which is played by boys and young men. Two boys or more start out with long arrows, throwing them high in the air to as great a distance as possible and the boy who throws his arrows the farthest beats [wins] the game. It is believed that the sign for "chief" originated from this game as it represents the arrow falling beyond.

---

8 The Kiowa name of the game is Jòâugà (Tipi Game) and not Jòâugà (Moccasin Game). Today on the southern plains the game is popularly called Hand Game. To my knowledge, the Kiowas have no tradition of playing the game with the use of moccasins, as found in the northeastern plains–Great Lakes region.

[MISCELLANEOUS TRIBAL INFORMATION]

When the Kiowas lived in the north and first grew up they fought everybody except the Apaches. After that they were friends with Crows, the [24] Blackfeet [Blackfoot], and the Commen—the Gros Ventres. There used to be men up there we call "Face Ring (Painted, Tattooed) on the Cheekbone" (Mandan?).[9] I do not know where they lived. Also some men we called "Rabbit (ears back and forth) Robe Men (Crees, Bannocks?)."[10] The old Kiowas up there saw them and after did not see them again. The Rees [Arikaras] lived toward the east from the Kiowas. They visited the Rees, it was not far.

He Dog, etc., Pine Ridge, Dakota, 1920

Kiowa Apaches. C'ikakize = rubbing two sticks together, the noise of wood on wood.

Also letter of James McLaughlin, Washington, Nov. 12, 1921.

> Dear Gen. Scott,
> The Sioux word for Apache is C'ikakize, which means rubbing two wooden sticks together. I got this from Amos Red Owl and Strange Horse, the two Sioux in Washington [who] attended the burial of the unknown soldier.
> Sincerely Yours, James McLaughlin.

Same from *Mythology of the Wichita*, George A. Dorsey, Carnegie Institution 1904, p. 17. "The chanting of the rituals (Wichita) was the chief feature up north [in] these ceremonies. The tune of the singing being marked by the drawing of a stick over a notched club, one end of which rested on a buffalo raw hide resonator. Both had their origin in the animal gods."

[27]

FOREWORD TO THE SCINDAY STORIES

The Kiowa, Comanche, and Kiowa Apache Indians compose their tribes friendly to each other, which live intermixed between the Washita and Red Rivers and about the Wichita Mountains in what was formerly known as

---

9 Clark (1885:238) and Mooney (1898:159) confirm this sign for the Mandans as referencing the tattooing of the chin and lower sides of the face. See also Meadows (2013:18).

10 Based on tribal synonymy for the Crees (Darnell 2001:650), whom several tribes called "Rabbits" or "Rabbit People," this Kiowa ethnonym probably refers to the Crees, whom they likely would have known or at least been aware of when residing in the northern plains. Although the account does not specify whether this refers to a spoken or signed name, the spoken form would most likely be Pòlá̱ hi̱kǎugàu (literally, Rabbit Robe/Hide Men) (Meadows 2013).

the Indian Territory but is now in the new state of Oklahoma. They were placed there in 1869, the result of the campaigns of Generals Sheridan and Custer with the 7th Cavalry.

ZOHN-AL OR AWL GAME OF THE KIOWAS AND KIOWA APACHES
[General Hugh L. Scott Collection Box 7: General Scott Diary, 1860–1931, Fort Sill Archives]

Zohn = Creek, Ahl = wood in Kiowa tongue. The cloth is called "awl cloth" and is divided into points by which the game is counted. The four sticks are called "al" or wood. Three of them have a red stripe down the middle and one a blue stripe. They are held in the hand together and struck on the rock on the ends and allowed to fall as in our game of jackstraws.

If all the sticks fall with plain sides up it is called "white" and counts ten.
If sticks fall with one blue and three red = five and called "red."
If sticks fall with one blue and two red = 3.
If sticks fall with three red = 3.
If sticks fall with one blue and one red = 2.
If sticks fall with two red = 2.
If sticks fall with one blue = 1.
If sticks fall with one red = 1.

The curved lines are called "knees" because they represent the knees of the players as they kneel around the awl cloth. The parallel lines [on the cloth] between [the numbers] 1 and 1 and 20 and 20 = (II) are called "the creek" and those at right angles [on the cloth] (=) are called the "little branches."

The game is played only by girls and women and it is said to be very old. The players, who may consist of any even number of females, half on one side and half on the other, divided on the dotted line N.S. [north and south], kneel around the edge of the cloth. The flat stone is placed in the middle. The two awls are "in the creek at S" [south]. The person opposite the left one of the awls makes the first throw and counts the result by sticking the awl in the cloth, just beyond the number made in the throw, going around by the left, the other side counting and marked by the right. If white or red are made, in addition to the 10 or the five counted that person has another throw. The throwing progresses from right to left around the circle in the direction of the hands of a watch. If the awl of either side gets "in the creek" that side is set back to the

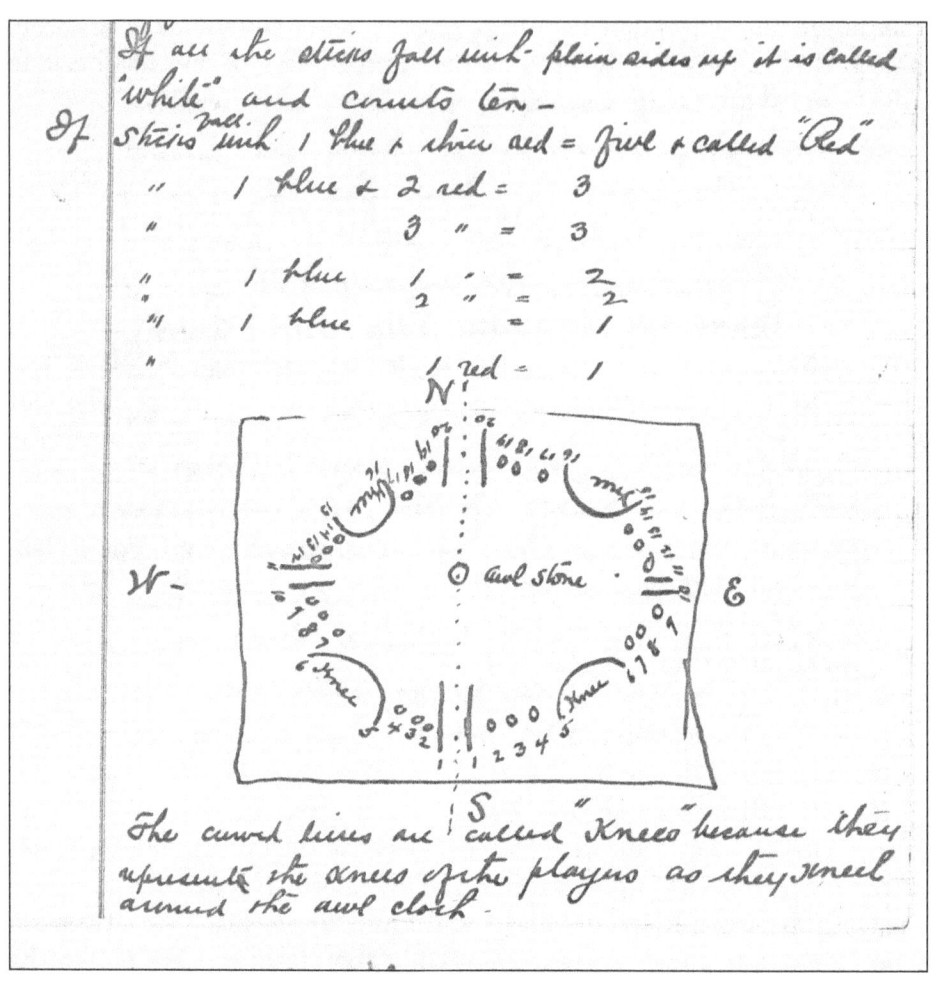

Ledger image of diagram of Kiowa awl game.
General Hugh L. Scott Collection Box 7: General Scott Diary, 1860–1931.
Courtesy of Fort Sill National Historic Landmark and Museum Archive and Wade Popp.

beginning, the object being to jump over the creek. For instance if one side has made and counted 19, and that side at the next throw should make but one, that side is then in the creek and is set back to 0 again. If the creek is jumped the counting goes on around. If the two awls should meet at any station the one that is there first is "killed" or "whipped" and set back to the beginning.

When either side makes a complete circle before the other it receives one of the eight sticks which are used as counters. If one side is set back for any cause it has to forfeit a counter to the other side, and the side which has the most counters when the game breaks up from any outside cause or the side which wins all the counters is entitled to the prize, which may be anything from a few nickels to a pony.

Often a great excitement arises over this game when many persons are engaged in playing for large prizes. They have a custom of wetting the fingers with the tongue, slapping them on a [the] stone before a throw, and calling out "white, white" or "red, red" according to the number they desire to count or if the opposite party needs but one to throw it in "the creek," they wet the first finger and draw it over the stone and call out "parko, parko" or "one, one." If any individual has had bad luck in her throws she rubs the sticks all together between the palms of her hands to get a chance of luck.[11]

The Comanches have a similar game, which is played with 8 sticks. The Cheyennes and Arapahoes have still another, which is played with sticks two feet long and over.

---

11 Scott appears to have misheard some of the terminology associated with the game. The typical name of the game is Chóáu (Awl/Stick Game), abbreviated from chóáugà, in reference to marking one's position with an awl on the game cloth. The syllable *cho* means awl, while the compound *auga* refers to any form of game, play, or gambling. "Awl cloth" would be *chòkáui*. Sticks, wood, and trees are *ą́ dàu* (s) and *ą́* (d/t). In Kiowa these expressions called out during play would be *thą́i, thą́i* (white, white) and *gúldą́u, gúldą́u* (red, red). The expression "parko, parko" would be *fą́gàu, fą́gàu* (one, one).

APPENDIX

Troop L, 7th Cavalry Rosters, Fort Sill

LIST 1
INDIAN MEMBERS OF TROOP L, 7TH CAVALRY, FORT SILL
(TROOP L, 7TH U.S. CAVALRY 1929)

*[Tribal affiliations: C (Comanche), FSA (Fort Sill Apache),
K (Kiowa), Ke (Keechi). English translations of Indian names
in parentheses as recorded by the army are not always accurate.
Tentative tribal affiliations were provided by the author.]*

A.G.062.14
Troop L, 7th Cavalry
(1-2-29) ORD

*List of the Names of Indian Members of Troop L,
7th United States Cavalry, between June 30, 1891, and May 31, 1897*

Joseph Hunter (Husk-day-haste, Man Hunter) trumpeter.	[FSA?]
Calvin Kiowa [Calvin Kauley] saddler.	[K]
Edgar Keahbone (living) wagoner.	[K]
Lucius Aitsan (Aitsan-hoodle-ah, He Bribes) private, later sergeant.	[K]
Mark Auchchiah (Looks Out Of Lodge) private.	[K]
Ah-heh (Tell You Something) private.	[K]
James Ai-site (Tear It Up) private.	[K]
Bay-e-lah (Half-breed Mexican) private.	[K]
Burgess (Mo-ne-wer-te-qua, Strike With The Hand) private.	[C]
George Brizzle (Ton-kodle-ke, Red Foliage) private.	[K]
Cha-ve (Little Boy) private.	[K?]

455

456 APPENDIX

Docto (Quer-ke-ya, Born Starting On Buffalo Hunt) private.	[C?]
Domat (Caller) private.	[K]
Wirt Davis (Udle-quo-quo, Curing Scalps) private, later sergeant.	[K]
James Dodone, private, later sergeant.	[K]
Dow-a-ton (Medicine Bearer) private, [later] sergeant.	[K]
Frederick D. Eagle (Quo-mahn, Bob Tail) private.	[C]
E-ah-pah (Baby) private.	[K]
Ee-ho-tah (Buffalo Killer) private.	[K]
Ea-agoo (Two Red) private.	[K]
E-man-ah (Sleeping Bear) private.	[K]
Guy (Aut-do, Mourner) private.	[K]
Haw-gone (Silver Horns) private.	[K]
Honameahtah (Charging Man) private, later sergeant.	[K]
Honantz (Blind Man) private.	[?]
I-see-o (Plenty Fires) private, later 1st sergeant.	[K]
I-za-chi (Two Men) private.	[FSA]
John Kibben (Eta-with-ta-qua, Strike You With A Bow) private.	[C]
Satanta Kaardly (Bitter, White Bear) private.	[K?]
Kicking Bird, private, later sergeant.	[K]
George Maddox (Pur-su-su-wite-yer-queth, I Do As I Please) private, later corporal.	[C]
Luke Mauhe (Lame Boy) private.	[K]
Michacho (Boy) private.	[K]
Na-chon-ko (Strike The Enemy) private.	[C?]
Nas-cha-na-ni (Yellow Buffalo) private.	[C?]
Odle-pah (Buffalo Bird)	[K]
Pahsita (Hairless)	[C]
Poa-que (Find Something)	[C]
Pohd-lohk (Wolf-Bear) private.	[K]
William Patterson (Cha-dle-yah, Pick Him Up) private.	[K]
George Ross (Marbone, Looker) private.	[C]
Soh-kone (Moses) private.	[K]
Tcha-ka (Bread) private.	[K/Ke]
Tonacho (Turtle) private.	[K]
Tone-moh (Water Drinker) private.	[K]
To-es-sit (Black Roan Horse) private.	[C]
Tso-da-ha (Stand In Water) private.	[K?]
Tabahorty (Sweat House)	[K]
Ti-eh (Morning Star) private.	[K]

Toan-ko-ko (Bird's Tail) private.   [K]
Wohaw (Beef) private.   [K]
Pearly Whitemore (Wa-si-wit-ah, Short Curly Hair) private.   [C]
We-he (Butcher Knife) private.   [C]
Woodle-quoe (Bob-Tailed Bay Horse) private.   [C]

Additional Members after February 29, 1892

Ho-bah-teth-ka (Coffee Drinker) wagoner.   [C]
Nem-o-quo-u-a (Taking Cloth Off) ferrier.   [C]
William Jackson, trumpeter.   [FSA]
In-dagh-ta-ah (Singing Man) private.   [K]
E-dle-ta-hay (I Will Do It) private.   [K]
Jim Mam-i-ah (Poke With [A] Stick) private.   [C]
Nan-i-mah (Belly) private.   [C?]
Tap-i-to-sa (White Sun) private.   [C]
Tap-i-yet-sa (Rising Sun) private.   [C]
Tab-i-tad (Sun Shine) private.   [C]
Po-chan-ki (Punch With A Stick) private.   [C?]
Eustace Essaypoyhet (Running Wolf) private.   [C]
Goh-see-bahno (Brain All Over His Head) private.   [C]
Tessie-lo-qyati (Strike) private.   [C]

[Fort Sill Apache Members, after 1894]

Duncan Balatchu, private.
Martin Kayihtah, private.
Frank Mangus, private.
Simeon Nahdelte, private.
James Russell, private.
Jim Sage, private.
Allen Yezos, private.
Horace Songbean, private.
Burdette Tesuah, sergeant.
Roger Toclanny, sergeant.
Christain Naiche, sergeant.
Jacob Kaahteney, sergeant.
Ambrose Chachu, sergeant.
Louis Lemnioux, private.

Sam Havzous, trumpeter.
James Nicolas, trumpeter.
Borgia Aanitso, private.
Benjamin Asstoyeh, private.
Clarance Bailtso, private.
Samuel Binday, private.
Alfred Chato, corporal.
William Coonie, private.
Mike Dahkuja, private.
Ben Francis, private.
Harold Dick, private.
Joseph Dominick, private.
Lot Eyelash, private.
David Fatty, private.

458 APPENDIX

Paul Geydelkon, private.
Frederick Gokliz, private.
Talbot Gooday, private.
Firah Jose, private.
Stephen Kyzha, private.
Tim Kaydahzinne, private.
Arnold Kinzhuna, private.
Carl Mangus, corporal.
Lawrence Mithlo, private.
Leo Nahnalzhuggi, private.
George Noche, corporal.

Leon Perico, corporal.
John S. Kuyyuggi, private.
Erick Spitty, private.
Jewett Tissuelthtos, private.
Chiricahua Tom, private.
Albert Tovisquah, private.
Evans Tzozone, private.
Waldo Tseedekizin, private.
Henry Williams, private.
Edwin Yanozha, private.
Charles Martine, private.

War Department
The Adjutant General's Office
January 9, 1929.

LIST 2
LIST OF THE NAMES OF INDIAN MEMBERS OF TROOP L.
7TH UNITED STATES CAVALRY, BETWEEN
JUNE 30, 1891, AND MAY 31, 1897
*[English translations of Indian names in parentheses
as recorded by the army are not always accurate.
Kiowa Indian Agency spellings of names added
in brackets (or tribe if name spellings are the same).]*

Captain Hugh L. Scott, Commanding.
Lieutenant Ernest Stecker, Training Officer.

[Kiowas]
Calvin Kiowa/saddler.	[Calvin Kau-ley]
Edgar Keahbone (living) wagoner.	[Edgar Keah-bone]
Lucius Aitsan (Aitsan-hoodle-ah, He Bribes) pvt., later sgt.	[Lucius Ait-san]
Mark Auchchiah (Looks Out Of Lodge) private.	[Mark Au-chia-ah]
Ah-heh (Tell-You Something) private.	[Ah-haitty]
James Ai-site (Tear It Up) private.	[Jim Asah]
Bay-e-lah (Half-breed Mexican) private.	[Bay-la-kah]
George Brizzle (Ton-kodle-ke, Red Foliage) private.	[George Tan-quodle]
Cha-ve (Little Boy) private.	[K?]

Domat (Caller) private. [Do-mat. D. 1892]
Wirt Davis (Udle-quo-quo, Curing Scalps)
   private, later sgt. [K]
James Dodone, private, later sergeant. [James To-dome]
Dow-a-ton (Medicine Bearer) pvt., [later] sgt. [Jack Doyeto]
E-ah-pah (Baby) private. [E-pah (Baby)]
Ee-ho-tah (Buffalo Killer) private. [Harry A-hote]
Ea-agoo (Two Red) private. [Yeah-quo?]
E-man-ah (Sleeping Bear) private. [Em-mau-a (Setemmaua)]
Guy (Aut-do, Mourner) private. [Aut-dau (Guy Ware)]
Haw-gone (Silver Horns) private. [Hau-goon (Silverhorn)]
Honameahtah (Charging Man) private, later
   sergeant. [Hone-a-mea-tah,
   aka Bau-dai]
I-see-o (Plenty Fires) private, later 1st sgt. [Tah-bone-mah]
Satanta Kaardly (Bitter, White Bear) private. [K?]
Kicking Bird, private, later sergeant. [Aun-gope (KB II)]
Luke Mauhe (Lame Boy) private. [Luke Ma-ha]
Michacho (Boy) private. [Mo-cha-chi]
Odle-pah (Buffalo Bird) [Odle-paugh]
Pohd-lohk (Wolf-Bear) private. [Kiowa George Poolaw]
William Patterson (Cha-dle-yah, Pick Him Up)
   private. [Chard-le-ah]
Soh-kone (Moses) private. [Moses Tso-kone]
Tcha-ka (Bread) private. [Chock-ah]
Tonacho (Turtle) private. [Ton-a-cho]
Tone-mah (Water Drinker) private. [Tone-mah]
Tso-da-ha (Stand In Water) private. [K]
Tabahorty (Sweat House) [Tape-e-do]
Ti-eh (Morning Star) private. [Ti-edle]
Toan-ko-ko (Bird's Tail) private. [Tone-kau-ko-ah]
Wohaw (Beef) private. [Wo-haw]
In-dagh-ta-ah (Singing Man) private. [Em-do-to-a]
E-dle-ta-hay (I Will Do It) private. [aka Boat-tal-le]
Joseph Hunter (Husk-day-haste, Mah Hunter)
   trumpeter. [FSA]
I-za-chi (Two Men) private. [FSA]
Frederick D. Eagle (Quo-mahn, Bob Tail)
   private. [C]

Docto (Quer-ke-ya, Born Starting On Buffalo
    Hunt) private. [C?]
Na-chon-ko (Strike The Enemy) private. [C?]
Nas-cha-na-ni (Yellow Buffalo) private. [C?]
Pahsita (Hairless) [C]
Poa-que (Find Something) [C]
George Maddox (Pur-su-su-wite-yer-queth,
    I Do As I Please) private, later corporal. [C]
John Kibben (Eta-with-ta-qua, Strike You
    With A Bow) private. [C]
George Ross (Marbone, Looker) private. [C]
To-es-sit (Black Roan Horse) private. [C]
Pearly Whitemore (Wa-si-wit-ah, Short Curly
    Hair) private. [C]
We-he (Butcher Knife) private. [C]
Woodle-quoe (Bob-Tailed Bay Horse) private. [C]
Ho-bah-teth-ka (Coffee Drinker) wagoner. [C]
Nem-o-quo-u-a (Taking Cloth Off) farrier. [C]
William Jackson, trumpeter. [FSA]
Jim Mam-i-ah (Poke With [A] Stick) private. [C?]
Nan-i-mah (Belly) private. [C?]
Tap-i-to-sa (White Sun) private. [C]
Tap-iyet-sa (Rising Sun) private. [C]
Tab-i-tad (Sun Shine) private. [C]
Po-chan-ki (Punch With A Stick) private. [C?]
Eustace Essaypoyhet (Running Wolf) private. [C]
Goh-see-bahno (Brain All Over His Head)
    private. [C]
Tessie-lo-qyauti (Strike) [C]
Burgess (Mo-ne-wer-te-qua, Strike With The
    Hand) private. [C]

[The List of Comanche Veterans at the Comanche Nation Complex also contains Ane-po-ti-yerp, Tabbytite (possibly Tab-i-tad), Te-es-it, Tessi-lo-qyauti (possibly Essaypoyhet), and Ti-eh as Troop L members.]

References

ARCHIVAL SOURCES

Alice Marriott Papers
    1935–37   Kiowa Fieldnotes. University of Oklahoma, Western History Collections, Norman, Oklahoma.

Ananti Odlepaugh Calendar
    n.d.   Fort Sill Ledgerbook D-1049. Ananti Calendar (1851–1945). Fort Sill Museum Archives, Fort Sill, Oklahoma.

Arlington National Cemetery
    2010   Hugh Lenox Scott, Major General, United States Army. Arlington National Cemetery website online at www.arlingtoncemetery.net/hlscott.htm.

Diker, Charles
    n.d.   Letter entitled "The Pictures of Silverhorn, Kiowa Indian." Museum of New Mexico, Museum of Indian Arts and Culture/Laboratory of Anthropology, Santa Fe, New Mexico.

Doris Duke Oral History Collection
    1968   Guy Quoetone to Julia A. Jordan, Meers, Oklahoma, Apr. 30, 1968. DD-T-642. Western History Collections. Norman, University of Oklahoma.

Iseeo
    n.d.a   SGT I-SEE-O Enlistments and Data, Gillette Griswold, May 1971, Iseeo Folder, FSA.
    n.d.b   Iseeo Military Career File, Biography/Indian, FSA.

John R. Brennan Family Papers
    1882–1972   South Dakota State Historical Society, Pierre, South Dakota.

Kiowa Family Record
    1901   Fiscal Year 1900, June 1901. Bureau of Indian Affairs. Copy from Parker P. McKenzie in possession of the author.

Kiowa Tribal Census
- 1879 Bureau of Indian Affairs, Kiowa Indian Agency, Anadarko, Oklahoma.
- 1880 Bureau of Indian Affairs, Kiowa Indian Agency, Anadarko, Oklahoma.
- 1881 Bureau of Indian Affairs, Kiowa Indian Agency, Anadarko, Oklahoma.
- 1889 Bureau of Indian Affairs, Kiowa Indian Agency, Anadarko, Oklahoma.
- 1895 Bureau of Indian Affairs, Kiowa Indian Agency, Anadarko, Oklahoma.
- 1899 Bureau of Indian Affairs, Kiowa Indian Agency, Anadarko, Oklahoma.
- 1920 Bureau of Indian Affairs, Kiowa Indian Agency, Anadarko, Oklahoma.

La Barre, Weston
- 1935 Kiowa Fieldnotes. Santa Fe Laboratory of Anthropology Expedition. Unnumbered manuscript in Weston La Barre Collections, Series 1, Boxes 1–4, National Anthropological Archives, Smithsonian Institution, Washington, D.C.

McKenzie, Parker Paul
- 1977 *Vocabulary of Kiowa Terms for Mammals, Birds, Insects, Reptiles & Fishes*. Privately published. Copy in possession of the author.
- 1987 Descendants of Tah-Bone-Mah (I-See-O), B/1849; D/3-11-[19]27. Unpublished manuscript written 4/6/1987. Copy in possession of the author. Copy, Parker P. McKenzie Files. Oklahoma History Center, Oklahoma City.
- 1991 *Kiowa Disyllables*. Privately published. Copy in possession of the author.
- n.d. Kiowa Police at the Kiowa, Comanche, & Wichita Agency—1880 to 1895. Compiled by Parker Paul McKenzie. Copy in possession of the author.

Mooney, James
- n.d. Kiowa Field Notes. National Anthropological Archives. MS 2531, vols. 1, 6, 11; MS 2538, Box 2, Folder 1. Smithsonian Institution, Washington D.C.

Museum of the Plains Indian Arts and Crafts Center
- 1979 *Plains Indian Sign Language. A Memorial to the Conference September 4-6, 1930, Browning, Montana*. U.S. Department of the Interior, Museum of the Plains Indian Arts and Crafts Center, Browning, Mont.

Scott, Gen. Hugh L.
- ca. 1874–1934 Papers of Hugh L. Scott. Manuscript Division, Library of Congress, Washington D.C.
- n.d.a Ledgerbook, Vols. I–IV (ca. 1889–97). Collection No. 266, Box 19, 21, Fort Sill Museum Archives, Fort Sill, Oklahoma.
- n.d.b MS 2932, Manuscript Collection, Box 2, Kiowa, Box 3, Kiowa. MS 4396, Box 1, Personal Letters Received 1897–98. MS 4525. [Accompanying Notes] Manuscript Collection. National Anthropological Archives, Smithsonian Institution, Washington, D.C.
- n.d.c "Notes on the Sign Language of the Plains Indians." *Americanists Report* 8025:87–91 (ca. 1915). Reprinted in Umiker-Sebeok and Sebeok (1978:53-68).
- n.d.d "Notes on the Sign Language of the Plains Indians." Manuscript 1799, dated November 5, 1915. National Anthropological Archives, Smithsonian Institution, Washington, D.C.
- n.d.e "Tales of the South Plains (Legends of Sinday and Other Fables)" [ca. 1920s]. Edited with an introduction by Gillette Griswald [ca. 1970]. Unpublished manuscript, 101 pp. National Anthropological Archives, Smithsonian Institution, Washington, D.C.
- n.d.f "Tales of the South Plains (Origins, the Warpath, Customs, and Adventure)" [1920]. Museum of New Mexico, Museum of Indian Arts and Culture/Laboratory of Anthropology, Santa Fe, New Mexico. Unpublished manuscript, edited by Gillette Griswold [ca. 1970]. National Anthropological Archives, Smithsonian Institution, Washington, D.C.
- n.d.g General Hugh L. Scott, Diary, 1860–1931. General H. L. Scottt Collection No. 266, Box 7. Fort Sill Museum Archives, Fort Sill, Oklahoma.

Swett, Master Segeant Morris J.
- n.d. "Sergeant I-see-o, Kiowa Indian Scout." Unpublished manuscript, Field Artillery Library, Fort Sill, Oklahoma.

Troop L, 7th U.S. Cavalry
- 1929 List of the Names of Indian Members of Troop L. 7th, United States Cavalry, between June 30, 1891, and May 31, 1897. Kiowa Misc. File, Fort Sill Museum Archives, Fort Sill, Oklahoma.
- 2010 http://sill-www.army.mil/museum/Troop%20L.htm.

United States Military Academy
- n.d. Military Record of Colonel Hugh L. Scott, U.S. Army. Superintendent, U.S. Military Academy, No. 32. West Point, N.Y.

Wilkinson, James
- 1805 Letter to Thomas Jefferson, December 23. Thomas Jefferson Papers, folio 27050. Library of Congress, Washington, D.C.

Books, Articles, and Manuscripts

American Indian Sign Language Conference
- 2012 — Advertisement flyer. Printed August 3. Copy courtesy of Dr. Jeffrey Davis. See also pislresearch.com.

Axtell, Julia L.
- 1891 — *The Indian Sign Language and the Invention of Mr. Lewis Hadley, as Applied to the Speedy Christian Civilization and Education of the Wild Adult Indians.* Chicago: Western Label Company.

Battey, Thomas C.
- 1875 — *The Life and Adventures of a Quaker among the Indians.* Boston: Lee and Shepard. Reprinted Williamstown, Mass.: Corner House Publications, 1972.

Battison, Robin M.
- 1978 — *Lexical Borrowing in American Sign Language.* Silver Spring, Md.: Linstock Press. Reprinted 2003.

Beebe, Chaplain Milton O.
- 1931 — "I-See-O, The Last of the Fort Sill Indian Scouts." *Field Artillery Journal* (Fort Sill, Okla., July–August): 356–61.

Bell, William Gardner
- 2010 — *Commanding Generals and Chiefs of Staff, 1775–2010: Portraits and Biographical Sketches of the United States Army's Senior Officers.* Washington, D.C.: Center of Military History, United States Army.

Blaylock, Fred Frank
- 1980 — "Last of the Fort Sill Indian Scouts—Plenty Fires." *Frontier Times* 54(4), new series 126 (June–July): 6–11.

Blee, Lisa
- 2007 — "The 1925 Fort Union Indian Congress: Divergent Narratives, One Event." *American Indian Quarterly* 31(4):582–612.

Boyd, Maurice
- 1983 — *Kiowa Voices.* Vol. 2. Fort Worth: Texas Christian University Press.

Burnet, David G.
- 1824 — "Indians of Texas." *Cincinnati Literary Gazette,* May 8.
- 1840 — "Indians of Texas: A Series of Letters Originally Addressed to Col. John Jamison, Deceased, Late Indian Agent at Nacogdoches." *Telegraph and Texas Register,* July 1.
- 1851 — "The Comanches and Other Tribes of Texas." In *Historical and Statistical Information Respecting the History Conditions and Prospects of the Indian Tribes of the United States,* edited by Henry R. Schoolcraft. 229–41. Vol. 1. Philadelphia: Lippincott, Grambo.

Campbell, Lyle
　1997　　　　　*American Indian Languages: The Historical Linguistics of Native America*. New York: Oxford University Press.

Catlin, George
　1841　　　　　*Letters and Notes on the Manners, Customs, and Conditions of the North American Indians*. 2 vols. London: Published by the author, printed by Tosswill and Myers. Reprinted London: David Bogue, 1844; and as *North American Indians*, Edinburgh: John Grant, 1926; also New York: Dover Publications, 1973; New York: C. N. Potter, distributed by Crown, 1975.

Clark, Blue
　1999　　　　　*Lone Wolf v. Hitchcock. Treaty Rights & Indian Law at the End of the Nineteenth Century*. Lincoln: University of Nebraska Press.

Clark, William Philo
　1885　　　　　*The Indian Sign Language, with Brief Explanatory Notes of the Gestures Taught Deaf-Mutes in Our Institutions for Their Instruction, and a Description of Some of the Peculiar Laws, Customs, Myths, Superstitions, Ways of Living, Code of Peace and War Signals of Our Aborigines*. Philadelphia: L. R. Hamersly and Company. Reprinted as *The Indian Sign Language*. Lincoln: University of Nebraska Press, 1982.

Cody, I. E.
　1952　　　　　*How: Sign Talk in Pictures*. Hollywood: H. H. Boetler Lithography.

Cohen, Matt
　2009　　　　　*The Networked Wilderness: Communicating in Early New England*. Minneapolis: University of Minnesota Press.

Corwin, Hugh D.
　1958　　　　　*The Kiowa Indians: Their History and Life Stories*. Lawton, Okla.: Privately published.
　1959　　　　　*Comanche and Kiowa Captives in Oklahoma and Texas*. Guthrie, Okla.: Cooperative Publishing Company.
　ca. 1962　　　"Fifty Years with the Kiowas, 1850–1900." Unpublished manuscript, copy in possession of the author.

Covey, Cyclone
　1993　　　　　*Cabeza de Vaca's Adventures in the Unknown Interior of America*. Albuquerque: University of New Mexico Press.

Darnell, Regna
　2001　　　　　"Plains Cree." In *Handbook of North American Indians*, Vol. 13, *Plains*, edited by Raymond J. DeMallie, 638–51. Washington, D.C.: Smithsonian Institution Press.

Davidson, Levette J.
　1950　　　　　"Some Current Folk Gestures and Sign Language." *American Speech* 25(1):3–9.

Davis, Jeffrey
 1997 "North American Indian Signed Language Varieties: A Comparative Historical Linguistic Assessment." In *Sign Languages in Contact,* edited by David Quinto-Pozos, 83–122. Washington, D.C.: Gallaudet University Press.
 2005a "Code Choices and Consequences: Implications for Educational Interpreting." In *Educational Interpreting: From Research to Practice,* edited by M. Marschark, R. Peterson, and E. Winston, 112–41. Oxford: Oxford University Press.
 2005b "Evidence of a Historical Signed Lingua Franca among North American Indians." *Deaf Worlds: International Journal of Deaf Studies* 21(3):42–72.
 2005c "Teaching Observation Techniques to Interpreters." In *Advances in Teaching Sign Language Interpreters Series,* edited by C. Roy, 22–48. Vol. 1. Washington, D.C.: Gallaudet University Press.
 2005d "Working with Sign Language Interpreters in Human Service Settings." *Human Service Education* 25:41–52.
 2006 "A Historical Linguistic Account of Sign Language among North American Indians." In *Multilingualism and Sign Languages: From the Great Plains to Australia,* edited by C. Lucas, 3–35. Washington, D.C.: Gallaudet University Press.
 2007 "North American Indian Signed Language Varieties: A Comparative Historical Linguistic Assessment." In *Sociolinguistics in Deaf Communities,* edited by David Quinto-Pozos, 85–122. Vol. 13. Washington, D.C.: Gallaudet University Press.
 2010 *Hand Talk: Sign Language among American Indian Nations.* Cambridge: Cambridge University Press.

Davis, Jeffrey E., and Melanie McKay-Cody
 2010a Hand Talk. Online at pislresearch.com.
 2010b "Signed Languages of American Indian Communities: Considerations for Interpreting Work and Research." In *Sign Language Interpreting in Multilingual and Multicultural Contexts,* edited by Rachel L. McKee and Jeffrey E. Davis, 119–57. Washington, D.C.: Gallaudet University Press.

Davis, Jeffrey, and S. Supalla
 1995 "A Sociolinguistic Description of Sign Language Use in a Navajo Family." In *Sociolinguistics in Deaf Communities,* edited by C. Lucas, 77–106. Washington, D.C.: Gallaudet University Press.

Davis, Richard Harding
 1903 *The West from a Car Window.* New York: Harper and Brothers.

DeMallie, Raymond J., ed.
 2001 *Handbook of North American Indians,* Vol. 13: *Plains.* Washington, D.C.: Smithsonian Institution Press.

Dodge, Col. Richard Irving
- 1877 — *The Plains of the Great West.* New York: G. P. Putnam and Sons. Reprinted as *The Plains of North America and Their Inhabitants.* Ed. Wayne R. Kime. Newark: University of Delaware Press, 1989.
- 1882 — *Our Wild Indians: Thirty-Three Years' Personal Experience among the Red Men of the Great West.* Hartford, Conn.: A. D. Worthington and Company.

Dorsey, George A.
- 1904 — *Mythology of the Wichita.* Publications of the Carnegie Institution of Washington, No. 221. Washington, D.C.: Carnegie Institution.

Dunbar, William
- 1809 — "On the Language of Signs among Certain North American Indians." *Transactions of the American Philosophical Society* 6 (pt. 1, no. 1):1–8.

Dunlay, Thomas W.
- 1982 — *Wolves for the Blue Soldiers: Indian Scouts and Auxiliaries with the United States Army, 1860–90.* Lincoln: University of Nebraska Press.

Ewers, John C.
- 1978 — "Richard Sanderville, Blackfoot Indian Interpreter. Blackfoot, ca. 1873–1951." In *American Indian Intellectuals*, edited by Margot Liberty, 116–26. St. Paul, Minn.: West Publishing Company.

Farnell, Brenda
- 1991 — "Nakota Makoc'e: An American Storytelling Performance." In *Yearbook of International Council for Traditional Music*, 79–99.
- 1995a — *Do You See What I Mean?: Plains Indian Sign Talk and the Embodiment of Action.* Austin: University of Texas Press.
- 1995b — "Where Mind Is a Verb: Spatial Orientation and Deixis in Plains Indian Sign Talk and Assiniboine (Nakota) Culture." In *Action Sign Systems in Cultural Context: The Visible and the Invisible in Movement and Dance*, edited by Brenda Farnell, 82–111. Metuchen, N.J.: Scarecrow Press.
- 1995c — *WIYUTA: Assiniboine Storytelling with Signs.* Interactive multimedia CD-ROM. Austin: University of Texas Press.
- 1996 — "Sign Language." In *Encyclopedia of North American Indians*, edited by Frederick E. Hoxie, 589–90. New York: Houghton Mifflin Company.

Flores, Dan L.
- 1985 — *Journal of an Indian Trader: Anthony Glass and the Texas Trading Frontier, 1790–1810.* College Station: Texas A&M University Press.

Foley, Tommy
    2007   *The Indian Sign Language*. Directed by Raymond Evans. Narrated by Major General Hugh L. Scott. U.S. Department of the Interior, Office of Indian Affairs. Indian Sign Language and Plains Indian Sign Language Conference 1930, Browning. Dick West's Lord's Prayer.

Foner, Jack D.
    1970   *The United States Soldier between Two Wars, 1865–1898*. New York: Humanities Press.

Foreman, Carolyn Thomas
    1949   "Lewis Francis Hadley: 'The Long-Haired Sign Talker.'" *Chronicles of Oklahoma* 27(1):41–55.

Gelo, Daniel J.
    2000   "Comanche Land & Ever Has Been: A Native Geography of the Nineteenth-Century Comancheria." *Southern Historical Quarterly* 103(3):272–307.
    2012   *Indians of the Great Plains*. Upper Saddle River, N.J.: Pearson Education.

Goddard, Ives
    1979   "The Languages of South Texas and the Lower Rio Grande." In *The Languages of Native America: Historical and Comparative Assessment*, edited by L. Campbell and M. Mithun, 70–132. Austin: University of Texas Press.
    2001   "The Languages of the Plains: Introduction." In *Handbook of North American Indians,* Vol. 13, Part 1, *Plains*, edited by Raymond J. DeMallie, 61–70. Washington, D.C.: Smithsonian Institution Press.

Goff-Paris, Damara, and Sharon Kay Wood
    2002   *Step into the Circle: The Heartbeat of American Indian, Alaska Native and First Nation Deaf Communities*. Monmouth, Ore.: AGO Publications.

Gordon, Raymond G., Jr.
    2005   *Ethnologue: Languages of the World*. 15th ed. Dallas: SIL International. Online at www.ethnologue.com.

Greene, Candace S.
    1996   "Exploring the Three 'Little Bluffs' of the Kiowa." *Plains Anthropologist* 41(157):221–42.
    2001   *Silver Horn: Master Illustrator of the Kiowas*. Norman: University of Oklahoma Press.
    2009   *One Hundred Summers: A Kiowa Calendar Record*. Norman: University of Oklahoma Press.

Greene, Candace, and Frederick Reuss
    1993   *Saynday Was Coming Along* (exhibit booklet). Washington, D.C.: Smithsonian Institution Traveling Exhibition Service.

Grinnell, George B.
    1906   "Cheyenne Stream Names." *American Anthropologist* 8:15–22.
    1923   *The Cheyenne Indians: Their History and Ways of Life.* 2 vols. New Haven: Yale University Press.
    1956   *The Fighting Cheyennes.* Norman: University of Oklahoma Press, Norman (originally printed by Charles Scribner's Sons, 1915).

Hadley, L. F.
    1890   *A Lesson in Sign Talk.* Fort Smith, Ark.: Hadley Publishing.
    1893   *Indian Sign Talk.* Chicago: Baker and Company.

Hagan, William T.
    1976   *United States–Comanche Relations: The Reservation Years.* New Haven: Yale University Press.
    1993   *Quanah Parker, Comanche Chief.* Norman: University of Oklahoma Press.

Harper, James W.
    1968   "Hugh Lennox Scott: Soldier Diplomat, 1853–1917." Ph.D. diss. University of Virginia.

Harrington, John Peabody
    1928   *Vocabulary of the Kiowa Language.* Smithsonian Institution. Bureau of American Ethnology Bulletin 84. Washington, D.C.: United States Government Printing Office.
    1938   "The American Indian Sign Language [Pt. 2]." *Indians at Work* (Washington, D.C.) 5(7):8–15; 5(11):28–32; 5(12):25–30; 6(3):24–29. Reprinted in *Aboriginal Sign Languages of the Americas and Australia,* edited by D. Jean Umiker-Sebeok and Thomas A. Sebeok, 2:109–42. 2 vols. New York: Plenum Press, 1978.

Henry, Thomas H.
    1931   "U.S. Pays 40-Year Debt to Indian Who Stopped Cult Revolution." *Evening Star* (Washington, D.C.), May 12, 1–2.

Hibben, Capt. Paxton
    1928   "The Story of a Soldier's Life: A Half Century of Army Service." *Mentor* 16(8), serial no. 307 (September): 1–10.

Hofsinde, Robert (Grey Wolf)
    1941   "Talk without Talk." *Natural History* 47:32–39.
    1956   *Indian Sign Language.* New York: William Morrow and Company.

Hoig, Stan
    2000   *The Kiowas and the Legend of Kicking Bird.* Boulder: University Press of Colorado.

Hollis, Maj. Gen. Robert P.
    1977   "The Army's Legendary Sgt. I-See-O." *Army* (Washington Association of the U.S. Army, June): 41–45.

Holm, Tom
    1996   *Strong Hearts, Wounded Souls: Native American Veterans of the Vietnam War.* Austin: University of Texas Press.

Howard, James H.
    1957   "The Mescal Bean Cult of the Central and Southern Plains: An Ancestor of the Peyote Cult?" *American Anthropologist* 59(1):75–87.

Humfreville, J. Lee
    1899   *Twenty Years among Our Hostile Indians.* New York: Hunter and Company. Republished Mechanicsville, Pa.: Stackpole Books, 2002.

Hyde, George E.
    1968   *The Life of George Bent, Written from His Letters.* Ed. Savoie Lotinville. Norman: University of Oklahoma Press.

Jacobs, Jan
    1969   "I-See-O, 'Stone-Age Product' Bridged White, Indian Gap." *Lawton Constitution Morning Press.* January 5, 10E.

John, Elizabeth A. H.
    1985   "An Earlier Chapter of Kiowa History." *New Mexico Historical Review* 60:379–97.

Johnson, Robert E.
    1994   "Sign Language and the Concept of Deafness in a Traditional Yucatec Mayan Village." In *The Deaf Way: Perspectives from the International Conference of Deaf Culture,* edited by C. Erting, R. Johnson, D. Smith, and B. Snider, 102–109. Washington, D.C.: Gallaudet University Press.

Kavanagh, Thomas W.
    1996   *Comanche Political History: An Ethnohistorical Perspective, 1706–1875.* Lincoln: University of Nebraska Press.
    2001   "Comanche." In *Handbook of North American Indians,* Vol. 13, Part 2: *Plains,* edited by Raymond J. DeMallie, 886–906. Washington, D.C.: Smithsonian Institution Press.

Kavanagh, Thomas W., comp. and ed.
    2008   *Comanche Ethnography: Field Notes of E. Adamson Hoebel, Waldo R. Wedel, Gustav G. Carlson, and Robert H. Lowie.* Lincoln: University of Nebraska Press, Lincoln.

Kelly, Walter P., and Tony L. McGregor
2003 "Keresan Pueblo Indian Sign Language." In *Nurturing Native Languages*, edited by J. Reyhner, O. Trujillo, R. L. Carrasco, and L. Lockard, 141–48. Flagstaff: Northern Arizona University Press.

Kracht, Benjamin
1989 "Kiowa Religion: An Ethnohistorical Analysis of Ritual Symbolism, 1832–1987." Ph.D. diss. Southern Methodist University, Dallas.

Kroeber, Alfred L.
1958 "Sign Language Enquiry." *International Journal of American Linguistics* 24(1):1–19.

Lassiter, Luke E.
1998 *The Power of Kiowa Song.* Tucson: University of Arizona Press.

Levy, Jerrold
2001 "Kiowa." In *Handbook of North American Indians*, Vol. 13: *Plains*, edited by Raymond J. DeMallie, 907–25. Washington, D.C.: Smithsonian Institution Press.

Linderman, Frank Bird
1962 *Plenty-Coups, Chief of the Crows, 1848–1932.* Lincoln: University of Nebraska Press (originally published in 1930).
1972 *Pretty-Shield, Medicine Woman of the Crow.* Lincoln: University of Nebraska Press (originally published in 1932).

Ljung, Magnus
1965 "Principles of a Stratificational Analysis of the Plains Indian Sign Language." *International Journal of American Linguistics* 31:119–27.

Long, J. Schuyler
1908–10 "The Sign Language: A Manual of Signs." *American Annals of the Deaf* 53–55(1):230–49; 2:438–48; 3:23–37; 4:140–60; 5:213–81; 6:239–47; 7:420–38; 8:142–55.
1918 *The Sign Language: A Manual of Signs; Being a Descriptive Vocabulary of Signs Used by the Deaf of the United States and Canada.* Reprint of 2nd ed. Washington, D.C.: Gallaudet College.

Long, Stephen H.
1823 *Account of an Expedition from Pittsburgh to the Rocky Mountains.* 3 vols. Ann Arbor, Mich.: University Microfilms.

Mallery, Garrick

1880a   *A Collection of Gesture Signs and Signals of the North American Indians with Some Comparisons.* Washington, D.C.: Smithsonian Institution. Reprinted in Umiker-Sebeok and Sebeok 1978:1:77–406.

1880b   *Introduction to the Study of Sign Language among the North American Indians as Illustrating the Gesture Speech of Mankind.* Washington, D.C.: Bureau of Ethnology. Reprinted in Umiker-Sebeok and Sebeok 1978:1:1–76.

1880c   "The Sign Language of the Indian of the Upper Missouri, in 1832." *American Antiquarian* 2(3):218–28.

1881   "Sign Language among North American Indians, Compared with That among Other Peoples and Deaf-Mutes." In *1st Annual Report of the Bureau of [American] Ethnology [for] 1879–'80*, 263–552. Washington, D.C.: Government Printing House. Reprinted (with articles by A. L. Kroeber and C. F. Vogelin) in *Approaches to Semiotics* 14. The Hague: Mouton, 1972.

1882   "The Gesture Speech of Man." *Proceedings of the American Association for the Advancement of Science, 30th Meeting (August 1881)*, 283–313. Salem, Mass.: Salem Press.

Marcy, Randolph B.

1866   *Thirty Years of Army Life on the Border.* New York: Harper and Brothers.

Marquis, Thomas Bailey

1962   *Wooden Leg: A Warrior Who Fought Custer.* Lincoln: University of Nebraska Press (originally published as *A Warrior Who Fought Custer.* Minneapolis: Midwest Company, 1931).

1974   *Memoirs of a White Crow Indian.* Lincoln: University of Nebraska Press (originally published as *Memoirs of a White Crow Indian.* New York: Century Company, 1928).

McAllister, Gilbert J.

1937   "Kiowa-Apache Social Organization." In *Social Organization of North American Tribes*, edited by Fred Eggan, 97–169. Chicago: University of Chicago Press.

1965   "The Four Quartz Rocks Medicine Bundle of the Kiowa-Apache." *Ethnology* 4(2):210–24.

1970   *Daveko: Kiowa-Apache Medicine Man.* Bulletin 17. Austin: Texas Memorial Museum.

McCoy, Tim

1946   *Injun Talk.* www.youtube.com/watch?v=a6aGVQwdxQk.

McKay-Cody, M.

1997   "Plains Indian Sign Language: A Comparative Study of Alternate and Primary Signers." Master's thesis. University of Arizona.

McKee, R., and Jeffrey Davis, eds.
    2010   *Sign Language Interpreting in Multilingual and Multicultural Contexts: Studies in Interpretation.* Washington, D.C.: Gallaudet University Press.

Meadows, William C.
    1999   *Kiowa, Apache, and Comanche Military Societies.* Austin: University of Texas Press.
    2006   "Black Goose's Map of the Kiowa-Comanche-Apache Reservation in Oklahoma Territory." *Great Plains Quarterly* 26(4):265–82.
    2008   *Kiowa Ethnogeography.* Austin: University of Texas Press.
    2010   *Kiowa Military Societies: Ethnohistory and Ritual.* Norman: University of Oklahoma Press.
    2013   "Kiowa Ethnonymy of Other Populations." *Plains Anthropologist* 58(226):5–30.

Meadows, William C., and Kenny Harragarra
    2007   "The Kiowa Drawings of Gotebo (1847–1927): A Self-Portrait of Cultural and Religious Transition." *Plains Anthropologist* 52(202):229–44.

Meadows, William C., and Parker P. McKenzie
    1999   "The Parker P. McKenzie Kiowa Orthography: How Written Kiowa Came into Being." *Plains Anthropologist* 46(177):233–48.

Medicine Lodge
    1994   Peace Treaty, Medicine Lodge, Kansas. Dede-Morgan-Vick, "Peace Treaty: The Product of a Town Working Together." Online at www.cyberlodge.com/mlcity/peacetreaty.html.

Miller, Katrina R., ed.
    2004   "Circle of Unity: Pathways to Improving Outreach to American Indians and Alaska Natives Who Are Deaf, Deaf-Blind, and Hard of Hearing." University of Arkansas Rehabilitation Research and Training Center for Persons Who Are Deaf and Hard of Hearing. Little Rock, Ark.

Mithun, Marianne
    1999   *The Languages of Native North America.* Cambridge: Cambridge University Press.

Mooney, James
    1896   *The Ghost-Dance Religion and the Sioux Outbreak of 1890.* Part 2, Fourteenth Annual Report of the Bureau of [American] Ethnology, 1892–93. Washington, D.C.: Government Printing House
    1898   *Calendar History of the Kiowa Indians.* Seventeenth Annual Report of the Bureau of American Ethnology, 1895–96. Washington, D.C.: Government Printing House.

Moore, John H.
    1987   *The Cheyenne Nation.* Lincoln: University of Nebraska Press.
    1996   *The Cheyenne.* Cambridge, Mass.: Blackwell Publishers.

Moore, John H., Margot P. Liberty, and Terry Straus
    2001   "Cheyenne." In *Handbook of North American Indians*, Vol. 13: *Plains* edited by Raymond J. DeMallie, 863–85. Washington, D.C.: Smithsonian Institution Press.

Morgan, E. Buford
    1973   *The Wichita Mountains: Ancient Oasis of the Prairies*. Waco: Texian Press.

Moses, Lester George
    1996   *Wild West Shows and the Images of American Indians, 1883–1933*. Albuquerque: University of New Mexico Press.

Nabokov, Peter, and Lawrence Loendorf
    2004   *Restoring a Presence: American Indians and Yellowstone National Park*. Norman: University of Oklahoma Press.

Newell, L. E.
    1981   "A Stratificational Description of Plains Indian Sign Language." *Forum Linguisticum* 5:189–212.

Nye, Col. Wilbur S.
    1937   *Carbine and Lance: The Story of Old Fort Sill*. Norman: University of Oklahoma Press.
    1962   *Bad Medicine and Good: Tales of the Kiowa*. Norman: University of Oklahoma Press.

Palmer, Gus, Jr.
    2009   "Kiowa Glossary and Guide to Pronunciation." In *One Hundred Summers: A Kiowa Calendar Record*, edited by Candace Greene, 195–202. Lincoln: University of Nebraska Press.

Parsons, Elsie Clews
    1929   *Kiowa Tales*. Memoirs 22. New York: American Folklore Society.

Peery, Dan W.
    1935   "Gen. Hugh L. Scott." *Chronicles of Oklahoma* 13(3):355–56.

Pfening, Fred D., Jr.
    1955   *Col. Tim McCoy's Real Wild West and Rough Riders of the World: Complete History and Official Route Book*. Columbus, Ohio: Pfening and Snyder.

Powell, Peter J.
    1981   *People of the Sacred Mountain: A History of the Northern Cheyenne Chiefs and Warrior Societies 1830–1879, with an Epilogue, 1969–1974*. 2 vols. San Francisco: Harper and Row.

Robinson, Lila Wistrand, and James L. Armagost
    1990   *Comanche Dictionary and Grammar*. Summer Institute of Linguistics and the University of Texas at Arlington, Publications in Linguistics 92. Dallas: Summer Institute of Linguistics.

Ruxton, George F.
    1848   *Adventures in Mexico and the Rocky Mountains.* 1st American ed. New York: Harper and Brothers; originally published London: John Murray, 1847. Reprinted Glorieta, N.Mex.: Rio Grande Press, 1973.

Samarin, William J.
    1987   "Demythologizing Plains Indian Sign Language History." *International Journal of American Linguistics* 53:65–73.

Sanderville, Richard
    1934   Contributions to Hugh L. Scott's "Film Dictionary of the North American Indian Sign Language." Filmed by Paul D. Hellyer. Washington, D.C.: Smithsonian Institution Archives.

Sayce, A. H.
    1880   Sign Language among the American Indians. *Nature* 22(5):93–94.

Schnell, Stephen
    1994   "The Kiowa Homeland in Oklahoma." Master's thesis, University of Kansas, Lawrence.
    2000   "The Kiowa Homeland in Oklahoma." *Geographical Review* 90(2):155–76.

Schweinfurth, Kay Parker
    2002   *Prayer on Top of the Earth: The Spiritual Universe of the Plains Apache.* Boulder: University Press of Colorado.

Scott, Hugh L.
    1892   "The Messiah Dance in the Indian Territory: Essay for the Fort Sill Lyceum, Fort Sill, Oklahoma." March.
    1898   "The Sign Language of the Plains Indians." In *The International Folk-Lore Congress of the World's Columbian Exposition, Chicago 1893: Archives of the International Folk-Lore Association*, edited by Helen Wheeler Bassett and Frederick Starr, 1:206–20. Chicago: Charles H. Sergel Company. Reprinted in Umiker-Sebeok and Sebeok 1978:2:53–67.
    1907   "The Early History and the Names of the Arapaho." *American Anthropologist* 9:545–60.
    1911   "Notes on the Kado, or Sun Dance of the Kiowa." *American Anthropologist* 13(3):345–79.
    1928   *Some Memories of a Soldier.* New York: Century Company.
    ca. 1930   "Indian Sign Language." *Kentucky Standard.* Reprinted from the *Iowa Hawkeye.*
    1934   "Film Dictionary of the North American Indian Sign Language." Record Group 106.13, 106.14, 106.15, National Archives Audiovisual Division, Washington, D.C.

Seton, Ernest Thompson
- 1918 — *Sign Talk: A Universal Signal Code, without Apparatus, for Use in the Army, Navy, Camping, Hunting, and Daily Life—The Gesture Language of the Cheyenne Indians*. New York: Doubleday, Page, and Company.

Spivey, Towana
- n.d. — *Warriors in Blue: The Indian Soldiers of Troop L, 7th U.S. Cavalry, Fort Sill, Oklahoma Territory* (Fort Sill National Historic Landmark brochure). Fort Sill, Oklahoma.

Standing Bear, Luther
- 1975 — *My People the Sioux*. Lincoln: University of Nebraska Press.
- 1978 — *Land of the Spotted Eagle*. Lincoln: University of Nebraska Press.
- 1988 — *My Indian Boyhood*. Lincoln: University of Nebraska Press.

Stewart, Omer C.
- 1987 — *The Peyote Religion: A History*. Norman: University of Oklahoma Press.

Stokoe, William C.
- 1960 — *Sign Language Structure: An Outline of the Visual Communication Systems of the American Deaf*. Studies in Linguistics, Occasional Papers 8 (revised 1978). Silver Spring: Linstock Press.
- 1972 — *Semiotics and Human Sign Languages*. The Hague: Mouton.
- 1980 — "Sign Language Structure." *Annual Review of Anthropology* 9:365–90.

Swett, Morris
- 1935 — "Sergeant I-See-O, Kiowa Indian Scout." *Chronicles of Oklahoma* 13(3):341–54.

Tate, Michael L.
- 1986 — "From Scout to Doughboy: The National Debate over Integrating American Indians into the Military, 1891–1918." *Western Historical Quarterly* 17 (October): 417–37.

Taylor, Alan R.
- 1975 — "Non-verbal Communication in Aboriginal North America: The Plains Indian Sign Language." In Umiker-Sebeok and Sebeok 1978(2):223–46.
- 1996 — "Non-speech Communication Systems." In *Handbook of North American Indians*, Vol. 17: *Languages*, edited by Ives Goddard, 275–89. Washington, D.C.: Smithsonian Institution Press.

ten Kate, H. F. C.
- 1885 — "Notes ethnographiques sur les Comanches." *Revue d'Ethnographie* 4:120–36.

Thom, James Alexander
- 2000 — *Sign-Talker: The Adventure of George Drouillard on the Lewis and Clark Expedition*. New York: Ballantine Books.

Tomkins, William
   1926   *Universal Indian Sign Language of the Plains Indians of North America*. San Diego: FRYB and Smith. Reprinted New York: Dover Publications, 1969.
   1927   *Universal Indian Sign Language of the Plains Indians of North America*. 2nd ed. San Diego: FRYB and Smith.

Umiker-Sebeok, Donna Jean, and Thomas Sebeok, eds.
   1978   *Aboriginal Sign Languages of the Americas and Australia*. 2 vols. New York: Plenum Press.

United States, Office of Indian Affairs
   1891   "Report of the Kiowa, Comanche, and Wichita Agency. Anadarko, Ok., Aug. 20, 1891" (Charles E. Adams). In *Annual Report of the Comissioner of Indian Affairs for the Year 1891 (Part 1)*. Washington, D.C.: Government Printing Office.

Van De Logt, Mark
   2010   *War Party in Blue: Pawnee Scouts in the U.S. Army*. Norman: University of Oklahoma Press.

Vaughn-Roberson, Glen
   2007   "Texas-Oklahoma Boundary Controversies." *Oklahoma Encyclopedia of History*, Oklahoma Historical Society, Oklahoma City. Online at okhistory.org/publications/enc/entry.php?entry=TE025.

Vestal, Paul A., and Richard Evans Schultes
   1939   *The Economic Botany of the Kiowa Indians, as It Relates to the History of the Tribe*. Cambridge, Mass.: Harvard University Botanical Museum.

Viola, Herman J.
   1999   *Little Bighorn Remembered: The Untold Indian Story of Custer's Last Stand*. New York: Times Books.

Voegelin, Carl F.
   1958   "Sign Language Analysis: One Level or Two?" *International Journal of American Linguistics* 24:71–77.

Walker, Deward E., Jr.
   1998   "Nez Perce." In *Handbook of North American Indians*, Vol. 12: *Plateau*, edited by Deward E. Walker, Jr., 420–38. Washington, D.C.: Smithsonian Institution Press.

Walker, Jerell R.
   1953   "The Sign Language of the Plains Indians of North America." *Chronicles of Oklahoma* 31(2):168–77.

Weatherwax, Marvin
   2002   *Indian Sign Language*. VHS. Department of Blackfeet Studies, Blackfeet Community College, Browning, Montana.

Webb, Walter P.
 1931 "The Sign Language of the Plains Indians." In *The Great Plains*, 68–84. Boston: Ginn and Company.

West, La Mont, Jr.
 1960 "The Sign Language: An Analysis." 2 vols. Ph.D. diss. Indiana University, Bloomington. (Ann Arbor, Mich.: University Microfilms International, 1977.)

White, W. Bruce
 1968 "The Military and the Melting Pot: The American Army and Minority Groups, 1865–1924." Ph.D. diss. University of Wisconsin.
 1976 "The American Indian as Soldier, 1890–1919." *Canadian Review of American Studies* 7 (Spring): 15–25.

Wied-Neuwied, Alexander Philipp Maximilian (Prinz zu Wied-Neuwied)
 1843 *Travels in the Interior of North America, 1832–1834*. Translated from the German by H. Evans Lloyd. 2 vols. London: Ackermann and Company (originally published in German: J. Hoelscher, Coblenz, 1839–41; English ed. reprinted in vols. 22–24 [1906] of *Early Western Travels, 1748–1846*, edited by Reuben G. Thwaites: Cleveland: Arthur H. Clark, 1904–1907).

Wise, Jennings C.
 1931 *The Red Man in the New World Drama: A Politico-Legal Study with a Pageantry of American Indian History*. Washington, D.C.: W. F. Roberts Company.

Wurtzburg, Susan, and Lyle Campbell
 1995 "North American Indian Sign Language: Evidence of Its Existence before European Contact." *International Journal of American Linguistics* 61(2):153–67.

Yandell, Kay
 2012 "The Moccasin Telegraph: Sign-Talk Autobiography and *Pretty-Shield, Medicine Woman of the Crow*." *American Literature* 84(3):533–61.

Index

abandonment, of people, 142, 207
Adams, Charles, E., 50, 55
Adams, Granger, 101
Adobe Walls Fight (1874), 133, 134, 142, 167–69, 180, 181, 282, 299, 301, 304, 322, 330, 370, 371, 372
adultery, 199; penalty for women, 276
Afraid of Bears. *See* Tsait-a-pay-ta / Tsait-ape (aka Afraid of Bears; Kiowa)
Afraid of Water (Comanche), 354, 421
Ahhaitty, Dan (Kiowa), 38
Ahpeatone, Ahpeahton, Ahpiatim, Ahpiaton (aka Wooden Lance; Kiowa), 53–54, 67, 68, 231, 360
Aitsan, Lucius (Kiowa), 177–78, 406
A-ke-a (Kiowa), 129
Àláhògàu. *See* Quapaw
alligator. *See* Zema-coon / Zemacouny / Zirracunny (Zémáutqùné / Zémáutqùnóp, Kiowa underwater monster[s])
allotment, 66–69, 75, 83, 85, 92, 99, 100, 109, 133, 147
American Philosophical Society, 15, 22
American Sign Language (ASL), 34, 37
animals. *See names of individual animals*
antelope, hunting of, 142, 212, 417–19, 426–27
Antelope Hills (Okla.), 174, 181, 195, 224, 226, 294, 329
Antelope Horn Hills (Deer's Ear), 224
Antelope Medicine, 142, 417–19, 426–27
Apache (Indians), as prisoners of war, 60, 65–66, 98

Apache Creek, 292, 394
Apache John (Naishan Apache), 5, 66, 67, 70, 111, 113, 155, 473, 475
Arapaho (Indians), 328–30, 331, 334–35, 420; death customs, 330; divisions, 328–29; Flat Pipe, 328; migration to obtain horses, 329, 334; origins of, 335; peace with Kiowa, 423–24; soldier bands (military societies) of, 329
Arickaree Fork: 1868 Cheyenne battle at, 332; Cheyenne sign for, 299
Arikara (Indians; aka Ree), 26, 44, 45, 46, 265, 299, 320, 334, 403, 420, 429, 450
Arkansas River, 281, 296, 298, 299, 305, 331
Arko (Comanche), 293
Arnold, A. V., 107, 108
arrow games, 448–49
arrowheads, 220–21, 299, 329, 330
arrows, 108; fletching of, 184; gluing of, 198; tribal styles of, 233, 253–55, 265, 332, 335
Ash Creek, 331, 374
Asphalt Spring, 191, 422
Assiniboine Boy (Gros Ventre), 26
A-tong-ty (Kiowa), 123
Atta-kanick (aka Attocknie; Comanche), 270
Auchiah, James (Kiowa), 109
Auchiah, Mark (Kiowa), 94
Áulbéáuihyà (aka Many Scalps, One of Many Scalps). *See* Ten Medicines (Kiowa Medicine Bundles, aka *Áulbéáuihyà* or One of Many Scalps)

479

awl game, 451–53

Ba-lah-kah (Kiowa), 199
Baldwin, Frank D., 71, 72, 96, 97
Balmer, Jesmond D., 114, 118
Baptists, Kiowa names for, 326
Bat-chaddle (Kiowa), 114
Battey, Thomas, 266
Bayelah, 199
bears, 161, 196, 200, 218, 222, 339, 348, 349, 359, 395
Bear Butte (S.Dak.), 223–24, 225, 294
Bear Lodge Mountains. *See* Bear Lodge Tower (Devil's Tower, Wyo.)
Bear Lodge Tower (Devil's Tower, Wyo.), 224–26, 242, 264–65, 420; name of, 223, 294. *See also* Pleiades (constellation)
Bear Play (Sétyáiàum; Kiowa game), 264–65, 335
Bear Woman, 362, 363, 365
Bell, J. Franklin, 71
Belle Fourche River (Wyo.), 143, 223, 297
Bell's Palsy, 284
Benteen, Frederick W., 46
Bent's Fort (Colo.), 281, 290, 299, 305; sign for, 322
Bent, George, 168, 169, 290
Bent, William, 281
Benteen, Frederick W., 46
Berry, Tennyson (Plains Apache), 111
Big Black Tripe. *See* Kom-au-day / Kom-au-dy (aka Black Stomach / Big Black Tripe; Kiowa)
Big Bow (Kiowa), 56, 70, 123, 126, 146, 160; and Bull Medicine shields, 376; in herding ritual, 388, 402; shield of, 231; society leader, 278, 357, 359; visits Utes, 204, 209; war journeys of, 231
Big Bow, Joe (Kiowa), 132
Big Cow (Comanche), 50; biographical sketch of, 135–36
Big Dipper (Jack Rabbit), 195–96
Big Foot (Lakota), 52
Big Horse. *See* Pe-ah-bo
Big Horse Dance (Comanche), 168
Big Leg (Kiowa), 375–76

Big Looking Glass (Comanche), 67
Big Mountain (Mount Scott, Okla.), 182, 188, 190–91, 257, 258, 290, 294, 375
Big Mouth. *See* Zema-coon / Zemacouny / Zirracunny (Zę́máutqṳ̀né / Zę́máutqṳ̀nóp, Kiowa underwater monster[s])
Big Plume (Sarcee), 26
Big River (Rio Grande), 174, 205, 295, 332, 440, 468
Big Wolf (Comanche), 258
Big Young Man (Kiowa), 187–88
Big Tree (Kiowa), 397–98, 406
Bird Appearing (Kiowa), 436
Bird Rattler (Blood), 26; photo of, 29
Bird Who Travels Back And Forth On Ridge (Kiowa), 376
bison (buffalo): ages of, 316; pledges with dung chips of, 200; as offerings, 188; corrals, drives, and surrounds, 212–13; dance, 328; Euro-American hunters, 167–70, 181–82; guarding and holding of, 164–66, 211–12, 359–60; holes, 224; hunting of, 202, 211–13, 235–36; surrounds on foot, 212–13; taboo for hunting albino, 236, white bison (albino), 235–36
Bison Bull Coming Out / Emerging (aka Lives a Long Time; Kiowa), medicine of, 181–82, 358, 360–61
Biter. *See* Arikara Tribe
Bitter Root Jim (aka Bear Road; Flathead), 26
Bittle, William, 154
black-eared horses, 195
Blackfeet Indians, 450
Blackfoot Sioux, 308
Black Goose (Kiowa), 142, 264, 280
Black Horse (Comanche), 272, 279
Black Horse (aka Tsenkongia; Kiowa), 166–67
Black Kettle (Cheyenne), 176, 367, 423
Black Hills (S.Dak.), 141, 143, 176, 222–24, 225, 294, 329, 334, 335, 337, 420, 429
Black Leggins / Leggings (Kiowa Warrior Society), 128, 207, 277–79; Comanche use of name, 171, 328

INDEX   481

Blee, Lisa, 37, 76, 77
Blind Man and His Wife (story of), 404–405
Boat-tah-le (Kiowa), 203
Bolaute. *See* Poolant, Bob (aka Approaching/Crawling Snake; Kiowa)
Bone Earring (Kiowa man), 417–18, 427
Bonee, 250–52
Botone (Kiowa), 177
Bowstring Society (Cheyenne), 126, 394
Boy Scouts of America, and sign language, 20, 25
Brazos River (Tex.), 274, 296, 299, 368, 399, 421
Brennan, John, 25
Brewster, General Alden F., 103, 107
Browning, Daniel, 67
buffalo. *See* bison (buffalo)
Buffalo, Mary (Kiowa), 251
Buffalo Bull Medicine, 160, 374–76
buffalo bull skulls, 176–77
Buffalo Cow Woman, 407–409
buffalo holes, 225
Buffalo Medicine Men, 124, 160, 162
buffalo surround: on foot, 142, 190, 212, 419; on horse, 419
Buffalo Tail Shield Medicine, 162
Buffalo Tree (Kiowa Medicine Site), 263–64
Bull Comes Out Of His Lodge (aka Lives a Long Time), medicine of, 181–82, 358, 360–61
Bull Dance (Comanche), 328, 355
Bull Tail Medicine. *See* Buffalo Bull Medicine
Bull Woman (Kiowa), 375
Bureau of American Ethnology (BAE), 18, 22, 29, 31, 71, 75, 78, 139, 150, 439
Bureau of Indian Affairs (BIA), 75
burials, 179; of Snapping Turtle, 187, 206–207, 450

Cabaya (Comanche), 10, 135
Cabeza de Vaca, Alvar Núñez, 7
Cache Creek (Okla.), 103, 134, 149, 151, 168, 189, 231, 257, 270, 296, 298, 406, 421, 422
Caddo (Indians), 286, 298, 300, 430; bands, 273; enemies of, 274; fights with Kiowas, 393–94; foods of, 273–74; movements of, 273–74; origins, 273; peace with Kiowa, 435–36; sign language use by, 274
Caddo Jake, 146, 273
Caddo Mausape (Kiowa), 216
Caddo Spring, 261, 298
Calumet Dance (Kiowa-Pawnee), 89, 261, 266–71, 325; counting coup in, 268; ritual capture of child in, 267–68, sign for, 266
Camp Crier, Kiowa name of, 183, 266; sign for, 306, 355, 426
Campbell, Lyle, 7, 9
Canadian River (Okla., Tex.) 8, 143, 226, 296, 298, 329, 330, 331
cannibalism, ritual, 428–29
Carlisle Indian School, 66, 68, 84, 131
Carrither's Mission, 257, 292
Carlton, Caleb Henry, 46, 54, 55
Carries Firewood On His Back (Comanche), in Kiowa-Comanche Peace, 352–54
Carson, Kit: Kiowa fight with, 126, 370–71, 374; sign language name of, 290
Castañeda, Pedro de, 7
Catholics, Kiowa names for, 326
Catlin, George, 189, 191 198, 270, 271, 363
Cavalry Creek, 260
Chaddlesone, Sherman (Kiowa), 437
Chaka. *See* Tchaka (Kiowa)
Chalepah, Alfred, 163
Chandler Creek (aka Kobi or Wild Horse Creek), 394, 436
Cheevers (Comanche), 134, 187, 292
Cherokee (Jerome) Commission, 66–68, 69, 92, 133, 147
Cheevers (Comanche), 187
Cheyenne (Indians), 195, 330–36, 420; divisions of, 332; enemies of, 333–34; Dog Soldier Society, 332; 1837 Bowstring Society Fight location, 436; horticulture of, 334; migration to obtain horses, 334; military societies (policing), 221, 332; names for, 265; names of streams, 331–32; names of tribes, 331; oaths of, 335–36; party killed by Kiowa and others (1837), 436; origins of, 332–33;

Cheyenne (Indians) *(continued)*: origins of sign language attributed to, 233, 430–31; and Palo Duro Rock, 335–36; peace with Kiowa, 423–24; Pleiades's story of, 335–36; Sacred Arrows of, 220, 330, 334; sign for, 233; sign language among, 430–31; signs for other tribes, 233; smallpox among, 220–21; Sweet Medicine, 333; women, 380–81

Cheyenne Massacre. *See under* Cheyenne

Chief River, 296, 299, 331

chiefs, 109, 171–73; breaking a bad Chief's Road, 410; elections of, 360; in hand game, 449; on war parties, 367–77

Chihuahua, Kiowa raids into, 174, 208

cholera, 125, 141, 221–22, 306

Christians, 130, 290; Kiowa names for, 319–20, 326

Cimarron River (Kans., Okla.), 143, 208, 292; sign language name of, 296

Clancy, Thomas, 59, 83, 145; death of, 275

Clark, Ben, 70, 136, 145, 169, 223, 225; on Cheyenne Medicine Arrows, 330, 374

Clark, William P., 6, 11, 16–18, 39, 44, 71

Cleveland, Grover, 68, 70

Cloud Chief (Okla.), 312, 260, 436

Cochetethkas (Comanche Division), 421

Cody, I. E., 20

Cody, William F., 18, 25, 70, 76, 95

Cohen, Matt, 21

colds, cures for, 293

Comanches, 371; Bull Dance, 328, 355, constellations and stars, 234; death customs, 234; defensive earthworks of, 203; divisions of, 134–36, 231–33, 327, 421, 422–23; fables, 235; ghosts and whirlwinds, 234; horses among, 228, 421; name of, 231, 233, 234, 320, 421; names of months, 327; names of tribes, 320; origins of, 232–34; origin of buffalo, 233; raid on Kiowas, 377–80; rattlesnake bites and cures, 272–73, 293; separation with Shoshones, 232, 421–23; sign language used by, 139–40; military societies of, 327–28; vision quest sites, 262. *See also* Kiwash (aka Nim Kiwash, "Deceitful Man," Comanche Trickster)

Comes Over A Ridge (Pea-goo-ah; Kiowa), owl medicine of, 371–74

consumption (tuberculosis), 215

Coolidge, Calvin, 112–14

coup / counting coup (striking a blow to an enemy), 89, 127, 173, 186; at dance, 355; in hunting bison for Sun Dance, 384, 388; in oath, 200, 205, 236, 268; on women, 380

Coronado, Francisco Vázquez de, 7, 433

cottonwood, 242, 262; sign for, 276, 306; in Kiowa Sun Dance, 276, 306, 329, 331, 378, 379, 385; and Smoky Hill River, 299

cranes (birds), 226

Crook, George, 147, 281

crossing streams, 368–70

Crow (Indians), 4, 17, 18, 32, 35, 47, 336–37, 420; and Cheyennes, 334; hair extensions of, 356; intermarriage with Kiowa, 306; Kiowa accounts of, 336–37, 420, 429, 450; Kiowa name for, 320; Kiowa visits to, 261, 450; moccasins of, 337; in northern Plains, 141, 439; pledges of, 200; relations with Kiowas, 336; reservation of, 25; salvaging drowned bison, 336; scouts, 45, 65; sign language consultants, 6, 11, 13, 14, 21; signs for mountains, 294, 295, 297; *Táimé* medicines of, 124, 176–77, 285, 389. *See also* Goes Ahead (Crow); Goes Together (Crow); Plenty Coups (Crow)

Custer, George A, 14, 21, 43, 45, 47, 58, 225, 281, 291, 451

Cuthead Pass (Okla.), 257

Cuthead Spring (Okla.), 257

Cut Off Head Mountain. *See* Cutthroat Mountain (Okla.)

Cutthroat Mountain (Okla.), 142, 209, 257–62, 263, 290, 294, 298

cyclones. *See* tornadoes

Dagoi (Kiowa), 400

Daley Ranch (Cache Creek, Okla.), 135, 421, 422

Daveko (Plains Apache), 373

Davis, Jeffrey, 33–36

INDEX   483

Davis, Richard H., 81–82
Dawes Act, 66. *See also* Cherokee (Jerome) Commission
Day, George, 66–67
death. *See* burial; fainting; finger cutting; trance
De Smet, Pierre Jean, 290
deaf and mute people, 300; as good sign talkers, 300
Deibert, Ralph C., 114
Deer Nose (Crow), 26
descendants of Troop L, 7th U.S. Cavalry, 121
Devil's Lake (N.Dak.), 333–34, 341
Devil's Tower (Wyo.; aka Xòâi, Rock Tree, Rock That Grew Upward, Up a Rock), 141, 195, 196, 222–23, 242, 261, 286, 287, 363, 420. *See also* Bear Lodge Tower (Devil's Tower, Wyo.); Pleiades (constellation)
Dickson, Billy, 168, 281
Different Tribes / All Tribes (Kiowa woman), 357
Diker, Charles, 145, 153
Docto (aka Tonakaut; Kiowa): medicine of, 2, 186–87; Troop L member, 187, 199
doctors (Indian), and medicine, 187
Dodge, Richard I., 15, 16, 17, 70, 168, 223, 333, 407
Dodge City (Kans.), 168
dogs, 227, 234
Dog Eater (Comanche), 272
Dohausen. *See* Done-pi (aka Dohausen; Kiowa); Tohausen (aka Dohausen, *Jòhâusàn*; Kiowa)
Dohauty / Dowhainte / Doyhauty / Doyharty (aka Walks On A Cloud, Mamanti; Kiowa), 178–80, 185–86
Domat (Kiowa), 132, 207, 219; name of, 456, 459
Domebo, Harry (Kiowa), 363
Done-pi (aka Dohausen; Kiowa), 112, 127, 186, 270; pipe of, 388
Dorsey, George, 189
Double Mountain (Tex.), 149, 151, 167, 292, 294, 377
Doyeto, Jack (Kiowa), 13, 14, 200, 217, 459

Drags Wolf (Hidatsa), 26
Drouillard, George, 7
Dunbar, William, 15
Dunlay, Thomas, 18, 64, 95, 100, 119, 147, 148

Eagle, James (Arikara), 26
eagles: in Antelope Medicine, 426–27; on calumets, 266, 270; catching of, 69, 131, 183–85, 210; in doctoring, 187; eggs of, 289; fans, 309; feathers of, 284, 288, 417, 426; golden eagle, 289; in Kiowa origins story, 240; Medicine Eagle, 404, 411; in Omaha Dance, 185; in peyotism, 215; on shields, 160; in Sun Dance, 363, 386, 389, 391, 392; in Ten Medicine Bundle, 363; types of, 288; in Wichita vision quest, 191
Eagle Heart (Kiowa), camp of, 257, 394, 435
Eapah (aka Baby; Kiowa), 372
earache, cure for, 293
earthworks, defensive, 201
Eddy, John R., 64
Ehota (aka A-hote, Buffalo Killer; Kiowa), 363
elk, 212, 227–28, 240–41, 249, 250, 300, 366, 403, 415–15, 435
Elk Creek (Okla.), 168, 178,180, 182, 190, 258–59, 296–98, 407
Elk Soldier Arrow, 205, 278
Elk Tongue (aka Tom Mobeadleky; Kiowa): as consultant for Scott, 146; in making feathered bonnet, 69; in peyote meeting, 215; picture of, 129; relatives of, 201, 421; and signals, 291, 447; on trip with Scott, 50, 128
Emaa / Eemahan (aka Gives Food; Kiowa), 178
E-mau-ah, Captain Scott (Kiowa), 62
E-mau-tah (Kiowa), 62, 120; name of, 360
Eonah (aka Eueanah or Unap, Trailing the Enemy; Kiowa), 363
Esaquitas. *See* Mescalero Apache
Esati (Comanche), 168, 170
Eschiti (aka Isati / Isatai; Comanche), 131, 180, 183
Ewers, John C., 26, 28, 31

Ezkiminzin (Eskimazin; Apache), 65–66

fainting, 178. *See also* trance
Fane, John, 111
Farnell, Brenda, 32
Fine Young Man (Sarcee), 26
finger cutting, in mourning, 201, 379
Foner, Jack, 63
Foolish Woman (Mandan), 26
Fort Abraham Lincoln, 43, 46, 225
Fort Berthold (N.Dak.), 45–46
Fort Buford, 225
Fort Custer, 47
Fort Dodge, 374, 393, 436
Fort Elliot (Tex.), 168, 368
Fort Larned (Kans.), 88, 372, 374
Fort Lynn, 167
Fort Marion (Fla.), 60, 178, 186, 235, and Kiowa prisoners, 131, 147
Fort Meade, 47
Fort Reno (Okla.), closing of, 70–71, 81, 136, 145, 259, 292, 329, 435, 436, 440; sign language name of, 282
Fort Sill (Okla.), 49–155, 167–68, 179, 186, 188, 189, 191, 229, 259, 262, 270, 281–82, 284, 300, 405–407, 418, 423, 436, 440
Fort Supply (Okla.), 66, 175, 261, 282, 335
Fort Totten, 47, 341
Fort Union Indian Congresses, 76–77
Fort Washakie, 328
Fox Quirt Dance or Fox Whip Dance (Comanche Dance), 168, 171
fox skin quirt handles, 284
Frizzle Head (Kiowa man), 125; biographical sketch of, 128, 141, 145, 146; saves White Bear, 167, 277, 360

Gallaudet, Thomas H., 15
game, division of, 439
Garlington, E. A., 46
Garza, José Venustiano Carranza (governor of Coahuila), 84
Gassaway, B. F., 130
Geikaunmah, Bert (Kiowa), 15
German silver, 436
Geronimo (Apache), 65, 66

geysers (Yellowstone area), and early Kiowa history, 141, 289, 420, 436
ghosts, 190, 191, 284, 310, 372, 395; and whirlwinds (Comanche), 234
Ghost Dance, 50–54, 361
Gie-san (aka Little Child; Kiowa-Apache), 146; account from, 412–17; biographical sketch of, 136
Girard, F. F., 46
Given, Frank (Kiowa), 217
Given, Joshua (Kiowa), 67
Glacier National Park, 28
Glennan, J. D., 83–84
Glass, William, 89
glue: making of, 198; signs for, 309; in hair extensions, 356, 357
Goes Ahead (Crow), 14
Goes Together (Crow), 11, 21
Goff-Paris, Damara, 35
Good Road / Trail (Kiowa), 357
Goombi, Lutie (Kiowa), 37, 117
Goomdaw, Olive (Kiowa), 15
Grant, Ulysses S., 42
Grantham, David, 51
Grauman's Chinese Theater, 28
gray fox (pelts for quirt handles), 284
Great Northern Railway, 47, 76
Greene, Candace, 152, 253
Grinnell, George B., 155, 200, 247, 290, 331, 335, 344, 351, 371, 394, 446
Gros Ventre (Indians), 329, 341, 450

Hadley, Lewis F., 19–20
hairpipes (bone necklaces), 169, 301
hair swatches, 356–57
Hand Game, 449; signs used in, 38
hanging, of people, 196–97
Harney's Peak, 225, 281
Harrington, John P., 24, 25
Haun-goo-pah (aka Never Got Shot; Kiowa), 131
Hau-vaht (aka Slope / Hillside; Kiowa), 112, 127
Hawgone. *See* Silverhorn
Having Horns (Kiowa), 130
Hazen, William B., 113
He Bear (Comanche), 168, 170

Heart Eater (Kiowa), basis of name, 429
Heidsick (Kiowa), 70, 418; Black Leg's Society leader, 141, 145, 146, 126–27, 278; and Calumet Ceremony, 261, 270; naming of daughter by, 357; obtains peyote from Mescaleros, 214; war dress of, 288
Hill, John, 66
Hinds, Ernest, 107, 109
Hoffman, Walter J., 18
holding camp (by Kiowa military societies), in 1834, 207–208
holding the buffalo (by Kiowa military societies), 164–66, 211–12; and Kicking Bird, 359
Hollis, Robert, 56
Honameatah (aka Hanameatah, Unafraid of Danger; Kiowa), 91, 127–28, 201; biographical sketch of, 130–31
hoop and pole game, 238–39, 333. *See also* Wheel Game (Kiowa)
horses: acquired from Comanches, 228; acquiring, 227–28; origins of (Kiowa), 227–28, 420, 433
Howard, James, 189
Hueco Tanks (Tex.), 124, 128, Kiowa sieged at in 1839, 208–10, 211, 230–31, 243, 398–402
Humfreville, J. Lee, 16
Hunt, Ernest (Kiowa), 113
Hunt, George (Kiowa), 88, 109, 111, 112, 113, 114, 326, 399
Hunter, Andrew, 41
Hunter, David, 42
Hunting Horse. *See* Tsa-toke / Tsatoke (Hunting Horse; Kiowa)

Íàumcùngà (Child-Making Dance, Kiowa name of Calumet Dance). *See* Calumet Dance (Kiowa-Pawnee)
Ickes, Harold L., 28
Indian Scouting Program (late 1800s), 57–65
Indian Sign Language Councils, 25–28, 36. *See also* Plains Indian Sign Language (PISL)
Indian women, and courting customs, 380–81

insanity, 214, 271
inheritance, 205
Iron Creek, 298, 424
Iron Whip (Sioux), 26
Ironheart, Charlie (Sioux), 341
Irwin, George Le R., 112, 113
Isati / Isa-ti (Comanche), 180, 181, 182
Iseeo (Plenty Of Round Fireplaces; Kiowa), 49, 52, 55, 56, 59, 69, 358, 437; allotment of, 100; biography and life of, 87–122; commemorations of, 121; cottage built for, 102–103; death and funeral of, 114–17; dress of, 102, 109; family of, 87–88, 114; father of, 440; and Ghost Dance, 101–105; horse medicine of, 440–41; lifetime enlistment, 100; military service of, 118–20; names of, 88, 279, 358; Peace Treaty Pageant, 113; peyotism and, 109; photos of, 90, 93, 115, 116; and Ripley's Believe it or Not, 120; relationship with Hugh L. Scott, 41–83, 91–109, 112–13, 121–22, 146–48; remarriage of, 112; as Ten Medicine Bundle Keeper, 109; Texas-Oklahoma Boundary Dispute, 110–12; in Troop L, 91–99; wife of, as half-Wichita, 266; World War I citation and, 113
Island Mountain, 176

J*á*ifègàu Society (Kiowa military society), 277–79; in Sun Dance preparation, 383. *See also* military societies
Jefferson, Thomas, 15, 19, 140
Jerome Commission. *See* Cherokee (Jerome) Commission
Jones, Horace P., 55, 274, 407
Joseph (aka Chief Joseph; Nez Perce), 45–46
judges, 199–200
July 4th (Big Medicine Day), 440

Kavanagh, Thomas, 132, 155, 180, 200, 231, 328, 353, 421
Káuiqáunhól (aka Dragonfly; Kiowa), 55
Keahbone, Edgar (Kiowa), 120
Keahbone, Mark (Kiowa), 219
Ke-ah-ve (Kiowa), 203
Keechi (Indians), 397
Keechi Joe, biographical sketch of, 131, 132

486 INDEX

Keechei Hills (Caddo Co., Okla.) 97, 257; and Keechi village, 295
Keyes, Major, 176
Kicking Bird (Kiowa), 89; as chief, 359–60; and Fort Marion prisoners, 178, 186, 201, 210, 224, 229; and policed hunt law, 164–66, 359
Kicking Bird II, Paul, 50, 94, 120; biographical sketch of, 130–31
Killed A Mountain (Kiowa man), 406
killing, accidental, 199, 283, 300–302, 431; herders at Ft. Sill, 405–407
Kingfisher Creek, 261
Kintadl (aka Moth; Kiowa), 127, 217
Kiowa (Indians): afterlife, 197; agriculture among, 418; anger among, 224–25; attacked by Pawnee, 424–26; awl game of, 451–53; bands of, 194–95, 265–66; courting customs, 380–81; curses among, 224; defensive earthworks of, 201, 325; early history and land of, 435–40, 450; death and mourning, 201, 206–207; and eating bears, 200; electing chiefs, 360; enemies of, 420; fights with Cheyenne, 368, 371; and finger cutting, 201; hair customs of, 197–98; language classification of, 440, 468; levirate among, 205; lost group of, 438–39; marriage customs, 194, 205, 265; medicine dance (Sun Dance) of, 195; military societies of, 207–208, 211–12, 277–79, 359, 382–83; name for sign language, 14–15; name for deaf-mutes, 15; names of tribes, 319–20, 429; naming practices, 357–58; origins of, 436–40; in Northland, 336–37; origins of horses, 352–56, 420; Osage Massacre of, 122–23, 207, 257–62, 290; peace with Caddo, 445–46; peace with Cheyenne and Arapaho, 261–62, 423–24; peace with Comanche, 352–57; peace with Pawnee, 229–30; pipes, 230; range of, 435–37, 450; river crossing incident, 368–70; separation of, in north, 437–40; sororal polygyny among, 205; suicide, 196–97; Sun Dance, 377–79, 381–93; tails, 411–12; tattoos of, 201; term for scalping, 204; tipi making, 202–203; women, 380–81
Kiowa-Apaches (Plains Apaches), 371, 412–17, 419, 420; Medicine Lake Story, 413–17, 420; name of, 450; underwater monster, 414–16
Kiowa Bill (Kiowa), 111
Kiowa Mountains, 290, 429, 436
Kiowa Sun Dance ($Q\hat{a}uj\acute{o}$), 381–93; bison hunt in, 201, 236; brush dragging, 382–86; bull used in, 236; camp formation, 265; Kiowa Sun Dance Leaders ($Q\hat{a}uj\acute{o}q\grave{\imath}$), 381–93; mud fight, 386; timber fight, 386
Kiwash (aka Nim Kiwash, "Deceitful Man," Comanche trickster), 190, 223, 233–35; and Comanche origins, 233; and Euro-Americans, 234–35; How Kiwash Deceived the White man, 234–35
Ko-au-de. See Kom-au-day / Kom-au-dy (aka Black Stomach / Big Black Tripe; Kiowa)
Kobe / Kobi (Wild Horse, Kiowa chief) creek named after, 300; Comanche name of, 188, 394; death of, 393–94, 436
Koh-marty / Koh-marty (aka Big Head; Kiowa), 183, 217, 219, 265, 393
Kokoyden (Elk Tongue). See Elk Tongue (aka Tom Mobeadleky; Kiowa)
Ko-le-ah-ty (Kiowa), 217
Kom-au-day / Kom-au-dy (aka Black Stomach / Big Black Tripe; Kiowa), 125, 230–31, 243, 358, 393; Hueco Tanks fight, 231, 243, 399–402; shield of, 231, 399–402
Ko-yante (Kiowa), 125
Kroeber, Alfred E., 22–23; references to works of, 139, 150, 160, 344, 349, 351, 365, 366, 403, 446

Lakota Indians, 43–45, 62
Lee, Jesse, 59
Lean Old Man (Kiowa), vision of, 226
Leforge, Thomas H., 21
Left Hand (Arapaho), 329
Lewis, Meriwether, 7
Lewis and Clark, expedition of, 7
lightning, 159, 206, 342, 367; sign for, 286, 309
Lincoln, Abraham, 42
Linderman, Frank B., 11, 21

Lipan-Apache (Indians): area of, 377; sign for, 313
Little Bluff. *See* Tohausen (aka Dohausen, Jòhâusàn; Kiowa)
Little Chief (Cheyenne), 225, 330
Little Child. *See* Gie-san (aka Little Child; Kiowa-Apache)
Little Man (Cheyenne), 330
Little Plume (Piegan), 26
Little Raven (Arapaho), 335
Little Robe (Kiowa), 376
Little Washita (river), 259
Little Wolf (Northern Cheyenne), 18
Lives A Long Time (aka Jáudèkáu, Kept His Name a Long Time, Bison Bull Coming Out / Emerging; Kiowa), medicine of, 181–82, 358, 360–61
Ljung, Magnus, 23
Loco (aka Mokin; Kiowa captive), 177, 405, 406
Lone Traveler / Travels Alone (Kiowa), 357
Lone Wolf (aka Mammedaty; Kiowa), 67, 68, 89
Lone Wolf (Kiowa, d. 1879), 89, 206, 229, 366, 427–28; death of, 406–407; hunting skill of, 235
Lone Wolf, Delos K. (Kiowa), 109
Lone Wolf, Ida Wansey (Kiowa), and sign talking, 300
Lone Wolf v. Hitchcock (1903), 68
Long. J. Schuyler, 34
Long, Stephen H., 11, 15
Long Foot (Kiowa), 358
Lowie, Robert H., 135, 139, 150

Mackenzie, Randall, 133
Maddox, George (aka Pesuwiyeckwit, Comanche George), 50, 135
Mallery, Garrick, 16–18
Mamanti / Mamante (Kiowa), 178–80, 185–86
Mandan (Indians), 315
Many Scalps Medicines (Kiowa Medicine Bundles). *See* Ten Medicines (Kiowa Medicine Bundles, aka *Áulbéáuihyà* or One of Many Scalps); scalping
March, Payton C., 100–101

Marquis, Thomas, 21
marriage, 7, 37, 194; sororal polygyny, 205
Marriott, Alice, 88, 109, 132, 154, 181, 399
Matopaha (Grizzly Bear Butte), 223
Mato Ti, 222, 223, 297
Màuchàchê (aka Muchacho; Kiowa), 55
McAllister, Gilbert J., 155, 216, 361, 373
McCoy, Tim, 24–25, 32
McKay-Cody, Melanie, 33–36
McKenzie, Parker P. (Kiowa), observations of sign language, 14–15, 62, 91, 114, 122, 124, 125, 127, 131, 132, 172, 176, 77, 178, 217, 231, 281, 286, 299, 307, 318, 349, 370
medicine (supernatural power): "Going to the Medicine," 187–88; "Man having Medicine," 180–83; Rain Medicine, 202. *See also* Buffalo Bull Medicine; Buffalo Tail Shield Medicine; Kiowa Sun Dance
Medicine Arrow (Cheyenne), 330
Medicine Bluff Concavity (Mount Rochester, Tex.), Kiowa name for, 226, 294
Medicine Bluffs (Comanche Co., Okla.), 262
Medicine Butte (Tex.), 226, 294
Medicine Horse (Mancayaa or cyclones), 366–67
Medicine Lake (N.Dak.), 337–41
Medicine Dance / Lodge. *See* Kiowa Sun Dance
Medicine Lodge Creek (Timber Hill Creek), 296
Medicine Lodge Treaty, 66, 88, 110, 173, 296, 440
Medicine Wolf, 428
Merrill, Lewis, 47
Merritt, Wesley, 53, 54
mescal. *See* peyote / peyotism
mescal bean (*sophora secundiflora*): from Mexico, 189; Wichita Red Bean Ceremony, 142, 189
Mescalero Apache (Indians), 98, 174, 212; Comanche names of, 320, 413; and peyote, 214, 267, 377
Messiah Dance. *See* Ghost Dance
Methodists (aka *Áultạ́dóp*, Hair Wetters), Kiowa name of, 305
Methvin, Frank (Plains Apache), 111
Methvin, John J., 67

Meyer, Albert J., 16
Mexico: Kiowa raids into, 87, 123, 146, 167, 173, 175, 187, 230, 234, 372, 399; mescal beans in, 189; native languages in, 7; war trail into, 376–77
Miles, Nelson A., 18, 44, 66, 70, 72, 85, 94, 97, 168, 186, 214, 281
military societies: Arapaho, 221; Cheyenne, 221; Comanche, 327–28; Kiowa, 211, 277–79, 359, 383
Miller, Katrina, 35
mirages, 315, 429
Mirey or Boggy Creek (*Chènvǎu*, aka Rainy Mountain Creek, Okla.), 51 122, 136, 159, 182, 197, 257, 258, 259, 260, 296, 314, 412, 413
Missouri River, 8, 19, 44, 53, 63, 141, 189, 289, 297, 329, 331, 334–37, 420, 439
Mithun, Marianne, 4
Mobeadleky, Tom (Kiowa). *See* Elk Tongue (aka Tom Mobeadleky; Kiowa)
Moccasin Game. *See* Hand Game
Molay-tay-quop, Comanche name of Hugh L. Scott, 50, 62, 280
moon, 163, 171, 315, 316, 327, 362, 391, 392, 421
Mooney, James (BAE ethnologist), 67, 77–79; *Calendar History* of, 77, 79
Moore, John H., 155
Moses, Lester, 24
Mosquito Hawk, 447
Motokis (Blackfeet), 290
Mount Scott (Okla.), 257, 258; Comanche vision quest site, 262, 271, 290, 292, 294, 375
Mount Sheridan (Okla.), 100; name of, 194, 262, 290, 292, 294–95
Mountain Calf (aka Stone Calf; Cheyenne), 280; basis of name, 225
mountains. *See names of individual mountains*
Mountain Chief (Piegan), 26
morning star, 88, 175, 195, 234, 280, 358, 366
mourning customs. *See under* Kiowa
Moving About With Lodges (Kiowa), 88, 89, 440

Mud (Kiowa). *See* Sain-a-quo / Sin-ah-quo (aka Nose Mucous, Mud; Kiowa)
mulberry (robe paint), 314
Museum of the Plains Indian, 258
mute, 11, 15, 17, 231, 300; sign for, 303, 307. *See also* deaf and mute people

Naiche (Apache), 66
names: giving of, 88, 357–58; men's, 130, 210, 279–82; tribal names, 163–64, 265, 319
National Park Service, 28
Native American Church, 37, 133
Native American Indian Sign Language (NAISL), 33
Navajo (Indians), 35, 70, 74, 79, 88, 104, 113, 137, 139, 173, 195, 205, 218, 258, 272; and sign language, 276–77, 287, 320, 357, 369, 376–77, 466
Navajo Mountain (Okla.), 258, 272, 368
Neum, name for Comanche. *See* Comanches
Newell, L. E., 24
new items, signs for, 318
Nez Perce (Indians), 273
Niastor (Wichita), 188
Night Shoots (Piegan), 26
Noconi / Nokoni (Comanche Division), 422–23
North, Frank, 95
North American Indian Sign Language (NAISL), 33
North Star (Pawnee Star or Star Does Not Move), 195, 234
Nye, Wilber S., 53, 56, 106, 108, 119, 125, 153–54

oaths, 199–200, 335–36
O-be-in, Mollie (Kiowa), 131
Odlety, Nellie (Kiowa), 127
offerings, 370; Cheyenne, 335–36
Oheltoint, Charley (Kiowa), 127
Old Fort Rice, 225
Old Lady Bison Bull (Kiowa), 160–61
Old Man Black Beard (Cheyenne), 169
Old Men Trail, 376–77
Old Spider Woman, 238, 240; cultivates gourd, 289, 418

Olla (Spanish name of Comanche man), 422
Ollar-ho, 270
Omaha Dance (aka Grass / War Dance), 185
omens, 210
Onsoti (aka Tonanti, Long Foot; Kiowa), 178, 358–59
Osage (Indians), 191, 193, 203, 204, 205, 242, 271, 274, 275, 286, 357, 397, 423, 429; arrows of, 253; bow wood, 331; capture of Kiowa Táimé, 358; lookout of, 295; Massacre of Kiowa, 122–23, 142, 207, 209, 257–62, 290, 294, 298, 303, 423; names of, 317, 320; and persimmons, 275, 289, 318; shaved heads of, 270, tattoos of, 397
O-tah-ty (later wife of Iseeo), 112
Otter Belt (Comanche), 168
Owl Medicine, of Comes Over A Ridge, 178, 185, 371–74
owls, 190, 284, 330; and whirlwinds, 330

Pahsita (Comanche), 204, 456, 460
Pah-tuy-y-ya (aka Afraid Of Water; Comanche), 353, 354, 421
Paint / Paint Mines, 292, 356, 357, 425; sign for, 318
Palmer, Gus, Sr. (Kiowa), 107, 123
Palo Duro Creek (Tex.), 299, 370
Palo Duro Rock (Tex.), 335–36, 370
parfleches (rawhide storage containers), 195, 292, 420; sign for, 318, 337; Taime in, 391, 393; Ten Medicine Bundles in, 363–64
Parker, Cynthia Ann, 132
Parker, Quanah (Comanche), 51, 59, 68, 70, 121, 142, 144, 146, 149, 151, Adobe Walls Fight, 167–68; biographical sketch of, 132–33; death of, 275, 279, 282; doctoring for rattlesnake bite, 272, 292–93, 296, 298, 319, 328, 360; made chief by whites, 432; peyote use, 213–14, 257, 258, 270; signaling, 170, 180, 181; threatens to kill Hugh L. Scott, 68
Parker, White, 114
Parker-Iseeo American Legion Post, 107
Paruasumuno (aka Ten Bears; Comanche), 134
Paugh-ti (Kiowa), 114

Páuìyoi (Descendants or Offspring of the Bison Bull), 160, 376
Pau-to-mah (Kiowa / Wichita): as wife of Iseeo, 89; death of, 112
Pawnee (Indians), 65, 95, 159, 171, 220, 241, 242, 286, 294, 338, 363, 391, 393, 424, 445; arrows of, 253; attack on Kiowa camp, 424–26; Calumet Dance of, 266–71; capture of Cheyenne Sacred Arrows, 220; capture of Kiowa woman, 374–76; Cheyenne and Arapaho name for, 331; Comanche name for, 163, 320; early location of, 357; and Frank North, 95; and horses, 433; origins, 241; Kiowa name of (Cûiqàgàu or Wolf People), 261, 287, 320; Pawnee Star (Kiowa name for North Star), 195; locations named for, 294, 299, in Medicine Lake story, 338–39; Peace with Kiowa, 229–30; relations with Wichita, 188–92, 195; in Sainday Story (Kiowa), 347–48; scouts, 17, 65; sign language use by, 286; signs for, 318, 325; warfare with, 159, 167, 171, 218, 242, 338, 363–64, 391, 393
Pawnee Star (North Star), 195
P. B. Hearst Museum, 167
Pea-goo-ah. *See* Comes Over A Ridge (Pea-goo-ah; Kiowa)
Pe-ah-bo (aka Big Horse; Kiowa), 123
Peah-mah (Kiowa), 123
Pecos River, 8, 143, 323, 377
Peneteckas (Comanche Division), 421
Peta Nokona (Comanche), 132
Pershing, John J., 74, 84, 101
persimmons, 300, 411; Caddo use of, 274; Kiowa use of, 275; Osage Indians' use of, 275; and Sainday, 412; sign for, 289, 318
Petter, Randolph, 76
Pewo, Wilbur (Comanche), 111
peyote / peyotism, 53, 83, 109, 126, 213–16
Pike, Albert, 150, 169
Pine Hills, 223
pipes, 160, 162, 330, 359, 367, 373, 388; Apache Medicine Lake story, 338; Arapaho Flat Pipe, 328; asking favors with, 413; Buffalo Shield keeper taboo (Kiowa), 230, 359; Calumet pipe, 266–71;

pipes *(continued)*: divination, 373; in making peace, 260, 262; with medicine bundles, 217–18, 362–63, pipe stems, 162; in Sainday stories, 350, 447; in soliciting war party, 133, 166, 168, 171–72, 174, 180–81, 185, 187, 207, 291, 327; smoked towards tornadoes, 367; straight pipe, 363, 388; in Sun Dance, 382, 388; in turning storms, 367

Plains Indian Sign Language (PISL), 3–40; 1930 Sign Language Conference, 25–28; adequacy of, 433–34; and Caddo, 274; current uses of, 37–38; dialects of, 13, 23; differences among Caddos, 274; factors of decline, 36–37; Far Northern or Storytelling Dialect, 23; forms of, 5; Kiowa use of, 14–15; North American history of, 3–15; origins of, 6–11; Plains Standard dialect, 23; recent research on, 32–38; revival programs of, 35; relationship to American Sign Language, 34; sign for (hand talk), 322; Southern Plains use of, 37–38; studies of, 15–24; use by deaf Native Americans, 9, 35–37; use in warfare, 13–14; uses of, 11–15; visual sources of, 24–25. *See also* Plains Indian Sign Language signs

Plains Indian Sign Language signs: birds, 287–89; descriptions of signs that may be forgotten, 282–87; expressions, 301–303, 312–13, 431–32; letters A–J, 303–12; letters K–N, 313–16; letters O–Q, 317–19; letters R–Z, 321–25; men's names, 279–82; modern signs, 325–26; mountains and hills, 294–95; people at Bent's Fort, 290; place names, 282, 289–90; plants, 284–87, 289; rivers, 295–97, 298–300; signs that may be forgotten, 282–87; snakes, 289; trees, 276, 284–87; weather, 282, 284, 286–87

plants: names of, 98, 124, 237, 287, 289, 331; tan (pomme blanche), 236

Platte River, 122, 143, 228, 231, 232, 374, 377, 379, 381; names of, 285, 297, 331

Pleiades (constellation), 195–96, 264–65, 335–36. *See also* Star Girls

Plenty Bears (Kiowa), 178

Plenty Coups (Crow), 14

Plenty Stars (aka Got No Moccasins; Kiowa): as Táimé keeper, 178; as war party leader, 366

Plummer, Edward H., 103

Poco, Comanche name of prairie dog owl, 234

Pohoi, Comanche name of Shoshone, 421

policing. *See under* military societies

Ponca (aka Bushy Bang Men), 83, 137, 213

Pong-quodle (Kiowa), 300

Poolant, Bob (aka Approaching / Crawling Snake; Kiowa), 56, 183

Pope-tsait-ke (aka Spotted Horse; Kiowa), 98, 114, 182

Poolaw, Kiowa George (Kiowa), 120

Poor Boy, antelope medicine of, 417–18, 426–27

Poor Buffalo (Kiowa), 51, 265; biographical sketch of, 128; as Black Legs Society leader, 128, 145, 146, 277; camp of, 210; discourages cavalry enlistments, 59, 70; resisting surrender, 127; as Ten Medicine Bundle Keeper, 217, 435

porcupine: in Kiowa origins story, 236; range of, 381; in Sainday story, 411; sign for, 317

Porter, Mel, 89

prairie (concept / term): and accidents, 301; gifts, 99, 229, 325; in killing, 199, 283, 301; in lying, 303; in looking, 312, 330; in marriage, 205; in return of captive, 260; in thought, 302; with no medicine, 419; without / with no reason, 419, 431, 433

Powell, John Wesley, 71

Pratt, Richard H., 84, 187

Pretty Shield (Crow), 6, 11, 13, 14, 21

Proctor, Redfield, 58

property rights, 205

Pueblo (Indians), 317

Pway-ti-ya, Comanche term for ghost, 234

Qóichégàu Society (Kiowa), 128, 123, 277

Quahada (Comanche Division), 127, 133, 168, 175, 180, 207, 208, 231, 232, 270, 328, 377, 421, 422

Quay, A. G. Clayton, 62, 68, 83, 377

Quay, Matt, 68
Que-ton (Kiowa captive), 14, 178, 299, 370
Quinette's Store, 270
Quoetone, Guy (Kiowa), 111, 113, 461
Quoetone, Jimmy (Kiowa), 109
Quo-haw-ty (Kiowa), 88, 114
Quo-to-tai (aka Eagle on Top; Kiowa), 89

rain, 202, 367; making of by Kee-ar-by, 203; sign for, 202
Rainy Mountain (Okla.), Kiowa camp in 1833, 260; sign for, 296
Rainy Mountain Creek (Okla.), Ghost Dance site, 51; paint mine near, 292
rattlesnakes, bites and cures, 271, 272–73, 292–93
Read, J. L., 114
Red Bean (mescal bean) Ceremony (Wichita), 142, 189
Red Bluff, 370
Red Cloud (Lakota), 46
Red Hill, 370, 372, 374
Red Mud (Kiowa), 195
Red Neck (Cheyenne translator), 223, 330; and Euro-American trader, 168, 169, 282, 301; and Edward H. Wyncoop, 282, 330; and Kiowa agent J. Lee Hall, 182
Red River (Big Sandy River), 435–36
Red Sleeve(s) (aka Shirt With Red Sleeves; Comanche), 374, 393
Ree Indians. *See* Arikara (Indians, aka Ree)
Remington, Frederick, 70
Republican River, 143, 159, 296, 298, 299, 331, 334, 424
Rides Black Horse (Assiniboine), 26
Ring or Spear Game (Kiowa), 447–48
Ripley's Believe It Or Not, 9, 120
Rio Grande River, 113, 143, 174, 205, 295, 332, 440, 468
Rises From the Water (Kiowa), 270
rivers: Cheyenne, Comanche, Kiowa names of, 295–97, 298–300; Wichita names of, 298
Robinson, Lila, 134
Roman Nose (Cheyenne), 332
Roosevelt, Theodore, 70

Sac and Fox. *See* Sauk and Fox
saddles, 276
Saddle Mountain (Okla.), 96, 125 128, 130, 187, 199, 257, 295, 298, 406
sage, medicinal use of, 214
Sain-a-quo / Sin-ah-quo (aka Nose Mucous, Mud; Kiowa), 207, 435, 437; biographical sketch of, 132
Sainday / Saynday / Scinday / Sinday (Kiowa trickster), 243–48, 249–50, 253, 255, 257, 264, 389, 409; and Ant, 344–47; and Antelope, 250; Boy Who Killed Eagle, 253, 255; and origin of intertribal warfare, 242; foreword to stories on, 450–51; gives speech to Indians, 241–42; How Crow Came to be Black, 249; How Scinday Became Blind, 446; How Scinday Broke His Legs and Mended Them, 441; How Scinday Deceived Panther, 441–42; How Scinday's Lodge Burned Up, 442–43; Sainday and the Bald Headed Eagle, 256–57; Sainday and the Beavers, 256; Sainday and Coon, 342–43; Sainday and Ghost / Whirlwind, 395; Sainday and Hashmeats / Why the Cat Has No Nose and a Short Tail, 350–52, 365–66; Sainday and Porcupine, 411; Sainday, Sapoodle, and the "Cheet" Bird, 396–97; Sainday's Laws, 346–47; Scinday, Bear, and the Tight Tree, 395–96; Scinday and his Daughter, 347–48; Scinday and his Mother-in-Law, 346; Scinday and Pawnee, 347–48; Scinday and Red Horse, 366; Scinday and Sapoodle, 412; Scinday and the Antelope Kid, 443; Scinday and the Boy, 349–50; Scinday and the Bison Hunt, 443; Scinday and the Elk's Head, 403; Scinday and the Fight Tree, 348–49; Scinday and the Girl, 349; Scinday and the Split Boys, 365–66; Scinday and the White Eagle's medicine, 404; Scinday Kills Deer Woman, 445–46; Scinday Let Out the Buffalo, 446–47; Scinday's Race with Sapoodle, 402–403; sign language, 6–7
Sain-to (Horse Looker). *See* Tsa-toke / Tsatoke (Hunting Horse; Kiowa)
Saingko (Kiowa), 326

Salt Fork Red River, 242–43, 296, 299, 359; Kiowa Crossing at High Water, 368–70
Samarin, William, 7
Sanderville, Richard (Blackfeet), 26–29, 31–32; 1930 Sign Language Council film, 28–32
Sand Hills (Okla.), 178, 422
Sankadota (Kiowa), bitten by rabid wolf, 271
Sa-pin, Rose (Kiowa), 131
Sapoodle (Kiowa ogre), 344–46, 396–97, 402–403, 412
Satanke, death of, 397–99
Satanta. *See* White Bear (aka Santanta; Kiowa)
Sateavo (Saukeahho). *See* Sauk and Fox
Satickee. *See* Sauk and Fox
Satsevo. *See* Sauk and Fox
Sauk and Fox (Indians), 87, 167, 271, 358, 402
Sayce, A. H., 20
scalping, 173, 236, 339; on bundles, 216, 217–20, 358, 361–63, 426; painting of, 393; on shirts, 385; survivors of, 203–204
Schofield, John M., 57, 64
Schultes, Richard Evans, 98, 331
Scinday. *See* Sainday / Saynday / Scinday / Sinday (Kiowa trickster)
Scott, David Hunter, 42, 47
Scott, Hugh L.: assistance to Indians, 79–84; autobiography of, 77; BAE appointment, 71; biographical information on, 41–86; and capturing eagle, 69; Cheyenne name of, 62; civic service of, 75–77, 79; Comanche name of, 50, 62, 280; commemorations of, 85; criticism of Army and American Society, 80–84; death of, 84; descriptions of by others, 81–82, 85; education of, 42–43; family of, 41–42; at Fort Sill, 49–71; and Ghost Dance, 50–54; introduction to PISL, 44–45; and James Mooney, 77–79; and Kiowa-Comanche-Apache allotment, 66–68; Kiowa names of, 62, 280; marriage of, 47; and measles outbreak, 83; military assignments and promotions, 86; and 1930 Sign language Conference, 25–28; and noted Indian leaders, 70; and noted political and western figures, 70; in Philippines, 73; Plains service, 43–72, 68–69; and Poolant incident, 56; publications by, 151–53; sign language research of, 18–19, 25–31; in Spanish American War, 72–73; theoretical approach, 79; and Three Kiowa Boys incident, 55–56; transfer to 7th Cavalry, 43; use of sign language by, 76–77; views towards Indians, 75, 79–84; at West Point, 42–43, 73
Scott ledgers: characteristics of, 136–44; consultants for, 122–36, 144–46; context and unique features of, 140–48; editing of, 150–51; focus by tribe, 137–40; potential uses of, 154–55; prior use of, 153–54; writing and grammatical style of, 148–50
scouts, 227
seasons, 201, 316
Sebeok, Thomas, 23–24
Séthái̯dè (aka Small Intestine; Kiowa), 55
Seton, Ernest Thompson, 20
Shakespeare, William (Arapaho), 22
Sham Battle, at Kiowa Sun Dance, 385–87
Sheridan, Philip, 17, 44, 45, 57, 70, 72, 223, 281, 451
shield keepers, fears of, 358–59
shields (Kiowa): Bird Shields, 359; Buffalo Shields, 160, 359, 376; Táimé Shields, 358–59
Shirly, William, 274
Short Face (Piegan), 26
Shoshone (Indians), 232, 234, 320, 327, 335, 420, 421, 429
Sickel, H. G., 47
sign language. *See* Plains Indian Sign Language (PISL)
Signal Mountain (Okla.), 406
signals, long distance signaling, 227, 291–92
Silverhorn (aka Hawgone; Kiowa), 98, 99, 120, 127, 145, 152, 153, 270, 446, 459
sinew, 220, 237, 240–41, 253; sign for, 321, 447
Sioux, Kiowa name for, 265, 319
Sit-a-pa-tah (aka Afraid of Bears; Kiowa), 216–17
Sitting Bear (aka Satanke; Kiowa), death of, 397–99
Sitting Down Rock. *See* Palo Duro Rock

Sitting Bull (Arapaho), and Ghost Dance, 51, 70, 183, 185, 361
Sitting Bull (Lakota), 45, 53, 69
Sitting in the Saddle (Kiowa), 407
skin offerings, 187–88
Sleeping Wolf (Kiowa), and Kiowa-Comanche Peace, 352–56
smallpox: Caddo losses from, 274; Cheyenne prevention of, 177, 220–21; Kiowa losses from, 141, 221; among Arapaho, 329, 341, 416; Sun Dance named for, 393, 436
Smoky (Kiowa), 406
Smoky Hill River (Kans.), 143, 296, 298, 299, 331
snakebite, and Comanches, 272–73, 293
So-he (aka Hairy, Comanche), 136
Sok-kone. *See* Tso-kone (aka Moses Black Stone; Kiowa)
sorcery, 186–87
Spear Game, 447–48
Speechless One (Kiowa), 231. *See also* Big Bow, Joe (Kiowa)
spider bites, cure for, 293
Spider Woman, 237–41, 418; and Crow, 249, 448
Spivey, Towana, 63, 121, 167, 219
Split Boys (aka Twin Boys; Kiowa culture heroes), 7, 238–41, 361–63, 365, 366
Spotted Bird (Kiowa), 111
Spotted Horse (aka Pop-Tsait-ke; Kiowa), 114
Spotted Horse Sun Dance (Kiowa), 98, 182, 195
Standing Bear, Luther (Lakota), 14, 20
Stands In The Middle (Kiowa), prophetic medicine of, 182–83, 263, 303, 361, 376
Staked Plains (Llano Estacado, Tex.), 174–75, 208, 212, 270, 285, 294, 353, 356, 376; name of, 294, 299, 318; Quahada Comanches and, 232, 421
Stanford, Leland, 25
stars, 195–96; in Comanche stories, 233, 421; constellations, 195; 1833 meteor shower, 10, 22, 195, 419; Milky Way, 195, 196, 286, 315; morning star (North star), 195; in Wichita vision quest, 190. *See also* Morning Star; Pleiades (constellation); Star Girls
Star Girls, 195, 196, 223, 264–65, 335–36, 366

Star Woman, 242–43; creek named after, 243, 296, 299, 368–69
Stecker, Ernest, 59, 83, 275
Stinking Creek. *See* Zoo-dle-tone
Stirling, Matthew W., 29
Stokoe, William, 22, 24
Stone, Forrest R., 26
Stone Calf (aka Mountain Calf), 280; basis of name, 225
Strange Owl (Cheyenne), 26; photo of, 29
Strong Spring, 262
Strong Wood Sundance, 243
Stumbling Bear (Kiowa), 70, 125–26, 144, 145, 146, 167, 182, 209, 224, 225, 226, 229, 258, 291, 292, 336, 357, 359, 366
Sturgis, Samuel D., 46
Sturm, J. J., 133
Sugar Creek: in Caddo Co., Okla., 191, 193, 199, 273, 436, 295, 296; on Kiowa Co., Okla., 271, 294, 413
suicide, 196–97
sun, 186–89, 195, 200, 203, 218, 224, 227, 232, 241, 244, 272, 278, 286, 287, 292, 308, 361, 362, 384, 388, 390, 428, 414, 421, 445
Sunboy: Kiowa cultural hero, 361–62; Kiowa man, bandleader in 1880s, 214, 271, 362
Sun Dance. *See* Kiowa Sun Dance
Sun Dance Creek. *See* Palo Duro Creek (Tex.)
Sun Father, 228
Sun Medicine, 177
Sun Shield, 176–77
Sunwater Springs (Tex.), 376–77
surrounds. *See* buffalo surround
Sweat, Morris, 101, 109, 113, 117
sweat lodges, 200–201, 217–20
Sweet Medicine (Cheyenne culture hero), 333
Sweet Water Creek. *See* Sugar Creek
synonyms, 434

T'au (Kiowa religious item), 124–25
Tabaharty (Sweat Lodge, Kiowa), 178
Tabananaka (Comanche), 59, 187; biographical sketch of, 134
Taft, Howard, 70
Tahbonmah (aka Sees The Morning Star). *See* Iseeo

494   INDEX

Tahbonemah, Luke (Kiowa), 98, 114
Tahpony/Tah-pon-y (Comanche), 144, 146, 421–23; biographical sketch of, 134–35
Táimé (Kiowa Sun Dance Medicine Bundle), 176–78, 187, 195, 220, 230, 236, 285, 361, 381–83, 401,402; capture by Osage, 261, 316, 342, 388–94; capture by Ute, 176; origins of, 177–78; taboos, 358–59
Táimé Shields, 390, 392
Táimédè (aka One Who Is Táimé, Taimeday, Standing Táimé; Kiowa), 177–78
Táiméqì̀ (Táimé Keeper, Kiowa), 87, 125, 177–78, 187, 200, 358–59, 381–83, 388–94
Tằlyîdàui (Paternal Grandmother Medicine)/Tàlyîdàui (Boy Medicine), 217
tan (pomme blanche), 236–37
Ta-ne-oh-keah (Good Eagle, Kiowa), 123
tanning (hides), 202–203
Tape-day-ah (Kiowa), 119, 372–74
Tattooed Faces. See Wichita (Indians)
tattoos, 89, 190–94, 198–201, 315, 319, 325, 397–98, 433, 450. See also under Kiowa; Wichita (Indians)
Taybodle (aka Teybodle; Kiowa), 70; age of, 336, 352, 356, 357, 364, 412; biographical sketch of, 122–28, 142, 144, 146, 162, 163; in Black Legs Society, 277, 280, 303, 313; Cutthroat Massacre account, 257–61, 164, 265; on horse raids, 377, 402, 418, 419; name of, 177, 194; and origin of horses, 141, 228, 420, 251; role in Sun Dance, 201, 222
Taylor, Alan, 24
Tay-nay-dau (Tenedooah; Kiowa), 125
Tchaka (Kiowa): on trip with Scott, 50, 69, biographical sketch of, 131–32, 146, 360, scars of, 361; on raids, 405–407
Tee, George (aka Luke Tahbonemah; Kiowa), 114
Tee, Harry (Kiowa), 114
Ten Medicine Keeper (Kiowa Medicine Bundle Keeper), 393–94; Pawnee attack on keeper and two other lodges, 424–26
Ten Medicines (Kiowa Medicine Bundles, aka Áulbéáuihyằ or One of Many Scalps), 216–21, 361–65, 424–26; and bears, 200, 218; and Bear Woman, 362–63; and dispute settlement, 199–200; names of, 216, 217; origin of, 236–42; and porcupine, 236; renewing the parfleches of, 363–65; and scalps, 216–20, 426; and Sainday, 241, 361–62; and Spider Woman, 237–41; Split Boys, 238–41; and sweat lodges, 200–201, 217–20; and tan plant, 236–37; use in warfare, 362–64; water taboo of, 202, and wheel and stick game, 238–39
Terry, Alfred, 45
Texas-Oklahoma boundary dispute, 110–12
Texas Rangers, 89
Tháumgá (Kiowa name of sign language), 14–15
Thàumhátdằu (deaf people, Kiowa), 15
Thomas, Elmer, 112–13
Thunder (Big Throat Man), 206, 341–42
thunder and lightning, 206, 341–42
Thunder Bird, 206, 309
Tichaneuas (Comanche division), 421
Timber Mountain and Creek (Kans.), 173, 298, 373
Timber Mountain Treaty (Kans.), 208. See also Medicine Lodge Treaty
time, concepts of, 303, 305, 309, 310, 316
tipis: making, 202–203; painted, 341
Tocana (Dark House People), 194, 423
Todome, Jim (Kiowa), 94
To-haddle, Carrie (Kiowa), 114
Tohausen (aka Dohausen, Jòhâusằn; Kiowa): band affiliation of, 265; basis of name, 280, 283, 305; after Cutthroat Massacre, 257–62; death of in 1866, 359; family of, 91, 127; at Hueco Tanks Fight, 208–10, 265, 368, 399–400; as leader of raid, 174–75; painted tipi of, 126; rise as chief, 207–208. See also Hueco Tanks (Tex.)
To-koy-ty (Kiowa), 122
Tomkins, William, 20
Tonacho I (Snapping Turtle, Kiowa), 187
Tonacho II (Snapping Turtle, Kiowa), 199
Tonanti (aka Onsoti; Kiowa), 178, 358–59
Tonemah (Kiowa), 62, 96, 120
Tonemah, Scott (Kiowa), 62
Tonemah, Quay (Kiowa), 62
Tonkawa/Tonkaways (Indians), 149, 151,

167, 168, 194; massacre of, 193, 298; names of, 320, 323, 369, 428–29, 436; ritual cannibalism of, 428–29
tornados (cyclones), 366–67; pipes smoked towards, 367
trance, 141, 178–80. *See also* fainting
travois, 419
trees, signs for, 276, 284, 287, 303, 304, 306, 308, 310, 314, 315, 317
Troop L, 7th Cavalry, 57–65; army views of, 63–65; disbandment of, 63; functions of, 60–62; leadership and, 63; rosters of, 455–60; success of, 64–65
Tsaitanke (aka Sitting Bear; Kiowa), death of, 397–99; death of son of, 399
Tsaitante (aka White Bear; Kiowa), 96, 128, 164, 359; arrest of, 397; band association of, 265; medicine arrow (lance) of, 173; name of, 279; shield of, 77, 122, 166–67
Tsaitkopeta, Paul (aka Mountain Bear), biographical sketch of, 131, 186; name of, 210, 310
Tsait-a-pay-ta / Tsait-ape (aka Afraid of Bears; Kiowa): keeper of Ten Medicine bundle, 216–17, 362–63, 365; name of, 217n62
Tsa-toke / Tsatoke (Hunting Horse; Kiowa), 89, 109, 262; wives of, 132
Tso-aa. *See* Devil's Tower
Tso-kone (aka Moses Black Stone; Kiowa), 363
Tsoodle, Henry, Jr. (Kiowa), 363
Tsoodle, Henry, Sr. (Kiowa), 363
tuberculosis (consumption), 215
Twin Boys (Kiowa culture heroes), 6–7
Tylor, Billy, 168

Umiker-Sebeok, Donna Jean, 23–24
Ute (Indians), 187, 201, 204, 218, 221, 242, 257, 291, 352, 373, 390, 391, 393; in Kit Carson Fight, 370; 1868 fights with Kiowa, 176, 178, 370–71, 373; Kiowa name of, 429

Vestal, Paul, 98, 331
Villa, Pancho, 74
visions, 188; by Comanche, 262; by Kiowa man, 226, 261; by Kiowa woman, 263, 374–75; by Plains Apache, 337; by Wichita, 190–91
vision quest sites: at Bear Butte, 223–24; Comanche, 262; Kiowa, 261, Wichita, 191
Voegelin, Carl, 22–23
Voegelin, Erminie, 22
vomiting (induced): and buckeye nuts, 262; and sulphur water, 262
Vomit Springs (Sulphur Spring). *See* Zoo-dle-tone

Wakoare (father peyote button, Comanche), 214
Walker, Francis A., 57
Walnut Creek (North Fork Red River), 175, 181, 186, 207, 259, 276, 286, 296, 300, 331
Wapeton (Sioux Indians), 341
war bonnets, 169, 184, 386, 422
Ware, Louis (Kiowa), 111
war parties, 170, 171–72, 201, 283, 291, 355
war trails, 376–77
Washakie, Dick (Shoshone), 26
Washita River (Tex., Okla.), 143, 176, 178, 242; sign language sign of, 295; Wichita name, 298
water containers, 376, 379
Weeks, John Wingate, 112
West, Dick (Southern Cheyenne), 32
West, La Mont, Jr., 22–23
Wheel Game (Kiowa), 411, 416. *See also* hoop and pole game
Wheritt, Barton, 55
White Bear (aka Santanta; Kiowa), arrest of, 397–98; band affiliation, 265; medicine arrow of, 173; name of, 279; political orientation of, 359; shield of, 167–68
White Bear (Northern Cheyenne) 46
white buffalo (albino), 235–36
White Calf, Jim (Blackfeet), 26
white flags, 259, 309, 422
White Horse (Kiowa), 279, 368–69, 406
Whitehorse, Charley (Kiowa), 128
Whitehorse, Roland (Kiowa), 128
White Horse, Tom (Arapaho), 26
White Shield (Cheyenne), 430–21; village of, 229

White Wolf, Howard (Comanche), 134
White Wolf / Old Man White Wolf
  (Comanche), 59; biographical sketch of,
  134; death of, 275
Wichita (Indians), 89, 137, 188–94, 198–99,
  232, 234, 241, 242, 258, 259, 261, 274,
  286, 295, 421, 423, 429, 436, 440;
  burials of, 207; cache pits of, 192–93;
  Calumet Ceremony of, 266–71; earth
  lodges among, 189; fortifications of,
  191–92; gardens of, 192; Ghost Dance of,
  185; grass houses of, 189; horses among,
  189–90; *Ishtick*, 189; name of Mountain
  range, 290; names by other tribes, 163,
  192, 194, 319, 320; names of streams,
  298; pumpkins (braiding of), 192; Red
  Bean (mescal bean) Ceremony of, 142,
  189; tattoos of, 194, 198–99, 397–98,
  433; village sites of, 191, 193, 423; visions
  among, 190–91
Wichita Mountains (Okla.), 174, 189, 191,
  194, 232, 242, 261, 270, 290, 294, 295,
  421, 423, 435, 450; location of, 143;
  Scott's experiences in, 49, 61, 69, 70, 104,
  128
Wild Horse (Comanche). *See* Kobe / Kobi
  (aka Wild Horse; Kiowa chief)
wild horses, 188, 250, 334, 435, 440–41. *See
  also* horses
Wild West shows, 24, 76
Wilkinson, James, 140
Wilson, Wilburn L., 25
Wilson, Woodrow, 70
wind: names of four winds, 293; what makes
  the wind blow, 160
Wise, Jennings C., 64
Wissler, Clack, 139, 150, 247, 344, 349, 351,
  403, 446
Wohaw (Kiowa), 60, 91, 457, 459
Wolf: Wolf Helped A Man to See, 160–61,
  427–28; Wolf and the Rock, 248
Wolf Creek (Okla.), 145, 282, 296, 436; 1838
  fight at, 261, 262, 335, 368, 371, 422,
  423–24
Wolf Lying Down (Kiowa), 353, 421
wolves, and rabies, 271
Woman's Heart (Kiowa), 210

women. *See* Indian women
Wood, Leonard, 70, 72
Wood, Sharon Kay, 35
Wooden Leg (Northern Cheyenne), 21
World's Congress of Ethnologists, 18
Wounded Knee Battle Site (South Dakota),
  25, 50, 52, 53, 104, 107
Wovoka (aka Jack Wilson; Paiute), 51, 53–54
Wum-pan-to-da (Kiowa), 260
Wurtzburg, Susan, 7, 9
Wyncoop, Edward W. (aka Red Neck), 330

Yandell, Kay, 4, 14, 21
Yapainʉʉ (Yapparikas, Comanche Division),
  134, 135, 136, 231, 232, 327, 421
Yàpfàhêgàu (Temporary Police / Guards,
  Kiowa), 211. *See also* military societies
Ye-ah-some (aka They Viewed Him Twice;
  Kiowa), 123
Yellow Bull (Arapaho), 59
Yellow Fish (Comanche), 111
Yellowstone area (Wyo.), 6, 8, 46, 47, 76,
  141, 143, 225, 289, 297, 420, 436, 439.
  See also geysers (Yellowstone area)
Young Mustang Colt (Kiowa captive), 123,
  251
Young Whirlwind (Cheyenne), 270
Young Wolf Heart (Kiowa), 407

Záidètàlyì̀ (Half, Split, or Twin Boys), 238,
  361, 363, 365, 366
Zeadle-ke-ah (Kiowa), 123
Zebile (aka Big Arrows; Kiowa), 162; and
  Calumet ceremony, 270
Zema-coon / Zemacouny / Zirracunny
  (*Zę́máutqų̀né / Zę́máutqų̀nóp*, Kiowa
  underwater monster[s]), 236, 240, 265,
  306, 322, 333, 338–41, 345–46, 432; and
  the Kiowa Girl, 444–45; in Kiowa origin
  story, 239; Plains Apache account of,
  414–17; name of Kiowa woman, 417, 418;
  and scalps, 338, 339; in vision, 186
Zę́máutqų̀némà̀ (Kiowa), 418
Zoo-dle-toon: Stinking Creek, Kiowa Co.
  Okla., 55, 142, 258–59, 262, 270; Sulphur
  Creek, 296, 298

www.ingramcontent.com/pod-product-compliance
Lightning Source LLC
Chambersburg PA
CBHW081532300426
44116CB00015B/2597